Leipziger Altorientalistische Studien

Herausgegeben von
Michael P. Streck

Band 12

2022
Harrassowitz Verlag · Wiesbaden

Nathan Wasserman, Elyze Zomer

Akkadian Magic Literature

Old Babylonian and Old Assyrian Incantations: Corpus – Context – Praxis

2022
Harrassowitz Verlag · Wiesbaden

Drawing on the cover: Pnina Arad, Jerusalem (based on BM 97877).

Bibliografische Information der Deutschen Nationalbibliothek
Die Deutsche Nationalbibliothek verzeichnet diese Publikation in der Deutschen Nationalbibliografie; detaillierte bibliografische Daten sind im Internet über https://dnb.de abrufbar.

Bibliographic information published by the Deutsche Nationalbibliothek
The Deutsche Nationalbibliothek lists this publication in the Deutsche Nationalbibliografie; detailed bibliographic data are available in the Internet at https://dnb.de.

For further information about our publishing program consult our website https://www.harrassowitz-verlag.de

Printed on permanent/durable paper.
Printing and binding: Memminger MedienCentrum AG
Printed in Germany

ISSN 2193-4436
ISBN 978-3-447-11765-4

Table of Contents

List of Tables

Preface and Acknowledgements

Some words about the title of this book. Magic is a multifarious phenomenon, a chiaroscuro of the known and the unknown, where the here-and-now stretches to the far-and-beyond. In the sphere of magic, words and actions conjoin. Pain is soothed through words and fumigation, fears are quelled through hushed blessings and jangling amulets, and disease healed through the application of formulae and arcane pastes.
Classifying magic as 'literature' might therefore seem to unnecessarily delimit the boundaries of this rich field. And yet, when talking about cuneiform sources, appending 'literature' to magic is inevitable – but at the same time, debatable.[1] 'Inevitable', since ancient Mesopotamian magic – its practitioners, clients, *materia magica* and magic implements, as well its arcane *modes opératoires* – is buried under the oceans of time, leaving behind shell-strewn beaches in the shape of hundreds, if not thousands, of fragmentary texts that afford but a glimpse into the complex cultural enterprise of Mesopotamian magic.

But beyond the textual dimension, linking 'magic' and 'literature' is not immediately obvious, since many would argue that texts dealing with Mesopotamian magic are *technical* rather than literary. This question cannot be resolved by applying accepted linguistic criteria, but has to address the question of what literature is – in general, and in ancient cultures in particular. Our position is clear: the literary qualities of second-millennium Akkadian incantations are very real. The main argument against the inclusion of incantations in the realm of literature, viz. their *being used* in practices and procedures, is immaterial, as the concept of 'pure' literary texts, did not exist in ancient Mesopotamia. It is with this conviction that the main title for the present study was chosen.

'Old Babylonian and Old Assyrian Incantations' is self-explanatory. The period ca. 2000–1500 BCE, the formative phase of later Mesopotamian magic, yields fascinating incantations. The Akkadian incantations of the second part of the second millennium – Middle Babylonian and Middle Assyrian incantations – were studied by Zomer (2018a), whereas the Akkadian magic texts of the late third millennium, viz. Old Akkadian, Ur III period and especially Ebla incantations, still require systematic study (cf. Krebernik 1984). As for the early Sumerian incantations, Cunningham (1997) presented a preliminary catalogue of the Sumerian, Akkadian and alloglot incantations of the third and early second millennium and Rudik (2015) presented an analysis of the Early Dynastic and Ur III corpus. A detailed study of the vast corpus of Old Babylonian Sumerian incantations would be welcome.

Finally, the triad 'Corpus – Context – Praxis'. These three terms denote that our study aims not only to present the texts in a sound philological manner, but also to understand the actual way they were used in early second millennium Mesopotamia.

This study commenced in 2013 with N. Wasserman's three-year project financed by the Israel Science Foundation ("The Reality of Magic: The Corpus of Old Babylonian and Old Assyrian Incantations in their socio-historical and literary Context", grant no. 116/13). A

1 On this question, cf. Schwemer 2014, 266–268.

delay in completing the project worked in our favour since two important works were in the meantime published, expanding our scientific understanding of early Akkadian incantations: A.R. George's *Mesopotamian Incantations and Related Texts in the Schøyen Collection* (2016) and E. Zomer's *Corpus of Middle Babylonian and Middle Assyrian Incantations* (2018a). To bring this ambitious project to completion, E. Zomer started working on the project in autumn 2018. The present study is the fruit of collaboration of the two authors.

We would like to thank the following colleagues for their help on this book: Yigal Bloch, Yoram Cohen, Jeanette Fincke, Irving Finkel, Andrew George, Jacob de Ridder, Ulrike Steinert, Michael Streck, Yulia Tulaikova and Klaus Wagensonner. Thanks also to members of the SEAL project (*Sources of Early Akkadian Literature*: https://seal.huji.ac.il/), in Leipzig, in Jerusalem, and elsewhere. Thanks are also due to Ami Asyag, Jerusalem, for his technical aid. Susan Kennedy copy-edited our text.

We take this opportunity also to extend our gratitude to the curators of the following collections: The British Museum in London, Yale Babylonian Collection (New Haven); and Vorderasiatisches Museum (Berlin).

The *Publikationsfonds des Zentrums für Gender Studies und feministische Zukunftsforschung* at the Philipps-University Marburg covered part of the publishing costs of this monograph, and The Hebrew University of Jerusalem's Mandel Scholion Interdisciplinary Research Center offered a generous support for this project in its final stages. We are grateful to them all.

Nathan Wasserman
Jerusalem

Elyze Zomer
Marburg

Abbreviations

A	Tablets in the collections of the Oriental Institute
AbB	Altbabylonische Briefe in Umschrift und Übersetzung
adj.	adjective
AfO	Archiv für Orientforschung
AHw	W. von Soden, *Akkadisches Handwörterbuch*, Wiesbaden 1959–81
Akk.	Akkadian
AMD	Mesopotamian Magic. Textual, Historical, and Interpretative Perspectives (Ancient Magic and Divination)
AML	Akkadian Magic Literature. Old Babylonian and Old Assyrian Incantations: Corpus – Context – Praxis (= LAOS 12)
AMT	R. C. Thompson, *Assyrian Medical Texts from the originals in the British Museum*, London 1923
AO	Museum siglum Louvre
AOAT	Alter Orient und Altes Testament
AoF	Altorientalische Forschungen
ARM	Archives royales de Mari
AS	Assyriological Studies
ASJ	Acta Sumerologica
Ass.	Assyrian
AUAM	Tablets in the collections of the Andrews University Archaeological Museum
AuOr Suppl.	Aula Orientalis Supplements
Bab.	Babylonian
BaF	Bagdhader Forschungen
BAM	Die babylonisch-assyrische Medizin in Texten und Untersuchungen
BBVO	Berliner Beiträge zum Vorderer Orient
BM	Museum siglum of the British Museum, London
BiMes	Bibliotheca Mesopotamica
BIN	Babylonian lnscriptions in the Collection of J. B. Nies
BiOr	Bibliotheca Orientalis
Bod	Ashmolean Museum, Bodleian Collection, Oxford
Bogh.	Boghazköi/Boghazkale
BPOA	Biblioteca del Proximo Oriente Antiguo
BSOAS	Bulletin of the School of Oriental (and African) Studies
Bu	Museum siglum of the British Museum (Budge)
BWL	W.G. Lambert, *Babylonian Wisdom Literature*, Oxford 1959
BZAW	Beihefte zur Zeitschrift für die alttestamentliche Wissenschaft
CAD	The Assyrian Dictionary of the University of Chicago
CBS	Museum siglum of the University Museum in Philadelphia

CCT	Cuneiform Texts from Cappadocian Tablets in the British Museum
CDA	Concise Dictionary of Akkadian
CDLI	Cuneiform Digital Library Initiative
CHANE	Culture and History of the Ancient Near East
CM	Cuneiform Monographs
CRRAI	Proceedings of the Rencontre assyriologique internationale; Compte rendu de la Rencontre Assyriologique Internationale
CT	Cuneiform Texts from Babylonian Tablets in the British Museum
CUNES	The Cornell University Collection in Ithaca, New York
CUSAS	Cornell University Studies in Assyriology and Sumerology
Ecc.	Ecclesiastes
ETCSL	Electronic Text Corpus of Sumerian Literature
f.	feminine
FAOS	Freiburger Altorientalische Studien
FM	Florilegium Marianum
Fs. Hirsch	A.A. Ambros/M. Köhbach (eds.), *Festschrift für Hans Hirsch zum 65. Geburtstag gewidmet von seinen Freunden, Kollegen und Schülern* (= WZKM 86), Wien 1996.
Fs. Pope	J.H. Marks/R.B. Good (eds.), *Love & Death in the Ancient Near East*, Guilford 1987
Fs. de Meyer	H. Gasche/M. Tanret/C. Janssen/A. Degraeve (eds.), *Cinquante-deux réflexions sur le Proche-Orient ancien: offertes en hommage à Léon De Meyer* (= MHEO 2, 1994)
Fs. Stol	R.J. van der Spek (ed.), *Studies in Ancient Near Eastern World View and Society. Presented to Marten Stol on the occasion of his 65th birthday*, Bethesda 2008
Fs. Wilcke	W. Sallaberger/K. Volk/A. Zgoll (eds.), *Literatur, Politik und Recht in Mesopotamien. Festschrift für Claus Wilcke* (= OBC 14, 2003)
GAG[3]	W. von Soden, *Grundriss der Akkadischen Grammatik* (= AnOr 33/47, 1995 [1952])
Gilg.	The Gilgameš Epic
GKT	K. Hecker, *Grammatik der Kültepe-Texte* (= AnOr 44)
HANES	History of the Ancient Near East
Heb.	Hebrew
IB	Ishan Bahriyat, Isin excavation sigla
IM	Museum siglum of the Iraq Museum in Baghdad
JA	Journal Asiatique
JCS	Journal of Cuneiform Studies
JEOL	Jaarbericht van het Voor-Aziatisch-Egyptisch-Gezelschap
Jer.	Jeremiah
JMC	Le Journal des Médecines Cunéiformes
JNER	Journal of ancient Near Eastern Religions
JNES	Journal of Near Eastern Studies
KAR	E. Ebeling, *Keilschrifttexte aus Assur religiösen Inhalts I/II* (= WVDOG 28, 1919; 34, 1923)
KBo	Keilschrifttexte aus Boghazköi

Kt	Inventory numbers of Kültepe tablets
KUB	Keilschrifturkunden aus Boghazköi
LANE	Languages of the Ancient Near East
LAOS	Leipziger Altorientalische Studien
LB	Tablets in the de Liagre Bohl Collection (Leiden)
l.e.	Left edge
LE	Laws of Ešnunna
LH	Laws of Hammurapi
LSS	Leipziger Semitistische Studien
m.	masculine
M.	Siglum Mari Excavations
MA	Middle Assyrian
MB	Middle Babylonian
MC	Mesopotamian Civilizations
MHEO	Mesopotamian History and Environment
MIO	Mitteilungen des Instituts für Orientforschung
MLC	Morgan Library Collection, siglum of the Yale Babylonian Collection, New Haven
MS	Manuscript Schøyen; object signature, Schøyen Collection Oslo and London
MSL	Materials for the Sumerian Lexicon; SS = Supplementary Series
NA	Neo-Assyrian
NABU	Nouvelles Assyriologiques Brèves et Utilitaires
NBC	Nies Babylonian Collection, siglum of the Yale Babylonian Collection, New Haven
OA	Old Assyrian
OAkk.	Old Akkadian
OB	Old Babylonian
OBC	Orientalia Biblica et Christiana
OBO	Orbis Biblicus et Orientalis
Obv.	Obverse
Odys.	Odysseus
OECT	Oxford Editions of Cuneiform Texts
OIP	Oriental Institute Publications
OLP	Orientalia Lovaniensia periodica
OLZ	Orientalistische Literaturzeitung
OPKF	Occasional Publications of the Samuel Noah Kramer Fund
Or.	Orientalia, NS = Nova Series
PANS	Proceedings of the National Academy of Sciences
PBS	University of Pennsylvania, Publications of the Babylonian Section
pf.	perfect
PIHANS	Publications de l'Institut historique-archéologique néerlandais de Stamboul
PIPOAC	Publications de l'Institut du Proche-Orient ancien
pl.	plural

PRAK	H. de Genouillac, *Premieres recherches archeologiques a Kich*, Paris 1925
pres.	present
Ps.	Psalms
r.	Reverse
RA	Revue d'Assyriologie et d'Archéologie Orientale
RIMB	The Royal Inscriptions of Mesopotamia, Babylonian periods
RINAP	The Royal Inscriptions of the Neo-Assyrian Period
RlA	Reallexikon der Assyriologie (und Vorderasiatischen Archäologie)
SAACT	State Archives of Assyria Cuneiform Texts
SAM	Studies in Ancient Medicine
SANER	Studies in Ancient Near Eastern Records
SB	Standard Babylonian
SEAL	Sources Early Akkadian Literature
sg.	singular
SpTU	Spätbabylonische Texte aus Uruk
St. Pohl	Studia Pohl
Sum.	Sumerian
TAPS	Transactions of the American Philosophical Society
TIM	Texts in the Iraq Museum
TSO	Texte und Studien zur Orientalistik
TUAT	Texte aus der Umwelt des Alten Testaments
U.	Find siglum, Ur (London/Philadelphia/Baghdad)
UAVA	Untersuchungen zur Assyriologie und Vorderasiatischen Archäologie
u.e.	Upper edge
UET	Ur Excavations. Texts
UF	Ugarit-Forschungen
UIOM	Tablets in the collections of the Univ. of Illinois Oriental Museum
VAT	Museum siglum of the Vorderasiatisches Museum, Berlin
VS	Vorderasiatische Schriftdenkmäler der (königlichen) Museen zu Berlin
WAW	Writings from the Ancient World
WO	die Welt des Orients
WZKM	Wiener Zeitschrift für die Kunde des Morgenlandes
YBC	Tablet siglum, Yale Babylonian Collection
YOS	Yale Oriental Series, Babylonian Texts
ZA	Zeitschrift für Assyriologie und Vorderasiatische Archäologie

Conventions

ar-ḫu-um e-ri-a-at	Texts in italics are Akkadian
DUMU^{meš}	Texts in capitals are Sumerograms, while small written syllables in superscript mark determinatives
ka-inim-ma ur-gi$_7$-ti-la	Texts in lowercase not in italics and expanded spacing are unilingual Sumerian passages
ku-ul si-ḫa-ra ku-ul si-ik-ra	Texts in lowercase not in italics and normal spacing denote alloglot passages
ar pa ḫa *ap-pi-*⸢*ša*⸣	When the exact reading is uncertain in Akkadian passages, signs are rendered in lowercase separately
TUK ga-ri-im-⸢ma⸣-a-ni	When the exact reading is uncertain in Sumerian passages, signs are rendered in capitals
{x}	Indicates an erasure
⸢x⸣	Indicates that there are some traces of a sign, which cannot be identified due to damage
li-ib-bi-[*k*]*i*	Square brackets are used to indicate damaged signs
[(x)]	Indicates that there is a possible place for an extra sign
[…]	Ellipsis marks a lacuna of an uncertain number of signs
I	Indicates the use of a word divider
qa$^{?}$*-mu-um*	A question mark in superscript indicates an uncertain reading
ḫi-iṣ$^{!}$(IŠ)*-ba-am*	An exclamation mark in superscript indicates erroneous use or depiction of a sign
li-iš-ku-‹un›-ka	Signs omitted by ancient scribes are indicated by angle brackets
[*a*]-⸢*na mu-uḫ*⸣*-ḫi* ‹‹ḫi››	Signs erroneously inserted by the ancient scribes, i.e., dittography, are indicated by double angle brackets

Concordances

1. Text numbers and corresponding individual texts. Texts that are not edited are marked by an asterisk (*). They are listed in the List of Excluded Texts.

№ 1	Fs. Larsen 397/399b
№ 2	BiOr 75, 15f.
№ 3	BiOr 75, 19f.
№ 4	BM 115745
№ 5	CCT 5, 50e
№ 6	CUSAS 32, 26a
№ 7	CUSAS 32, 28a
№ 8	CUSAS 32, 29c
№ 9	Fs. Larsen 397/399a
№ 10	RA 70, 135/137
№ 11	SANER 9, 77
№ 12	VS 17, 34
№ 13	YOS 11, 17
№ 14	YOS 11, 86a
№ 15	BiOr 75, 21f.
№ 16	CT 4, 8
№ 17	CUSAS 32, 7c
№ 18	CUSAS 32, 7m // CUSAS 32, 8f
№ 19	CUSAS 32, 7o // CUSAS 32, 8i
№ 20	CUSAS 32, 7p // CUSAS 32, 8j
№ 21	CUSAS 32, 8d
№ 22	CUSAS 32, 8h
№ 23	CUSAS 32, 25a
№ 24	CUSAS 32, 26c
№ 25	CUSAS 32, 30a
№ 26	CUSAS 32, 30b
№ 27	CUSAS 32, 32a
№ 28	CUSAS 32, 32b
№ 29	CUSAS 32, 32c
№ 30	Fs. de Meyer 75/83d
№ 31	JEOL 47, 58b
№ 32	OECT 11, 3
№ 33	PBS 7, 87
№ 34	VS 17, 9
№ 35	YOS 11, 11
№ 36	YOS 11, 12a

№ 37	YOS 11, 13
№ 38	UET 5, 85
№ 39	YOS 11, 14c
№ 40	AMD 14, 191b
№ 41	YOS 11, 14b
№ 42	YOS 11, 69c
№ 43	YOS 11, 16b
№ 44	YOS 11, 7
№ 45	JNES 14, 15
№ 46	YOS 11, 3
№ 47	YOS 11, 12c
№ 48	YOS 11, 29a
№ 49	CT 42, 32
№ 50	CT 44, 32(+)33t
№ 51	CUSAS 32, 7e
№ 52	CUSAS 32, 22a
№ 53	Fs. Stol 150
№ 54	JCS 9, 9
№ 55	JCS 9, 10
№ 56	RA 88, 161c
№ 57	Semitica 61, 13f.
№ 58	YOS 11, 8
№ 59	YOS 11, 9a
№ 60	YOS 11, 10
№ 61	AMD 1, 243 (fig. 1)
№ 62	AMD 1, 243 (fig. 2)a
№ 63	AMD 1, 286b
№ 64	AMD 14, 197b
№ 65	BiOr 11 Pl. II (fig. 1)
№ 66	BiOr 11 Pl. II (fig. 2)
№ 67	CUSAS 32, 29a
№ 68	CUSAS 32, 29b
№ 69	Fs. Hirsch 427
№ 70	Fs. Pope 87
№ 71	OECT 11, 4
№ 72	PIHANS 44 No. 302
№ 73	TIM 9, 73a
№ 74	VS 17, 8
№ 75	ZA 71, 62c
№ 76	Fs. de Meyer 75/83b
№ 77	CUSAS 32, 50b
№ 78	CUSAS 32, 51
№ 79	YOS 11, 5f
№ 80	YOS 11, 6
№ 81	PRAK 2 Pl. III (C1)

№ 82	YOS 11, 69d
№ 83	AMD 1, 247 (fig. 11)
№ 84	BM 97331a
№ 85	BM 97331b
№ 86	CUSAS 10, 19
№ 87	CUSAS 32, 21l
№ 88	CUSAS 32, 24a
№ 89	CUSAS 32, 24b
№ 90	CUSAS 32, 27c
№ 91	CUSAS 32, 30c
№ 92	CUSAS 32, 30d
№ 93	CUSAS 32, 49
№ 94	CUSAS 32, 50a
№ 95	Elamica 10, 65c
№ 96	RA 66, 141b
№ 97	RA 88, 161a
№ 98	Semitica 62, 15f.
№ 99	Semitica 62, 19
№ 100	YOS 11, 1
№ 101	YOS 11, 2
№ 102	YOS 11, 4b
№ 103	YOS 11, 4c
№ 104	YOS 11, 35
№ 105	AMD 1, 245 (fig. 5)
№ 106	CUSAS 32, 27a
№ 107	CUSAS 32, 48
№ 108	Fs. Wilcke 62
№ 109	OECT 15, 260
№ 110	TIM 9, 65 // TIM 9, 66a
№ 111	VS 17, 4
№ 112	YOS 11, 19b
№ 113	YOS 11, 5a
№ 114	YOS 11, 5b
№ 115	YOS 11, 41
№ 116	TIM 9, 72
№ 117	UET 6/2, 399
№ 118	ZA 75, 184
№ 119	ZA 75, 198–204h
№ 120	AoF 45, 196
№ 121	CUSAS 32, 31e
№ 122	OECT 11, 2
№ 123	RA 36, 4a
№ 124	ZA 71, 62b
№ 125	AMD 1, 273a

№ 126	CUSAS 32, 55
№ 127	CUSAS 32, 56
№ 128	CUSAS 32, 57
№ 129	TIM 9, 73b
№ 130	BM 115743
№ 131	CUSAS 10, 11
№ 132	CUSAS 32, 23b
№ 133	OECT 11, 11
№ 134	VS 17, 23
№ 135	YOS 11, 21c
№ 136	YOS 11, 87
№ 137	ZA 75, 198–204b
№ 138	ZA 75, 198–204c
№ 139	ZA 75, 198–204d
№ 140	ZA 75, 198–204e
№ 141	ZA 75, 198–204f
№ 142	ZA 75, 198–204i
№ 143	ZA 75, 198–204j
№ 144	RA 36, 3a
№ 145	YOS 11, 21b
№ 146	AMD 1, 287b
№ 147	PBS 1/2, 122
№ 148	UET 6/2, 193a
№ 149	YOS 11, 15 // YOS 11, 29b
№ 150	AoF 35, 146
№ 151	CUSAS 32, 7g // CUSAS 32, 8c
№ 152	CUSAS 32, 21f
№ 153	CUSAS 32, 31b
№ 154	CUSAS 32, 31c
№ 155	CUSAS 32, 31d
№ 156	Fs. de Meyer 86
№ 157	ZA 71, 62a
№ 158	AMD 1, 286a
№ 159	BIN 2, 72
№ 160	BIN 4, 126
№ 161	Fs. de Meyer 89
№ 162	Or. 66, 61
№ 163	TIM 9, 63d
№ 164	YOS 11, 19a
№ 165	YOS 11, 20
№ 166	YOS 11, 92
№ 167	CUSAS 32, 20d
№ 168	CT 42, 6e
№ 169	JEOL 47, 58a
№ 170	NABU 1996/30

№ 171	CUSAS 32, 58
№ 172	Fs. de Meyer 87
№ 173	YOS 11, 12d
№ 174	YOS 11, 16a // YOS 11, 77b
№ 175	YOS 11, 67a // NABU 2019/43a
№ 176	AMD 1, 243 (fig. 2)b*
№ 177	AMD 1, 247 (fig. 12)*
№ 178	CUSAS 32, 20a*
№ 179	Finkel (*forthcoming*)/a*
№ 180	Finkel (*forthcoming*)/b*
№ 181	Finkel (*forthcoming*)/c*
№ 182	TIM 9, 67a*
№ 183	TIM 9, 67b*
№ 184	YOS 11, 12b*
№ 185	YOS 11, 14a*
№ 186	YOS 11, 21a*
№ 187	YOS 11, 77a*
№ 188	ZA 75, 198–204g*

2. Individual texts in alphabetical order. Texts that are listed in the List of Excluded Texts are marked by an asterisk (*).

AMD 1, 243 (fig. 1)	№ 61
AMD 1, 243 (fig. 2)a	№ 62
AMD 1, 243 (fig. 2)b*	№ 176
AMD 1, 245 (fig. 5)	№ 105
AMD 1, 247 (fig. 11)	№ 83
AMD 1, 247 (fig. 12)*	№ 177
AMD 1, 273a	№ 125
AMD 1, 286a	№ 158
AMD 1, 286b	№ 63
AMD 1, 287b	№ 146
AMD 14, 191b	№ 40
AMD 14, 197b	№ 64
AoF 35, 146	№ 150
AoF 45, 196	№ 120
BIN 2, 72	№ 159
BIN 4, 126	№ 160
BiOr 11 Pl. II (fig. 1)	№ 65
BiOr 11 Pl. II (fig. 2)	№ 66
BiOr 75, 15f.	№ 2
BiOr 75, 19f.	№ 3
BiOr 75, 21f.	№ 15
BM 97331a	№ 84

BM 97331b	№ 85
BM 115743	№ 130
BM 115745	№ 4
CCT 5, 50e	№ 5
CT 4, 8	№ 16
CT 42, 6e	№ 168
CT 42, 32	№ 49
CT 44, 32(+)33t	№ 50
CUSAS 10, 11	№ 131
CUSAS 10, 19	№ 86
CUSAS 32, 7c	№ 17
CUSAS 32, 7e	№ 51
CUSAS 32, 7g // CUSAS 32, 8c	№ 151
CUSAS 32, 7m // CUSAS 32, 8f	№ 18
CUSAS 32, 7o // CUSAS 32, 8i	№ 19
CUSAS 32, 7p // CUSAS 32, 8j	№ 20
CUSAS 32, 8d	№ 21
CUSAS 32, 8h	№ 22
CUSAS 32, 20a*	№ 178
CUSAS 32, 20d	№ 167
CUSAS 32, 21f	№ 152
CUSAS 32, 21l	№ 87
CUSAS 32, 22a	№ 52
CUSAS 32, 23b	№ 132
CUSAS 32, 24a	№ 88
CUSAS 32, 24b	№ 89
CUSAS 32, 25a	№ 23
CUSAS 32, 26a	№ 6
CUSAS 32, 26c	№ 24
CUSAS 32, 27a	№ 106
CUSAS 32, 27c	№ 90
CUSAS 32, 28a	№ 7
CUSAS 32, 29a	№ 67
CUSAS 32, 29b	№ 68
CUSAS 32, 29c	№ 8
CUSAS 32, 30a	№ 25
CUSAS 32, 30b	№ 26
CUSAS 32, 30c	№ 91
CUSAS 32, 30d	№ 92
CUSAS 32, 31b	№ 153
CUSAS 32, 31c	№ 154
CUSAS 32, 31d	№ 155
CUSAS 32, 31e	№ 121
CUSAS 32, 32a	№ 27
CUSAS 32, 32b	№ 28

CUSAS 32, 32c	№ 29
CUSAS 32, 48	№ 107
CUSAS 32, 49	№ 93
CUSAS 32, 50a	№ 94
CUSAS 32, 50b	№ 77
CUSAS 32, 51	№ 78
CUSAS 32, 55	№ 126
CUSAS 32, 56	№ 127
CUSAS 32, 57	№ 128
CUSAS 32, 58	№ 171
Elamica 10, 65c	№ 95
Finkel (*forthcoming*)/a*	№ 179
Finkel (*forthcoming*)/b*	№ 180
Finkel (*forthcoming*)/c*	№ 181
Fs. de Meyer 75/83b	№ 76
Fs. de Meyer 75/83d	№ 30
Fs. de Meyer 86	№ 156
Fs. de Meyer 87	№ 172
Fs. de Meyer 89	№ 161
Fs. Hirsch 427	№ 69
Fs. Larsen 397/399a	№ 9
Fs. Larsen 397/399b	№ 1
Fs. Pope 87	№ 70
Fs. Stol 150	№ 53
Fs. Wilcke 62	№ 108
JCS 9, 9	№ 54
JCS 9, 10	№ 55
JEOL 47, 58a	№ 169
JEOL 47, 58b	№ 31
JNES 14, 15	№ 45
NABU 1996/30	№ 170
OECT 11, 2	№ 122
OECT 11, 3	№ 32
OECT 11, 4	№ 71
OECT 11, 11	№ 133
OECT 15, 260	№ 109
Or. 66, 61	№ 162
PBS 1/2, 122	№ 147
PBS 7, 87	№ 33
PIHANS 44 No. 302	№ 72
PRAK 2 Pl. III (C1)	№ 81
RA 36, 3a	№ 144
RA 36, 4a	№ 123
RA 66, 141b	№ 96
RA 70, 135/137	№ 10

RA 88, 161a	№ 97
RA 88, 161c	№ 56
SANER 9, 77	№ 11
Semitica 61, 13f.	№ 57
Semitica 62, 15f.	№ 98
Semitica 62, 19	№ 99
TIM 9, 63d	№ 163
TIM 9, 65 // TIM 9, 66a	№ 110
TIM 9, 67a*	№ 182
TIM 9, 67b*	№ 183
TIM 9, 72	№ 116
TIM 9, 73a	№ 73
TIM 9, 73b	№ 129
UET 5, 85	№ 38
UET 6/2, 193a	№ 148
UET 6/2, 399	№ 117
VS 17, 4	№ 111
VS 17, 8	№ 74
VS 17, 9	№ 34
VS 17, 23	№ 134
VS 17, 34	№ 12
YOS 11, 1	№ 100
YOS 11, 2	№ 101
YOS 11, 3	№ 46
YOS 11, 4b	№ 102
YOS 11, 4c	№ 103
YOS 11, 5a	№ 113
YOS 11, 5b	№ 114
YOS 11, 5f	№ 79
YOS 11, 6	№ 80
YOS 11, 7	№ 44
YOS 11, 8	№ 58
YOS 11, 9a	№ 59
YOS 11, 10	№ 60
YOS 11, 11	№ 35
YOS 11, 12a	№ 36
YOS 11, 12b*	№ 184
YOS 11, 12c	№ 47
YOS 11, 12d	№ 173
YOS 11, 13	№ 37
YOS 11, 14a*	№ 185
YOS 11, 14b	№ 41
YOS 11, 14c	№ 39
YOS 11, 15 // YOS 11, 29b	№ 149
YOS 11, 16a // YOS 11, 77b	№ 174

YOS 11, 16b	№ 43
YOS 11, 17	№ 13
YOS 11, 19a	№ 164
YOS 11, 19b	№ 112
YOS 11, 20	№ 165
YOS 11, 21a*	№ 186
YOS 11, 21b	№ 145
YOS 11, 21c	№ 135
YOS 11, 29a	№ 48
YOS 11, 35	№ 104
YOS 11, 41	№ 115
YOS 11, 67a // NABU 2019/43a	№ 175
YOS 11, 69c	№ 42
YOS 11, 69d	№ 82
YOS 11, 77a*	№ 187
YOS 11, 86a	№ 14
YOS 11, 87	№ 136
YOS 11, 92	№ 166
ZA 71, 62a	№ 157
ZA 71, 62b	№ 124
ZA 71, 62c	№ 75
ZA 75, 184	№ 118
ZA 75, 198–204b	№ 137
ZA 75, 198–204c	№ 138
ZA 75, 198–204d	№ 139
ZA 75, 198–204e	№ 140
ZA 75, 198–204f	№ 141
ZA 75, 198–204g*	№ 188
ZA 75, 198–204h	№ 119
ZA 75, 198–204i	№ 142
ZA 75, 198–204j	№ 143

3. Texts and tablet sigla in alphabetical order.

AMD 1, 243 (fig. 1)	BM 79125
AMD 1, 243 (fig. 2)	BM 79938
AMD 1, 245 (fig. 5)	CBS 7005
AMD 1, 247 (fig. 11)	FM 22878
AMD 1, 247 (fig. 12)	U.30503
AMD 1, 273	H 72
AMD 1, 286	YBC 8041
AMD 1, 287	MLC 1614
AMD 14, 191	A 663
AMD 14, 197	A 704
AoF 35, 146	Kt 94/k 520

AoF 45, 196	IM 160096
BIN 2, 72	NBC 1265
BIN 4, 126	NBC 3672
BiOr 11 Pl. II (fig. 1)	LB 1001
BiOr 11 Pl. II (fig. 2)	LB 2001
BiOr 75, 15f.	–
BiOr 75, 19f.	–
BiOr 75, 21f.	–
BM 97331	BM 97331
BM 115743	BM 115743
BM 115745	BM 115745
CCT 5, 50e	BM 113625
CT 4, 8	BM 92518
CT 42, 6	BM 15820
CT 42, 32	BM 17305
CT 44, 32(+)33	BM 78249 (+) 78253
CUSAS 10, 11	MS 2920
CUSAS 10, 19	MS 3949
CUSAS 32, 7	MS 3097
CUSAS 32, 8	MS 3085
CUSAS 32, 20	MS 3086
CUSAS 32, 21	MS 3084
CUSAS 32, 22	MS 3105/1
CUSAS 32, 23	MS 3062
CUSAS 32, 24	MS 3059
CUSAS 32, 25	MS 2780
CUSAS 32, 26	MS 3387
CUSAS 32, 27	MS 2791
CUSAS 32, 28	MS 3067
CUSAS 32, 29	MS 3082
CUSAS 32, 30	MS 3093
CUSAS 32, 31	MS 3103
CUSAS 32, 32	MS 2822
CUSAS 32, 48	MS 3070
CUSAS 32, 49	MS 3060
CUSAS 32, 50	MS 3073
CUSAS 32, 51	MS 3061
CUSAS 32, 55	MS 3388
CUSAS 32, 56	MS 3380
CUSAS 32, 57	MS 3334
CUSAS 32, 58	MS 3323
Elamica 10, 65	–
Finkel (*forthcoming*)	–
Fs. de Meyer 75/83	IM 95317
Fs. de Meyer 86	IM 90648

Fs. de Meyer 87	IM 90647
Fs. de Meyer 89	CBS 10455
Fs. Hirsch 427	Kt a/k 611
Fs. Larsen 397/399	Kt 90/k 178
Fs. Pope 87	AUAM 73.2416
Fs. Stol 150	LB 1000
Fs. Wilcke 62	Sb 12360
JCS 9, 9	Spurlock Museum 1913.14.1465
JCS 9, 10	AUAM 73.3092
JEOL 47, 58	Kt 91/k 502
JNES 14, 15	Ish-35-T.19
NABU 1996/30	Kt a/k 320
NABU 2019/43	MLC 334
OECT 11, 2	Bod AB 215
OECT 11, 3	Bod AB 214
OECT 11, 4	Bod AB 217
OECT 11, 11	Ashmolean 1932.156g
OECT 15, 260	Ashmolean 1932.382
Or. 66, 61	Kt 94/k 821
PBS 1/2, 122	CBS 332
PBS 7, 87	CBS 1690
PIHANS 44 No. 302	A 21959
PRAK 2 Pl. III (C1)	AO 10621
RA 36, 3	–
RA 36, 4	–
RA 66, 141	AO 7682
RA 70, 135/137	AUAM 73.3094
RA 88, 161	M. 15289
SANER 9, 77	Kt 94/k 429
Semitica 61, 13f.	CUNES 48–06–263
Semitica 62, 15f.	CUNES 49–02–218
Semitica 62, 19	CUNES 49–03–357
TIM 9, 63	IM 21180_x
TIM 9, 65	IM 51292
TIM 9, 66	IM 51328
TIM 9, 67	IM 21180, 21
TIM 9, 72	IM 51207
TIM 9, 73	IM 52546
UET 5, 85	U.17204C
UET 6/2, 193	–
UET 6/2, 399	U.16892D
VS 17, 4	VAT 8363
VS 17, 8	VAT 8355
VS 17, 9	VAT 2681
VS 17, 23	VAT 8354

VS 17, 34	VAT 8539
YOS 11, 1	YBC 5620
YOS 11, 2	YBC 5090
YOS 11, 3	NBC 8957
YOS 11, 4	YBC 4593
YOS 11, 5	YBC 4616
YOS 11, 6	YBC 7967
YOS 11, 7	YBC 5640
YOS 11, 8	NBC 6321
YOS 11, 9	YBC 5619
YOS 11, 10	YBC 1970
YOS 11, 11	YBC 9897
YOS 11, 12	YBC 4625
YOS 11, 13	YBC 9117
YOS 11, 14	YBC 4599
YOS 11, 15	YBC 4588
YOS 11, 16	YBC 5328
YOS 11, 17	YBC 5630
YOS 11, 19	YBC 4601
YOS 11, 20	YBC 9846
YOS 11, 21	YBC 4598
YOS 11, 29	YBC 4597
YOS 11, 35	YBC 9899
YOS 11, 41	YBC 5638
YOS 11, 67	MLC 640
YOS 11, 69	YBC 4594
YOS 11, 77	YBC 9898
YOS 11, 86	YBC 4603
YOS 11, 87	MLC 1299
YOS 11, 92	YBC 9841
ZA 71, 62	BM 122691
ZA 75, 184	Tell Asmar 1930–117
ZA 75, 198–204	IB 1554

4. Tablet sigla and texts in alphabetical order.

–	BiOr 75, 15f.
–	BiOr 75, 19f.
–	BiOr 75, 21f.
–	Elamica 10, 65
–	Finkel (*forthcoming*)
–	RA 36, 3
–	RA 36, 4
–	UET 6/2, 193
A 663	AMD 14, 191

A 704	AMD 14, 197
A 21959	PIHANS 44 No. 302
AO 7682	RA 66, 141
AO 10621	PRAK 2 Pl. III (C1)
Ashmolean 1932.156g	OECT 11, 11
Ashmolean 1932.382	OECT 15, 260
AUAM 73.2416	Fs. Pope 87
AUAM 73.3092	JCS 9, 10
AUAM 73.3094	RA 70, 135/137
BM 15820	CT 42, 6
BM 17305	CT 42, 32
BM 78249 (+) 78253	CT 44, 32(+)33
BM 79125	AMD 1, 243 (fig. 1)
BM 79938	AMD 1, 243 (fig. 2)
BM 92518	CT 4, 8
BM 97331	BM 97331
BM 113625	CCT 5, 50e
BM 115743	BM 115743
BM 115745	BM 115745
BM 122691	ZA 71, 62
Bod AB 214	OECT 11, 3
Bod AB 215	OECT 11, 2
Bod AB 217	OECT 11, 4
CBS 332	PBS 1/2, 122
CBS 1690	PBS 7, 87
CBS 7005	AMD 1, 245 (fig. 5)
CBS 10455	Fs. de Meyer 89
CUNES 48–06–263	Semitica 61, 13f.
CUNES 49–02–218	Semitica 62, 15f.
CUNES 49–03–357	Semitica 62, 19
FM 22878	AMD 1, 247 (fig. 11)
H 72	AMD 1, 273
IB 1554	ZA 75, 198–204
IM 21180$_x$	TIM 9, 63
IM 21180, 21	TIM 9, 67
IM 51207	TIM 9, 72
IM 51292	TIM 9, 65
IM 51328	TIM 9, 66
IM 52546	TIM 9, 73
IM 90647	Fs. de Meyer 87
IM 90648	Fs. de Meyer 86
IM 95317	Fs. de Meyer 75/83
IM 160096	AoF 45, 196
Ish-35-T.19	JNES 14, 15
Kt 90/k 178	Fs. Larsen 397/399

Kt 91/k 502	JEOL 47, 58
Kt 94/k 429	SANER 9, 77
Kt 94/k 520	AoF 35, 146
Kt 94/k 821	Or. 66, 61
Kt a/k 320	NABU 1996/30
Kt a/k 611	Fs. Hirsch 427
LB 1000	Fs. Stol 150
LB 1001	BiOr 11 Pl. II (fig. 1)
LB 2001	BiOr 11 Pl. II (fig. 2)
M. 15289	RA 88, 161
MLC 334	NABU 2019/43
MLC 640	YOS 11, 67
MLC 1299	YOS 11, 87
MLC 1614	AMD 1, 287
MS 2780	CUSAS 32, 25
MS 2791	CUSAS 32, 27
MS 2822	CUSAS 32, 32
MS 2920	CUSAS 10, 11
MS 3059	CUSAS 32, 24
MS 3060	CUSAS 32, 49
MS 3061	CUSAS 32, 51
MS 3062	CUSAS 32, 23
MS 3067	CUSAS 32, 28
MS 3070	CUSAS 32, 48
MS 3073	CUSAS 32, 50
MS 3082	CUSAS 32, 29
MS 3084	CUSAS 32, 21
MS 3085	CUSAS 32, 8
MS 3086	CUSAS 32, 20
MS 3093	CUSAS 32, 30
MS 3097	CUSAS 32, 7
MS 3103	CUSAS 32, 31
MS 3105/1	CUSAS 32, 22
MS 3323	CUSAS 32, 58
MS 3334	CUSAS 32, 57
MS 3380	CUSAS 32, 56
MS 3387	CUSAS 32, 26
MS 3388	CUSAS 32, 55
MS 3949	CUSAS 10, 19
NBC 1265	BIN 2, 72
NBC 3672	BIN 4, 126
NBC 6321	YOS 11, 8
NBC 8957	YOS 11, 3
Sb 12360	Fs. Wilcke 62
Spurlock Museum 1913.14.1465	JCS 9, 9

Tell Asmar 1930–117	ZA 75, 184
U.16892D	UET 6/2, 399
U.17204C	UET 5, 85
U.30503	AMD 1, 247 (fig. 12)
VAT 2681	VS 17, 9
VAT 8363	VS 17, 4
VAT 8354	VS 17, 23
VAT 8355	VS 17, 8
VAT 8539	VS 17, 34
YBC 1970	YOS 11, 10
YBC 4588	YOS 11, 15
YBC 4593	YOS 11, 4
YBC 4594	YOS 11, 69
YBC 4597	YOS 11, 29
YBC 4598	YOS 11, 21
YBC 4599	YOS 11, 14
YBC 4601	YOS 11, 19
YBC 4603	YOS 11, 86
YBC 4616	YOS 11, 5
YBC 4625	YOS 11, 12
YBC 5090	YOS 11, 2
YBC 5328	YOS 11, 16
YBC 5619	YOS 11, 9
YBC 5620	YOS 11, 1
YBC 5630	YOS 11, 17
YBC 5638	YOS 11, 41
YBC 5640	YOS 11, 7
YBC 7967	YOS 11, 6
YBC 8041	AMD 1, 286
YBC 9117	YOS 11, 13
YBC 9841	YOS 11, 92
YBC 9846	YOS 11, 20
YBC 9897	YOS 11, 11
YBC 9898	YOS 11, 77
YBC 9899	YOS 11, 35

I. Akkadian Incantations of the Early Second Millennium: An Overview

1.1 Definition of the Corpus

The definition of the corpus in this study is straightforward: it includes all Akkadian incantations from the OB and OA periods.[2] Indeed, all Akkadian incantations known to us (some of which unpublished), whose date of composition falls within this timeframe, were collected.[3] Some texts, notably bilingual or alloglot texts,[4] required serious deliberation. YOS 11, 67a // NABU 2019/43a (№ 175), e.g., counts an even number of lines in Sumerian and in Akkadian. It was included in AML. Contrariwise, the Sumerian spells CUSAS 32, 7f and 8b (George 2016, 105) contain Akkadian phrases, but these are fixed formulae ("N.N. son of N.N. whose god is N.N."), not free Akkadian sentences.[5] These incantations were excluded from the corpus. A borderline case was YOS 11, 41. Most of it is in Elamite, but it nonetheless contains one non-formulaic Akkadian line which tipped the scales in favour of its inclusion in AML.[6]

---

2 Contrary to many other Mesopotamian genres, incantations are generically self-referential, namely they contain typical subscripts and/or rubrics which designate them as incantions (ka-inim-ma, (tu$_6$-) én-é-nu-ru or *šiptum*, see below § 1.4.5). These paratextual comments refer to the verbal part of the magical act, the *dicenda*. In some cases, the *what-to-do* section, the *agenda,* follows the magical words. This part, too, often has a paratextual tagging *kikkiṭṭaša/kikkittaša* (KÌD.KÌD.BI and variants). Against the common usage, we chose to call this part **procedure**, thus distinguishing it from **ritual**. The reasons for this decision are set out in Wasserman 2020c and will not be described here in full. Suffice to say that a **ritual** is a cyclical religious practice, with a fixed scheme of action which carries deep religious meaning for the individual and the community. By contrast, a **procedure** is a technical series of steps meant to achieve a specified external result. In other words, a procedure is an instrumental process which can be replaced by another, more efficient one, whereas the meaning of a ritual and its cultural value are inherent to it. The *what-to-do* sections in second millennium BCE incantations are succinct technical instructions aimed at alleviating a client's suffering; they do not carry intrinsic religious meaning. Their instrumental character is clear and therefore they ought to be called **procedures**.

3 OB texts which comprise only procedures, without spells, are not part of the corpus. Such are, e.g., BM 79022 (Wasserman 2010) which contains three Sumerian incantations with Akkadian procedures, or LB 1002 (Wasserman 2020c) an Akkadian procedure followed by an Elamite incantation. We were also careful to separate incantations from therapeutic or diagnostic texts (such as, e.g., YOS 11, 28 // YOS 11, 29: 8–11, see Krebernik 2018, 38). The latter are also not included in the present work.

4 The present corpus contains 4 bilingual incantations, i.e., CT 4, 8 (№ 16), PBS 1/2, 122 (№ 147), PRAK 2 Pl. III (C1) (№ 81), and RA 70, 135/137 (№ 10). Alloglot spells are otherwise commonly referred to as 'abracadabra'-incantations, see Veldhuis 1999, 46–48; Schwemer 2014, 266. For a recent study of alloglot incantations, see Krebernik 2018.

5 Another case excluded from the present corpus is CUSAS 32, 30f, a syllabic Sumerian incantation appended with an Akkadian legitimation formula.

6 Non-Akkadian incantations with Akkadian subscript, such as RA 36, 2 – a Hurrian incantation with an Akkadian subscript – were not included in the corpus.

Another matter was chronology. We decided at the outset not to deal with third millennium incantations. Thus, incantations from Ebla (Krebernik 1984), as well as Old Akkadian incantations, and even Ur III Akkadian spells,[7] were excluded from this study. OA incantations from Kaneš were clear-cut, but some OB texts were included after deliberation. A case in point is AMD 1, 243 (fig. 1) (№ 61) which appears to be Late Babylonian (perhaps a copy of an OB incantation). YOS 11, 15 // YOS 11, 29b (№ 149) may also be post-OB. In questionable cases, we preferred to include the texts, even if it meant deviating from our definition of the corpus.

The main issue with our corpus is not such unavoidable loose ends, but its exclusive focus on Akkadian texts and exclusion of unilingual Sumerian incantations. Limiting the corpus to Akkadian (or bilingual) incantations prevents us from a comprehensive explication of the system of magic texts of the period. In the first half of the second millennium BCE, Akkadian and Sumerian incantaions were not separate corpora but complementary. Our rationale for the restriction was practical; namely our belief that dealing in addition with Sumerian incantations was too large and complex a project.

Texts that are broken or whose Akkadian is beyond understanding (as, e.g., TIM 9, 67a and TIM 9, 67b) were not presented in edition and translation, but were mentioned in the List of Excluded Texts at the end of this volume, which amounts to 13 texts.

As of summer 2021, this study amounted to 188 incantations.[8] Quantitively speaking, incantations are the most prolific genre in the entire OB (and probably also in the lesser known OA) literary system, so it is likely that new texts will be found in museums, private collections and as a result of future archaeological excavations.[9]

1.2 Thematic Division of the Corpus

In order to gain a panoramic view of OB and OA Akkadian incantations, a thematic analysis was deemed necessary. To this end, we have divided the corpus into five main categories, according to the cause of trouble or concern: (I) Specific Diseases and Medical Problems, (II) Animals, (III) Humans, (IV) Supernatural Entities, and (V) Inanimate Objects. Incantations whose category was hard to discern were collected under (VI) Miscellaneous.

We further divided each category into sub-groups. When possible, this sub-division was based on the ancient designations (e.g., ka-inim-ma munus ù-tu-da-kam "incantation for a woman giving birth", ka-inim-ma ^{d}*Lamaštu* "incantation (against) Lamaštu", or *šiptum ša īn*[*im*] "incantation (against the Evil) Eye"). In cases where these subscripts were not preserved, or were absent in the original, we made a necessarily subjective designation. Incantations with typical phrases and key-words, such as incantations against snakes, scorpions, dogs, or for a woman in labour, were easy to classify. But in other cases, it was not easy to determine to which group a given text belonged, especially when the language

7 A possible Ur III period Akkadian incantation is the unpublished NBC 11470 (against *liʾbum*).

8 We count incantations, i.e., compositions, not tablets. Note further, that we refer to duplicate texts as one. In the corpus, we have 8 incantations in the corpus, which – fully or partially – duplicate each other (CUSAS 32, 7m // CUSAS 32, 8f; CUSAS 32, 7o // CUSAS 32, 8i; CUSAS 32, 7p // CUSAS 32, 8j; TIM 9, 65 // TIM 9, 66a; YOS 11, 15 // YOS 11, 29b; CUSAS 32, 7g // CUSAS 32, 8c).

9 About twenty years ago, Wasserman 2003, 176 catalogued 128 incantations.

was allegoric, using a wide array of images – many times unparalleled or unique. One such case is the OA incantation JEOL 47, 58a (№ 169), which speaks of *diqārum* "(brewing) pot". Similar vessels, esp. *namzītum*, are known to stand metaphorically for a diseased or bloated belly. We hesitated whether to classify this text under Gastrointestinal Problems. After lengthy discussions we decided to place the text in the small group of incantations for Foods and Drinks. On the other hand, the "she-goat" in Fs. Larsen 397/399b (№ 1) was taken as a metaphor for bile. We would not be surprised if scholars in the future deem it necessary to alter our thematic classification.

According to our division, the largest thematic category is § 2.1 Specific Diseases (59 incantations). Then comes § 2.2 Animals (52 incantations), § 2.3 Humans (34 incantations),[10] § 2.4 Supernatural Entities (18 incantations), § 2.6 Miscellaneous (5 incantations)[11] and § 2.5 Inanimate Objects (4 incantations). The largest sub-groups in the corpus are § 2.1.4 Gastrointestinal Problems (22 incantations) and § 2.2.6 Scorpions (22 incantations), § 2.2.1 Dogs (15 incantations), § 2.3.4 Love and Sexual Atttraction (14 incantations) and § 2.1.2 Childbirth (13 incantations).

1.3 Geographical Setting and Archaeological Context

The geographical distribution of incantations whose provenance is known is as following:

Southern Mesopotamia: Larsa and Larsa area (> 50), Isin (9),[12] Ur (4), Adab (2)[13]
Central Mesopotamia: Sippar (7), Kiš (3), Tell Duweihes (3),[14] Nippur (2), Lagaba (1[?])
The Diyala region: Šaduppûm (5), Ešnunna (2), Nērebtum (2), Mēturan (1)
Upper Mesopotamia: Kaneš (11), Mari (4)
Periphery of Mesopotamia: Susa (1)

This list, accidental to a large extent,[15] covers the principal Mesopotamian urban centres in the first half of the second millennium. This wide geographical distribution bolsters the unsurprising notion that incantations were common and that their production and use were not restricted to a specific area or social setting.

10 Plus 3 texts in the List of Excluded Texts.
11 Plus 11 texts in the List of Excluded Texts.
12 On a single tablet.
13 On a single tablet.
14 On a single tablet.
15 Many of the incantations in the corpus arrive from the antiquity market and are therefore unprovenanced. So is the large, over forty-strong, group of incantations published in CUSAS 32, see George 2016, 29. As for BM 115743 (№ 130) and BM 115745 (№ 4), both tablets were bought simultaneously by the British Museum in 1923 from I Élias Géjou; BM 97331 (№ 84–85) was acquired by the British Museum in 1902 from A.P. Samhiry and F.A. Shamash.

1.3.1 Southern Mesopotamia

Larsa (mod. Tell as-Senkereh)

It is important to note the large number of texts stemming from southern Mesopotamia, in particular Larsa and its vicinity. This arises from the fact that all the texts published in YOS 11 (44 Akkadian incantations)[16] were considered to come from the area of Larsa (see van Dijk/Goetze/Hussey 1985, 2f.). If this is indeed the case, then Larsa can be regarded as an important hub for the production of magic texts. One might go so far as to suggest that this activity took place at the Enki temple in Larsa, for "The Enki temple was not only the depository of archives but also the central library of the city in the period of independence under Rīm-Sîn and under the Babylonian domination [….].[17] This large library contained literary compositions, liturgical poetry, incantation charms, divinatory handbooks, penitential prayers, and mathematical texts" (Goodnick Westenholz/Westenholz 2006, 7f.).

This premise is supported by YOS 11, 21, which is a collective tablet ending with a colophon mentioning the names of two people who probably commissioned the tablet, one of which is Balāye (Balmunamḫe), descendant of the well-documented Larsian administrator also called Balmunamḫe of the Enki temple.[18]

Isin (mod. Ishan-baḥriyat)

A rather unique archaeological context is found for ZA 75, 198–204 (№ 119, 137–143, 188) from Isin. This tablet was deliberately cut and broken in antiquity and subsequently buried in a jar and placed in the corner of a residential wall (see Wilcke 1985, 187–191 with Hrouda 1987, Pl. 6), which reflects the use of this tablet in an actual magic context, see § 1.4.3.

Ur (mod. Tell el-Muqayyar)

Three incantation tablets were recorded to have been found at No. 1 Broad Street, which are most likely UET 6/2, 193a, UET 6/2, 399 and AMD 1, 247 (fig. 12) (№ 148, 117 and 177 respectively).[19] This house was simultaneously a school run by a priest called Igmil-Sîn.[20]

UET 5, 85 (№ 38) was found in a domestic context at no. 4 Store Street in the AH-district.[21]

16 To this group one should add CUSAS 32, 28a (№ 7) (see George 2016, 47), Semitica 62, 15f. (№ 98) and Semitica 62, 19f. (№ 99) (see Guichard 2020a), which are probably also from the Larsa area.

17 That a temple for Enki existed in Larsa was suggested by Dyckhoff 1999. No archaeological evidence for its existence exists, however. Wagensonner 2019a, 51 raised the idea that the name of Qīšti-Ea, a scribe known to be active in Larsa, whose name appears on different scholarly tablets, could offer further support for Dyckhoff's hypothesis.

18 A structural study of the archive of Balmunamḫe was provided in the unpublished dissertation of Dyckhoff 1999. For a discussion of the figure of Balmunamḫe, see van de Mieroop 1987 and Veenhof 2005, XIX (with additional literature).

19 Following Charpin 2020.

20 Woolley 1976, 136f. For an overview and study of the curricular tablets, see recently Delnero 2019, 179–186.

21 Woolley 1976, 248.

Adab (mod. Tell Bismiya)
Excavations by The Oriental Institute of the University of Chicago at Tell Bismiya during 1903–1905 yielded two OB incantation collectives: AMD 14, 191 and AMD 14, 197 (№ 40 and 64 respectively), both without an exact findspot.[22]

1.3.2 Central Mesopotamia

Sippar (mod. Tell Abu Ḥabbah)
The incantation tablets Fs. de Meyer 75/83 (№ 30 and 76), Fs. de Meyer 86 (№ 156) and Fs. de Meyer 87 (№ 172) were found in a private domestic house (room 115, stratum IV below layer I) together with a lexical bird list IM 90646 (Black/Al-Rawi 1987) and a small trade-archive belonging to Ipiq-Išḫara and his wife Nīši-inīšu (Cavigneaux 1994, 73 fn. 2). This lot has a rather early date, around the reign of Sîn-muballiṭ (1812-1793 BCE).[23] It is noteworthy that the incantations are said to have been found with the remains of two persons.[24]

PBS 7, 87 (№ 33), previously misunderstood as a letter, is said to come from Sippar (Ungnad 1920, 5). Although their exact provenance remains unknown, CT 4, 8 and CT 44, 32 (+) 33 (№ 16 and 50, respectively) are also thought to come from Sippar.[25]

An interesting uninscribed magic object from OB Sippar is the magic figurine published by Gasche 1994, 97–101 (see § 1.5.5).

Kiš (mod. Tell el-Uhaymir & Tell Ingharra)
PRAK 2 Pl. III (C1) (№ 81), a bilingual incantation against a goat was found in Tell el-Uhaymir during de Genouillac's survey in 1912. AMD 1, 247 (fig. 11) (№ 83) was discovered during the first season of the joint expedition of The Field Museum-Oxford in 1923 – both unfortunately without a recorded findspot.

OECT 11, 11 (№ 133), a love incantation, was found in Tell Ingharra, the ancient Ḫursagkalama complex in Kiš, in trench C-15 among various OB scribal exercises.[26]

---

22 See Lauinger 2012, 176f. and Farber 2018, 189, on earlier observations by Gelb, who states that it cannot be excluded that A 663 may have been purchased by Banks in Iraq, not excavated at Tell Bismiya.

23 Based on textual evidence, see Charpin 2005, 157f.

24 Al-Rawi/Dalley 2000, 6.

25 Both tablets belong to the group Bu 88-5-12, which was purchased by E.A.T Wallis Budge during his expedition to Iraq in 1887–1888, the majority of which is known to have come from Sippar (see Leichty/Finkelstein/Walker 1988, xiv–xvii).

26 Ohgama/Robson 2010, 222.

Nippur (mod. Nuffar)

AMD 1, 245 (fig. 5) and Fs. de Meyer 89 (№ 105 and 161) are recorded as coming from Nippur, but without an exact findspot.

Tell Duweihes

The provenance of ZA 71, 62 (№ 75, 124, 157) is registered at the British Museum as Tell Duweihes, an otherwise unknown site, said to be located near Nippur.[27]

Lagaba

As noted by Böhl (1954, 81), both square tablets with spells against dogs, i.e., BiOr 11 Pl. II (fig. 1) (LB 1001) (№ 65) and BiOr 11 Pl. II (fig. 2) (LB 2001) (№ 66), were bought by him from the same dealer in Baghdad together with administrative documents from Larsa and Lagaba. Both incantation texts are thus thought to be from the same origin.

1.3.3 The Diyala Region

Šaduppûm (mod. Tell Ḫarmal)

Van Dijk (1976) states in his catalogue that TIM 9, 65 and TIM 9, 66 (№ 110), TIM 9, 72 (№ 116) and TIM 9, 73 (№ 73 and 129) stem from Šaduppûm. No excavation reports are known.

Ešnunna (mod. Tell Asmar)

During the excavations conducted by The Oriental Institute of the University of Chicago in 1930, a single magic text, ZA 75, 184 (№ 118), an incantation against anger, was found on the surface ground (Whiting 1985, 179 with exact coordinates).[28]

Based on palaeographic and orthographic analysis, von Soden (1954, 338) tentatively suggested that BIN 2, 72 (№ 159), a single incantation tablet against Lamaštu, may also come from Ešnunna.

Nērebtum (mod. Ishchali)

Among the texts excavated at Nērebtum by the Chicago Expedition, two incantation tablets were found: JNES 14, 15, an incantation against styes and PIHANS 44 No. 302, against a dog (№ 45 and 72, respectively). Both tablets are reported to have been found in proximity to the temple complexes. JNES 14, 15 near the small Šamaš Temple (5V31)[29] and PIHANS 44 No. 302 from the Kititum Temple Archive (6S29).[30]

---

27 See Cunningham 1997, 99 fn. 4. Farber 1981, 61 argues for a South Babylonian orthography.

28 For the peculiarities of this tablet, see § 1.4.4.

29 Landsberger/Jacobsen 1955, 15.

30 Greengus 1979, 57 with deJong-Ellis 1986, 768 fn. 56. A suggestion was raised that a *šangû*-priest was the chief administrator of this archive which was dated to the reigns of Dannum-taḫaz, Daduša and Ibâl-pi-el II (deJong-Ellis 1986, 765 and Greengus 1979, 14–22).

Mēturan (mod. Tell Haddad)
All magic texts, including the sole Akkadian incantation AMD 1, 273a (№ 125) that were excavated in Mēturan, come from Area II 'Unit B' rooms 10 and 30. They were found together with private documents of Bēlšunu, son of Lu-Lisina (room 10), and one Zimri-Addu (room 30), residents of this building. The relation between these two gentlemen is unknown. The fact that a large group of Sumerian literary texts was found in the same building suggests that it was used for educational as well as practical purposes (Cavigneaux 1999, 256–258).

1.3.4 Upper Mesopotamia

Kaneš (mod. Kültepe)
All incantation texts coming from Kaneš, for which an archaeological provenience is known, are found in private commercial archives belonging to Assyrian merchants (Barjamovic 2015, fig. 5).

The amulet Or. 66, 61 (№ 162), an incantation against Lamaštu, was found in the archive of a merchant, Šalim-Aššur, son of Issu-arik. SANER 9, 77, an incantation aiding childbirth and AoF 35, 146, against the Evil Eye (№ 11 and 150), were probably found in the archive of Irma-Aššur, son of Nide-pani. Fs. Larsen 397/399, containing incantations for an easy childbirth and against bile (№ 9 and 1), comes from the archive belonging to Šumi-Abiya, son of Puzur-Ištar. JEOL 47, 58 (Kt 91/k 502) containing incantations against gastrointestinal problems and for the preparation of food (№ 169 and 31) comes from the same house as the archive of the trader Elamma, son of Iddin-Suen.

More intriguing are Fs. Hirsch 427, against a dog (№ 69), and NABU 1996/30, for the consecration of a reed (№ 170), which are found in the house of Uzua in the context of commercial archive and, more importantly, a group of educational texts (Barjamovic 2015, 65–68), see § 1.4.3.

Mari (mod. Tell Ḫariri)
Among the many thousands of tablets discovered in the palace archives in Mari, only six incantation tablets were found. It is noteworthy that Hurrian, not Akkadian, appears to be the dominant language of magic here. The texts first published by Thureau-Dangin (1939) are stated to come from 'salle 108' of the Mari palace. RA 36, 1; RA 26, 2 and RA 36, 5 are Hurrian single incantation tablets, of which not much can be said except that RA 36, 1 contains a Hurrian version of the famous tooth worm incantation.[31] Both RA 36, 3a, against a rival in a trial (№ 144) and RA 36, 4a, an incantation to help a baby with ear ache (№ 123), contain a Hurrian spell on the reverse.[32]

31 Already Thureau-Dangin 1939, 1–5. A recent edition was provided by Campbell/Fischer 2018.

32 Although this is a known format for bilingual texts from the second millennium (Zomer 2018a, 126 fn. 443), it appears that the Hurrian is not a translation of the Akkadian. For a recent edition of the Hurrian incantations RA 36, 3b and RA 36, 4b, see Krebernik 2018, 36. Note that the duplicate of RA 36, 4b is described as *šipat gergiššim* "incantation against the *gergiššu* (skin) disease" (Krebernik 2001, no. 379).

Another magic tablet from Mari was published by Cavigneaux (1994). It contains, besides an unidentified alloglot (most likely Hurrian) incantation (RA 88, 161b), two Akkadian spells: RA 88, 161a (№ 97), against scorpions, and RA 88, 161c (№ 56), against various diseases. This tablet is reported to have been found among administrative documents in 'salle R (= 52)' of the palace.[33]

1.3.5 Periphery of Mesopotamia

Susa (mod. Shush)

Fs. Wilcke 62 (№ 108), a snake incantation, is registered in the Louvre as stemming from Susa.

1.4 Physical Properties of Tablets Containing Incantations

1.4.1 Classification of Tablets

The present corpus amounts to a total of 134 tablets containing 196 incantations (188 taking duplicates in account). In order to investigate the use of incantations, it is imperative to determine their compositional organization on the tablets in which they occur.

Single-Incantation Tablets

Tablets that contain a single incantation (with or without accompanying procedures), coined here **single-incantation tablets**, and the present corpus contains 72 such tablets. Notably, in 16 (ca. 20%) the reverse is left uninscribed. This, in our opinion, may suggest that these tablets were prepared for a specific aim and for a specific client, see § 1.4.3.

Table 1: Single-Incantation Tablets

Tablet	**Subject**
AMD 1, 243 (fig. 1)	Dogs
AMD 1, 245 (fig. 5)	Snakes
AoF 35, 146	Evil Eye
AoF 45, 196	Baby
BIN 2, 72	Lamaštu
BIN 4, 126	Lamaštu
BiOr 11 Pl. II (fig. 1)	Dogs
BiOr 11 Pl. II (fig. 2)	Dogs
BiOr 75, 15f.	Childbirth
BiOr 75, 19f.	Childbirth
BiOr 75, 21f.	Child Disease
BM 115743	Love
CCT 5, 50e	Childbirth
CT 4, 8	Gastrointestinal
CT 42, 32	Various Diseases
CUSAS 10, 11	Love
CUSAS 10, 19	Scorpions
CUSAS 32, 48	Snakes

33 Cavigneaux 1994, 155 fn. 1.

Tablet	Subject
CUSAS 32, 49	Scorpions
CUSAS 32, 51	Flies/Bees
CUSAS 32, 55	Empowerment
CUSAS 32, 56	Empowerment
CUSAS 32, 57	Empowerment
CUSAS 32, 58	Miscellaneous
Fs. de Meyer 86	Evil Eye
Fs. de Meyer 87	Miscellaneous
Fs. de Meyer 89	Lamaštu
Fs. Hirsch 427	Dogs
Fs. Pope 87	Dogs
Fs. Stol 150	Various Diseases
Fs. Wilcke 62	Snakes
JCS 9, 9	Various Diseases
JCS 9, 10	Various Diseases
JNES 14, 15	Stye
NABU 1996/30	Reed
OECT 11, 2	Baby
OECT 11, 3	Gastrointestinal
OECT 11, 4	Dogs
OECT 15, 260	Snakes
Or. 66, 61	Lamaštu
PBS 1/2, 122	Witchcraft
PRAK 2 Pl. III (C1)	Goat
RA 70, 135/137	Childbirth
SANER 9, 77	Childbirth
Semitica 61, 13f.	Various Diseases
Semitica 62, 15f.	Scorpions
Semitica 62, 19	Scorpions
TIM 9, 65	Snakes
TIM 9, 72	Anger
UET 5, 85	Jaundice
UET 6/2, 399	Anger
VS 17, 4	Snakes
VS 17, 8	Dogs
VS 17, 9	Gastrointestinal
VS 17, 23	Love
VS 17, 34	Childbirth
YOS 11, 1	Scorpions
YOS 11, 2	Scorpions
YOS 11, 3	Worms/Leeches
YOS 11, 6	Flies/Bees
YOS 11, 7	Pox
YOS 11, 8	Various Diseases
YOS 11, 10	Various Diseases
YOS 11, 11	Gastrointestinal
YOS 11, 13	Gastrointestinal
YOS 11, 15	Witchcraft
YOS 11, 17	Childbirth
YOS 11, 20	Lamaštu
YOS 11, 35	Scorpions
YOS 11, 41	Worms/Leeches
YOS 11, 87	Love
YOS 11, 92	Wardat-lilî

Incantation Collectives

Alternatively, different incantations can be found on one tablet. We call these tablets **incantation collectives**, of which 55 are found in the present corpus. Even tablets which contain two separate incantations, as, e.g., AMD 1, 286a (№ 158) and AMD 1, 286b (№ 63) are considered by us as collectives.[34]

Incantation collectives may have a shared theme, e.g., TIM 9, 73 (№ 73 and 129) (Lamaštu); TIM 9, 66 (№ 110) (snakes/scorpions); YOS 11, 69 (№ 42 and 82) (agricultural). Some collectives may occasionally contain incantations with procedures ending with a positive prognosis, i.e., "he will be well" designated with *baliṭ* (AMD 1, 286) or *iballuṭ* (Elamica 10, 65, YOS 11, 29 and YOS 11, 67 // NABU 2019/4), reminiscent of therapeutic and diagnostic texts.[35] But other times, the logic behind the grouping of the different incantations eludes us.

Collectives may be unilingual Akkadian (or Sumerian), bilingual Akkadian-Sumerian, or alloglot incantations (as YOS 11, 4 where Elamite and Akkadian incantations are found together).[36]

Cognisant of the process of serialization of material dealing with magic that began during the second half of the second millennium BCE, and accelerated during the first millennium, we were keen to see whether OB incantation collectives were precursors of later canonical series of incantations. We do not have a clear answer. Whereas some incantation collectives from the MB, or MA period can be shown to be forerunners to later standardized series, as, e.g., Udugḫul and Lamaštu (Zomer 2018a, 7), only one such case could perhaps be found in the present corpus: Finkel (*forthcoming*) (№ 179–181), which presents three non-canonical forerunners to first-millennium Egalkura incantations. We thus conclude that the commencement of first millennium serialization took place later than our corpus, in post-OB times.[37]

Table 2: Incantation Collectives

Tablet	Subject
AMD 1, 243 (fig.2)	Dogs/ Miscellaneous
AMD 1, 273	Empowerment/Evil Tongue
AMD 1, 286	Lamaštu/Dogs
AMD 1, 287	Lamaštu/Witchcraft
AMD 14, 191	Miscellaneous /Maškadu
AMD 14, 197	Miscellaneous /Dogs
BM 97331	Scorpions
Finkel (*forthcoming*)	Egalkura

34 As long as it is not proven that the Hurrian incantations on RA 36, 3 and RA 36, 4 are translations of the Akkadian, both tablets are regarded as containing two incantations and considered incantation collectives.

35 The obverse of YOS 11, 29 contains medical prescriptions. It should be stressed that other Akkadian medical texts from the OB period do not contain full-blown incantations (BAM 393; CUSAS 32, 72; CUSAS 32, 73; Iraq 55, 104; YOS 11, 25; YOS 11, 26; YOS 11, 27). Note that YOS 11, 28 contains an *in extenso* alloglot incantation. For MB/MA incantations in therapeutic texts, see Zomer 2018a, 10f.

36 E.g., CT 42, 6; CUSAS 32, 20; Fs. de Meyer 75/83; YOS 11, 5.

37 This statement does not refer to OB collectives of unilingual *Sumerian* incantations. These were not studied in the present volume.

Tablet	**Subject**
CT 42, 6	Miscellaneous /Foods & Drinks
CT 44, 32(+)33	zi – pà /Various Diseases
CUSAS 32, 7	Travel/Gastrointestinal/Dogs/Evil Eye/Bile
CUSAS 32, 8	Dogs/Evil Eye/Gastrointestinal/ Miscellaneous
CUSAS 32, 20	Miscellaneous/Snakes/Scorpions/Bitumen
CUSAS 32, 21	Witchcraft/Childbirth/Evil Eye/Snakes/Scorpions
CUSAS 32, 22	Various Diseases/Miscellaneous /Lamaštu
CUSAS 32, 23	Bones/Love/Miscellaneous
CUSAS 32, 24	Scorpions/Miscellaneous
CUSAS 32, 25	Gastrointestinal/Snakes
CUSAS 32, 26	Childbirth/Miscellaneous/Gastrointestinal
CUSAS 32, 27	Snakes/Bones/Scorpions
CUSAS 32, 28	Childbirth/Miscellaneous/Lamaštu
CUSAS 32, 29	Dogs/Childbirth
CUSAS 32, 30	Gastrointestinal/Scorpions/Miscellaneous/Bones
CUSAS 32, 31	Evil Eye/Baby (Crying)
CUSAS 32, 32	Gastrointestinal
CUSAS 32, 50	Scorpions/Bees
Elamica 10, 65	Scorpions
Fs. de Meyer 75/83	Dead Deity/Fish/Dog/Gastrointestinal
Fs. Larsen 397/399	Childbirth/Bile
JEOL 47, 58	Food/Gastrointestinal
NABU 2019/43	Miscellaneous
RA 36, 3	Trial/Miscellaneous
RA 36, 4	Baby/*gergiššu* condition
RA 66, 141	Miscellaneous/Scorpions
RA 88, 161	Scorpions/ Miscellaneous/Various Diseases
TIM 9, 63	Lamaštu
TIM 9, 66	Snakes/Scorpions
TIM 9, 67	Snakes or Scorpions?/Miscellaneous
TIM 9, 73	Dogs/Empowerment
UET 6/2, 193	Witchcraft/Snakes and Scorpions?
YOS 11, 4	Scorpions
YOS 11, 5	Worms/Bees
YOS 11, 9	Various Diseases/Samānu
YOS 11, 12	Gastrointestinal/Miscellaneous /Tooth
YOS 11, 14	Miscellaneous/Maškadu/Jaundice
YOS 11, 16	Miscellaneous/Orthopaedic Problems
YOS 11, 19	Lamaštu/Snakes
YOS 11, 21	Miscellaneous/Trial/Love
YOS 11, 29	Tooth/Witchcraft
YOS 11, 67	Miscellaneous
YOS 11, 69	Agricultural
YOS 11, 77	Miscellaneous
YOS 11, 86	Childbirth/Lamaštu
ZA 71, 62	Evil Eye/Baby (Crying)/Dogs
ZA 75, 198–204	Anger/Love/Miscellaneous

Incantations and Mathematical Texts

A unique case is BM 115745 (№ 4), which combines an incantation for an easy birth with a mathematical text, and is most likely a student exercise (see § 1.4.3).

Table 3: Incantations and Mathematical Texts

Tablet	Subject
BM 115745	Childbirth

Uncertain Classification

Six tablets in the corpus are so fragmentary that their compositional organization remains unclear.

Table 4: Uncertain Classification

Tablet	Subject
AMD 1, 247 (fig. 11)	Scorpions
AMD 1, 247 (fig. 12)	Miscellaneous
OECT 11, 11	Love
PBS 7, 87	Gastrointestinal
PIHANS 44 No. 302	Dogs
ZA 75, 174	Anger

1.4.2 Format of Tablets

Following Wasserman (2014a, 52), the corpus of incantations can be divided according to the format of tablets. Those tablets whose length: width ratio falls beween 1 and 2, are designated **portrait-oriented tablets**; those tablets having a ratio of ≥ 2 are classified **elongated tablets**; tablets with a ratio of < 1 are regarded as **landscape-oriented tablets**; and those having a ratio of ca. 1 are considered **square tablets**. Rarely, amulet-like incantations may be shaped with a "handle", hereby called ***tabula ansata***.

This division, in turn, can be further differentiated between single- and multi-column tablets. The importance of the physical difference in format is that it might indicate the way a given tablet was used, i.e., did it serve curricular purposes, was it a work of reference, or was it used in a private context (see Wasserman 2014a; Zomer 2018a, 14–25).[38]

Based on the above analysis, Wasserman (2014a, 56) postulated that small, especially square and landscape-oriented tablets, generally without procedures, were most likely fabricated for private magic use (e.g., VS 17, 4 = № 111, VS 17, 8 = № 74, and VS 17, 23 = № 134). This theory was examined by Zomer (2018a, 79), yielding similar results for the MB/MA corpus. Support for this notion comes from a much later period. Finkel (2000, 146), showed that Babylonian scribes of the Achaemenid period used different formats for tablets of different genres. Texts belonging to *asûtu* (therapeutic texts) were usually portrait-oriented, while tablets belonging to *āšipūtu* (exorcistic texts), tended to be written on landscape-oriented tablets.

The present corpus holds in total **134** individual tablets: **80** portrait-oriented tablets, **10** elongated tablets, **31** landscape-oriented tablets, **8** square tablets and **1** *tabula ansata*. The format of **4** fragmentary tablets cannot be determined.

---

38 Similar approaches have been conducted for other genres in cuneiform literature, e.g., Gesche 2001, 44–51; Robson 2008, 99f.

Portrait-Oriented Tablets

Of the **80** portrait-oriented tablets, **73** tablets are single-column.[39]

Table 5: Portrait-Oriented Tablets

Tablet	Classification	Subject	Measurements l × w cm
AMD 1, 273	Inc. collective	Empowerment/Evil tongue	–
AMD 1, 286	Inc. collective	Lamaštu/Dogs	5.2 × 3.8
AMD 1, 287	Inc. collective	Lamaštu/Witchcraft	7.8 × 4.8
AMD 14, 191	Inc. collective	Miscellaneous/Maškadu	10.1 × 6.7
AMD 14, 197	Inc. collective	Miscellaneous/Dogs	7.3 × 5.2
AoF 35, 146	Single inc.	Evil Eye	–
AoF 45, 196	Single inc.	Baby	10.4 × 5.1
BIN 2, 72	Single inc.	Lamaštu	6.7 × 4.5
BiOr 75, 15f.	Single inc.	Childbirth	5.8 × 3.9
BM 115743	Single inc.	Love	6.6 × 4.7
BM 115745	Inc./Math.	Childbirth	7.62 × 5.0
CCT 5, 50e	Single inc.	Childbirth	–
CT 4, 8	Single inc.	Gastrointestinal	9.5 ×5.4
CT 42, 6	Inc. collective	Miscellaneous/Foods & Drinks	10.9 × 9.1
CT 44, 32(+)33	Inc. collective	zi – pà /Various diseases	–
CUSAS 32, 7	Inc. collective	Travel/Gastrointestinal/Dogs/Evil Eye/Bile	25.0 × 24.0
CUSAS 32, 8	Inc. collective	Dogs/Evil Eye/ Gastrointestinal/Miscellaneous	16.5 × 9.3
CUSAS 10, 11	Single inc.	Love	9.5 × 5.4
CUSAS 32, 20	Inc. collective	Miscellaneous/Snakes/Scorpions/Bitumen	15.5 × 6.5
CUSAS 32, 21	Inc. collective	Witchcraft/Childbirth/Evil Eye/Snakes/Scorpions	18.5 × 9.5
CUSAS 32, 22	Inc. collective	Various Diseases/Miscellaneous/Lamaštu	15.0 × 13.0
CUSAS 32, 24	Inc. collective	Scorpions	5.7 × 4.5
CUSAS 32, 25	Inc. collective	Gastrointestinal/Snakes	6.8 × 4.9
CUSAS 32, 27	Inc. collective	Snakes/Bones/Scorpions	15.0 × 7.0
CUSAS 32, 28	Inc. collective	Childbirth/Miscellaneous/Lamaštu	9.8 × 5.0
CUSAS 32, 29	Inc. collective	Dogs/Childbirth	18.5 × 7.5
CUSAS 32, 30	Inc. collective	Gastrointestinal/Scorpions/Miscellaneous/Bones	13.5 × 12.0
CUSAS 32, 31	Inc. collective	Evil Eye/Baby (Crying)	12.5 × 11.5
CUSAS 32, 32	Inc. collective	Gastrointestinal	10.0 × 6.0
CUSAS 32, 49	Single inc.	Scorpions	7.5 × 4.4
CUSAS 32, 51	Single inc.	Flies/Bees	7.8 × 4.3
Elamica 10, 65	Inc. collective	Scorpions	9.4 × 6.1
Finkel (*forthcoming*)	Inc. collective	Egalkura	–
Fs. de Meyer 75/83	Inc. collective	Dead Deity/Fish/Dog/Gastrointestinal	–
Fs. de Meyer 86	Single inc.	Evil Eye	–
Fs. de Meyer 89	Single inc.	Lamaštu	–
Fs. Larsen 397/399	Inc. collective	Childbirth/Bile	5.3 × 4.2
Fs. Pope 87	Single inc.	Dogs	–
JCS 9, 9	Single inc.	Various Diseases	8.5 × 4.5
JNES 14, 15	Single inc.	Stye	–
OECT 11, 2	Single inc.	Baby	7.7 × 5.3

39 With the exception of CT 42, 6; CUSAS 32, 7; CUSAS 32, 8; CUSAS 32, 22; CUSAS 32, 30 and CUSAS 32, 31, which are incantation collectives and multi-column. Note that presently, IB 1554 (see ZA 75, 198–204), the famous tablet of love incantations from Isin, has a ratio of ≥ 2, but originally it had at least three columns since it was purposely broken in antiquity (Wilcke 1985, 90). Its original ratio is estimated to correspond with that of a portrait-oriented tablet.

Tablet	Classification	Subject	Measurements l × w cm
OECT 11, 3	Single inc.	Gastrointestinal	7.7 × 4.8
OECT 11, 4	Single inc.	Dogs	7.0 × 4.6
OECT 11, 11	Uncertain	Love	5.7 × 4.8
OECT 15, 260	Single inc.	Snakes	9.4 × 5.1
PRAK 2 Pl. III (C1)	Single inc.	Goat	13.2 × 7.36
PIHANS 44 No. 302	Single inc.	Dogs	3.8 × 5.6
RA 36, 3	Inc. collective	Trial/Miscellaneous	7.0 × 5.5
RA 36, 4	Inc. collective	Baby/*gergiššu* condition	9.0 × 4.8
RA 66, 141	Inc. collective	Miscellaneous/Scorpions	7.5 × 4.4
RA 88, 161	Inc. collective	Scorpions/Miscellaneous/Various Diseases	–
SANER 9, 77	Single inc.	Childbirth	–
Semitica 62, 15f.	Single inc.	Scorpions	–
Semitica 62, 19	Single inc.	Scorpions	–
TIM 9, 63	Inc. collective	Lamaštu	10.5 × 7.0
TIM 9, 66	Inc. collective	Snakes/Scorpions	8.5 × 5.0
TIM 9, 67	Inc. collective	Snakes or Scorpions?/Miscellaneous	10.0 × 7.0
TIM 9, 72	Single inc.	Anger	6.5 × 4.0
TIM 9, 73	Inc. collective	Dogs/Empowerment	6.5 × 5.0
UET 5, 85	Single Inc.	Jaundice	4.6 × 3.4
UET 6/2, 193	Inc. collective	Witchcraft/Snakes and Scorpions?	7.7 × 6.5
UET 6/2, 399	Single inc.	Anger	7.0 × 4.6
YOS 11, 1	Single inc.	Scorpions	5.4 × 4.4
YOS 11, 2	Single inc.	Scorpions	6.6 × 5.4
YOS 11, 3	Single inc.	Worms/Leeches	7.1 × 5.2
YOS 11, 4	Inc. collective	Scorpions	8.7 × 5.5
YOS 11, 6	Single inc.	Flies/Bees	6.4 × 4.5
YOS 11, 7	Single inc.	Pox	7.9 × 4.9
YOS 11, 10	Single inc.	Various Diseases	7.9 × 4.9
YOS 11, 11	Single inc.	Gastrointestinal	6.4 × 4.6
YOS 11, 12	Inc. collective	Gastrointestinal/Miscellaneous/Tooth	17.2 × 7.6
YOS 11, 16	Inc. collective	Miscellaneous/Orthopedic Problems	6.8 × 5.3
YOS 11, 19	Inc. collective	Lamaštu/Snakes	11.6 × 6.3
YOS 11, 21	Inc. collective	Miscellaneous/Trial/Love	10.4 × 6.7
YOS 11, 29	Inc. collective	Tooth/Witchcraft	9.3 × 7.9
YOS 11, 69	Inc. collective	Agricultural	9.0 × 5.0
YOS 11, 77	Inc. collective	Miscellaneous	7.5 × 5.0
YOS 11, 87	Single inc.	Love	9.5 × 5.5
ZA 71, 62	Inc. collective	Evil Eye/Baby (Crying)/Dogs	8.9 × 6.4
ZA 75, 198–204	Inc. collective	Anger/Love/Miscellaneous	25.5 × 8.0

Elongated Tablets

10 tablets in the present corpus are elongated in form, the majority of which (7) are single-incantation tablets.

Table 6: Elongated Tablets

Tablet	Classification	Subject	Measurements l × w cm
AMD 1, 247 (fig.12)	Uncertain	Miscellaneous	10.3 × 4.7
CUSAS 32, 23	Inc. collective	Bones/Love/Miscellaneous	12.0 × 4.5
CUSAS 32, 48	Single inc.	Snakes	9.0 × 4.4

Tablet	Classification	Subject	Measurements l × w cm
Fs. Stol 150	Single inc.	Various Diseases	–
JCS 9, 10	Single inc.	Various Diseases	12.8 × 6.2
PBS 1/2, 122	Single inc.	Witchcraft	15.9 × 7.2
RA 70, 135/137	Single inc.	Childbirth	–
Semitica 61, 13f.	Single inc.	Various Diseases	–
YOS 11, 86	Inc. collective	Childbirth/Lamaštu	13.5 × 5.5
YOS 11, 92	Single inc.	Wardat-lilî	11.0 × 5.0

Landscape-Oriented Tablets

31 tablets in the corpus are landscape oriented, the majority of which (22) are single-incantation tablets. [40]

Table 7: Landscape-Oriented Tablets

Tablet	Classification	Subject	Measurements l × w cm
AMD 1, 243 (fig.2)	Inc. collective	Dogs/Miscellaneous	4.7 × 5.7
AMD 1, 245 (fig. 5)	Single inc.	Snakes	–
BM 97331	Inc. collective	Scorpions	5.1 × 6.6
BiOr 75, 21f.	Single inc.	Childhood Disease	4.2 × 6.0
CT 42, 32	Single inc.	Various Diseases	6.6 × 8.1
CUSAS 10, 19	Single inc.	Scorpions	3.5 × 5.3
CUSAS 32, 50	Inc. collective	Scorpions/Bees	4.9 × 5.8
CUSAS 32, 55	Single inc.	Empowerment	7.2 × 10.0
CUSAS 32, 56	Single inc.	Empowerment	6.6 × 11.0
CUSAS 32, 57	Single inc.	Empowerment	5.5 × 10.0
CUSAS 32, 58	Single inc.	Miscellaneous	7.2 × 8.0
Fs. Wilcke 62	Single inc.	Snakes	–
NABU 1996/30	Single inc.	Reed	3.0 × 4.0
NABU 2019/43	Inc. collective	Miscellaneous	5.43 × 6.6
TIM 9, 65	Single inc.	Snakes	5.7 × 8.0
VS 17, 4	Single inc.	Snakes	4.0 × 6.0
VS 17, 8	Single inc.	Dogs	3.7 × 5.0
VS 17, 9	Single inc.	Gastrointestinal	5.5 × 7.5
VS 17, 23	Single inc.	Love	5.0 × 7.0
VS 17, 34	Single inc.	Childbirth	5.0 × 7.0
YOS 11, 5	Inc. collective	Worms/Bees	7.6 × 8.3
YOS 11, 8	Single inc.	Various Diseases	6.8 × 8.7
YOS 11, 9	Inc. collective	Various Diseases/Samānu	5.5 × 7.0
YOS 11, 13	Single inc.	Gastrointestinal	3.5 × 4.6
YOS 11, 14	Inc. collective	Miscellaneous/Maškadu/Jaundice	7.5 × 10.6
YOS 11, 15	Single inc.	Witchcraft	6.2 × 7.7
YOS 11, 17	Single inc.	Childbirth	4.1 × 6.4
YOS 11, 20	Single inc.	Lamaštu	5.2 × 7.3
YOS 11, 35	Single inc.	Scorpions	4.5 × 6.4
YOS 11, 41	Single inc.	Worms	4.0 × 6.0

40 The reverse of NABU 2019/43 is arranged in columns and the orientation of the reverse differs 180 degrees from the obverse. Note that different orientations on both sides of one tablet is known for Kassite scribal exercises, see Bartelmus 2016, 23–36 (with previous literature). This format may suggest that the tablet was a scribal exercise.

Tablet	Classification	Subject	Measurements l × w cm
YOS 11, 67	Inc. collective	Miscellaneous	5.53 × 8.31

Square Tablets

Following Wasserman (2014a, 56), square tablets with incantations are prime candidates to be considered private magic texts, i.e., tablets prepared for, and handed over, to a client by the expert in magic, see § 1.4.3. In the present corpus, we find 8 square tablets (4 of which are concerned with dogs).[41] As for the findspots of the square tablets, it is noteworthy that BIN 4, 126 (№ 160); Fs. Hirsch 427 (№ 69) and JEOL 47, 58 (№ 31 and 169) all come from private merchant archives in Kaneš.[42]

Table 8: Square Tablets

Tablet	Classification	Subject	Measurements l × w cm
AMD 1, 243 (fig.1)	Single inc.	Dogs	4.6 × 4.7
BIN 4, 126	Single inc.	Lamaštu	–
BiOr 11 Pl. II (fig.1)	Single inc.	Dogs	3.0 × 3.0
BiOr 11 Pl. II (fig.2)	Single inc.	Dogs	2.9 × 3.1
BiOr 75, 19f.	Single inc.	Childbirth	4.0 × 4.5
Fs. de Meyer 87	Single inc.	Miscellaneous	–
Fs. Hirsch 427	Single inc.	Dogs	5.0 × 5.0
JEOL 47, 58	Inc. collective	Food/Gastrointestinal	4.8 × 4.8

Tabula Ansata

Tabula ansata, also known as T-shaped, or amulet-shaped tablets (i.e., tablets with a "handle"), are well-known from later periods of Mesopotomia (see Heeßel 2014; Panayotov 2018). They can be made out of clay, stone, or metal and are not restricted to the genre of incantations.[43] Almost all magic *tabulae ansatae* are directed against the demoness Lamaštu and they frequently carry visual depictions of the demoness on the obverse, and a spell on the reverse.[44] *Tabula ansata* served as apotropaic texts and could have been worn around the neck, or hung in a domestic context (see § 1.4.3).

As for the present corpus, only one example can be found: Or. 66, 61 from Kaneš, an almost square clay tablet with a spell against Lamaštu (no drawing).

41 Only one MB/MA incantation on a square tablet is known, see Zomer 2018a, 16. Note the therapeutic text CUSAS 32, 72 (without incantation) which is also square (George 2016, 164f.).

42 See Barjamovic 2015, 69.

43 For Late Bronze Age examples of *tabulae ansatae* of other genres, see Zomer 2018a, 20 fn. 53.

44 Exceptions can be found in the two Sumerian exorcistic amulets (not T-shaped) against any evil, published by Lambert 1976 in Iraq 38 fig. 2 and fig. 3. For an overview of Lamaštu amulets from the Bronze Age, see Zomer 2018a, 22f.

Table 9: Tabula Ansata

Tablet	Classification	Subject	Measurements l × w cm
Or. 66, 61	Single inc.	Lamaštu	5.3 × 5.0

Tablets of Uncertain Format

The format of 4 tablets in the present corpus cannot be determined. A case in point is CUSAS 32, 26. As described by George (2016, 46), this tablet "has been cut down from a piece from the middle of a multi-column tablet and backed with new clay in order to make a squarish, bun-like tablet attractive to the antiquities market".

Table 10: Tablets of Uncertain Format

Tablet	Classification	Subject	Measurements l × w cm
AMD 1, 247 (fig. 11)	Uncertain	Scorpions	–
CUSAS 32, 26	Inc. collective	Childbirth/Miscellaneous /Gastrointestinal	5.7 × 5.2
PBS 7, 87	Uncertain	Gastrointestinal	–
ZA 75, 174	Uncertain	Anger	–

1.4.3 Use of Tablets

Private Magic Texts

Commissioning of magic texts for private clients was no doubt common in antiquity. However, this practice left little trace in second millennium Mesopotamia, so much so that it remains almost impossible to determine which tablets were made for private use. One may assume that amulet-shaped tablets (*tabulae ansatae*), which could be hung around the neck or in a domestic context, were prepared for private use. In our corpus, one such case exists (Or. 66, 61 = № 162). But what about regular tablets? Some indications for a private use can be suggested, first and foremost by the archaeological context of a given tablet, notably if it was found in a domestic setting, in foundation deposits, or in a burial context (see Zomer 2018a, 78f.).[45] Secondly, tablets in particular formats are more likely to have been produced for private use (Wasserman 2014a). Finally, in rare cases, the name of the client, or the individual against whom the magic text was commissioned, is indicated on the tablet, vouching that the tablet was specifically used by the named person or against him. Such is the famous incantation collective from Isin ZA 75, 198–204 (IB 1554). It contains a variety of incantations concerned with aggressive magic, trying to gain control over a person – in amorous relations, or in a legal trial. The tablet was purposely broken in antiquity;[46] one piece was placed in a jar and buried in the corner of a residential wall.[47] Earlier scholars argued that the breaking of the tablet was meant to nullify its effects (Wilcke 1985, 191; Hecker 2008, 67), but, with Mertens-Wagschal (2018, 164), we believe that the opposite is true,

45 A possible magical use of the Susa Funerary Texts was suggested by Wasserman 2019.

46 Another tablet that was purposely broken, but in modern times, is CUSAS 32, 26 (see above).

47 See Wilcke 1985, 188.

namely that the breaking and burying of the tablet was part of the magic procedure which accompanied recitation of the spell. An interesting aspect of the Isin tablet is that most of its incantations are written from the perspective of an unidentified jealous woman.[48] Two of her male victims are indicated by name: Erra-bāni and Iddin-Damu. The latter is described as having a 'big-mouth' and being 'curly-eared', making this magic text even more personal.[49]

As for the tablets' formats, Wasserman (2014a, 56) has argued that second millennium private magic texts are ideally small single-incantation, square or landscape-oriented tablets, generally without procedural instructions. This hypothesis can now be examined. Let us turn first to the lot of magic texts with the clearest archaeological context, namely the incantations found in the private archive of the Assyrian merchant from Kaneš (see Barjamovic 2015). It contained square tablets (BIN 4, 126 = № 160; Fs. Hirsch 427 = № 69; JEOL 47, 58 = № 31 and 169), as well as the sole example of *tabula ansata* (Or. 66, 61 = № 162), and one landscape-oriented tablet (NABU 1996/30 = № 170). Except for the incantation collective JEOL 47, 58, all texts are single-incantation tablets. As for the landscape-oriented tablets in the corpus, 23 out of 32 are single-incantation tablets, agreeing with the above hypothesis.

An especially interesting sub-group of incantations is that of CUSAS 32, 55 (№ 126); CUSAS 32, 56 (№ 127) and CUSAS 32, 57 (№ 128), all landscape-oriented, single-incantation tablets. Thematically they are entwined with motifs of mythical self-legitimation, containing conspicuous alloglot passages. The private function of one of them is confirmed by an explicit dedication to the clients – Sîn-iddinam, and his unnamed wife (CUSAS 32, 56: 15–16 = № 127): "Living and life in the house of lordship, I am the *very best*! (For) the life of Sîn-iddinam and the life of [his] wi[fe]".

Although there is enough evidence to corroborate our view that privately used incantations are typically small, single-incantation tablets, one can point to some incantation collectives which probably functioned as private magic texts: JEOL 47, 58 from Kaneš, the tablet of love incantations from Isin (see above), and YOS 11, 21, whose colophon presents the commissioners of the text (see § 1.4.5).

A different aspect which should be considered here concerns the relatively large group of portrait- and landscape-oriented tablets whose reverse is largely left uninscribed (**19** in number, see Table 11 below).[50] In our opinion, these one-sided tablets were prepared in advance, to be used *ad hoc*, with texts that were at times too short for the tablet. The writers of these client-oriented texts did not bother to prevent further writing on the back of these tablets, a fact which may hint that they were delivered to illiterate clients. Only in one case (YOS 11, 17 = № 13), a large X-sign is drawn on the uninscribed reverse (see § 1.4.4).

Another group of tablets that we assume were written for private clients are those written clumsily, in a crude script, such as the landscape tablets CUSAS 10, 19 (№ 86) and YOS 11, 20 (№ 165) and the square tablet PIHANS 44 No. 302 (№ 72).[51] These gauchely written texts were probably written by the healers themselves whose scribal proficiency was limited.

---

48 Wilcke 1985, 200 has interpreted the subscript of ZA 75, 198–204e (№ 140) to contain the name of a jealous priestess called Eṭirtum. This interpretation was rejected by Scurlock 1989–90.

49 See Wasserman 2016, 24.

50 See Wasserman 2014a, 55 fn. 24 and Wilhelm 2019, 1182.

51 Cf. also BM 115745 (№ 4) which could be the product of a student.

Table 11: Tablets with (Largely) Uninscribed Reverse

Publication	Format	Classification	Subject	Measurements l × w cm
AoF 45, 196	Portrait	Single inc.	Baby	10.4 × 5.1
BiOr 75, 15f.	Portrait	Single inc.	Childbirth	4.0 × 4.5
BM 115743	Portrait	Single inc.	Love	6.6 × 4.7
CUSAS 10, 11	Portrait	Single inc.	Love	9.5 × 5.4
CUSAS 32, 29	Portrait	Inc. collective	Dogs/Childbirth	8.9 × 6.4
CUSAS 32, 51	Portrait	Single inc.	Flies/Bees	7.8 × 4.3
Fs. Wilcke 62	Landscape	Single inc.	Snakes	–
OECT 11, 3	Portrait	Single inc.	Gastrointestinal	7.7 × 4.8
Semitica 62, 19	Portrait	Single inc.	Scorpions	–
VS 17, 4	Landscape	Single inc.	Snakes	4.0 × 6.0
VS 17, 8	Landscape	Single inc.	Dog	3.7 × 5.0
VS 17, 9	Landscape	Single inc.	Gastrointestinal	5.5 × 7.5
VS 17, 23	Landscape	Single inc.	Love	5.0 × 7.0
YOS 11, 7	Portrait	Single inc.	Pox	7.9 × 4.9
YOS 11, 11	Portrait	Single inc.	Gastrointestinal	6.4 × 4.6
YOS 11, 17	Landscape	Single inc.	Childbirth	4.1 × 6.4
YOS 11, 19	Portrait	Inc. collective	Lamaštu/Snakes	11.6 × 6.3
YOS 11, 41	Landscape	Single inc.	Worms/Leeches	4.0 × 6.0
YOS 11, 92	Portrait	Single inc.	Wardat-lilî	11.0 × 5.0

The statement that private magic texts are generally unanccompanied by procedural instructions seems also to be correct. Noteworthy exceptions are AMD 1, 243 (fig. 1) (№ 61), YOS 11, 15 (№ 149) and YOS 11, 35 (№ 104), the first being a square tablet, and the other two landscape-oriented tablets. Interestingly, YOS 11, 15 is duplicated in the incantation collective YOS 11, 29b (№ 149), a fact supporting our idea that private magic texts could be excerpted from reference texts (see below).

Magic Texts as Reference Works

When attending to his patient, the magic expert could consult a master text which collected different recitations and procedural *agenda* suitable for specific cases (Wasserman 2014a, 59, after Gager 1992). These master texts were mostly, we believe, incantation collectives which reflect the intention of grouping some incantations purposefully. These text collectives could have had their origins in a curricular context, but without definitive archaeological provenance, this possiblity is hard to prove (cf. Zomer 2018a, 82). That incantations could have been written by a magic expert, who at the same time was a scribe with students, is demonstrated by Bēlšunu, son of Lu-lisina and Zimri-Addu from ancient Mēturan. In the house of these two gentlemen, several incantations (all Sumerian, except for the Akkadian AMD 1, 273a = № 125) were found, together with a variety of other literary texts (Cavigneaux 1999), see § 1.3.4.

Those incantation collectives with a clear common theme are easier to define as reference works, e.g., TIM 9, 73 (Lamaštu); TIM 9, 66 (snakes/scorpions); YOS 11, 69 (agricultural). In many cases, however, the principle behind the organization of these collective texts eludes the modern scholar.

The idea that private magic texts could be copied from a master text was recently proven by Finkel (2018). Based on evidence from the first millennium BCE, Finkel has shown that incantations inscribed on amulets had their counterparts in incantation collectives accompanied by instructions on how to produce these amulets. In our corpus, two similar cases are found. The snake incantation TIM 9, 65 (№ 110) and the anti-witchcraft incantation YOS 11, 15 (№ 149) are both small landscape single-incantation tablets which may qualify as private magic texts. Both are duplicated in incantation collectives: the former in TIM 9, 66 (snakes and scorpions), the latter in YOS 11, 29 (various diseases).[52]

Magic Texts in a Curricular Context

How did one become a healer? How was one trained, what tests did one have to take before being recognized as a magician? Who were the teachers or mentors who ordained them? These questions remain hidden from us – not only because of insufficient documentation, but, more likely, because these processes were mostly oral. But not entirely so. One text, CUSAS 32, 54 allows a rare peek into the education of an OB magic expert – or, rather, of scribes schooled in writing magic texts. The text, written in crude but clear signs on a small landscape-format tablet (4.0 × 5.4 × 2.3 cm), resembles various short incantations in the corpus (see Table 7, above). Yet unlike other single-text incantation tablets, this bilingual text – Sumerian on the obverse; Akkadian on the reverse – does not result in a consistent incantation.[53] Moreover, although the two sides of the tablet do not contain different texts, the Akkadian is not a direct translation of the Sumerian: it offers an exegetical interpretation of it (see commentary in George 2016, 159–160). As George (ibid) concludes: "the Akkadian would be the teacher's oral explanations, noted down by an apprentice".

Besides this exceptional curricular text, some incantations in the corpus are probably student texts.[54] BM 115745 (№ 4) is a portrait-oriented tablet on whose reverse an incantation for difficult labour is found. Its obverse contains a mathematical text. With its numerous mistakes and crude handwriting, this is likely a school product. TIM 9, 67 (№ 182–183) is another badly written incantation (against reptiles[?]). Its reverse contains another text, probably not an incantation, and may be a scribal exercise as well.[55] Different writing directions on the obverse and reverse suggest that this is a scribal exercise.[56] Besides BM 115745, just mentioned, NABU 2019/43 (№ 175) also shows this 90° shift in writing direction. The use of the correction gloss kúr in CUSAS 32, 58: 4 (№ 171) suggests that this tablet belongs to a school context.

As observed in § 1.3, the following incantations were found in an educational context: UET 6/2, 193a (№ 148), UET 6/2, 399 (№ 117) and AMD 1, 247 (fig. 12) (№ 177), which

52 The obverse of YOS 11, 29 contains four medical prescriptions: against *miqtum* (epilepsy), *urbatum* disease, *baskiltum* (rectal disease), and a malaise attacking the head. Its reverse contains two incantations with procedures against toothache and against witchcraft.

53 The text goes as follows: a-gu$_{10}$ šub-ú / zi-pàd-dè / nam-giš-{ras.}-pàd sikil-la / tu-ra íb-zi-zi-dè // ⌜*mu*⌝-*ú-a ra-bu-tum* / [*p*]*a-at-tu-ú na-pi-iš-ti* / *bu-ur-ti el-le-tum* / *mu-na-*⌜*sí-ḫa-at mu-ur*⌝*-ṣi* (Sum.:) "Throw my water! Take an oath! The pure invocation will disperse the diseases"; (Akk.:) "My massive water – a bucket of life; My pure cistern – the disperser of diseases" (George 2016, 159 differently).

54 On Sumerian incantations being part of the curriculum in OB schools (as OECT 5, 55, a lentil-shaped tablet with a Sumerian Lamaštu incantation), see Michalowski 1978, 345.

55 A similar example from the MB period is Emar 737. It contains an incantation concerned with gastrointestinal ailments followed by a lexical list, see Zomer 2018a, 12/83.

56 For Kassite scribal exercises displaying this phenomenon, see Bartelmus 2016, 23–36.

come from the school of Igmil-Sîn in Ur, and OECT 11, 11 (№ 133), that was found together with scribal exercises.

As for OA incantations, let us note that Fs. Hirsch 427 (№ 69) and NABU 1996/30 (№ 170) come from the house of Uzua, where besides a commercial archive, a group of educational texts were found (Barjamovic 2015, 65–68).[57] A similar case is depicted in the archive of Ipiq-Išḫara from Sippar, where incantations and a lexical list of birds are found together with monetary documents. The fact that we find in both groups examples for square- (Fs. Hirsch 427 and Fs. de Meyer 87) and landscape-oriented tablets (NABU 1996/30) suggests that these texts are private magic texts, see § 1.4.3

Magic Texts as Palimpsests

In the present corpus, we find three cases of incantations written on re-used tablets: BiOr 75, 15f. (№ 2), BM 115745 (№ 4), CUSAS 32, 24 (№ 88–89) and ZA 75, 198–204 (№ 119, 137–143, 188).[58]

57 On the question of Uzua's house being a school, see Hecker 1993, 281. An important observation that needs to be made regarding OA incantations is that although they are written in the Assyrian dialect, their orthography shows some peculiarities. The use of the sign LA_1 instead of LA_2 is very rare in OA (Kryszat 2015, 112), but is attested in 5 out of the 10 incantation tablets from Kaneš (CCT 5, 50e; SANER 9, 77; JEOL 47, 58; AoF 35, 146 and BIN 4, 126). As argued by Kryszat 2015, 112, LA_1 is rather archaic, similar to the use of, e.g., BI/BE_2 instead of BE, TI instead of DÍ and AB instead of AB_2. Such signs are likely to be used in Kaneš by those who received a thorough education in Assur (or even in southern centres), as the letter of Sueyya, son of Pušukēn (Larsen 1976, 305 fn. 47).

58 For BiOr 75, 15f. and BM 115745 as re-used tablets, see Wasserman 2018, 15 fn. 2. For ZA 75, 198–204, see Wilcke 1985, 190.

1.4.4 Drawings on Tablets

Contrary to the magic praxis in first millennium AD Mesopotamia, where drawings are common in incantation bowls (Vilozny 2017), it is very rare to find any drawing in our corpus.[59] Only one such case stands out: YOS 11, 17 (№ 13) a small landscape-oriented tablet whose uninscribed reverse contains a large X-sign. The meaning of this clumsily incised X is unclear: a geometric diagram enhancing the power of the written incantation, or to eradicate blank space and prevent further writing.[60]

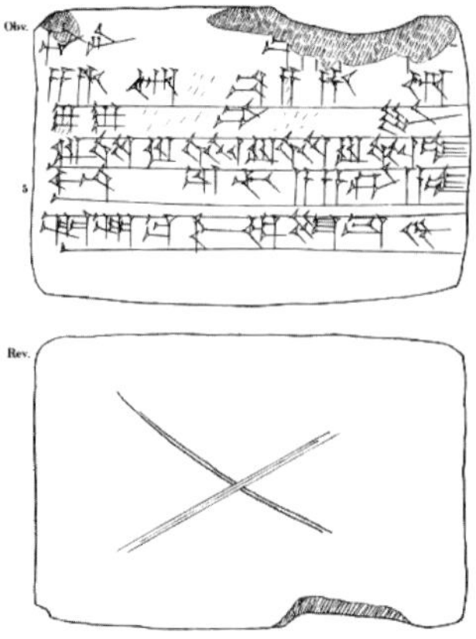

Original copy of YOS 11, 17

Another text that ought to be mentioned here is ZA 75, 184 (№ 118). As its publisher notes, its back "is smooth and shows marks of a cloth. In addition, it shows traces of two parallel vertical wedges and two converging oblique wedges arranged to form the stylized representation of the neck and snout of an animal as in the contemporary ANŠE or AZ signs....". It probably was not intended to be a drawing, since, "apparently two lumps of previously used clay had been pressed together to make the tablet, and when the tablet broke, it separated into two original pieces" (Whiting 1985, 179–180).

1.4.5 Paratextual Comments

Ancient Mesopotamian scribes often classified incantations with self-referential designations.[61] Many of these textual markers, here named rubrics, are variants of tu$_{6}$-én-é-nu-ru. They are mostly found at the start or at the end of the incantation. Additionally, a subscript such as ka-inim-ma, *šipat* ... or *šiptum ša* ... or simply *ša* ... is commonly found below the incantation, denoting its specific function. A different kind of rubric could be used to indicate accompanying procedures – usually following the incantation. This is marked by *kikkittaša/kikkiṭṭaša*(KÌD.KÌD.BI/DÙ.DÙ.BI). Finally, tablets can be concluded with colophons containing additional editorial and personal references.

---

59 On drawings on cuneiform tablets in general, see Finkel 2011. For additional examples of drawings on medico-magic tablets from the first millennium, see Zilberg/Horowitz 2016 and Arbøll 2019.

60 These diagrams are quite rare in Mesopotamian incantations. Another OB example can be found in the Sumerian incantation collective YOS 11, 66. A MB tablet with the St. Andrews cross is found in Iraq 54 Pl. XIV (see Zomer 2018a, 26). More on this, see Reiner 1960, 151f.; Maul 1994, 175–181; Wasserman 1994, 54; Wasserman 2014a, 54f.

61 In addition to rubrics and subscripts, we find similar self-referential designations in the spells themselves, e.g., *luddikum šiptam ṭāridat kala murṣê* "May I cast on you a spell driving out all diseases" (CT 42, 32: 1 = № 49), or *sikkūr awâtum dīnum tûm* "The words – the lock! The incantation – the verdict!" (Semitica 62, 15f.: 19–20 = № 98). Note the contrast between the 'spell of life' (e.g., *liddikum Ea šipat balāṭim* "May Ea cast on you (m.) a spell of life" in Fs. Stol 150: 1 № 53) and the 'spell of death' (e.g., *ina šiptim serram niṣabbat u zaqīqībam sipat mūtim* "We seize the snake with a (simple) spell, but the scorpion – (with) a spell of death!" (Semitica 62, 15f.: 5–6 = № 98)).

Rubrics

(tu₆-)én-é-nu-ru

The use of this rubric goes back to the earliest incantations from the Early Dynastic period, from Fāra and Ebla, where it appears in various orthographic variations.[62] Starting in the OB period, the rubric is normalized to tu₆-én-é-nu-ru, and could be further abbreviated as én-é-nu-ru. The strongly abbreviated version én (common in later periods)[63] is found once in the present corpus (YOS 11, 29a: 19 = № 48).[64]

As in later periods, this rubric can appear with phonetic variants, e.g., en-ne-nu-ri (YOS 11, 12a: 15 = № 36), te-e!-en-nu!-ri-e (AMD 1, 287b: r. 9 = № 146), tu-⸢ú-e-ni⸣-in-nu-ri (AMD 1, 286a: 4 = № 158).[65]

Contrary to post-OB texts, where this rubric (and its variants) can be found in initial and/or final position (Zomer 2018a, 28–31), our corpus uses this designation mainly in final position with the exception of YOS 11, 29a: 19 (№ 48) and YOS 11, 20: 13a–b (№ 165), where the rubric hold simultaneously the initial and final position.[66]

Interestingly, this rubric is also attested outside of the textual body of incantations. In a recently published OB literary letter from the area of Larsa, a certain Nūr-Kūbī wrote to his dead ancestors, asking them to help him in his grave illness. The letter cites briefly a Sumerian incantation, ending with this paratextual comment, spelled tu₁₁-én-⸢ru⸣uru (Guichard 2020b, 153: 13).

KÌD.KÌD.BI /DÙ.DÙ.BI

Incantations with accompanying procedures can be introduced with a rubric, generally rendered KÌD.KÌD.BI.[67] In later periods, this rubric only occurs logographically,[68] but in the present corpus we find several examples for Akkadian *kikkittaša*/*kikkiṭṭaša*.[69] In fact, KÌD.KÌD.BI is found only once (CUSAS 32, 29c: 30 = № 8), otherwise it is found with its phonetic variants: KI.KI.BI (YOS 11, 67a // NABU 2019/43a: 7 = № 175), and KIN.KIN.BI

62 Krebernik 1984, 197–207.
63 Zomer 2018a, 27.
64 én here is MIN+AN, not the common ŠÚ+AN. For similar variants of én, see Zomer 2018a, 28.
65 For this rubric in MB and MA incantations, see Zomer 2018a, 28.
66 Other exceptions in the present corpus are AMD 14, 191b (№ 40), where the rubric appears in penultimate position (l. 14); AMD 1, 243 (fig. 1) (№ 61), where the rubric is used twice. See further CUSAS 32, 7m // CUSAS 32, 8f (№ 18), where the rubric appears *in medias res* (l. 5) and again in final position (l. 10).
67 Not all procedures are introduced with an individual rubric: AMD 1, 243 (fig. 1) (№ 61), CT 4, 8 (№ 16), CUSAS 32, 29a (№ 67), CUSAS 32, 29c (№ 8), RA 66, 141b (№ 96), YOS 11, 9a (№ 59), YOS 11, 12c (№ 47), YOS 11, 15 (№ 149), and YOS 11, 35 (№ 104). In ZA 75, 198–204b (№ 137) procedural instructions are inserted within the incantation, separated by a single horizontal ruling. In RA 66, 141, the instructions directly follow the spell, on the reverse.
68 See Zomer 2018a, 31f.
69 *ki-ik-ki-ta-ša* (YOS 11, 4b: 20 = № 102), [*k*]*i*!-*i*[*k*!]-*ki-ta-ša* (YOS 11, 14c: 12 = № 39), *ki-ki-ṭa-ša* (AMD 1, 286a: 6 = № 158), *ki-ki-ṭa-ša* AMD 1, 286b: 13 = № 63) and *ki-ik-ki-it-tum* (CUSAS 32, 8d: ii 10' = № 21).

(YOS 11, 21a: 10 = № 186). The rubric DÙ.DÙ.BI is quite rare in the second millennium and occurs only once in the present corpus, i.e., CUSAS 32, 30c: i 24 = № 91).[70]

Subscripts

A different kind of self-referential designation of incantations is the use of a subscript, usually introduced by ka-inim-ma[71] "incantation" (lit. "saying") followed by a designation explaining the purpose of the preceeding incantation.[72] Contrary to the incantations of the first millennium, those of the second millennium display additional possibilities besides ka-inim-ma to denote a subscript, introduced by *šipat*... *šiptum ša* ... and simply *ša* ...[73] Unique for this corpus is the apparent use of *awāt* ... as a subscript (see below).

Akkadian subscripts can occur after Sumerian and alloglot incantations; these, as already mentioned, are not included in the present discussion.[74]

ka-inim-ma

The most common subscript is ka-inim-ma, which is written throughout with very little orthographic variation.[75] Whereas in post-OB texts subscripts with ka-inim-ma are usually separated from the incantation by a ruling, this is not yet consistent in the present corpus.[76]

Some texts show atypical use of this subscript. VS 17, 8 (№ 74) terminates with three ka-inim-ma subscripts, and in CUSAS 32, 29a (№ 67), the ka-inim-ma subscript is repeated *after* the procedure. The most intriguing case perhaps is YOS 11, 92 (№ 166), where the subscript is rather a hyperscript, i.e., at the very start of the incantation.

Commonly, a designation in Sumerian follows the Sumerian subscript ka-inim-ma, but there are cases in the present corpus with a (partial) Akkadian designation, e.g., ka-inim-ma *alpum*(GU_4) *immerum*(UDU.NÍTA) *em-ru-um*! (CUSAS 32, 8d: ii 9' = № 21).

šipat ...

In eleven cases, the subscript consists of the construct state of *šiptum*, i.e., *šipat* "incantation (against/of) ...".[77] In post-OB texts, only one case of this subscript is known so far: KBo 1,

---

70 The other two examples known for the MB/MA corpus are BAM 4: 10' and LAOS 9, 227 (VAT 13226: 17), see Zomer 2018a, 32. According to Maul 2009, there is no apparent difference in use of *kikkittaša*/*kikkiṭṭaša* (KÌD.KÌD.BI) and *dudubûm* (DÙ.DÙ.BI). Both are later equated with Akkadian *epištašu*/*epuštašu*.

71 For reading ka-inim-ma as opposed to inim-inim-ma, see Schramm 1981, 90; with addition of ka-i-ni-ma in BM 79949: 5, see Finkel 1999, 230.

72 Note the occurrence of individual subscripts, i.e., *šipat libbiya* "incantation for my belly" (Fs. de Meyer 75/83d: 40–41 = № 30) and *šipat kaššapiya* "incantation against my witch" (AMD 1, 273b: r. 10). On one occasion the rubric is simply omitted, providing only the designation of the spell, i.e., AMD 1, 243 (fig. 1): 12 (№ 61). Similar examples can be found in the late second millennium, see Zomer 2018a, 32.

73 An overview of subscripts in MB/MA incantations is found in Zomer 2018a, 32–35.

74 As, e.g., *ša zuqiqīpim* (TIM 9, 66: 35), *šipat tūltim* (YOS 11, 4: 3) – both after an alloglot spell, or *mû mušapšiqtum* (JNES 43, 312: r. 6') – after a Sumerian spell.

75 The abbreviated form ka-inim is found in CUSAS 32, 29a: 11/18 (№ 67), CUSAS 32, 29b: 19a (№ 68) and VS 17, 8: 8 (№ 74).

76 Alternatively, note YOS 11, 7 (№ 44), where the subscript is found on the lower edge, and TIM 9, 63d (№ 163), where the subscript is on the left edge, separated by a vertical ruling from the last lines of the incantation.

77 AMD 1, 247 (fig. 11): r. 4 (№ 83), AMD 1, 286b: 22 (№ 63), AMD 1, 287b: r. 10 (№ 146), BM 115745:

18 (see Zomer 2018a, 34f.).[78] Remarkably, this subscript is rarely separated by a ruling[79] and it is consistently rendered phonetically, with minor variations.[80] In AMD 1, 286a (№ 158) and AMD 1, 286b (№ 63), the subscript is found after the procedure.

šiptum ša ...

Alternatively, we find the subscript *šiptum ša* "incantation against/of…". This subscript is found twice in the present corpus, on the same tablet: ZA 71, 62a: 18' (№ 157)[81] and ZA 71, 62b: r. 12' (№ 124).[82]

ša

An abbreviated version of *šiptum ša*, is the use of the relative-determinative pronoun *ša* alone. It is attested in YOS 11, 14c: r. 11 (№ 39), and UET 6/2, 399: 24 (№ 117), and cf. Semitica 62, 15f.: 28 (№ 98). It occurs also after OB Sumerian and alloglot spells.[83]

awāt ...

A rare subscript in the corpus is the construct state of *awātum*, i.e., *awāt* "word (of) …". It is found twice: YOS 11, 12c: 37 (№ 47) and OECT 11, 3: 11 (№ 32).[84]

Colophons

Colophons are scarcely attested in the present corpus.[85] The most telling one is found in YOS 11, 21, where we find a rare colophon mentioning the name of two persons, who most likely commissioned the tablet (see § 1.5.2).[86] Some tablets provide information regarding their content. YOS 11, 69d: r. 20' (№ 82) indicates the total number of incantations on it: 4 ka-inim-ma "(total) of 4 incantations". Similarly, CT 42, 6: iv 32 has: [N.N. ka]-⌜inim-

---

r. 15 (№ 4), CT 4, 8: 21 (№ 16), CUSAS 32, 24a: 8 (№ 88), Fs. de Meyer 75/83b: 27 (№ 76), Fs. de Meyer 75/83d: 40–41 (№ 30), Fs. de Meyer 86: 22' (№ 156), UET 5, 85: 9–10 (№ 38), YOS 11, 4b: 19 (№ 102).

78 For this subscript after OB Sumerian and alloglot incantations, see van Dijk/Hussey/Goetze 1985, 5.

79 AMD 1, 247 (fig. 11): r. 4 (№ 83). Note that the post-OB examples in KBo 1, 18 are also not separated by a ruling, see Zomer 2018a, 35. In the case of Fs. de Meyer 86: 22' (№ 156), the subscript is found on the lower edge.

80 Plene spelling in UET 5, 85: 9–10 (№ 38) and *ši-‹pa›-at*[!] in Fs. de Meyer 75/83b: 27 (№ 76).

81 On the lower edge of the tablet.

82 Previously discussed in Zomer 2019, 1262. For the occurrence of this subscript in the MB/MA corpus, see Zomer 2018a, 34.

83 See van Dijk/Hussey/Goetze 1985, 5; Cunningham 1997, 157/159. As for post-OB evidence, this subscript is only attested in KBo 1, 18, see Zomer 2018a, 34 and Zomer 2019, 1263f.

84 Another possible example may be found in Fs. de Meyer 87: 9 (№ 172).

85 Designations for the identity of the scribe, generally introduced with ŠU ("hand of") PN, are not found in the present corpus, but a good example is displayed in a contemporary Elamite magic text with an Akkadian procedure (Sb 12353) from Susa: ŠU *E-lum-da-ti* DUB.SAR TUR "Hand of Elum-dati, the junior scribe", see Cavigneaux 2020, 56.

86 Reading: *aš-šum* DINGIR-*šu-a-bu-šu* ŠEŠ *ma-an-nu-um-ki-ma*-[d]UTU DUMU [id]UD.KI[B.NUN …] *i-na* É *Nu-ra-tum* DUMU *Bé-la-nu-um* AGRIG *aš-šum* BALA-*e* DUMU *I-din-É-a* PISAN.DUB.BA *ša un-ne-du*-⌜x⌝ […] "On behalf of Ilšu-abušu, the brother of Mannum-kīma-Šamaš, the son of Purattum […], at the court[?] of Nūrātum, son of Bēlānum the steward; on behalf of Balāye, the son of Iddin-Ea the accountant of the letters", see Wasserman 2014a, 57.

ma⌉.[87] An interesting case is CT 4, 8: 26 (№ 16) whose closing statement is: 2 EME *ša li-ib-bi* "two tongues (i.e., languages) against the belly", referring to the bilinguality of the text.[88]

A possible dating is found in RA 70, 135/137: 61 (№ 10): [iti] gu₄ "[the month] Gusisa" and in AMD 1, 247 (fig. 12): l.e. 25' (№ 177): ⌈iti x x⌉ [...].[89]

Only one tablet in the corpus contains an editorial note regarding the number of lines: On the left edge of ZA 75, 198–204 we find the summary "120 lines".[90]

An enigmatic statement is found in TIM 9, 73b: 9–10 (№ 129): *rēš šipti*. This might be a scribal remark designating the incipit of a (collection of) incantation(s). A practice otherwise unknown in the present corpus (see commentary № 129).

---

87 Other contemporary examples are found in the unilingual Sumerian incantation collectives VS 17, 10 and FAOS 12 pls. 1–2, see Zomer 2018a, 176 fn. 592.

88 A similar designation is found in VS 17, 10: vi 1'–2' šu-nigin 22 ka-inim-ma gír-tab eme-gi₇ "total of 22 incantations concerning scorpion(s) – Sumerian".

89 Examples of other OB incantations known to have a dating outside the present corpus are LB 1003, which dates 23/XI/Samsuiluna (see Wasserman 2020c), and YOS 11, 64, which reads iti-1 u₄-10 èše ᵈUTU-*ga-mil* É ᵈUTU-*ga-mil* mu-1-kam É ᵈNin-a-zu šà é-gíd-da (see Prechel/Richter 2001, 335f.). Another post-OB example from the second millennium is found on the prism KBo 1, 18 from Hattuša, see Zomer 2019, 1260.

90 See ZA 75, 198–204j (№ 143). The line numbering includes the spell an mul ki mul-mul.

1.5 The Praxis

1.5.1 *Ex opere operantis:* The Magic Practitioners

The professionals performing magic were designated *wāšipum,*[91] *mašmaššum,*[92] *pāširum*/*pāširtum,*[93] and *emqum asûm* "wise physician" or simply *emqum* "wise (man)".[94] Judging by the grammar, the practitioners were male (but note the *pāširtum* in BM 97331a: 3/4 = № 84 and CUSAS 32, 49: 27 = № 93). Practitioners of non-official magic, that is, magicians who were not backed up by the centres of hegemonic power in society, were stereotyped as "witches" or "sorcerers".[95]

Unlike in later periods, little is known about magic experts in the OB period. Even in daily-life texts, the magician (*w*)*āšipum* or *mašmaššum*, is rarely mentioned.[96] Another healing profession, that of the *asû* "physician", is documented in legal and daily-life texts, but its attestation in therapeutic tablets is likewise limited (see above and Geller 2010, 69f.).[97] While often appearing in first-person voice ("May I cast on you a spell driving out all diseases" CT 42, 32: 1 = № 49 or "I am the weapon of Ningirsu!" CUSAS 32, 55: 7 = № 126), the magic practitioners remain nameless.[98]

First millennium magic experts are mostly attested in the public domain (the royal court and temples).[99] Early second millennium material presents the opposite picture. Indirect

91 AMD 1, 245 (fig. 5): 14 (№ 105), CUSAS 32, 49: 32 (№ 93). The occurrence of the female counterpart of *wāšipu*, i.e., (*w*)*āšiptu*, is to our knowledge used only in later periods, see Schwemer 2007, 76.

92 CT 42, 32: 18 (№ 49).

93 BM 97331a: 3 (№ 84), CUSAS 32, 49: 26/27/28 (№ 93) and possibly AMD 1, 247 (fig. 11): 3 (№ 83). Note that the designation *pāširu*/*pāširtu* in the present corpus is restricted to scorpion incantations. In later corpora, it plays a dominant role in incantations to arouse sexual desire, e.g., LAOS 9, 227 (VAT 13226) and the šaziga spells (Biggs 1967). Another term for the magic practitioner could be *laḫḫāsum* (and *laḫḫastum*) "the whispering-one". Attested in only one incantation (YOS 11, 69c = № 42, against *maškadu*), this designation refers probably to the healer, since whispering goes well with magic charms, and "whispering-ones" can hardly describe the sick person or the sick milking cows mentioned in the incantation.

94 OECT 15, 260: 15, 16 (№ 109, against snakes).

95 A male sorcerer is found in AMD 1, 287b: r. 10 (№ 146). For witchcraft, witches, trials and accusations, see Schwemer 2007, 69–87 and 132 and Zomer 2017, 223.

96 Two Mari letters mention magic experts. In ARM 26, 44 *wāšipū* are listed together with *mussirū* (professional purifiers) and in ARM 26, 263 *mašmaššū* cooperate with *mār kalê* "lamentation priests". Additionally, the *Seleucid List for Kings and Scholars* mentions the names of two OB scholars (*ummânū*) serving in the reign of Abī-ešuḫ: Gimil-Gula und Tāqiš-Gula (Lenzi 2008, 142). Besides their scholarly work, the *ummânu*s are known to have worked in magic, similar to the (*w*)*āšipu* (Zomer 2018a, 70–72).

97 OB therapeutic tablets are BAM 393; CUSAS 32, 72; CUSAS 32, 73; Iraq 55, 104; YOS 11, 25; YOS 11, 26; YOS 11, 27; YOS 11, 28 and YOS 11, 29.

98 Ali/Geller 2020, 6–10 have recently argued that the inserted names of Aššur-šāliṭ, Balassi and Aššur-mudammiq in Maqlû-related texts are self referential, i.e., that these are the names of the *āšipu*s.

99 For the NA period, the N4 Library in Aššur, the *Haus der Beschwörungspriesters*, offers a good example. Its study shows that various male members of the family were active in the Aššur temple over several generations (see May 2018). Indications for magic experts performing purification rites in the palace in the third millennium (^{lú}mu$_{13}$-mu$_{13}$) were studied by Sallaberger 2002, 165. See further Zomer 2018a, 74f.

textual and direct archaeological evidence suggests that practice of magic in that period took place mainly in a domestic context (but note the incantations found at the palace of Mari and the temple archives at Nērebtum, § 1.3.3).

The (*w*)*āšipu* used to visit the house of the patient. This is patently clear from the incipit of the medical diagnostic series Sakikkû: *enūma ana bīt marṣi āšipu illiku* "when a magician goes to the house of the patient" (Heeßel 2000, 13). In our corpus there is no mention of a payment, but there is little doubt that the magic expert was reimbursed for his efforts. Possible allusions to fees can be found in *Kultmittelbeschwörungen* from later periods, where *materia magica* are addressed with payment formulae, as *šīmki maḫrāti* "You (the potter's clay) have received your price!" or *qīšta(m) maḫrāta aplāta* "You (a lamp) have received (your) gift, you are paid!" (Zomer 2018a, 107). Even clearer are the *quid-pro-quo* formulae addressed to healing goddesses in post-OB spells: DN *bulliṭī mār apkalli* (var. *ummâni*) *qīštam limḫur* "DN restore his (= the patient's) health, so that the expert may receive (his) fee!" or DN *bulliṭī qīštam leqī* (var. *muḫrī*) "DN restore (his) health, receive (your) gift!" (Zomer 2018a, 64 fn. 217).[100]

Were the magic experts literate? Did they write the spells that we have in our hands today? The considerable number of written incantations from this period would suggest that indeed some of them could write. The fact that a number of texts in the corpus are clumsily written would reinforce this assumption, see § 1.4.3.[101] Wasserman (2012, 182) proposed the 'one person – two functions' model, suggesting that some of the magic practitioners were graduates of scribal schools, able to copy, or even compose, tablets on their own. If this indeed was the case, then we can imagine an illiterate magic practitioner asking a scribe to set down his knowledge in writing, or alternatively, a trained scribe taking an incantation – which he himself knew, or learned from an illiterate magician – and adding it to his scribal repertoire.[102] The figures of Bēlšunu, son of Lu-lisina and Zimri-Addu from Mēturan, could serve as examples of this model: the personal archives of these gentlemen consisted of both incantations and literary texts (see §§ 1.3.3 and 1.4.3). Similarly, in Igmil-Sîn's Ur-based school, magic texts were found in the scribal context (see § 1.3.1).

A possible indication of the participation of trainees or helpers in the magic performance may be found in cases where an unknown crowd, referred to in the second or third voice plural, is addressed.[103] These persons are requested to speak to Asalluḫi and to describe the unfortunate events: "Now, tell (pl.) Asalluḫi, the son of Enki, that he r[eleas]es the heart of

---

100 Geller 2010, 93f. suggests that the gift is in fact the fee paid to the expert.

101 The inscriptions imitating Sumerian spells on Lamaštu amulets also suggest that laymen were trying to produce magic texts (Zomer 2018a, 26 fn. 74).

102 The 'one person – two functions' model suggested for ancient Mesopotamian incantations is found, *mutatis mutandis*, in later Jewish/Aramaic magic in Babylonia. In a recent study, Manekin-Bamberger 2020, 253 argues that Jewish magic bowls were written by "scribes [who] were part of a professional guild of *soferim* that engaged in different forms of Jewish writing…." and "that these bowl scribes were […] professional Jewish writers, producing biblical and liturgical scrolls as well". In other words, there was no schism between magicians or exorcists on the one hand and Rabbinic scribes on the other, but rather a mixed-used writing zone in which the same person could compose an official divorce document in the morning and a magic spell in the afternoon.

103 For examples from later periods, see Zomer 2018a, 63 fn. 212.

Sîn in the sky, the heart of Šamaš etc." (CUSAS 32, 7o // CUSAS 32, 8i: 22–38 = № 19)[104], or "Place (pl.) the […] into his mouth and slap (pl.) his cheek, so that […] he goes down again and again!" (CUSAS 32, 20d: 16'–17' = № 167),[105] and still "A man … whom a scorpion … They will make him drink water … and he will get well" (Elamica 10, 65c = № 95).

1.5.2 The Clients

Personal names are rare in Mesopotamian incantation literature. The identity of the clients is therefore almost never disclosed. This situation stands in stark contrast to other magic literary bodies (Greek and Latin *defixiones* and Aramaic magic bowls), which contain many personal names. This has to do with the fact that the majority of Mesopotamian magic texts were used as works of reference in a curricular or scholarly context (see § 1.4.3). Another reason for the paucity of personal names in our corpus is that Mesopotamian magic texts, or objects, that were actually used (and had the client's name inscribed on them) were often destroyed in the process of their activation.[106] For these and other reasons, we often find the formula "N.N. son of N.N." (*annanna mār annanna*, sometimes extended to *ilšu annanna ištaršu annanītum* "whose (personal) god is N.N., whose (personal) goddess is N.N."), instead of the client's name.[107] When preparing a private magic text for a client, his or her name was inserted by the magic expert in the *locum tenens*.

Some personal names, however, are found in the corpus: [108]

> *Living and life in the house of lordship, I am the very best! (For) the life of Sîn-iddinam and the life of* [*his*] *wi*[*fe*]*. The paths of the land I put in place. Great is my name! Advisor, handsome one, protector am I.*[109]

The name of the client can be found in the tablet's colophon. In the case of YOS 11, 21: 34–35 we find evidence that this tablet was commissioned by two gentlemen, Ilšu-abušu and Balāye:

> *On behalf of Ilšu-abušu, the brother of Mannum-kīma-Šamaš, the son of Purattum* […]*, at the court*? *of Nūrātum, son of Bēlānum the steward; on behalf of Balāye, the son of Iddin-Ea the accountant of the letters* […].[110]

The figure Balāye, which is a hypercoristicon of Balmunamḫe, is the grandson of the more famous Balmunamḫe, son of Sîn-nūr-mātim, a known entrepreneur and public figure in the

104 Cf. CUSAS 32, 24a: 3–7 (№ 88) and (Fs. Pope 87: 4 (№ 70).

105 Cf. CUSAS 32, 21f: 13' (№ 152), Fs. de Meyer 87: 6–8 (№ 172) and ZA 71, 62a: 15'–16' (№ 157).

106 See PBS 1/2, 122: 8 (№ 147).

107 Note the variant in CUSAS 32, 25a: 6–7 (№ 23): ne-nam dumu ne-n[am] dingir-bi ne-nam ù ama-^{d}innin-[bi] ne-nam "N.N., son of N.N., whose god is N.N., and whose goddess is N.N."

108 Two names are found on one love-related magic text: Erra-bāni (ZA 75, 198–204j: 117 = № 143) and Iddin-Damu (ZA 75, 198–204i: 100 = № 142), see § 1.5.1. In a recently published group of post-Old Bablonian fever amulets (Finkel 2018), the name of the female patient, with her mother's name, is found.

109 CUSAS 32, 56: 15–18 (№ 127). Could this be Sîn-iddinam, the king of Larsa? Hardly. First, Sîn-iddinam is a common personal name in the OB period. Secondly, this monarch used to write his name in Akkadian, not in Sumerian as in our incantation.

110 See Krebernik 2018, 38.

city of Larsa.[111] Textual evidence suggests that the same activities were carried out by his descendants.[112] Ilšu-abušu and Balāye may have been public figures in Larsa, but YOS 11, 21, which contains spells for love and help in a trial, suggests that the tablet was commissioned for private purposes.

As observed in § 1.3.4, all OA magic texts come from private houses belonging to Assyrian merchants at Kaneš.[113] This does not mean that all these magic tablets were commissioned for, or used by, the men who lived in this archaeological context. In the case of Or. 66, 61 (an amulet against Lamaštu = № 162), SANER 9, 77 (childbirth = № 11), and Fs. Larsen 397/399 (childbirth/bile = № 9 and 1), the clients were women and children – perhaps the merchant's immediate family. So also, the magic tablets from the house of the Sippar-based merchant Ipiq-Išḫara and his wife Nīši-inīšu.[114]

Clients are more often referred to by general terms, such as *marṣum* "patient" (lit. "sick one"),[115] *rēšum* "patient" (lit. "head, slave"),[116] *maḫṣum* "stricken one",[117] or simply *awīlum* "man",[118] *zikarum* "man",[119] *eṭlum* "young man",[120] or *māri awīlūtim* "son of mankind".[121]

In childbirth incantations and in spells against a difficult labour, the patient was naturally a woman. In other instances, female clients can be deduced from the grammar: ‹*ina*› *muḫḫi šinniša marušti* "*on the top*? of her aching tooth" (YOS 11, 12c: 33 = № 47), and *tamḫaṣi pānūša tušbalkiti pūša* "You (f.) have hit her face and you (f.) have turned upside down her mouth" (YOS 11, 14c: 7 = № 39).[122] The stereotypical designation *wardatum* "maiden" is found in lists depicting all kinds of targets, and is therefore less indicative of the client's sex. In one case, however, it does seem to refer specifically to a woman: "Oh belly where are you going? To smite a maiden?" (JEOL 47, 58b: 20–23 = № 31). Another case where a woman is explicitly mentioned is CUSAS 32, 32c (№ 29), where a dialogue between a young man and a bartender is found, alluding probably to Gilgameš and Siduri, and more concretely to the masculine healer and his female patient (see § 1.7.4).

Pregnant women and newborns were the main targets of the demoness Lamaštu (§ 2.4.2). The vulnerability of infants is found in BiOr 75, 21f. (№ 15), a spell for a young child whose life is in danger, *dādummi dādum ukkupamma* "the beloved child, beloved child is about (to

111 For discussion of the archives of Balmunamḫe, son of Sîn-nūr-mātim and his grandson Balmunamḫe, son of Iddin-Ea, see Van de Mieroop 1987. For a restoration of the family tree, see Charpin 1987.

112 See Veenhof 2005, XIXf.

113 But other incantations were unearthed in non-private contexts: the spells found in the palace in Mari (§ 1.3.4) and those in the temples at Nērebtum (§ 1.3.3).

114 Fs. de Meyer 75/83 (№ 30 and 76), Fs. de Meyer 86 (№ 156) and Fs. de Meyer 87 (№ 172).

115 OECT 15, 260: 20 (№ 109).

116 CUSAS 32, 25a: 5 (№ 23).

117 CUSAS 32, 30d: 14/16 (№ 92).

118 E.g., AMD 1, 243 (fig. 2)a: 10 (№ 62), CUSAS 32, 7g // CUSAS 32, 8e: 5/6 (№ 151), Elamica 10, 65c: 21 (№ 95), OECT 11, 3: 9 (№ 32).

119 E.g., YOS 11, 3: 4 (№ 46).

120 E.g., JNES 14, 15: 27 (№ 45) and Fs. Hirsch 427: 6 (№ 69).

121 E.g., YOS 11, 4b: 13 (№ 102) and BM 97331b: 12 (№ 85).

122 Note YOS 11, 15 // YOS 11, 29b (№ 149), where YOS 11, 29b: 23 specifies that the patient is female. In AMD 1, 286b: 20 (№ 63) the scribe uses the fem. suffix to denote the otherwise male rendered patient, probably by mistake.

die)".[123] In two spells, YOS 11, 5a: 5 and YOS 11, 5b: 11 (№ 113 and 114), a child (*ṣeḫrum*) is said to be infested by worms, and in a different example, YOS 11, 4b: 16/17 (№ 102), we find a young boy (*ṣuḫārum*), who is stung by a scorpion. A group of incantations deals with crying toddlers who disturb their exhausted parents' sleep.

Animals too are treated as patients in our corpus. Explicit examples of veterinary medicine are YOS 11, 7 (№ 44), for sheep struck by the *sikkatum*-disease, perhaps pox, and CUSAS 32, 8d (№ 21), intended to treat the bloated stomach of an ox or a sheep. Some spells serve as remedies for both humans and animals, as is evident from CT 4, 8 (№ 16), dealing with gastrointestinal problems.[124]

The arcane knowledge of healing is in the hands of the magician, but occasionally, the client is asked to join forces with the expert in the process. The client's participation is evident from passages where the expert addresses him directly: "Raise your eyes (and see)!" (Fs. de Meyer 86: 9' = № 156).

In the procedures, the instructions for the magic expert are consistently in the second-person and the client is referred to in the third-person voice, as is demonstrated in AMD 1, 286a: 6–9 (№ 158):[125]

> *You tie up a lump of salt in a piece of cloth. You tie (it) on his neck. He will be well.*

Even when the patient himself is to perform certain actions, he, or she, is still referred to in the third-person voice, as in YOS 11, 29a: 22–23 (№ 48):[126]

> [*He will apply*] *myrrh on the tooth which the w*[*orm has eaten*]. *He will place the myrrh* [*on the …*] *and he will be well.*

Having said that, it is not uncommon to find incantations written in the first person, merging the perspectives of the expert and the client. Such spells speak in a personal tone and are emotionally charged. Good examples can be found in spells concerning love-related matters, as CUSAS 32, 23b: 7–16 (№ 132):[127]

> *I have torn the thorn, I will be sowing a vine! I have poured water onto the fierce fire! Love me as your lamb! Encircle me as your small cattle! Look at me!*

---

123 See Wasserman 2018, 21–23.

124 Ancient Mesopotamian medicine and magic understood zoonotic diseases spreading from animals to humans. Some diseases raining down from heaven are said to affect animals, mostly sheep, and humans alike, i.e., JCS 9, 9: 11–12 (№ 54), JCS 9, 10: 11–13 (№ 55), RA 88, 161c: 12'–13' (№ 56), Semitica 61, 13f.: 9–11 (№ 57) and YOS 11, 8: 10–11 (№ 58). Another zoonotic ailment may be *maškadum* (Brucellosis?), for which see Wasserman 2012.

125 Cf. AMD 1, 243 (fig. 1): 12–17 (№ 61), AMD 1, 286b: 13–21 (№ 63), RA 66, 141b: 10–14 (№ 96), YOS 11, 4b: 20–22 (№ 102), YOS 11, 15 // YOS 11, 29b: 19–20 and 22–24 (№ 149), YOS 11, 67a // NABU 2019/43a: 7–10 (№ 175). The same situation is found in MB/MA incantations, see Zomer 2018a, 78–79.

126 See also YOS 11, 14c: 12 (№ 39).

127 Other examples can be found among the spells for gastrointestinal disorders, i.e., Fs. de Meyer 75/83d (№ 30), and in YOS 11, 41 (№ 115) against worms/leeches.

1.5.3 Location of Magic Praxis

Our study indicates that magic texts are strongly connected to the domestic sphere. Mention of the client's house (*bītum*) is found in the accompanying instructions to anti-witchcraft spells UET 6/2, 193a: 14'–16' (№ 148) and YOS 11, 15 // YOS 11, 29b: 19–20/22–23 (№ 149). In the latter case, the house is part of the magic procedure: the *materia magica* (listed in ll. 17–18) are to be buried in the socket of a doorpost of the client's house, and a brick from his threshold is to be placed in his stove in order to release him from his woes. Indirect references to the private domestic context can be detected in passages describing the location of attack by the malevolent entity. Examplary are the actions of the Evil Eye, vividly depicted in ZA 71, 62a: 4'–11' (№ 157):

> *Passing through the tots' door, she brought about a quarrel between the tots; Passing through the door of the birthing women, she strangled their babies. She entered the vessels' storeroom, broke the sealing bullae; She scattered the fireplace, the place of safety; She turned the house full of (happy) noise into a ruin. Having struck down the chapel, the god of the house went out.*

Spells against Lamaštu and Wardat-lilî offer a similar picture. Both demonesses slip into their victim's house, wreaking havoc in the household. Consequently, magic actions against these female demons strive to prevent them from entering the client's house: "You will not enter to the house which I enter! [Where] I spit you will not touch!" (YOS 11, 92: 28–31 = № 166).

Raging or rabid dogs are also considered primarily a domestic menace, connected to the threshold (*askuppatum*) of the house.[128] Other marauding animals, such as scorpions, are active in the courtyard of a house (*kisallum*),[129] or are active outside in the street (*šullûm*).[130] Snakes are said to come from the drain-pipes (*naṣṣabum*).[131]

Admittedly, the above examples speak not of the location of the magic practice against evil, but reveal rather that men and women were primarily *attacked* in their domestic surroundings. In the absence of contrary evidence, we assume that the fight against the malevolent agent took place where the attack occurred, namely at home or near it.

That magic praxis was mainly carried out in domestic surroundings may further be substantiated by archaeological finding. The prime examples being the collection of love-related spells from Isin (IB 1554, see ZA 75, 198–204) which was intentionally cut and broken and buried in a jar hidden in the wall of a private home, as well as the many magic texts from Kaneš unearthed in domestic context (§ 1.3.4).

Some magic texts, however, were found in public buildings. The temple at Nērebtum (§ 1.3.3), or the royal archives in Mari (§ 1.3.4) are clear cases. These incantations may have served as reference works with educational function, but one cannot exclude that they were

128 E.g., OECT 11, 4: 5 (№ 71) and VS 17, 8: 4 (№ 74). A possible exception is the OA incantation with the black dog lurking on a tell (Fs. Hirsch 427 = № 69), but note the common presence of dogs in Kaneš and other Anatolian towns (Barjamovic 2015, 52 with additional literature).

129 E.g., RA 88, 161a: 4 (№ 97). Note additionally, YOS 11, 35 (№ 104) where Anum is invoked to purify the house against a scorpion.

130 BM 97331b: 11 (№ 85).

131 E.g., CUSAS 32, 27a: 2 (№ 106).

actually used for magic praxis, proving that, functionally speaking, private and non-private contexts were not entirely separated (see § 1.4.3).[132]

1.5.4 Geographical Horizon in Magic Texts

In any discussion of toponyms in magic texts, one must keep in mind that the available corpus, albeit not insignificant in size, is only a fraction of what existed in the past, and that the data at hand is arbitrary to a large extent. With this caveat, the examination of the toponyms in the corpus reveals two important observations. First, the geography displayed by the magic texts does not correspond to the historical geography of the period. The main OB cities, as Babylon, Sippar, Isin or Larsa, play no role in the magic texts available to us – a fact which calls for special attention, as all but few of our texts stem from the large urban centers of central Mesopotamia. Three exceptions should be noted though: Sippar is alluded in the name of the healing agent called 'Sipparian-tree' in AMD 14, 197b: 9 (№ 64), and Ur and Nippur are anecdotally mentioned in CUSAS 32, 20d: 14' (№ 167) and in YOS 11, 5b: 10 (№ 114).[133]

The second observation is that the corpus, as it is available to us, shows a strong bent to toponyms and river names located in Eastern Mesopotamia.[134] To put it bluntly, it seems that OB magicians were looking to the periphery,[135] more accurately eastward, to Elam.

Table 12: Overview of Geographical and River Names

Geographical Names	River Names
Dilmun (1)	*Araḫtum*-canal (3)
Elam (1)	Lagaš-canal (1)
Eridu (4)	LU.UḪ.DA (1)
Kudimšum (1)	Tigris (5)
Meluḫḫa (1)	Ulaya (1)
Magan (1)	
Nippur (1)	
Paraḫšum (1)	
Sippar (1)	
Susa (1)	
Ur (1)	

132 The paucity of references to temples in the corpus should be marked. Only Esikila in CUSAS 32, 51: 5 (№ 78) and possibly an unspecified temple in CUSAS 32, 58: 1/2 (№ 171) are attested. The absence of major temples tells that the practice of magic was not connected to sanctuaries.

133 The traditional occurrence of Eridu in the corpus is conneced directly to the divine magical couple Enki/Ea and Asalluḫi/Marduk (e.g., Fs. Stol 150: 21–22 = № 53).

134 The Esikila temple (CUSAS 32, 51: 5 = № 78) is probably the temple of Ninazu-Tišpak in Ešnunna, but it could refer to the chapel within the perimeter of the É-kur in Nippur, see George 1993, 141 nos. 987–989.

135 Three southern loci are found: Dilmun (CUSAS 32, 29a: 5 = № 67), Magan (Fs. de Meyer 75/83b :16 = № 76) and Meluḫḫa (CUSAS 32, 58: 4 = № 171).

The origin of fearsome dogs is ascribed to Elam: once in connection with the *maškadu*-disease which attacks like "an Elamite-dog" (YOS 11, 14b: r. 3 = № 41), and once in a spell against a dog-bite, where it is stated that "between Kudimšum and Paraḫšum, a dog has bitten a man" (Fs. Pope 87: 1–3 = № 70).[136] Elam is mentioned also in the love spell VS 17, 23 (№ 134), where various materials for the production of kohl are said to come from Susa, via the river Tigris. Fs. Wilcke 62 (№ 108), the sole incantation in the corpus found in Susa, tells that the river Tigris bore a snake and that the river Ulaya raised it. The latter watercourse was leading to the Netherworld in Babylonian cosmology (see Wiggermann 1996, 212). The area between the Tigris and the canal of Lagaš was the area where a scorpion was active, according to YOS 11, 4c: r. 23 (№ 103). Anger incantations connect the Tigris with burst of anger, in possible analogy with its violent seasonal tides and turbulent nature (UET 6/2, 399 and ZA 75, 198–204h = № 117 and 119). To this significant accumulation of data let us add the fact that the river Euphrates, along which all main urban centers of the period were concentrated, is not mentioned in our corpus. An important canal leading from the Euphrates, however, does appear: the *Araḫtum*-canal which is mentioned in some birth incantations[137] (BM 115745, Fs. Larsen 397/399a, SANER 9, 77 = № 4, 9 and 11).[138] Its mention, however, is explicated through a wordplay with *arḫum* "cow" and *arḫiš* "quickly" – two keywords in this group of spells.[139]

This tendency of *Magi ex oriente* is no doubt connected with the fact that not a few of our texts contain Elamite, or pseudo-Elamite, passages.[140]

1.5.5 Time of Magic Praxis

Not much can be safely said about the time that magic procedures were to be performed. From later prayers and rituals, we know that the nocturnal setting, and especially the transition points of dusk or dawn, were of great importance in Mesopotamian magic.[141] Most explicit in this regard is the anti-witchcraft spell UET 6/2, 193a (№ 148), where witchcraft is to be resolved on the "day of the disappearance of the moon", "the first day of the moon", "the seventh day (of the moon)" and the "fifteenth day (of the moon)", i.e., on the waning crescent, on the new moon, when the moon is waxing, and on the full moon.[142]
Nocturnal activity of the magic practitioner is hinted at BM 97331a: 4 (№ 84, against scorpions): "My female releaser in the night (lit. her night) [...]".

Some incantations whose aim is to quiet a crying baby reveal nocturnal setting, as the astral designation "One-walking-behind-the-cattle" in OECT 11, 2: 25 (№ 122). Indeed, it stands to reason that the magical actions to put babies to sleep were taken at night. Occasional

---

136 For a discussion of geographical identification of both toponyms, see Durand/Guichard 1997, 22 fn. 25; for their parallels in later MB incantations, see Zomer 2018a, 258.

137 For the *Araḫtum*-canal in previous literature, see Blaschke 2018, 360–365.

138 Cf. also YOS 11, 19a (№ 164).

139 See Steinert 2017a, 224f.

140 Krebernik 2018.

141 For witchcraft and anti-witchcraft nocturnal rituals, see Schwemer 2007, 63f.; 102; in Maqlû-ceremony, see Schwemer 2007, 39. For the role of celestial objects in Mesopotamian prayers and incantations, see Reiner 1995, 15–24. A general discussion of nocturnal rituals: Schwemer 2007, 133–143.

142 Cf. Sm 352(+), an anti-witchcraft procedure referring to the first, seventh and fifteenth day of the month, see Schwemer 2007, 105 fn. 193.

allusion to constellations in other incantation may be also indicative to night-time magical activities, as "the soaring one of the sky", referring to the constellation Scorpio (RA 88, 161a: 1 and CUSAS 32, 49: 3 = № 97 and № 93, both against scorpions). Stars are mentioned in BM 97331a (№ 84, against scorpions), CT 42, 6e (№ 168, to get food), YOS 11, 12c (№ 47, against toothache) and ZA 75, 198–204j (№ 143, for love).

1.5.6 *Materia Magica*

In order to achieve the desired effect, the *recitanda* in magic practice were accompanied by specific actions, ordered accurately, the *agenda*. This part of the magical process is usually unknown to us, but glimpses of it are revealed in the instructions which follow the incantations, generally introduced with an indicative rubric (see § 1.4.5). In some cases, the-what-to-do section is woven into a mythical narrative, historiola (see § 1.7.4), most commonly the Marduk-Ea Dialogue. A specific type of incantation to activate and consecrate objects for their magic purpose is the so-called *Kultmittelbeschwörung*.[143]

The materials and substances used in the magic process – the *materia magica* – are of great variety: victuals, beverages, wild plants, minerals, metals and metallic powders, animal substances, and domestic utensils. These *materia magica* can be of a practical nature (as salt used for enema), or may have a symbolic relation with the *recitanda* (as a torch representing the scorpion's sting).

A clear example of *materia magica* with a practical nature is YOS 11, 29a (№ 48), where the remedy for a client suffering from tootache is myrrh (*murrum*). Even nowadays myrrh is used in toothpaste and is known for its antiseptic and analgesic qualities.[144]

Salt is known as a purgative for different digestive disorders. CT 4, 8: 17–21 (№ 16) reads:

> *(As for the patient) – be it a human being, an ox or a sheep – ex*[*tract*?] *a lump of salt and thyme!* [*May he drop (it)*] *in the form of excre*[*ment*]*!* [*May he eject it*] *in the form of a b*[*elch*]*!* [*May he make it go out*] *in the form of w*[*ind!*].[145]

Besides the practical use of saline solutions in treating gastrointestinal problems, salt carried a symbolic meaning. It could "terrify plants in heaven and on earth" (VS 17, 1: iv 17) and as such, was effective against gallbladder inflammation described as malign plants that break the surface of the earth (George 2016, 8).

Another use of salt for practical reasons is found in CUSAS 32, 58 (№ 171), where it serves as a remedy for loss of fluids. ZA 75, 198–204h (№ 119), a spell against love-related anger, terminates with the subscript k a - i n i m - m a l a g - m u n - k a m "Incantation of the salt lump". Here salt is used symbolically: it was probably dissolved, or burned, in a manner analogous to relenting anger.[146] Another symbolic use of salt is found in AMD 1, 286a (№

143 Also known as *Weihungstyp* (Falkenstein 1931). In the present corpus we have examples for bitumen (CUSAS 32, 20d = № 167), foods and drinks (CT 42, 6e = № 168; JEOL 47, 58a = № 169), and reeds (NABU 1996/30 = № 170). More on *Kultmittelbeschwörungen*, see Zomer 2018a, 2 fn. 7.

144 The use of myrrh against toothache was also used in ancient Greece, see Carter 1990, 6. As for the modern therapeutic value and uses of myrrh, see El Ashry/Rashed/Salama *et al*. 2003.

145 Cf. CUSAS 32, 8d (№ 21) and Fs. Larsen 397/399b (№ 1). For the application of salt and thyme in digestive disorders, see George 2016, 6–9 and Steinert/Vacín 2018, 713/726f.

146 Similar analogy is found in anti-witchcraft practices, see Schwemer 2007, 97/143.

158, against Lamaštu) where a lump of salt is bound up in cloth and hung around the neck of the patient. The symbolic meaning of this act is not clear, however.[147]

Scorpion bites could be healed by applying dough to the wound, armpits and groins (CUSAS 32, 30d: 16–26 = № 92):[148]

> *If the stricken one has come (to you), you place dough in is armpits and groins. If the messenger comes to you, you cast an incantation over the water and he drinks it.*[149]

This, no doubt, was a practical method to relieve the bite and calm the lymph nodes. But at the same time, it had a symbolic meaning of transposing the pain inflicted by the scorpion into the dough which absorbed it.[150]

The use of donkey's earwax on the lesion of a scorpion sting (YOS 11, 4b = № 102) is less clear. Most likely, the lardy substance had a soothing effect.[151] Similar is the use of oil in RA 66, 141b: 10–14 (№ 96, against a scorpion) and the combination of oil and ghee against a dog bite in AMD 1, 243 (fig. 1): 13–14 (№ 61). A different approach to treat a dog bite is displayed in CUSAS 32, 29a (№ 67), where a mixture of various botanical ingredients is boiled down in a cauldron before being applied in a bandage.[152] In AMD 1, 286b (№ 63), in another incantation against a dog bite, dirt? from the foundation wall of a tavern is supposed to be smeared on the bite before it is bandaged. This act, we assume, is symbolic, as stray dogs are typically found by taverns and city walls.

As for birth incantations, the reference to the milk of a pure cow and the cream of a lactating cow in RA 70, 135/137: 44–45 (№ 10) finds parallels in other birth-related texts where it is said to be smeared on the woman's vagina to ensure a fast and safe delivery.[153] These materials are directly connected with the prevalent metaphor of the pregnant woman as a cow in Mesopotamian magic literature.[154]

Later texts against witchcraft present a wide array of *materia magica* used in the magic processes (Schwemer 2007, 199–237). The present corpus, however, shows only a few examples where objects are used against witchcraft. The fragmentary spell UET 6/2, 193a: 9'–16' (№ 148) lists a torch, mottled barley, sulphur of a *maštakal*-plant, the 'magic-stick'-plant, the *šalālum*-reed, tamarisk, and young date palm, and calls them the 'pure ones' denoting their inherent cleansing capacities, used to expel sorcery from the client's house.[155] In YOS 11, 15 // YOS 11, 29b: 17–19 (№ 149), the entire household is bewitched. The action

147 An overview and discussion on the use of salt in Mesopotamia: Streck 2006–2008.

148 Cf. CUSAS 32, 30c (№ 91).

149 Drinking water to heal a scorpion bite is found also in Elamica 10, 65c: 27–29 (№ 95).

150 George 2016, 175 noted that the instructions in the OB therapeutic text CUSAS 32, 72 are almost identical to CUSAS 32, 30c and CUSAS 32, 30d (№ 91 and № 92).

151 On the ways to heal a scorpion's sting in first millennium texts, see George 2016, 165.

152 Similar ingredients are found in a poultice for a bone fracture in CUSAS 32, 30f, see George 2016, 139f.

153 See Finkel 1980, 47f.

154 See BiOr 75, 19f. (№ 3), CCT 5, 50e (№ 5), Fs. Larsen 397/399a (№ 9), SANER 9, 77 (№ 11), VS 17, 34 (№ 12). On the historiola 'Cow-of-Sîn' in birth incantations, see Veldhuis 1991.

155 In another anti-witchcraft spell (PBS 1/2, 122: 23–26 = № 147), we find a s a ḫ a r-vessel with water, tamarisk, i n n u š-soapwort, 'horned' alkali, s u l ḫ i-reed, juniper, white cedar and a variety of stones. The healing power of the tamarisk is made clear by YOS 11, 19a: 15 (№ 164), where Lamaštu is said to be tied by the gods to a tamarisk in the middle of the sea.

to be taken mentions that 8 *hallūrum*-peas, 7 *kiššēnum*-peas, 9 (grains of) *šegušsum*-barley, 7 grains of *sikillum*-plant, beerwort and vinegar are to be buried in the socket of the doorpost. The same text continues with instructions concerning a troubled man. He is to tear out a brick from his own threshold and place it in his stove and his troubles "will be torn out as well" (YOS 11, 15 // YOS 11, 29b: 21–23).

Human body fluids, such as urine and spittle, used as *materia magica,* are common in later witchcraft-related texts.[156] We find prophylactic use of one's spittle in YOS 11, 92: 28–31 (№ 166), a spell against Wardat-lilî: "You will not enter to the house which I enter! [Where] I spit you will not touch!".

Small seeds are used to attack the evil entity, the demoness Lamaštu. BIN 2, 72: 16–19 (№ 159) reads:

> *With dust your mouth, with a whirl-wind your face, with cress seeds finely ground I will verily fill your eyes!*

These pulverized materials are meant to disable Lamaštu's speech and sight. A similar strategy is found in ZA 71, 62a: 8'–16' (№ 157), a spell against the Evil Eye, where salt and ashes are used:

> *She entered the vessels' storeroom, broke the sealing bullae; she scattered the fireplace, the place of safety; she turned the house fall of (happy) noise into a ruins; having struck down the chapel, the god of the house went out. Strike her cheek! Make her turn back! Fill (pl.) her eyes with salt! Fill (pl.) her mouth with ashes!*

The choice of salt and ashes to drive away the Evil Eye aims to reverse the damage caused. Having broken the bullae in the storeroom, where salt was probably stored, and having scattered the fireplace spreading ashes all over, these very items are now used to oust her.

Fragmentary instructions in a spell to catch a scorpion (YOS 11, 35: 6–7 = № 104) mention a torch (*dipārum*).[157] This appears to be of both a practical and a symbolic nature. A customary way of catching scorpions is by encircling them in a ring of fire; metaphorically, the scorpion's tail is called a torch, referring to the burning effect of its sting (CUSAS 32, 211: 30'; CUSAS 32, 49: 11–12; YOS 11, 35: 11–12 = № 87, 93 and 104, respectively).

In the subscript of a love-related incantation, the *maštakal*-plant is mentioned (ZA 75, 198–204i = № 142). As suggested by Wasserman (2016, 271), the different parts of the plant were used, by means of an analogy, to gain control over the object of the spell, a person named Iddin-Damu.

Some incantations which concern love and sex contain references to beer. This figurative language may hint at the use of alcoholic beverages as an aphrodisiac, see ZA 75, 198–204b (№ 137) "(Just like) Seraš binds her drinkers, (so) I have bound you (m.) with my hairy mouth, with my drooling mouth".

The objects mentioned in VS 17, 23: 4–7 (№ 134) are unique, where a desired woman is to be won over with the gift of charcoal, *sangû*, copper and lead from Susa. Wasserman (2015) suggested that these materials are intended for the preparation of kohl, eye-liner, and serve here as a gift of courtship.

156 See Schwemer 2007, 18f.; 100f.

157 A torch to counteract the scorpion's sting is found also in Elamica 10, 65c: 20 (№ 95).

As for actual archaeological evidence for *materia magica*, it is not surprising that nothing remains. The materials used are perishable in nature and were often secretly buried, or destroyed on purpose.[158] Only one clear example for the OB period stands out: the remains of a magic figurine found in Sippar (Tell ed-Dēr), first published by Gasche (1994). As argued by Schwemer (2007, 212–214), this figurine can directly be connected with (anti-)witchcraft practices.

1.5.7 Deities

Deities played a significant role in Mesopotamian incantations. They served as healers in the face of the malicious being; they were called upon to support the magic expert as guarantors of divine oaths, and they bestowed on the practitioner the necessary authority to confront evil by means of officiation formulae. Most historiolae revolve around gods who were the main actors in minor mythical scenes (see below).

As expected, Enki/Ea, Asalluḫi/Marduk, and Ningirim, the magic experts of the Mesopotamian pantheon, crop up frequently in our corpus.[159] Almost equally important are deities with medical expertise, such as Gula, Ninkarrak, and Damu. The modern dichotomy between magic and medicine does not apply in ancient Mesopotamia, where *āšipūtu* and *asûtu* were complementary strategies.[160] Exorcistic deities are frequently described as *bēl*(*et*) *šipātim* "lord(/lady) of the incantations". Once we find the title *mašmaš ilī* "exorcist of the gods" implicitly used for Ea (*šar Apsî* "king of the Apsû") in CT 42, 32: 18 (№ 49). Therapeutic deities are described as gently applying compresses to the wounds of the patient and soothing him (Ninkarrak: CT 42, 32: 8 = № 49, CUSAS 32, 22a, 5'–6' = № 52, Fs. Stol 150: 3 = № 53). They grant health and are called *bēl balāṭim* "lord of life" (Damu, in AMD 1, 243 (fig. 2)a: 7 = № 62) and *ilat balāṭim* "goddess of life" (Ninkarrak, in Fs. Stol 150: 19 = № 53). The former god is *bēl takkalātim* "lord of craftiness" (an ambiguous term which may be understood also as *bēl tākalātim* "lord of the pouches, i.e., stomach" (CUSAS 32, 25a: 9 = № 23, against stomach-ache). The prominent healing goddess, Gula, is called *asût awīlê* "(female) physician of men" (CUSAS 32, 25a: 11 = № 23), and the mother goddess, Bēlet-ilī, is called *asûtum* in a birth incantation (YOS 11, 86a: 18 = № 14), which may be a mistake for *šabsūtum*, "midwife" (George 2016, 141).

Specific circumstances call for specific gods. In love-related matters, Ištar, Dumuzi and Nanāya make an appearance,[161] and in the event of childbirth, the mother goddess – Bēlet-ilī, Šassūr, Ninḫursag – is invoked.[162] To fight witchcraft spells, deities related to the Netherworld are invoked: Gilgameš and Ningišzida,[163] as well as the fire-related Gibil and

158 This practice is especially known from anti-witchcraft texts, see Schwemer 2007, 97–100. A different example can be found in instructions against the demon Any Evil (*mimma lemnu*), see Schwemer 2020.

159 Exorcistic abilities are also ascribed to Adad, Šakkan, Nāru, Šamaš, and Ḫursānu, and the holy gods of the steppe (Fs. Stol 150: 5 = № 53, cf. CT 42, 32: 13 = № 49).

160 Geller 2007, 393.

161 Ištar: CUSAS 10, 11: 16 (№ 131); ZA 75, 198–204b: 14 (№ 137); ZA 75, 198–204d: 44 (№ 139). Nanāya: ZA 75, 198–204d: 45 (№ 139); ZA 75, 198–204h: 98 (№ 119). Dumuzi: ZA 75, 198–204b: 14 (№ 137).

162 Bēlet-ilī: CUSAS 32, 28a: 13 (№ 7); YOS 11, 86a: 18 (№ 14). Šassūr: CCT 5, 50e: 10' 18 (№ 5); Fs. Larsen 397/399a: 9 18 (№ 9); SANER 9, 77: 9 (№ 11). Ninḫursag: CUSAS 32, 26a: 8' (№ 6).

163 PBS 1/2, 122: r. 1'/r. 24' (№ 147).

divine river-ordeal Idlurugu.[164] To be rid of vermin, Kusu, Indagar and Ninkilim are called upon.[165]

Divine Oaths

Promissory oaths mentioning deities are known in Sumerian and Akkadian incantations.[166] The common formula in Sumerian incantations is zi DN … ḫé-pà "(By) the life of DN … you are conjured!" (// *nīš* DN … *lū tamâta* in bilinguals). In our corpus, however, promissory oaths are formulated differently, the speaker actively administering the oath: *utammīka* DN_1 (*u* DN_2) "I conjure you by DN_1 (and DN_2)".[167] In two OA spells, an impersonal formulation is used: *tammuʾāti* DN_1 (*u* DN_2) "You are conjured by DN_1 (and DN_2)" (AoF 35, 146: 20 an JEOL 47, 58a: 8 = № 150 and 169, respectively).

The threatening being (a demon, a disease, or a menacing animal) are often adjured by reference to primordial deities, such as Anum and Antum, Laḫmum and Dūrum.[168] Enšēda and Ḫadaniš instead of Laḫmum and Dūrum appear in YOS 11, 92: 25–27 (№ 166). As observed by van Dijk/Goetze/Hussey (1985, 51), this pair is likely to be identified with ^{d}LUM-ma and Ḫadaniš, both are known guardian deities of the Ekur.[169] Cosmological entities are also used in such oaths: the Earth (*erṣetum* in YOS 11, 12a: 8 = № 36; AoF 35, 146, 22 = № 150), or bodies of water (*ḫammû* "lakes" in YOS 11, 12a: 8 = № 36), or *naʾilū* "watercourses" in AoF 35, 146: 23 and JEOL 47, 58a: 10 = № 150 and 169).

Non-primordial deities are also found. A snake is conjured by Ištar and Dumuzi in Fs. Wilcke 62: 8–9 (№ 108). The opening lines of this spell state that the snake was born to the river Tigris and raised by the river Ulaya which is known, in Babylonian cosmology, as the border to the Netherworld.[170] The chthonic character of the reptile is confirmed in ll. 6–7, where Nergal is said to have invested it with the capacity to crawl (and roaring Adad gave it the ability to shout). This explains the invocation of Ištar and Dumuzi, two deities with seasonal sojourns in the Netherworld.

The adjuration of Lamaštu by Ea in BIN 2, 72: 20 (№ 159) can be similarly explained. It is Anum who begot this demoness, but Ea is said to have raised her (BIN 2, 72: 1). For this reason, the speaker threatens her with Ea's name (BIN 2, 72: 10–13).

Ninkarrak appears in an oath in a spell against flies (YOS 11, 6: 9 = № 80). The healing goddess was chosen in this case as flies symbolize death.[171]

Šamaš appears in an oath in JCS 9, 10: 28 (№ 55). Following lines ll. 29–31, this deity, in his role as divine judge, is chosen to conjure the different disease.

---

164 PBS 1/2, 122: r. 15 ' (№ 147).

165 Kusu and Indagar: CUSAS 32, 24b; 11 (№ 89). Ninkilim: YOS 11, 35: 1 (№ 104).

166 See Cunningham 1997, 30/57/117.

167 On one occasion, the phrase is extended with *māmītum* "oath": *utammīki māmīt* ^{d}*Ea* "I conjure you by the oath of Ea!" (BIN 2, 72: 20 = № 159).

168 See Lambert 2013, 411 and 417.

169 On ^{d}LUM-ma – Enšēda: Marchesi 2006, 37–39.

170 See Wiggermann 1996, 212.

171 See Veldhuis 1993, 44; Kilmer 1987; Thomsen 2018.

Divine Support

In order to reinforce a spell, and add divine authority to it, phrases such as *ina pī* DN_1 (*u* DN_2) or *ina qibīt* DN_1 (*u* DN_2) "by the command of DN_1 (and DN_2)" are used.[172] To a similar effect, an enumeration of deities may be found at the end of some spells.[173] It is not surprising that Enki/Ea/Nudimmud and Asalluḫi/Marduk, the main deities of Mesopotamian magic, are called upon in such cases, as, e.g.: *ina qibīt Enki Asalluḫi u Ensigal-Abzu maḫṣum libluṭma qibīt Enki līšir* "By the command of Enki, Asalluḫi and Ensigal-Abzu, may the stricken one get well and may the command of Enki be true!" (CUSAS 32, 30d: 12–15 = № 92).[174] On one occasion, Enki and Marduk are backed up by two healing goddesses, Gula and Ninkarrak (BiOr 75, 21f.: 10–11 = № 15).[175] In other cases, senior deities of the Mesopotamian pantheon are invoked: Anum (PBS 1/2, 122: r. 18', YOS 11, 35: 1 = № 147 and 104) and Nunnamnir, i.e., Enlil (Fs. Stol 150: 2 = № 53).

It is not surprising to find Nazi, i.e., Nanše, in a spell destined to help in fishing (*ina pī Nazi abarakkatim ša Ningal liṣiʾamma* "By the command of Nazi, the stewardess of Ningal, may it (the fish) come out to me!", Fs. de Meyer 75/83b: 24–25 = № 76), for this goddess is directly connected to marshes and fish.[176]

The learned enumeration of Inšušinak, Sagkud and Mes-sanga-Unug in CUSAS 32, 57: 4 (№ 128) is exceptional. The first two gods, Sagkud and Mes-sanga-Unug, are found in the Ningirsu/Ninurta section of the OB Weidner Godlist (AfO 2, 13: 14–15). The Elamite Inšušinak is also known to have been identified with Ninurta (cf. Hinz 1976–1980, 118).[177] Thus, the authorative formula in this spell appears to revolve around the figure of Ningirsu/Ninurta.[178]

Divine Legitimation

The legitimation formula *šiptum ul yattun šipat* DN_1 *u* DN_2 "the incantation is not mine, it is the incantation of DN_1 and DN_2" was studied by Lenzi (2010). The following gods are found in our corpus: Gula (YOS 11, 5b: 14 = № 114), Ninkil[il] (JEOL 47, 58b: 31 = № 31), Asalluḫi (Fs. Stol 150: 22 = № 53), Ea (AoF 35, 146: 19 = № 150) and Ningirim (CUSAS 32, 8d: ii 5'and AMD 1, 247 (fig. 12): 24 = № 21 and 177, respectively).[179] When a pair of deities is referred to, then a male–female pair tend to appear: Ninkilil and Ninkarrak (Or. 66, 61: 18–20 = № 162), Damu and Gula (AMD 1, 243 (fig. 1): 8 = № 61); YOS 11, 5a: 8 = № 113), Ea and Ištar (CUSAS 10, 11: 16 = № 131), with the male deity in the leading position. Once, in an OA incantation, we find Ninkilil instead of Ningirim (Or. 66, 61: 18 = № 162).[180]

172 A similar authoritative formula is *Besiyata Dishmaya* (בְּסִייַעְתָּא דִשְׁמַיָּא, often abbreviated בס"ד). This Aramaic phrase, meaning "with the help of Heaven", is routinely placed by observant Jews at the top of every written document.

173 BiOr 75, 21f. (№ 15), CT 44, 32(+)33t (№ 50), CUSAS 32, 57 (№ 128). See further, Zomer 2019, 1264.

174 For Ensigal-Abzu, see George 2016, 115.

175 Possibly followed by Ningirim, see BiOr 75, 21f. (№ 15).

176 Heimpel 1998–2000, 152f.

177 The alloglot passage may suggest an Elamite origin.

178 See also CUSAS 32, 55: 7 (№ 126).

179 In YOS 11, 3: 10–13 (№ 46) we find Enlil and Šamaš in two consecutive legitimation formulae.

180 Probably to be restored also in Fs. Larsen 397/399a: 21 (№ 9) and in JEOL 47, 58b: 31 (№ 31).

Ningirim is a female deity, as the epithet *bēlet šipātim* "lady of the incantations" proves (e.g., CUSAS 32, 8d = № 21). Ninkilil, by contrast, is a male god, referred to as *bēl šipātim* "lord of the incantation" (Or. 66, 61 = № 162). As Ninkilil is otherwise unknown in the Mesopotamian pantheon, this name is probably an amalgamation of Ningirim and Ninkilim, the latter a male deity frequently associated with vermin and wildlife (George 1999, 297f.).[181] Single-sex combinations are also found: the feminine duo Ningirim and Ninkarrak in AoF 45, 196: 18–19 (№ 120), the male triad Enki, Asalluḫi and Ensigal-Abzu in CUSAS 32, 30d: ii 10–11 (№ 92), and Ningirim, Enki and Asalluḫi in JCS 9, 9: 32–33 (№ 54).[182]

The frequent occurrence of Ningirim in the corpus continues the early Sumerian magic tradition of the third millennium, where all spells are attributed to this deity (Rudik 2015, 30f.). In later periods, other gods join in.[183]

Legitimation formulae, such as "I am the man of DN_1" or "I am the magician of DN_1" or "I am the messenger of DN_1", known from contemporary Sumerian spells (Cunningham 1997, 118), are not found in our Akkadian corpus.[184] We do find, however, a similar expression "I am the weapon of Ningirsu!" in CUSAS 32, 55: 7 (№ 126).[185]

Divine Protection

Contrary to hymns, laments, or literary letters, direct reference to divine protection is rarely found in the body of incantations studied by us. Only on one occasion (YOS 11, 21b: 23–24 = № 145) does the speaker assert divine protection:

> *The hand of Šamaš is my protection, Ištar, Ningirgi[lum?], and Nin-MAŠ are the commanders? – you will not approach to ...*

Deities in Historiolae

As historiolae are set in mythical times, deities are the main protagonists to feature in them (see § 1.7.4), where they may stand for a primeval victim. Plucking the poisonous 'heart-plant', Šamaš caused a long chain of contamination.[186] In another story, Sîn is stung by a scorpion while building a house.[187] What is common to these patients is their celestial position. The 'heart-plant' grows across the mountains (YOS 11, 11: 1–9 = № 35). It is thus natural that the Sun-god would transfer it from East to West. The fact that the Moon-god Sîn was the second victim to catch the disease, corroborates the astral origin of the toxic plant. By the same token, it seems that the Moon-god was stung by the scorpion as a result of a celestial encounter between the moon and the constellation Scorpio. Another interesting case

---

181 See further, Krebernik 1984, 260–262.

182 Enki and Ningirim may be found in CUSAS 32, 31d: iii 2'–3' (№ 155). In OECT 11, 11: r. 4' (№ 133), read perhaps I[štar? and Ea?].

183 See Zomer 2018a, 61 fn. 203.

184 These formulae are more frequent from the late second millennium (Zomer 2018a, 64) and become dominant in the first millennium, e.g., Udugḫul III 124–127 (Geller 2016, 114f.) and Ḫulbazizi no. 4 (Finkel 1976, 84).

185 Allusions to narratives where Ningirsu/Ninurta is the main protagonist (Lugale and The Return of Ninurta to Nippur) can also be found in a group of Sumerian incantations from the first millennium, see Zomer 2020, 359.

186 E.g., CUSAS 32, 7o // CUSAS 32, 8i (№ 19), YOS 11, 11 (№ 35), YOS 11, 13 (№ 37).

187 CUSAS 32, 21l (№ 87), CUSAS 32, 49 (№ 93), YOS 11, 4c (№ 103).

of a joint appearance of Sîn and Šamaš comes in JNES 14, 15 (№ 45). In this spell, against a stye, Sîn is described as reaping and Šamaš harvesting. It is hard to avoid the interpretation that the lunar crescent of Sîn resembles a sickle and the shining solar halo of Šamaš resembles stacks of barley or wheat.

The Moon-god is purposely throwing harmful creatures at a human victim, a child suffering from worms in his nose and eyes (YOS 11, 5b = № 114). It is the healing goddess Gula who comes to the rescue of mankind in this case. Standing on the healing side, Sîn is often mentioned in birth incantations as assisting the cow in her difficult labour. This role may be assumed also by Enlil (BiOr 75, 19f.: 9–10 = № 3) and Šamaš (VS 17, 34: 4–6 = № 12).[188]

In the common *mannam lušpur* formula, the speaker tries to get help from deities. As discussed by Farber (1990b), the Daughters of Anum (*mārāt Anim*) are most frequently sought out.[189] They are described as a kind of divine fire brigade extinguishing the inflammation and soothing the patient.

> *Whom should I send and assign to the Daughters of Anum, seven and seven, whose vessels are gold, their jars pure lapis-lazuli? Let them take for me their vessels of gold, their jars of pure lapis-lazuli! Let them draw for me pure water of the se*[*as*]*! let them sprinkle, let them extinguish the sikkatum-disease, fever, the ašû-disease, the ziqtu-disease, bad collapse, the šamagum-disease, the samānu-disease, the gergiššum-disease, the sernettum-disease, the sweet simmu-disease, the ekketum-disease, the rišītum-disease, the bloody feces, shivering, the šagbānu-disease, the šaššaṭu-disease!* (JCS 9, 9: 13–29 = № 54)

Not much is known about the benevolent Daughters of Anum. In fact, in the first-millennium anti-witchcraft series Maqlû, malevolent Daughters of Anum aid the witch in her sorcery.[190] Similar groups of goddesses are found in OA incantations, where we find formulae with the Daughters of Šassūr and the Daughters of Ea. Šassūr ('Womb') is a mother goddess and occurs in birth incantations (CCT 5, 50e: 5'–11', Fs. Larsen 397/399a: 8–10 and SANER 9, 77: 6–10 = № 5, 9 and 11, respectively).[191] As for the Daughters of Ea in a spell against a dog (Fs. Hirsch 427 = № 69), this appellation can be linked to another *mannam lušpur* formula from Babylonia, where an appeal is made to "the dweller of the great Apsû" (YOS 11, 11: 10–12 = № 35, against gastrointestinal disorders). The dweller of the Apsû is Enki/Ea, and he appears in *mannam lušpur* formulae in his capacity as a senior magician deity.[192]

Two other deities are found in the *mannam lušpur* formulae. In OECT 11, 2: 15–18 (№ 122, for a crying baby), Enkidu appears with the nocturnal appelation "the creator of the three night watches". Gilgameš's dead friend became the authority for nightly disturbances. In the

188 Weeping Enlil is also found in the birth incantation CUSAS 32, 29c: 27 (№ 8). The epithet *ellamê* for Šamaš, used in VS 17, 34 (№ 12), is known to describe Sîn. On the weeping of Sîn, *ellamê* and the possible relation to a lunar eclipse, see Civil 1974, 334 and Stol 1992, 275ff.

189 See CUSAS 10, 11 (№ 131), CUSAS 32, 211 (№ 87), JCS 9, 9 (№ 54), JCS 9, 10 (№ 55), JNES 14, 15 (№ 45), RA 36, 4a (№ 123), Semitica 61, 13f. (№ 57), YOS 11, 8 (№ 58).

190 E.g., Maqlû III 63 (Abusch 2016, 306). For a discussion of the Daughters of Anum in the late-Hellenistic incantation "Philinna Papyrus", *mystodokos* and the dark-eyed maidens, see Faraone 1995.

191 For Šassūr as a mother goddess, see Krebernik 1993–1995, 507.

192 Farber 1990b, 303.

beautiful snake incantation CUSAS 32, 48: 14–20 (№ 107), Ningirsu crops up. This god, so the incantation says, is capable of ensnaring the great gods, making him the perfect choice to control a snake.

Last but not least, we ought to mention here the experienced Enki/Ea and his prodigal son Asalluḫi/Marduk. These two divine magicians join forces in texts known – after Falkenstein (1931) – as the Marduk-Ea incantations. This is the power couple of Mesopotamian magic, and no other god can better address an acute situation.[193]

193 For other dialogues between a senior and a junior god, see Rudik 2015, 95 and Zomer 2018b, 38.

1.6 *Ex opere operato*: Magic Strategies

Some incantations are meant to procure a much-needed entity. Such are the incantations to catch a fish (§ 2.2.2) and the incantations related to honeybees (§ 2.2.3). Another group of incantations focus on the healer himself, aiming to charge him with superhuman power (§ 2.3.3). But most incantations counteract a threat or a problem, be it the Evil Eye or a frightening demon, a disease or dangerous animal, a trial or a resistant would-be lover. In this section we shall treat incantations that were used to counteract problems and threats – and examine the different magic methods employed by them.

It is remarkable that prophylactic actions are totally absent in our corpus. No preventive magic measures are taken against coming misfortune. All incantations act *ex post facto*, in a retroactive manner: first, the misadventure strikes and then, and only then, does the magic process take place. This attitude is in a sharp contrast to later Mesopotamian magic literature where, based on bad omens, precautionary, even pre-emptive, actions were often taken. It is also of interest that the principles of *similia similibus curantur* and *similibus curentur* cannot really be found in our corpus. Perhaps the closest to these – originally neo-Platonic – essential concepts of healing are expressions like "As the *signs* of dignity do not stay overnight, may the labour pain not stay overnight in your belly!" in BiOr 75, 15f.: 1–4 (№ 2) (childbirth), or "Like calves run off to the cows (and) goat-kids run off to the she-goats, may the brewing jar, the daughter of Enki, run off to the beer jugs!" in CUSAS 32, 32b: 2'–4' (№ 28) (gastrointestinal problems).[194] But such comparisons are figures of speech belonging to rhetoric; they do not present a magico-medical doctrine according to which 'like is cured by like'.

Faced with evil, the OB or OA magician could take different means of action: (1) Direct confrontation; (2) Indirect approach; (3) Offering a way out; (4) Ignoring evil.

In the following, we furnish examples for each of these magic strategies. Let us be aware that different magic methods can be used concomitantly within a single incantation.

194 Cf. TIM 9, 73b: 6–7 (empowerment).

1.6.1 Direct Confrontation

The healer can take direct action through words – by uttering wishes and commands – or physically. In the latter case, what we have are his declarations, performative statements (usually in first-person verbs in the past tense: "I have done so-and-so") which presumably accompanied his actions, or replaced them. The practitioner may act unaided, or in enhanced fashion using *materia magica*.

Verbal actions

Uttering a wish or command

"May it (the newborn) fall to the ground! The cow, may she rise […]!" (BiOr 75, 15f.:18–20 = № 2, childbirth), or "Do not oppose it! Go out of the (patient's) belly!" (YOS 11, 14c: 10 = № 39, jaundice).

Physical action, unassisted or with the help of *materia magica*

Stepping over, crossing above

"Let me pass back and forth through you like (through) an *Arkabinnu*-door! Let me hang above you like a lintel! Like (with) a restraining-rope, let me curb your step!" (TIM 9, 72: 10–16 = № 116, anger), or "[I will tr]ead on you like a reed of the path! [I will cr]oss over you like (over) the threshold!" (CUSAS 32, 31e: 18–21 = № 121, crying baby).

Holding back, binding, locking, blocking, enveloping

"I hold you (m.) back just like Ištar held back Dumuzi, (Just like) Seraš binds her drinkers, (so) I have bound you (m.) with my hairy mouth, with my drooling mouth", or "I locked your thighs" (ZA 75, 198–204b: 14–18 = № 137 and ZA 75, 198–204i: 105 = № 142, both for love), or still "Stars, I detain you! Heavens, I detain you! Earth, I detain you! Anum, I detain you! Enlil, I detain you!" (CT 42, 6e: 2–6 = № 168, food), and "I have blocked it (anger)" (UET 6/2, 399: 12 = № 117) (anger), or "I have enveloped you like a f[og]" (RA 36, 3a: 2 = № 144, trial).

Smashing, tossing, attacking

"I smote the *parkulla*, even the *parakulla*-snake…" (AMD 1, 245 (fig. 5): 10–11 = № 105, snake), or "…I have thrown you down (on) your buttocks!... I have attacked you like a wolf!" (RA 36, 3a: 3, 5 = № 144, trial).

Throwing objects

"I threw at her a weapon… I threw at her a shepherd staff… I threw at her beer bread, thyme, and salt – I verily did turn her over from her root" (Fs. Larsen 397/399b: 29–33 = № 1, bile).

Seizing

"I will seize the snake in the reed-bed! I will seize the viper in the rushes!" (CUSAS 32, 48: 7–8 = № 107, snake).

Tearing, pulling out

"I have torn the thorn, I will be sowing a vine!" and "I pulled out? your heel, I took the … of your heart" (CUSAS 32, 23b: 7–8 = № 132 and ZA 75, 198–204i: 103–104 = № 142, both for love).

Extinguishing the burning

"I have poured water onto the fierce fire!" and "Let me throw on your (m.) heart ice (and) frost!" (CUSAS 32, 23b: 9–11 = № 132 and YOS 11, 21c: 27 = № 135, both love).

Silencing

"I have taken a bowstring; I have fastened your lips" (RA 36, 3a: 4 = № 144, trial).[195]

Blinding

"With dust your mouth, with a whirl-wind your face, with cress seeds finely ground I will verily fill your (the demoness') eyes!" (BIN 2, 72: 16–19 = № 159, Lamaštu) and perhaps also "I have thrown my excrement over you (the legal opponent) like a lion!" (RA 36, 3a: 6 = № 144, trial).

1.6.2 Indirect Approach

The healer may act indirectly, asking deities, natural forces or living entities for help or to work for him. He may compel evil to obey by pronouncing divine names, or swearing divinely-enforced oaths. Or he may try and control evil by proxy, i.e., by acting on a related object which is manageable *in lieu* of attempting to handle the cause of trouble.

Divine intervention

"May the god of the house throw the eye out to the outside!" (CUSAS 32, 31c: 19–20 = № 154, Evil Eye), or "Reed-bed of Sîn! Reed of Magan! Sîn my lord! Pull out your reed-mat!" (Fs. de Meyer 75/83b: 16–17 = № 76, to catch a fish), or still "… Ea noticed him (the baby in the womb). Asalluḫi opened for him the path, made the road ready for him, (saying:) 'May Šamaš set you to freedom!'" (BM 115745: 11–13 = № 4, childbirth).

Divine legitimation for action

"The incantation is not mine! It is the incantation of Enlil! The incantation is not mine! It is the incantation of Šamaš! I am the wild bull of the mountains (and) I cast the incantation on my body!" (YOS 11, 3: 10–18 = № 46, toothache), or "Since Damu has cast his incantation – he got well, (now) I will cast my incantation so that he will get well" (YOS 11, 16b: 6–7 = № 43, orthopaedic problems). Here we may mention also the magic pattern of "just as *in illo*

195 Silencing the enemy finds parallels in anti-witchcraft incantations, e.g., "I have seized your mouth so that it cannot speak evil against me, with a seal of *šubû*-stone and (a seal) of *šadânu*-stone I have sealed your lips, so that they cannot utter my name!" (Abusch/Schwemer 2011, 143: 42–44), "I have seized your mouth, I have dried out your tongue, I have seized your hands, I have put a (muzzle) of thread in your mouth! I have now opened your mouth, I have now torn out the tongue from your mouth, so that you are not able to slander me, so that you are not able to distort my words!" (Abusch/Schwemer 2011, 363: 1–5).

tempore, so *in hoc tempore*": "Just as Anum, king of heaven, inseminated the herd of Šakkan, may I impregnate and pour magic over the patient" (CUSAS 32, 25a: 4–5 = № 23, gastrointestinal problems).

Calling for natural healing elements, healing materials or artifacts

"May the Sippirûm-tree? cross the river hither! May it go down to me! May it ascend from its subterranean water!" and "May the date palm from Dilmun cross the sea hither! May it go down to me, may it get across from (its) subterranean water!" (AMD 14, 197b: 9–12 = № 64 and CUSAS 32, 29a: 5–6 = № 67, both against dogs), or "A torch, mottled barely, sulfur of a *maštakal*-plant, the 'magic-stick'-plant, the *šalālum*-reed, tamarisk, a young date palm – the pure ones (= the above plants) will come along [in order] to re[lease] the house of the man, [so that] the so[rcery?] will [c]ome out" (UET 6/2, 193a: 9'–16' = № 148, witchcraft).[196]

Compelling oaths involving deities

"You are adjured by Anum and Anatum, Laḫmum and Dūrum, the earth and its watercourses: 'You shall not return! You shall not snatch her!'" (AoF 35, 146: 20–24 = № 150, Evil Eye), or "(By) Enki and Marduk! (By) Gula, Ninkarrak (and) Nin[girim?]!" (BiOr 75, 21f.: 10–11 = № 15, childhood disease).

Offering ex votos

Rarely we find the strategy of *do ut des* "I give (you, the god) so that you give me". Namely, the patient convinces the gods to help him in his misery by promising them lavish *ex votos*: "May I keep carefully placing solar-disks on the pedestals of the great gods appropriately!" (YOS 11, 7 = № 44, against pox in sheep).

Compelling oaths not involving deities

"I swear by entering the threshold of the house!" (CUSAS 32, 32c: 15' = № 29, gastrointestinal problems),[197] and the interesting threat in YOS 11, 3: 6–9 = № 46 (against toothache): "Until there will be joy and the dead man revives from the Netherworld, you shall not rise!".

---

196 In a recently published OB Sumerian incantation, a fish and a bird are summoned as vehicles to carry sorcery off to the sky and the deep water (Wagensonner 2020). This method appears also in later texts, as in the *Lipšur Litanies* (Reiner 1956, 140–141: 22'). The method of getting rid of evil by animals that carry it off is not unknown in the Babylonian Talmud. In Bab. Shabbat 66b we read: "Abaye also said: Mother told me: For a daily fever one must take a white *zuz* (a small coin), go to a salt deposit, take its weight in salt, and tie it up in the nape of the neck with a white twisted cord. But if this is not [possible], let one sit at the cross-roads, and when he sees a large ant carrying something, let him take and throw it into a brass tube and close it with lead, and seal it with sixty seals. Let him shake it, lift it up and say to it, 'Thy burden be upon me and my burden be upon thee.' Said R. Aha son of R. Huna to R. Ashi: But perhaps [another] man had [previously] found it and cast [his illness] upon it? Rather let him say to it, 'My burden and thy burden be upon thee' (Trans. Soncino edition).

197 The magical role of the threshold may be alluded by the prophet Zephaniah (1: 8–9), describing foreign and improper habits occurring in the Temple: "And it shall come to pass in the day of the Lord's sacrifice that I will punish the princes, and the king's sons, and all such as are clothed with foreign apparel. In the same day also will I punish all those that leap over the threshold, that fill their master's house with violence and deceit" (transl. JPS Tanakh).

Threatening evil with implements

"Go out *maškadum* before the flint razors of Gula will reach you!" (YOS 11, 14b: 5 = № 41, Maškadum, cf. BIN 2, 7: 12, against Lamaštu).

Calling for an analogical natural element

"Oh my …! Oh my sta[r …]! … [my] [*ach*]*ing to*[*oth*$^?$]! You (or: she) will say three times, as following: '[Oh s]tar! my star! my tooth is aching! Carry away [the pa]in of my tooth!'" in YOS 11, 12c: 31–37 (№ 47) (toothache). The malevolent agent causing the toothache is *tūltum* "worm". A constellation by this name is known. The spell probably asks the analogical astral worm to counteract the worm in the tooth. See also: "The South-wind, the North-wind, the East-wind, the West-wind have risen (and) seized the mouth of the brewing-vat" in CUSAS 32, 32a: 17–18 (№ 27) (gastrointestinal problems). Here flatus causes internal troubles and the four winds of the compass are invoked to serve as a solution. The internal wind is relieved by the analogical external winds.

Manipulation by proxy

"… You are placed on a stand. You are furnished with a *kittu*, a stopper (and) a plug. With Ištar's (help), I removed from you the stoppers, (thus) made the feast go out; I pulled out the plug, (thus) created wind. I turned your draff into a recitation; the water (with) which you have rinsed I made into an incantation", or "Wood of god; water-skin of humanity! Let the wood stand, let the water-skin be smashed!" (CUSAS 32, 32a: 7–14 = № 27 and CUSAS 32, 30b: 11–14 = № 26, both for gastrointestinal problems). In both cases, liquid-containing vessels – a brewing vat or the water-skin – stand for the man's aching belly. The healer is acting upon those containers, and by analogy, the sick organ gets better.

1.6.3 Offering a Way Out

The magician may choose an aikido-like strategy, viz. meeting the attack with avoidance, containing it, and offering it a way out.

Releasing evil

"Get out, wind, affluence of the people! From the head get out, wind! From the eye get out, wind! From the mouth get out, wind! From the ear get out, wind! From the anus get out, wind! Let the man rest" (OECT 11, 3: 3–9 = № 32, gastrointestinal problems), or "the door socket is wide (enough) for you, open are the doors: Go, walk about the steppe!" (BIN 2, 72: 14–15 = № 159, Lamaštu), and "You (the worm eating the tooth) should go up into the mountains!" (YOS 11, 3: 3 = № 46), and simply "get out!" said to a scorpion (Semitica 62, 15f.: 17 = № 98).

Sending evil back to its origin

"Chase away the Eye! Drive away the Eye! Make the Eye go out to your (m.) …! May the Eye go back to its own[er!]" (Fs. De Meyer 86, 15'–16'/20' = № 156, Evil Eye), or "May you (f.) rejoin the eye(s) of your (m.) father and mother! May you (f.) be tied up in your (m.) house!" (CUSAS 32, 31d: 4–6 = № 155, Evil Eye), or still "[To] your (DN's) hold [may] they (the diseases) return (back to their heavenly origin)!" (JCS 9, 10: 30–31 = № 55, various diseases). In YOS 11, 8: 7–9 (№ 58, against various diseases), a severe skin disease which descended from heaven and darkened its victims is ordered to leave like smoke and cloud. Though formally only a simile ("like x, like y"), smoke and cloud were chosen as analogical natural elements that will carry the pathogen back to its place in heaven. An interesting case is the call to send evil back not to its spatial origin, but to its day of creation: "May his (the rabid dog's) mouth become as it was on the day he was born!" (BiOr 11 Pl. II (fig. 1): 7–9 = № 65, dogs).[198]

Flattering evil, honouring it

In some rare cases, it seems that the magician is trying to be nice, cajoling evil to comply: "Get out wind, the son of god! Get out, wind, affluence of the people!" (OECT 11, 3: 1–2 = № 32, gastrointestinal problems), or "Let the Tigris carry for you (the unyielding woman) charcoal, *sangû*, copper, lead of Susa! Let it carry hither *sangû*! Oh you, who pierces your (f.) eyes!" (VS 17, 23: 4–7 = № 134, for love), and "Oh threshold! Keep letting your sons enter!" addressing honeybees (CUSAS 32, 51: 2 = № 78).

1.6.4 Ignoring Evil

Incantations devoid of any strategy to combat evil

Some incantations contain no clear method of combating or dispersing evil. All they do is describe the harming agent, as BIN 4, 126 and YOS 11, 20 (№ 160 and № 165, both against Lamaštu). Similarly, historiola can be told, recounting a successful encounter with the harming agent in the mythological past, as YOS 11, 19a (№ 164, also against Lamaštu).

There is more to say on the subject of Mesopotamian magic strategies, and the authors hope to present a more detailed study in the future.

198 See Wasserman 2005b.

1.7 Literary Devices

Incantations intend to control reality and manipulate it by verbal means. Through words – their meaning and their sound – and through particular actions, the magic practitioner aims to direct a given situation towards a desired point. It is therefore of little surprise that incantations are inventive and expressive texts. In this study, philological in essence, a thorough investigation of the style and form of incantations is not possible.[199] In the following, the reader will find an outline of some of the most elementary stylistic devices employed.

1.7.1 Sound-Based Devices

Alliteration

The vocal aspect of incantations, any incantation in any cultural setting, is a vital part of their performance. The transfiguration spell in J. K. Rowling's *Harry Potter* offers a good starting point: *Amato Animo Animato Animagus*. The repeated vocables add a non-lexical layer to the spell, augmenting thus its effect beyond the meaning of the uttered words. A fine example from our corpus comes from an OA incantation for a woman in labour: ***arḫ****um* ***araḫ Araḫ****tum* ***arḫa****t* ***arḫ****iš tarri* ***arḫ****iš tullad* ***arḫ****iš illukū mā'ū ipiša* "A cow, Oh cow! The *Araḫtum*-canal is quick! Quickly, she is pregnant! Quickly, she is giving birth! Quickly, the water is coming from her afterbirth!" (Fs. Larsen 397/399a: 1–5 = № 9). The sequence ARḪ not only throbs rhythmically beneath the words, but adds polysemic force, for ARḪ is the consonantal base found in "moon", "month", "quick" and "cow", all of which are thematically relevant. Note also the beginning of the OA incantation against bile, Fs. Larsen 397/399b:24–28 (№ 1), where the vocable ERQ is repeated, accompanied by the percussion of the **t**: ***erqum eriq eriq****ṯum* ***erqa****ṯ iṣṣilli miṯraṯim* ***eriq****ṯem ezzum barumaṯum ṯarṯe''e* "The verdure is yellow-green. The vegetation is yellow-green. The shade of the yellow-green irrigated orchard, a speckled she-goat keeps pasturing". A maze-like alliteration, based on the shushing **š**, is found in an incantation against scorpions: *waruq* ***ša*** *ṣē[rim] ṣalim* ***ša*** *bītim muttapriš* ***šam****[āʾī]* *aruḫ* ***ša*** *baštim* ***ša*** *ina eper* ***šadîš****[****u****]* *ballu* "It (the scorpion) is the yellow of the steppe, it is the black of the house, it is the soaring one of the sky, it is the rushing one of the shrubs. The one spread with the dust of its mountain of origin" (CUSAS 32, 49: 1–6 = № 93), and also in another incantation against scorpions, where the consonants **š** and **k**/**q** alternate: *nimmelillaššu ina qātīni šuḫut qarnī liškun qaqqar****šu*** "We play with it (the scorpion) in our hands. May it place the anger of (its) horns towards the ground!" (Semitica 62, 15f.: 7–9 = № 98).

A no less pronounced case of alliteration is found in an incantation against a scorpion, where **b**/**p** and **d**/**t**/**ṭ** are contrasted: ***b****ūḏāšu li****b****iṯṯum li****bb****ašu nāḏum liḫ‹ḫe›****pi*** *li****b****iṯṯum liššariṭ nāḏum li****b****li ḏi****p****ār zi****bb****aṯišu u qannīšu* "Its shoulders – a brick, its middle part – a water-skin. May the brick be broken! May the water-skin be torn! May the torch of its tail and its two horns be extinguished!" (CUSAS 32, 49: 7–12 = № 93). A line from a bilingual incantation

199 Various aspects of style and form in OB incantations were presented by Wasserman 2003.

against the demoness Lilītum shows subtle alliteration: a kar sikil-la-ta [dug]sáhar ù-ba-e-ni-si /// ***mê** karri **ellim** ina **mullīmma*** "Fill (a porous pot) with water from a pure quay" (PBS 1/2, 122: 23 = № 147). The sonorant **m** and the liquids **l** and **r** imitate the sound of flowing water described in this line. Another fine example where phonetics and semantics lean on each other is *ḫussīnima kīma ašnugalli liḫšušū pānūki kīma rīmtim* "Think of me as an *Ašnugallum*-snake! May your face rejoice as a wild cow" (CUSAS 10, 11: 8–9 = № 131, for love). *ḫasāsum* "to think, to remember" and *ḫašāšum* "to swell, be happy" are used to strengthen the message of the male lover: if you remember me, you will rejoice.

Alliteration in alloglot passages ought not to be overlooked for this is where they were most important. The foreign tongue passages were most likely unintelligible to the Mesopotamian magician or patient. Their effect resulted from their strong musicality and strange sounds which increased the speaker's authority. The *Harry Potter* series may serve to illustrate this point, for Latin was often used in the English-speaking Hogwarts School of Witchcraft and Wizardry. Two examples of alliteration in alloglot passages can be supplied: *[ku]l kimḫa kul kimmaḫa kul sihara kul sikra kuli rabika kuli rabika* (YOS 11, 41: 1–4 = № 115), and *[zazali] zazali zal u zazal … ⸢u za⸣lizal zalizal u zazal*, and *[udd]ul ulla uddul ulla* (CUSAS 32, 55: 1–2, and 9 = № 126). On the different aspects of alloglot passages in first millennium incantations and medical texts, see Baragli (2019), where the term *vox magica* is used.

Paronomasia, jeu de mots, double entendre

Puns are not a distinguishing feature of incantations. Conspicuous cases of this trope seem to be more typical of longer compositions. A *locus classicus* is Gilg. XI 39–47, the famous speech of Enki to Atraḫasīs in the opening of the story of the Flood.[200] Still, some cases of *jeu de mots* or *double entendre* based on homonyms can be detected in our corpus. The short love incantation CUSAS 32, 23b: 7–8 (№ 132) begins with *assuḫ baštam azarru karānam* "I have torn the thorn, I will be sowing a vine!". The vivid image of replacing wild thorns with a wanted productive plant is expanded once we realize that *baštum* "thorn" is a homonym of *bāštum* "(sexual) dignity". The implication is clear: what the speaker has in mind is a manipulation of the woman's emotions to make her sexually desirous of him (Wasserman 2016, 248). A similar use of a homonyimic couple is found in the birth incantation which ends with the request *kīma dādim šūṣi ramānka* "Come out by yourself like a good boy!" (YOS 11, 86a: 26–27 = № 14). The word *dādum* is used here in its two meanings: "darling, beloved one", and "an aquatic animal with a shell", conveying the wish that the neonate will come out easily and that the birth will end in a healthy baby.[201] In a spell against scorpions, the dangerous pincers are likened to a (male) goat's horns (*eddā qarnāka kīma urīṣi*). A few lines later it is said that the mouth of the scorpion is furious (*ez pīka*). The formally non-

200 See Worthington 2020 where the term 'bitextuality' is introduced. Other significant puns in the Epic of Gilgameš were identified by Parpola 1997, XCII–XCIII, related to Enkidu's sexual role in the epic: *kiṣru* ≈ *kezru* and *ḫaṣṣinu* ≈ *assinnu*. In the Sargon Birth Legend as well, a sex-related pun is found: the king is said to be born in *Azupirānu*, an invented toponym which means "like *azupīru*", a plant known to induce abortion. This wordplay points ironically to the tradition according to which Sargon's mother was an *Ēntu*-priestess not supposed to have children (Goodnik Westenholz 1997, 39)

201 See also BM 115745: 3 and 8 (№ 4), an incantation for an easy birth, where *šerrum* "baby" and *šīru* "flesh" lean on each other.

complete form *ez* (instead of *eziz* or *ezi*) is most likely used because of its play on *ezzum*/*enzum* "she-goat" (Semitica 62, 15f.: 1, 4 = № 98). So here, too, a homonymic pun is used ("furious" – "she-goat"). Finally, the Evil Eye is said to cause disharmony between friends: *īmur bukīnam mūdâm umarrir* "She (the Eye) saw the trough, embittered an acquaintance" (CUSAS 32, 31c: 4–5 = № 154). Now, as suggested by George (2016, 96), *bukīnum* "bucket" is used here with double meaning, playing on *pû kīnum* "loyal talk".

1.7.2 Syntagmatic Devices

Repetition

The reduplication of a key-word is a literary device which tends to appear at the beginning of incantations. Consider the love incantation which begins with *[pitarr]assī pitarras‹sī›* "[Keep] her apart! keep [her] apart!" (CUSAS 10, 11 = № 131), the spell against a stye which opens with *erṣetummi erṣetummi* "Earth – they say – earth…" (JNES 14, 15 = № 45), the incantation against flatus whose first line is *ṣī šārum ṣī šārum* "Get out, wind! Get out, wind!" (OECT 11, 3 = № 32), and the incantation against anger, where each section begins with *uzzum uzzum* "Anger! Anger!" (ZA 75, 198–204h: 78/85/95 = № 119).[202] A case of an ever-extending repetition is found in a partially broken incantation for a child, in the midst of which we read *ruʾ ruʾ ruʾ ruʾtum* "Spit, spit, spit - spittle!" (YOS 11, 17: 4 = № 13).[203]

Keywords

When a noun, or a verbal root, carrying crucial meaning are repeated in the text, one may speak of keywords. CT 42, 6e (№ 168), an incantation destined to procure a food ration, uses this device in an effective manner. The hungry and angry speaker is halting the stars, the heavens, and the earth, employing the verb *kalûm* "to detain" (*akallākunūti*, *akallāki*, *akallāka*). The universe can move again only when he takes (*leqûm*) his food and drink – thus, alliteration is reinforcing the rhetorical message. Another wonderful case of keywords, based on the root AḪZ and the noun *īnum* "eye", is the beginning of an incantation against the Evil Eye: *inūma īnum* ***īḫuzu āḫizam*** *u Enki* ***āḫizam īḫuz īḫuz*** *ibbarum īn Šamši u īnum bīt awīlim* ***īḫuz*** "When the eye seized the Seizer – Enki seized the Seizer. Mist seized the eye of the sun and the eye seized man's household" (CUSAS 32, 7g // CUSAS 32, 8c: 1–5 = № 151).[204]

Enumeration

Lists in general, and lists of items which incantations treat directly in particular, are typical of magic texts (Wasserman 2021). Clear cases of such lists, or enumerations, are found in incantations against snakes and dogs, creatures which must be specified in order to be properly fended off. Note TIM 9, 65 // TIM 9, 66a: 1–4 (№ 110), an incantation against snakes, which begins with a long, lexical-like, catalogue of reptiles: "I seized the mouth of

202 And YOS 11, 69c: 9' (№ 42); YOS 11, 69d: 16' (№ 82).

203 A similar, modern example of an ever-extending repetitive utterance with clear magic function is the famous formula of the Breslover Hasidim *Na Nach Nachma Nachman Me'uman*, based on the name of the founder of this religious group, Rabbi Nachman of Breslov.

204 Minor variations between the two texts are disregarded.

all snakes, even the *Kurṣindu*-snake, a snake impervious to spell(s), the *Aš*(*šu*)*nugallu*-snake, the *Burubalû*-snake, the *Šanapšaḫuru*-snake, of spackled eyes, the eel snake, the hissing snake, (even) the hisser, the snake at the window!". A regrettably broken incantation against dogs enumerates canines of different colour: "A blac[k dog, a whi]te [dog], a yellow dog, a red [do]g, [a speckled] dog…" (PIHANS 44 No. 302: 1–4 = № 72). Enumeration can also be used as an organizing thread, as in the following incantation against a sick belly, where body parts are listed from the head downwards: "Get out, wind! Get out, wind! … From the head get out, wind! From the eye get out, wind! From the mouth get out, wind! From the ear get out, wind! From the anus get out, wind! Let the man rest…" (OECT 11, 3: 1–9 = № 32).

Chain

A chain (or *anadiplosis*) is a construction in which the last word in a clause is immediately repeated in the following one, resulting in a hinge of recurring lemmas (see Veldhuis 1993 and Wasserman 2021). This trope, carrying a strong cohesive effect, is typical of historiolae describing a process of creation.[205] Consider the opening of the stye incantation: "Earth – they say – earth bore the dirt, the dirt bore the stalk, the stalk bore the ear, the ear bore the stye…" (JNES 14, 15 = № 45).[206] Descriptions of sequences of action also make use of chains, as in the spell against an irritating insect: "I hit you (the fly) at (my) cranium, from the cranium to (my) forehead, from the forehead to (my) ear, from the ear to the nostril of (my) nose" (YOS 11, 6 = № 80). A sequence of actions expressed by a chain is found also in a beautiful incantation against a snake: "When it (the snake) was thirsting for sustenance, the shore shook. The shore shook and it went into the reed-bed" and further: "He (the snake) cried out and approached the mountain; he approached the mountain and split a rock. He split a rock…" (CUSAS 32, 48: 5–7 and 11–12 = № 107). This exceptional chain (…*inūš kibru inūšma kibrum*… and *iššīma šadâm īkip šadâm īkip abnam ilte abnam iltēma*…) has a mimic function: it imitates the serpentine movement of the mythological snake from the depth of the sea, where it was born, as it crawls ashore to the rocks and thence up to the trees.

A more complex chain is found in an incantation destined to remedy internal disease whose malevolent agent is the magic plant: "Šamaš brought over the (magic) plant across the mountain. It seized the heart of Šamaš who brought it across; It seized the heart of Sîn in the sky; It seized the heart of the ox in the stall; It seized the heart of the sheep in the fold; It seized the heart of the lad in the street; It seized the heart of the maiden in the dance..." (YOS 11, 11 = № 35).[207] The series of victims of the plant (Šamaš, Sîn, ox, sheep, lad, maiden) is encased in a fixed formula which starts with *libbi*..., 'the heart of...' and ends with *iṣṣabat*, 'it seized'. A powerful rhetorical effect is achieved: a developing chain of contamination and of growing ailment is traced back to its origin: the magic plant which seized whatever it came in contact with.

205 As other devices, this trope is not restricted to literary texts but found, on occasion, also in the non-literary context. The Laws of Ešnunna § 49 present a good example: *šumma awīlum in wardim šarqim amtim šarqim ittaṣbat* ***wardum wardam amtum amtam*** *iredde* "If a man should be seized with a stolen slave or a stolen slave woman, a slave shall lead a slave, a slave woman shall lead a slave woman" (Roth 1995, 66).

206 See also YOS 11, 5a (№ 113, against a worm).

207 See also CUSAS 32, 7o // CUSAS 32, 8i (№ 19).

Rhyming Couplets

The non-ubiquity of rhymes – more exactly, homeoteleutic, or end-rhymes – in Akkadian literature, is discussed by Wasserman (2003, 157–158).[208] Rhyming couplets as a rhetorical sign at the end of incantations is striking (Wasserman 2003, 162–165). Clear examples are BIN 2, 72 (№ 159); Fs. Pope 87 (№ 70); OECT 11, 4 (№ 71); YOS 11, 87 (№ 136); YOS 11, 92 (№ 166). A fine case of rhyming couplet, not in a final position, is *būḏāšu* ***libiṯṯum*** *libbašu* ***nāḏum*** | *liḫ‹ḫe›pi* ***libiṯṯum*** *liššariṯ* ***nāḏum*** "Its shoulders – a brick, its middle part – a water-skin. May the brick be broken! May the water-skin be torn!" (CUSAS 32, 49: 7–12 = № 93, against a scorpion). This rhyming unit opens the manipulative section in which the healer is faced with the predatory arachnid. The importance of the utterance is further emphasized by its chiastic construction.

Expanding Rhyme

This stylistic device is rare in the genre of incantations.[209] It can be found in RA 70, 135/137 (№ 10), a long bilingual incantation for a woman in labour. Its opening lines end with the repeated phrase *kīma eleppi īteʾʾel* "the (pregnant) woman wobbled like a boat" (1–11, partially broken). Then, the lines start expanding: *kīma elep rīqī rīqī maliat* | *kīma elep erēni erēnam maliat* | *kīma elep rīqī erēni rīqī erē*[*nam maliat*] | *kīma elep sāmtim u uqnîm sām*[*tam u uqnâm maliat*] "Like a boat (carrying) aromatics, she is filled with aromatics. Like a boat (carrying) cedar, she is filled with cedar. Like a boat (carrying) aromatics and cedar, [she is filled] with aromatics and cedar. Like a boat (carrying) carnelian and lapis-lazuli, [she is filled] with carne[lian and lapis lazuli]" (12–19). This literary device creates a compelling litany-like effect.[210] Another case of expanding rhyme is found in a sadly broken text, YOS 11, 19b (= № 112, against a snake), where the lines open with *saḫḫum... saḫḫum... ina bamtika... ina bamat īnīka...* "The meadow... the meadow... in the middle... in the middle of your eyes...".

Chiasmus

We understand this stylistic device in the broader sense, namely, a syntactic construction, or phrase, with a symmetrical X-like form. Consider the following example, from an incantation against a rabid dog, where the wings of the chiastic construction are marked: ***izâb*** *<u>mūtum</u> ina pīšu naši nīlšu ašar iššuku <u>mārašu</u>* ***īzib*** "(From his teeth) death oozes. He carries his semen in his mouth – wherever he bit, he left his offspring" (AMD 14, 197b: 6–8 = № 64). A similar case of pronounced wings is found in an incantation against scorpions: *kīma* ***ṭābtim*** *u kasîm*

208 Rhyming couplets may occur, sporadically, in non-literary texts, reflecting popular speech. The Laws of Ešnunna § 36 (Roth 1995, 64) read: *šumma awīlum būšēšu ana napṭarim ana maṣṣartim iddimma* ***bītum lā pališ sippu lā ḫališ aptum lā nasḫat*** *būšē maṣṣartim ša iddinušum uḫtalliq būšēšu irīabšum* "If a man gives his goods to a *napṭarum* for safekeeping and he (the *napṭarum*) then allows the goods which he gave to him for safekeeping to become lost – without evidence that the house has been broken into, the doorjamb scraped, the window forced– he shall replace his goods for him".

209 It occurs more in longer compositions. See, e.g., SB Gilg. XI: 81–84: [*mimma īšû*] *eṣēnši mimma īšû eṣēnši kaspa mimma ī*[*šû*] *eṣēnši ḫurāṣa mimma ī*[*šû eṣē*]*nši zēr napšāti kalāma* "[Whatever I had] I loaded on her (the boat): Whatever silver I had, I loaded on her; whatever gold I had, I loaded on her. Whatever seed, of all living creatures, I loaded on her" (Wasserman 2020, 107; 116).

210 For expanding, litany-like rhymes in first-millennium incantations, see Schwemer 2014, 274–276.

eli muštemmiya lū ***ṭābāku*** "May my words (lit. I) be flavourful to my listener as salt and mustard!" (Semitica 62, 15f.: 17–19 = № 98). In another case, an incantation to ward off witchcraft is the axis of the chiastic construction that is made distinct, carrying a moral message: *ēpiš* ***lemnētim lemnētušu*** *ul išettašu* "The evildoer, his evil deeds will not leave him" (YOS 11, 15: 1 // YOS 11, 29b: 1 = № 149). Other cases of chiastic axis (involving paronomasia) are *ištēniš qarnī* ***ṭeri tari*** *zibassu* "simultaneously it (the scorpion) is rooting up (the ground) with (its) two horns, [its] ta[il] is curled up" (BM 97331b: 13 = № 85, against a scorpion) and *ša Ea šar Apsîm u* ***ṣērim ṣarram*** *Ištar* "(I come with the message) of Ea, king of the Apsû and the steppe, the eager one of Ištar" (CUSAS 32, 32c: 9'–10' = № 29, for gastrointestinal problems).

Hypallage

Morier, *Dictionnaire de poétique et de rhétorique*[4e] (1989, 520) defines this trope as "figure qui attribue à un objet l'acte ou l'idée convenant à l'objet voisin". There are some cases in our corpus which fit this definition. In an incantation against Lamaštu, the baby-killer demoness is said to strangle "the small-ones" and compel "the big ones to drink the amniotic fluid" (YOS 11, 20: 10–12 = № 165). Clearly, it is the unborn fetuses, the small-ones, who drink the amniotic fluid, while the bigger babies, the unweaned children, are those who risk dying in their sleep, strangled, presumably, by the demoness. Thus, the action attached to the first unit belongs logically to the second, and vice-versa.

In two incantations for easy birth, the woman in labour is compared to a cow. The incantations start with "The cow is pregnant, the cow is giving birth". Later, however, the text describes Enlil crying "over [his] cow, not deflowered, (over) [his] kid who never gave birth". Here, too, a *hypallage* is at work, and the attributes of the two animals should be switched: the cow, i.e., the young woman, is obviously not a virgin, since she is giving birth (for the first time?), while the kid – added hyperbolically for reasons of emphasis – is the one who was not deflowered (BiOr 75, 19f.: 1, 14–15 and VS 17, 34: 1, 9–10 = № 3 and 12, respectively).

Towards the end of a bilingual incantation against a bleating goat (with possible humoristic intentions) we find the request "may the goat die as if it is sleeping!" (PRAK 2 Pl. III (C1): 15 = № 81). Since the main problem is not the very existence of the goat, but its noise which disturbs the tired shepherd's sleep, it is unlikely that the incantation wishes the goat to die. Evidently, a semantic reversal, an intentional one, took place, and what the incantation means is "may the goat sleep as if it is dead".

1.7.3 Semantic Devices

Similes

Comparing A to B is perhaps the most fundamental of all literary devices (Wasserman 2003, 99). Indeed, incantations are especially rich in simile (Wasserman 2003, 178). The amniotic fluid is "like a wave"; the baby-boy is "like a wild ram" while a baby-girl is "like a wild cow" (CUSAS 32, 29c: 23 and SANER 9, 77: 17–21= № 8 and 11, respectively, both for a woman in labour). A certain disease should depart "like a fox", or ascend back to heaven "like smoke" (UET 5, 85: 6–8, against jaundice and YOS 11, 8: 8, against various diseases = № 38 and 58, respectively). The scorpion's pincers are "like a wild ram's horns" (BM 97331b: 12 = № 85, against scorpion) and anger comes "like a wild bull" (TIM 9, 72: 1 = № 116, against anger). A woman, resisting the advances of her suitor, is asked to come out like "an orchard fruit", and the resisting male lover should rejoice "like a harp" (VS 17, 23: 3, to attract a woman and ZA 75, 198–204b: 24, to attract a man, № 134 and 137, respectively).

Metaphors

What distinguishes similes from metaphors is much discussed. For our purpose, however, suffice to say that similes contain a comparative component (*kīma*, *kī*, *–iš*, *–āni*, etc., see Wasserman 2003, 131–135) and metaphors do not (Streck 1999, 30–31). Still, this rule does not imply that a simile simply denotes a comparison while a metaphor denotes an equivalence. Rather, similes form a partial relation between two entities, an association based on a specific trait which links the two items (e.g., a king is like a lion because they are both awe-inspiring), while metaphors offer a deeper connection between A and B, so that A is conceptualized through B (e.g., in Christian theology, *agnus dei* represents god's ultimate sacrifice leading to redemption). Furthermore, similes describe two approaching entities which approximate each other, whereas metaphors create a semantic juxtaposition, even blending, of two entities.

Some metaphors in incantations stand out. A woman in labour is a boat struggling in high waters (RA 70, 135/137 = № 10). The womb is a dark tomb where the embryo is confined (ZA 71, 62b: r. 1' = № 124, for an easy birth). A bloated belly is a fermentation vat (CUSAS 32, 32a = № 27, for gastrointestinal problems). An evil-doer is "a torn-eyed wolf" (YOS 11, 15 // YOS 11, 29b: 5 = № 149, against witchcraft). A scorpion is "the bull of the earth",[211] but in another text, "the soaring one of the sky", referring to the constellation Scorpio (RA 88, 161a: 1 and CUSAS 32, 49: 3, against scorpion, № 97 and 93, respectively). Less self-explanatory but no less powerful are the metaphors in an incantation dealing with honeybees: "The temple of Esikila, its threshold is (made of) juniper. Ea, the stag, dwells in it. The house is flesh, the threshold a bull" (CUSAS 32, 51: 5–7 = № 78).

1.7.4 Thematic Devices

Fixed Formulae

OB and OA incantations are non-formulaic texts. In fact, they are characterized by their inventiveness and free imagination. Still, some formulae show up in our corpus. First, the well-known *mannam lušpur* formula (Farber 1990b), as, e.g., "Whom should I send to the dweller of the great Apsû (saying)..." (YOS 11, 11: 10–12 = № 35, against gastrointestinal problems), or "Whom should I send to the Daughters of Ea, seven [and] seven, (saying)..." (Fs. Hirsch 427: 8–11 = № 69, against a dog). Another fixed formula is the legitimation, or better, officiation formula, *šiptum ul yattun šipat* DN... (Lenzi 2010). See, e.g.: "The incantation is not mine; it is the incantation of Asalluḫi, the son of Ea of Eridu" (Fs. Stol 150: 21–22 = № 53, against various diseases), or "The incantation is not mine, it is the incantation of Ningirim, Enki (and) Asalluḫi, which Ningirim has cast and [I] have taken it" (JCS 9, 9: 31–35 = № 54, against various diseases). It is worth noting that these two formulae share an important feature: the sudden appearance of the magic practitioner, breaking the narrative texture of the incantation with his first-person voice.

211 This case proves that metaphors and similes are closely related, for, as we have seen, the scorpion is likened to a wild bull through similes as well.

Dialogues

The typical speech acts in incantations are **assertives** ("the situation is so-and-so"), **directives** ("you should do so-and-so"), **commisives** ("I swear that so-and-so") and **performative declarations** ("here and now it is so-and-so!"). In other words, incantations describe reality – either impersonally ("the diseases descended from heavens"), or from the point of view of the healer ("the woman in labour is in pain") – and they also contain different modal utternaces ("may the wind depart!", "go up to the mountains!"). In some incantations, however, short dialogues burst onto the surface of the texts. The better-known dialogues are between Enki/Ea and his son Marduk/Asalluḫi (see below, in Historiolae). It makes good sense that the exchange of questions and answers between the two gods represents the hesitant young healer asking his senior mentor for advice. The appearance of the practitioner in a dialogue is somewhat clearer in VS 17, 34 (№ 12, for a woman in labour), where the healer speaks to Šamaš:

> *When Šamaš saw her he was crying, when the pure-of-rites saw her, his tears were flowing down (saying:)*
>
> – *"Why does Šamaš cry? The tears of the pure-of-rites flowing down?"*
>
> – *"(Over) my cow, not deflowered, (over) my kid, never giving birth!"*

A surprising dialogue is found in CUSAS 32, 32c: 6'–12' (№ 29). This incantation, aimed at solving gastrointestinal problems, begins as a play, where two figures, a female bartender and a young man, talk to each other:

> – *"Young man from where you come?"*
>
> – *From the steppe! I intend to go to the tavern-keepster!*
>
> – *"On whose instruction?"*
>
> – *Of Ea, king of the Apsû and of the steppe, the eager one of Ištar!*
>
> – *"Look at the pellet of dirt and the spiny thorn of the steppe that are in my hands!"*

It is hard not to note that this conversation echoes the encounter between Gilgameš and Siduri (more on that in the commentary to the text).

Historiolae

Short or truncated stories embedded in incantations, with a mythical reference, identified or not, are a well-known feature of magic texts in various ancient Near Eastern and Mediterranean cultures. These short stories, historiolae, can be divided into two types: abridged stories of longer mythical or religious narratives (in later periods, many times, the Bible), and *ad hoc* stories which were composed, or assembled, by the magic expert based on knowledge, shared by him and his clients. The meaning and function of these narratives-within-incantations were recently treated by Waller (2014),[212] where a detailed survey of previous literature regarding the function of historiolae can be found.

212 Waller 2014, 263–280.

Faraone (1988, 284), focusing on Greek spells, stated that "these short mythological stories provide a paradigm for a desired magic action".[213] What this 'paradigm' means was further explicated by Sanders (2001, 432) who took historiolae to "channel 'power' from a primeval time or place into our world".[214] In the same direction, historiolae were said to "connect mythic time and space to present time and space," Waller (2014, 264).

These observations, gathered from the study of the Greco-Roman magic tradition, dating from the Classical times to Late Antiquity and early Middle Ages, are also valuable for our corpus. Let us examine one case, a complete and fully developed historiola: YOS 11, 5b (№ 114), an incantation destined to heal a child suffering from worms in his nose and eyes:

> *When Gula was walking in bravery, (her) dogs were walking behind her. – "Worms! To (my) side! To me!" – Supplication(s) and Laughter that were walking behind her. When Sîn came out of Nippur he released the [fly$^{?}$/ee]l$^{?}$ and the scorpion to the head. My lord threw the larva to the child's nose. May the child not experience (any more of) his illness, may he not experience (any more of) his distress, (of) his anxiety! I have sealed (his) nose and (his) ear. I have sealed the sutures of his skull that Allatum has loosened. She threw (him$^{?}$/it$^{?}$) in between her breast. This incantation is not mine: (it is) the incantation of Gula.*

The incantation begins with two temporal clauses ("when" ...), referring to a couple of seemingly separate occasions when Gula and Sîn went out (presumably of their abode). The Moon-god, Sîn, was accompanied by a scorpion and some kind invertebrates, while Gula, the healing goddess, went out with her emblematic dogs (which, as suggested by Wasserman 2008, 81–83, may stand for leeches). The motivation behind these divine outings remains untold, but they do not seem to be part of a momentous mythological event. Hence, one may conclude that YOS 11, 5b contains an *ad hoc* historiola.[215] So terse is the short story that it is not said explicitly that an encounter between the two deities occurred, but it stands to reason that the gods did meet and that Sîn's harmful creatures were confronted with Gula's healing skills. If this is the case, the historiola presents a mythological precedent to the actual situation in which the healer challenges the worms that infected the little boy. And so, the historiola conjoins a mythological episode in the most ancient of times (*in illo tempore*) with the concrete event taking place now (*in hoc tempore*). This collision of times coincides with the performance of the magic act, when the practitioner casts the incantation and performs the therapeutic procedure.

Two points should be marked. First, that the mythological example – paradigm, if we are to use Faraone's term – does not describe a successful recovery. Nothing in the historiola guarantees that the healer will be efficacious in his deed. What is said is only that the confrontation that takes place here-and-now already occurred in the divine realm. Put

213 Faraone 1988, 279–286.

214 Sanders 2001.

215 A word of caution is in place. In the Mesopotamian context, it is very difficult, if not impossible, to distinguish an *ad hoc* historiola from historiolae that refer to (or 'echo', in Waller's words) a full-scale mythological narrative. This inability results from the fact that our knowledge of ancient Mesopotamian mythology is far from being complete. It is quite possible that what initially looks like an *ad hoc* historiola may turn out to be a reference to a fully developed mythological text that was previously unknown, as, e.g., the *Song of Bazi* which was entirely unknown until its publication (George 2009, no. 1).

differently, the players are different, but the play is known. Secondly, the historiola presents a confrontation between two sides which are on the same scale. The etiology of the disease, as hinted by the historiola, carries no moral designation. It is not Evil which is the source of the problem; the trouble results from an interplay of worldly powers, embodied in two members of the pantheon. The healer, naturally, strives to prevail, but the historiola does not necessarily favour the sufferer.

The theme of divine trips appears also in other historiolae. In a badly damaged incantation mentioning bitumen, we find: "[When? (s)he] went up to Ur ... [(s)he ....] ... the stewardesses. Bitumen. They have soaked the qu[ay?] with water" (CUSAS 32, 20d: 14'–15' = № 167) and an incantation for a sick stomach also describes a divine voyage: "... they were walking together. When they were crossing the river, they singled him out and left the belly behind. Asalluḫi turned his favor to them and resuscitated the belly" (CUSAS 32, 30a: 1–9 = № 25). Let us note that nowhere in these voyage-historiolae is a temple mentioned. This is an important indication for the non-dependence of ancient magic on temple priesthood and administration (see § 1.5.3).

Other historiolae point at primordial cosmological events. An incantation for an aching belly reads: "Just as Anum, king of heaven, inseminated the herd of Šakkan, may I impregnate and pour magic over the patient..." (CUSAS 32, 25a: 4–5, cf. CUSAS 32, 7m // CUSAS 32, 8f: 2–4 = № 23 and 18, respectively) – a clear case of a historiola which denotes 'as it was then, so may it be now' (Waller 2014, 267, 275). Historiolae relating a process of creation are also known, e.g.: "Anum begot the sky, the sky bore the earth; The earth bore the stench, the stench bore the mud; The mud bore the fly, the fly bore the worm" (YOS 11, 5a: 1–3 = № 113, against worms) – a good example of historiolae that investigate the inception of the specific problem encountered by the magician. The opposite dynamic is also known, namely, mythological stories that relate the progression of the problem, listing all the victims of the particular evil. To this category belong the historiolae of 'heart-plant'. See, e.g.: "Šamaš brought over the (heart) plant across the mountain – It seized the heart of Šamaš who brought it across; It seized the heart of Sîn in the sky; It seized the heart of the ox in the stall; It seized the heart of the sheep in the fold; It seized the heart of the lad in the street; It seized the heart of the maiden in the dance..." (YOS 11, 11: 1–9 = № 35, for gastrointestinal problems). A description of a progressive illness is known in incantations dealing with various diseases that "came down from the ziggurat of heaven, burned up the sheep, the lambs, caused the children on the shoulders of the nurse to be somber". The historiola offers a solution to these fiery diseases falling from heaven by summoning "the Daughters of Anum, seven and seven, whose vessels are gold, their jars pure lapis-lazuli" (JCS 9, 9: 10–12, 13–16 = № 54).

Most historiolae recount episodes from the life of gods or demons. A couple of Lamaštu incantations present mythological snapshots from the youth of this horrifying demoness: "Anum created her, Ea brought her up, a face of a lioness Enlil fixed for her" (BIN 2, 72: 1–2 = № 159) and "(She is a) daughter of a god. Daughter of Anum. Because of her malevolent intention(s), her blasphemous decision(s), Anum, her father, smashed her down to earth from heaven" (BIN 4, 126: 5–15 = № 160). These biographical shortcuts serve to explain the demoness' malice and evil actions. Another incantation ends with Lamaštu's banishment to a remote location, a story which comes as the reassuring promise of a successful magic act: "When the two gods saw her, they threw her out of the window. They made her slink through the door socket. They have tied her to a *tamarisk*? in the middle of the sea" (YOS 11, 19a:

12–15 = № 164). The early life of the succubus Wardat-lilî is recounted in YOS 11, 92 (№ 166). As a young maiden, she broke her nuptial arrangement, ran away with a lover and did not bear children.

Other historiolae talk of an incident that happened to the Moon-god: "While building the house, while turning over the brick pile, the scorpion stung Sîn's little finger" (CUSAS 32, 211: 31', CUSAS 32, 49: 13–17 and Semitica 62, 19: 19 = № 87, 93, and 99, respectively. Cf. also YOS 11, 4b = № 102, all against scorpions). It is Sîn, the Moon-god, whom the scorpion bites because scorpions are nocturnal or crepuscular. A more intricate astral reasoning motivating this story is plausible, since the scorpion appears in the sky as the constellation *Scorpio*. In another spell, Sîn is described fishing (Fs. de Meyer 75/83b = № 76). A group of incantations relate how Šamaš encountered a magic plant (the 'heart-plant'), plucked it, and was seized by it, triggering a long line of contamination: "[The] heart-plant, [its] beauty [was entic]ing [...]. Šamaš noticed it: he [plucked it and took it] up to heaven. It seized the heart of Sîn, it seized the heart of Šamaš, its plucker, (it seized) the heart of Earth, its burier, (It seized) the heart of the ox in the stall etc." (CUSAS 32, 7o // CUSAS 32, 8i = № 19, for gastrointestinal problems).

Ningirsu's killing of the mythological one-eyed *igitelûm* is mentioned *en passant* in CUSAS 32, 55: 12 = № 126.

A mythological scene which warrants consideration here is the dialogue between Enki and his son Asalluḫi.[216] The Enki-Asalluḫi (or Ea-Marduk) motif is typical of Sumerian and bilingual incantations.[217] Indeed, in our corpus it occurs on three occasions, all in bilingual texts: RA 70, 135/137: 28–40 (№ 10, for a woman in labour), PBS 1/2, 122: 13–21 (№ 147, against Lilītum and her witchcraft) and in CT 4, 8: 8–16 (№ 16, for gastrointestinal problems) which reads: "Oh my father! (There is an) aching belly… Ea answers Marduk: 'My son, what do you not know? What can I add to it? What I know, you know; What you know, I know!'". It must be noted that this exchange between Enki, the old magician of the pantheon, and Asalluḫi, his brilliant son and successor, is nowhere found outside of the magic corpus. In other words, this historiola, so widespread in all periods of Mesopotamian magic, does not lean, as far as we know, on any mythological scene.[218]

Less common, but very interesting, are historiolae which talk not about gods, but about mythological animals. CUSAS 32, 48 (№ 107) describes a mythological snake with marine origins attacking the earth. The powerful description goes as follows:[219]

> *Broad of shoulder, dead of glance – a snake, cord of moonshine, whom they created in the bitter sea and placed in the hand of Ea. When he was thirsting for sustenance, the shore shook; the shore shook and he went into the reed-bed! I will seize the snake in the reed-bed! I will seize the viper in the rushes! The viper, six are his mouths, seven are the tendons that are moving in his body! He cried out and approached the mountain; he approached the mountain and split a rock. He split a rock and dried up a poplar. He made wither away the roots of the oak.*

216 For other deities appearing in divine dialogues, see Zomer 2018b.
217 As already observed by Falkenstein 1931.
218 On the topos of a senior deity instructing a junior, see Rudik 2015, 95 and Zomer 2018b, 38.
219 See also OECT 15, 260 (№ 109, against snakes).

In some incantations descriptions of nature are found. The purpose of these lyrical historiolae is not fully clear; it is difficult to decide whether they refer to specific mythological moments. Consider: "The wind went out (flying over) the (different) seas. The Sea was looking at it. It plowed the way of the seas…" (CUSAS 32, 7c: 19'–22' = № 17, against flatus$^{?}$), or "[The] Daughters of Anum, the lights of heaven, [*in day-ti*]*me*$^{?}$ purified the sky of Anum" (CUSAS 10, 11: 2–4 = № 131, for love), or "Mist seized the eye of the sun" (CUSAS 32, 7g // CUSAS 32, 8c: 3–4 = № 151). A pastoral image is found in Fs. Larsen 397/399b:24–28 (№ 1), an OA incantation against bile: "The verdure is yellow-green. The vegetation is yellow-green. In the shade of the yellow-green irrigated orchard, a speckled she-goat keeps pasturing".

But perhaps the most intriguing historiolae are those containing references to identifiable literary compositions. An incantation destined to quiet a crying baby alludes to the Epic of Gilgameš: "Whom should I send to Enkidu, the creator of the three night watches, (saying:) 'He who caught the deer may catch him (too) (i.e., the baby)! He who bound the gazelle may bind him (too)! May his fellow (i.e., Gilgameš) in the field give him his sleep! May (the constellation of) the One-walking-behind-the-cattle leave for him his sleep!' Until his mother wakes him up, may he not awake!" OECT 11, 2: 15–28 (№ 122). Another clear allusion to the same epic is found in CUSAS 32, 32c (№ 29, for gastrointestinal problems) where the meeting between the expert and the (female$^{?}$) patient echoes the meeting between Gilgameš and the bartender Siduri. In an incantation in which the magic expert asks for legitimation, a reference to the opening line of Atraḫasīs is found: "When the gods were like men (*inūma ilū kīma awīlī*), I was the strongest! They were heaping mountains, (but) I made (them) give up (their) labour!" CUSAS 32, 55: 15–16 (№ 126).[220] Finally, an incantation against snakes alludes to the Epic of Etana, mentioning a snake, a bird, a tree, and the "snake's son crying in the ground" OECT 15, 260: 4–5 (№ 109).

It is clear by now that historiolae cannot be considered just another literary device. To a greater degree than syntactic constructions or alliterative ornamentations, these short, at time enigmatic stories, are powerful thematic engines, which – alongside other crucial traits of incantations, such as the confrontation between the healer and the malicious agent or the mention of *materia magica*, and the summoning of divine help – are the quintessence of the magic discourse.

220 For the incorporation of Ningirsu/Ninurta narratives such as Lugale in magic texts in Sumerian incantations of the first millennium, see Zomer 2020, 359.

II. The Texts

The texts in this volume are named after their source, that is by the publication place of their **copy**, or, if there is no copy, by their **photo**. Unpublished texts are named by their **museum number**. We have numbered all the texts in the volume, so that each text has its own running number (**№ NN**). When referring to a given text, usually both its name and its running number are used. Concordances of **text numbers → text names** and **text names → text numbers** are found at the outset of the book (pp. XIX–XXXIII). The reader is encouraged to use these concordances when locating a specific text. As explained above (§ 1.2), the texts are ordered thematically: (I) Specific Diseases and Medical Problems, (II) Animals, (III) Humans, (IV) Supernatural Entities, (V) Inanimate Objects, and (VI) Miscellaneous incantations. Within each thematic section, the texts are arranged in alphabetic order of their name.

2.1 Specific Diseases and Medical Problems

2.1.1 Bile

Since an increase of bile is known to cause jaundice in patients, the yellowish appearance of the skin and eyes is metaphorically ascribed to goats in therapeutic incantations against bile from the first millennium BCE (Collins 1999, 97). The OA spell Fs. Larsen 397/399b (№ 1) uses the same image of the she-goat, but yellowness is here ascribed to her immediate surroundings.

№ 1: Fs. Larsen 397/399b

SEAL No.: 7223
Copy: Michel 2004, 397/399
Tablet Siglum: Kt 90/k 178
Photo: Michel 2004, 397/399
Edition: Michel 2004
Studies: Wasserman 2003 Cat. No. 31; Michel 2003, 138; Hecker 2008, 65f.; Steinert/Vacín 2018, 713
Collection: Anadolu Medeniyetleri Müzesi, Ankara
Provenance: Kaneš
Measurements: 5.3 × 4.2 cm
Procedure: No

Introduction

This incantation collective (containing also a childbirth incantation, Fs. Larsen 397/399a = № 9) was found in the archive of the OA trader Šumi-Abiya, son of Puzur-Ištar. The spell is addressed against a she-goat, but with George (2016, 7) and Steinert/Vacín (2018, 713), who noticed its close resemblance to BAM 578: iii 45–49 (Collins 1999, 231), we understand this incantation to be destined against bile.

Reverse

24 *e-er-qú-um e-ri-iq*
25 *e-ri-iq-tum e-er-qá-at*
26 *i-ṣí-li* | *mì-iṭ-ra-tem*
27 *e-ri-iq-tem e-zu-um*
28 *ba-ru-ma-tum ta-ar-té-/e*

Lower Edge

29 *a-dí-šé-em kà-kà-a-am*
30 *lá a-ba-ra-ší* | *a-dí-šé-em / ší-*bi_4*-r[a-a]m*

Left Edge

31 *lá a-ṣa-áb-ta-ší* | *a-[d]í-šé-em ba-pì-ra-/am*
32 *ḫa-šu-a-am ù [ṭá]-áb-tám i-na*
33 *[š]u-ur-ší-ša šu-ba-al-ku-tu[m] uš-ba-al-k[i-s]í*

Translation

24–25 The verdure is yellow-green. The vegetation is yellow-green.
26–27 In the shade of the yellow-green irrigated orchard,
27–28 a speckled she-goat keeps pasturing.
29–30 I threw at her a weapon – but did not catch her.
30–31 I threw at her a shepherd staff but did not get hold of her.
31–32 I threw at her beer bread, thyme, and salt –
32–33 I verily did turn her over from her root.

Commentary

31–32: For the use of the combination of thyme and salt, cf. CT 4, 8: 18 (№ 16). See Steinert/Vacín (2018, 713, 726f.).

2.1.2 Childbirth

This thematically discrete group of incantations serves to ensure a positive outcome following a difficult birth. Some incantations show more concern with the mother in labour, others with the baby struggling to be born. Still others are concered with both. There are no fixed phrases in this group of incantations, but images of young cow anguishing in her travail and heavily loaded boat – both referring to the woman in labour – can be found. The baby is described as a *homunculus* obstructed in a dark cell (the womb), wishing to see the sun.

№ 2: BiOr 75, 15f.

SEAL No.: 7062
Copy: –
Tablet Siglum: –
Photo: Wasserman 2018, 15f.
Edition: Wasserman 2018, 15–18
Studies: –
Collection: Private Collection
Provenance: Unknown
Measurements: 5.8 × 3.9 cm
Procedure: No

Introduction

This incantation is specifically designed to relieve labour pains (*ḫīlum*, *ḫīlū*). The back of this tablet was coated in a secondary layer of clay, covering the previously inscribed reverse.

Obverse

1 *ki-ma* ⸢*la*⸣ *ba-*⸢*i-ta*⸣*-at*
2 *i-ta-*⸢*at*$^{!}$⸣(LA) *ba-aš-ti-im*
3 ⸢*ḫi*⸣*-lum a i-bi-it*
4 *i-na li-bi*$^{?}$*-ki*
5 *ki-ma it-ba-ru-tum*$_8$(tim)
6 *ba-a-at*
7 *ka-li šam-mi*
8 *ḫi-il-ki lu ba-i*

Reverse uninscribed

Translation

1–2 As the *signs* of dignity do not stay overnight,
3–4 may the labour pain not stay overnight in your belly!
5–8 As partnership passes, – Oh all plants – may your labour pain pass!

Commentary

2: Although the third sign looks like LA, which is possibly a copying-mistake from the LA in the previous line, *ittāt bāštim* seems the only plausible reading. For a discussion of this reading, see Wasserman (2018, 17).

4: Following Wasserman (2018, 17), the image of *itbārūtum* "partnership (of a specific type)" is to be explained in the present context as something that dissolves quickly, the desired outcome in the case of labour pains too.

№ 3: BiOr 75, 19f.

SEAL No.: 7063
Copy: –
Tablet Siglum: –
Photo: Wasserman 2018, 19f.
Edition: Wasserman 2018, 18–20
Studies: –
Collection: Private Collection
Provenance: Unknown
Measurements: 4.0 × 4.5 cm
Procedure: No

Introduction

With its stenographic style, the text may have served as an *aide-memoire* (see Wasserman 2018, 18f.). Noteworthy is the ruling after the incipit in l. 1. Another example of such a ruling is found in the MB incantation LAOS 9, pl. I–III (VAT 13226), where the rubric (én-é-nu-ru) opens the text and is separated by a ruling from the rest of the incantation.

Obverse

1 *[l]i-ti-mi*

----

2 *[l]i-ti*
3 *li-ti tu-la-da-am*
4 *li-ti iṭ-ḫe-am*$^{?}$
5 *[l]i-ti i-qá-da*$^{?}$*-da*$^{?}$
6 *[q]á-qá-ra i-*⸢*sà*⸣*-r[a-aq]*
7 *li-ti* ⸢*i-sú*⸣*-u[q*$^{?}$*]*
8 ar pa ḫa *ap-pi-*⸢*ša*⸣

Reverse

9 *i-mu-‹ur›-ši* ⸢^{d}*En-líl i-ba*⸣*-[ki]*
10 ^{d}*En-líl i-*⸢*la-ka di-ma-šu*⸣
11 *a-mi-ni-*⸢*mi*⸣ ^{d}*En-*⸢*líl*⸣
12 *a-*⸢*mi*⸣*-‹ni›* ^{d}*En-líl* ⸢*i-ba-ki*⸣
13 *ṭa-ba-at*
14 *li-ti-ia la* ⸢*pé-ti-tim*⸣
15 ⸢*ú*⸣*-ni-qí-ia la wa-*⸢*li-tim*⸣
16 ⸢{x x} *ma-na-mi*⸣ *lu*$^{?}$*-*⸢*uš*⸣*-pu*$^{?}$*-ur*$^{?}$

Upper Edge

17 *[lu-wa]-*⸢*e*⸣*-ra-[am]*
18 *[l]i-im-qú-tam qá-qá-‹ar›-šu*

Left Edge
19 ⌜*li-tum*⌝
20 ⌜*li-li a*⌝*-na a-aš-*[…]

Translation
1 Oh my cow!

2–4 My cow, my cow is giving birth, my cow drew near (the appointed time).
5–6 My cow is bending down, she is sprink[ling the gr]ound (with her tears?)
7–8 My cow *brushes* the … with her nose.
9–10 Enlil saw her (and) was crying, Enlil, his tears were flowing.
11–12 – "Why is Enlil, why is Enlil crying?"
13 – she is good! –
14–15 – "(Over) my cow, not deflowered, (over) my kid who never gave birth".
16–17 – "… Oh whom should I send and instruct?"
18–20 May it fall to the ground! The cow, may she rise to […]!

Commentary
5: The reading *i-qá-da*?*-da*? follows Wasserman (2018, 18). The verb *qadādum* is now differentiated from *gadādum* (Sum. te - ḫar) "to lacerate" (Gabbay 2019). A play between *littu* "cow" and *lētu* "cheek", typically used with the latter verb, may be intended here. In later incantations, it is *kamāsu* which describes the kneeling cow, as, e.g., [gu4]ÁB *ik-ta-mi-ṣi~i-ḫa-al* in AS 16, 287f.c: ii 26 (MA); *ta-aḫ-ti-me-iš ta-ḫa-al* in Iraq 31 pls. V–VIb: 57 (MA), see Zomer (2018a, 151/153).
7: The verb *esēqum* "to incise" is further attested in OA birth incantations, i.e., CCT 5, 50e: 2' (№ 5) and Fs. Larsen 397/399a: 6 (№ 9).
20: A phrase *ana išdīša* or *ana ašriša* is anticipated A similar phrase may be restored in CCT 5, 50e: l.e. 1'' (№ 5).

№ 4: BM 115745

SEAL No.: 7054
Copy: Steinert (*forthcoming*)
Tablet Siglum: BM 115745
Photo: –
Edition: Steinert (*forthcoming*)
Studies: Steinert (*forthcoming*)
Collection: British Museum, London
Provenance: Unknown
Measurements: 7.62 × 5.0 cm
Procedure: No

Introduction

This incantation for an easy childbirth, to be published by U. Steinert,[221] is probably the work of a student, as can be deduced from the numbers, perhaps an arithmetic exercise, on its obverse which is oriented at a 90° angle to the reverse.[222] Indicative are also the large and crude signs and the numerous mistakes in the text,[223] the unusual rubric tu-en-ni-in-nu-ra and the subscript *šipat aruḫtim*. Other texts in this group use ka-inim-ma munus ù-tu-da-ka.

Reverse

1	[*i-na me*]*-e na-ki*$^{!}$(DI)*-im*
2	*ib-ba-ni e-ṣe-em-tum*
3	*ši-ru-*⸢*ú*⸣ *še-er-ḫa-nu-*⸢*ú*⸣
4	*ib-nu li-li-da-am*
5	*i-na me-e a-a-ba ša-am-*⸢*ru*⸣*-tim*
6	*ša-ru-uḫ-tim*
7	*i-na me-e an-za-nu-zi ru-qú-tim*
8	*a-ša-ar* ⸢*še*$_{20}$*-er-ru*⸣*-um*
9	*ku-us-sa i-da-šu*
10	*ka-at-ma i-na-šu la i-da-ga-la* ⸢*nu*$^{!?}$*-ra*⸣-‹‹am››*-am*
11	*i-mu-ur-šu-ma*$^{!}$ {x} *É-a* ^{d}*Asal-lu-ḫa*
12	*ip-te-šu pa-da-na-*⸢*am*⸣ *uš-ta-sí-iq-šu ṭù-dam*
13	*a-na mi-ša-ri-im* ^{d}*Šamaš*(UTU) *li-iš-ku-‹un›-ka*

221 The present edition is based on photos and notes sent to us by U. Steinert (Oct. 2016).

222 The British Museum online database mentions that the tablet was "re-used", that the different texts on the obverse and the reverse are not necessarily a sign that it is a student's work, but of a palimpsest. https://www.britishmuseum.org/collection/object/W_1923-0113-26.

223 See l. 1: DI instead of *ki* (in *nâkim*); l. 6: *šaruḫtim* for *šarḫūtim*; l. 10: *nūram* written ⸢*nu*$^{!?}$*-ra*⸣-‹‹am››-*am*; l. 11: a badly written *-ma* (next to erasure); l. 11: Asalluḫi written ^{d}*Asal-lu-ḫa*; l. 13: *liškunka* written *li-iš-ku-‹un›-ka*; l. 15: *aruḫtim*, probably a conflated form of *arītum*, "pregnant" and *arḫum*, "cow".

Lower Edge

14 tu-en-ni-in-nu-ra

Left Edge

15 *ši-pa-at a-ru-uḫ-tim*

Translation

1–2 In the fluid of conception the substance was created.

3–4 The flesh (and) the tissue have created the *homunculus*.

5–7 In the water of the ocean, so fierce, so *powerful*, in the subterranean body of water, so remote,

8–11 in the place where the little-one, his hands are bound, his eyes are covered, not seeing the *light*, (there) Ea noticed him.

11–13 Asalluḫi opened for him the path, made the road ready for him, (saying:) "May Šamaš set you to freedom!"

14 tu-en-ni-in-nu-ra

15 Incantation for a *pregnant woman*.

Commentary

3–4: Contrary to YOS 11, 86a: 4 (№ 14), where *lillidum* is created passively within the fleshy tissue (*ibbani*), this incantation describes the mysterious process as actively performed by two engendering entities *šīru* and *šerʾānu*, following perhaps the motif of the chain of creation.

7: *anzanuzû*: Until now, the rare and poetic word *anzanuzû* (*anzanunzû*), designating subterranean water or abyss, was known only from post-OB literary texts (CAD A/2, 152f.). Parallel incantations employ more common words: YOS 11, 86a: 5–7 (№ 14): *tiāmtim ruqûtim*; CUSAS 32, 28a: 2–3 (№ 7): *ina mê Apsîm ruqûtim*. (The relevant lines are missing in CUSAS 32, 26a = № 6).

8: *šerrum* vs. *šīru* (l. 3): This *jeu de mots*, connecting flesh and baby, is found also in OB Gilg. P: i 7 (see Wasserman 2011, 9).

10: *katmā īnāšu lā idaggalā* ⸢*nu*!?⸣-⸢*ra*⸣-‹‹am››-*am*: Parallel texts have *katmā īnāšu mūṣâm išēʾam*, "he was looking for a way out", but this cannot be read here. We suggest instead that the last word, overrun to the reverse, is a badly written *nūram* which goes well with *dagālum*.[224]

11: Asalluḫi … Ea…: Although syntactically not impossible, *īmuršuma Ea Asalluḫi iptēšu*… seems like a scrambled sentence. All parallel incantations mention Asalluḫi as the sole helping protagonist. We assume that YOS 11, 86a: 11 (№ 14), which mentions explicitly ᵈ*Asalluḫi māri* ᵈ*Enki*, may explain the awkward sentence in BM 115745. – Note the PNs *Ḫadi-āmer-Šamaš* (AbB 9, 1: 9 and 19)

224 U. Steinert (private communication) reads this complex as *ḫa-ra-na-am*, noting that "…the vertical wedge of NA overlaps with the beginning of AM, and the ḪA is not nicely written". In our view, the penultimate sign has too many wedges for NA, while the assumed ḪA has sufficient wedges. Finally, *harrānam dagālum* is less obvious in this context which stresses that the baby's eyes are covered.

and *Ḫadi-āwer-Šamaš* (AbB 5, 175: 14) "Happy is the one seeing the sun", names for a child whose process of birth was hard and long.

12: *uš-ta-sí-iq-šu ṭūdam*: This reading follows U. Steinert who turned our attention to OB Gilg. iii 259–261 (= George 2003, 204–206) where *nasāqum* Št is found in similar expression: *liptēkum padānam peḫîtam ḫarrānam li-iš-ta-sí-iq ana kibsīka šadâ li-iš-ta-sí-iq ana šēpīka*, "May he (Šamaš) open for you the paths that are shut, may he ready the road for your footsteps! May he make ready the mountain for your feet!"

13: The phrase *ana mīšarim Šamaš lišk‹un›ka*[225] does not fit this context of childbirth (and is missing from parallel incantations). The trigger for its appearance might, again, be YOS 11, 86a (№ 14), notably in ll. 8–10: *ašar ṣeḫrum kussâ īdāšu qirbissu lā ušnawwaru īn Šamšim*. The description of the baby, tied up and locked in as a prisoner in his mother's womb, followed by the mentioning of Šamaš (as a source of light) could motivate the writer of BM 115745 to insert here the well-known – but irrelevant! – motif of Šamaš as responsible for redemption in the judicial sense (If verb *ešērum* is found in YOS 11, 86a: 17, this could also explain the use of *ana mīšarim* here, see commentary ad YOS 11, 86a: 17 (№ 14).

15: Although *a-ru-uḫ-tim* can grammatically be explained from *arḫum* I (f. *aruḫtum*) "fast, quick (one)", it is most certainly a play on *arītum* "pregnant (woman)", *arḫum* "quick", *arḫum* "cow", (*w*)*arhum* "month" and the *Araḫtum*-canal. Note in this regard the start of the OA spell Fs. Larsen 397/399a: 1–5 (№ 9). For the notion of *aruḫtum* (Ass. *araḫtum*) as a designation for a 'woman in travail' (lit. 'hastened one'), see Steinert (2017, 224f.).

225 *li-iš-ku-‹un›-ka*: hardly an assimilation. The only other example of /nk/ > /kk/ in final position in OB texts known to us is *a-na-ad-di-ku-nu-ti* ARM 2, 94: 19 (courtesy M. P. Streck).

№ 5: CCT 5, 50e

SEAL No.: 7217
Copy: CCT 5, 50e; Kouwenberg/Fincke 2013, 143
Tablet Siglum: BM 113625
Photo: Kouwenberg/Fincke 2013, 143
Edition: Kouwenberg/Fincke 2013; Barjamovic 2015, 75
Studies: Barjamovic 2015; Zomer 2018a, 233f.
Collection: British Museum, London
Provenance: Kaneš
Measurements: 2.9 × 3.85 cm
Procedure: No

Introduction
This OA incantation shares direct similarities with the two other birth incantations from Kaneš (Fs. Larsen 397/399a = № 9 and SANER 9, 77= № 11), see Barjamovic (2015, 57).

Obverse
1' *[i-n]a* ⸢*a-pí*⸣-[*ša*]
2' [*q*]*á-qá-ra-am* ⸢| *té*⸣-[*sú-uq*?]
3' ⸢*i*⸣-*na dí-im-a-té-š*[*a*]
4' *ta-sà-ra-aq*
5' *bītam*(É-*tám*) | *ma-na-ša-/am*
6' *la-áš-pu-ur*

Lower Edge
7' *ma-na-ša-am*
8' *lu-e-e-er*

Reverse
9' *a-na ma-ru-*⸢*a*⸣-[*a*]*t*
10' *Ša-su-ur* ⸢7⸣
11' *ù* 7-*ma* | *ma-re-ki-/na*
12' *ta-áp-šu-kà-té-ki-na*
13' [*l*]*e-qí-a-ni-ma*
14' [x (x)] ⸢x x dí | ga⸣ […]
(*breaks*)

Left Edge
1'' […] ⸢x⸣(-)*ri-ša*

Translation

1'–2'	With her nose she *brushes* the ground.
3'–5'	With her tears she sprinkles the house.
5'–11'	Whom should I send (and) whom should I instruct (with orders) to the seven and seven Daughters of Šassūr (saying:)
11'–13'	"Take (f. pl.) your spades and baskets and [...]!
14'	[...]
1"	[... *to*?] her [...]

Commentary

L.E. 1": In the edition of Kouwenberg/Fincke (2013, 142) this line was wrongly placed in the edition of Fs. Larsen 397/399a (№ 9). It should in fact be here in CCT 5, 50e.

№ 6: CUSAS 32, 26a

SEAL No.: 7055
Copy: George 2016 Pl. LXXII
Tablet Siglum: MS 3387
Photo: CUSAS 32 Pl. LXXII; CDLI P252328
Edition: George 2016, 142
Studies: Zomer 2018a, 234
Collection: Schøyen Collection, Oslo
Provenance: Unknown
Measurements: 5.2 × 5.7 cm
Procedure: No

Introduction

George (2016, 46) describes this incantation collective as having "… been cut down from a piece from the middle of a multi-column tablet and backed with new clay in order to make a squarish, bun-like 'tablet' attractive to the antiquities' market". The childbirth incantation is followed by a badly broken unidentified Sumerian incantation and an Akkadian incantation against toothache.

i'

1'	[*ṣe-eḫ-ru-um ku-us-sa-a i*]-⸢*da*⸣-[(*a*)]-⸢*šu*⸣
2'	[*ka-at-ma i-na-šu mu*]-*ṣa-a i-še*$_{20}$-*i*
3'	[*i-mu-ur-šu-ma* ^{d}*Asa*]*l-lú-ḫi*
4'	[*pa-da-na*]-*am ip-te-šu*
5'	[*iš-ku-un-šu ṭù*]-*da-am*
6'	[*pe-ti pa-d*]*a-nu-um*
7'	[*ša-ki-in-ku ṭ*]*ù-ú-du-um*
8'	[*wa-aš-ba-at-ku*] ⸢^{d}⸣*Nin-ḫur-sag-gá*
9'	[*a-sú-tum b*]*a-ni-a-at*
10'	[*a-wi-lu-t*]*i-im*
11'	[*mi-it-ḫa-aṣ*$^{?}$ *it-ti ši-r*]*i-im ù e-ṣé/-*[*e*]*m-ti-im*
12'	[*ki-ma da-di-im šu-lu-u*]*p ra-ma-an-ka*
13'	[ka-inim-ma munus ù-t]u-ud-da-kam

Translation

1'–2'	[The baby], his hands [*were* bound, his eyes *were* covered]. He *was* looking for the way [out].
3'–5'	[(There) Asall]uḫi [noticed him]. He opened for him the path, set for him the road, (saying:)
6'–10'	"The path is open for you! The road is set for you! Ninḫursag [is sitting for you, the *medicine woman*/*midwife*, the *cr*]*eatrix* of mank]ind:
11'–12'	[wrestle with tiss]ue and substance! [Pull ou]t yourself [like a good boy!"]
13'	[Incantation (for) a woman in la]bour.

Commentary

1': *ṣeḫrum* seems secure, but note that BM 115745 (№ 4) has *šerrum*.

9'–10': George (2016, 142) proposes [*um-mu-um b*]*a-ni-a-at* [*a-wi-lu-t*]*i-im*, but YOS 11, 86a (№ 14): 18 has (following George) *wa-aš-ba-at-ku-*⌜*um*⌝ *Bēlet-ilī*(^d⌜MAḪ⌝) *a-sú-tum*, which makes *asûtum* (for *šabsūtum*?) preferable also here.

№ 7: CUSAS 32, 28a

SEAL No.: 7056
Copy: George 2016 Pl. LXXVII
Tablet Siglum: MS 3067
Photo: CUSAS 32 Pl. LXXVI; CDLI P252076
Edition: George 2016, 140f.
Studies: George, CUSAS 32, 140f.; Zomer 2018a, 234
Collection: Schøyen Collection, Oslo
Provenance: Larsa area[226]
Measurements: 9.8 × 5.0 cm
Procedure: No

Introduction
This childbirth incantation is followed by an unidentified incantation and a Sumerian incantation against Lamaštu. The same sequence, an Akkadian childbirth incantation followed by a Sumerian Lamaštu incantation, is found in YOS 11, 86a (№ 14).

Obverse
1 ⸢*i*⸣-[*na me*]-⸢*e*⸣ *na-ki-im ib*-[*ba-ni* (*e-ṣe-em-tum*)]
2 *i-na* ⸢*me-e ap-sí-im*⸣ *ru-qú-t*[*im*]
3 *i-na me-e a-a-ba ti-me-tim ra-a*[*p-ša-tim*]
4 *a-ša-ar ma-am-ma-an la* ‹*i*›-*du*-[*ú*]
5 *qé-re-eb-ša ṣe-eḫ-ru-um ku-u*[*s-sà-a*]
6 *i-da-šu ka-at-ma i-na*-⸢*a*⸣-[*šu*]
7 *mu-ṣa-a-am i-še*$_{20}$-⸢*e*⸣-[*am*]
8 *i-mu-ur-šu-ú-ma* ^{d}*Asal-lú*-[*ḫi*]
9 *ip-te-šum ṭù-da-am pa*-[*d*]*a-n*[*a-am*]
10 *iš-ku-un-šu*[*m*]
11 *ša-ki-in-kum pa-da-nu-u*[*m*]
12 *pe-ti-ku-um ṭù-ú-d*[*u-um*]
13 *wa-aš-ba-at-ku-um Bēlet-ilī*(^{d}M[AḪ])
14 *ba-ni-a-at a-wi-lu-tim*
15 ⸢*mi-it-ḫa*⸣-*aṭ* [*i*]*t-ti e-ṣe*-⸢*em-tim*⸣
16 *ù ši-ir-ḫa*-⸢*ni*⸣-*im*
17 *ki-ma da*-⸢*di*⸣-*im*
18 *šu-lu-up ra-ma-an*-⸢*ka*⸣
----
19 ka-inim-ma [*a-li-it*]-*tum*

226 See George 2016, 47.

Translation

1 In the fluid of conception the [*substance*] was cr[eated].

2–5 In the water of the Apsû, so remote, in the water of the ocean, the seas, so wi[de], (in) a place whose interior nobody knows,

5–7 the baby, his hands are bound, his eyes are covered. He is looking for the way out.

8 (There) Asalluḫi noticed him.

9–10 He opened for him the road, set for him the path, (saying:)

11–14 "The path is set for you! The road is open for you! *Bēlet-ilī* is sitting for you, the *creatrix* of mankind:

15–18 Wrestle with substance and tissue! Pull out yourself like a good boy!"

19 Incantation (for) [a woman giving bir]th.

Commentary

1: George's (2016, 141) *eṣemtum* is followed here. What *eṣemtum* means, however, is not a bone in the strict sense (i.e., the hard piece making the skeleton), but the dense, undefined organelle within the womb, namely the embryo. A similar use is found in Ecc. 11: 5 which employs the cognate Heb. word *ʿeṣem*. Contrary to different translators who took the Heb. כַּעֲצָמִים בְּבֶטֶן הַמְּלֵאָה to denote bones,[227] the Masoretic text speaks of nuclei of living creatures, the embryos.[228]

15: Following George (2016, 141) *mitḫaṭ* stands for *mitḫaṣ* (cf. *atbatka* for *aṣbatka* in RA 36, 3a: 1 = № 144).

17–18: For a possible allusion to Gilgameš in this couplet, see George (2016, 141).

227 The New American Standard Bible: "Just as you do not know the path of the wind and how bones *are formed* in the womb of the pregnant woman, so you do not know the activity of God who makes all things".

228 The New Jewish Publication Society of America Tanakh is in the right direction: "Just as you do not know how the lifebreath passes into the limbs within the womb of the pregnant woman, so you cannot foresee the actions of God, who causes all things to happen".

№ 8: CUSAS 32, 29b

SEAL No.: 7057
Copy: George 2016 Pl. LXXIX
Tablet Siglum: MS 3082
Photo: George 2016 Pl. LXXVIII; CDLI P252091
Edition: –
Studies: George 2016, 47f.
Collection: Schøyen Collection, Oslo
Provenance: Unknown
Measurements: 18.5 × 7.5 cm
Procedure: Yes

Introduction

This childbirth incantation comes in the tablet after spells concerned with dogs. The reverse is blank. A line on the bottom of the obverse marks presumably a subscript. MA and SB incantations offer thematic parallels (see below). This, as well some grammatical features, suggest that it is a late-OB text.

20 [*kar pu-u*]*š-qí-im ik-ta-la e-le-ep-pi*
21 [*bu*]-⸢*uš-ta*⸣-*am ú-ul i-šu-ú-ma*
22 [x (x)] ⸢x x⸣ *úr-tam-mi*
23 [x x] ⸢x *ki*⸣-*ma a-gi-im i-ši-il-li*
24 [x x *i*$^{?}$-*ša*$^{?}$]-⸢*a*$^{?}$⸣-*as-sú-ú li-ib-bu-ú-a*
25 [*an-nu-ú*] *me-ḫu-ú e-li-ia*
26 [*il*$^{?}$]-⸢*ka*$^{?}$⸣-*am* ^{d}*Šamaš*(UTU) *ku-uš-da-an-ni*
27 [x x x]-*mi ša di*-⸢*ma-at*⸣ ^{d}*En-líl*
28 [x x x] ⸢*la*$^{?}$⸣-*ma-ku-mi*
29 [x x x] {x x x} en
----
30 [ka-inim-ma munu]s-ù-tu KÌD.KÌD.BI ì-giš

Translation

20 [A quay of] danger has detained my boat!
21–23 She has no dignity and she has untied [...] she *submerges* [...] like a wave.
24 – [...] that screams in my belly: –
25–26 "[*This*] violent storm is upon me! [*Come*$^{?}$] to me! Šamaš reach for me!
27–28 [...] of the weeping of Enlil [...] I am surrounded!"
29 [...]
30 [Incantation for a woma]n in labour. Its procedure: oil.

Commentary

21: A similar phrase is found in the MA birth incantation Iraq 31 pls. V–VIa: 45 reading *bu-ul-ta ul ti-šu* (Zomer 2018a, 254). Note further the occurrence of *bāštum* in BiOr 75, 15f. (№ 2).

22: The image of loosening clothes is found in Iraq 31 pls. V–VIa: 44–45 *ul sāqat irassa sappuḫū kullūlūša puṣunni ul paṣṣunat* "her breast is not restrained, her headbands are loosened, she wears no veil" and cf. BiOr 75, 15f. (№ 2). The verb *ramû* D is describing the undressing of Šamḫat in SB Gilg. I 188 *urtammi Šamḫat dīdāša* "Šamḫat untied her skirts" (George 2003, 548f.).

23: The image expressed here is that of a huge wave drowning the woman. We interpret *i-ši-il-li* to be a wrong form of *šalû* (one expects *išalli*).

25: This line finds direct parallels with the NA birth compendium BAM 248: ii 46 *annû meḫû lamâku kuldanni* "This is a violent storm, I am surrounded, reach for me!" and again the MA incantation Iraq 31 pls. V–VIa: 47 *annû tēšû lamâkuma kuldanni* "This is chaos, I am surrounded, reach for me!". These agitated words are spoken by the trapped baby, see Lambert (1969, 36); Finkel (1980, 45); Zomer (2018a, 256).

26: [*il*$^{?}$]-⌜*ka*$^{?}$⌝-*am* is tentative. Following BAM 248: ii 44 and Iraq 31 pls. V–VIa: 46, we expect *izizzam*(*ma*) "stand by me!", a call to the helping deity (here Šamaš, in later parallels Marduk), see Zomer (2018a, 255f.).

27: Enlil is weeping in a birth scene, also in BiOr 75, 19f. (№ 3).

28: The reading ⌜*la*$^{?}$⌝-*ma-ku-mi* follows the later parallels presented above (l. 25). Note the change of /w/ > /m/, generally considered a post-OB feature.

№ 9: Fs. Larsen 397/399a

SEAL No.: 7218
Copy: Michel 2004, 397/399
Tablet Siglum: Kt 90/k 178
Photo: Michel 2004, 397/399
Edition: Michel 2004; Barjamovic 2015, 74
Studies: Michel/Wasserman 1997; Michel 2003; Wasserman 2003 Cat. No.17; Hecker 2008, 65f.; Barjamovic 2015; Steinert 2017a, 224f.; Zomer 2018a, 233f.
Collection: Anadolu Medeniyetleri Müzesi, Ankara
Provenance: Kaneš
Measurements: 5.3 × 4.2 cm
Procedure: No

Introduction

This OA incantation, with similarities to the other birth incantations from Kaneš (CCT 5, 50e = № 5 and SANER 9, 77= № 11), was found together with an incantation against bile (Fs. Larsen 397/399b = № 1).

Obverse
1 *ar-ḫu-um a-ra-aḫ*
2 *A-ra-aḫ-tum ar-ḫa-at*
3 *ar-ḫi-iš | ta-ri-i | ar-ḫi-iš*
4 *tù-lá-ad ar-ḫi-iš | i-lu-ku*
5 *ma-ú i-pí-ša | i-na*
6 *a-pí-ša | qá-qá-ra-am | té-sú-uq*
7 *i-zi-bi-tí-ša | ta-ša-bi-iṭ*
8 *bé-tám ma-na-me | lá-áš-pur*
9 *ú lu-wa-e-er a-me-er$^{!}$-ú-at Ša-sú-ra-tem*
10 *7 ù 7-ma | ma-ri-ki-/na*
11 *ù ta-áp-šu-kà-tí-ki-na*
12 *le-qí-a-nim-ma | ba-áb*
13 *A-ra-aḫ-tem ḫa-ba-tum*

Edge
14 *ḫu-ub-ta | šu-ma | za-kàr*
15 *e-tù-da-ni šu-ma*

Reverse
16 *sí-ni-ša-at ša-pá-ra-ni*
17 *šu-ma | sà-ak-pu-um | sà-ki-ip*
18 *i-li-šu | li-šé-lá-ma | k[i$^{?}$]-i*
19 *ṣa-ru-ú | ki-ra-nim | li-i[m-q]ú-tám*
20 *qá-qá-ar-šu | ší-ip-tu[m]*

21 *lá i-a-tum ší-pá-at Ni-ki-l*[*i-il*$_{5}$]
22 *be-el ší-pá-tem ù be-el tí-i-i*[*m*]
23 *be-lá-at ša-sú-ra-tem l*[*i-dí*]

Translation

1–2 A cow, oh cow! The *Araḫtum*-canal is quick!

3–5 Quickly, she is pregnant! Quickly, she is giving birth! Quickly, the water is coming from her afterbirth!

6–7 With her nose she *brushes* the ground. With her tail she sweeps the house.

8–10 Whom should I send and whom should I instruct (with orders) to the seven and seven Daughters of Šassūr (saying:)

10–14 "Take (f. pl.) your spades and baskets and take (f. pl.) it (the baby) forcefully out of the gate of the *Araḫtum*-canal!"

14–20 If it is a boy – like a wild ram, if it is a girl – like a wild cow, if it is a miscarriage – rejected by its god, may they (f. pl., the Daughters of Šassūr) let it come up and like a vine-snakes may it (the baby) fall down to the ground!

20–23 The incantation is not mine. (It is) the incantation of Ninkilil, lord of the incantations and lord of the spells. May the lady of wombs (i.e., Šassūr) cast it (i.e., the spell)!

Commentary

1–5: For the double meaning of *araḫtum* in the context of birth incantations, see Steinert (2017a, 224f.).

5: *ma-ú i-pí-ša* is interpreted as *māʾū ipiša* "water from her afterbirth", namely water breaking (see CAD I/J, 173, s.v. *ipum* "memebrae, afterbirth"). However, this phrase could also be read *māʾū ippīša* (<*in*(*a*) *pīša*) "water from her mouth", where mouth could refer metaphorically to the vulva, also a sign of labour.

18: *Pace* Hecker (2008, 65 fn. 24), who interprets *liššillam* from *našlulum* N (Bab. *našallulum*) "to slither out", *li-šé-lá-ma* is to be derived from *elûm* Š "to let come up" with the Daughters of Šassūr as the subject, in opposition to *limqutam* (l. 19). If so, this is a Babylonian verbal form, see de Ridder (2019, 131).

№ 10: RA 70, 135/137

SEAL No.: 7058
Copy: M. Cohen 1976, 135/137
Tablet Siglum: AUAM 73.3094
Photo: CDLI P249267
Edition: M. Cohen 1976, 136–139; Bergmann 2008, 28f.
Studies: Veldhuis 1989; Cunningham 1997 Cat. No. 314; Wasserman 2003 Cat. No. 142; Zomer 2018a, 132/234
Collection: Siegfried H. Horn Museum, Institute of Archaeology, Andrews University, Michigan
Provenance: Unknown
Measurements: –
Procedure: No (but note the instructions in the divine dialogue)

Introduction

One of the few examples of a bilingual incantation in the present corpus. The English translation follows the Akkadian, except for the places it does not appear – in which cases the translation is based on the Sumerian.

Obverse

1 [én-é-nu-ru]
2 [munus du-da-a-ni ma-gi$_4$ a mi-ni-ri]
3 [...]
4 [... munus du-da-a-ni ma-gi$_4$ a mi-ni]-ri
5 [...] *ki-ma e-le-pí i-te-i-il*
6 [munus du-da-a-ni ma-gi$_4$ a mi]-ni-ri
7 [... *a-ta-al-lu*]*-ki-ša ki-ma e-le-pí i-te-i-il*
8 [... munus du-d]a-a-ni ma-gi$_4$ a mi-ni-ri
9 [...] *i-na a-ta-al-lu-ki-ša ki-ma e-le-ep-pí i-te-i-il*
10 [x an-ú]r du-da-a-ni ma-gi$_4$ a mi-ni-ri
11 [*i-ši*]*-id ša-me-e ù er-ṣe-tim i-na a-ta-lu-ki-ša ki-ma e-le-pí i-te-i-il*
12 ⸢ma-še⸣-ma-ta še-em im-mi-in-si
13 *ki-ma e-le-ep ri-qí ri-qí ma-li-a-at*
14 ma-e-re-na-ta e-re-en im-mi-in-[si]
15 *ki-ma e-le-ep e-re-ni e-re-na-am ma-li-*[*a-at*]
16 ma-še-em-e-re-na-ta še-em-e-re-na im-mi-[in-si]
17 *ki-ma e-le-ep ri-qí e-re-ni ri-qí e-re-n*[*a-am ma-li-a-at*]
18 ma-gu-ug-za-gi-na gu-ug-za-gi-na im-mi-i[n-si]
19 *ki-ma e-le-ep sa-am-tim ù uq-ni-im sa-am-t*[*a-am ù uq-na-am ma-li-a-at*]
20 ù gu-ug nu-zu ù za-gi-i[n nu-zu]
21 *ù sa-am-tum ú-ul i-di ù uq-nu-ú-um ú-u*[*l i-di*]
22 ma kar za-la-na kar-ta ba-an-ta-ge$_4$

23 *a-na ka-ar ta-ši-la-tim i-te-i-i*[*l*]

24 ^{d}Asal-lú-ḫi i-gi im-ma-an-s[um]

25 [^{d}]⸢*Marduk*⸣(AMAR.UTU) […]

26 [a-a-ni ^{d}En-ki-ra é-a ba-an-ši-ku$_4$ gù mu-na-an-dé-e]

27 […]

28 [a-a-gu$_{10}$ munus du-da-a-ni ma-gi$_4$ a mi-ni-ri]

29 [… munus du-da-a-ni ma-gi$_4$ a mi-ni-ri]

30 [… munus du-da-a-ni ma-gi$_4$ a mi-ni-ri]

31 [a-rá-min-na-kám-ma-aš-šu-ub-du]

32 […]

Reverse

33 [^{d}En-ki ^{d}Asal-lú-ḫi dumu-ni-ra mu-na-ni-íb-gi$_4$-gi$_4$]

34 […]

35 [^{d}Asal-lú-ḫi a-na ma-ra-bé a-na a-ra-ab-daḫ]

36 […]

37 [ì-ga-zu-mu ù za-e nì-gá-zi]

38 […]

39 [ù za-e ì-ga-zu]-a [gá-e nì-gá-zi]

40 [… *ti*]-*du-ú a-na-ku lu*-⸢x x⸣ (...)

41 gen-na ⸢dumu⸣-[gu$_{10}$] (Akk.) *al-kam* […]

42 gi-sú-ug-bàn-da-eri$_4$-du$_{10}$-ga šu [ù-me-ti]

43 *qá-na-a ša Sú-ug-bàn-da ša Eri*$_4$*-du*$_{10}$*-ga i-na* [*le-qí-i*]

44 ia-ab-kù-ga ga-ra-ab-ši-il-la-ma šà-ba [ù-me-ni-dub]

45 *ša-ma-an li-it-tim el-le-tim li-iš-da-am* […] *šu-pu-uk*

46 saḫar sila-⸢lam$_4$⸣-bi (Akk.) *e-pí-ir su-qí er-be-t*[*i*]

47 ⸢x⸣ [x x] id li ib [x] giš ⸢x x⸣ zi (…)

48 ⸢x⸣ [x x (x)] ⸢x⸣ tim ša ⸢x⸣ ni im

49 […] ba ⸢x⸣ […] ⸢x⸣du$^{?}$ ki ta (x)

50 […] nu nu tim ḫa ⸢ma⸣am mi im ⸢x x⸣ im me [x]

51 […]-*e mi-it-ḫa-ri-iš bu*-⸢*ul*⸣-*li-il* ⸢x⸣ […]

52 […] ⸢x⸣ ḫé-en-[x]-ge$_4$

53 [*e-li a-bu-un-na-ti*]-*ša he-pé-e-ma*

54 [tukum-bi dum]u$^{?}$-ta kalag tukul-a-ni igi [mu-u]n-ši-in-bar

55 [*šum-ma*] ⸢*ma*⸣-*ar a-na ka-ki šu-a-ši* [*ip-pa*]-⸢*li-su*⸣

56 [tukum-bi dumu-munus-ta] ⸢kalag⸣ TUK ga-ri-im-⸢ma⸣-a-ni igi
[mu-un-ši-in]-bar

57 [*šum-ma ma-r*]*a-at a-na* ⸢x⸣-[*...šu*]-*a-‹ši› i-*[*ip-pa*]-⸢*li-su*⸣

58 […] til la ḫé a sa ⸢x⸣

59 […] ^{d}Utu-kam ḫé-⸢em⸣-ma-ra-⸢è⸣

60 […] ⸢x⸣-*tim li-it-ta-aṣ-‹ṣi›*

61 [ka-inim-ma munus ⸢ù-tu-da⸣
[iti] gu$_4$

Translation

1 [én-é-nu-ru]:
2–3 [The woman, when walking about, she wobbled like a boat],
4–5 [… the woman$^{?}$, when walking about], she wobbled like a boat,
6–7 [… the woman$^{?}$, when walking] about, she wobbled like a boat,
8–9 [… the woman$^{?}$], when walking about, she wobbled like a boat,
10–11 The horizon, when she is walking about, she wobbled like a boat.
12–13 Like a boat (carrying) aromatics, she is filled with aromatics,
14–15 Like a boat (carrying) cedar, she is filled with cedar,
16–17 Like a boat (carrying) aromatics and cedar, [she is filled] with aromatics and cedar,
18–19 Like a boat (carrying) carnelian and lapis-lazuli, [she is filled] with carne[lian and lapis lazuli],
20–21 Is it carnelian? She knows not; is it lapis-lazuli? She knows not.
22–23 She wobbled towards the quay of celebrations.
24–25 Marduk [observed this],
26–27 (Sum.) [to his father Enki, into the house he came in, calling to him …]:
28–30 (Sum.) – "[My father: the woman, about to give birth, leads the boat in the water; the woman, about to give birth, leads the boat in the water]"
31–32 (Sum.) [When saying this for the second time…],
33–34 (Sum.) [Enki answers his son Asalluḫi]:
35–36 (Sum.) – "[Asalluḫi, what could I say to you? What could I add to you? …]"
37–38 (Sum.) [What I know, you (also) know yourself …],
39–40 [What] you know [yourself], I [know] (too).
41 Come [Marduk],
42–43 When [taking] (Sum:) a little reed from the marsh (Akk: a reed from the little marsh) of Eridu,
44–45 pour the fat-milk of a pure cow, and the cream of [a mother cow],
46 dust from a crossroads,
47–50 …
51 "[…] mix together […]
52–53 break it [above her navel]!"
54–55 [If] it is a (Sum. strong) boy, they [look]ed at his "weapon",
56–57 [If] it is a (Sum. strong) g[irl], they [look]ed at [h]er ["*crucible*"$^{?}$],
58 (Sum.) …
59–60 May he come out [(*to the light*$^{?}$)]
61 [Incantation] for [a woman] in labour.
62 [The month] Gusisa.

Commentary

4–5: Following M. Cohen (1976, 140), Sum. (^{giš}ma)… ri // Akk. *eʾēlum*, "to coagulate$^{?}$" (CAD E, 41) is rendered as "to undulate, wobble" (*i-te-i-il* is Gtn preterite).

11: *išid šamê u erṣetim* is the subject of the sentence (M. Cohen 1976, 139 differently). The undulating movement of the boat (= the pregnant woman) is so strong that the horizon itself seems to be unstable.

18–21: For carnelian and lapis lazuli as symbolizing the gender of the baby to come, see Civil (1974, 331–336); Barrett (2007, 26); Bergmann (2008, 43–44) and Simkó (2014, 118–119).[229]

20–21: Akk. takes the Sum. ù gu-ug nu-zu ù za-gi-in nu-zu as a question and an answer: *u samtum ul īdi u uqnum ul īdi*. (M. Cohen 1976, 139 translated: "… she knows not if it is carnelian/lapis lazuli", but this would be *samtam/uqnam ul īdi*).

42–43: For similar instructions concerning reed, see Steinert (2017b, 336 fn. 135).

46: We follow here Steinert's (2017b, 336–339) interpretation which takes into account the commentary 11N-T3: 9–12 (Civil 1974, 332), explaining BAM 248, including a later version of this incantation. For dust taken from crossroads, see Finkel (1980, 48 fn. 25).

52–53: Reading follows Steinert (2017b, 336).

54–57: For the formula "if it is a boy... if it is a girl..." see Michel/Wasserman (1997). Both the "weapon" of the boy, and the "crucible" of the girl are euphemistic terms referring to the male and female sex organs. – In the Akk. version it is the parents who are looking at the neonate (*ippalisū*; *pace* M. Cohen 1976, 140 ad ll. 54–55). The first glance of both parents, symbolizing their acceptance of the new child, is mentioned in Ištar Louvre i 42 (Streck/Wasserman 2018, 17), and in a Mari letter (Marello 1992, 117: 36, for which see Wasserman 2016, 39 fn. 144).

56: With Cohen (1976, 140) ga-ri-im for garin = *agarinnum*, "womb, crucible".

62: Restoration follows Cohen (1976, 138f.). A date formula in incantations is rarely found but note ITI *ša re-ši* in the colophon of KBo 1, 18, a four-sided prism with a longitudinal hole, containing a collection of Sum. and Akk. incantations from Ḫattuša (see Schwemer 2013, 154; Zomer 2018a, 37; Zomer 2019), and LB 1003, an Elamite incantation which ends with a colophon with the date 23 XI Samsu-iluna 26 (see Wasserman 2020c).

229 Note that the association of red/pink ≈ girl, and blue ≈ boy is a recent cultural equation, found mainly in the Western world (see Frassanito/Pettorini 2008, 881). Bergmann (2008, 43–44) convincingly argues in favour of the opposite equation in this incantation, namely carnelian ≈ boy and lapis lazuli ≈ girl.

№ 11: SANER 9, 77

SEAL No.: 7219
Copy: –
Tablet Siglum: Kt 94/k 429
Photo: Barjamovic 2015, 77
Edition: Barjamovic 2015, 75f.
Studies: Zomer 2018a, 233
Collection: Anadolu Medeniyetleri Müzesi, Ankara
Provenance: Kaneš
Measurements: –
Procedure: No

Introduction

This OA incantation is related to the two other birth incantations from Kaneš (CCT 5, 50e = № 5 and Fs. Larsen 397/399a = № 9). In comparison with its other parallels from Kaneš, this version appears to be written defectively.[230] Since the photo presented in SANER 9 is barely readable and no copy is offered, some readings remain questionable.

1 *ar-ḫu-um* | *A-ra-aḫ-tum*
2 *ar-ḫi-iš* | *ta-ri-i*
3 [*ar-ḫ*]*i-iš* | *tù-la-ad*
4 ⸢*ar*⸣*-ḫi-iš* | (x$^{?}$-)*ma-id*
5 *ma-ú* | *pu-*⸢x x-*ša*⸣
6 *a-ma-ni-mì* | *la-áš*$^{!?}$*-pu-ur*
7 *a-ma-nim lu-wa-i-ir*
8 *a-na ma-ru-a-at*
9 *Ša-sú-ra-tem*
10 *7 ú 7-ma*
11 *ma-re-ki-na-mì*
12 *ú ta-áp-šu-kà-té-ki-na*
13 *le-qí-a-nim* ⸢ḫa x (x)⸣
14 ⸢x⸣-*ḫa-am*
15 SIG$_5$-*a-tám*
16 *šu-ul-ḫa-nim*
17 *šu-ma* | *z*[*a-k*]*à-ar*
18 *e-tù-da-ni* | ‹‹*šu-ma*››
19 *šu-ma* | [*s*]*í-ni-ša-at*
20 *ša-pá-ra-ni*
21 *li-šé-lam i-na ṣé-er*
22 *ki-ra-nim* | *ki-i* | ^{še}GIG

230 Note the use of dative *a-ma-ni-mi* (l. 7) and *a-ma-nim* (l. 8) and the possible confusion of Bab. *ṣer karānim* / Ass. *ṣar kirānim* with the preposition *ina ṣēr* in *i-na ṣé-er ki-ra-nim*, see Barjamovic 2015, 58.

23 *a-ša-ar-šu*
24 *li-iṣ-ba-at*

Five lines badly broken

Translation

1 The cow, the *Araḫtum*-canal –
2–5 quickly, she is pregnant! Quickly, she is giving birth! Quickly, the water(s) *become plentiful* [in] her v[ulva].
6–10 To whom should I send (the patient)? To whom should I dispatch (her)? To the seven and seven Daughters of Šassūr (saying:)
11–16 "Take (f. pl.) your spades and baskets … pull out (f. pl.) the good …!"
17–21 If it is a boy – like a wild ram! If it is a girl – like a wild cow, may it get out!
22–24 May it take its place on top of the vine-snake like wheat!

Commentary

5: Considering that the other OA parallel reads *ar-ḫi-iš* I *i-lu-ku ma-ú i-pí-ša* (Fs. Larsen 397/399a = № 9), it is not impossible to restore *pu-*⌜x x-*ša*⌝ as a locative.

21: *li-šé-lam* and *li-šé-lá-ma* (Fs. Larsen 397/399a: 18 = № 9) are interpreted as precatives 3.sg/3.pl.f. of *elûm* Š. Barjamovic (2015, 58 fn. 6; 74), following Hecker (2008, 65 fn. 24), derives both forms from *našlulum* N (Bab. *našallulum*) "to slither out". This suggestion cannot be accepted, for this analysis should result in *liššalil*(*am*), see Kouwenberg (2010, 302).

№ 12: VS 17, 34

SEAL No.: 7059
Copy: van Dijk 1971 Pl. XV
Tablet Siglum: VAT 8539
Photo: –
Edition: van Dijk 1972, 343–345; Bergmann 2008, 22
Studies: Röllig 1985; Farber 1987, 274–277; Veldhuis 1991; Cunningham 1997 Cat. No. 367; Michel/Wasserman 1997; Stol 2000, 63f.; Wasserman 2003 Cat. No. 209; Kogan 2004; Foster 2005, 170f.; Bergmann 2008, 21f.; Hecker 2008, 72; Steinert 2017a, 223f.; Zomer 2018a, 233f.
Collection: Vorderasiatisches Museum, Berlin
Provenance: Larsa area
Measurements: 5.0 × 7.0 cm
Procedure: No

Introduction
Text collated on 3/2/2011 (NW).

Obverse
1 *ar-ḫu-um e-ri-a-at ar-ḫu-um ul-la-ad*
2 *i-na ta-ar-ba-ṣi-im ša* ^{d}*Šamaš*(UTU)
3 *sú-pu-ú-úr* ^{d}*Šákkan*
4 *i-mu-ur-ši-i-ma* ^{d}*Šamaš*(UTU) *i-ba-ak-ki*
5 *i-mu-ur-ši-i-ma el-lam-me-e i-il-la-ka*
6 *di-i-ma-a-šu*
7 *am-mi-nim-mi* ^{d}*Šamaš*(UTU) *i-ba-ak-ki*
8 [*e*]*l-lam-me-e i-il-la-ka di-ma-šu*
9 [*a-n*]*a ar-ḫi-ia-mi la-a pe-ti-i-tim*
10 *ú-ni-qí-ia la wa-li-it-tim*

Reverse
11 [*ma-na*]*-am-mi lu-u*[*š-pu-ur*]
12 [*ù lu-w*]*a-e-*[*er*]
13 [*a-na ma-ra-a*]*t A-ni-im se-bi ù s*[*e-bi*]
14 [*li-...*] *a*$^{?}$*-ma karpassina*(DUG-*as-sí-n*[*a*]) *ša* [...]
15 *li-še*$_{20}$*-ši*$^{!}$(WI)*-ra-nim še*$_{20}$*-er-ra-a*[*m*]
16 *šum-ma zi-ka-ar a*$^{?}$*-tu-da-ni*
17 *šum-ma sí-in-ni-ša-at / na-ap-ṭ*[*á*]*-ar-ta-ni*
18 *li-im-qú-ta-am qá-aq-qá-ar-*[*šu*]*m*
19 tu$_{6}$-én-é-nu-ru
20 ka-inim-ma munus ù-tu-[da-k]am

Translation

1–3	The cow is pregnant, the cow is giving birth, in the stall of Šamaš, the pen of Šakkan.
4–6	When Šamaš saw her, he was crying, when the pure-of-rites saw her, his tears were flowing down (saying:)
7–8	– "Why does Šamaš cry? The tears of the pure-of-rites flowing down?
9–10	– "(Over) my cow, not deflowered, (over) my kid, never giving birth!"
11–13	– ["Wh]om should I se[nd and sum]mon the Da[ughters] of Anum, seven and se[ven]?"
14–15	Let them [take for me] their vessels of [*gold*], let them cause the child to be delivered effortlessly!
16–18	If it is a male – like a wild ram, if it is a female – like a *napṭartu*-woman, may it fall (safely) to the ground!
19	tu$_6$-én-é-nu-ru
20	Incantation for a woman in labour.

Commentary

15:	Restoration after Farber (1990b, 308, 2.6). Durand (1988, 295 fn. c) maintains *li-še$_{20}$-wi-ra-nim* (< *šuwwurum*), explaining it as "dénominatif sur *šewêrum* «anneau» = «encercler»": "entourer (un enfant) de ses bras".
16:	For *a-tu-da-ni*, see Michel/Wasserman (1997) and Stol (2000, 64 fn. 100).
18:	For *maqātum* describing the final stage of giving birth in other OB incantations, see BiOr 75, 19f. (№ 3), Fs. Larsen 397/399a (№ 9); for later, MB/MA incantations, see AS 16, 287f.c and KUB 4, 13a. Note especially BiOr 11 Pl. II (fig. 1) (№ 65), where an afterbirth of a dog is mentioned. This idiom appears also in epistolary context, see Marello (1992, 117: 36) and Wasserman (2016, 39 fn. 144).

№ 13: YOS 11, 17

SEAL No.: 7060
Copy: van Dijk/Goetze/Hussey 1985 Pl. XX
Tablet Siglum: YBC 5630
Photo: https://collections.peabody.yale.edu/search/Record/YPM-BC-019695
Edition: –
Studies: Cunningham 1997 Cat. No. 393; Wasserman 2003 Cat. No. 247
Collection: Yale Babylonian Collection, New Haven
Provenance: Larsa area
Measurements: 4.1 × 6.4 cm
Procedure: No (but see l. 4)

Introduction

A fragmentary incantation, whose subscript reveals that it is for a woman in labour. No parallel texts are known. On the reverse a large "X" sign is inscribed.

Obverse

1 *bi-ni* ⸢x x x⸣
2 *ṣa-ḫa-ar-ša ṣa-ḫa-ar*
3 *lu-lu bi-in*
4 *ru-uʾ*$_4$ *ru- uʾ*$_4$ *ru- uʾ*$_4$ *ru- uʾ*$_4$*-tum*
5 *ši-na iš-ti-a ṣa-bi-a-tum*
6 ka-inim-ma munus ù-tu-da-kam

Reverse uninscribed, but with an "X" sign)

Translation

1 A son of ...
2 *Her small one is small*!?
3 The *primeval man is a boy*!
4 Spit, spit, spit – spittle!
5 They (f. pl.) drank, the gazelles.
6 Incantation (for) a woman in labour.

Commentary

1/3: *bīnum*, must be "son", or "boy" (a rare word attested in OAkk and in post-OB literary texts, AHw 127a, s.v.), and not "tamarisk" which makes little sense here (note *lullû* in l. 3).

2: *ṣa-ḫa-ar-ša ṣa-ḫa-ar*: the vocalization *ṣaḫar* seems to indicate an early OB date (similarly the uncontracted vowels in *ṣabiātum* in l. 5).

4: *ru*-ÚḪ-*tum* is the OB spelling of *ruʾtum* "spittle" (cf. *ru-uʾ*$_4$*-tim* CUSAS 32, 32a: 16 = № 27; *ru*-ḪA-*tim* ZA 75, 198–204b: 18 = № 137). The imperative *ru-uʾ*$_4$ is so far anattested (probably denominative of *ruʾtum*). See Kogan (2001, 276).

№ 14: YOS 11, 86a

SEAL No.: 7061
Copy: van Dijk/Goetze/Hussey 1985 Pl. LXXVII
Tablet Siglum: YBC 4603
Photo: https://collections.peabody.yale.edu/search/Record/YPM-BC-018668
Edition: van Dijk 1973, 503–507; Bergmann 2008, 32
Studies: Scurlock 1991, 141; Cunningham 1997 Cat. No. 404; Veldhuis 1999, 39–41; Wasserman 2003 Cat. No. 262; Foster 2005, 171f.; Bergmann 2008, 128/152; Hecker 2008, 72f.; Zomer 2018a, 234f.; Polinger Foster 2020, 131
Collection: Yale Babylonian Collection, New Haven
Provenance: Larsa area
Measurements: 13.5 × 5.5 cm
Procedure: No

Introduction
An elongated incantation collective: a childbirth incantation on the obverse and a Sum. incantation against Lamaštu on its reverse. This incantation is the longest of the four known parallel childbirth incantations and could perhaps be the one which served as a textual model for the writer of BM 115745 (№ 4).

Obverse
1 *i-na me-e na-a-ki-im*
2 *ib-ba-ni e-ṣé-em-tum*
3 *i-na ši-i-ir* [*še*$_{20}$]*-er-ḫa-nìm*
4 *ib-ba-ni* [*l*]*i-il-li-du-um*
5 *i-na me-e ayabba*(A.AB.BA) *ša-am-ru-tim*
6 *pa-al-ḫu-ú-tim*
7 *i-na me-e ti-a-am-tim ru-qú-ú-tim*
8 *a-šar ṣe-eḫ-ru-um ku-us-sà-a i-da-a-šu*
9 *qí-ir-bi-is-sú la-a uš-na-wa-ru*
10 *i-in ša-am-ši-im*
11 *i-mu-ur-šu-ú-ma* ^{d}*Asal-lú-ḫi ma-ri* ^{d}*En-ki*
12 *ip-ṭù-ur ma-ak-sí-i-šu*
13 *ku-uṣ-ṣú-ru-ú-tim*
14 *ṭù-ú-da-am iš-ku-un-šum*
15 *pa-a-da-na-am ip-te-e-šum*
16 [*pu*$^{?}$*-ut*$^{?}$]*-tu-ku-um ṭù-ú-du*
17 *pa-a-da-nu p*[*u-uṭ-ṭù-u*]*r-ku-um*
18 *wa-aš-ba-at-ku-*⸢*um*⸣ *Bēlet-ilī*(^{d}⸢MAḪ⸣) *a-sú-tum*
19 *ba-a-ni-a-at* [*mi*$^{?}$*-n*]*a*$^{?}$*-mi-i-i*[*m*]
20 *ba-ni-a-at ka-li-i-ni*
21 *a-na ši-ga-ri-im*
22 *ta-aq-ta-bi wu-uš-šu-*⸢*ra-at*⸣

23 [*pa-a*]*ṭ-ru sí-ik-ku-ru-*[(x)]
24 [*ru-um*]*-ma-a da-la-t*[*u-*(x)]

Reverse
25 [*li*]*-im-ḫa-aṣ* [*si-ip-pí*]
26 *ki-ma da-di-*[*im*]
27 *šu-ṣí ra-ma-an-ka*
----
28 ka-inim-ma munus ù-tu-da-⌜kam⌝

Translation

1–2 In the fluid of conception the substance was created.
3–4 In the fleshy tissue the *homunculus* was created.
5–7 In the water of the ocean, so fierce, so frightening, in the water of the sea, so remote,
8–10 a place where the little-one, his hands are bound, a place which is not lit by the eye of the sun –
11 (there) Asalluḫi, the son of Enki, noticed him.
12–15 He loosened his shackles so tight, set for him the road, opened for him the path, (saying:)
16–17 "The road is [op]en for you, the path is c[*leared up*?]for you!
18–19 Bēlet-ilī, the female physician, is sitting for you, the *creatrix* of everything,
21–22 the *creatrix* of all of us said to the bolt:
22–27 "You are released! [un]bolt are the bars, loosened are the door[s]!", "[May] he break the [*door jambs*]!", "Come out by yourself like a good boy!"
----
28 Incantation for a woman in labour.

Commentary

1: The verb *niākum*/*nâkum* describes mostly illicit sexual relations, see Wasserman (2016, 36 and *passim*), but here, and in the other parallel texts, *mê nâkim* denotes the anatomical environment of the baby, resulting from any intercourse, with no moral judgement.

17: Reading *padānu p*[*u-uṭ-ṭù-u*]*r-ku-um* "the path is cleared up for you" or *p*[*u-ut-t*]*u-ku-um* "is opened up for you", was suggested by U. Steinert (private communication).

18: This line is now made clear by George (2016, 141), who suggested further that *asūtum* is a mistake for *šabsūtum*, "midwife".

19: [*mi*?*-n*]*a*?*-mi-i-i*[*m*]: Examining the copy and photos of the tablet, the half broken sign before *-mi* seems like [*n*]*a*. If so, *mīnamîm*, a by-form of *mīnummê*, "all (of), whatever, everything" (CAD M/2, 97) comes to mind (but note that this indefinite pronoun is attested only in post-OB texts). Another possibility (suggested by U.

Steinert, private communication) is to read *bāniat* [*d*]*a-mi-i-im*, which fits well but "DN the creatrix of blood" is unanticipated.

22: *wuššurāt*(*a*), "you are released" (a shortened 2 m. stative form). U. Steinert's suggestion to read *wuššurka*, "your release", cannot be sustained.

25: [*li*]-*im-ḫa-aṣ* [*si-ip-pe*] is tentative, based on the preceding *sikkurū* and *dalātu*. This phrase has no parallel in the corresponding texts.

26: *kīma dād*[*im*]: A play between the homonyms *dādum* A ("object of love, darling") and *dādum* B "an aquatic animal with a shell" (attested only in post-OB texts), could be intended. The boy is expected to go out of the aquatic surrounding of the womb "like a darling" and "(as smoothly) as a shellfish".[231]

231 Support for this idea can be found in Ps 58: 9: "Like a snail that melts away as it moves; like a woman's stillbirth, may they never see the sun!" (The New Jewish Publication Society of America Tanakh). Even if used for a different goal, the Psalmist finds it useful to compare the baby in the womb with a molluscan creature.

2.1.3 Childhood Disease

The present corpus holds a rare example of an incantation that specifically aims 'to revive a beloved child', i.e., BiOr 75, 21f. (№ 15). As for references to children outside the thematic group of Childbirth (§ 2.1.2), note the spells against Worms and Leeches (§ 2.2.8).

№ 15: BiOr 75, 21f.

SEAL No.: 7052
Copy: –
Tablet Siglum: –
Photo: Wasserman 2018, 21f.
Edition: Wasserman 2018, 21–23
Studies: –
Collection: Private Collection
Provenance: Unknown
Measurements: 4.2 × 6.0 cm
Procedure: No

Introduction

This incantation on a landscape-oriented tablet reflects a grave moment: a small child suffering from a critical ailment (see Wasserman 2018).

Obverse

1 *da-du-um-mi da-du-um*
2 *uk-ku-pa-ma*
3 *da-da-ru-um*
4 *ši-ni-ih-šu* {x} *mu-tu-um*
5 *am-ma-at mu-tu-um*
6 *ú-uṭ ba-*⸢*la*⸣*-ṭú*
7 *ši-in ši-z*[*i*]-⸢*i*⸣

Reverse

8 *a-ma-ru ša* DINGIR-[*šu*]
9 *ú-da*$^{?!}$*-am-mi-q*[*á-am/aš-šu*]
10 ⸢$^{d+}$*En-ki*⸣ *ù* ^{d}*Marduk* (⸢$^{d?}$AMAR$^{?}$.UTU⸣) ^{d}⸢*Gu-la*⸣
11 ⸢^{d}*Nin*$^{?}$*-ka*$^{?}$*-ra-ak*$^{?}$⸣ ^{d}⸢*Nin*⸣-[*girim*$^{?}$]
12 ka-inim-ma [*da*$^{?}$*-du*$^{?}$]*-um*
13 ti-la-kam

Translation

1–2	The beloved child, beloved child is about (to die).
3–4	The ill-smelling *daddarum*-thorn, its blockage (in the child's throat) is death.
5–8	Death – one cubit; life – half-cubit; two times one-third cubit – the (caring) glance of [his] deity!
9	It (god's glance) made [him] better!
10–11	(By) Enki and Marduk! (By) Gula, Ninkarrak (and) *Nin*[*girim*?]!
12–13	Incantation to revive a [*beloved ch*]*ild*?.

Commentary

7–8:	Following Wasserman's interpretation (2018, 23), *šin šizî* "two times one-third cubit" refers to the seeing eyes of the personal deity (*amāru ša ili*[*šu*]).
10–11:	Similar occurences of the abbreviated authorative formula "(By) DN_1, DN_2, DN_3 etc." are found in KBo 1, 18, see Zomer (2019, 1266).

2.1.4 Gastrointestinal Problems

This large group of incantations concerns different disorders of the digestive system and the inner organs which are referred to generally as *libbum*, lit. heart". An important sub-group of these texts contain the so-called 'heart-plant' motif, i.e., CUSAS 32, 7o // CUSAS 32, 8i (№ 19), CUSAS 32, 26c (№ 24), YOS 11, 11 (№ 35) and YOS 11, 12a (№ 36).[232]

Typical to this group of incantations is the description of the *libbum* as a kind of brewing or fermentation vat, i.e., *kakkullum*/gakkùl (CT 4, 8 = № 16) and *namzītum*, i.e., CUSAS 32, 32a (№ 27), CUSAS 32, 32b (№ 28), CUSAS 32, 32c (№ 29) and PBS 7, 87 (№ 33).[233]

№ 16: CT 4, 8

SEAL No.: 7065
Copy: Pinches 1898 Pl. 8a; Steinert/Vacín 2018, 717/719
Tablet Siglum: BM 92518
Photo: Steinert/Vacín 2018, 716/718
Edition: Sullivan 1980, 131–134; Steinert/Vacín 2018, 720–732
Studies: Alster 1972, 354; Cohen S. 1976, 102f.; Foster 1993 II.19, 12; Cunningham 1997 Cat. No. 311; Wasserman 2003 Cat. No. 57; Steinert/Vacín 2018; Zomer 2018a, 124 fn. 440/134/176 fn. 592.
Collection: British Museum, London
Provenance: Sippar$^{?}$
Measurements: 9.5 × 5.4 cm
Procedure: Yes

Introduction

This interlinear bilingual incantation ends with the unusual notation 2 EME *ša libbi* (see commentary to l. 26). Steinert/Vacín (2018) assume that the text is composed of two consecutive incantations: a long one (ll. 1–21), ending with the compressed rubric *šipat* KA ... "incantation *of the opening of* [...]", and a shorter incantation (ll. 22–25) with no rubric of its own. The final subscript – read by Steinert/Vacín as 2 ka-‹inim-ma› *ša libbi* – supposedly summarizes the two incantations. We differ and understand ll. 22–25 not as a separate incantation, but as procedures in which a magic call (or an incipit of a separate incantation) is embedded: *libbī libbī šamû erṣetum* "Oh my belly! Oh my belly! Heaven (and) earth!" (l. 22). According to our understanding, 2 EME *ša libbi* refers not to two successive incantations, but to the two languages of the text, i.e., "Two tongues (i.e., languages) concerning the belly". As Steinert/Vacín (2018, 732–737) have noted, this OB bilingual incantation continued to be transmitted into the first millennium, where a unilingual Sumerian version of it is known.

232 Primarily discussed by Reiner 1985, 94–100 and Veldhuis 1990. A corrupt variant of this motif is found in CUSAS 32, 29a (№ 67, against dogs).

233 The *diqārum*, a large vessel which was used for brewing beer, in JEOL 47, 58a (№ 169) is another variant of this image. On vessels as metaphor in incantations, see Steinert 2013.

Obverse

1 šà gig-ga ‹‹⸢in⸣›› gi-pisan$^{!}$-gin$_7$ kéš-da
li-ib-bu ma-ar-ṣú ša ki-ma pí-ša-an-ni ka-at-m[*u*]

----

2 a íd-da-gin$_7$ al-du-un nu-zu
ki-ma me-e na-ri-im e-ma i-il-la-ku ú-⸢*ul*⸣ [*i-di*]

----

3 a pú-gin$_7$ a-ge$_6$-a ‹‹⸢gin$_7$⸣›› nu-tuku
ki-ma me-e bu-ur-ti a-gi-a ú-ul i-šu

----

4 gakkùl-gin$_7$$^{!}$ ⸢ka-bi⸣ ba-dul
ki-ma ka-ak-ku-li [*pí*$^{?}$*-šu*$^{?}$] *ka-ti-im*

----

5 a nu-mu-un-da-ku$_4$-ku$_4$ ninda nu-mu-un-da-ku$_4$-ku$_4$
a-ka-lu ù mu-ú ú-ul i-ir-ru-bu-šum

----

6 ^{d}Asal-lú-ḫi igi-ni im-ma-an-sì
^{d}*Marduk*(AMAR.UTU) *ip-pa-li-ís-su-ma*

----

7 a-a-ni ^{d}En-ki-ke$_4$ gù mu-un-na-dé-e
a-na a-bi-šu ^{d}*É-a i-*⸢*ša*⸣*-ás-si*

----

8 a-a-ni šà gig-ga ‹‹in›› gi-pisan-gin$_7$ kéš-da
a-bi li-ib-bu ma-ar-ṣú ša ki-ma pí-ša-an-ni ka-at-mu

----

9 a íd-da-gin$_7$ al-du-un nu-zu
ki-ma me-e na-ri-im e-ma i-il-la-ku ú-ul i-di$^{!}$(ŠU)

----

10 a pú-gin$_7$ a-ge$_6$-a ‹‹gin$_7$›› nu-tuku
ki-ma me-e bu-ur-ti a-gi-a ú-ul i-šu

====

Reverse

11 ⸢gakkùl⸣-[gin$_7$ ka-b]i$^{?}$ ba-⸢dul$^{?}$⸣
ki-ma ka-⸢*ak-ku*⸣*-l*[*i*] *p*[*í*$^{?}$*-šu*] *ka-ti-im*

----

12 a nu-mu-un-da-ku$_4$-ku$_4$ ninda nu-mu-un-da-ku$_4$-ku$_4$
akalu(NINDA) *ù mu-ú ú-ul i-ir-ru-bu-šum*

----

13 ^{d}En-‹‹líl››-ki-ke$_4$ ^{d}Asal-lú-ḫi mu-un-na-ni-íb-gi-gi
^{d}*É-a* ^{d}*Marduk*(AMAR.UTU) *i-ip-pa-al*

----

14 dumu-gu$_{10}$ a-na-àm nu$^{!}$(NE)-zu a-na-àm ma-ra-ab-daḫ-e
ma-ri mi-i-na la ti-di-ma mi-i-na-am lu-ṣi-ib-šu

----

15 níg ge$_{26}$-e zu-gu$_{10}$ ù za-e gá-zu

ša a-na-ku i-du-ú ‹‹ú›› *at-ta ti-di*

----

16 ù za-e gá-zu níg ge$_{26}$-e zu-gu$_{10}$
ša at-ta ti-du-ú a-na-ku i-di

----

17 lú ḫé-a ⸢gu$_{4}$ ḫé-a⸣ udu ḫé-a
lu-ú a-wi-lu-tum lu-ú al-pu lu-ú im-me-ru

----

18 lag mun ù ḫa$^{!}$-še-na ù-un-daḫ ù-bí-⸢in⸣-[šub]
ki-ir-ba-an ṭa-ab-ti ù ḫa-ši-i us-ḫa-a[*m* x x x]

----

19 še$_{10}$-‹gin$_{7}$› ki-šè ḫé-si-il-le *ki-ma ši-it-*[*ti-im liddi*$^{?}$]
20 bu-lu-úḫ-gin$_{7}$ ḫé$^{?}$-si-il-le *ki-ma g*[*i-šu-ú-tim li-ig-šu*]
21 tu$_{15}$-gin$_{7}$ gu$^{!}$(ŠE)-du-šè è-íb-ta *ki-ma š*[*a-ri-im li-še-ṣi*]
ši-pa-at ka [...]

----

22 *ša-ri-ìš* 4 *libbi*(ŠÀ-*bi*) *libbi*(ŠÀ) *šamê*(AN) *erṣetim*(KI) *t*[*u*$^{?}$-x x x x]
23 *i-nu-ma a-na awīlim*(LÚ) *qáb-la-*‹‹DU››-*t*[*um*] *lu-*⸢x⸣-[x x x]
24 [*i*]-*na-ad-di-šu-ú dišpam*(LÀL$^{?}$) *i-le-em-m*[*a* x x x x x x]
25 *li-ib-bu i-na-aḫ l*[*i*-x x x x x]

====

26 2 EME *ša li-ib-bi*

Translation

(Akk. only)
1–3 Aching belly which is covered like a box, like the water of a river it does not know where to go, like the water of a well it has no flow.
4–5 Its [*opening*$^{?}$] is covered like a brewing vat: food and water cannot enter into it.
6–7 Marduk observed it and called to his father, Ea (saying):
8–12 – "Oh my father! (There is an) aching belly which is covered like a box, like the water of a river it does not know where to go, like the water of a well it has no flow. Its opening is covered like a brewing vat: food and water cannot enter into it".
13 Ea answers Marduk:
14–16 – "My son, what do you not know? What can I add to it? What I know, you know; What you know, I know!
17–18 (As for the patient) – be it a human being, an ox, or a sheep – *ex*[*tract*$^{?}$] a lump of salt and thyme!
19–21 [May *he drop* (*it*)] in the form of excre[ment]! [May *he eject it*] in the form of a *b*[*elch*]! [*May he make it go out*] in the form of w[ind!]"
Incantation *of the opening of* [...]
22 To the wind (*say*) four times: "Oh my belly! Oh my belly! Heaven (and) earth [...]"
23 When into the (sick) person, the middle of the body ... [...]
24 *He will drop it.* He will consume *honey*$^{?}$.

25 The belly will come to rest; The b[elly will recover].

====

26 Two tongues (i.e., languages) against the belly.

Commentary

17: Other gastrointestinal incantations destined for either man or animal are CUSAS 32, 26c and CUSAS 32, 8d (№ 24 and 21, respectively).

18: Alternatively one may read *uṣ-ṣa-a*[*b*] “he will add”, corresponding to Sumerian d a ḫ. Note, however, that we would expect in the instructive part of the divine dialogue either a 2.sg. *tuṣṣab* “you will add”, or an imperative. – For thyme and salt in magico-therapeutic texts, see Steinert/Vacín (2018, 711/713).

21: It is not impossible to read *ši-pa-at* ka as *šipatka* “your incantation”, for a similar phrase, *tûka* “your incantation”, is found in a couple of MB incantations against various diseases (Ugaritica 5, 17a, see Zomer 2018a, 246–249 and Ugaritica 5, 17b, see Zomer 2018a, 249–252). Yet *tûka* in these MB incantations refers to Asalluḫi, not to the patient, as in our case. We prefer to see here a subscript denoting the end of the incantation, whereas ll. 22–25 contains the accompanying procedure.

22: *ša-ri èz-za libbi*(ŠÀ-*bi*), suggested by Steinert/Vacín (2018, 721), is difficult both orthographically and syntactically.

22–25: *Pace* Steinert/Vacín (2018, 721 and 730), we suggest that this section contains procedures, starting with the command to recite four times the magic call, or an incipit of another incantation, “Oh my belly! Oh my belly! Heaven (and) earth!”. It is likely that the speaker had to face each of the four cardinal points while saying this sentence (see CUSAS 32, 32a: 17–18 = № 27). Speaking to the wind is found also in Fs. Pope 87: 4–5 (№ 70). – “My heart” in the first-person voice is found also in Fs. de Meyer 75/83d: 40–41 (№ 30).

23: Steinert/Vacín (2018, 721) read *ana awīlim*(LÚ) *qáb-la-tím*$^{!}$(TÚM *erasure*), but it is unlikely that the scribe would use TÚM (= DU) in this period. In fact, after DU the beginning of TUM, or perhaps TIM, can be seen.

24: Steinert/Vacín (2018, 721 and 731) suggest [*i*]-*na-ad-di šu-šam*^{am} “licorice”. This spelling is difficult. Our LÀL, after [*i*]-*na-ad-di-šu-ú*, is uncertain, and another sweet edible, meant to overcome the bitter taste of the salt in l. 18, may be there.

26: Steinert/Vacín (2018, 699) took this colophon to be a short form of 2 k a - ‹ i n i m - m a › *ša libbi*. We take the sign previously read as KA to be EME (see photo below), hence: 2 *lišānū ša libbi* “two tongues (i.e., languages) concerning the belly”, referring to the fact that the tablet is bilingual.

№ 17: CUSAS 32, 7c

SEAL No.: 7066
Copy: George 2016 Pls. XXII
Tablet Siglum: MS 3097
Photo: George 2016 Pls. XXI; CDLI P252106
Edition: George 2016, 151f.
Studies: George (*forthcoming*)
Collection: Schøyen Collection, Oslo
Provenance: Unknown
Measurements: 25.0 × 24.0 cm
Procedure: No

Introduction

Sadly, only the beginning of this incantation with its lyrical description of the wind over the sea has reached us. Since the text is found in an incantation collective containing Sumerian and Akkadian incantations, this description could be a historiola of an incantation against 'wind', flatus.

i
19' *ša-rum ti-me-a-tim ú-ṣi-i-ma*
20' ⸢*ù*⸣ *ti-a-me-tum ip-pa-al-la-‹sú›-šum*
21' [*im*]-*ḫa-aṣ ú-ru-*{x}-*uḫ*
22' [*ti*]-*wi-a-tim*
23' [x x x x] ⸢x *ap*⸣-*pa-ra-*⸢*ti*⸣
24'ff. (*traces*)

Translation

19'–22' The wind went out (flying over) the (different) seas. The Sea was looking at it. It plowed the way of the seas.
23' […] marshes
(*remainder lost*)

Commentary

19'/20'/22': Oddly, two different spellings for "sea" are used here: *timiātum* or *tiwiātum* and *tiamêtum*.

21': *maḫāṣum* is used metaphorically, with the meaning "to plow" (CAD M/1, 79f.), although in this meaning the verb *mayārum* is almost always used. – The construct form *uruḫ* can be derived from *uruḫḫum* "hair" (CAD U/W, 270) or *urḫum* "way". George (2016, 151) prefers "the sea's hairline" – a beautiful poetic image, but unknown elsewhere. By contrast, the co-location *urḫu* and *tâmtu* "seaway" is quite common in first millennium royal inscriptions: *ina tâmti u nābali itti ummānīya urḫu padānu ušaṣbissunūti* "I made (those kings, together with their forces and boats), take the road (and) path with my troops by sea and dry land" Ashurbanipal 11: i 73f. (Novotny/Jeffers 2018, 232f., cf. CAD U/W, 219a), and similarly,

Ashurbanipal 23: 43 (Novotny/Jeffers 2018, 302). The image is clear: the sea is quiet, but then the wind blows and cuts waves through it.

№ 18: CUSAS 32, 7m // CUSAS 32, 8f

SEAL No.: 7116
Copy: George 2016 Pl. XXV; Pls. XXVIII
Tablet Siglum: MS 3097; MS 3085
Photo: George 2016 Pl. XXVI, CDLI P252106); Pl. XXVII, CDLI P252094
Edition: George 2016, 128f.; Krebernik 2018, 41
Studies: Krebernik 2018, 19
Collection: Schøyen Collection, Oslo
Provenance: Unknown
Measurements: 25.0 × 24.0 cm (MS 3097); 16.5 × 9.3 cm (MS 3085)
Procedure: Yes

Introduction
This spell is attested in two incantation collectives. The subscript is almost entirely lost, but its resemblance to the other incantations on these tablets and its phraseology suggest that it is destined to ease a stomach pain (George 2016, 128).

Text A = CUSAS 32, 7m; Text B = CUSAS 32, 8f

1	A v 38	lú sag-ga-ak-ra-áš sà$^{!}$(A)-bu-ra
	B ii 21'	lugal sag-ga-ak-ra-áš sa-bu-ra
2	A v 39	*ša-mu-ú er-ṣe-ta-am ir-ḫu-ú*
	B ii 22'	*ša-mu-ú er-ṣe-ta-am ir-ḫu-ú*
3	A v 40	*b[u]-ul* ^{d}*Šákkan ir-ta-ak-*⸢*bu*⸣
	B ii 23'	*bu-ul* ^{d}*Šákkan i-na ṣe-ri-im ir-ta-ak-bu*
4	A v 41	*e-ri-iš ta-am-ma-ga-[a]r*
	B ii 24'	*e-ri-iš ta-am-ma-ga-*⸢*ar*⸣
5	A v 42	én-⸢é⸣-nu-ru
	B ii 25'	én-é-nu-ru
6	A v 43	⸢*an*⸣*-[na-an-n]a māri*(DUMU) *an-na-an-*⸢*na*⸣
	B ii 26'	*an-na-an-*⸢*na māri*(DUMU⸣) *an-na-*
7	A v 44	[*ša il*(DINGIR)*-šu*] *an-na-an-*[*na*]
	B ii 26'	*ša il*(DINGIR)*-šu an-na-an-na*
8	A v 45	[*iš-ta-a*]*r-šu an-na-ni-*[*tum*]
	B ii 27'	*iš-ta-a*[*r-šu*] *an-na-ni-tum*
9	A v 46	[x x x] ⸢x x x-*tim*$^{?}$⸣ *ši-ti-a-*[*am*]

10	A v 47	[tu$_6$-é]n-é-nu-ru
	B ii 28'	⸢tu$_6$-én⸣-[x x x x x x] ⸢x x x⸣
11	A v 48	[ka-inim-ma šà-gig *pa-ša-r*]*u-u*[*m*]
	B ii 29'	[…]

Translation

1	*Lu(gal) saggak-raš sabura.*
2–3	Heaven inseminated Earth, the herds of Šakkan mounted one another.
4	Ask! (– and your request) will be granted!
5	én-é-nu-ru.
6–8	Oh N.N., son of N.N., whose god is N.N., whose goddess is N.N.
9	drink the … !
10	tu$_6$-én-é-nu-ru.
11	[Incantation] to undo [stomach-ache].

Commentary

1: Alloglot passage in an unidentified language, see Krebernik (2018, 19/41).

№ 19: CUSAS 32, 7o // CUSAS 32, 8i

SEAL No.: 7117
Copy: George 2016 Pl. XXV; Pls. XXVIII-XXIX
Tablet Siglum: MS 3097; MS 3085
Photo: George 2016 Pl. XXVI, CDLI P252106; Pls. XXVII/XXX, CDLI P252094
Edition: George 2016, 130f.
Studies: Wasserman 2021
Collection: Schøyen Collection, Oslo
Provenance: Unknown
Measurements: 25.0 × 24.0 cm (MS 3097); 16.5 × 9.3 cm (MS 3085)
Procedure: No

Introduction
A fully developed example of the 'heart-plant' motif with a prime example of the literary device of chain (see Wasserman 2021).

Text A = CUSAS 32, 7o; Text B = CUSAS 32, 8i

	(A 4–8 lost)	
1	B ii 40'	[*ša-am-m*]*u-um ša li-i*[*b-bi-im*]
2	B ii 41'	[*šu-sú*]-⸢*um*⸣ *da-ma-aq-*[*šu*]
3	B ii 42'	(*traces*)
4	B iii 1	⸢^{d}*Šamaš*(UTU)⸣ *i-mu-ur-*⸢*šu* {x}⸣ *i*[*s-sú-uḫ-šu-ma*]
5	A vi 9	*a-na ša-m*[*e-e ú-še*$_{20}$*-li-a-aš-šu*]
	B iii 2	[*a*]*-na ša-me-e ú-še*$_{20}$-[*li-a-aš-šu*$^{?}$]
6	A vi 10	*li-ib-*⸢*bi*⸣ ^{d}*Sîn*(EN.ZU)] ⸢*iṣ*⸣*-ṣa-ba-a*[*t*]
	B iii 3	*li-ib-bi* ^{d}*Sîn*(EN.ZU) *iṣ-*[*ṣa-ba-at*]
7	A vi 11	*li-ib-bi* ⸢^{d}*Šamaš*(UTU) *na-si*⸣*-ḫi-*⸢*šu*⸣ *iṣ-ṣa-ba-a*[*t*]
	B iii 4	*li-ib-bi* ^{d}*Šamaš*(UTU) *na-sí-ḫi-šu i*[*ṣ-ṣa-ba-at*]
8	A vi 12	*li-ib-bi er-ṣe-tim qé-*⸢*bi*⸣*-ir-ti-šu / iṣ-ṣa-‹ba›-at*
	B iii 5	*li-ib-bi er-ṣe-tim qé-*⸢*bi*⸣*-i*[*r-ti-šu*]
9	A vi 13	⸢*li*⸣*-ib-bi al-pi-im i-na sú-pu-ri-im*
	B iii 6	*li-ib-bi al-pi-im i-na s*[*ú-pu-ri-im*]
10	A vi 14	*li-ib-bi im-me-ri-im i-na ta-ar-ba-/*⸢*ṣi*⸣*-im*
	B iii 7	*li-ib-bi im-me-ri-im i-na* [*ta-ar-ba-ṣi-im*]
11	A vi 15	*li-ib-*⸢*bi*⸣ *ka-al-bi-im i-na ru-ub-ṣi-šu*
	B iii 8	*li-ib-bi ka-al-bi-im i-na* [*ru-ub-ṣi-šu*]

12	A vi 16	*li-ib-bi ša-ḫi-im i-na er-re-ti-šu*
	B iii 9	*li-ib-bi ša-ḫi-im i-na* [*er-re-ti-šu*]
13	A vi 17	*li-ib-bi eṭ-lim i-na šu-le-em*
	B iii 10	*li-ib-bi eṭ-lim i-na* [*šu-le-em*]
14	A vi 18	*li-ib-bi wa-*⸢*ar-da*⸣*-tim i-*⸢*na*⸣ *me-*⸢*lu-lim*⸣
	B iii 11	*li-ib-bi wa-*⸢*ar-da*⸣*-tim i-na* [*me-lu-lim*]
15	A vi 19	*li-ib-bi nu-nim* ⸢*i*⸣*-na ap-sí-im*
	B iii 12	*li-ib-bi nu-nim i-na a*[*p-sí-im*]
16	A vi 20	*li-ib-bi iṣ-ṣú-*⸢*ri*⸣*-im i-na ap-pa-ri-im*
	B iii 13	*li-ib-bi iṣ-ṣú-ri-im i-na a*[*p-pa-ri-im*]
17	A vi 21	*l*[*i-i*]*b-bi ra-*[*a*]*q-qí-im i-na ru-šu-um-tim*
	B iii 14	*li-ib-bi ra-aq-qí-im i-na r*[*u-šu-um-tim*]
18	A vi 22	*li-ib-bi ši-le-ep-pi-im i-na sà-aḫ/-sà-aḫ-tim*
	B iii 15	*li-ib-bi ši-e-le-ep-pi-im i-*[*na sà-aḫ-sà-aḫ-tim*]
19	A vi 23	*li-ib-bi an-na-an-na māri*(DUMU) *an-na-an-na*
	B iii 16	*li-ib-bi an-na-an-na māri*(DUMU) *an-n*[*a-an-na*]
20	A vi 24	*ša il*(DINGIR)-[*š*]*u an-na-an-na*
	A vi 25	⸢*iš*⸣*-ta-ar-šu an-na-ni-tum*
	B iii 17	*ša il*(DINGIR)*-šu an-*⸢*na-an*$^{!}$⸣*-na iš-ta-*[*ar-šu an-na-ni-tum*]
21	A vi 26	*iṣ-ṣa-ba-at*
	B iii 18	*iṣ-ṣa-*[*ba-at*]
22	A vi 27	*a-*[*n*]*u-um* ⸢*a*⸣*-na* ⸢^{d}⸣[*A*]*sal-lú-ḫi māri*(DUMU) ^{d}*En-ki*
	A vi 28	*qí-bi-a-ma*
	B iii 19	*a-nu-um-ma* ⸢*a*⸣*-na* ^{d}*As*[*al-lú-ḫi māri*(DUMU) ^{d}*En-ki qí-bi-a-ma*]
23	A vi 29	*li-ib-bi* ^{d}*Sîn*(EN.ZU) *i-na ša-me-e*
	B iii 20	*li-ib-bi* ^{d}*Sîn*(EN.ZU) [*i-na ša-me-e*]
24	A vi 30	*li-ib-bi* ^{d}*Šamaš*(UTU) *na-sí-ḫi-šu*
	B iii 21	*li-*⸢*ib-bi* ^{d}*Šamaš*(UTU)⸣ [*na-sí-ḫi-šu*]
25	A vi 31	*li-ib-bi er-ṣe-tim qé-bi-ir/-ti-šu*
	B iii 22	⸢*li-ib*⸣*-bi* ⸢*er-ṣe*⸣*-*[*tim qé-bi-ir-ti-šu*]
26	A 32	[*li-ib-bi al-pi-im i-n*]*a* ⸢*sú-pu-ri*⸣*-/-im*
	B iii 23	⸢*li-ib-bi al*⸣*-pi-im* [*i-na sú-pu-ri-im*]

27	A vi 33	*li-ib-bi im-me-ri-im i-na ta-ar-ba/-ṣi-im*
	B iii 24	*li-ib-⸢bi im-me⸣-ri-im i-n[a ta-ar-ba-ṣi-im]*
28	A vi 34	*li-ib-bi ka-al-bi-im i-na ru-ub-ṣí-šu*
	B iii 25	*li-ib-bi [ka]-al-bi-im i-⸢na⸣ r[u-ub-ṣi-šu]*
29	A vi 35	*li-ib-bi ša-ḫi-im [i-n]a er-re-ti-šu*
	B iii 26	*li-ib-bi [ša]-⸢ḫi⸣-im i-na ⸢er-ṣe-ti⸣-š[u]*
30	A vi 36	*li-ib-bi eṭ-lim i-na šu-le-em*
	B iii 27	*li-ib-b[i e]ṭ-lim i-⸢na šu⸣-[le-em]*
31	A vi 37	*[l]i-⸢ib-bi wa-ar⸣-da-tim i-na me-lu-lim*
	B iii 28	*⸢li⸣-ib-⸢bi wa-ar-da⸣-tim i-[na me]-l[u-lim]*
32	A vi 38	*[li]-⸢ib⸣-[bi n]u-nim i-⸢na ap-sí⸣-im*
	B iii 29	*⸢li-ib⸣-[bi] nu-nim i-⸢na⸣ ap-s[í-im]*
33	A vi 39	*[li-ib-bi i]ṣ-⸢ṣú⸣-r[i-im i-na a]p-pa-ri-im*
	B iii 30	*⸢li-ib⸣-bi iṣ-ṣú-ri-i]m i-⸢na ap⸣-pa-r[i-im]*
34	A vi 40	*[li-ib-bi ra-aq-qí-im i-na] ru-šu-um-tim*
	B iii 31	*⸢li-ib⸣-bi ra-⸢aq-qí⸣-im i-na ru-⸢šu⸣-[um-tim]*
35	A vi 41	*[li-ib-bi ši-le-ep-pi-im i-na sà-aḫ-sà-aḫ]-tim*
	B iii 32	*[li]-ib-bi ši-e-le-ep-pi-im i-na i-na s[à-aḫ-sà-aḫ-t]im*
36	B iii 33	*[l]i-ib-bi ⸢an-na-an-na māri*(DUMU) *an⸣-na-[an-na]*
37	B iii 34	*[š]a il*(DINGIR)*-šu ⸢an-na-an⸣-n[a [Iš-ta-a]r-[šu an-na-ni-t]um*
38	B iii 35	*l[i-wa-aš-š]i-[ir]*
39	B iii 36	[tu$_{6}$-é]n-⸢é⸣-[nu-ru]
40	B iii 37	ka-inim-m]a ⸢šà⸣-[gig-ga]

Translation

1–5 [The] heart-plant, [its] beauty [was entic]ing [...]. Šamaš noticed it: he [plucked it and took it] up to heaven.

6–8 It seized the heart of Sîn, it seized the heart of Šamaš, its plucker, (it seized) the heart of Earth, its burier,

9–12 (It seized) the heart of the ox in the stall, the heart of the sheep in the fold, the heart of the dog in its lair, the heart of the pig in its pigpen,

13–14 (It seized) the heart of the lad in the street, the heart of the maiden in the dance,

15–18 (It seized) the heart of the fish in the deep water, the heart of the bird in the wetland, the heart of the dry-land turtle in the mud, the heart of the freshwater turtle at the water's edge,

19–21 It seized the heart of N.N., son of N.N., whose god is N.N., and whose goddess is N.N.

22–25 Now, tell (pl.) Asalluḫi, the son of Enki, that he r[eleas]es the heart of Sîn in the sky, the heart of Šamaš, its (the heart-plant) plucker, the heart of Earth, its (the heart-plant) burier,

26–29 the heart of the ox in the stall, the heart of the sheep in the fold, the heart of the dog in its lair, the heart of the pig in its pigpen (so A; B: in his land),

30–31 the heart of the lad in the street, the heart of the maiden in the dance,

31–35 the heart of the fish in the deep water, the heart of the bird in the wetland, the heart of the dry-land turtle in the mud, the heart of the freshwater turtle at the water's edge,

36–38 the heart of N.N., son of N.N., whose god is N.N., and whose goddess is N.N.!

39 [tu$_6$-é]n-é-[nu-ru]

40 Incantation (against) stomach[-ache].

Commentary

1–5 The Epic of Etana also tells of a magical plant – "the plant of giving birth" (*šammu ša alādi*) – related to Šamaš and heavens (e.g., II 141, 142, 148 and *passim*, see Novotny 2001, 19).

2 [*šūsu*]*m damāq*[*šu*] following George (2016, 131).

18 For *saḫsaḫtum* "land near a watercourse", see George (2016, 132).

№ 20: CUSAS 32, 7p // CUSAS 32, 8j

SEAL No.: 7118
Copy: George 2016 Pls. XXIV-XXV; Pl. XXIX
Tablet Siglum: MS 3097; MS 3085
Photo: George 2016 Pl. XXVI, CDLI P252106; Pl. XXX, CDLI P252094
Edition: George 2016, 132f.
Studies: –
Collection: Schøyen Collection, Oslo
Provenance: Unknown
Measurements: 25.0 × 24.0 cm (MS 3097); 16.5 × 9.3 cm (MS 3085)
Procedure: No

Introduction

The subscript of this fragmentary incantation is almost entirely broken, but its designation against stomach-ache seems certain, as it is found between other incantations against gastrointestinal problems on two incantation collectives.

Text A = CUSAS 32, 7p; Text B = CUSAS 32 8j

	A vi	(*beginning lost*)
	B iii 38	(*traces*)
	B iii 39–40	(*broken*)
1'	A vii 1	*qá-at-ku-nu la t*[*u-pa-aš-ša-ra*]
	B iii 41	[… *n*]*a-ap-šu-*⸢*ru*⸣
2'	A vii 2	*a-di li-ib-bi an-n*[*a-an-na mār*(DUMU) *an-na-an-na*]
	B iii 42	[…] ⸢lum?⸣
3'	A vii 3	*ša il*(DINGIR)-*šu an-*[*na-an-na*]
	B iii 43	[…] ⸢x⸣
4'	A vii 4	⸢*iš-ta-ar-šu an-na*⸣-[*ni-tum*]
	B iii 44	[…] ⸢x⸣
5'	A vii 5	[*tu-wa-aš-ša-ra*]
	B iii 45	[…]-*ka-ma*
6'	A vii 6	[tu$_6$-én-é-nu-ru]?
	B iii 46	[…]

7'	A vii 7	⸢ka-inim-ma šà⸣-[gig-ga]
	B iii 47	[…] ⸢x x⸣

Translation

1'–5' (DN$_1$ DN$_2$) do not release your (pl.) hand until you set free the belly of N.N., son of N.N., whose god is N.N., and whose goddess is N.N … [you will release].

6' [tu$_6$-én-é-nu-ru]$^?$

7' Incantation (against) stomach-[ache].

№ 21: CUSAS 32, 8d

SEAL No.: 7067
Copy: George 2016 Pl. XXVIII
Tablet Siglum: MS 3085
Photo: George 2016 Pl. XXX; CDLI P252094
Edition: George 2016, 133f.
Studies: –
Collection: Schøyen Collection, Oslo
Provenance: Unknown
Measurements: 16.5 × 9.3 cm
Procedure: Yes

Introduction

This incantation is destined primarily, or solely, to cure ruminating animals. Other gastrointestinal incantations with veterinary use are CT 4, 8 (№ 16) and CUSAS 32, 26c (№ 24). After the break, the magician turns to an unknown healing agent and asks for a release of the wind from the animal's digestive tract. A legitimation formula and detailed procedures follow.

ii
1' *(traces)*
2' *ša-ra-am le-‹em›-na-am*
3' *im-ta-am le-mu-ut-ta-am ša li-⸢ib⸣-bi-im*$^{!}$
4' *ši-ip-tum ú-ul ia-tum*
5' *ši-pa-at* ^{d}*Nin-girim*$_{x}$(TAR.ḪA.DU) *be-le-et ši-pa-tim*
6' ^{d}*Nin-girim*$_{x}$ *iq-bi-i-⸢ma⸣*
7' *a-na-ku ad-di*
8' tu$_{6}$-én-é-nu-ru

9' ka-inim-ma *alpum*(GU$_{4}$) *immerum*(UDU.NÍTA) *em-ru-um*$^{!}$
10' *ki-ik-ki-it-tum a-na* 1 *qa me-e*
11' ⅓$^{?}$ *qa ṭābtam*(MUN$^{!}$) *ta-na-ad-di-ma*
12' *ta-ša-aq-qí-šu-ma*
13' *mu-da-ab-bi-ba-am i-na pi-šu ta-ša-ak-ka-an*
14' *ú-ba-an-ka a-na qí-in-na-ti-⸢šu tu⸣-ub-ba-al-ma*
15' *ši-ni-šu ši-ip-ta-am ta-na-ad-di-⸢šum⸣-ma*
16' *i-na šu-bu-ur-ri-šu ú-wa-aš-ša-ra-am*

Translation

2'–3' [... Release] the bad wind (and) bad venom of the belly!
4'–7' The incantation is not mine, it is the incantation of Ningirim, the lady of incantations. Ningirim has pronounced it; I have cast (it).
8' tu$_{6}$-én-é-nu-ru.

9' Incantation (for?) a bloated ox (or) sheep.

10'–14' The procedure: You throw ⅓ kg of salt into 1 litre of water. You let it drink by placing a funnel (lit. 'loudspeaker') in its mouth and bring your finger into its rump.

15'–16' You recite to it twice the incantation and it will release (flatulence) through his anus.

Commentary

14': For the expression *ubānam ana* X *wabālum*, see George (2016, 134).

№ 22: CUSAS 32, 8h

SEAL No.: 7119
Copy: George 2016 Pls. XXVIII
Tablet Siglum: MS 3085
Photo: George 2016 Pls. XXVII; CDLI P252094
Edition: –
Studies: –
Collection: Schøyen Collection, Oslo
Provenance: Unknown
Measurements: 16.5 × 9.3 cm
Procedure: No

Introduction
Very broken incantation, only the last part of which remains.

ii
33' ⸢x⸣ [x x x x] bi ḫ̮é$^{?}$ ⸢x⸣ [x x]
34' ⸢x⸣ [x x x x-*m*]*a-am-ma* ⸢x⸣ [x x]
35' ⸢x x⸣ *li-iṣ-ba-*[*at*]
36' *a*[*n-na-a*]*n-na mār*(DUMU) *an-na-an-na ša il*(DING[IR)-*šu an-na-an-na*]
37' ⸢*iš-ta*⸣*-ar-šu an-na-an-*[*ni-tum*]
38' giš uk šu [(x x)]
39' ka-inim-ma šà-[gig-ga]

Translation
33'–34' …
35' … may he seize.
36'–38' N.N. the son of N.N. whose god is N.N. whose goddess is N.N. …
39' Incantation against stomach-ache.

№ 23: CUSAS 32, 25a

SEAL No.: 7120
Copy: George 2016 Pl. LXXI
Tablet Siglum: MS 2780
Photo: George 2016 Pl. LXXI; CDLI P251829
Edition: George 2016, 127
Studies: George 2016, 46
Collection: Schøyen Collection, Oslo
Provenance: Unknown
Measurements: 6.8 × 4.9 cm
Procedure: No

Introduction
A rectangular tablet with two incantations, each on a different side of the tablet. The obverse is destined to cure an aching heart, i.e., belly, switching between Sumerian and Akkadian, with a passage for the name of the patient (ll. 6–7). On the reverse: an incantation against a snake in a non-identified language (see George 2016, 118 II.D.14).

Obverse
1 ú-a ab-gig lú-b[u]
2 ú-‹a› ab-gig gig an-ta su[r-ra]
3 ki-te-x+KAK in-nu-z[i$^{?}$-(x)]
4 *ki-ma An-nu šar ša-me-e ir-*⸢*ḫu*⸣-[*ú*]
5 *bu-ul* ^{d}*Šákkan rēšam*(SAG) [*l*]*u-šu-ri-ma*
6 ne-nam dumu ne-n[am] dingir-bi ne-nam
7 *ù* ama-^{d}innin-[bi] ne-nam
8 *lu-ra-ḫi-mi i-di ši-ip-tam*
9 ^{d}*Da-mu be-el ta-ka-la-tim*
10 *Bēlet-ilī*(^{d}MAḪ) *be-le-et re-mi-im*
11 ^{d}*Gu-la a-sú-ut a-wi-le-e*
12 ⸢*kap*⸣*-pa-šu lu-pu-ut*
13 *zu-qá-as-sú i-ši ti-bé-e*$^{!}$*-mi / qí-bi-šum*
14 k[a$^{!}$-i]nim-ma$^{!}$ šà-gig-ga

Translation
1–3 Alas! that man is sick! Alas! He is sick! A sickness oozing from above, from below *it is rising*$^{?}$.
4–5 Just as Anum, king of heaven, inseminated the herd of Šakkan, may I impregnate and pour magic over the patient (lit. slave, "head") (whose name is)
6–8 N.N., son of N.N., whose god is N.N., and whose goddess is N.N.! Cast the incantation!
9–11 Oh Damu, lord of the craftiness! Oh Bēlet-ilī, lady of the womb, Oh Gula, physician of men!

12–13 Touch (sg.) his hand, lift his chin! Order him: "Stand up!"
14 Incantation against stomach-ache.

Commentary

4–5: Two options for the insemination motif are known: The first is self-insemination, (e.g., *araḫḫi araḫḫi pagri kīma nārum irḫû kibrīša* "I will inseminate myself, I will inseminate my body, just like the river inseminates its banks" YOS 11, 2: 1–2 = № 101, see also ZA 75, 198–204j: 115–116 = № 143). The second is progressive insemination, found in the cosmic chain of creation (as *šamû erṣetam irḫû būl* ^{d}*Šakkan ina ṣērim irtakbū* "The sky inseminated the earth, the animals of Šakkan mounted one another" CUSAS 32, 7m // CUSAS 32, 8f: 2–3 = № 18, see also YOS 11, 5a: 1 = № 113). Here an abbreviated variant of the second kind is found.

5: The first-person voice refers to the healer, while the expression *rēšam [l]ušūrīma* (*arû* Š) alludes to the patient: an actual slave (*rēšum*), or an unusual designation for any man.

9: ^{d}*Damu bēl ta-ka-la-tim*: George (2016, 127) translates "lord of the pouch" (CAD T, 61, s.v. *takaltu* "bag, pouch, sheath" and "stomach"), but as the form is in the plural, we prefer *takkalātu* (< *nakālum*) "clever, ingenious behaviour" (with LAOS 7.2, 55). A *double entendre* is no doubt at work: Damu, the lord of craftiness is also the lord of the (aching) belly.

9–11: The joint mentioning of Damu, Bēlet-ilī, and Gula is unique. No other incantation known to us contains this divine triad.

12f.: The three imperatives are all in the singular which means that they refer probably to the healer, not to the three gods just mentioned. It is hard to read these lines without recalling Mark 5: 41–42: "Then He took the child by the hand, and said to her, 'Talitha, cumi', which is translated, 'Little girl, (I say to you,) arise!' Immediately the girl arose and walked, for she was twelve years of age" (New King James Version).

13: *tibē-mi* here (also l. 5) offer a fine example for the use of the particle *-mi* in literary texts, serving as an apostrophe (see Wasserman 2012a, 188).

№ 24: CUSAS 32, 26c

SEAL No.: 7121
Copy: George 2016 Pl. LXXII
Tablet Siglum: MS 3387
Photo: George 2016 Pl. LXXII; CDLI P252328
Edition: George 2016, 138f.
Studies: George 2016, 46
Collection: Schøyen Collection, Oslo
Provenance: Unknown
Measurements: 5.7 × 5.2 cm
Procedure: No

Introduction
This incantation collective was cut into its present state in antiquity. It contains an incantation with the motif of the 'heart-plant', only that this time the plant is not attacking the heart, i.e., the middle body (as, e.g., in YOS 11, 11 = № 35), but the head and teeth of the patients. Its place in the category of gastrointestinal problems is therefore open to question. Note that the incantation is destined to both man and ox (cf. CT 4, 8 = № 16 and CUSAS 32, 8d = № 21).

ii'
1' *⸢ša-am-ma-am ša⸣ š[a$^{?}$-di-im]*
2' *i-iš-l[a-up$^{?}$]*
3' *mi-nu-um ša-am-mu-u[m an-nu-ú-um]*
4' *i-lum ⸢mu⸣-ši-ri-is-sú [i-ku-ul-šu-ma]*
5' *qá-aq-qá-as-sú [iṣ-ba-at]*
6' *ši-in-na-šu [iṣ-ba-at]*
7' *al-pu-um ⸢i$^{!}$⸣-k[u-ul-šu]*
8' *qá-aq-qá-as-sú [iṣ-ba-at]*
9' *ši-in-na-šu [iṣ-ba-at]*
10' *an-na-an-na māri*(DUMU) *[an-na-an-na]*
11' *ša il*(DINGIR)*-šu an-na-an-na [iš-ta-ar-šu] / an-na-n[i-tum]*
12' *i-ku-ul-šu-[ma]*
13' *qá-aq-qá-as-sú [iṣ-ba-at]*
14' *ši-in-na-šu [iṣ-ba-at]*
15' *al-pu-⸢um⸣* [x x x x]
(*broken*)

Translation

1'–3'	(Šamaš) pulled out the plant of [*the mountain*, (asking)]: "What plant [is this?]"
4'–6'	The god who brought it down [ate it and it seized] his head, [it seized] his tooth.
7'–9'	An ox [ate it and it seized] its head, [it seized] its tooth.
10'–11'	N.N., son of [N.N.,] whose god is N.N., [whose goddess is] N.[N.]
12'–14'	ate it [and it seized] his head, [it seized] his tooth.
15'	The ox […]

Commentary

1': ⸢*ša-am-ma-am ša*⸣ *š*[*a*$^{?}$*-di-im*] (or *ša* Ḫ[UR.SAG]) after YOS 11, 11: 1 (№ 35).

№ 25: CUSAS 32, 30a

SEAL No.: 7122
Copy: George 2016 Pl. LXXXI
Tablet Siglum: MS 3093
Photo: George 2016 Pl. LXXX; CDLI P252102
Edition: George 2016, 134
Studies: –
Collection: Schøyen Collection, Oslo
Provenance: Unknown
Measurements: 13.5 × 12.0 cm
Procedure: No

Introduction
All that is left of this broken incantation is the end of a historiola where Asalluḫi acts as the saviour. Another incantation for the intestines (libiš) follows, see CUSAS 32, 30b (№ 26).

Obverse
i

1	(*traces*)
2	[x x] bi ⸢x x⸣-*du*-⸢*ud*⸣
3	[*pu-ḫ*]*u-ur i-la-ku*
4	[*na-ra*]*-am i-na e-bé-ri-šu-nu*
5	[*ú*]*-wa-ḫi-du-šu-ú-ma*
6	[*li-i*]*b-ba-am i-te-ez-bu*
7	[*i-n*]*u-un-šu-nu-ti-i-ma*
8	ᵈ*Asal-lu-ḫi*
9	*li-ib-ba-am ub-ta-al-li-iṭ*
10	ka-inim-ma libiš(ÁB.ŠÀ)

Translation

2–3	… they were walking together.
4–6	When they were crossing the river, they singled him out and left the belly behind.
7–9	Asalluḫi turned his favour to them and resuscitated the belly.
10	Incantation for the stomach.

№ 26: CUSAS 32, 30b

SEAL No.: 7123
Copy: George 2016 Pl. LXXXI
Tablet Siglum: MS 3093
Photo: George 2016 Pl. LXXX; CDLI P252102
Edition: George 2016, 134
Studies: –
Collection: Schøyen Collection, Oslo
Provenance: Unknown
Measurements: 13.5 × 12.0 cm
Procedure: No

Introduction

Second of two consecutive incantations for the gut, this incantation is constructed of two pithy expressions describing wood (an unspecified healing tree or a magic wand) and a water-skin (a metaphor for a swollen inner organ of the patient, cf. *šumma martu kīma nādi mêša išaḫḫal* "if the gall bladder filters? its liquid like a water-skin" KAR 423 iii 19, cited in CAD N/1, 101a).

i

----

11 *i-ṣú-um ša ilim*(DINGIR)
12 *na-du-um ša a-we-lu-tim*
13 *li-iz-zi-iz i-ṣu-um*
14 *li-iḫ-ḫe-pi na-du-um*
15 ⸢tu$_6$-én⸣-é-nu-ru
16 ka-inim-ma libiš(ÁB.ŠÀ)

Translation

11–12 Wood of god; water-skin of humanity!
13–14 Let the wood stand, let the water-skin be smashed!
15 tu$_6$-én-é-nu-ru
16 Incantation for the stomach.

Commentary

11: *iṣum ša ilim* may be a general designation for a tree as a healer. Two incantations against rabid dogs mention specific trees as healers: AMD 14, 197b (№ 64) mentions a *Sippirûm*-tree, and CUSAS 32, 29a (№ 67) a date palm from Dilmun.

11–14: Note the parallelism: *iṣum ša X nādum ša Y* ↔ Precative$_1$ *iṣum* Precative$_2$ *nādum*.

№ 27: CUSAS 32, 32a

SEAL No.: 7068
Copy: George 2016 Pls. LXXXIX
Tablet Siglum: MS 2822
Photo: George 2016 Pls. LXXXVIII; CDLI P251869
Edition: George 2016, 136
Studies: –
Collection: Schøyen Collection, Oslo
Provenance: Unknown
Measurements: 10.0 × 6.0 cm
Procedure: No

Introduction

An incantation addressed to *namzītum*, a fermentation vat whose effervescence symbolizes bloated, flatus-full, bowels.

Obverse

1 [x x x (x)]$^{\text{ḫi.a}}$ *ku-un* [x]-⸢x *ú*⸣*-a*
2 [*ki-ir-ba-a*]*n eqlim*(A.ŠÀ^{lim}) *za-ap-pi* ⸢*ša*⸣*-ḫi-im*
3 [*mu-ṣa*]*-a-am ú-ul* ⸢*i-šu*⸣
4 [^{d}*En-l*]*il* ⸢*ib-ni*⸣*-ki* ^{d}*En-ki ú-*⸢*ra*⸣*-bi-ki*
5 [*iš-k*]*u-*⸢*un*⸣*-ki* ^{d}*Nuska a-na ku-*⸢*ši*⸣*-ri*
6 [*a*]-⸢*na mu-uḫ*⸣*-ḫi* ‹‹ḫi›› *ta-li*[*m*] *ša É-a É-a ir-ka*$^{!}$*-ab*
7 *il-qé-e-ki sà-bi-tum ku-ru-*⸢*pu-ú-ki*⸣ *ma-aš-ḫu*
8 ⸢*ša-ak*⸣*-na-a-at i-na ka-an-nim*
9 *ša-ak-nu ki-it-tu*$^{!?}$ *a-pa-ri-ku ù* ⸢*pu*⸣*-ru-us-su*
10 *i-na li-ib-bi-*[*k*]*i*
11 *ú-še-et-bi-ki it-ti* ⸢*Iš*$_{8}$$^{?}$*-tár*$^{?}$⸣ *a-*⸢*pa*⸣*-ri-ki* ⸢*uš*$^{!}$⸣*-te-ṣi-a-am* / ⸢*qé*⸣*-ri-i-tam*
12 *pu-ru-us-sà-am aš-lu-um-ma ša-ra-am aš-ku-un*
13 *ut-te-e-er tu-uḫ-ḫi-ki a-na mi-nu-tim*
14 *me-e ša ra-as-na-at a-*⸢*na*⸣ *ši-ip-tim-ma aš-ku-un*
15 *i-na qí-bi-tim ša É-a ù* ^{d}*Asal-lú-ḫi*
16 *i-na pi-i ez-zi-im i-na ru-uḫ-tim le-mu-ut-tim* / *ša a-wi-lu-tim*
17 *šu-ú-tum il-ta-nu ša-ad-du-ú-um a-mu-ur-ru*
18 *it-bu-ú iṣ-ba-tu pi-i na-am-zi-tim*
19 tu-en-ni-nu-ri

Translation

1 [*In* the …], my […] is placed.
2–3 Field's lump! pig's bristle! It has no [out]let!
4–6 [Enl]il created you (f.), Enki raised you, Nuska [ma]de you successful. Ea was riding over Ea's litter:
7–8 The ale-wife took you; your cases for (soaked) grain are well-measured; you are placed on a stand.

9–10 A *kittu*, a stopper (and) a plug are placed in you.
11–12 With Ištar's (help), I removed from you the stoppers, (thus) made the feast go out; I pulled out the plug, (thus) created wind.
13–14 I turned your draff into a recitation; the water (with) which you have rinsed I made into an incantation.
15–16 By the order of Ea and Asalluḫi, by the furious mouth and evil sorcery of humankind:
17–18 The South-wind, the North-wind, the East-wind, the West-wind have risen (and) seized the mouth of the brewing-vat.
19 tu-en-ni-nu-ri

Commentary

1: George (2016, 136 "driven by context"): [*i-na eperī*(SAḪAR)$^{?}$]$^{\text{ḫi.a}}$ *ku-un* [*pû*(K]A$^{!}$)-*ú-a* "My [mouth] is stuck [in dirt...]".

1–2: For similar phrases, swear words or maledictions, cf. YOS 11, 2: 3–6 (№ 101) and YOS 11, 14c: r. 8–9 (№ 39), and see George (2016, 137).

3: Most likely this is an abbreviated variant of a riddle-like description of the malevolent entity, cf. e.g., *qaqqadam ula īšu* "it has not head" CUSAS 10, 19: 1 (№ 86). Alternatively, since *īšu* can be analyzed also as a third-person, it may refer to the speaker's own predicament.

4: Rather than [*ru-bu*]-*ú* (George 2016, 136), we read [^{d}*En-l*]*íl*, having in mind BIN 2, 72: 1–2 (№ 159): *Anum ibnīši Ea urabbīši pānī labbatim išīmši Enlil.*

9: We derive *aparikku*, unattested so far, from *parākum* and translate "stopper" *vel sim* (George offers no translation).

11: Ištar is active with the fermentation vat also in a later magic text: *Ištar ummidī qātki in kanni u namzīti* "Oh Ištar, place your hand on the stand and the vat" (ZA 32, 172: 35 dupl. KAR 144: 21, cited in CAD N/1, 257b).

13: George (2016, 136) translates: "I have returned your spent grain to the reckoning", but the next line shows a clear parallel between *minûtum* and *šiptum*, hence *minûtum* is taken to denote magic recitation.

16: It is not easy to tell whose mouth is furious and whose sorcery is evil. Note that the previous line mentions Ea and Asalluḫi.

№ 28: CUSAS 32, 32b

SEAL No.: 7111
Copy: George 2016 Pls. LXXXIX/XCI
Tablet Siglum: MS 2822
Photo: George 2016 Pls. LXXXVIII/XC; CDLI P251869
Edition: George 2016, 137
Studies: –
Collection: Schøyen Collection, Oslo
Provenance: Unknown
Measurements: 10.0 × 6.0 cm
Procedure: No

Introduction

A partly broken incantation which seems to ease an intestinal blockage. The *namzītum* 'fermentation vat' is mentioned.

Obverse

----

20 *tu-ú-*⸢x⸣ [(x) x] ⸢x x⸣*-ku-ú*
21 ⸢x⸣ […] ⸢x x x⸣ is
22 […] ⸢x⸣ aḫ
(*broken*)

Reverse

(*broken*)
1' ⸢*li-pa-aṭ-ṭi-ru*⸣ [x x x x x x]
2' [*k*]*i-ma bu-ru-ú id-*⸢*da*⸣*-a*[*r-ru-ú*] / *a-na li-a-ti*[*m*]
3' *id-da-ar-ru-ú la-lu-ú a-na en-*⸢*zé*⸣*-*[*tim*]
4' *na-am-zi-tum mārat*(DUMU.MUNUS) ^{d}*En-ki li-da-ri-ir* / *a-na te-er-ḫi-ša*
5' tu-en-ni-nu-ri
(*blank space*)

Translation

20–22 (*too fragmentary*)
1' May they dispel […].
2'–3' Like calves run off to the cows (and) goat-kids run off to the she-goats,
4' may the brewing jar, the daughter of Enki, run off to the beer jugs!
5' tu-en-ni-nu-ri

Commentary

2'–3': The young domestic animals running off, or roaming freely (*darārum* N) to their mothers (calves to cows, kids to she-goats), is a lively metaphor meant to describe the felicitous release of the obstructed belly.

4': Two kinds of vessles connected to beer are found here: *namzītum*, where beer is fermented, and the poorly attested *terḫum* (CAD T, 425 s.v. *tirḫum*) which seems to be a container from which beer is served. If this is indeed the case, the image is again that of discharge and relief.

№ 29: CUSAS 32, 32c

SEAL No.: 7112
Copy: George 2016 Pl. XCI
Tablet Siglum: MS 2822
Photo: George 2016 Pl. XC; CDLI P251869
Edition: George 2016, 137f.
Studies: –
Collection: Schøyen Collection, Oslo
Provenance: Unknown
Measurements: 10.0 × 6.0 cm
Procedure: No

Introduction
Although not stated directly, the present text, like the other spells on this tablet, is concerned with gastrointestinal problems. Again, it mentions the *namzītum*, a metaphor for the human stomach and digestive tract. Note that the spell begins with an extraordinary dialogue which echoes the encounter between Gilgameš arriving from the steppe and Siduri, the *sābītum*.

Reverse

6'	*eṭ-lu-um a-a-nu-um ta-al-la-ka-am*
7'	*iš-tu ṣe-ri-im a-na na-ga-aš sà-bi-tim / pa-nu-ú-a ša-ak-nu*
8'	*ši-pi-ir-tum ša ma-an-ni-im*
9'	*ša É-a ša-ar ap-sí-im*
10'	*ù ṣé-e-ri-im ṣa-ar-ra-am* ᵈ*Ištar*(INANNA)
11'	*am-ra-a ša qá-ti-ia ku-up-ta-ti-in*
12'	*ṭi-i-di-im ù a-ša-ag ṣe-ri-im*
13'	*i-ba-ak-ki sà-bi-tum eḫ-te-pe-e na-am-zi-tam*
14'	*qú-ú-lam at-ta-di e-li ku-sí-a-tim*
15'	*as-ku-up-pa-at bi-tim e-re-ba-am / ú-ta-am-mi*
16'	[t]u-en-ni-nu-ri

Translation

6'	– "Young man from where you come?"
7'	– From the steppe! I intend to go to the ale-wife!
8'	– "On whose instruction?"
9'–10'	– Of Ea, king of the Apsû and of the steppe, the eager one of Ištar!
11'–12'	– "Look at the pellet of dirt and the spiny thorn of the steppe that are in my hands!"
13'	The ale-wife is weeping.
13'–14'	"I have broken (her) fermenting vat! I have cast silence on the (bar) stools!
15'	I swear by entering the threshold of the house!"
16'	[t]u-en-ni-nu-ri

Commentary

6'–7': The ale-wife's question "Young man from where you come?" reverberates the opening of Siduri's speech to Gilgameš: *Gilgameš êš tadâl* "Oh Gilgameš, where are you wandering"? (Gilg. OB iii 1, see George 2003, 278–279), and the young man's answer *ištu ṣērim ana nagāš sābītim* also alludes to this passage in the epic, viz. Gilgameš's description of his restlessness after Enkidu's demise *attanaggiš kīma ḫābilim qabaltu ṣēri* "… I wandered like a trapper through the midst of the wild" (Gilg. OB ii 11').

9'–13': Note that in the preceeding incantation, CUSAS 32, 32a (№ 27), a similar connection between Enki/Ea and Ištar's tavern is found.

9'–10': The connection of Ea with the Apsû is natural, but the god's relation to the steppe is surprising. This neologism is caused by the fact that the figure of the young man, the *eṭlum*, embodies two persons, mythological and real: Gilgameš, who was roaming in the *ṣērum* after Enkidu's death, and the magic practitioner, who is connected to Ea by virtue of the latter being the god of magic. The welding point of this complex thematic merging is the word *ṣērum*. The alliteration between *ṣērum* and *ṣarrām Ištar* should not be ignored.

11'–12': Pellets made of dirt are known to be used in magic procedures, esp. those meant to resolve sexual problems, see Wasserman (2010, 337). Note further the anticipatory genitive (*ša qātīya kuptatin ṭīdim* …), a rare syntactic construction in the corpus and in OB in general (see Wasserman 2011, 11 for more examples).

№ 30: Fs. de Meyer 75/83d

SEAL No.: 7069
Copy: Cavigneaux/Al-Rawi 1994, 83
Tablet Siglum: IM 95317
Photo: Cavigneaux/Al-Rawi 1994, 83
Edition: Cavigneaux/Al-Rawi 1994, 82–85
Studies: Wasserman 2003 Cat. No. 149
Collection: Iraq Museum, Baghdad
Provenance: Sippar
Measurements: 16.5 × 9.3 cm
Procedure: No

Introduction

This elongated tablet contains four incantations. Two in Akkadian (the present one and one to catch a fish = № 76); one in Sumerian and one in an unidentified language. An alloglot formula concludes this incantation (ll. 38–39).

32 *ši-ri ki-ma pa-at-ri-im*
33 *i-ta-ak-ki-ip ki-ma alpim*(G[U$_4^!$])*-im*
34 *ki-ma al-ma-at-ti-im*
35 *qú-tu-ru pa-nu-šu*
36 *ki-ma a-gi-im ú-ḫa-sí-ir ki-ib-ra-tim*
37 *i-pu-ḫa-an-ni ku-ku-id$^?$-ri*
38 b i - n i - i g - r i - i š k i - k i - l a - b i
39 k u - n u - š a - a m
40 *ši-pa-at*
41 *libbiya*(ŠÀ.GU$_{10}$)

Translation

32–33 My flesh is like a dagger: (pain) keeps goring me like an ox.
34–35 Its face is clouded like (that of) a widow,
36–37 It broke off the (river)-banks like a flood, my stomach set fire *in* me.
38–39 *binigriš kikilabi kunušam*
40–41 Incantation for my belly.

Commentary

37: It is tempting to render *napāḫum* here as "to be bloated, swollen", but this meaning is used in the stative only (CAD N/2, 265, one attestation).
40–41: The first-person voice reference to "my belly" is found also in CT 4, 8: 22 (№ 16).

№ 31: JEOL 47, 58b

SEAL No.: 7216
Copy: Kouwenberg 2018–2019, 58
Tablet Siglum: Kt 91/k 502
Photo: Kouwenberg 2018–2019, 58
Edition: Kouwenberg 2018–2019, 59f.
Studies: Wasserman 2003 Cat. No. 16; Michel 2003, 138; Barjamovic/Larsen 2008, 145/147; Barjamovic 2015, 52
Collection: Anadolu Medeniyetleri Müzesi, Ankara
Provenance: Kaneš
Measurements: 4.8 × 4.8 cm
Procedure: No

Introduction
The preceding incantation on this tablet (JEOL 47, 58a = № 169) addresses a *diqārum*, a large vessel probably used to brew beer (*namzītum* in OB), cf. Kouwenberg (2018–2019, 61). This, together with the fact that the present text addresses *libbum*, suggests that the entire tablet was concerned with digestive disorders.

Reverse
16 ǀ *li-bu-mì* ǀ *li-bu-um*
17 ǀ *li-bu-um* ǀ *da-an*
18 ǀ *li-bu-um qá-ra-ad*
19 ǀ *li-bu-um a-mu-ra-ta*
20 ǀ *e-na-šu* ǀ *li-bu-um*
21 ǀ *e-iš ta-lá-ak*
22 ǀ *a-na ur-de*$_8$*-tem*
23 ǀ *ni-a-re-em* ǀ šu ba lu ru
24 ǀ *iš-té* ǀ *ep-re-em*

Upper Edge
25 ǀ *i-dí-ma pu-ur-sí-tem*
26 ǀ *ša qá-té-kà e-ri-*⌜*a-té*⌝
27 *ša a-ḫe-kà e-ru-tem*

Lower Edge
28 ǀ *li-bu-um li-tur*$_4$
29 ǀ *a-na iš-ri-šu* ǀ *ší-ip-tum*
30 ǀ *lá i-a-tum* ⌜*ší-pá-at*?⌝ *be-el*
31 *Ni-*⌜*ki-li*?⌝*-*[*il*$_5$?]

Translation

16	Belly, Oh belly!
17–18	The belly is strong, the belly is heroic,
19–20	The belly, its two eyes are dazzling.
20–23	– "Oh belly where are you going? To smite a maiden?"–
23–27	Pour … with dust *into*? a bowl of your naked hands, of your … arms.
28–29	May the belly return to its (original) condition.
29–31	The incantation is not mine; It is the incantation of the lord ‹of incantations›, Ninkilil.

Commentary

16–18: Cf. the MB incantation against gastrointestinal disease Emar 737: v 1", see Zomer (2018a, 261).

№ 32: OECT 11, 3

SEAL No.: 7070
Copy: Gurney 1989, 43
Tablet Siglum: Bod AB 214
Photo: –
Edition: Gurney 1989, 21f.; Fish 1939, 184
Studies: Cunningham 1997 Cat. No. 354; Wasserman 2003 Cat. No. 113
Collection: Ashmolean Museum, Oxford
Provenance: Unknown
Measurements: 7.7 × 4.8 cm
Procedure: No

Introduction
An incantation against flatus, concatenated along enumerated body parts, *a capite ad calcem.*

Obverse
1 *ṣi-i ša-a-ru-um ṣi-i ša-a-ru-um*
2 *ṣi-i ša-a-ru-um ma-⸢ri i⸣-li*
3 *ṣi-i ša-a-ru-um nu-ḫu-uš ni-ši*
4 *i-na qá-qá-di-im ṣi-i ša-a-ru-um*
5 *i-na i-nim ṣi-i ša-a-ru-um*
6 *i-na pi-i-im ṣi-i ša-a-ru-um*
7 *i-na uz-nim ṣi-i ša-a-ru-um*
8 *i-na šu-bu-ur-ri-im ṣi-i ša-a-ru-um*
9 ⸢*li*⸣*-ip-ša-a*[*ḫ*$^{?}$ *a*]-⸢*wi*⸣*-lum*
10 ⸢*li*⸣*-nu*$^{?}$*-uḫ*$^{?}$ […] ⸢x⸣ ni ⸢*ša*$^{?}$*-ru*$^{?}$⸣-[*um*$^{?}$]
----
11 ⸢INIM *li-ib-bu*$^{!}$⸣*-um*

Reverse uninscribed

Translation
1 Get out, wind! Get out, wind!
2 Get out, wind, son of the gods!
3 Get out, wind, affluence of the people!
4 From the head get out, wind!
5 From the eye get out, wind!
6 From the mouth get out, wind!
7 From the ear get out, wind!
8 From the anus get out, wind!
9 Let the man rest.
10 Let the… repose, *wind*!
----
11 Incantation (*against*) *the belly.*

Commentary

11: The subscript is restored after the faint traces in the hand-copy.

№ 33: PBS 7, 87

SEAL No.: 7202
Copy: Ungnad 1915 Pl. LXI
Tablet Siglum: CBS 1690
Photo: CDLI P259022
Edition: Ungnad 1920, 57 (no. 87)
Studies: Cunningham 1997 Cat. No. 356; Wasserman 2003 Cat. No. 123
Collection: University Museum, University of Pennsylvania, Philadelphia
Provenance: Sippar
Measurements: –
Procedure: No

Introduction

At first, this text was mistaken for a letter (Ungnad 1920). As in CUSAS 32, 32a (№ 27), CUSAS 32, 32b (№ 28) and CUSAS 32, 32c (№ 29), the image of the fermentation vat (*namzītum*) appears here, symbolizing the bowels suffering from flatulence (*šārum*).

Obverse
(*broken*)

Reverse

1 *nam-zi-is-sú ḫa-ar-*⸢x-x-x⸣
2 *bi-il-la-as-sú ša-rum*
3 *ši-ip-tum an-ni-tum*
4 ⸢*ša*⸣ ^{d}*Marduk*(AMAR.UTU) *i-na ma-tim*
5 ⸢*ú*⸣*-ša-ab-šu-*⸢*ú*⸣
6 ⸢x⸣-*bi-šu ù si-*⸢x⸣ [x (x)]
7 [x] du *ar-ka-a*[*t* x (x)]
8 [x x] ⸢x *wa*⸣*-tá-rum la* [x x (x)]
(*broken*)

Translation

(*broken*)
1 Its mashtub is …
2 Its mixture is flatulence!
3–6 This spell that Marduk has created in the land … and …
7 … is long […]
8 … exceedingly not […]

Commentary

8: The syllabic value /tá/ is unusual and the reading is questionable.

№ 34: VS 17, 9

SEAL No.: 7204
Copy: van Dijk 1971 Pl. IV
Tablet Siglum: VAT 2681
Photo: cf. SEAL No. 7204
Edition: –
Studies: Cunningham 1997 Cat. No. 365; Wasserman 2003, 115/Cat. No. 207
Collection: Vorderasiatisches Museum, Berlin
Provenance: Larsa area
Measurements: 5.5 × 7.5 cm
Procedure: No

Introduction
The mid-body, *libbum*, is the subject of this non-standard incantation which shows complex metaphors: the inflammation is associated with the luminosity of the moon, and the patient's anal opening is compared to a window. The tablet was collated by NW in Feb. 2011.

Obverse
1 ⸢x⸣ [...]
2 *is-*[*s*]*i*$_{20}$*-il li-ib-bu-um i*[*m-mi*$^?$*-ir*$^?$]
3 *nam-ri-ri ma-li ki-i-ma w*[*a-ar-ḫi-im*]
4 *a-na a-ap-ti-šu ma-am-ma ú-u*[*l iṭeḫḫi*?]
5 *ša-ak-na-at-m*[*a*] *dan*$^?$*-nu šu-te-pu-u*[*š*]
6 *iṭ-ṭe*$_4$*-ḫa li-ib-bu-um*
7 [*mi*$^?$]*-i-ma ta-ri-bu i-ba-aš-ši e*$^?$*-š*[*i*$^?$*-iš*$^?$]
8 [tu$_{(6)}$-e]n-ni-in-nu-ra-am

Reverse uninscribed

Translation
1 (…)
2–3 The belly became blown-up, became *s*[*wollen*], radiating like the *m*[*oon*].
4–5 Nobody [...] to its opening.
5–6 Since (the opening) is well-placed, the strong one *is at work*$^?$: the belly was approached.
7 [*What*]*ever* you have replaced will be as *n*[*ew*]!
8 *It is a* [tu$_{(6)}$-e]n-ni-in-nu-ra

Commentary
2: Both *esēlum* and *emērum* may describe a bloated body.
3: This line, which according to our interpretation describes the inflamed belly, is partially cited in CAD N/1, 238b (no translation).
4: The verb *ṭeḫûm* is commonly used in magic and medical contexts, describing the approaching disease or demon, or the healer. – The 'window' follows the metaphor

of the radiance in the preceding line. It is probably a euphemism for the patient's rectum.

5: The 'strong one': a possible elliptic description for the healer at work.

6: If *libbum* is in nom. then *iṭṭeḫa* is in the N stem (almost unattested). Alternatively, *libbum* stands in the loc. adv. and the verb is in G perfect.

8: Alternatively, last sign may be rendered -bi, which would then be a possessive marker. Both copula -am as -bi are unparralled for the use of a rubric.

№ 35: YOS 11, 11

SEAL No.: 7124
Copy: van Dijk/Goetze/Hussey 1985 Pl. XII
Tablet Siglum: YBC 9897
Photo: cf. SEAL No. 7124
Edition: Gurney 1989, 21
Studies: van Dijk/Goetze/Hussey 1985, 22; Farber 1990b, 308f.; Veldhuis 1990, 27–44; Veldhuis 1993, 50–51; Cunningham 1997 Cat. No. 383; Wasserman 2003 Cat. No. 236; Foster 2005, 189 (II 25.a)
Collection: Yale Babylonian Collection, New Haven
Provenance: Larsa area
Measurements: 6.4 × 4.6 cm
Procedure: No

Introduction
A 'heart-plant' incantation with a *mannam lušpur* formula.

Obverse
1 ^{d}*Šamaš*(UTU) *ša-am-ma-am iš-tu š*[*adîm*](Ḫ[UR.SAG])
2 *ù-še*$_{20}$*-bi-ra-am*
3 *libbi*(ŠÀ) ^{d}*Šamaš*(UTU) *mu-še*$_{20}$*-bi-ri-šu*
4 *iṣ-ba-at*
5 *libbi*(ŠÀ) ^{d}*Sîn*(NANNA) *i-na ša-me-e iṣ-ba-at*
6 *libbi*(ŠÀ) *alpim*(GU$_{4}$) *i-na su-pu-ri-i*[*m*] *iṣ-ba-at*
7 *libbi*(ŠÀ) *immerim*(UDU) *i-na ta-ar-ba-ṣí-im iṣ-ba-at*
8 *libbi*(ŠÀ) *eṭlim*(GURUŠ) *i-na šu-li-i-im iṣ-ba-at*
9 *libbi*(ŠÀ) *wardatim*(KI.SIKIL) *i-na me-lu-ul-ti-im iṣ-ba-at*
10 *ma-an-na-am lu-uš-pu-ur*
11 *a-na wa-ši-ib ap-sí-im*
12 ⸢*ra*⸣*-bi-i-im*
13 ^{d}*Šamaš*(UTU) *ša-am-ma-am* [*i*]*š-tu šadîm*(ḪUR.SAG)
14 *ú-še*$_{20}$*-bi-ra-am-ma*
15 *libbi*(ŠÀ) ^{d}*Šamaš*(UTU) *mu-še*$_{20}$*-bi-ri-i-šu iṣ-*[*ba-at*]
16 *libbi*(ŠÀ) ^{d}*S*[*în*](NA[NNA]) *i-na š*[*a-me-e iṣ-ba-at*]
17 *libbi*(⸢ŠÀ⸣) *alpim*(G[U$_{4}$]) [...]
(*broken, several lines missing*)

Reverse
1' [...] ⸢x⸣ [...]
2' [... *ša-am-m*]*a-am*$^{?}$
3' [...] *ú-ša-ap-pí-i*[*l*]

Rest uninscribed

Translation

1–2 Šamaš brought over the (heart) plant across the mountain:
3–4 It seized the heart of Šamaš who brought it across,
5 It seized the heart of Sîn in the sky,
6 It seized the heart of the ox in the stall,
7 It seized the heart of the sheep in the fold,
8 It seized the heart of the lad in the street,
9 It seized the heart of the maiden in the dance,
10–12 Whom should I send to the dweller of the great Apsû (saying):
13–14 "Šamaš brought over a plant across the mountain:
15 It seized the heart of Šamaš who brought it across,
16 It sei[zed] the heart of Sîn in the s[ky],
17 It [seized] the heart of the o[x …],"

1' (*broken*)
2'–3' … [the pla]nt … he *brought down* …

Rest uninscribed

№ 36: YOS 11, 12a

SEAL No.: 7125
Copy: van Dijk/Goetze/Hussey 1985 Pls. XIII/XIV
Tablet Siglum: YBC 4625
Photo: cf. SEAL No. 7125
Edition: Veldhuis 1990, 28f./42f.
Studies: van Dijk/Goetze/Hussey 1985, 22f.; Veldhuis 1993, 51–52; Cunningham 1997 Cat. No. 384; Wasserman 2003 Cat. No. 237
Collection: Yale Babylonian Collection, New Haven
Provenance: Larsa area
Measurements: 17.2 × 7.6 cm
Procedure: No

Introduction

Another 'heart-plant' incantation (cf. CUSAS 32, 7o // CUSAS 32, 8i = № 19, CUSAS 32, 26c = № 24, and YOS 11, 11 = № 35).

Obverse

1 *[Šamaš šamma(m) š]a*$^{?}$ *li-ib-bi [ina šadî is-s]u-ḫa-am*
2 *[libbi Šamaš] na-si*$^{?}$*-ḫi-[šu iṣ-ṣa-ba-at]*
3 ⸢*re*$^{?}$*-i*$^{?}$ ^{d}⸣*Sîn*(EN.ZU) *iṣ-ṣa-[ba-at]*
4 *li-ib-bi al-pí i-na su-pu-ri iṣ-ṣ[a-ba-at]*
5 *li-ib-bi im-me-ri i-na ta-ar-[ba-ṣi] iṣ-ṣa-ba-at*
6 *li-ib-bi an-na-an-na mār*(DUMU) *an-na-an-na ša iš-šu an-na-an-na*
7 *iš-ta-ar-šu [an-na]-ni-tum iṣ-ṣa-ba-at*
8 *ut-ta-mi-ka er-ṣe-tam ù ḫa-am-mé-e*
9 ⸢*li-ib-bi*⸣ ^{d}*Šamaš*(UTU) *na-sí-ḫi-ka lu-ú tu-wa-ša-ar*
10 ⸢*re*$^{?}$⸣*-[i*$^{?}$ ^{d}*Sîn*(EN.Z]U) *lu-ú tu-wa-ša-ar*
11 *[li-ib-bi al-p]i* ⸢*i*⸣*-na su-pu-ri lu-ú tu-wa-ša-ar*
12 *[li-ib-bi im-me-ri] i-na ta-ar-ba-ṣi lu-ú tu-wa-ša-ar*
13 *[li-ib-bi an-na-an-na] mār*(DUMU) *an-na-an-na ša iš-šu an-na-an-na*
14 *[iš-ta-ar-šu an-na-ni]-tum lu-ú tu-wa-ša-ar*
15 [...] la [...] da su ra e n - n e - n u - r i

Translation

1 [Šamaš] tor[e off the plant-o]f-the-heart [in the mountain] –
2–3 It [sei]zed [the heart of Šamaš], who tore [it],
3 It sei[zed] (the heart) of Sîn the shepherd,
4 It sei[zed] the heart of the ox in the stall,
5 It seized the heart of the sheep in the fo[ld],
6–7 It seized the heart of N.N. son of N.N. whose god is N.N. (and) his goddess is N.N.,
8 I conjure you by the earth and the lakes:
9 "Release the heart of Šamaš who tore you off!

10 Release (the heart) of [Sî]n the sh[epherd]!
11 Release [the heart of the o]x in the stall!
12 Release [seized the heart of the sheep] in the fold!
13–14 Release [the heart of N.N.] son of N.N. whose god is N.N. (and) his [goddess is N.]N.!
15 [...] ... en-ne-nu-ri

Commentary

3/10: The first sign in both lines was collated by Farber (1985, 62) as ri. The ensuing reading suggestion *rēʾi* is not easy, as one expects *libbi Sîn*. OB PNs in which Sîn is referred to as a shepherd are known (CAD R, 310a), but this is not a typical appellation of the Moon-god. *rēʾi Sîn* remains difficult.

6/13: Note the assimilation /lš/ > /šš/ (*iš-šu* < *ilšu*). Similar cases are found in the bilingual proverb BWL Pl. 68: 2/5 (*a-ka-šu* for *akaššu* < *akalšu*), and the love-related composition MIO 12, 52f.: 11 (Wasserman 2016, 125/128): *kīma na-aš-ši* (*nalši*) *irimmu izannan* “Like dew charms (of love) rain down (on him)”.

8: For this merismatic pair *erṣetum - ḫammū*, see Wasserman (2003, 80).

№ 37: YOS 11, 13

SEAL No.: 7126
Copy: van Dijk/Goetze/Hussey 1985 Pl. XV
Tablet Siglum: YBC 9117
Photo: cf. SEAL No. 7126
Edition: –
Studies: van Dijk/Goetze/Hussey 1985, 23; Cunningham 1997 Cat. No. 387; Wasserman 2003 Cat. No. 240
Collection: Yale Babylonian Collection, New Haven
Provenance: Larsa area
Measurements: 3.5 × 4.6 cm
Procedure: No

Introduction

A poorly preserved tablet with different stock phrases known from magic literature. Its place in the category of gastrointestinal incantations is uncertain. Perhaps a draft or a memo. Following Farber's comments (in van Dijk/Goetze/Hussey 1985, 63), the obverse and the reverse of the text should be inverted.

Obverse$^{!}$
1 [*iš*$^{?}$*-t*]*a*$^{?}$*-ka-an libbi*(ŠÀ) ⸢du⸣ […] ⸢x⸣
2 *i-mu-ru-ka-ma* ^{d}*Šamaš*(U[TU) *ù* ^{d}*Sîn*(NANNA)]
3 *ú-ta-ru-*[*ú*]
4 ⸢*ša as*⸣*-sà-aḫ-ru-ú-ma*
5 *libbi*(ŠÀ) ^{d}*Šamaš*(UTU) *libbi*(ŠÀ) ^{d}*Sîn*(NAN[NA]) *iṣ-ba*$^{!}$(NI)*-at*$^{!}$(AB) ⸢x⸣
6 ⸢*ta-qá*⸣-[*ab*]-⸢*bi-šu*⸣-[*um*]
7 *ki-*⸢*ma*⸣ *a-na-an-*⸢*na*⸣ ‹(*mār*)DUMU› *a-na-an-n*[*a*]
8 *ta-ap-pa-aṭ-ru-*[*ú*]

Reverse$^{!}$
9 *a-na-an-na* ‹‹an na›› *mār*(DUMU) *an-na-a*[*n-na*]
10 *ša il*(DINGIR)*-šu an-na-an-na*
11 *lu pa-aṭ-ra-at*
12 *ki-ma bu-ul* ^{d}*Šákkan*
13 [*ir-t*]*a-ak-*‹‹⸢du⸣››*-bu-ú-ma*
14 [x x x x] ⸢x⸣*-šu a-na li-bi-šu*
15 […] ⸢x⸣ […]
16 […] ⸢x x x⸣ […]
17 […] ⸢x na x⸣ […]

Lower Edge
18 t[$u_6$$^{?}$-én-é-nu-ru]

Translation

1 *[It] continuously imposes the heart (of)*?[…]
2 Ša[maš *(and) Sîn*?] took notice of you!
3 They are tur[ning away…]
4 (that) which *I was looking for*? …
5 *It seized*? the heart of Šamaš, the heart of Sîn!
6 You will say to him:
7–8 – “Like N.N.n ‹son› of N.N. you will be released!
9–11 N.N., son of N.N. verily you are released!” –
12–13 Just as the animals of Šakkan mounted one another
14 … to his heart
15–17 (*broken*)
18 t[u_6?-én-é-nu-ru]

Commentary

5: With caution, the signs iṣ ni ab ⌜x⌝ at the end of the line, are interpreted for *iṣbat*. If correct, this line furnishes a link to the ‘heart-plant’ sub-group of the gastrointestinal incantations.

6: Tentative restitution, based on VS 17, 34: 7 (№ 12).

11: *lū paṭrāt*: stat. m. abbreviated ending with *-āt.*

12: Restoration after CUSAS 32, 7m // CUSAS 32, 8f: 2–3 (№ 18): *šamû erṣetam irḫû būl* ^{d}*Šakkan ina ṣērim irtakbū* “The sky inseminated the earth, the animals of Šakkan mounted one another”.

2.1.5 Jaundice

Two incantations in the present corpus are against a form of jaundice, *aw/murriqānum*.[234] Whereas UET 5, 85 (№ 38) equates jaundice with the supernatural, i.e., the saliva of the deity of pestilence Nergal, YOS 11, 14c (№ 39) locates the disease in the belly of the patient.

№ 38: UET 5, 85

SEAL No.: 7128
Copy: Figulla/Martin 1953 Pl XV
Tablet Siglum: U.17204C
Photo: –
Edition: Landsberger/Jacobsen 1955, 14
Studies: Landsberger 1969, 139; von Weiher 1971, 34; Cunningham 1997 Cat. No. 333; Veldhuis 1999, 37; Wasserman 2003 Cat. No. 181; Charpin 2020; Thavapalan 2020, 75f.; http://www.ur-online.org/subject/18194/
Collection: Iraq Museum, Baghdad
Provenance: Ur
Measurements: 4.6 × 3.4 cm
Procedure: No

Introduction

Found on a small single incantation tablet.

Obverse

1 *i-za-an-na-an*
2 *ki-ma ša-me-e*
3 *el-li-at*
4 ^{d}*Nergal*(NÈ.IRI$_{11}$.GAL)
5 *el-li-tu-šu*
6 *ki-ma še-li-/bi-im*

Reverse

7 *li-i-r*[*e-eq*]
8 *i-na a*$^{!}$*-wu-r*[*i-qá-nim*]
9 *ši-pa-a-*[*at*]
10 *a-wu-ri-qá-n*[*i*]*m*

---

234 Another condition, i.e., *aḫḫāzu*, is known as jaundice in Akkadian magico-medical texts. The main symptom characterizing both *aw/murriqānum* and *aḫḫāzu* is the yellow/green colour of the patient. For a summary of the discussions by previous scholars regarding the difference between the two conditions, see Couto-Ferreira 2018, 154f.

Translation

1–2 It is raining down like rain;
3–5 Its saliva is the saliva of Nergal.
6–8 May it depart like a fox through jaundice!
9–10 Incantation (against) jaundice.

Commentary

6: "Fox", with CAD I/J, 85; CAD A/2, 91 (and not "turtle" - as suggested in AHw, 1210; von Weiher (1971, 34); CAD Š/2, 271 1a), see commentary to l. 7.

7: *li-i-r*[*e-eq*]: The plene-spelling better suits a derivation from *warāqum*, "to be(come) green or yellow", but *līriq* (kept by all commentators, including Veldhuis 1999, 37) does not make sense here: why would the speaker ask the disease to become green or yellow? Is the person sick not yellow enough? A reading *lirēq*, from *rêqum*, "to withdraw, to go away, to depart", though not accounting for the long *i* in *li-i-r*[*e-eq*], makes better sense here. CAD R does not list this text s.v. *rêqum*, but note Landsberger/Jacobsen's reading in their *editio princeps li-i-ṣ*[*í-a*] (repeated in CAD A/2, 91, and translated "slip out", which finally was rejected in Landsberger 1969, 139 fn. 2). With the reading *lirēq* the question whether *še-li-BI-im* is a "fox" or a "turtle" seems to be solved: the speaker wishes that the disease will depart as (quick) as a fox, not as (slow) as a turtle.

8: *i-na a*$^{!}$*-wu-r*[*i-qá-nim*]: Correct CAD A/2, 91 which read *i-na ṣa-ar-*[*ri-*(*im*)].

№ 39: YOS 11, 14c

SEAL No.: 7129
Copy: van Dijk/Goetze/Hussey 1985 Pl. XVI
Tablet Siglum: YBC 4599
Photo: cf. SEAL No.: 7129
Edition: –
Studies: Farber 1985, 63; Cunningham 1997 Cat. No. 390; Wasserman 2003 Cat. No. 243; George 2016, 137
Collection: Yale Babylonian Collection, New Haven
Provenance: Larsa area
Measurements: 7.5 × 10.6 cm
Procedure: Yes

Introduction

Curiously, this incantation is destined for a woman and against a woman. One could perhaps imagine that the circumstances behind this incantation were that of a quarrel between two rival women, leading one of them to resort to magic. If this is the case, then ll. 8–9 would contain a list of curses, not *materia magica*. The "a spell for jaundice" (l. 11) could be explained if we assume that green/yellow-face were also sign of jealousy.

Reverse

7 [*tam*]*-ḫa-ṣi pa-nu-š*[*a*$^{?}$] *tu-uš-ba-al-ki-ti-ma pu-ša*
8 [*k*]*i-*⸢*ir*⸣*-ba-an eqlim*(A.ŠÀ^{lim}) *pa-ar ša-ḫi-i-im*
9 [*za*]*-ap-pu ši-ik-ke-e ṣú-ru-ut ar-ra-bi-im*
10 [*š*]*i*$^{!}$*-i*[*p*]$^{!}$*-tum*$^{!}$ *ša il-tu*[*m*$^{!}$ *i*]*š*$^{?}$*-ku-nu-ki e tu-uš*$^{!}$(UT)*-tam-ḫi-ri ṣi i-na li-ib-*[*bi*]*-im*
11 [x x] *ša a-mu-ur-ri-qá-nim*
12 [x (x) *k*]*i*$^{!}$*-i*[*k*$^{!}$]*-ki-ta-ša ka-ra-ši ú-ḫe-eš-še*$_{20}$*-e-ma ù* ni is *i-ša-tu*[*m*]

Translation

7–9 You (f.) have hit her face and you (f.) have turned upside down her mouth (saying:) – "field's clod! pig's hide! Mongoose's whiskers! Dormouse's fart!" –
10 A spell, which the goddess has created against you (f.), do not (f.) oppose it! Go out (f.) of the (patient's) belly!
11 (A spell) against jaundice
12 Its procedure: she will chop leeks, and … fire.

Commentary

8–9: Similar list of curses in YOS 11, 2: 3–6 (№ 101) and CUSAS 32, 32a: 2 (№ 27). Note that our [*k*]*i-*⸢*ir*⸣*-ba-an eqlim*(A.ŠÀ^{lim}) goes against Farber, 1985, 63 who suggested [*p*]*i-*[K]A*-an a-lu-lim* (reading based on photos).

10: *Pace* Farber (1985, 63) the sign is a clear IL (not AN-*tum*$^{!}$).

12: The verbal form *ú-ḫe-eš-še*$_{20}$*-e-ma* (if not a mistake for *tu-ḫe-eš-še*$_{20}$*-e-ma*) may refer to 1.sg. denoting a remark for the magic expert himself, but similar to YOS 11, 29a: 22–23 (№ 48), we assume a 3.sg. instruction for the client.

2.1.6 Maškadu

A group of incantations against a zoonotic disease attacking ruminant animals (cows and sheep) and humans – perhaps brucellosis (Wasserman 2012b). In later, post-OB sources, *maškadum* appears mainly in incantations which are part of the *Muššuʾu*-series, a cluster of ailments whose main symptoms were joint and muscle pain (cf. Arbøll 2018).

№ 40: AMD 14, 191b

SEAL No.: 7154
Copy: Farber 2018, 191
Tablet Siglum: A 663
Photo: –
Edition: Collins 1999, 234f.; Farber 2018, 192f.
Studies: Wasserman 2012b; Arbøll 2018; Farber 2018
Collection: Oriental Institute, Chicago
Provenance: Adab
Measurements: 10.1 × 6.7 cm
Procedure: No

Introduction

After an incantation in a non-identified language (ll. 1–7, see Farber 2018, 194) comes the incantation against *maškadum* which terminates with an alloglot-formula (l. 16) and the "incantation for loose bowels" (diarrhea[?]).

----

8 *ma-aš-ka-du-um ma-aš-ka-du-um ú-la ma-aš-ra šu-ú-um*
9 *iš-tu ša-mi ur-da-am*
10 *i-na ši-it-pi-im ma-an-za-zu-šu*
11 *i-na ki-bi-is al-pi-i-im ma-a-a-al-šu*
12 *e-re-eb bu-li-im i-ru-ab wa-ṣú bu-li-im iṣ-ṣí*
13 *ú-ta-mi-ka An ù An-tum a-šar ta-aṣ-ba-tu*
14 *lu tu-wa-ša*[!]*-ar* tu-en-ni-in-nu-ri
15 *ṣí-i ma-aš-ka-du ṣí šu-ḫu-ur*

====

16 ḫa-ap-pa-ḫa-zi ḫa-la-di[?] ḫa-pa-ḫa-zi

-----

17 ka-inim-ma *ir-ri i-ša-ru-tim*

Translation

8 *maškadum*! *maškadum*! – not *maškadum* (text: *mašra*): *šuʾum* (is its name)!
9 It came down from heaven.
10–11 In the pit is its location, in the track of the bull is its laying.
12–13 It enters with the entering of the herd; it goes out with the going out of the herd.

13–14 I conjure you by Anum and Antum: wherever you have grasped you will release!
14 tu-en-ni-in-nu-ri
15 Leave, *maškadum*, leave! Become still!
===
16 *ḫappaḫazi ḫaladi ḫappaḫazi*
----
17 Incantation (against) loose bowels.

Commentary

8: *ma-aš-ra* is a mistake for *ma-aš-ka-du-um*. The gloss-like comment "*maškadum*! *maškadum*! – no *maškadum*, *šuʾum* (is the correct name of the disease)" is found in other OB and post-OB *maškadum*-incantations (Collins 1999, 233ff.; Böck 2007, 290: 153–153a; 293: 167–168 and Reiner 1995, 59 fn. 248). We take this dual appellation as a scribal effort to match the original, probably Amorite, name of the disease, viz. *maškadum*, with its corresponding Akkadian term, *šuḫûm*/*šuʾum*, see Wasserman (2012b, 429).

12: Both *i-ru-ab* and *iṣ-ṣí* are mistaken forms. One expects *ir-ru-ub* (or *i-ru-ub*), and *uṣ-ṣí*, respectively, see Farber (2018, 195). Note, however, that in post-OB texts verbs primae-*w* show at times forms with prefix *i*- (e.g., *ibbal* instead of *ubbal*, cf. GAG[3] § 103n).

15: Reading and understanding after Farber (2018, 193/195).

16–17: Farber (2018, 196) compared the alloglot formula in l.16 and *irrī išarūtim* to the subscript in YOS 11, 21: 32, where the formula is concluded with ŠÀ.SI.SÁ.

№ 41: YOS 11, 14b

SEAL No.: 7155
Copy: van Dijk/Goetze/Hussey 1985 Pl. XVI
Tablet Siglum: YBC 4599
Photo: cf. SEAL No. 7155
Edition: van Dijk/Goetze/Hussey 1985, 23–24 (partial)
Studies: Cunningham 1997 Cat. No. 389; Wasserman 2003 Cat. No. 242; Foster 2005, 931 (II.23e); Wasserman 2012b; Arbøll 2018
Collection: Yale Babylonian Collection, New Haven
Provenance: Larsa area
Measurements: 7.5 × 10.6 cm
Procedure: No

Introduction

The second of three incantations (the first badly broken, the third against jaundice or jealousy, № 39), this spell is reminiscent of the previous one against *maškadum*, only ending with the invocation of Gula as a surgeon, and without a subscript.

Reverse

1 *[m]a-aš-ka-du-[um ma-aš-k]a-du-um ú-ul ma-aš-ka-du-um šu-ḫu-ú-um*
2 *i-na š[u-li]-im*! *na-ar-ba-ṣu-šu i-na ‹‹ma-an-za-as-sú›› i-me-ri m[a-an-z]a-zu-šu*
3 *na-ša-ak ba-ar-ba-ri-um i-na-aš-ša-ak ša-ḫa-aṭ kal-bi-im e-la-m[i]* ⸢*i-ša*⸣*-ḫi-iṭ*
4 *e-re-eb bu-lim i-ru-u[b w]a-ṣe-e bu-lim uṣ-ṣi*
5 *[ṣ]i-i ma-aš-*⸢*ka-du-um la*⸣*-a-ma ik-šu-du-ka ṣú-ur-ru na-ag-la-b[u (ša)* ^{d}*]Gu-la*
6 t[u$_6$]-én-é-nu-⸢ri⸣

Translation

1 *maškadu[m*! *mašk]adum*! – not *maškadum* (but) *šuḫûm* (is its name).
2 In the street is its lair; in between the sheep is its location.
3 It bites a wolf-bite; it attacks an Elamite-dog's attack.
4 It enters (with) the entering of the herds, it goes out (with) the going out of the herds.
5 Go out *maškadum* before the flint razors of Gula reach you!
6 t[u$_6$]-én-é-nu-⸢ri⸣

Commentary

1: For the disease name, see above, commentary to AMD 14, 191b: 8 (№ 40).
5: *lāma ikšuduka ṣurrū naglabu*: the same expression is found in AMT 12, 1: 47. A similar magical warning (*lāma ikšudakki epkallam šipir Ea qardu*) is found in BIN 2, 72: 10–12 (№ 159). – For the hendiadys *ṣurru naglabū* see Wasserman (2003, 11) and cf. Erra IV 57 (Cagni 1969, 110).

№ 42: YOS 11, 69c

SEAL No.: 7156
Copy: van Dijk/Goetze/Hussey 1985 Pl. LXVII
Tablet Siglum: YBC 4594
Photo: https://collections.peabody.yale.edu/search/Record/YPM-BC-018659
Edition: Cavigneaux/Al-Rawi 2002, 10f.
Studies: van Dijk/Goetze/Hussey 1985, 45; Cunningham 1997 Cat. No. 401; Wasserman 1999, 348f.; Wasserman 2003 Cat. No. 258; Wasserman 2012b; Arbøll 2018
Collection: Yale Babylonian Collection, New Haven
Provenance: Larsa area
Measurements: 9.0 × 5.0 cm
Procedure: No

Introduction

The third of four incantations, all concerned with agricultural matters: the first two in Sumerian, against field rodents and infesting birds; the fourth against wild asses in Akkadian. Broken and hard to construe, this incantation is different to the previous two *maškadum*-incantations. Milking cows are mentioned and Amorite words are probably used. This text is the only one in the group with a clear subscript identifying it as an incantation against *maškadum*.

Reverse
9' *la-ḫa-sú-um la-aḫ-si-a-tum*
10' *tu-ub-la* ‹*la*$^{?}$›*-ḫa-sú-um la-aḫ-si-a-tum*
11' *ar-ḫa-tu-ú-a ḫa-li-ba-tum*
12' *lu-uš-qà-*[*an*$^{?}$]*-ni lu-uš-qú-ul balāṭam*(TI)
13' *lu*$^{!}$*-la-a-ba-*[x x] [*l*]*i*$^{?}$-[*i*]*t*$^{?}$ *l*[*a-a*]*ḫ-si-a-tum*
14' ^{d}*Nin-girim*$_{x}$(ḪA.TAR.A.DU) [x *l*]*i*$^{?}$*-i*[*t*$^{?}$ *l*]*a*$^{?}$-[*aḫ-s*]*i*$^{?}$*-a-tum*

15' k a - i n i m - m a *ma-aš-ka-du-um*

Translation

9' *The whispering, the whispering-ones* (f.).
10' *She has brought to me. The whispering, the whispering-ones* (f.).
11' My milking cows!
12' Let me... let me ... *life*!
13' ... *cow*$^{?}$, *whispering-ones* (f.).
14' Ningirim (…) *cow*$^{?}$, [*whispering*]*-ones* (f.).

15' Incantation (against) the *maškadum*-disease.

Commentary

9': *la-ḫa-sú-um la-aḫ-si-a-tum*: with Cavigneaux/Al-Rawi (2002, 10f.), the root √LḪS is probably to be connected to *laḫāšum* "to whisper". Morphologically, *la-ḫa-sú-um* could stand for the infinitive *laḫāsum* "whispering" or *laḫḫāsum* "the whispering-one". The second lemma, *la-aḫ-si-a-tum*, is a f.pl. form of the hitherto unattested m. *laḫš/sûm*.

9'–10': Similar rhythmic repetitions with magical impact are known. See, e.g., YOS 11, 17: 1–4 (№ 13); YOS 11, 19b: 18–22 (№ 112) and YOS 11, 67a//NABU 2019/43a: 5–6 (№ 175).

2.1.7 Orthopaedic Problems

Incantations destined to resolve orthopaedic problems, notably mending broken bones, are well attested in Sumerian. They are usually referred to as ka-inim-ma ^{uzu}gìr-pad-rá (see George 2016, 139–140). In our corpus, a single specimen of this category is known, relating to repairing a sinew *šerʾānum*(SA).[235]

№ 43: YOS 11, 16b

SEAL No.: 7209
Copy: van Dijk/Goetze/Hussey 1985 Pls. XVIII/XIX
Tablet Siglum: YBC 5328
Photo: cf. SEAL No. 7209
Edition: van Dijk/Goetze/Hussey 1985, 24 (no translation); Krebernik 2018, 24
Studies: Cunningham 1997 Cat. No. 392a; Wasserman 2003 Cat. No. 245
Collection: Yale Babylonian Collection, New Haven
Provenance: Larsa area
Measurements: 6.8 × 5.3 cm
Procedure: No

Introduction

The second of two incantations (the first probably against a scorpion) aiming to remedy a damaged sinew (cf. l. 8). Not carefully written: erasures and omissions of signs exist.

Obverse
4 *ri-mu ri-ma-*{x}*-ni* / *še*$_{20}$*-le-bu la-ba-tu*
5 *in-ḫu ka-ab-ta-ti* / *da-du li-ib-bi*
6 ^{d}*Da-mu i-di-ma* / *ši-pa-as-sú ib-lu-uṭ*

Reverse
7 *a-na-ku ši-ip-ti* / *a-na-an-di li-ib-‹lu›-uṭ*
8 *ú-du-uš šerʾān*(SA) *ra-ma-ni-šu* / *lu la pa-ga-ar-šu* ‹‹nu››
9 *ka-al-bu si*$_{20}$(sup. ras.)*-im-mi* / *ra-ma-ni-šu-*{x}*-nu*
10 *li-li-i-ku*
11 tu-ú-e-ni-in-nu-ri

Translation

4 Wildest of bulls! Fox! Lioness!
5 The trouble of the mind, the darling of the heart:
6–7 (Since) Damu has cast his incantation – he got well, (now) I will cast my incantation so that he will get well:
8 Renewed is his sinew, if not his[!] (text: their) body –

235 Mending broken bones was also a subject of Germanic, pre-Christian incantations. For the Merseburg incantation and its later derivations, see Wasserman 2014b, 255.

9–10 Just as (lit: may) the dogs lick their own wounds.
11 tu-ú-e-ni-in-nu-ri

Commentary

4: The spell is destined to help heal a torn sinew, hence the enumeration of fast running wild animals.

6: Instead of the finite verb *ibluṭ*, perhaps emend to *libluṭ* as in the next line?

7: van Dijk/Goetze/Hussey (1985, 24) read *a-na* AN *di-li-ip-tam* (so also Wasserman 2003, 75). A better reading is *a-na-an-di li-ib-‹lu›-uṭ* (suggestion U. Gabbay). Note that the dissimilation *anaddi* > *anandi* may point to late-OB date.

8: Reading *u-du-uš šerʾān*(SA!) *ramānišu* corrects Wasserman (2003, 8). The confusion of the scribe at the end of this line (*lu la pa-ga-ar-šu* ‹‹nu››), was caused by *ra-ma-ni-šu-*{x}*-nu*, the end of l. 9. – As for the sequence *lū lā pagaršu*, we take it to denote a negative concession "if not...".

10: For *lêkum*, see also YOS 11, 87: 22 (№ 136).

2.1.8 Pox

The *sikkatum*-disease (udu-gag-šub-ba) occurs frequently in enumerations, often in first place (see JCS 9, 9 = № 54, JCS 9, 10 = № 55, RA 88, 161c = № 56, Semitica 61, 13f. = № 57, YOS 11, 8 = № 58, YOS 11, 9a = № 59, and Fs. Stol 150 = № 53), but only one incantation is specifically addressed against this form of pox.[236] The disease attacks sheep and humans alike, particularly when they are young.

№ 44: YOS 11, 7

SEAL No.: 7160
Copy: van Dijk/Goetze/Hussey 1985 Pl. VIII
Tablet Siglum: YBC 5640
Photo: cf. SEAL No. 7160
Edition: van Dijk/Goetze/Hussey 1985, 21
Studies: George 1987, 360; Edzard 1997, 426; Cunningham 1997 Cat. No. 378; Wasserman 2003 Cat. No. 232; Foster 2005, 183; Wasserman 2007, 54
Collection: Yale Babylonian Collection, New Haven
Provenance: Larsa area
Measurements: 7.9 × 4.9 cm
Procedure: No

Introduction

An elongated tablet with one incantation only. Sumerian subscript. Reverse left unwritten. The disease comes from heaven as fire. The spell ends with a rare reference to placing *ex votos* in the temple.

Obverse
1 *i-na ša-me-e* ⸢*e*$^{?}$⸣-[*lu*$^{?}$-*tim*$^{?}$]
2 *in-na-pi-iḫ i-ša-a-*⸢*tum*⸣
3 *sí-ik-ka-tum im-ta-qú-ut*
4 *e-li ka-li bu-li-im*
5 *úḫ-ta-am-mi-iṭ*
6 *la-a-le-e ka-lu-mi*
7 *ù ṣe-eḫ-ḫe-ru-tim i-na bu-*⸢*ú*⸣*-ud / ta-ri-i-tim*
8 *a-na um-mi-ia* ^{d}*Nin-girim*$_{x}$(ḪA.KUD.A.DU$^{!}$)
9 *qí-bí-a-ma*
10 *bu-lu-um li-wi-ru pa-nu-š*[*u*$^{!}$]
11 *li-iḫ-du* ^{d}*Šákkan*
12 *li-iḫ-du ša-am-mu-um*
13 *li-ri-iš šu-lu-ú-um*
14 *lu-uš-ta-ka-an ša-am-ša-a-tim*
15 *i-na šu-pa-a-at i-li ra-bu-tim*

236 For the suggestion that these enumerations are symptoms of the *sikkatum*-disease, see Kämmerer 1995.

16 *i-na te-ek-ni-i*

Lower Edge
17 ka-inim-ma udu-gag-šub-ba

Reverse uninscribed

Translation

1–2 Fire has been inflamed in the p[ure$^{?}$] heaven,
3–4 The *sikkatum*-disease (pox) has fallen over the entire herd,
5–7 burned up the kids, the lambs and the children on the shoulders of the nurse.
8–9 Speak to my mother, Ningirim:
10–13 "May the face of the herd be bright! May Šakkan rejoice! May the herb rejoice! May the path be happy!"
14–16 May I keep carefully placing solar-disks on the pedestals of the great gods appropriately!
17 Incantation for a sheep (infected) with *sikkatum*.

Commentary

8: For the different spellings of GIRIM, see Krebernik (1998–2001, 363f.).
15: For *šupāt ilī rabûtim*, see George (1987, 50).
17: For udu-gag-šub-ba = *šá sik-*[*ka-ti*], "a sheep (infected) with *sikkatum*", listed in an enumeration of different kinds of sheep, see Ura XIII 44 (MSL 8/1, 10) incl. OB unilingual forerunners.

2.1.9 Stye

Only one spell is known against *merḫu* in Mesopotamian incantation literature, i.e., JNES 14, 15, which was first published by Landsberger/Jacobsen (1955). Akkadian *merḫu* was here translated as 'ergot', a disease mainly of the eye. Later studies by Bottéro (1985, 286–288) and Farber (1987, 272f.) translate 'orgelet' and 'Gerstenkorn' respectively. Stol (1989, 165) argues *merḫu* rather to be stye, an inflammation of the eyelid, but following parallels in Late Antiquity, notes that trachoma could alternatively be meant here.

№ 45: JNES 14, 15

SEAL No.: 7184
Copy: Landsberger/Jacobsen 1955, 15
Tablet Siglum: Ish-35-T.19
Photo: –
Edition: Landsberger / Jacobsen 1955
Studies: Goetze 1955, 17f.; Landsberger 1958, 56f.; Bottéro 1985, 286–288; Farber 1987, 272f.; Stol 1989, 165; Farber 1990b, 300 fn. 10/306; Veldhuis 1993, 48–50; Cunningham 1997 Cat. No. 342; Wasserman 2003 Cat. No. 83; Foster 2005, 181; Lambert 2013, 399
Collection: Iraq Museum, Baghdad
Provenance: Nērebtum
Measurements: –
Procedure: No

Introduction

The tablet belongs to the lot of tablets from Ishchali, presently in Baghdad (see Greengus 1979, 2 fn. 5). An incantation combining the chain theme of creation (see Wasserman 2021) and the *mannam lušpur* formula. An astral mythological scene at the centre of the spell (ll. 12–13): Sîn is reaping (his lunar crescent resembling a sickle), while Šamaš is harvesting (his solar halo resembling stacks of barley or wheat).

Obverse

1 *er-ṣé-tum-mi er-ṣé-tum*
2 *ú-li-id lu-ḫa-ma*
3 *lu-ḫu-mu-ú*
4 *ú-li-*⸢*id*⸣ *i-ši-na*
5 *i-ši-nu-um ú-li-id*
6 *šu-bu-ul-tam* ‹‹am››
7 *šu-bu-ul-tum*
8 *ú-li-id me-er-ḫa*
9 *i-na-mi eqel*(A.ŠÀ) ^{d}*En-líl*
10 *mi-it-ḫa-ri-im*
11 70 IKU *eqlam*(A.ŠÀ)
12 ^{d}*Sîn*(EN.ZU) *i-ṣí-di*

Reverse

13 ^{d}*Šamaš*(UTU) *ú-ša-ap-ḫa-ar*

14 *a-na-mi īn*(IGI) *eṭlim*(GURUŠ)

15 *i-te-ru-ub*

16 *me-er-ḫu-um*

17 *ma-na lu-uš-pu-ur*

18 *ù lu-wa-ʾì-ir*

19 *a-na mārat*(DUMU.MUNUS) *An* 7 7

20 *li-il-qí-nim*

21 *agubbâm*(⸢E$^{?}$⸣.GUB) ⸢*ša*⸣ *sa-am-ti*

22 *karpatam*(DUG) *ša ḫu-la-lim*

23 *li-sa-ba-nim*

24 *me-e*$^{!}$ *tam*$^{!}$*-tim*

25 [*e*]*l-lu-tim me-er-ḫa*

26 [*l*]*i-še*$^{!}$*-li-*[*a*$^{?}$]

27 [*i*]*-na īn*(IGI) *eṭlim*(GURUŠ)

Translation

1–8 Earth – they say – earth bore the dirt, the dirt bore the stalk, the stalk bore the ear, the ear bore the stye.

9–11 In – they say – the field of Enlil, the square, 70 Iku of surface,

12–13 (when) Sîn was reaping (and) Šamaš was harvesting,

14–16 into – they say – the young man's eye entered the stye.

17–19 "Whom should I assign and send to the Daughters of Anum, seven (and) seven?

20–22 Let them take for me a vessel of carnelian, a pot of alabaster.

23–25 Let them draw for me pure water of the sea.

25–27 Let them take out the stye from the young man's eye!"

Commentary

1/9/14: On the use of the modal particle *-mi* in OB literary texts (as opposed to non-literary texts) see Wasserman (2012b). For *-mi* in this text, see Landsberger/Jacobsen (1955, 21) and Foster (2005, 181), whose translation "they say" is adopted here.

12: For the *i*-suffix, see GAG^{3} § 82e* with previous literature.

20/26: The verbal forms perhaps show the vowel contraction *ī-ā* > *ê*/*î*: *lilqênim* and [*l*]*išēlê*. Another example can be found in JCS 9, 9: 20 (№ 54).

2.1.10 Tooth

A small group of incantations is destined to alleviate acute toothache. The malevolent agent is a worm that is considered to be eating the tooth. A figurative language, rich in simile, is used.

№ 46: YOS 11, 3

SEAL No.: 7192
Copy: van Dijk/Goetze/Hussey 1985 Pl. III
Tablet Siglum: NBC 8957
Photo: cf. SEAL No. 7192
Edition: van Dijk/Goetze/Hussey 1985, 17f. (partial); Collins 1999, 271–274; Wasserman 2008, 74f.; Stadhouders 2018, 173–175
Studies: Cunningham 1997 Cat. No. 370; Wasserman 2003 Cat. No. 225; Wasserman 2005a, 598f.; Wasserman 2008
Collection: Yale Babylonian Collection, New Haven
Provenance: Larsa area
Measurements: 7.1 × 5.2 cm
Procedure: No

Introduction

Wasserman (2008) understood the worm mentioned in this text (l. 1) as referring to leeches, but following Stadhouders (2018), we consider the incantation as destined to remedy a toothache. A legitimation formula seals the text.

Obverse
1 *tu-ul-tum la t*[*a-ka-li*]
2 *níg-gal-la* ⸢*ša ṣur*⸣-[*ri-im*]
3 *t*[*e*]-*l*[*i*] ⸢*a-na ša-di*⸣-*i*
4 *tu-ṣa-li-mi* ⸢*pí*$^{?}$ NÍTA$^{?}$⸣ *ki* ŠE$_{10}$
5 *i-ti-li li-ṣa-li-lu*-⸢*ni-ik*⸣-*ki*
6 *a-di i-mi ri-š*[*a*]-⸢*tim*⸣-[*m*]*a*
7 *mi-tum iš-tu er-ṣ*[*e*]-*tim*
8 *i-ba-lu-ṭa-am-ma*
9 *la te-li*

Reverse
10 *ši-ip-tum ú-ul ia-a-tum*
11 *ši-pa-at* ^{d}*En-líl*
12 *ši-ip-tum ú-ul ia-a-tum*
13 *ši-pa-at* ^{d}*Šamaš*(UTU)
14 ^{d}*Šamaš*(UTU) *ši-ip-tam id-di*
15 *a-na-ku ri-mu*
16 *ka-ad-ru ša ša-d*[*i*]-*i*

17 *ad*-⸢*di*⸣ *š*[*i*]-*i*[*p*]-*t*[*am-m*]*a*
18 *a-na ra*-⸢*ma-ni*⸣-[*ia*]

Translation

1–2 Worm, you (f.) should not e[at] the sickle *of obsidian*!
3 You (f.) should go up into the mountains!
4 You (f.) have blackened *the mouth of the man* as if with excrement!
5 Lie (f.) down! May they put you (f.) to rest!
6–9 Until there will be joy and the dead man revives from the Netherworld, you shall not rise!
10–11 The incantation is not mine! It is the incantation of Enlil!
12–13 The incantation is not mine! It is the incantation of Šamaš!
14 Šamaš cast the spell!
15–16 I am the wild bull of the mountains
17–18 (and) I cast the incantation on my body!

Commentary

1–2: Interpretation follows Stadhouders (2018, 173f.). We reconstruct, however, *t*[*a-ka-li*], as verbal forms of 2. f. sg. are consistently used when addressing the worm.

3: The motif of expelling evil into the mountains (or another place outside the realm of society) is found in other Akkadian incantations (see e.g., the MB incs. AuOr Suppl. 23, 14a: 6 = Zomer 2018a, 259; MC 17, 443ff.: 17 = Farber 2014, 181). These extensive parallels show that in these faraway places, evil can feast on more delicious things, see Zomer (*forthcoming*).

4: Interpretation of this line follows Collins (1999, 271).

6: *īmi rīšātim*: *ewûm* + acc., esp. with abstract nouns, denotes “turning into...”. The phrase is ironic: the worm should remain idle until the dead are resurrected, namely – it should never rise again.

№ 47: YOS 11, 12c

SEAL No.: 7185
Copy: van Dijk/Goetze/Hussey 1985 Pls. XIII-XIV
Tablet Siglum: YBC 4625
Photo: cf. SEAL No. 7185
Edition: van Dijk/Goetze/Hussey 1985, 23 (partial); Krebernik 2018, 40
Studies: Farber 1985, 62; Veldhuis 1990, 42f.; Veldhuis 1993, 41f.; Cunningham 1997 Cat. No. 386; Wasserman 2003 Cat. No. 239
Collection: Yale Babylonian Collection, New Haven
Provenance: Larsa area
Measurements: 17.2 × 7.6 cm
Procedure: Yes

Introduction

The instigator of pain, no doubt *tūltum* "worm", is not mentioned in the text, or at least it is not preserved (cf. l. 29). The patient is a woman. The magic strategy of this spell involves calling upon a remote healing agent for assistance: a star is asked to carry away (*tabālum*) the trouble. The star is not specified by name – it is represented in the procedure by a star-shaped object – but let us note that a constellation "worm", MUL *tūltu*, is known (CAD T, 468a). The tooth worm and the astral worm had to be united, thus healing the patient.

Obverse
29 [*tūltum*$^{?}$ … *iṣ-ṣa*]*-ba-at*
30 […] ⸢x ba$^{?}$ x⸣

Reverse
31 [x x x] ⸢*a*⸣ *i*$^{?}$*-tu*$^{?!}$*-úr a-na aš-*⸢*ri*⸣ [x x x]
32 [x]-⸢x⸣-zi *ka-ak-k*[*a-b*]*i š*[*i*$^{?}$*-in*$^{?}$*-ni*$^{?}$]
33 [x x *š/t*]*a-am i-na-ad*$^{!}$(DA)*-di ‹i-na› mu-ḫi ši-ni-ša* ⸢*ma-ru-uš-ti*⸣
34 [*ka*]*-ak-ka-ab-ti-ša ta-la-ap-pa-ta-ma*
35 [*ša-l*]*a-*⸢*ši-šu*⸣ *ki-a-am ta-qá-ab-bi*
36 [*ka-ak-k*]*a-ab ka-ak-ka-b*[*i*] *ši-in-ni ma-ar-ṣa-*⸢*at*⸣
37 [*mu*]-⸢*ru*⸣*-uṣ ši-in-ni-ia ta-ba-al a-wa-tum a-wa-at bu-*[*ul*$^{?}$*-ṭim*$^{?}$]

Translation

29 … [the worm$^{?}$ *se*]*ized*$^{?}$
30 …
31 … May it/she not *return* to [its/her] place …
32–33 Oh my … ! Oh my sta[r …]! … [my] [*ach*]*ing to*[*oth*$^{?}$]!
33 *He/it is placing*$^{?}$ … *on the top*$^{?}$ of her aching tooth.
34 You (or: she) will touch her star-ornament
35 and you (or: she) will say three times, as following:

36 "[Oh s]tar! my star! my tooth is aching!
37 Carry away [the pa]in of my tooth!" The spell (lit. word) is a *h*[*ealing*] spell.

Commentary

32: If the traces of the last sign before the break is the beginning of ŠI, then, perhaps *š*[*i*$^{?}$-*in*$^{?}$-*ni*$^{?}$].

33: [*ma*$^{?}$-*ru*$^{?}$-*uš*$^{?}$-*t*]*a-am* comes to mind, but there is no room for that. – What follows is, with caution, a form of *nadûm* (for the use of this verb in a similar context, see CAD Š/3, 50a).

34–35: The verbal forms *talappatamma* and *taqabbi* can be analyzed as 3 sg. f. (the female patient) or, as we consider more likely, 2 sg. m., referring to the healer.

37: A similar designation of *awātum* for "incantation" is found in YOS 11, 15:4 // YOS 11, 29: 24 (№ 149) and cf. Fs. de Meyer 87: 9 (№ 172).

№ 48: YOS 11, 29a

SEAL No.: 7153
Copy: van Dijk/Goetze/Hussey 1985 Pls. XLVIII/XLIX
Tablet Siglum: YBC 4597
Photo: https://collections.peabody.yale.edu/search/Record/YPM-BC-018662
Edition: Cavigneaux 1998; Collins 1999, 274
Studies: Cavigneaux 1998; Collins 1999, 274–276
Collection: Yale Babylonian Collection, New Haven
Provenance: Larsa area
Measurements: 9.3 × 7.9 cm
Procedure: Yes

Introduction

The incantation is accompanied by a partly broken procedure where the worm is mentioned (l. 22). Interestingly, as noted already by Cavigneaux (1998) and Collins (1999, 274f.), the incantation employs phrases known from love incantations (cf. in YOS 11, 87: 18–20 = № 136). In the latter, the yearning lover asks his inamorata not to remain attached to her father's house but to leave her domestic duties for him, the lover. In this text, the same phraseology is used à l'inverse: the speaker orders the worm not to attach its house to the beloved (i.e., the tooth), and be ready to detach itself from its possessions (i.e., to leave the cavity in the tooth and depart). This could be a parody, but the fact that the text is followed by a procedure, makes this possibility less likely.

Reverse

19 én[!](MIN+AN) *dān*(KAL) *ḫurāṣum*(KÙ.GI) *ši-na i-ṭe₄-en-ni-a-am mu-ši ù ur-ri-im*
20 *at-ti a-na ra-mi-ia e tar-ku-si-im bi-it-*[*ki*]
21 *a-na dam-qí-im bi-ši qá-ti-i-ki e ta-ap-pa-al-s*[*í-im*]
----
22 *murram*(ŠIM.ŠEŠ) *i-na mu-úḫ-ḫi ši-in-ni ša t*[*u*]-⌜*ul-tum*⌝ [x x x x x]
23 ⌜*murram*(ŠIM.ŠEŠ) x x x x x⌝*-tim i-ša-ak-ka-an-ma i-ba-lu-uṭ*

Translation

19 Incantation: Strong is gold! It (the worm) is continually grinding the tooth, night and day.
20 You (f. = the worm) should not attach your house to my love!
21 You (f. = the worm) should not look favourably upon the possession of your hands!
----
22 [He will apply] myrrh on the tooth which the w[orm has eaten].
23 He will place the myrrh [on the …] and he will be well.

Commentary

19: Note the parallel in the later Egalkura incantation KAL-*an* URUDU KAL-*an* ZABAR (KAR 71: 12), see Klan (2007, 47). Metals are known in love incantations to be used as a metonymic reference to the male genital organs (see Wasserman 2016, 41), but in the present context it refers to the worm instead. – Collins (1999, 275) explained: "*šina* as referring to the two kidneys, and *itenniam* as the Gtn preterite of *enû*". But *ši-na* is a defective spelling of *šinna* "the tooth" (acc.) and the verb is *i-ṭe*₄*-en-ni-a-am* (*ṭênum* G present + ventive, namely, "it (the worm) is continually grinding the tooth, night and day".

20: *rāmiya*, or *râmiya* is the tooth.

2.1.11 Various Diseases

A large group of incantations are concerned with miscellaneous diseases. Some are directed against "all diseases" (*kala murṣê*), i.e., CT 42, 32 (№ 49), CUSAS 32, 22a (№ 52) and Fs. Stol 150 (№ 53). These have parallels in later incantation series of the first millennium (Sag.gig VII/a and *Muššuʾu* IV/a), see Zomer (2018a, 200). Other incantations enumerate diseases that come down from heaven, i.e., JCS 9, 9 (№ 54), JCS 9, 10 (№ 55), RA 88, 161c (№ 56), Semitica 61, 13f. (№ 57), YOS 11, 8 (№ 58), YOS 11, 9a (№ 59). A third sub-group is less clear-cut. One large fragmentary incantation (CT 44, 32(+)33t = № 50) is a forerunner to a non-canonical Udugḫul incantation of the first millennium (JCS 31, 218f.: 1–26 and CT 51, 142) known to be directed against a variety of diseases. It ends with a description of a humanoid figure. CUSAS 32, 7e (№ 51) and YOS 11, 10 (№ 60) contain variants of this description.

№ 49: CT 42, 32

SEAL No.: 7071
Copy: Figulla 1959 Pl. 41
Tablet Siglum: BM 17305
Photo: Geller/Wiggermann 2008, 151;
https://www.britishmuseum.org/collection/object/W_1894-0115-19
Edition: von Soden 1961, 71f.; Geller/Wiggermann 2008, 156–160
Studies: Cunningham 1997 Cat. No. 350; Wasserman 2003 Cat. No. 63; Foster 2005, 279; Böck 2007, 147–180; Hecker 2008, 71; Zomer 2018a, 200/203/209
Collection: British Museum, London
Provenance: Unknown
Measurements: 6.6 × 8.1 cm
Procedure: No

Introduction

This incantation shares parallels with CUSAS 32, 22a (№ 52) and Fs. Stol 150 (№ 53) and is echoed in later series (Sag.gig VII/a and *Muššuʾu* IV/a), see Zomer (2018a, 200).

Obverse
1 *lu-di-kum šiptam*(TU$_{6}$) *ṭà-ri-da-at ka-la mu-úr-*⸢*ṣe-e*⸣
2 *ša* ^{d}*En-líl-bàn-da iš-ku-nu mu-ši-im ši-ma-tim*$^{!}$
3 *li-di-kum É-a šipat*(TU$_{6}$) *ba-la-ṭi*$_{4}$*-im*
4 ^{d}*Nu-‹dím›-mud ù* ^{d}*Nammu*(ENGUR) *e-le-et An-ni-im*$^{!}$(IḪ)
5 *li-di-kum šiptam*(TU$_{6}$) ^{d}*Nin-níg-erím-me-e be-le-et ši-pa*$^{!}$*-tim*$^{!}$(TUM)
6 *i-di šiptam*(TU$_{6}$) ^{d}*Nin-níg-érim-me-e be-le-et ši-pa-tim*
7 *i-te-bi mar-ṣú-um i-na tu-i-ša ú-ul ú-ša-na-ah*
8 *li-ir-ku-ús-ka* ^{d}*Nin-kar-ra-ak i-na ra-ba-tim qá-ti-ša*
9 ^{d}*Da-mu ma-na-ah-ta-ka li-še*$_{20}$*-te-eq el-ka*
10 *mar-tam pa-ši-tam* ^{d}*Lamaštam*(DÌM.ME) *ek-ke-em-tam ni-ši-ik*
kalbim(UR.GI$_{7}$.RA) *ši-in-ni / a-wi-lu-tim*

Lower Edge

11 *li-di-iš An-nu-ni-tum i-na tu-i-ša*

Reverse

12 ^{d}*Adad*(IŠKUR) ^{d}*Šákkan* ^{d}*Nisaba*(ŠE.NAGA) ^{d}*Šamaš*(UTU) ^{d}*Nārum*(ÍD) *Ḫur*$^{?}$-⸢*sa-an*⸣

13 *ilū*(DINGIR.RA) *qá-aš-du-tum*$^{!}$: *šu-nu li-il*$_{5}$*-li-lu-ka*

14 *el-le-et* ^{d}*Enlil*(EN.LÍL.LÁ) *li-il*$_{5}$*-li-lu-ka*

15 *Māšum*(MAŠ) *ù Maš-tum mārū*(DUMU^{meš}) ^{d}*Sîn*(EN.ZU) ^{d}*Šamaš*(UTU) *ù Iš*$_{8}$*-tár*

16 *dab-bi-‹bu› ša-ba-ši-tum dal-pu-um ep-ša-tum ù gún-nu-ṣum*

17 *ù la li-bi i-la e-li-ka li-iš-bu-ús*

18 *šar*(LUGAL) *Apsîm*(ZU.AB) *maš-maš ilī*(DINGIR.RA) *el-lu* ‹‹TU$_{6}$-*a*››

19 *šiptam*(TU$_{6}$) *ša la ta-pa*$^{!}$(AP)*-ra-sú li-di-kum*

20 *li-še*$_{20}$*-bi-ir ana sú-rím ma-na-ah-ta-ka-*⸢*ma a-na erṣetim*(KI⸣-[*t*]*im*)

21 *ad-di-kum šiptam*(TU$_{6}$) *ṭà-ri-da-at ka-la* ⸢*mu-ur-ṣé*⸣

Translation

1–2 May I cast on you (m.) a spell driving out all diseases, which Enlilbanda, the one deciding all fates, placed (for me)!

3 May Ea cast on you (m.) a spell of life!

4–6 May Nudimmud, and Nammu, (with) the authority of Anum, cast a spell on you (m.)! Ningirim, the lady of incantations cast a spell, Ningirim, the lady of incantations!

7 The patient is getting up through her incantation, he suffers no more.

8 May Ninkarrak compress you (m.) with her gentle hands!

9 May Damu let your misery pass by you!

10–11 As for the murderous bile, Lamaštu, the Snatcher-demon, dog bite, (or) human tooth, may Annunītum trample (them) through her incantation!

12–13 Adad, Šakkan, Nisaba, Šamaš, Nāru, Ḫursānu, the holy gods, may they purify you (m.)!

14–15 (With) the authority of Enlil may they purify you (m.), the twin-brother and twin-sister, the children of Sîn, Šamaš and Ištar!

16–17 Should either the gossiping man, the irate woman, the sleepless man, sorceresses or the sneering person, or one rejected by (his personal) god be angry with you,

18–19 may the king of the Apsû, the pure exorcist of the gods, cast a spell that you can not stop upon you!

20 May it bring your suffering immediately to the Netherworld!

21 I cast a spell upon you (m.) driving away all diseases!

Commentary

13: For the use of the *Glossenkeil*, see Geller/Wiggermann (2008, 158).

14: *el-le-et* ^{d}*Enlil*: we do not follow Geller/Wiggerman (2008, 158) who saw here *illatu* A “troop”.

№ 50: CT 44, 32(+)33t

SEAL No.: 27074
Copy: Pinches 1963 Pls. XXIII-XXV
Tablet Siglum: BM 78249 (+) 78253
Photo: –
Edition: Geller 2016, 54–57 (ms. c_1)
Studies: Zomer 2018a, 217/221/224
Collection: British Museum, London
Provenance: Sippar$^{?}$
Measurements: –
Procedure: No

Introduction

This incantation can be regarded as a forerunner to a non-canonical Udugḫul incantation of the first millennium (JCS 31, 218f.: 1–26 and CT 51, 142) and is found at the end of an incantation collective with forerunners to Gattung I (zi – pà formulae), see Zomer (2018a, 224). A contemporary abbreviated version of this spell can be found in YOS 11, 10 (№ 60) and a variation thereof in CUSAS 32, 7e (№ 51). For its OB dating, see Geller (2016, 44).

Reverse
vii$^{?}$
5'' é-n-é-nu-ru
6'' an imin ⸢ki⸣ imin [...]
7'' bar imin [bar-t]a$^{?}$ ⸢imin⸣ [...]
8'' ⸢igi⸣ i[min ...]
9'' ⸢x⸣ [...]
(*gap of ca. 5 lines*)
10''' ⸢x x⸣ [...]
11''' *mu-ru-ṣi* [...]
12''' *a-pi-at* ^{d}*Adad*(I[ŠKUR]) [...]
13''' *a-pi-at* ^{d}*Nergal*(NÈ.IRI$_{11}$$^{!}$.GAL) *ša i-na libbi*(Š[À]$^{?}$) [...]
14''' *ši-ip-tum ša*$^{!}$ ^{d}MAŠ.[TAB.BA]
15''' *ḫi-mì-iṣ ṣe-ṭim ù ši-*⸢*bi-iṭ*⸣ [...]
16''' *ṣi-bi-it*$^{!}$(DU) *Li-i-li*$^{!?}$ *ù Li-i-l*[*i*$^{!?}$*-ti*]
17''' *Šu-la-ak ša*$^{?}$ si ⸢ti⸣ ia
18''' ⸢*mu-šul-lu*⸣ *Ḫa-ia-ṭú aṣ-ṣa-ba-*⸢*at*$^{!}$⸣
19''' *qí-it-ma ša-ap-ta-š*[*u*]
20''' *ka-lu-ú pa-nu-š*[*u*]
21''' *pi-i-šu mi-iq*$^{!}$(KU$^{?}$)*-tum ki-ša-a*[*s-sú*]
22''' ⸢GIN$_7$$^{!?}$⸣ *mi-ra-a-*[*ḫu*]
23''' [*a*]-⸢*tal*⸣*-lu-uk-šu ḫ*[*u*$^{!?}$*-ur-ba-šu*]
24''' [...] ⸢x x⸣ [...]
(*broken*)

viii$^?$

1	[*arki ú-pu-un-t*]*i*-⌜*ka*⌝
2	[n]íg gar níg gar níg nu-gar-ra
3	[šaga]-me-en ge$_6$-a-DU.DU
4	[dab]-da-zu-dè
5	[gìr]i-⌜zu⌝ ús-sa-ab
6	[^{d}Ut]u Maš-tab-ba$^!$
7	[igi] m[i]-n[i]-⌜in$^{?!}$⌝-bar-ra
8	[tu$_6$]-⌜én⌝-é-nu-ru

9	⌜x⌝ [...]

Translation

vii$^?$

5''	én-é-nu-ru
6''–9''	Heaven 7, Earth 7, [...], Back 7, from Back 7, [...] Eye 7, [...]
10''	...
	(*broken*)
11'''–13'''	[*Strange*] *illnesses*, the *apiātu*-disease of Adad [...], the *apiātu*-disease of Nergal from the middle of [*the mountains*]!
14'''	(*By*) a spell of the Twin Deities,
15'''	*Ḫimiṭ ṣētim*-disease, *šibiṭ* [*šāri*-disease,]
16'''	seizure by *Lilû*$^?$ and *Lilītu*$^?$
17'''	(and) Šulak of ...,
18'''	the hurling *Ḫayyattu*-demon *I have been seized*!
19'''–20'''	Black paste are its lips! Yellow-ochre paste is its face!
21'''–22'''	Its mouth is the *miqtum*-disease! Its neck is *like* a little snake!
23'''–24'''	Its roaming is *t*[*error*!] ...
	(*broken*)

viii$^?$

1	[*After*] your [*flour offering*!]
2	(*You are*) *the one, who does not calm and sooth everything!*
3	You are [the wronged person] who goes around at night!
4–5	Go forward to that which you have seized!
6–7	(By) Šamaš, who took notice of the Twin Deities!
8	[tu$_6$]-⌜én⌝-é-nu-ru
9	...

Commentary

vii$^?$ 11''': We prefer *mu-ur*$^!$(RU)-*ṣi* over *mu-ru-iṣ*$^!$, as parallels show *mur-ṣi*, see Geller (2016, 54).

vii$^?$ 12'''f.: For the notion of *apâtu* (*apiātu*) "numerous" as a disease, see CAD A/2, 168b.

vii$^{?}$ 14''': Later parallels read *šiptum ša qāt*(ŠU) ^{d}MAŠ.TAB.BA "Spell which is against the Hand of the Twin Deities". As for ŠU ^{d}MAŠ.TAB.BA as a common diagnosis in the diagnostic handbook Sakikkû, see Heeßel (2000, 165 fn. 32).

vii$^{?}$15''': Note the assimilation *ṣṭ* > *ṣṣ* in *ḫi-mì-iṣ ṣe-ṭim* for *ḫimiṭ ṣētim*.

vii$^{?}$ 16''': Interpretation remains tentative and follows LÍL.EN.NA *ù* MUNUS.LÍL.EN.NA of the later parallels, see Geller (2016, 55).

vii$^{?}$ 17''': Later parellels read ^{d}*Šulak ša mu-un-ze-e-ti*, see Geller (2016, 55).

vii$^{?}$ 18''': *šalû*-D is otherwise unattested (but note Dt-forms listed in CAD Š/1, 273a).

vii$^{?}$ 19'''–23''' Note the contemporary parallels in CUSAS 32, 7e: ii 7'–11' (№ 51) and YOS 11, 10 (№ 60).

vii$^{?}$21''': Our reading differs from Geller (2016, 55). Note the abbreviated versions of this spell (CUSAS 32, 7e: ii 9' = № 51 and YOS 11, 10: 4/7 = № 60), also from the OB period, which equate the demon's mouth with the *miqtum*-disease, whereas the first millennium exemplars read *šumšu* "its name".

viii$^{?}$ 2: As stated by Geller (2016, 419 fn. 111), the expressions níg-gar-ra and níg-nu-gar-ra in Udugḫul are problematic, as is its appearance in the OB forerunners. Geller's (2016, 57) interpretation of this line follows the bilingual version of Udugḫul III 165 (níg gar-ra níg-gar-ra níg-bi ki gar-gar-ra-e-dè // *mu-ni-iḫ mim-ma šum-šú mu-pa-áš-šiḫ mim-ma šum-šú šá ina šip-ti-šú mim-ma šum-šú i-pa-áš-šá-ḫu*),[237] namely he takes it to describe the benevolent actions of the deity Ea. In our text, however, this expression denotes the malevolent nature of the addressed evil entity. Therefore, we interpret this line as a negative counterpart to Udugḫul III 165.

viii$^{?}$ 9: Anticipated is a subscript starting with ka-inim-ma, similar to other incantations on this tablet, but the traces do not support this reading. Perhaps a colophon?

237 For lexical evidence for the expression ki -- gar // *pašāḫu*/*nâḫu* see Geller 2016, 125 fn. 165.

№ 51: CUSAS 32, 7e

SEAL No.: 7072
Copy: George 2016 Pl. XXII-XXV
Tablet Siglum: MS 3097
Photo: George 2016 Pl. XXI/XXVI; CDLI P252106
Edition: –
Studies: –
Collection: Schøyen Collection, Oslo
Provenance: Unknown
Measurements: 25 × 24 cm
Procedure: No

Introduction

Partially parallels YOS 11, 10 (№ 60) and its extended version CT 44, 32(+)33t (№ 50).

Obverse
ii

7'	*qit*$^{!}$*-ma ša-ap-ta-šu*
8'	*ka-lu-um pa-*⸢*nu*⸣*-šu*
9'	⸢*pī*(KA$^{?}$)⸣*-šu mi-*[*iq-tum le-em-n*]*u*$^{!?}$*-um*
10'	⸢*ki-ma*$^{?}$⸣ *pi-it-n*[*im*] ⸢*ša*-x-*šu*⸣
11'	[x (x)] *ka-ra-*⸢*šu*$^{?}$⸣
12'	[*i*$^{?}$]*-ka-al ḫa-šu-*⸢*ta-am*$^{?}$⸣
13'	*ni-ra-am* [(x x)] ⸢x x⸣*-am*
14'	*ma-ḫi-iṣ* ⸢*mu*⸣*-uḫ-ḫi-i*[*m*]
15'	*mu-bi-il li-*[*iq pi-i*]*m*
16'	*ma-ḫi-iṣ bi-ir-ti a-ḫi-im*
17'	*mu-ra-am-mi ši-ir-ḫa-an a-ḫi-im*
18'	*e ta-am-ḫa-aṣ mu-uḫ-ḫa-a*[*m*]
19'	*e tu-ub-bi-il li-iq pi-i*[*m*]
20'	*e* ⸢*ta-am-ḫa*⸣*-aṣ bi-ir-ti a-ḫi-im*
21'	*e tu-ra-am-*⸢*mi*⸣ *ši-ir-ḫa-an a-ḫi-im*
22'	⸢*a*⸣*-li-ik* ⸢*e*$^{?}$⸣*-li-ma*
23'	[x] ⸢x x x⸣ [x] ⸢x x⸣ [x x(x)]
	(*broken*)

Translation

7'–8'	Black paste are its lips! Yellow-ochre paste is its face!
9'–11'	Its [*mouth*$^{?}$] is the [evi]l *mi*[*qtum*-disease]! Its … is like a *box*, *its … is …*
12'–13'	[It] is *eating ḫašūtum*-plant, a *yoke*$^{?}$ …, the ….
14'–15'	Who strikes the head, who scorches the palate,
16'–17'	Who strikes the middle of the arm, who paralyzes the sinew of the arm –
18'–19'	Do not strike the head, do not scorch the palate!
20'–21'	Do not strike the middle of the arm, do not paralyze the sinew of the arm!

22'–23' Go and *ascend* (*to*) …

Commentary

ii 7': *qit*[!]*-ma* (du. corresponding to *šaptāšu*), instead of *ag-ma* "angry", suggested by George (2016, 35). Our reading follows parellels in CT 44, 32(+)33t: 19''' (= № 50) and JCS 31, 218f. and CT 51, 142 (see, Geller 2016, 55: 16).

ii 9': For the mouth as the *miqtum*-disease, see YOS 11, 10: 4/7 (№ 60) and CT 44, 32(+)33t: iii 21''' (№ 50).

ii 12': Note the occurrence of the *ḫašūtum*-plant in BiOr 11 Pl. II (fig. 1): 1–2 (№ 65): *līkul uzzašu kīma ḫašūtim* "May he (i.e., the rabid dog) eat his anger like a *ḫašūtum*-plant!".

№ 52: CUSAS 32, 22a

SEAL No.: 7073
Copy: George 2016 Pl. LXVII
Tablet Siglum: MS 3105/1
Photo: George 2016 Pls. LXVI/LXVIII; CDLI P252114
Edition: –
Studies: –
Collection: Schøyen Collection, Oslo
Provenance: Unknown
Measurements: 15.0 × 13.0 cm
Procedure: No

Introduction
This incantation shares parallels with CT 42, 32 (№ 49) and Fs. Stol 150 (№ 53) and partly resembles the later series Sag.gig VII/a and *Muššuʾu* IV/a.

Obverse
i

(*broken*)
1' [*id-di šipat*(TU$_6$) ^{d}*Nin*]-*gìri*[*m*]
2' [*be-le-et*] *ši-pa-tim*
3' [*i-na šipti*(TU$_6$)-*ša*] *ma-ar-ṣum i-te/-eb-bi*
4' [*ú-ul ú-ša*]-{a}-*na-aḫ*
5' [*li-ir-ku-u*]*s-ka* ^{d}*Gu-la*
6' [*i-na ra-b*]*a-tim qá-ti-ša*
7' [x x x] ⸢*mar*$^{?}$-*tam*$^{?}$ *pa*$^{?}$⸣-*ši*$^{!}$(EŠ)-*tam ù di-ḫa-am*
8' [x x x] ⸢x⸣ ŠUB-*tam*
9' [DN] ^{d}*Núska* ^{d}*Nisaba*(ŠE.NAGA)
10' [^{d}*Šamaš*(UTU)$^{?}$ ^{d}*Nārum*(ÍD)$^{?}$] ^{d}*Ḫu-ur-sag*
11' [x x x *li-i*]*š*-⸢*ši*⸣-*pu-ka*
12' […] ⸢*eb*$^{?}$⸣-*bu-um*
13' […] ⸢kur⸣
14' […]
15' [… i]k$^{?}$
16' […] ⸢bi$^{?}$⸣ i ⸢ri$^{?}$⸣
17' […] ⸢x x x⸣
18' […] ⸢x⸣ ma
19' [… a]m$^{?}$
20' […] ⸢x x⸣
21' […] ir
22' […] ⸢x⸣ [(x)]-*Za-am*
23' […] ⸢x is$^{?}$⸣ ŠUB-*tam*
24' […]-*a-am*

25' [...]-⸢x⸣-*ni-tam*
26' [...] ⸢a/za⸣-*na-am*
27' [...](-)*bu-lum*
28' [...] ⸢x x x⸣
(*broken*)

Translation

(*broken*)
1'–2' [Nin]girim, [the lady of] incantations [cast a spell],
3'–4' [with her spell] the patients rises (again), [he suf]fers [no more].
5'–6' [May Gula bin]d you [with] her [so]ft hands!
7' [...], *murderous bile*? and the *diʾum*-disease,
8' [...] the *miqtum*-disease,
9'–11' [May DN] Nuska, Nisaba, [Šamaš, Nāru], Ḫursānu [... cu]re you with exorcism!
12'–28' (*too fragmentary for translation*)

Commentary

1'–6': Cf. CT 42, 32: 6–8 (№ 49).
9': CT 42, 32: 12 (№ 49) starts the list of gods with Adad, Šakkan, Nisaba.
10': Cf. a parallel list of deities in CT 42, 32: 12 (№ 49).
11': After Fs. Stol 150: 5 (№ 53). In CT 42, 32: 13 (№ 49) the verbal form is *li-il*$_5$*-li-lu-ka*.
22'–26': Probably another enumeration of diseases. In l. 23' ŠUB-*tam* "*miqtum*-disease". In l. 24' most likely [*a-ši*]-*a-am* "*ašû*-disease".

№ 53: Fs. Stol 150

SEAL No.: 7074
Copy: Geller/Wiggermann 2008, 150
Tablet Siglum: LB 1000
Photo: CDLI P355903 (obverse only)
Edition: Geller/Wiggermann 2008, 153–156
Studies: Böhl 1934; Böhl 1954; von Soden 1961, 71f. Cunningham 1997 Cat. No. 339; Stol 2000, 143 fn. 197; Wasserman 2003 Cat. No. 6; Zomer 2018a, 61 fn. 203/200/203/209.
Collection: Netherlands Institute for the Near East, Leiden
Provenance: Larsa
Measurements: –
Procedure: No

Introduction
As CT 42, 32 (№ 49), this incantation is also echoed in the later series (Sag.gig VII/a and *Muššuʾu* IV/a), see Zomer (2018a, 200).

Obverse
1 *li-id-di-kum É-a ši-pa-at ba-la-ṭim*
2 *i-na pī*(KA) ^{d}*Nu-dim-mu-ud ù* ^{d}*Nu-nam-nir / e tu-uš-ta-ne-eḫ*
3 *li-iṣ-mi-id-ka* ^{d}*Nin-kar-ra-ak / i-na ra-ab-ba-tim qá-ti-ša*
4 ^{d}*Da-mu li-is-sú-uḫ di-a-am ù a-ši*$^{!}$(DI)*-a-am /*
ša zu-um-ri-ka
5 ^{d}*Adad*(IŠKUR) ^{d}*Šákkan* ^{d}*Nārum*(ÍD) ^{d}*Šamaš*(UTU) *ù Ḫu-ur-sa-nu / i-lu qá-aš-du-tum*
ka-lu-šu-nu ša ša-di-im li-iš-ši-pu-ka
6 *el-lu-tum I-gi-gu li-il-il-lu-ka*
7 *Ma-šum ù Ma-aš-tum mārū*(DUMU^{meš}) ^{d}*Sîn*(EN.ZU) */ La-ma-aš-tam mar-tam pa-ši-it-tam /* ⸢*ek-ke-em*⸣*-tam sí-ik-ka-tam i-ša-tam /*
⸢*mi-iq-tam*⸣ *ša-na-dam šu-ru-up-pa-am a-sa-ak-kam / a-ia ú-ṭe*$_{4}$*-eḫ-ḫu-ú a-na ši-im-ti-ka*
8 *a-ia iṭ-ḫi-kum eb-be-tum ša-ga-aš-tum*
9 *a-ia i-še-er mu-uš-ta-ab-ba-ab-bu-um / i-na mu-uḫ-ḫi-ka ša ‹ki-ma› mé-ḫe-e-em / i-zi-qá-am ša-ru-um le-em-nu-um*
10 *ši-ib-bu mu-ur-ṣum mu-ru-uṣ li-ib-bi-im / ki-is li-ib-im /*
di-iʾ qá-aq-qá-di-im / mu-ru-uṣ zu-um-ri-im

Reverse
11 ^{d}*Nanše šar-ra-at a-gi-i-im / a-ia ú-ṭa-aḫ-ḫi-a-ak-kum /*
a-na zu-um-ri-ka
12 *mi-nam ša-at-ti-ša-am ma-aḫ-ṣum ku-ub-bu-súm ṭe*$_{4}$*-bi-kum /*
ù la li-ib-bi i-la e-li-ka ib-ši
13 *e-*⸢x⸣-[x (x) *mi-i*]*m-ma bu-un-na-ne-e qá-ti-ka*
14 *e-*⸢x⸣-[x (x) *i-l*]*a-at a-bi-šu* [*š*]*a tu-ul-di-šu*

15 *Ištar um-mi-šu ba-ni-at i-la-tim*
16 *i-li ḫa-li-šu re-mé-nu-um e-ṭe*$_4$*-er-šu / i-na pu-uš-qí-im*
17 *er-ra-am ṣa-ap-ra-am re-eš ku-uk / li-ib-bi-im*
18 *is-sú* ^{d}*Nin-kar-ra-ak*
19 *ú-ba-li-iṭ* DINGIR DIN.NA
20 tu-in-ne-nu-ri
21 *ši-ip-tum an-ni-tum ú-ul i-ia-at-tum*
22 *ši-pa-at* ^{d}*Asal-lú-ḫi mār*(DUMU) *É-a / ša Eridu*^{ki}

Translation

1–2 Let Ea cast for you a spell of life and by the command of Nudimmud and Nunamnir, you shall weary not more.
3 Let Ninkarrak compress you with her hands so gentle,
4 Let Damu remove the migraine (*diʾum*-disease) and headache (*ašû*-disease) of your body!
5–6 May Adad, Šakkan, Nāru, Šamaš, and Ḫursānu, all the holy gods of the steppe, cure you with exorcism! May the pure Igigū purify you!
7 May the twin-brother and twin-sister, children of Sîn, prevent Lamaštu, the murderous bile, the Snatcher, pox, fever, falling, *šanadum*-disease, shivering, the *asakku*-disease from bringing (you) to your destiny!
8 May the bright slaughter-demoness not approach you!
9 May the Flasher not come straight at you, he who blows (against you) ‹like› a storm, the evil wind!
10 As for the *šibbu*-disease, illness, internal illness, heart attack, headache, or (any other) physical illness –
11 may Nanše, the crowned queen, not let (them) approach your body!
12 Why has (someone) who is yearly stricken and trodden upon risen (suddenly) against you, and (a person) rejected by (his) god appeared (before you)?
13 … [an]y features (created by) your hand!
14–18 … [the god]dess of his father who gave him birth, the goddess of his mother, the *creatrix* of his kinfolk, the merciful god of his uncle who keeps him out of trouble, have driven away the 'pressed gut', the top of the stomach,
18–19 Ninkarrak cured him, the goddess of life.
20 tu-in-ne-nu-ri
21–22 The incantation is not mine; it is the incantation of Asalluhi, the son of Ea of Eridu.

Commentary

11: We take *agûm* in *Nanše šarrat agîm* to denote "crown", not waves. The same epithet is used for Ningišzida in UET 6/2, 395: 5/7/11.

12–16: After listing many demons and diseases, the text moves to the social sphere. Note the wordplay *iltum* (*ilat abīšu*) vs. *illatum* (*bāniat illatim*).

13–14: Geller/Wiggerman (2008, 154) restitute *e-n*[*i-iš*] at the beginning of this couplet ("Weakened is whatever you have created, ‹O god of his clan›, weakened is the one you gave birth to, Oh goddess of his father"), but the result is syntactically difficult and the meaning unclear to us.

17: For *ku-uk libbim*, see Geller/Wiggerman (2008, 156).

№ 54: JCS 9, 9

SEAL No.: 7075
Copy: Goetze 1955, 9
Tablet Siglum: Spurlock Museum 1913.14.1465 (previously: UIOM 1059)
Photo: CDLI P274661
Edition: Goetze 1955, 8–11
Studies: Farber 1990b; Stol 1993, 11f.; Cunningham 1997 Cat. No. 351; Wasserman 2003 Cat. No. 76; Foster 2005, 177f.; Wasserman 2007; Zomer 2018a, 201/203; Zomer 2021, 166
Collection: Spurlock Museum, University of Illinois at Urbana-Champaign
Provenance: Larsa$^{?}$ or Babylon$^{?}$
Measurements: 8.5 × 4.5 cm
Procedure: No

Introduction
An incantation describing diseases coming down from heaven (see Wasserman 2007 and Zomer 2021) with the *mannam lušpur* formula.

1 *[sí-ik-ka-tum i-š]a-tum*
2 *a-[šu-ú-um z]i-iq-tum*
3 *⸢mi-iq-tum⸣ ṣé-nu*
4 *ša-ma-gu sa-ma-nu*
5 *ge-er-gi-šu ṣe-ni-tum*
6 *sí-mu ma-at-qum e-ke-tum*
7 *ri-ši-tum ni-ṭù*
8 *šu-ru-pu-ú ša-ag-ba-nu*
9 *ù ša-ša-ṭù*
10 *iš-tu zi-qú-ra-at ša-me-e ur-du-ni*
11 *úḫ-ta-mi-iṭ i-me-ri ka-lu-mi*
12 *uḫ-ta-di-‹ir$^{?}$/ru$^{?}$› ṣú-ḫa-re-e i-na bu-ud ta-ri-tim*
13 *ma-an-na lu-‹uš›-pu-ur ù lu-wa-ir*
14 *a-na ma-ra-at A-ni* 7 *ù* 7
15 *ša ka-nu-ši-na ḫurāṣum*(KÙ.GI) *ka-‹ar›-pa-tu-ši-na*
16 *uq-nu-ú el-lu*
17 *li-‹il›-qí-a-ni ka-ni-ši-na ša ḫuraṣim*(KÙ.GI)
18 *ka-‹ar›-pa-ti-ši-na ša uq-ni e[l-li]*
19 *li-sà-ba-ni me-e ta-⸢me⸣-[tim] e-lu-ti*

Reverse
20 *li-is-lu-ḫa li-bé-le-e*
21 *sí-ik-ka-tam i-ša-tam*
22 *a-ša-a zi-iq-ta*
23 *mi-iq-ta ṣé-na*

24 *ša*$_{4}$*-ma-ga-am sa-ma-na*
25 *ge-er-gi-ša ṣé-er-ni-tam*
26 *sí-ma ma-at-qá-a*
27 *e-ke-tam ri-ši-tam*
28 *ni-ṭa šu-ru-pa-a*
29 *ša-ag-ba-na ù ša-ša-ṭa*
30 *tu-tu ellu*(KÙ) *ša* ^{d}*Da-mu ù* ^{d}*Nin-ni-ka-ra-ak*
31 *ši-ip-tum ú-ul ia-a-tum*
32 *ši-pa-at* ^{d}*Ni-gi-ri-ma*
33 ^{d}*En-ki* ^{d}*A-sa-lú-ḫi*
34 *ša Ni-gi-ri-ma i-du-ma*
35 [*a-na-k*]*u el-qú-ú*

Translation

1–9 [The *sikkatum*-disease (pox), fe]ver, the *ašûm*-disease, the *ziqtum*-disease, bad collapse, the *šamagu*-disease, the *samānu*-disease, the *gergiššu*-disease (skin disease), the *ṣennettum*-disease (leprosy$^{?}$), the sweet *simmu*-disease, the *ekketum*-disease (scabies$^{?}$), the *rišītum*-disease (redness), bloody faeces, shivering, the *šagbānu*-disease and the *šaššaṭu*-disease (joint sickness$^{?}$)

10–12 came down from the ziggurat of heaven, burned up the sheep, the lambs, caused the children on the shoulders of the nurse to be sombre.

13–16 Whom should I send and assign to the Daughters of Anum, seven and seven, whose vessels are gold, their jars pure lapis-lazuli?

17–18 Let them take for me their vessels of gold, their jars of pure lapis-lazuli!

19–29 Let them draw for me pure water of the se[as]! Let them sprinkle (and) let them extinguish the *sikkatum*-disease, fever, the *ašû*-disease, the *ziqtu*-disease, bad collapse, the *šamagum*-disease, the *samānu*-disease, the *gergiššum*-disease, the *sernettum*-disease, the sweet *simmu*-disease, the *ekketum*-disease, the *rišītum*-disease, the bloody faeces, shivering, the *šagbānu*-disease, the *šaššaṭu*-disease!

30 A pure spell of Damu and Ninkarrak.

31–35 The incantation is not mine, it is the incantation of Ningirim, Enki (and) Asalluḫi, which Ningirim has cast and [I] received it!

Commentary

10: For the cosmological meaning of *ziqqurrat* of heaven, see Zomer (2021, 183f.).

13–20: A complete example of the *mannam lušpur* motif see (Farber 1990b).

№ 55: JCS 9, 10

SEAL No.: 7076
Copy: Goetze 1955, 10
Tablet Siglum: AUAM 73.3092
Photo: CDLI P249272
Edition: Goetze 1955, 8–11
Studies: Farber 1990b; Cunningham 1997 Cat. No. 352; Wasserman 2003 Cat. No. 77; Foster 2005, 177f.; Stol 2007; Wasserman 2007; Zomer 2018a, 201/203; Zomer 2021, 168f.
Collection: Siegfried H. Horn Museum, Institute of Archaeology, Andrews University, Berrien Springs, Michigan
Provenance: Unknown
Measurements: 2.8 × 6.2 cm
Procedure: No

Introduction
Diseases descending from heaven. A truncated *mannam lušpur* formula. Unusually, Šamaš is called upon for help.

Obverse
1 *sí-ka-tum i-ša-a-tum*
2 *a-šu zi-iq-tum mi-iq-tum*
3 *ša-na-du ⸢sa-ma⸣-nu-um*
4 *[ge$_4$]-er-gi$_4$-šu sí-mu ma-at-qú*
5 *[e-ke]-tum ri-šu-tum*
6 *[ni]-ṭù-um ṣé-nu-um ṣí-i-tum*
7 *[ša]-ag-ba-nu ša-wi-nu-um*
8 *[šu]-ru-pu-um le-e-em-nu-um*
9 *[e-p]e-e-qé-nu ù [bu-š]a-nu-um*
10 *[iš]-tu ṣé-re-et [š]a-me-e*
11 *ur-du-ni uḫ-ta-mi-⸢ṭù⸣*
12 *i-mé-ri ka-lu-mi*
13 *uḫ-ta-mi-ṭù ṣé-ḫe-ru-tim ⸢i-na⸣ bu-ud ta-ri-tim*
14 šà$^?$ el *li-su-ni*$^?$ *mārat* (DUMU.‹MUNUS$^?$›) *Anim*(AN.NA) 7 *ù* 7
15 *ša ka-nu-ši-na ša ḫurāṣim*(KÙ.GI)
16 *ka-ar-pa-tu-ši-na uq-nu el-lu ‹‹li-sà››*
17 *⸢li⸣-sà-ba-ni me-e ti-ma*$^!$*-ti*
18 *li-is-lu-ḫa li-ba-li-a*
19 *[sí-k]a-ta i-ša-ta*

Reverse
20 *⸢a-ši⸣-a zi-iq-ta mi-i[q-ta]*
21 *ša-na-da sa-ma-na*
22 *ge$_4$-er-gi$_4$-ša sí-ma ma-at-qá*

23 *e-ke-e-ta ri-šu-ta-am*
24 *ni-ṭa-am ṣé-na-am ṣi-i-ta-am*
25 *ša-ag-ba-na ša-wi-na-am*
26 *šu-ru-pa-am le-em-na-*⸢*am*⸣
27 *e-pe-qé-na-am ù bu-ša-na-*[*am*]
28 [*ú-t*]*a-mi-ka* ^{d}*Šamaš*(UTU) *qú-r*[*a*]*-da*
29 [^{d}*Šamaš*(UTU)$^{?}$] *ú*$^{?}$*-sà-la i-la da-*⸢*a*⸣*-a-na*
30 [*a-na*] *ṣi-ib-t*[*i*]*-ka*
31 [*li*]*-tu-ru-ú-ma*
32 [*ga-a*]*m-la-a-ti bu-*⸢*li*⸣*-sú*
33 [*a-n*]*a-ku ši-ip-ta lu-ú-di*

Translation

1–11 The *sikkatum*-disease (pox), fever, the *ašû*-disease, the *ziqtum*-disease, collapse, the *šanadu*-disease, the *samānum*-disease, the [*ge*]*rgiššu*-disease (a skin-disease), the sweet *simmu*-disease, the [*ekke*]*tum*-disease (scabies$^{?}$), the *rišûtum*-disease (redness), evil [blo]ody faeces, sun-heat, the *šagbānu*-disease, the *šawinum*-disease, bad shivering, the *epeqēnu*-disease (skin disease) and the *bušānum*-disease (bad smell) descended from the leading rope of heaven!

11–13 They burned up the sheep, the lambs, burned up the small ones on the shoulders of the nurse.

14–16 *May the summon here*… Daughters of Anum, seven and seven, whose vessels are of gold, their jars pure lapis-lazuli?

17–27 Let them draw for me pure water of the seas, let them sprinkle, let them extinguish [the *sikk*]*atu*-disease, the fever, the *ašû*-disease, the *ziqtu*-disease, coll[apse], the *šanadu*-disease, the *samānu*-disease, the *gergiššu*-disease, the sweet *simmu*-disease, the *ekketu*-disease, the *rišûtum*-disease, the evil bloody faeces, sun-heat, the *šagbānu*-disease, the *šawinum*-disease, bad shivering, the *epeqēnum*-disease and the *bušānum*-disease!

28 [I] conjure you (sg.), by Šamaš the hero!

29–31 I beseech (you) [Šamaš] the divine judge! [To] your hold [may] they (the diseases) return!

32 You are [mer]ciful, so make him recover!

34 [As for] me – let me cast the spell!

Commentary

6: For *ṣē/ītum* "sun-heat", see Stol (2007, 22–39).

8: For *šuruppû* "shivering, fever", see Stol (2007, 19).

10: For *ṣerretu* "leading rope" (and not *ṣertu* "udder"), see Horrowitz (1998, 262f. and 265). On the use of *ṭurru* "string" in MB incantations as a parallel to *ṣerretu* "leading rope", see Zomer (2021, 181f.).

14: Corrupt text for the *mannam lušpur* formula (with Farber 1990b, 307, so already Goetze 1955, 14, fn. 42).

17: *ti-ma*$^{!}$*-ti* may be sg. or pl.

28: Note the unexpected sg. *-ka*.

29: *ú*[?]*-sà-la* is tentatively derived from *sullûm*.

32: For the stative *gamlāti* with *-āti*, less common in OB (but normal in OA), see Kouwenberg (2017, 488). Cf. CUSAS 32, 30d: 26 (№ 92).

№ 56: RA 88, 161c

SEAL No.: 7077
Copy: Cavigneaux 1994, 161
Tablet Siglum: M. 15289
Photo: –
Edition: Cavigneaux 1994, 156f.
Studies: Wasserman 2003 Cat. No. 144; Wasserman 2007; Zomer 2018a, 201 fn. 770; Zomer 2021, 166
Collection: Deir ez-Zor Museum
Provenance: Mari
Measurements: –
Procedure: No

Introduction

Incantation collective on a landscape-oriented tablet, which also contains an Akkadian incantation against a scorpion (ll. 1–r. 4' = № 97) and an alloglot incantation against an unknown agent (ll. r. 5'–9'). An imperfect *mannam lušpur* formula seals the text.

Reverse

10' *sí-ka-tum i-ša-tum mí-iq-tum ša-an-a-du-um a*$^{?}$*-šu*$^{?}$ / *ù ša-ma-nu-um*
11' *i-na zu-qú-ra-an ša-me-e ur-da-ma*
12' *im-qú-ut sí-ka-tum in-na-pí-iḫ i-sa*$^{?}$*-t*[*um*]
13' ‹*i*$^{?}$›*-ta-ku-ul i-ma-ra ka-lu*$^{!}$*-ma-am* / *ù ṣú-ḫa-ra-am i-li-im*$^{?}$*-mi*$^{?}$

Left Edge

14' *qú-tu-úr bu-lu-um la* i ta wi ⸢*ú*⸣ [...]
15' *ma-na-am lu-uš-pu-úr a-na* ^{d}*N*[*in*$^{?}$-...]
16' *li-di*$^{?}$*-na k*[*a-ar*]*-pa-at bu-l*[*i*...] [(x)] *ù*$^{?}$ *ba-la-*[*ṭi*$^{?}$...]

Translation

10'–11' The *sikkatum*-disease (pox), fever, falling, the *šanudû*-disease, the *ašûm*-disease, the *šamānum*-disease descended from the *height*$^{?}$ of heaven.
12' The *sikkatum*-disease (pox) has fallen down, fever had been ignited,
13' has *devoured* the sheep, the lamb, and *encircled*$^{?}$ the child.
14' The herd is gloomy, not [...]
15'–16' "Whom should I send to Nin[...], so that they will give$^{?}$ *extinguishing* jars ... and of well-[being]?"

Commentary

10'/12': For the list of diseases, see Stol (1993, 11f.) and Wasserman (2007). Note the š / s alternations: *šamānum* for *samānum*, and *isātum* for *išātum*. For the *sāmānu*-disease, see Finkel (1998) and Kinnier-Wilson (1994).

11': *zuq(q)urān šamê* is otherwise not attested. Each of the parallel texts read differently. YOS 11, 8: 5 (№ 58) has *kakkab šamê*; JCS 9, 9: 10 (№ 54) reads *ziqqurāt šamê*; and JCS 9, 10: 10 (№ 55) *ṣerret šamê*. For these heaven-related historiolae, see Zomer (2021).

13': *‹i?›-ta-ku-ul* following Cavigneaux. As for *ṣú-ḫa-ra-am i-li-im?-mi?* at the end of the line, parallel texts suggest prepositional phrase ("on the shoulders of the nurse", etc.) rather than another verb.

№ 57: Semitica 61, 13f.

SEAL No.: 26467
Copy: –
Tablet Siglum: CUNES 48–06–263
Photo: Guichard 2019, 13f.
Edition: Guichard 2019, 8–12
Studies: Zomer 2021, 165f.
Collection: Cornell University Collection, Ithaca
Provenance: Larsa area
Measurements: –
Procedure: No

Introduction

Here too, diseases descend from heaven and the *mannam lušpur* formula appear. Note the unusual orthography: /šúm/ for šum and /lú/ for lu.

Obverse

1 *ša-⸢mu⸣-um a-šu-um*
2 *mi-iq-tum na-ša-du*
3 *i-ša-tum sa-ma-nu-um*
4 *sí-kà-tum gi-ir-gi-šúm*
5 *up-ta-ḫa-ḫi-⸢ru⸣-ni-im-ma*
6 *iš-tu ša-me-im*
7 *ur-⸢du-ni-im⸣*
8 *⸢i-ku*$^{?}$*⸣-um na-ba-lu*
9 *uḫ-ta-mi-iṭ*
10 *im-me-ri-i*
11 *ṣú-ḫa-ri-i*

Reverse

12 *ma-na-am lú-uš-pu-/ur*
13 *⸢a⸣-na ma-ra-at*
14 *A-ni-im ša kà-ar-pa-tu-/ši-na*
15 *sí-⸢pa⸣-ru-ú*
16 *⸢ù*$^{?}$ *kà-nu-ši-na uqnû*(ZA.GÌN⸣-*nu*) *me el-/‹lu-ti›-⸢im⸣*
17 *li-sà-ba-ni-im*
18 *me-e ti-me-tim*
19 *el-lu-tim*
20 *lu as-pu-u[ḫ*$^{?}$ *sí]-kà-tum / i-⸢ta⸣-ba-al*
21 *ša-mu-um li-mu-ut i-na / iš-ri-šu*
22 *i-ša-tum li-ta-la-ak*
23 *a-na ša-di-ša* ‹‹diš››

Translation

1 The *šam(m)um*-disease, the *ašûm*-disease,
2 *miqtum*-disease, *šanadu*[!]-disease (text: *na-ša-du*)
3 *išātum*-disease, *sāmānum*-disease,
4 *sikkatum*-disease (pox), *gergiššum*-disease
5–7 gathered and descended from heaven.
8 The cultivated land is arid land!
9–11 It (i.e., the disease) burned up the sheep and little ones.
12–15 Whom should I send to the Daughters of Anum, whose vessels are bronze
16–17 and whose jars are lapis lazuli? May they draw for me pure water!
18–20 Verily I dispersed the water of the seas (and) the *sikkatum*-disease (pox) will disappear!
21 May the *šam(m)um*-disease die in its place (of origin)!
22–23 May the *išātum*-disease go back to its mountains!

Commentary

5: Following Guichard (2019, 9), the verbal form *up-ta-ḫa-ḫi-*⸢*ru*⸣*-ni-im-ma* can be explained as a Dtr of *paḫārum* (see Kouwenberg 2010, 440).

15: Note that the Daughters of Anum here carry bronze vessels, whereas in all the parallels the vessels are made of gold.

№ 58: YOS 11, 8

SEAL No.: 7078
Copy: van Dijk/Goetze/Hussey 1985 Pl. IX
Tablet Siglum: NBC 6321
Photo: CDLI P289353; cf. SEAL No. 7078
Edition: Goetze 1955, 11
Studies: Farber 1990b, 307f.; Wasserman 2003 Cat. No. 233; Foster 2005, 177f.; Wasserman 2007; Zomer 2018a, 201; Zomer 2021, 169
Collection: Yale Babylonian Collection, New Haven
Provenance: Larsa area
Measurements: 6.0 × 8.7 cm
Procedure: No

Introduction
Having descended from heaven and darkening the patients' countenance, the diseases are ordered to go back like smoke and cloud. With the typical *mannam lušpur* formula.

Obverse
1 *sí-ka-tum i-ša-tum mi-iq-tum ša-nu-du-ú*
2 *a-šu-ú-um sa-ma-nu-ú-um*
3 *e-ep-qé-nu ša-la-at-ti-nu-um*
4 *ù gi-ir-gi-iš-šu-um*
5 *iš-tu kakkab*(MUL) *ša-me-e ur-du-nim*
6 *an-na-nu-um er-ṣe-tum šu-nu-ti im-ḫu-ur*
7 *ti-bi gi-ir-gi-iš-šum la ta-ra-ab-*⸢*bí-iṣ*⸣
8 *ki-ma qù-ut-ri-i*[*m*] *e-l*[*i*] *š*[*a*]*-ma-n*[*i*$^{?}$]
9 *ki-ma ib-b*[*a-ri-im* x x x]

Reverse
10 *tu-uš-ta-aḫ-di-ir bu-*[*ul ṣe-ri-im*]
11 *ka-lu-mé-e ṣe-eḫ-ra-am i-na b*[*u-ud*] *ta-ri-tim*
12 *ma-an-na-am lu-uš-pu-ur a-na ma-ar-ti A-*[*ni*]*-im*
13 *li-bé-el-lu-nim*
14 *sí-ik-ka-tam i-ša-tam mi-iq-tam ša-nu-du*
15 *a-šu-ú-um sa-ma-nu-ú-um*
16 *e-ep-qé-nu ša-la-at-ti-nu-um*
17 *ù gi-ir-gi-iš-šum*
18 tu-ú-en-nu-nu-ru

Translation
1–6 The *sikkatum*-disease (pox), fever, falling, the *šanudû*-disease, the *ašûm*-disease, the *samānum*-disease, the *epqēnum*-disease, the *šalattinum*-disease, and the *girgiššum*-disease have descended from the star of heaven – here the earth has received them.

7 Rise *girgiššum*-disease, do not lie down!

8–9 Ascend to heaven like smoke, like a cloud [...].

10–11 You have caused the herds of the field, the lambs, the child on the shoulders of the nurse to be entirely dark.

12–13 "Whom should I send to the Daughters of Anum so that they will put out

14–17 the *sikkatum*-disease (pox), fever, falling, the *šanudû*-disease, the *ašûm*-disease, the *samānum*-disease, the *epqēnum*-disease, the *šalattinum*-disease, and the *girgiššum*-disease?"

18 tu-ú-en-nu-nu-ru

Commentary

1–4: For the list of diseases, see Stol (1993, 11f.) and Wasserman (2007). On the *sāmānu*-disease, see Finkel (1998) and Kinnier-Wilson (1994).

6: *annānum erṣetum šunūti imḫur*: the independent acc. pronoun (rather than the expected attached acc. pron.) emphasizes that the earth has received these diseases (and not others).

8: *ki-ma qù-ut-ri-i*[*m*] *e-l*[*i*] *š*[*a*]*-ma-n*[*i*$^{?}$]: with Farber's coll. in van Dijk/Goetze/Hussey 1985, 61 (CAD Q, 326d, differently). For the suffix *-āni* with the terminative function, see Wasserman (2003, 116 fn. 105).

9: Restoration following CAD I/J 107.

10: *tu-uš-ta-aḫ-di-ir*: The parallel text RA 88, 161c: 14' (№ 56) has *qú-tu-úr bu-lu-um* and YOS 11, 7: 10 (№ 44) has *bu-lu-um li-wi-ru pa-nu-š*[*u*$^{!}$], which prove that (*ḫ*)*adārum* Štn means "to darken" (not "to cause unrest, fear", as suggested by AHw, 11b "immer wieder in Furcht setzen"). So also in JCS 9, 9a: 12 (№ 54).

11: *b*[*u-ud*] *ta-ri-tim* (with JCS 9, 9: 12) follows AHw, 1330, 1a. Note that CAD P, 550b, 4a and CAD T, 232b, 1a understand *ina pūt* as prepositional phrase.

14–17: The first two diseases are in the acc., depending on the verb *li-bé-el-lu-nim* (l. 13), while the rest of enumerated diseases are in the nom., mirroring the list at the beginning of the incantation.

№ 59: YOS 11, 9a

SEAL No.: 7079
Copy: van Dijk/Goetze/Hussey 1985 Pl. X
Tablet Siglum: YBC 5619
Photo: https://collections.peabody.yale.edu/search/Record/YPM-BC-019684
Edition: –
Studies: Cunningham 1997 Cat. No. 380; Finkel 1998, 85; Wasserman 2003 Cat. No. 234; Wasserman 2007; Zomer 2021, 182 fn. 21
Collection: Yale Babylonian Collection, New Haven
Provenance: Larsa area
Measurements: 5.5 × 7.0 cm
Procedure: Yes

Introduction

The reverse of the tablet contains a Sumerian incantation against the *samānum*-disease, see Finkel (1998, 85). The *samānum*-disease is mentioned, among other diseases, in l. 2 and in the procedure in l. 9.

Obverse

1 *sí-ka-tum i-ša-tum mi-iq-tum bé*-[*nu-um*]
2 *šu-ru-up-pu-ú-um ù sa-ma-nu*-[*um*]
3 *iš*$^{?}$*-tu*$_{4}$ *kakkabim*(MUL$^{!}$) {x$^{?}$} *ur-da an-n*[*a*$^{?}$*-nu-um*]
4 NÍG.GU$_{7}$$^{!?}$ NU.TUKU ⸢x x x x⸣
5 ⸢x x⸣ ^{d}*Šamaš*(UTU)
6 ⸢x x x x⸣ ^{d}*En-ki* ^{d}[…]
7 t[u$_{6}$]-én-é-nu-[ru]

====

8 ka-inim-ma *ni-ip-šum* ⸢di$^{?}$ nam$^{?}$ x⸣ [x (x)]
9 ⸢*sa*⸣*-ma-nu-um* ^{ú}BÁPPIR ⸢x⸣

Translation

1–4 The *sikkatum*-disease (pox), fever, falling, epilepsy, shivering, and the *samānum*-disease from a star it came down.
4 He[re] (on earth) it has nothing to eat …
5 … Šamaš
6 … Enki D[N…]
7 t[u$_{6}$]-én-é-nu-[ru]

====

8 Incantation *against a (foul) smell*, …
9 The *samānum*-plant, beer-bread, …

Commentary

3: Tentative reading based on YOS 11, 8: 5–6 (№ 58).

4/6: The signs are unintelligible on the photo and they do not correspond with the copy.

№ 60: YOS 11, 10

SEAL No.: 7080
Copy: van Dijk/Goetze/Hussey 1985 Pl. XI
Tablet Siglum: YBC 1970
Photo: cf. SEAL No. 7080
Edition: –
Studies: Cunningham 1997 Cat. No. 382; Stol 1998, 348; Wasserman 2003 Cat. No. 235; Wasserman 2007, 44f.; Geller 2016, 55
Collection: Yale Babylonian Collection, New Haven
Provenance: Larsa area
Measurements: 7.9 × 4.9 cm
Procedure: No

Introduction

Partially parallels CUSAS 32, 7e (№ 51) and contains an abbreviated version of CT 44, 32(+)33t (№ 50).

1 *[qitmā]*
2 *[š]a-ap-ta-š[u-ú]*
3 *[ka]-lu-ú pa-nu-šu-ú*
4 *[kišāssu*(GÚ$^{?}$].BI) *mi-ra-ḫu-um pīšu*(KA-*šu*-⸢*ú*⸣)
5 *[m]i-iq-tum a-ta-al-lu-*⸢*ku*⸣
6 *[ḫ]u-ur-ba-*⸢*šu*⸣*-ú*
7 *pīšu*(KA-*šu-ú*) *mi-iq-tum*
8 *šu-ru-pu-um bu-da-šu*
9 *[u]l*$^{!?}$*-da-šu-ú šu-pu-ul-ma*
10 *um-ma-a-šu mu-*⸢*wa*⸣*-‹li›-tum*
11 *[i]š-ta-ka-a[n] i-ṣi-ri-im*
12 *[a-š]a-ma-*⸢*ša*⸣*-t[u*$^{?}$*]* ⸢*i-li*⸣*-ba-l[i-im]*
13 *i[š*$^{?}$*]-ta-ka-an tu-qú-um-ta*

====

Rest of obverse and reverse too damaged

Translation

1–3 [Black paste] are its lips! Yellow-ochre paste is its face!
4–5 Its [neck] is a little snake! Its mouth is the *miqtum*-disease!
5–7 (Its) roaming is terror! Its mouth is the *miqtum*-disease!
8 Frost are its shoulders!
9–10 (Even) its mother, the one who delivered (it), bore it in the depths!
11–12 In the steppe it keeps forming dust storms!
12–13 In the centre of town it keeps forming a battle!

Commentary

1–3: Restored after CT 51, 142: 16–17; CT 44, 33 iii: 10'–13' and JCS 31, 218: 16–17. – For *qitmum*, "black paste" and *kalûm*, "yellow-ochre paste", see Stol (1998, 347f.). Cf. CUSAS 32, 7e: ii 7' (№ 51): *ag-ma ša-ap-ta-šu.*

10: *mu-*⸢*wa*⸣*-‹li›-tum* follows *a-lit-ti* of its later parallel CT 51, 142: 19. Note that the other parallel JCS 31, 218f.: 20 reads here *a-ši-im-tu*$_4$.

12: ⸢*i-li*⸣*-ba-l*[*i-im*] follows Geller (2016, 55): *ina libbi ālim* in later parallels.

2.2 Animals

2.2.1 Dogs

Akkadian magic took a great interest in dogs. As one would expect, rabid dogs were a chief concern of ancient Mesopotamian healers (and even lawmakers, cf. Laws of Ešnunna § 56). Mesopotamians were well aware that rabies was caused by a dog bite and regarded rabid dogs as carrying the disease in their saliva, seen as semen. A sick dog was, as the incantations have it, producing puppies, i.e., spreading rabies, through biting.

But even healthy dogs, most likely wild or semi-wild, were considered a threat (see Sibbing Plantholt 2017), and incantations to fence them in are found (e.g., PIHANS 44 No. 302 = № 72 and ZA 71, 62c = № 75). Common to such incantations is the description of the main physical features of the dog, using Tamyīz constructions (Wasserman 2003 29–43, esp. 33f.), as, e.g., *uggur šēpīn aruḫ lasāmam bubūtam mād etniš akālam* "Twisted of leg, quick of running, great of hunger, very weak by (lack of) food" (OECT 11, 4: 1–4 = № 71). These descriptions are similar, but not identical, suggesting that this magic tradition had an oral background.

Interestingly, dogs in incantations are occasionally referred to by their nicknames: in ZA 71, 62c: 15 (№ 75) we find *Errēšûm* "Nagging" and *Našpûm* "Noisy", and in YOS 11, 5b: 10 (№ 114), an incantation against worms, the healing goddess Gula is accompanied by two dogs (= leeches?) called *Suppû* "Supplication(s)" and *Ṣūḫum* "Laughter" (Wasserman 2008, 81f.). Descriptive names of dogs are found in other literatures as well. In the Dog stela of Antef II (d. 2069; the 11th dynasty), the Pharaoh is depicted surrounded by five of his dogs, their names (probably of foreign origin) indicated.[238] Three of the names are understood: 'Gazelle', 'Black-one', 'Cooking-pot' (i.e., gluttonous). In Classical Greek literature, many dogs are named. The most famous is *Argos*, Odysseus' old hound who dies after seeing his master return home (Odys. 17: 290–327).[239] A long list of dog names is found in Ovid's Metamorphoses 3: 206–252. Actaeon, having seen the goddess Diana bathing in her nakedness, is turned by the furious goddess into a deer. He is pursued and killed by his own hounds, whose names are fully catalogued: "First 'Black-foot', Melampus, and keen-scented Ichnobates, 'Tracker', signal him with baying, Ichnobates out of Crete, Melampus, Sparta. Then others rush at him swift as the wind, 'Greedy', Pamphagus, Dorceus, 'Gazelle', Oribasos, 'Mountaineer', all out of Arcady: powerful 'Deerslayer', Nebrophonos, savage Theron, 'Whirlwind', and Laelape, 'Hunter' …".[240]

First millennium Akkadian rituals show a different tradition: elaborate and artificial dog names which tell of their function in the ritual. The standardized series of Lamaštu lists seven figurines of dogs that had to be placed in the house with the apotropaic purpose of guarding against the demoness: *Šaruḫ-tībušu* "Fast-is-his-attack", *Uṣur-mūša-ṭurud-Mārat-Anu*

238 Their names are apparently not Egyptian, but of foreign origin, probably early Berber, see Kossmann 2011.

239 More on dogs' names in Classical sources, see Ch. Hünemörder, "Dog", in: Brill's New Pauly: http://dx.doi.org/10.1163/1574-9347_bnp_e518400 (last visited 4 October 2020).

240 See http://ovid.lib.virginia.edu/trans/Metamorph3.htm#476975707 (last visited 22 July 2019).

"Watch-(all)-night, fend-off-the-Daughter-of-Anu!", *Urruḫ-tībušu* "Very-swift-is-his-attack", *Ana-maṣṣartika-lā-teggi* "Don't-be-negligent-in-your-watchfulness", *Ē-tamtal(l)ik-epuš-pīka* "Without-hesitation-use-your-muzzle!", *Sikip-lemna* "Overthrow-the-wicked-one!" and *Sîn-rēʾi-kalbī* "Sîn-is-the-herdsman-of-the-dogs" (Farber 2014, 170f.: 75–82; see discussion in Farber 2007a). More names of apotropaic dogs are known from written rituals and actual figurines: *Mušēṣû-lemuttim* "Expeller-of-evil", *Mušēribu-damqāti* "Bringer-of-good-things", *Kāšid-ayyābi* "Defeater-of-the-enemy", *Munaššiku-gārêšu* "Biter-of his-opponent", *Dan-rigimšu* "His-shout-is-strong", *Ē-tamtal(l)ik-ušuk* "Bite-without-hesitation!", *Aruḫ-napištašu* "Destroy his life!", *Ṭārid-Asakki* "The-one-who-drives-away-the-Asakku demon", and *Sākip-irat-lemni* "Overthrower-of-the-enemy's-breast" (Rittig 1977, 198f. and Corfù/Oelsner 2018, 131–138). When dog names are found in OB incantations, they carry unassuming daily nicknames, not the grandiose names typical of later rituals.

In some dog incantations, one finds the subscript ka-inim-ma ur-gi₇-ti-la. This formula cannot mean "incantation for resurrecting a thoroughbred dog" (Sigrist 1987, 86), or "Es ist eine Beschwörung des lebenden Hund" (Groneberg 2007, 93), but, with Farber (1987, 256): "Beschwörung, um (im Falle eines) Hund(erbisses) zu heilen" – an incantation to revive (a patient bitten) by a dog (just as ka-inim-ma muš-ti-la in VS 17, 4:7 (№ 111), means "an incantation to revive (a patient bitten) by a snake").

№ 61: AMD 1, 243 (fig. 1)

SEAL No.: 7082
Copy: Finkel 1999, 243 (Fig. 1)
Tablet Siglum: BM 79125
Photo: https://www.britishmuseum.org/collection/object/W_1889-0426-422
Edition: Finkel 1999, 215–218
Studies: Wasserman 2003 Cat. No. 96
Collection: British Museum, London
Provenance: Unknown
Measurements: 4.6 × 4.7 cm
Procedure: Yes

Introduction
An almost square tablet whose cursive script, unusual – even cryptic – orthography, and its extensive use of Sumerograms, suggests a late, perhaps even Late Babylonian, dating.

Obverse
1 *urruk*([G]ÍD.DA.GÍD-*uk*) ⸢*bir*⸣-*ki*
2 *šar-úh lá-an-šu*
3 *ištanaḫḫiṭ*(GUD.DA) *ašar*(KI) *išširu*(SI.‹SÁ›) *illak*(DU)
ašar(KI) *illaku*(DU) *iṣabbat* (⸢DAB⸣)
4 *ina pīšu*(KA-*šu*) *nà-ši ne-el*ₓ?(ŠID)-*šu*
5 *ašar*(KI) *iš-šu-ku me-ra-nam íb-ni*
6 tu₆(KA×UD)-é-én-nu-ru

7	*šiptum*(TU$_{6}$-*tum*) *ul*(NU) *ia-át-tum*$_{4}$
8	*šipat*(TU$_{6}$-*át*) ^{d}*Da*$_{7}$(UD)-*mu ù* ^{d}*Gu-*⸢*la*⸣
9	^{d}*Gu-la iqbi*(BÍ.IN.DUG$_{4}$)-⸢*ma*⸣
10	*a-na-ku ád-di*

Reverse

11	tu$_{6}$(KA×UD)-é-én-nu-ru
12	*a-na libbi*(ŠÀ) *ne-ši-ik kalbim*(UR)
13	*qabal*(MURUB$_{4}$$^{?}$) *pūrim*(BUR) *šamnam*(Ì) *tapaššaš*(ŠÉŠ$^{?}$-*ša-aš*)
14	*hé-me-tam tašakkan*(GAR.RA-*an*)
15	*šiptam*(TU$_{6}$) *á-ni-tam*
16	*tà-nà-di-ma*
17	*i-ne-e-eš*

Translation

1–3	Long of knee, proud of form, it keeps jumping!
3	Where it *prospers*, he goes! Where he goes he seizes!
4–5	In his mouth he carries his semen – wherever he bit, he bore a whelp.
6	tu$_{6}$-é-én-nu-ru
7–8	The incantation is not mine! It is the incantation of Damu and Gula.
9–10	Gula said (it) – I recited (it).
11	tu$_{6}$-é-én-nu-ru
12	(Incantation) against *the inside of* a dog-bite.
13–14	You anoint the … with *oil from a bowl*. You apply ghee.
15–17	Recite this incantation, and he will recover.

Commentary

6:	KA×UD for TU$_{6}$ is considered by Rudik (2015, 30–32) as a late feature.
12:	Cf. RA 66, 141b: 10 (№ 96).

№ 62: AMD 1, 243 (fig. 2)a

SEAL No.: 7083
Copy: Finkel 1999, 243 (Fig. 2)
Tablet Siglum: BM 79938
Photo: https://www.britishmuseum.org/collection/object/W_1889-1014-486
Edition: Finkel 1999, 218f.
Studies: Finkel 1999, 213–250; Wasserman 2003 Cat. No. 97
Collection: British Museum, London
Provenance: Unknown
Measurements: 4.7 × 5.7 cm
Procedure: No

Introduction

The script and orthography suggest a late-OB dating (*ana* and TI in l. 8). If correctly understood, the god Damu represents the healer, invoking Šala and Adad to carry off with the wind the malignant semen of the rabid dog.

Obverse

1	[*u*]*r-ru-uḫ bi-ir-ki-i*
2	*ḫa-mu-uṭ la-sa-ma-am*
3	*bu-bu-tam a*$^{!?}$*-li-ip a-ka-la-am* ⸢*e*⸣*-*[*eṣ*]
4	*i-na ši-*[*i*]*n-ni-šu na-ši ni-il-šu*
5	*e-ma iš-šu-ku ma-ra-šu*
6	*i-iz-zi-ib*
7	^{d}*Da-mu be-el ba-la-ṭi*
8	*ana balāṭi*(TI) ‹‹*ana*›› ^{d}*Ša-la ša-il-ma*

Reverse

9	⸢^{d}⸣*Adad(*IŠKUR) *li-*⸢*il*$^{?}$*-qu*$^{?}$⸣*-nim-ma*
10	*li-ib-lu-*[*uṭ a-wi*]*-*⸢*lu*$^{?}$⸣

Translation

1–3	Swift of knee, fast-running, distorted by hunger, sho[rt] of food.
4–6	In his teeth he carries his semen:
5–6	Wherever he bit he leaves his offspring.
7–8	Damu, the lord of life, asks Šala for (the patient's) life!
9–10	May Adad take it (i.e., the 'offspring'$^{?}$) away, so that *the man*$^{?}$ may live!

Commentary

3: Finkel (1999, 218) reads *a-li*-IB, without translation. Taking into consideration the similar incantation BiOr 11 Pl. II (fig. 2): 4 (№ 66) which reads *et-nu-uš a-ka-lam*, we prefer *alāpum* "to be/make immovable, paralyze part of the body" that is similar in meaning to *enēšum* "to be weak".

8: Grammatically, the use of *šâlum* is such that the one who is approached is in acc., while the desired thing is usually preceded by the prep. *ana* (cf. CAD Š/1, 279 f–g). Hence, *ana* DN is probably a mistake. Šala is not a deity usually found in such a context. Steinkeller (2005, 44) explained Šala's appearance as resulting from her being Adad's wife: she is to convince Adad… "[to] carry the deadly 'puppies' of the rabid dog away". The alliteration *šâlum* – Šala is certainly not accidental.

9: The pl. verb form tells that the subject of *li-⸢il-qú?⸣-nim-ma* is more than one deity, i.e., Damu and Šala.

10: Cf. Fs. Pope 87: 11 (№ 70).

№ 63: AMD 1, 286b

SEAL No.: 7084
Copy: Hallo 1999, 286
Tablet Siglum: YBC 8041
Photo: https://collections.peabody.yale.edu/search/Record/YPM-BC-022109
Edition: Hallo 1999, 277f.; Hallo 2010, 647f.
Studies: Wasserman 2003 Cat. No. 102
Collection: Yale Babylonian Collection, New Haven
Provenance: Unknown
Measurements: 5.2 × 3.8 cm
Procedure: Yes

Introduction

Following A. R. George (private communication, April 2014), the incantation is against a dog (UR.IGI for UR.GI$_{(7)}$ = *kalbi*), not *ur-ši* "bedchamber" as suggested by Hallo. Still, the appearance of Lamaštu in l. 12 (if reading is correct) needs explanation.

Obverse
10 *ú*$^{!}$(RI)-*ri*$^{!}$(Ú)-*da*$^{!?}$-*am-ma* ⸢ri/ḫu⸣ bé e ta? ⸢x⸣
11 *ú*$^{!}$(⸢RI⸣)-*ri*$^{!}$(Ú)-*da-am* i ni im lem ⸢x⸣ [x (x)]

Reverse
12 ŠU GÍD ^{d}⸢DÌM.ME⸣
13 *ki-ki-ṭa-ša mu-*⸢*uḫ-ḫi*⸣
14 *ni-iš-ki i-na* KUŠ.⸢DÙG$^{?}$.GAN$^{?}$⸣
15 *ta-na-aṭ-ṭù-ma*
16 *a-sú-ur bīt*(É) *aš-ta-am-*⸢*mi*$^{?}$⸣
17 *te-le-eq-qé*$^{?}$-[*e*$^{?}$]-*ma*
18 *mu-uḫ-ḫi ni-iš-ki-im*
19 *te-sé-e-er te-ṭe-eḫ-ḫi*
20 *ta-ra-ak-ka-as-ša*
21 *ba-li-iṭ*
22 *ši-pa-at kalbi*(UR.GI$^{!}$: text: igi)

Translation

10 *It came down and …*
11 *It came down …*
12 *Long of hand*(*s*) (*just as*) Lamaštu!
13–15 Its procedure: You *strike*$^{?}$ the top of the bite with a leather *bag*$^{?}$;
16–17 You take ‹*dirt*$^{?}$› from the foundation wall of a tavern;
18–19 You smear it on the bite;
19–21 You draw near, you bandage her^{sic} – and he will get better.
22 Incantation (against the bite of) a dog.

Commentary

15: *ta-na-aṭ-ṭù-ma*: from *naṭû* (u/u) "to beat, whip" (not *nadû* whose vocalization is i/i). If understood correctly, the healer is supposed to tap the bite with a leather object, perhaps a leather strap.

16: The key ingredient appears to have been omitted by mistake: probably dirt, or tin. Grammatically, one expects *asurî bīt aštammi*. Cf. the use of *eper bāb aštammi* in the procedures against Lamaštu (e.g., Farber 2014, 105: 61).

20: Note the unassimilated /s/ before /š/ in *ta-ra-ak-ka-as-ša*.

№ 64: AMD 14, 197b

SEAL No.: 7081
Copy: Farber 2018, 197 (by R. Whiting)
Tablet Siglum: A 704
Photo: –
Edition: Wu 2001, 34; Farber 2018, 199f.
Studies: Wasserman 2003 Cat. No. 14; Whiting 1985, 179-187, Finkel 1999; 213–250; Wu 2001
Collection: Oriental Institute, Chicago
Provenance: Adab
Measurements: 7.3 × 5.2 cm
Procedure: No

Introduction

An elongated, well-written tablet with two incantations. The first may be in syllabic Sumerian; the second, in Akkadian, against a rabid dog. A healing tree is called for help (cf. CUSAS 32, 29a = № 67).

Reverse

===

3 *ar-ḫu še-eḫ-ṭù-šu*
4 *ga-še-er ni-ši-ik-šu*
5 *i-na ši-in-na-ti-šu*
6 *i-za-a-ab mu-tum*
7 *i-na pi-šu na-ši ni-il-šu*
8 *a-šar iš-šu-ku ma-ra-šu i-zi-ib*
9 *sí-ip-pi-ru-ú-um*
10 *li-bi-ra-am-ma na-ra-am*
11 [*l*]*i-ir-da-am li-ta-l*[*i*]*-a-am*
12 [*i/a-n*]*a na-ag-bi-šu*
13 tu-en-ni-nu-ri

Translation

3–4 His jumps are swift, strong is his bite.
5–6 From his teeth death oozes.
7–8 He carries his semen in his mouth – wherever he bit, he left his offspring.
9–10 May the *Sippirûm*-tree[?] cross the river hither!
11–12 May it come down to me! May it ascend from its subterranean water!
13 tu-en-ni-nu-ri

Commentary

6: Note the alliterative chiastic construction *izâb mūtum* ↔ *mārassu īzib* which strengthens the notion that the dog's progeny means death.

8: For the collocation of *ezēbum* with semen and giving birth, see the OB prayer CT 15, 5–6: ii 2; vii 8–9 (SEAL no. 7514).

9–10: Farber (following Wu 2001) reads *Zi-ip-pi-ru-ú-um*. Noting correctly that *Sippirûm* cannot be the name of a river or a canal, for a feminine form is called for, he translates "*the one from Sippar*". But who might this mysterious Sipparian be? We submit that *sippirrum* is a by-form of *sibbirrum* "(a tree and an aromatic product obtained from it)" (CAD S, 230, attested in SB medico-magical context), or *sippirû* "(a fruit tree)" (CAD S, 300, attested only lexically), paralleling gišḫašḫur.UD.KIB.NUN.KI. Reading *sippirrum* explains the appearance of the river (l. 10) and *nagbišu* (l. 12), for the magical trees are portrayed as growing near water courses and growing their roots deep down to the subterranean water. Another healing tree, the date palm from Dilmun, is summoned as a purifying or healing agent in the dog incantation CUSAS 32, 29a: 5–6 (№ 67). Note also *īṣum ša ilim* in a spell against gastrointestinal problem, see CUSAS 32, 30b: 11 (№ 26). Trees as healing agents are known elsewhere, mostly in magico-therapeutic texts. The tamarisk describes himself in the *Dialogue Between Tamarisk and Date Palm* as "I am the *mašmaššu*-priest; I renew/purify the temple of the god" (*mašmaššākuma bīt ilim uddaš/ullal*, Wilcke (1989, 173/180); Streck (2004, 256), and in the canonical series Udugḫul the date palm is called "the purifier of the body" (su dadag-ga // *mullil zumur*, Geller (2016, 469: 122f.).

11: Perhaps read *li-ta-ḫ*[*i*?]-*a-am* "let him get close, reach"? But cf. Farber 2018, 200.

№ 65: BiOr 11 Pl. II (fig. 1)

SEAL No.: 7085
Copy: Wasserman 2020c, 456
Tablet Siglum: LB 1001
Photo: Böhl 1954 Pl. II; CDLI P355904
Edition: Böhl 1954, 82
Studies: Böhl 1934, 7; Cunningham 1997 Cat. No. 338; Stol 2000, 128f.; Wasserman 2003 Cat. No. 5; Foster 2005, 191; Wasserman 2005b, 21f.
Collection: Netherlands Institute for the Near East, Leiden
Provenance: Larsa? or Lagaba?
Measurements: 3.0 × 3.0 cm
Procedure: No

Introduction

A short incantation without the description of the threatening dog, opening with the wish section. With Stol (2000, 128), we understand the phrase "let it/he return to the day that it/he was born" (ll. 8–9) as a magical statement destined to return the dog to his earlier days when he was an innocent puppy, but one cannot rule out the notion that the incantation is in fact against anger (*uzzum*).

Obverse

1 *li-ku-ul uz-za-šu*
2 *ki-ma ḫa-šu-tim*
3 *si-li-is-sú*
4 *li-im-qù-ut*
5 *pa-ni-šu*

Lower Edge

6 *li-iḫ-ri-im*

Reverse

7 *pí-šu li-tu-úr*
8 *a-na u$_4$-mi-im*
9 *ša i-wa-al-du*
10 tu-en-ni-nu-ri

Translation

1–2 May he (the rabid dog?) eat his anger like a *ḫašūtum*-plant!
3–4 May his afterbirth drop off!
5–6 May he cover his face.
7–9 May his mouth become as it was on the day he was born!
10 tu-en-ni-nu-ri

Commentary

2: For another occurrence of the *ḫašūtum*-plant, see CUSAS 32, 7e: ii 12' (№ 51).

3: *silītu* is "afterbirth" (against CAD S, 264c sub *siliʾtu* "illness").

4: For *maqātum* in a context of birth-giving, see e.g., VS 17, 34: 18 (№ 12).

№ 66: BiOr 11 Pl. II (fig. 2)

SEAL No.: 7086
Copy: Wasserman 2020c, 455
Tablet Siglum: LB 2001
Photo: Böhl 1954 Pl. II
Edition: Böhl 1954, 82; Whiting 1985, 182f.
Studies: Cunningham 1997 Cat. No. 348; Finkel 1999, 214; Wu 2001; Wasserman 2003 Cat. No. 43; Foster 2005, 191
Collection: Netherlands Institute for the Near East, Leiden
Provenance: Unknown
Measurements: 2.9 × 3.1 cm
Procedure: No

Introduction

A short incantation which consists only of the description of the rabid dog. No magical means of confronting the threat, nor any therapeutic procedure against it, are mentioned.

Obverse

1 *ur-ru-uk bi-ir-ki-šu*
2 *a-ru-uḫ la-sa-ma-am*
3 *i-iṣ bu-bu-tam*
4 *et-nu-uš a-ka-lam*

Reverse

5 *i-na ši-in-ni-šu*
6 *e-ʾì-il ni-il-šu*
7 *a-šar iš-šu-ku*
8 *ma-ra-šu*
9 *i-zi-ib*
10 tu-en-ni-nu-ri

Translation

1–4 Long of knee, swift-running, short of victuals lacking in food.
5–9 From his teeth dangles his semen: wherever he bit he leaves his offspring.
10 tu-en-ni-nu-ri

№ 67: CUSAS 32, 29a

SEAL No.: 7087
Copy: George 2016 Pl. LXXIX
Tablet Siglum: MS 3082
Photo: George 2016 Pl. LXXVIII; CDLI P252091
Edition: –
Studies: George 2016, 47
Collection: Schøyen Collection, Oslo
Provenance: Unknown
Measurements: 18.5 × 7.5 cm
Procedure: Yes

Introduction
An Akkadian incantation with a short alloglot passage starting with the motif of the 'heart-plant'. A healing date palm from Dilmun is called to alleviate the patient's wound (see AMD 14, 197b = № 64). The procedure gives detailed instructions for the preparation of a soothing ointment (ll. 11–16; George 2016, 47 calls it text 'b'). A preliminary edition of the text was sent to us by George.

Obverse

1 ⸢*šammi*$^{?}$(Ú)⸣ ^{d}*Šamaš* {x} *ra-bi-im da-an-nim* ‹*ištu* ḪUR.›SAG.GÁ ⸢*ù*$^{?}$⸣-[*še-bi-ra-am*]
2 [*tu-š*]*a-li-ša-am-ma na-ši-ka-am ta-na-aš-ša-*‹‹ša››*-ak*
3 [*am*]*-mi-nim te-el-te-qé-a-*[*a*]*m ši-ir e-ne-tim*
4 [x *g*]*a*$^{?}$*-ar bi-ši-im ma-aš-ki pa-ri-im*
5 [$^{giš?}$*T*]*i-il-mu-nu-ú li-bi-ra-am te-a-am-ta-am*
6 [*li-i*]*r-dam li-še*$_{20}$*-bi-ra-am i-na na-ag-bi*
7 [x] ⸢x⸣ e da la ‹‹nu›› *te-gá* aš
8 [x i]n$^{?}$ ne ep ki di
9 [x] ⸢x⸣-zi-ir šu-bi-ir ka-la ti-la-ḫi ka-la pi-ra-ḫi
10 [x-ḫ]i *li-te-er-ka* ⸢tu$_6$⸣-én-é-n[u-r]u / ka-inim ur-gi$_7$-ra

====

11 [x] ⸢x⸣ *qá-du-tam si-ḫa*$^{!}$(ZA sup. ras.)*-am kupsam*(DUḪ.ŠE.GÌŠ.Ì)
12 [*šam*]*nam*([Ì.GI]Š) *ḫalṣam*(BÁRA) *bulluḫam*(^{šim}BULUḪ)
13 [*ta-ḫ*]*a-aš-ša-*‹*al*› *ta-na-ap-pi-i-ma*
14 [x] ⸢x⸣ *i-na ru-qí ta-ra-ba-ak-ma*
15 [*iš-ti*]*-šu ù ši-ni-šu ta-ṣa-mi-is-sú-ú-ma*
16 [x *ni-iš*]*-ki-im da-mi-iq* / ka-inim ur-gi$_7$-ra

Translation

1 [The *plan*]*t*$^{?}$ of Šamaš the great, the powerful, ‹he (Šamaš) brought over across› *the mountain.*

2 For the third time [you (the dog) ha]ve bitten a bite!

3–4 Why have you taken the meat of sin, the bad …, the skin of a mule?

5 May the date palm from Dilmun cross the sea hither!

6 May it go down to me, may it get across from (its) subterranean water!

7–8 … *do not be lazy*! …

9 … *zir šubir kala tilaḫi kala piraḫi*

10 May it turn you back! tu$_{6}$ én-é-n[u-r]u

Incantation (against) a dog.

====

11–13 You crush and sift … silt, wormwood, a residue (*of linseed*$^{?}$), pressed oil, (and) the *Bulluḫu* aromatic plant.

14–15 You boil down (the ingredients) in a cauldron. You apply (a bandage with the mixture) to him (the patient) once and twice,

16 – the [*wound*] of the bite will be fine.

Incantation (against) a dog.

Commentary

1: George (private communication) read here: [UR.G]I$_{7}^{?}$ ^{d}*Šamaš* {x} *ra-bi-im da-an-nim* SAG.GÁ *a*[*r*$^{?}$-x]. The first line, however, seems to contain a corrupt version of the motif of the magic plant of Šamaš (see YOS 11, 11: 1–2 = № 35): ^{d}*Šamaš*(^{d}UTU) *šammam ištu š*[*adîm*] (Ḫ[UR.SAG]) *ù-še*$_{20}$*-bi-ra-am*.

4: *maški pa-ri-im*: The incantation concerns a violent dog. It is therefore expected that the dog would bite living creatures and so *pa-ri-im* stands for *parûm* "mule" (CAD P, 206f.) or *parrum* "young lamb" (CAD P, 192). Note that non-plene spelling is found also in l. 14 *ru-qu* for *ruqqum* "cauldron". – The signs at the beginning of the line are clear, but [x *g*]*a*$^{?}$*-ar bi-ši-im* remains difficult.

5–6: Another healing tree is found in AMD 14, 197b: 9–12 (№ 64, against a dog).

10: *târum* D with the meaning of compelling evil to leave is found also in ZA 75, 184: 7' (№ 118, against anger) (Ref. courtesy George, private communication).

№ 68: CUSAS 32, 29b

SEAL No.: 7089
Copy: George 2016 Pl. LXXIX
Tablet Siglum: MS 3082
Photo: George 2016 Pl. LXXVIII; CDLI P252091
Edition: Krebernik 2018, 40
Studies: George 2016, 47
Collection: Schøyen Collection, Oslo
Provenance: Unknown
Measurements: 18.5 × 7.5 cm
Procedure: No

Introduction

A short and broken incantation identified as relating to a dog only by its subscript. George (2016, 47) notes that the language of this short incantation is unidentified (followed by Krebernik 2018, 19/40), raising the possibility that it contains a reference to the *igitelûm* "a monoculus". Since the subscript makes it clear that the incantation is against a dog (as the previous text on the same tablet), we take the text as Akkadian.

Obverse

----

17 [x] ⸢x⸣-bi *i-gi te-li-a*
18 [x x] *te-li-a*
19 [x x-*k*]*a*$^?$ *e-li-a*
19a ⸢ka-inim⸣ ur-gi$_7$-ra

Translation

17 … you climbed *my dike*$^{??}$,
18 You climbed […]
19 I climbed your […]
19a Incantation (against) a dog.

Commentary

17: *i-gi*: hard-pressed, *i-gi* could stand for *īku* "dike".
17–19: The verb involved is probably *elûm* with ventive, hence *tēlia* and *ēlia*.

№ 69: Fs. Hirsch 427

SEAL No.: 7220
Copy: Veenhof 1996, 427
Tablet Siglum: Kt a/k 611
Photo: –
Edition: Veenhof 1996, 426f.
Studies: Hirsch 1972 Nachträge 30b "Zu S. 82"; Cunningham 1997 Cat. No. 337; Michel 2003, 137; Wasserman 2003 Cat. No. 154; Foster 2005, 78; Groneberg 2007, 94; Hecker 2008, 66; Sibbing Plantholt 2017
Collection: Anadolu Medeniyetleri Müzesi, Ankara
Provenance: Kaneš
Measurements: 5.0 × 5.0 cm
Procedure: No

Introduction
This dog incantation is thematically unique as it reflects long-distance Assyrian trading. It continues with a variant of the *mannam lušpur* formula ('Daughters of Ea'), typical of Babylonian incantations.

Obverse
1 *da-mu-um* | *da-ma-mu-um*
2 *kà-al-bu-um*
3 *ṣa-al-mu-um*
4 *i-tí-li-im* | *ra-bi*$_4$*-iṣ*
5 *ú-qá-a ellatam*(ILLAT-*tám*)
6 *pá-ri-is-tám eṭ-lam*$_5$
7 *dam-qám* | *i-ta-na-áp-/l*[*i-sà*]
8 *e-na-šu ma-nam*
9 *lá-áš-pu-ur*
10 *a-na ma-ru-a-at É-/a*
11 4 [+3 *ù* 5+]2-*ma*
12 [*kàr-pá-tí*]-*ki-na*
13 *ša sà-am-tim ú kà-ni-ki-/na*
14 *ša ḫu-lá-li-im*
15 *le-qí-a-ma al-kà-ma*
16 *i-na na-ri-im*
17 [*ku*$^?$*-p*]*u-ra ma-i* [*e-lu-tim*]
18 [x x] ⸢x⸣ ga *a*[*l*-x (x)]
19 [x (x)]-*nim* [x x (x)]
20 [x x] ⸢x (x)⸣ [x x (x)]
21 [x x x] ⸢x⸣ [x x x (x)]
22 ⸢x x x x⸣ [x x x]

Lower Edge

23 *ṣí-i eṭ-lúm*

Left Edge

24 *[a-n]a iš-ri-kà* / *[t]ù-ur*

Translation

1–6 The dark howling (canine), the black dog is lying on the tell, waiting for the spread-out caravan.

6–8 Its eyes look around for a beautiful lad.

8–11 Whom should I send to the Daughters of Ea, sev[en and se]ven, (saying):

12–15 "Take your jars of carnelian and your pot-stands of chalcedony

15–17 and go and in the river [clean]se (them) in [pure] water!"

18–22 (*broken*)

23–24 Get out young man and return (in peace) to your place!

Commentary

1: The much-discussed opening *da-mu-um* | *da-ma-mu-um* (see Hirsch 1972 Nachträge 30b "Zu S. 82", citing Hecker GKT §59c.) is not translated by Veenhof (1996, 429) who, following Farber (1981, 70), takes it as an "untranslatable magic formula". A close parallel to this line is found, however in the OB dog incantation ZA 71, 62c: 13 (№ 75): *da-mu-um da-ma-nu-um* (cf. commentary). The mentioning of *kalbum ṣalmum* (ll. 2–3) prompts the reading *daʾmum* "dark-coloured", a description of *da-ma-mu-um*, probably a designation of a dog, or another canid.

17: *[ku?-p]u-ra*: Regardless of Veenhof's (1996, 430) reservations, we analyze this form as *kapārum* G imp. 2 pl. f.

№ 70: Fs. Pope 87

SEAL No.: 7094
Copy: Sigrist 1987, 87
Tablet Siglum: AUAM 73.2416
Photo: Sigrist 1987, 87; CDLI P249849
Edition: Sigrist 1987, 85f.
Studies: Cunningham 1997 Cat. No. 358; Durand/Guichard 1997, 22 fn. 25; Finkel 1999, 214; Wu 2001; Wasserman 2003 Cat. No. 157; Groneberg 2007, 98f.; Zomer 2018a, 62 fn. 208/97/257f.
Collection: Siegfried H. Horn Museum, Institute of Archaeology, Andrews University, Berrien Springs, Michigan
Provenance: Unknown
Measurements: –
Procedure: No

Introduction
An incantation against wild dogs, roving in the mountainous area East of Mesopotamia. A parallel is found in the MB spell Ugaritica 5, 17^{b}a // Ugaritica 5, 17d (see Zomer 2018a, 257f.).

Obverse
(*beginning deliberately erased*)

1 *[bi-r]i-it Ku-di-im-ši-im*
2 *ù Pa-ra-aḫ-ši-im*
3 *⸢ka⸣-al-bu-um a-wi-lam iš-šu-uk*
4 *⸢a-nu⸣-um-ma a-na ša-ri-im*
5 *a-li-ki-im qí-bi-a-ma*

Reverse
6 *ni-ši-ik ka-al-bi-im*
7 *me-ra-ni-e a i-ib-ni*
8 *šu-ri-ba ka-al-ba-am*
9 *a-na ṣí-bi-it-ti-im*
10 *ka-al-bu-um li-mu-ut-ma*
11 *a-wi-lum li-ib-lu-uṭ-⸢ma⸣*

Translation

1–3	Between Kudimšum and Parahšum, a dog has bitten a man.
4–5	Now say (pl.) to the blowing wind:
6–7	"May the dog's bite not produce puppies!
8–9	Cause (pl.) the dog to enter into custody!
10–11	May the dog die and the man live!"

Commentary

1–2: For the two toponyms, see Durand/Guichard (1997, 22 fn. 25).

4–5: On the healing role of the wind, i.e., Adad, see Steinkeller (2005, 44). For another example of speaking to the wind, see CT 4, 8: 22 (№ 16).

7: Sigrist (1987, 85 with fn. 2), reads *e ib-ni*, forgetting *i-* and assuming an erasure after *e*. Finkel (1999, 214) has *a-a*(!) *ib-ni*. The correct reading *me-ra-né-e a i-ib-ni*, confirmed by the photo as well as by the Akkadian grammar, is offered by Groneberg (2007, 98).

8: Sigrist (1987, 85), followed by Finkel (1999, 215), has *šu-ri-ma*. Groneberg (2007, 98) reads *šu-ri-ba* which better fits the sign form (cf. *-ma* l. 4).

№ 71: OECT 11, 4

SEAL No.: 7096
Copy: Gurney 1989, 43
Tablet Siglum: Bod AB 217
Photo: –
Edition: Gurney 1989, 22f.
Studies: Cunningham 1997 Cat No. 355; Finkel 1999, 215; Wu 2001; Wasserman 2003 Cat. No. 114; Groneberg 2007, 93f.
Collection: Ashmolean Museum, Oxford
Provenance: Unknown
Measurements: 7.0 × 4.6 cm
Procedure: No

Introduction
A typical description of the dog's physical features leading to a request that the dog would die and the man live. The incantation ends with the (broken) legitimation formula.

Obverse
1 *ú-ug-gu-ur še*$_{20}$*-pe-e[n*$_6$*]*
2 *a-ru-úḫ la-sà-ma-am*
3 *bu-bu-ta-am ma-ad*
4 *et-ni-i[š] a-ka-la-am*
5 *i-na as-[k]u-pa-tim*
6 *ir-ta-na-bi-iṣ*
7 *e-ma iš-šu-k[u m]e-ra-nam i-zi-ib*
8 *ú-su-úḫ ša-ar-k[a]-am*
9 *ša pa-ni-š[u]*
10 *ù pu-ul-ḫi-ta-am*
11 *ša ša-ap-ti-šu*
12 *ka-al-bu-um li-m[u-ut]*
13 *a-wi-lum li-ib-l[u-uṭ]*
14 *ši-pa*$^{?}$*-tum* ⸢*ú*$^{?}$⸣*-[ul ia-ti …]*

Lower Edge
(*not inscribed*$^{?}$)
15 […] ⸢x⸣ *ù* ⸢x⸣ […]
16 ⸢x x x⸣ [x x x] ḫi [(x x x)]
17 in ⸢x⸣ tu$_6$-⸢x⸣-[x x]
----
18 ka-inim-ma ur-⸢gi$_7$$^{!?}$ ti⸣-[la-kam]

Translation

1–2	Twisted of legs, quick of running,
3–4	great of hunger, very weak by (lack of) food,
5–6	constantly laying on the threshold.
7	Wherever he bit he left his puppy.
8–11	Remove the puss of his face, and the blister of his lips.
12–13	May the dog die! May the man live!
14	The incantation(s) is/are n[ot mine …]
15	[It is the incantation of …] and […]
16	[…]
17	[…] tu$_6$-⌜x⌝-[x x]

18	Incantation [to revive (someone) from a d]og (bite).

Commentary

10–11: *pulḫītum,* a blister on one's face resulting from hunger and physical stress, is found also in Atraḫasīs III iii 28'–29' [*pu*]-*ul-ḫi-ta ú-ka-la-la ša-ap-ta-ša* "(Nintu, the great lady,) her lips were covered with distress", see Wasserman (2020a, 25).

14: So, contra Gurney (1989, 22), who reads *ši-ú-tum* ("the neighbours…").

№ 72: PIHANS 44 No. 302

SEAL No.: 7095
Copy: Greengus 1979 No. 302
Tablet Siglum: A 21959
Photo: CDLI P355893
Edition: Farber 1981, 57
Studies: Farber 1981, 57f.; Greengus 1986, 91; Cunningham 1997 Cat. No. 343; Wasserman 2003 Cat. No. 110
Collection: Oriental Institute, University of Chicago, Chicago
Provenance: Nērebtum
Measurements: 5.6 × 3.8 cm
Procedure: No

Introduction

A badly preserved incantation which begins with a list of dogs of different colour. The phrases are clumsily arranged along the lines. On the reverse(?), Ninkarrak is mentioned and perhaps also the mythological Flood.

Obverse (?)

1	[*ka-al-bu-um ṣ*]*a*$^{!}$*-al-mu-um k*[*a*$^{!}$*-al-bu-um*]
2	[*pe*$^{?}$*-ṣu*$^{?}$]*-um ka-al-bu-um warqum*(SIG$_7$)
3	[*ka-al-bu*]*-um sa-mu-um ka-al-bu-um*
4	[*bu*$^{?}$*-ur*$^{?}$*-ru*$^{?}$*-mu*$^{?}$*-u*]*m*$^{!}$ *i-na ši-it-pi-im*
5	[*mu*]*-ša-bu-šu*
6	[*i-na as-ku-*(*up*)*-pa*]*-tim*$^{?}$
7	[*na-ar-ba-ṣú-š*]*u*$^{!}$

Reverse (?)

1'	[… *a*$^{?}$*-b*]*u-bi-im*
2'	[…] ⸢x⸣ *ma-ta-am*
3'	[…] ⸢*ma*$^{?}$⸣-[*l*]*i*$^{?}$*-im*
4'	[… ^{d}*Ni*]*n-kar-ra-ak*
5'	[…] ⸢x *uš*$^{?}$⸣*-š*[*u*]$^{?}$*-nu*
6'	[…] nim [(x)]*-ra*$^{?}$*-ni-im*
7'	[…] *bu*$^{?}$*-*[*tu*]*m*$^{?}$
8'	[tu]-en-n[e-nu-ri]

Translation

1–4	A blac[k dog, a whi]te [dog], a yellow dog, a red [do]g, [a speckled] dog –
4–7	its dwelling is in the pit, [in the thresho]ld [is] its [lair].
1'	… *of the flood*$^{?}$
2'	… *the land*$^{?}$
3'	… *of the tide*$^{?}$

4' … [Ni]nkarrak,
5'–7' (*too fragmentary*)
8' [tu]-en-n[e-nu-ri]

Commentary

1–4: The enumeration of the dogs of various colour in this incantation corresponds to *Enmerkar and the Lord of Aratta* 457–459 (ur na-an-gi$_6$-ge ur na-an-babbar-re ur na-an-su$_4$-e ur na-an-dara$_4$-e ur na-an-sig$_7$-sig$_7$-ge ur na-an-gùn-gùn-gú), see Mittermayer (2009, 142). For the semi-fixed list of colours in lexical texts, e.g., Ura XIV: 89–93 (MSL 8/2, 13–14, cf. also MSL 8/1, 16: 98–102).

1'–3' If our reading is correct, these fragmentary lines may contain a rare allusion in magic literature to the mythical Flood (cf. CUSAS 32, 55 = № 126 and CUSAS 32, 56 = № 127).

№ 73: TIM 9, 73a

SEAL No.: 7097
Copy: van Dijk 1976 Pl. LIX
Tablet Siglum: IM 52546
Photo: –
Edition: –
Studies: Cunningham 1997 Cat. No. 325; Wasserman 2003 Cat. No. 178
Collection: Iraq Museum, Baghdad
Provenance: Šaduppûm
Measurements: 6.5 × 5.0 cm
Procedure: No

Introduction
This badly preserved incantation with a list of dogs whose inner logic is unclear: belonging to gods, to a toponym, and defined by a colour.

Obverse
1 *ka-al-bu-um* [*ša*$^{?}$]
2 ^{d}*É-a ù* ^{d}[x-x-(x)]
3 *ka-la-ab Ḫa-aš*$^{?}$-[x (x)]
4 ⸢x⸣-[x]-*ka-šu*-⸢x⸣-[(x)]
5 [x x x]-*šu*$^{?}$ *a-ru-u*[*ḫ*$^{?}$ (x)]
6 *ik*$^{?}$ [x x] ⸢x⸣ *ne*-[x (x)]
7 [x x x *a*$^{?}$/*i*$^{?}$/*wa*$^{?}$]-*li-ti-šu*
===
8 ⸢x⸣ [...]
9 [*ka-al-b*]*u-um ṣalmum*([G]E$_{6}$)
10 [x] ⸢x x⸣

Reverse
11 [*i*$^{?}$-*n*]*a*$^{?}$ *bu-ul*$^{?}$ ^{d}*Šákkan*$^{!?}$
12 *ma-ḫi-ra-am ú-ul i-šu*
13 tu-en-ne-nu-ri$^{?}$

Translation

1	A dog [*of*?/*which*?]
2	Ea and of [...]
3	The dog of *Ḫaš*[...]
4	...
5	his... *swift*?
6	...
7	... his pack
===	
8	...
9	a black [do]g
10	...
11–12	In the herds of Šakkan it/he has no rival.
13	tu-en-ne-nu-ri?

Commentary

1–2: The "dog of Ea" is known from a Namburbi text: ur-zú-kud-da ^{d}En-ki-ga-ke$_4$ // *kalbu munaššsiku ša Ea* (STT 243: r. 8, cited in CAD K, 71f). Note also the OAkk. PN *Kalab-Ea* (MDP 2, 37: xi 4).

7: [*a*/*i*]-*li-ti-šu* is taken as a form of *illatum* (*illitu*, or *allatu*) "family group, clan", or "pack", when referring to dogs. Alternatively, a form of *a*/*ellītum*, "spittle" is possible (but cf. OECT 15, 260: 3 = № 109) with commentary.

13: The last sign in tu-en-ne-nu-ri? could be read as /ru/. The interpretation tu-en-ne-nu-ri follows other rubric from the area of Larsa.

№ 74: VS 17, 8

SEAL No.: 7098
Copy: van Dijk 1971 Pl. IV
Tablet Siglum: VAT 8355
Photo: cf. SEAL No. 7098
Edition: Sigrist 1987, 86
Studies: Whiting 1985, 183; Farber 1987, 256; Cunningham 1997 Cat. No. 364; Finkel 1999, 214; Wu 2001; Wasserman 2003 Cat. No. 206; Foster 2005, 190; Groneberg 2007, 193
Collection: Vorderasiatisches Museum, Berlin
Provenance: Larsa area
Measurements: 3.7 × 5.0 cm
Procedure: No

Introduction
A landscape-oriented tablet with the typical dog's drooling semen motif. The orthography indicates a southern origin (/pi/ in l. 5). Collated by NW in Feb. 2011.

Obverse
1 [*wa-ru*]*-úh bi-ir-ki-in da-an la-sà-ma-am*
2 [*pa-g*]*i-il ka-ab-ba-ar-ti-in ma-li i-ir-*[*tim*]
3 [*ṣi*]*-il-li du-ri-im mu-uz-za-zu-ú-šu*
4 *as-ku-pa-tum na-ar-ba-ṣu-šu*
5 *i-na pi-i-šu na-ši-i ni-il-šu*
6 *a-šar iš-šu-ku ma-ra-šu i-zi-ib*
7 ka-inim-ma ur-gi$_7$-ti-la
8 ka-inim gur-a-kam
9 ka-inim-ma ur-gi$_7$-ti-la-kam

Reverse uninscribed

Translation
1–2 Swift-kneed, fierce in running, [stro]ng-legged, full-chested.
3–4 His position is the shade of the city wall, his lying place is the threshold.
5–6 In his mouth he carries his semen: wherever he bit he left his offspring.
7 Incantation to revive (someone) from a dog (bite).
8 Incantation of turning away (a dog$^?$).
9 Incantation to revive from a dog (bite).

Commentary
7–9: The three subscripts which terminate this short text are unparalleled.

№ 75: ZA 71, 62c

SEAL no.: 7099
Copy: Farber 1981, 62
Tablet Siglum: BM 122691
Photo: https://www.britishmuseum.org/collection/object/W_1931-0413-4
Edition: Farber 1981, 63f.
Studies: Cunningham 1997 Cat. No. 329; Wasserman 2003 Cat. No. 268; Sibbing Plantholt 2017
Collection: British Museum, London
Provenance: Tell Duweihes
Measurements: 8.9 × 6.4 cm
Procedure: No

Introduction

The third incantation in an incantation collective (preceded by an incantation against the Evil Eye and an incantation to quiet a baby). The description of the two hostile dogs on the road is similar to the OA dog incantation in Fs. Hirsch 427 (№ 69). The end is broken.

Reverse

13	*da-mu-um da-ma-nu-um*
14	*ka-al-bu-um ru-bu-ṣú-um*
15	*e-re-šum na-aš-pu-um*
16	*še-na i-la-ku ur-ḫa-am*
17	*š[e-n]a i-[l]a-ku ḫa-[r]a-*‹‹na››*-na*
18	[…] ⸢x⸣ [x (x)] ⸢x⸣ na la/ad ba$^{?}$ ag
19	[…] ⸢na$^{?}$⸣

Translation

13–15	The dark wailing (canine), the lurking dog (whose names are) ‘Nagging’ (and) ‘Noisy’,
16–17	the two are walking on the path, the two are walking on the road.
18–19	(*too fragmentary*)

Commentary

13: *da-mu-um da-ma-nu-um*: Balkan (*apud* Hirsch 1972 Nachträge, 30b) translated “Blut und Jammer”, namely *dāmum damāmum*. Farber (1981, 70) saw this phrase as an untranslatable magical formula, similar to *da-mu-um da-ma-mu-um* which opens the OA dog incantation Fs. Hirsch 427 (№ 69), see Veenhof (1996, 428). Blood does not fit the context, hence *daʾmum*, “dark-coloured” (CAD D, 74f.), comes to mind. In SB texts, this adjective is mostly written with an aleph, *da-ʾ-mu-um*, but earlier sources have *da-a-mu-um*, which in non-plene spelling could result in *da-mu-um*. The partial parallel to the OA dog incantation just mentioned suggests that the next word, *da-ma-nu-um* (not listed in the dictionaries), is related to *damāmum* "to wail, moan", said also of animals. Considering the parallel construction of the first couple of lines, the "lurking dog" (l. 14) and "the dark wailing" (l. 13) refer probably to two members of the Canidae family, the former characterized by its bawling.

15: The pair of adjectives *Errēšûm* "(persistently) demanding" (CDA, 79) and "viel wünschend" (AHw, 243), i.e., 'Nagging', and *Našpûm* (< *šapûm* N) "getting loud", i.e., 'Noisy', are two appellations for the canines figuring in this incantation. Cf. the two dogs that were walking behind Gula in YOS 11, 5b: 10 (№ 114); Wasserman (2010, 81f.), whose names were *Suppû* 'Supplication(s)' and *Ṣūḫum* 'Laughter'.

16–17: Note the absence of the dual form in *šena illakū*.

2.2.2 Fish

Among the great variety of animals which incantations address, we find a unique example for catching a fish.

№ 76: Fs. de Meyer 75/83b

SEAL No.: 7114
Copy: Cavigneaux/Al-Rawi 1994, 83
Tablet Siglum: IM 95317
Photo: Cavigneaux/Al-Rawi 1994, 83
Edition: Cavigneaux/Al-Rawi 1994, 82f.
Studies: Cavigneaux 1996, 37f.; Wasserman 2003 Cat. No. 147
Collection: Iraq Museum, Baghdad
Provenance: Sippar
Measurements: Unknown
Procedure: No

Introduction

The present text is found in an incantation collective with another Akkadian spell against gastrointestinal problems (Fs. de Meyer 75/83d = № 30), a Sumerian incantation against 'a dead deity' (Fs. de Meyer 75/83a),[241] and an alloglot incantation against a dog (Fs. de Meyer 75/83c).

Obverse
16 *apum*(GIŠ.GI) *ša* ^{d}*Sîn qanûm*(GI) *ša* M á - g a n - n a
17 ^{d}*Sîn be-li ú-su-uḫ̮ zi-bi-in-ka*
18 *da-an-nu-um li-ri-id a-na libbi*(ŠÀ) ABZU$_{x}$(DÉ)-*e*
19 *bā᾽erum*(ŠU.ḪA) *i-ba-ar nūnam*(KU$_{6}$)
20 *am-me-nim a-di* ABZU$_{x}^{?}$(DÉ$^{?}$) *ṣú-ṣí* ‹‹im›› ‹‹aṣ›› *im-ḫ̮a-aṣ*
21 *al-su-um-ma ak-šu-‹da›-am-ma*
22 *il-su-ma-am-ma* ⸢*ú*⸣*-ul ik-šu-da-ni*
23 *Na-zi a-ba-ra-k*[*a-a*]*t* ^{d}*Nin-gal*
24 *i-na pí-i na-zi a-ba-ra-ka-tim*
25 *ša* ^{d}*Nin-gal li-ṣí-*⸢*a*⸣*-am-ma*
26 *nūnum*(KU$_{6}$) *ša ap-pa-ri-im li-ṣí-a-am*
27 t u - e - e n - n e - n u - r i *ši-‹pa›-at*$^{!}$ *ma-da-di-im*

Translation

16 Reed-bed of Sîn! Reed of Magan!
17 Sîn my lord! Pull out your reed-mat!
18 May the strong-one go down the midst of the Apsû!
19 The Fisherman is catching a fish:

241 For the resemblance of this spell to Sumerian incantations against Lamaštu, see Zomer 2018a, 192.

20 Why has he *cut* the reed-thicket until the Apsû?
21 I went fast and I reached (the fish):
22 It (the fish) went fast but did not reach me!
23 Nazi is the stewardess of Ningal.
24–25 By the command of Nazi, the stewardess of Ningal: may it (the fish) come out to me!
26 May the fish of the marsh come out to me!
27 tu-e-en-ne-nu-ri
Spell (against) (an) escaping (fish).

Commentary

17: For *zibnum*, see Cavigneaux (1996, 37).

20: Reading differs from Cavigneaux/Al-Rawi. At the end of the line, we suggest a partial dittography: ‹‹im›› ‹‹aṣ›› written twice, completing to *im-ha-aṣ* with the ḪA erroneously taken from the KU$_6$ above (l. 19).

27: The emendation of *ši-‹pa›-at*[!] follows another rubric on the same tablet (Fs. de Meyer 75/83b = № 76). – For *madādu* "to escape", see von Soden (1966, 14).

2.2.3 Flies and Bees

A small non-homogenous group of incantations against flying insects. YOS 11, 6 (№ 80) is aimed at catching an annoying fly (nim). The other three directed against ni-im-bu. George (2016, 117) suggested that ni-im-bu in the subscript of CUSAS 32, 50b (№ 77) stands for nim-bubbu(BUL+BUL) *ḫam/wītum* "a kind of wasp". This suggestion was followed by Wasserman (2020b, 308). And yet, if this small group of incantations concerns *Vespidae*, one wonders why the texts do not describe them as a threat. Simply put: how is it possible that the wasp's notoriously painful sting is not mentioned? In fact, contrary to George's interpretation (2016, 117), the texts do not present "some creature harmful to human beings that was a nuisance in the home", rather, one gains the impression that the ni-im-bu were welcomed, since the incantations explicitly call them not to leave ("Oh threshold! Keep letting your sons enter!" and "Oh long one! You should not go out! Oh short one! You should not depart!" (CUSAS 32, 51: 2, 9–10 = № 78). If not wasps, then what were the nim-bubbu? The natural candidate for this social insect is the honeybee. In support of the contention that honeybees are the subject of the first three incantations, come *nammaštu* "swarm" (CUSAS 32, 51: 8), *pī ḫurri* "the entrance of the hole" – probably the entrance to the hive (CUSAS 32, 51: 11), and *mê ramākim* "the water of bathing" (CUSAS 32, 51: 4), a preferred location for bees (as well as other flying insects). A valuable clue in support of this proposal is the mention of *arkum* "long-one" and *kurûm* "short-one" (CUSAS 32, 51: 9–10), both of which are requested not to leave, but rather stay. We submit that this couple stands for the queen of the hive and the drone, the male-bee, respectively.[242] Two difficulties, however, must be mentioned. First, lexically, the incantations do not speak of honey or wax, nor do they mention honeybees in any of their known terms (nim-làl = *nūbtum*, *nambūbtum*, or *lallartu*). They do not even describe them periphrastically, as the famous inscription of Šamaš-rēša-uṣur, where "the humming-creatures that collect honey" (*ḫabūbēti ša dišpu*(LÀL) *ilaqqatāni*) are found (Frame 1995, 281: iv 13–14, cf. Cammarosano et al. 2019, 126). The second difficulty is historical. As far as textual evidence goes, apiculture was not practiced in Mesopotamia before the first millennium. The clearest case is the account of Šamaš-rēša-uṣur, the 8th century governer of the lands of Sūḫu and Mari, who boasts of introducing beekeeping to his land after importing them from the land of Ḫabḫa, probably in the Zagros (Mazar 2020, 641 with previous literature). In other parts of the ancient Near East, however, beekeeping was known much earlier. In Egypt, bees were raised under royal tutelage already in the early kingdom (Kritsky 2015) and in Anatolia, the Hittites were also raising bees already in the second half of the second millennium (Bloch et al. 2010, 4–5). The dearth of evidence from Mesopotamia may be only accidental, but it may reflect real difficulties associated with raising bees in a hot climatic region (Crane 1999, 162–163). The unique discovery of the 10th century BCE apiary found *in situ* in Tel Rehov, Israel (Mazar 2020), would negate the climatic argument, as the temperatures in the Jordan Valley are very high. Notwithstanding these difficulties, in our opinion the purpose of this small group of

242 This is not to claim that ancient Mesopotamians understood the complexity of bee reproduction. Yet, being acute observers, it is not difficult to assume that those attending the hive were aware of the eusociality of the beehive, noting that there are different looking and differently functioning bees in every hive.

incantations was not to drive dangerous creatures away, but to provide magical help to achieve something difficult (similarly to the incantation destined to catch a fish, Fs. de Meyer 75/83b: 16–17 = № 76), namely raising honeybees.

№ 77: CUSAS 32, 50b

SEAL No.: 7107
Copy: George 2016 Pl. CXIX
Tablet Siglum: MS 3073
Photo: George 2016 Pl. CXIX; CDLI P252082
Edition: George 2016, 117; Krebernik 2018, 42
Studies: Wasserman 2020b, 308 fn. 11
Collection: Schøyen Collection, Oslo
Provenance: Unknown
Measurements: 4.9 × 5.8 cm
Procedure: No

Introduction

This incantation (a shortened version of CUSAS 32, 51 = № 78) comes after an incantation against scorpions (№ 94).

6 [li]-ri-ri-a i-ti-la
7 [*šu*]-*ul-ma-am ti-bi* ⸢*am*⸣-*ri-im*
8 [*šu-ṣ*]*e-e ra-ma-an-ki*
9 [*as*]-‹‹su$^?$››-*ku-up-pu šu-ri-bi* / *ma-re-e-ki*
10 [^{d}]Asal-lú-ḫi dumu Eridu^{ki}-ga-ke$_4$
11 [t]u-én-é-nu-ru
12 ka-inim-ma ni-im-bu

Translation

6 *Liriria itila*
7 Raise [pea]cefully and look at me!
8 [Get] yourself out!
9 Oh threshold, let your children enter!
10 Oh Asalluḫi son of Eridu!
11 [t]u-én-é-nu-ru
12 Incantation (*to grow*) *bees*$^?$.

Commentary

7: Despite George's (2016, 117) reservations, *šulmam* makes good sense here. The speaker encourages the bee not to be aggressive (cf. *tebûm* also in YOS 11, 6: 11 = № 80, against a fly). – The request *amrīm* "look at me!" is typical of love incantations (CUSAS 32, 23b: 16 = № 132; OECT 11, 11: 4' = № 133; ZA 75, 198–204b: 24 = № 137. Cf. also Semitica 62, 15f.: 14 and YOS 11, 87: 6 = № 98 and 136). This address seems to preclude the possibility that the incantation relates to a dangerous creature.

9: *askuppu* is not a locative (George 2016, 117: "over the threshold"), but a vocative. For the literary device of addressing doors in Akkadian literature, see Wasserman (2020b).

10: George (2016, 117) proposes [*a*$^{?}$-*na*$^{?}$ ^{d}] *Asal-lú-ḫi*…, "Take your children home, over the threshold [for$^{(?)}$] Asalluḫi", but there seems no room for *a-na*, hence we suggest an apostrophe: "Oh Asalluḫi son of Eridu!".

№ 78: CUSAS 32, 51

SEAL No.: 7108
Copy: George 2016 Pl. CXX
Tablet Siglum: MS 3061
Photo: George 2016 Pl. CXX; CDLI P252070
Edition: George 2016, 117f.; Krebernik 2018, 19/42
Studies: Wasserman 2020b, 308 fn. 13
Collection: Schøyen Collection, Oslo
Provenance: Unknown
Measurements: 7.8 × 4.3 cm
Procedure: No

Introduction
A longer version of CUSAS 32, 50b (№ 77). Of interest is the mention of the Esikila temple as the setting place of the incantation. At least two temples with this name are known. The better-known ones are the temple of Ninazu-Tišpak in Ešnunna and the chapel within the perimeter of the É-kur in Nippur.[243] Contrary to our intuition, beehives in antiquity were kept in walls, even in special buildings in the middle of town, as proven by the apiary at Tel Rehov. Raising bees was strongly related to cultic practice (Mazar 2020, 641). One can imagine a beehive taken care of by temple personnel eager to obtain honey and wax.

1 li-ri-a i-ti-la
2 *as-ku-up-pu-um šu-te-re-bi mārī*(DUMU^{meš})*-ki*
3 *mārat*(DUMU.MUNUS) *É-a* ^{d}*Asal-lú-ḫi*
4 *a-na me-e ra-ma-ki-im i-ir-ru-ub*
5 *bīt*(É) *E-sikil-la as-ku-pa-as-sú bu-ra-šu*
6 *É-a lu-li-mu-um wa-ši-ib libbi*(ŠÀ-*bi*)*-ša*
7 *ši-ir bītum*(É) *šu-ú-ur as-ku-pu*
8 *nam-ma-áš-ti šu*$^{!}$*-ṣi-i ra-ma-*⸢*an*⸣*-ki*
9 *ar-ku-um e tu-ṣa-a-am-ma*
10 ⸢*ku*⸣*-ru-ú-um e ta-at-ta-la-a*[*k*]
11 *i-na pī*(KA) *ḫu-ur-ri-i-*⸢*ki*⸣
12 ⸢*na*⸣*-ap-l*[*i*]*-*⸢*sú*⸣*-um l*[*i-*x x x]
13 ⸢tu⸣-[én-é-nu-ru$^{?}$]

243 George 1993, 141 nos. 987–989.

Translation

1 *Liria itila*

2 Oh threshold! Keep letting your sons enter!

3–4 The daughter of Ea – Oh Asalluḫi – is entering the bathing water.

5–6 The temple of Esikila, its threshold is (made of) juniper. Ea, the stag, dwells in it.

7 The house is flesh, the threshold a bull.

8 Oh my herd of crawling creatures, get yourself out!

9–10 Oh long one! you should not go out! Oh short one! You should not depart!

11–12 In the opening of your (f.) hole, let the *blinker*? …

13 ⸢tu⸣-[én-é-nu-ru?]

Commentary

2: As in CUSAS 32, 50b: 9 (№ 77), *askuppum* is a vocative.

3–4: The appellation "daughter of Ea" cannot refer to Asalluḫi who is Ea's son. The one "entering the bathing water" is the bee in receipt of this dignified pedigree. "The daughter of Enki", referring to a brewing jar, is found in CUSAS 32, 32b: 4' (№ 28). More on the the title "son of DN" in magic texts, see Wasserman (2008, 79–80).

6: Of note is the f. possessive pron. One expects *wāšib libbišu*.

9–10: For the suggestion that *arkum* "long-one" and *kurûm* "short-one" refer to the bee-queen and the drone, the male-bee, see introduction above (2.2.3). Note that grammatically, these two substantivized adjectives are m., while the creature which is the topic of CUSAS 32, 50b (№ 77) is grammatically f.

№ 79: YOS 11, 5f

SEAL No.: 7109
Copy: van Dijk/Goetze/Hussey 1985 Pls. VI-VII
Tablet Siglum: YBC 4616
Photo: https://collections.peabody.yale.edu/search/Record/YPM-BC-018681
Edition: van Dijk/Goetze/Hussey 1985, 20
Studies: Farber 1985, 61; Cunningham 1997 Cat. No. 375; Wasserman 2003 Cat. No. 230; Wasserman 2020b, 308 fn. 10
Collection: Yale Babylonian Collection, New Haven
Provenance: Larsa area
Measurements: 7.6 × 8.3 cm
Procedure: No

Introduction

As noted by George (2016, 116f), this short text also belongs to the group of incantations which we suggest relates to beekeeping.

27 *as-ku-up-pa-tum šu-te-ri-bi ma-re-e-ki*
28 ^{d}*Asal-lú-ḫi mār*(DUMU) ^{d}*En-ki i-ir-ru-ba-am*

Translation

27 Oh threshold! Keep letting your sons enter!
28 Asalluhi the son of Enki is entering.

№ 80: YOS 11, 6

SEAL No.: 7109
Copy: van Dijk/Goetze/Hussey 1985 Pl. VII
Tablet Siglum: NBC 7967
Photo: cf. SEAL No. 7109
Edition: van Dijk/Goetze/Hussey 1985, 21; Thomsen 2018, 773f.
Studies: Farber 1985, 61; Goetze 1957, 81f. (No. 22); Veldhuis 1993; Cunningham 1997 Cat. No. 376–377; Wasserman 2003 Cat. No. 231; Foster 2005, 931; Thomsen 2018; Polinger Foster 2020, 108
Collection: Yale Babylonian Collection, New Haven
Provenance: Larsa area
Measurements: 7.6 × 8.3 cm
Procedure: No?

Introduction

The body parts enumerated in the incantation belong not to the fly, as suggested by van Dijk/Goetze/Hussey (1985, 21), but to the man trying to get rid of the disturbing insect. A humoristic aspect is not impossible.

Obverse

1 *am-ḫa-aṣ-ka*
2 *i-na mu-ḫi-im*
3 *iš-tu mu-ḫi-im*
4 *a-na pu-ti-im*
5 *iš-tu pu-ti-im*
6 *a-na ḫa-ar-ḫa-sa-ni-im*
7 *iš-tu ḫa-ar-ḫa-sa-ni-im*
8 *a-na na-ḫi-ri-im ša ap-pí-im*
9 *ú-ta-mi-ka* d*Nin-kar-ra-ak*
10 *ti-bu-ti er-bi-im*
11 *lu te-te-bi-am*
12 *i-na ṣa-ab-ri-šu*

Reverse

1' [...]
2' [... -]*ri-šu*
3' [... -*k*]*a*?
4' [... -*t*]*i-im*
5' [... -*t*]*i-im*
6' [... d*Nin-kar-ra*]*-ak*

7' […] *a-pí-šu*
8' […] ⸢x⸣ na
9' […] ⸢x⸣ ru$^{?}$ na
10' *a-*⸢*na*⸣ [*ru*$^{?}$]*-ub-ṣí-ka*

11' ka-inim-ma nim-ma-kam
12' ka-kíši-re-da-kam

Translation

1–2 I hit you (the fly) at the cranium,
3–4 from the cranium to the forehead,
5–6 from the forehead to the ear,
7–8 from the ear to the nostril of the nose!
9 I conjure you by Ninkarrak:
10–12 You must rise a locust's rise *through* his *blinking*.
1'–5' (*too fragmentary*)
6' [*Ninkarr*]*ak*
7' […] of his nose!
8'–10' [… *go back*] to your dung.

11'–12' Incantation to tie a fly.

Commentary

12: *ina ṣa-ab-ri-šu* is difficult. Thomsen (2018, 773) reads *i-na za-ab-ri-šu* "von seiner Seite?". We prefer *ṣa-ab-ri-šu* having in mind *ṣabrum* "blinker, winker, one who blinks, winks" (CDA, 331) which could be a fly swatter.

9': Some form of *târum* is anticipated, but the final *na* (carried over mistakenly from the line above?) hinders such attempts.

10': Following Farber (1985, 61).

2.2.4 Goats

Goats are notably stubborn animals. One incantation, perhaps humoristic, against a noisy goat is found in the corpus.

№ 81: PRAK 2 Pl. III (C1)

SEAL No.: 7115
Copy: de Genouillac 1925 C 1
Tablet Siglum: AO 10621
Photo: –
Edition: de Genouillac 1925, 59-60; Lambert 1991
Studies: Cunningham 1997 Cat. No. 309; Geller 2002; Wasserman 2003 Cat. No. 124; Foster 2005, 198; Zomer 2018a, 132
Collection: Louvre, Paris
Provenance: Kiš
Measurements: 13.2 × 7.36 cm
Procedure: No

Introduction

As already observed by Lambert (1991, 418f.), the ending of this incantation is somewhat unusual. Instead of using a non-violent ritual action, Enki comes with the definitive solution of killing the poor noisy goat. Geller (2002) argued, therefore, that this text may be a parody of the traditional Sumerian incantation. Translation follows the Akkadian version.

Obverse

1 ud ^{d}En-[ki$^{?}$ ...] ⸢ma$^{?}$ ab$^{?}$⸣ [...]
i-nu-ma ^{d}E[n-ki$^{?}$ ...]

2 ^{d}En-líl [...]
^{d}En-líl [...] ⸢za$^{?}$⸣ [...]

3 níg úr-⸢limmu x⸣ [x (x)] ⸢an x⸣ [...]
i-na mi-im-ma ⸢x x⸣ [...]

4 ùz-e ⸢igi⸣ mu-[...]
e-za i-mu-ur-m[a ...]

5 ùz-e tu-ra ka-bi ⸢nu⸣-bi-[(x)]
e-zu ma-ar-ṣa-[a]t-ma pū/ī(KA)*-ša ú-*⸢*li*⸣ [...]

6 igi-lib sipa nu-dúr-dúru-na
i-da-al-li-ip re-e-ú ù-li i-ṣa-la-al

7 ka-pár-ri al-gi$_4$-ba
ka-pa-ri-šu [i]-da-li-ip

8 šú-šú-ba níg u$_4$ [ge$_6$$^{?}$] mu-un-lu-lu
ša i-[t]a-na-la-ku ú-mi ú mu-ši ir-te-e-ú

9 ^{d}En-ki-ke$_4$ igi du$_8$-ni-ta
^{d}En-ki i-na a-ma-ri-šu

10 lú-kù-zu gù ba-an-dé á-gal ba-an-ši-in-ak

e-em-qá-am i-si-ma ra-bi-iš ú-te-e-ir

11 ùz-e tùr-ra amaš-a ge$_6$ mu-sá-e

e-zu-um i-na ta-ar-[ba-ṣí (ù$^?$)] sú-pu-ri ú-š[a$^?$]-‹am›-ša i-da-li-pa-an-ni

12 gen-na na-ma-an-du$_{11}$-du$_{11}$-da

a-li-ik la i-da-al-li-pa-an-ni

13 šurim-bi šu ba-e-te

Reverse

ru-bu-sà le-eq-[e$^?$]

14 géštu-bi ù-mu-ni-in-gar

a-na uz-ni-ša ša šu$^!$(IŠ)*-me-li ‹li›-iš-ku-[u]n-ma*

15 ùz-e ù-sá-ni-gin$_7$ ḫ̮é-ug$_5$-ga

e-zu ki-ma ṣa-la-li-ša li-mu-ut

16 ^{d}Sumuqan lugal máš-anše$^!$-ke$_4$

^{d}*Šákkan be-el bu-li-im* ^{d}*Šákkan*

17 [níg]-nu-gar-ra na-ma-ni-gar

[x x] *mi-im-ma a-i iš-ku-un*

18 [ini]m$^?$-šè mu-ri-gi$_4$

a-na a-wa-a-tim la i-ṣa-ba-ta-an-ni

19 erín kalam-e ḫ̮é-si-li-dè

ṣa-bu ù ma-tum da-li-li-ka i-da-la-lu

20 nam-á-gal-zu dingir-gal-gal-e-ne si-li-TE

e-ú-ut-ka i-lu ra-bu-ut-tum i-da-al/-la-lu

Translation

1–2	When Enki […], Enlil […],
3–4	Among [all] four legged [creatures …], he saw a goat.
5	The goat is sick, it cannot [*close*$^?$] its mouth.
6	It keeps (everyone) awake, the shepherd cannot sleep.
7–8	It keeps the shepherd boys awake, those who go about shepherding day and night.
9–10	When Enki saw this, he called the clever one and instructed him grandly:
11–12	"The goat in the pen or fold is [spending the night (awake)], keeping me awake. Go, so that it should not keep me awake!
13–15	Take its dung, may he place it on its left ear! May the goat die as if it is sleeping!".
16–17	May Šakkan, lord of the beasts, hold nothing against me!
18–20	May he not take me to litigation! May the people of the land sing your praises! May the great gods praise your power!

Commentary

9–15: Normally in divine dialogues, it is the junior deity (i.e., Asalluḫi/Marduk) that observes the problem and reports back to the senior deity (i.e., Enki/Ea). In the present text, it is Enki who observes the noisy goat and orders the junior deity – presumably Asalluḫi/Marduk, here denoted by lú-kù-zu//*emqam* 'the clever one' – to quiet the animal down. Interestingly, Enki himself is silent on the fact that mankind can't sleep, but emphasizes instead that he himself can't sleep because of the noisy goat.

15: For a discussion of the intentional semantic reversal in this line, see *Hypallage* in § 1.7.2.

2.2.5 Pests

Agricultural problems such as pests were not uncommon in Mesopotamia and hence various magic texts address the issue. For the first millennium BCE, we find the ritual-series Zú buru$_5$ dab-bé-da (George 1999) which aims to counter evil arising from field pests that destroy crops. This topic is also widely addressed in the Sumerian incantations of the second millennium BCE, see Zomer (2018a, 226f.). Our corpus contains only one Akkadian example of this group.

№ 82: YOS 11, 69d

SEAL No.: 7157
Copy: van Dijk/Goetze/Hussey 1985 Pl LXVII
Tablet Siglum: YBC 4594
Photo: https://collections.peabody.yale.edu/search/Record/YPM-BC-018659
Edition: Cavigneaux/Al-Rawi 2002, 10f.
Studies: van Dijk/Goetze/Hussey 1985, 45; Cunningham 1997 Cat. No. 402; Wasserman 1999, 348f.; Wasserman 2003 Cat. No. 259; Zomer 2018a, 226
Collection: Yale Babylonian Collection, New Haven
Provenance: Larsa area
Measurements: 9.0 × 5.0 cm
Procedure: No

Introduction

Found amongst other spells concerned with agricultural problems in an incantation collective (YOS 11, 69a against mice (Sum.), YOS 11, 69b against a raven (Sum.), YOS 11, 69c against *maškadu* (№ 42)). The last line summarizes the four incantations on the tablet.

Reverse
16' *ḫa-a-ru ḫa-a-ru si-ru ḫi-a-su-um*
17' *am-ša*!(TA)*-lí pa-a mu-ša-nu-um*
18' *i-ta-ti-a* BÙR^{iku} *l[a*$^?$*-ma*$^?$*]-an i-ṭe*$_4$*-[eḫ]-ḫi*

19' ka-inim-ma lú-kúr lú-sa-gaz / *a-na* ŠE *la ṭe*$_4$*-ḫi-e-em*

20' 4 ka-inim-ma

Translation

16' Donkey, donkey, quick onager
17' – Yesterday, the winnower (blew) the chaff! –
18' [May (the equids) n]ot ap[p]roach the borders of the field!

19' Incantation to prevent the enemy and the plunderer from approaching the barley.

20' (Total of) 4 incantations.

2.2.6 Scorpions

Mesopotamians were troubled by scorpions that posed a constant threat to their daily life.[244] Indeed, scorpions were a chief topic in Mesopotamian magic, and these arachnids – with their horn-like pincers, poisonous sting rising like a torch at the top of their curved tail – fascinated the ancients' imagination. To date, 22 different Akkadian incantations against scorpions are catalogued, making this the largest thematic group in the corpus together with Gastrointestinal Problems (§ 2.1.4).

№ 83: AMD 1, 247 (fig. 11)

SEAL No.: 7161
Copy: Finkel 1999, 247 (fig. 11)
Tablet Siglum: FM 22878
Photo: –
Edition: Finkel 1999, 235
Studies: Wasserman 2003 Cat. No. 99
Collection: Field Museum, Chicago
Provenance: Kiš
Measurements: –
Procedure: No

Introduction
A badly broken fragment of a one-column tablet, probably its reverse.

Obverse
Not preserved

Reverse
1 *[a-]ru-uḫ ša*$^{!?}$ *b[a*$^{?}$*-aš-tim]*
2 *[b]i-iṣ-ṣú-úr ṣer-r[i-im]*
3 *pa-še-e[r...]*
----
4 *ši-pa-at zu-qí-[qí-pí-im]*

(blank)

244 A stone called NA$_4$ GÍR.TAB is listed in *abnu šikinšu*, see Schuster-Brandis 2008, 412.

Translation

1 It is the rushing one of the s[hrubs].
2 [The v]ulva of a sna[ke]
3 He is resolved […].
----
4 Incantation (against) a sc[orpion].

Commentary

1: Following CUSAS 32, 49: 4 (№ 93). Finkel (1999, 235), differently.

2: For the idea of "vulva of a snake" as a component of a magic or medical procedure, see Finkel (1999, 235). Note, however, the notion of "vulva of a bitch" in AMD 1, 273a: 4 (№ 125).

3: *pa-še-er*: a stative "he is resolved", or *pāširum*, "undoer, exorcist" (CAD P, 253) in *status constructus*, "the undoer of...". Note additionally the subscript of the MB spell KBo 1, 18k: D 23' *an-nu-tu*$_4$ *ša pa-ša-ar* ⸢GÍR$^{!}$⸣.TAB, see Zomer (2018a, 276; 2019, 1266).

№ 84: BM 97331a

SEAL No.: 7197
Copy: Plate I
Tablet Siglum: BM 97331
Photo: cf. SEAL No. 7197;
https://www.britishmuseum.org/collection/object/W_1902-1011-385
Edition: –
Studies: –
Collection: The British Museum, London
Provenance: Unknown
Measurements: 5.1 × 6.6 cm
Procedure: No

Introduction

The badly preserved obverse of this tablet contains an incantation destined, most likely, against scorpions. A *pāširum* and a *pāširtum* "male and female releaser" are mentioned, a profession which is connected to scorpions (see commentary below). On the better-preserved reverse, another incantation, also against scorpions, is found (BM 97331b = № 85).

Obverse

1	*aṣ-ba-at* ⸢*pí šamê*(AN$^{?}$)⸣ *aṣ-ba-at pí ka-ka-bi*
2	*i-na ša-ma-ia*
3	*pí* ⸢*pa-ši-ri ù*⸣ *pa-ši-ir-*⸢*tim*⸣
4	*pa-*⸢*ši-ir-ti*$^{?}$ *i+na li-li*⸣*-ša* ⸢x⸣ [(x)] ⸢x⸣
5	⸢x⸣ [x x (x)] ⸢GÍR$^{?}$.TAB$^{?}$⸣ [*š*]*a zi-iq-t*[*ì*$^{?}$]-⸢*šu*$^{?}$⸣
6	[x x x x] ⸢*í*$^{?}$*-na*$^{?}$⸣ ni ⸢x (x)⸣ ⸢mi$^{?}$ lu$^{?}$⸣ ⸢x (x)⸣

7	[x x x x] ⸢ar$^{?}$⸣ ma zi

8	[x x x]-⸢x⸣-*ri i-na bu-ud* ⸢*ta*⸣*-ri-*⸢*tim*⸣

Lower Edge

9	[…]*-ti za-aq-tu-um-ma*
10	[x x x] *li*$^{!}$*-ta-pa-aṣ pa-še-er-ša*

Translation

1–2	I seized the mouth of *the sky*$^{?}$! I seized the mouth of the stars above me (lit. my sky)!
3	The mouth of a male releaser, (the mouth of) a female releaser!
4	My female releaser in the night (lit. her night) […]
5–6	[…] *the scorpion of which its sting* […]
----	

7 […] …

----

8 […] on the shoulders of the (scorpion's) nurse,
9 […] the pointed one!
10 […] may her releaser smash it (the scorpion) aside!

Commentary

1: The incipit of this incantation is cited in CAD P, 460a, taking the broken sign after *aṣbat pî* as AN (already Finkel 1999, 225). Examining different photos of the tablet, doubts arise relating to this reading. If indeed the spell is against scorpions, one expects the predator itself to appear here, but admittedly, the sign does not allow such a reading. – The assertive *aṣbat* "Verily, I have seized, gained control over..." is found in the present corpus in snake incantations, e.g., CUSAS 32, 27a: 3 (№ 106): *aṣbat* … "I seized (an enumeration of snakes)", TIM 9, 65: 1// TIM 9, 66a: 1 (№ 110): *aṣbat pī ṣerrī kalima* "I seized the mouth of all the snakes". As for scorpions, we find MB *aṣbatka kīma šarriqi* "I seized you like a thief" KBo 1, 18k: D 21' (Zomer 2018a, 276). Note, additionally, CUSAS 32, 49: 30 (№ 93): *luṣbassum kakkam* "I will take up a weapon against it (the scorpion)". Besides animals, we find the assertive *aṣbat* in RA 36, 3a: 1 (№ 144): *atbatka*[sic] *kīma* ... "I seized you (my adversary in trial) like …", and in the unpublished OB Egalkura incantation (Finkel *forthcoming*/b = № 180): 11': *aṣbatki zittum* "I seized you, Oh (inheritance) portion!".

1–2: The nocturnal setting of this incantation comes as no surprise, for scorpions are largely active at night and find a hiding place in day-time. The opening of another incantation against scorpions, CUSAS 32, 49: 1–3 (№ 93), offers a good parallel to these lines: "It is the yellow of the steppe, it is the black of the house, it is the soaring one of the sky…". The appellation "the soaring one of the sky" must refer to the constellation Scorpio. Our incantation, which speaks of gaining control of the stars at night, also has the astral scorpion in mind, not only the terrestrial one.

3–4: The profession of *pāširum* appears also in CUSAS 32, 49: 26/27 (№ 93) and in AMD 1, 247 (fig. 11): 3' (№ 83), both against scorpions. One can mention also the MB incantation KBo 1, 18k: D 23' (cf. Zomer 2018a, 276) which terminates with: *annûtu ša pašār zuqiqīpi* "This (incantation) is to expel a scorpion". Thus, *pašārum* – besides its common meaning "to release, undo" (esp. sorcery, as in UET 6/2, 193a: 8' = № 148) – carries a specific nuance of magically confronting scorpions, mainly with the participle *pāširum*/*pāširtum*.

4: For *līlum* "evening" in OB texts, see Streck (2017, 600). Reading *i-na li-li ša…* "in the evening of…" is possible, but the use of attached personal pronouns to parts of the day or night, relating to the subject, are known to serve as definite markers, as in *ana ina mušītisu itti sinni*[*štim alākim*] "(this magic talisman is good) for [walking[?]] with a wo[man] at night" (LB 1002: 8 = Wasserman, 2020c). On this syntactic phenomenon, see Huehnergard/Pat-El (2012); Stol (1996, 416–418) and Mayer (2005, 56, fn. 5).

5: The general meaning of this line escapes us, but *ziqtum* "sting" is clear, and ⸢GÍR[?].TAB[?]⸣ is probable.

7: Since this line is separated by rulings from the rest of the text, it may contain a subscript or alternatively an alloglot passage.

8: We understand *tārītum* "nurse" to be related with the expression *tārīt zuqāqīpi* denoting the mother scorpion (lit. scorpion's nurse), see CAD T, 233a. The expression *ina būd tārītim* is found in YOS 11, 8: 11 (№ 58, against various diseases).

9: *zaqtum* is a substantivized adjective "the pointed-one", referring to the scorpion.

10: Two other scorpion spells employ the verb *napāṣum* "to smash": CUSAS 32, 27c: 21' (№ 90) – *li-da-⸢ap⸣-pa-aṣ* and CUSAS 32, 49: 26 (№ 93) – *li-⸢it⸣-ta-pa-aṣ*. In both, these verbs have a passive meaning (Dt or Ntn, see George 2016, 111). Since it is hard to imagine that the text asks for the *pāširum* to be crushed, we expect an active use of *napāṣum* Gt with a separative meaning: the *pāširum* crushes the scorpion away from the individual. The feminine pronoun remains unclear.

№ 85: BM 97331b

SEAL No.: 7604
Copy: Plate I
Tablet Siglum: BM 97331
Photo: cf. SEAL No. 7604;
https://www.britishmuseum.org/collection/object/W_1902-1011-385
Edition: –
Studies: –
Collection: The British Museum, London
Provenance: Unknown
Measurements: 5.1 × 6.6 cm
Procedure: No

Introduction

The second incantation against scorpions on this tablet. On the obverse, an incantation mentioning a *pāširu* and a *pāširtu*, gaining control over a scorpion (BM 97331a = № 84). The scorpion is called *našpar mūtim*, the messenger of death, an epithet known from the Mari incantation RA 88, 161a: 6 (№ 97).

Reverse
10 [GÍR$^{?}$.TAB$^{?}$ *i*]-⸢*na*⸣ *Ap-si-i-im na-aš-pa-ar mu-tim*
11 ⸢*ša*$^{?}$⸣ ^{d}*Lugal-Márad*(AMAR.DA)^{ki} ⸢*id-ku-uš*$^{?}$*-šu*$^{?}$⸣ *a-na* ⸢*šu*$^{?}$⸣*-li-im*
12 *mār*(DUMU$^{!}$) *a-wi-lu-tim ta*$^{!}$*-ar-ṣa qà-‹ar›-na-šu ki-ma a-*⸢*tu-di*$^{!}$⸣
13 *mitḫāriš*(TÉŠ.⸢BI) *qar*⸣*-ni ṭé-ri ta-ri zi-ba-*[(*as*)*-sú*]
14 ⸢*i+na*⸣ *ma-*⸢*tim ug-gá-ti ir*⸣*-ḫi-ma qá-mu-*⸢*ú*$^{?}$⸣ [*iq*$^{?}$*-mu*$^{?}$]
15 *ú-qá eṭ-*⸢*la-am ša*⸣ *il-šu la i-la-kam*
16 ⸢*it-ti*⸣*-šu*

====

Translation

10–12 [The *scorpion* i]n the Apsû, the messenger of death *which* Lugal-Marad *has pressed*$^{?}$*/unleashed*$^{?}$ to the street, (to) the person (lit. "son of mankind")!
12–13 Its horns are stretched out like a wild ram, simultaneously it is rooting up (the ground) with (its) two horns. It is curled up as to [its] ta[il].
14 It inseminated the country with anger and [it inflicted] complete annihilation (with fire).
15–16 It waits for the young man, whose god does not go with him.

Commentary

10: In the break, we assume a reference to the scorpion: be it direct (GÍR.TAB) or metaphorical, as e.g., *alap erṣetim*. In any case, there is room for no more than two signs, so *i-wa-li-id* or *ka-ri-iṣ* are excluded.

11: On Lugal-Marad, see Stol (1987–1990, 148f.). As for ⸢*id-ku-uš*$^{?}$*-šu*$^{?}$⸣, we either assume a non-grammatical form from *dakāšum* "to press in" (*idkussu*), or an aberrant form from *dekûm* "move s.o. (to)" (*idkušu*). An intransitive Gt *akāšum* "to go away" (*itkušu*) does not fit the present context.

12: *kīma atūdi* is another example of ovine imagery, typical to incantations against scorpions, see Cavigneaux (1994, 157–158) and Guichard (2018, 31).

13: The phrase *tari zibbassu* is also attested in RA 88, 161a: 7 (№ 97) and Semitica 62, 19: 10–11 (№ 99). The verb *tarûm* "to turn upward$^{?}$" is connected with tails of animals, particularly pigs and dogs, see CAD T, 249b. This, together with its two attestations in the present corpus (in scorpion incantations), proves that *tarûm* denotes the curled upward position of the scorpion's tail. Note the parallel use of *tarûm* D (intensive) in the MB scorpion incantation KBo 1, 19j: D 17'–19' *qannīšu ana patê sibbassu ana turri ul addinšu* "To open its pincers, to curl its tail, I do not allow it!", see Zomer (2018a, 275).

15–16: Cf. Semitica 62, 19: 13–14 (№ 99).

№ 86: CUSAS 10, 19

SEAL No.: 7162
Copy: George 2009 Pl. LXIII
Tablet Siglum: MS 3949
Photo: George 2009 Pl. LXIII; CDLI P253038
Edition: George 2009, 156; George 2016, 163f.
Studies: George 2010; George 2016, 163f.
Collection: Schøyen Collection, Oslo
Provenance: Unknown
Measurements: 3.5 × 5.3 cm
Procedure: No

Introduction

Although not directly referring to it by name, this cursively written, landscape-oriented small tablet describes a scorpion (George 2010). Note the similarities to the Mari incantation RA 88, 161a (№ 97). The lines are clumsily arranged. One word even spreads over two lines (*muttaḫlilum*, 6–7).

Obverse
1 *qá-qá-da-am ú-la i-šu*
2 *ú-ul-da-šu-ma*[!]
3 *a-sú-ru-um ge*$_6$*-eš-pa*[!]*-ar*
4 *pu-ti-im qá-ar-ni*

Lower Edge
5 *i-šu qá-qá-da-am*

Reverse
6 *ú-la i-šu mu-ut-ta-aḫ-*
7 *li-lu-um mu-ma-ṣi*
8 *i-ga-ra-tim*

Translation

1 It has no head.
2–3 The footing of the wall bore it.
3–6 The snare of the forehead – it has horns. It has no head.
6–8 A sneak-thief, able to reach walls.

Commentary

2–3: For the scorpion being born in the *asurrûm*, see CUSAS 10, 19: 2–3 (№ 86) and CUSAS 32, 211: 26' (№ 87).

3–4: For *gešpar pūtim* and its parallel *našpar mūtim* in RA 88, 161a: 6 (№ 97), see George (2010).

6–7: The scorpion as a “thief” is found also in KBo 1, 18k: D 21'–22' (see Zomer 2018a, 276; 2019, 1266).

№ 87: CUSAS 32, 211

SEAL No.: 7163
Copy: George 2016 Pl. LXV
Tablet Siglum: MS 3084
Photo: George 2016 Pl. LXIV; CDLI P252093
Edition: see below
Studies: –
Collection: Schøyen Collection, Oslo
Provenance: Unknown
Measurements: 18.5 × 9.5 cm
Procedure: No

Introduction
This broken incantation, written on a large incantation collective, is eclectic in nature: the Asalluḫi-Enki dialogue (l. 28'), followed by the *mannam lušpur* formula (ll. 32'–34'), leads to a historiola about Sîn being stung by a scorpion and hiding in a brick pile (l. 31'). For similar historiolae, see CUSAS 32, 49 (№ 93) and YOS 11, 4b (№ 102). Our edition makes use of preliminary notes sent to us by George.

====

24' [x x x x] ⌜x x x⌝ [x x x (x)] ⌜*ki*$^{?}$*-ma*$^{?}$⌝ *na-ri* ⌜*ù*$^{?}$ x x⌝-[*i*]*m*

25' [x x x x x x x x x x x x x x x x] ⌜x (x) x x⌝-*šu*

26' [x x x x x x x x x x] ⌜*ma*⌝*-ti-m*[*a i*]-⌜*na*$^{?}$⌝ *a*$^{?}$*-sú*$^{?}$*-ur*$^{?}$*-ri*$^{?}$⌝ *i-wa-li-id*

27' [x x (x)] *i-na be*-[x x] ⌜x⌝*-ga-am* ⌜x x*-tum*$^{?}$⌝ ⌜*i*⌝*-za-qar-ra-am a-wa-tam i-qá-ab-bi*

28' [*a*$^{?}$*-n*]*a*$^{?}$ *be-lí-š*[*u*] ⌜x⌝ [x] *ša ti* ⌜*šu*$^{?}$⌝ [x x x] ⌜x⌝ *ša a-na-ku i-du-ú at-ta ti-de*

29' [*l*]*i-li-kam*$^{!}$*-ma* ⌜x x x⌝ ^{lú}[KIN].⌜GI$_4$.A⌝ ⌜x⌝ [x] uk/as *li-*⌜*ip-pa-ṭi*$^{?}$⌝*-ir a-wa-as-sú*

30' ⌜x⌝ mu$^{?}$ ma ri im ⌜š/ta di$^{?}$⌝ im *qá-*⌜*an*$^{?}$*-ni*$^{?}$*-šu* x x⌝ [*d*]*i-*⌜*pa*$^{?}$*-ar*⌝ *zi-ib-ba-ti-šu* 7 *ù* 7

31' *i-na e-pe-eš bi-tim šu-ba-al-ku-ut a-ma-ri-im ú-*[*ba-an*] ^{d}*Sîn*(EN.ZU) *ṣeḫertam*(TUR.RA) *zuqiqīpum*(GÍR.TAB) *iz-qú-ut*

32' ⌜*ma-an-na-am*⌝ *lu-uš-pu-ur a-na mārāt*(DUMU.MUNUS^{meš}) *Anim*(AN^{nim}) 7 *ù* 7 *ša-*⌜*ap*⌝ *me-e li-il-qé-a-nim*

33' [*ka-an-ni-ši-na*] *ša ḫu-ra-ṣi-im ka-ar-pa-ti-ši-na ša uq-ni-im el-li-im*

34' [*li-iš-ku-na-ma me*]*-e bu-ra-tim el-lu-tim li-iš-ti ta ak* ⌜x x x x x x⌝

35' [x x x x x x] ⌜x⌝ *li-ša lim-*⌜*ma*$^{?}$ pi⌝ ru um *i-na zi-iq-ni-šu* ⌜x⌝ [x x x x x]

====

Translation

24' … *like river and …*

25' … his …

26' … *(of) the country*$^{?}$ and he was born *in the footing of the wall*$^{?}$

27' … he uttered a word, saying

28'–29' [to] his lord: … "that what I know, you know! May he come and … the messenger …, may his word be absolved!"

30' … of his horns … the torch of his tail(s), (which) are seven and seven.

31' While building the house, while turning over the brick pile, the scorpion stung Sîn's little finger.

32'–34' Whom should I send to the Daughters of Anum, seven and seven, so that they will take bowl of water, [so that they place their pot stands] of gold, their pots of pure lapis-lazuli, so that he (the client) drinks pure [wate]r of the cisterns?

35' … may he be succesful … in his beard …

Commentary

24': Another attestation of a river in a scorpion incantation can be found, in a broken context, in CUSAS 32, 49: 19 (№ 93).

26': For ⸢*i*$^{?}$*-na*$^{?}$⸣ ⸢*a*$^{?}$*-sú*$^{?}$*-ur*$^{?}$*-ri*$^{?}$⸣ *iwwalid*, see CUSAS 10, 19: 2–3 (№ 86) and RA 88, 161a: 6 (№ 97).

31': The same phrase, probably, is found also in YOS 11, 4b: 25–26 (№ 102).

№ 88: CUSAS 32, 24a

SEAL No.: 7164
Copy: George 2016 Pl. LXX
Tablet Siglum: MS 3059
Photo: George 2016 Pl. LXX; CDLI P252068
Edition: George 2016, 115f.
Studies: –
Collection: Schøyen Collection, Oslo
Provenance: Unknown
Measurements: 5.7 × 4.5 cm
Procedure: No

Introduction

Cursive early-OB signs (/la/ l. 6; /ma/ r. 6). The tablet is reused (see the leftover signs on the reverse and the space left before r. 1). The incantation shows parallels with CUSAS 32, 30d (№ 92).

Obverse

1 *[n]a-al-ba-⸢an⸣* ^{na4}*uqnîm*(ZA.⸢GÌN⸣.A)
2 *ke-eš-ki-ir-ri*$^{!}$ *eb-bi-i*
3 *a-na A-sà-lu-uḫ māri*(DUMU) *É-a*
4 *li-iq-bu-ú*
5 *ma-ri ši-ip-ri ša-pi-ir*
6 *la ka-li a-la-ka*
7 *li-pu-uš*
8 *ši-pa-at zuqiqīpim*(GÍR.TA[B$^{!}$])

Translation

1–2 Oh brick mould of lapis lazuli! Oh brick board of pure (*gold*)!
3–4 May they say to Asalluḫi, son of Ea:
5–7 "The messenger was sent off. He must not be detained! May he continue going!"
8 Incantation (against) a scorpion.

Commentary

2: Similarly, *nalbattum ša kaspim ⸢ki⸣-is-ki-[ir]-⸢ki*$^{!?}$*⸣ ša ḫurāṣim* (Elamica 10, 65c: 18–19 = № 95, against scorpions). Cf. George (2016, 116).

№ 89: CUSAS 32, 24b

SEAL No.: 13484
Copy: George 2016 Pl. LXX
Tablet Siglum: MS 3059
Photo: George 2016 Pl. LXX; CDLI P252068
Edition: George 2016, 115f.
Studies: –
Collection: Schøyen Collection, Oslo
Provenance: Unknown
Measurements: 5.7 × 4.5 cm
Procedure: No

Introduction

A short incantation on an incantation collective, with a line that could be in phonetic Sumerian. The Moon-god is called upon for help along with other gods. A few remaining signs on the reverse, written diagonally, suggest that this is a re-used tablet.

Reverse

(*few signs written diagonally*)

9 ^{d}Nanna Nanna
10 ki-si-ig si-li ér {x}
11 ku-ús-sa in-da-ag-ra
12 tu-re kúr-re
13 *a-na ši-ip-tim*
14 *ma-li i-ba-aš-šu-ú*

Upper edge
15 *in-na-di-/nu-šum*$^{?}$

Left edge
16 *ma-ri ši-ip-ri ša-pi-*[*ir*]
17 *zuqiqīpum*(GÍR.TAB) *íz-qù-*[*sú*] / {x}

Translation

9 Oh Nanna, Nanna!
10 *kisig sili er*
11–12 Oh Kusu and Indagar! A man is stung!
13–15 For the incantation, all that there is will be given to him.
16–17 The messenger was sent off – a scorpion stung [him].

Commentary

10: ki-si-ig could stand for kisig, *kispu* "funerary offerings" to which ér "weeping, mourning; tears" fits well.

12: Reading and interpretation with George (2016, 116).

14: Note the Sandhi spelling in *ma-li ibaššû.*

13–17: The closure mentioning a messenger, supplies the specific circumstances of this one-off spell.

№ 90: CUSAS 32, 27c

SEAL No.: 7165
Copy: George 2016 Pl. LXXV
Tablet Siglum: MS 2791
Photo: George 2016 Pl. LXXIII; CDLI P251837
Edition: George 2016, 110
Studies: –
Collection: Schøyen Collection, Oslo
Provenance: Unknown
Measurements: 15.0 × 7.0 cm
Procedure: No

Introduction
The third of three incantations on an elongated, one-column tablet: the first against a snake (CUSAS 32, 27a = № 106), the second, in Sumerian, is meant to heal broken bones (ll. r. 11'–r. 15'). Early-OB script. The speaker in this incantation stands for Enki: it is he who created the scorpion and therefore he is able to quash it.

Reverse

====

16' *[i-na li-i]b-bi-ia ab-ni-i-ka*
17' *[i-na ṭī]dim*([I]M) *ša qá-ti-ia*
18' *⸢e⸣-pu-uš-ka*
19' *[m]a-an-nu-um a-na ša-am-mi-im*
20' *[š]a mu-tim ú-te-er-ka*
21' *zuqiqīpum*(GÍR.TAB) *li-da-⸢ap⸣-pa-aṣ*
22' *a-wi-lum li-ib-lu-u[t]*
23' ^{d}*En-ki be-lí ki-a-am iq-bi*
24' tu$_6$-én-é-nu-ru
25' ka-inim-ma gír-tab

====

Translation
16'–18' "I have created you [inside me], I pinched you [from the di]rt of my hands.
19'–20' Who turned you into a 'plant of death'?
21'–22' May the scorpion be crushed! May the man live!"
23' Thus spoke Enki, my lord.
24' tu$_6$-én-é-nu-ru
25' Incantation (against) a scorpion.

Commentary

16'–18': The scorpion is also said to be pinched from the Apsû's clay in RA 88, 161a: 5 (№ 97). For other cases where Enki created creatures from the dirt of his hands, see George (2016, 111).

19'–20': A 'plant of death', here designating the scorpion's virulent venom, is not commonly found (but see, CAD Š/1, 320). It stands in apposition to *šammu ša alādi* and *šammu ša balāṭi* (CAD Š/1, 319).

21'–22': For the similar formula "may X die but may the man live!", see George (2016, 111) and Zomer (2018a, 61 with fn. 208).

21': For the irregular form of the verb *napāṣum*, see George (2016, 111). The expected form is found in CUSAS 32, 49: 26 (№ 93).

№ 91: CUSAS 32, 30c

SEAL No.: 13431
Copy: George 2016 Pl. LXXXI
Tablet Siglum: MS 3093
Photo: George 2016 Pl. LXXX; CDLI P252102
Edition: –
Studies: George 2016, 48
Collection: Schøyen Collection, Oslo
Provenance: Unknown
Measurements: 12.0 × 13.5 cm
Procedure: Yes

Introduction
Very fragmentary. Lapis lazuli is mentioned – perhaps referring to brick mould, as in CUSAS 32, 24a: 1 (№ 88).

i

17	[x x x] ⸢x⸣ ni
18	[x x x x] ⸢x⸣ i/a/uḫ ši
19	[x x x x x] ⸢x x⸣ mu un ka
20	[x] ⸢x x⸣ [x x x] i sà ak nu
21	[x] ⸢x x⸣ [x] ⸢x⸣ ^{na4}⸢*uq*$^{?}$⸣-*ni*
22	[tu$_6$]-én-⸢é⸣-nu-ru
23	ka-inim-ma gír-tab
24	[dù]-⸢dù⸣-bi *a-na me-e*
25	[*li*]-*ša-am ta-ma-*[*ḫa-a*]*ḫ-ma*
26	[x x x] ⸢x x x⸣ [...]

Translation

17–20	(*Unintelligible*)
21	… of lapis lazuli.
22	[tu$_6$]-én-⸢é⸣-nu-ru
23	Incantation (against) a scorpion
24–26	Its procedure: you moisten dough in water and …

№ 92: CUSAS 32, 30d

SEAL No.: 13429
Copy: George 2016 Pl. LXXXI
Tablet Siglum: MS 3093
Photo: George 2016 Pl. LXXX; CDLI P252102
Edition: George 2016, 114f.
Studies: George 2016, 48
Collection: Schøyen Collection, Oslo
Provenance: Unknown
Measurements: 12.0 × 13.5 cm
Procedure: Yes

Introduction

Opening with an invocation to the brick mould, the incantation continues not with Sîn, but with a messenger being stung (cf. CUSAS 32, 49: 13–17 = № 93). A legitimation formula mentioning Enki, Asalluḫi and Ensigal-Abzu follows. A detailed healing procedure seals the spell.

ii
1 *[na-al]-⸢ba⸣-[an] ⸢uq⸣-[ni-im]*
2 *⸢ki-iš⸣-ki-ir e-eb-b[i-im]*
3 *ša-⸢ap⸣-ra ma-ar ili*(DINGIR)-[*šu*]
4 *zuqaqīpum*(GÍR.TAB) *iz-qú-*[*sú*]
5 *⸢ma⸣-ar ši-ip-ri-[im]*
6 *me-e ši-qí-i-[ma]*
7 *a-⸢li⸣-ik ur-ḫi-im la ka-l[i]*
8 *a-la-ka-am li-pu-u[š]*
9 *ši-ip-tum ⸢ú⸣-ul ia-tum*
10 *ši-pa-at* ^{d}*En-ki* ^{d}*Asal-lú-ḫi*
11 *ù* ^{d}*En*$_{5}$*-si-gal-abzu*
12 *i-na qí-bi-it* ^{d}*En-⸢ki⸣*
13 ^{d}*Asal-lú-ḫi ù* ^{d}*En*$_{5}$*-si-gal-abzu*
14 *ma-aḫ-ṣú-um li-ib-lu-uṭ-ma*
15 *qí-bi-it* ^{d}*En-ki l[i-ši-i]r*
16 *šum-ma ma-aḫ-ṣú-um ⸢it⸣-ta-⸢al-kam⸣*
17 *li-ša-am a-na ša-ḫa-ti-⸢šu⸣*
18 *a-na ri-bi-ti-i-⸢šu⸣*
19 *ta-ša-ak-ka-an*
20 *šum-ma ⸢ma⸣-ar ši-ip-ri-im*
21 *i-la-ka-ak-kum*
22 *ši-ip-ta-am a-na me-e ta-na-ad-⸢di⸣-ma*
23 *i-ša-at-ti*
24 *ki-a-am ta-qá-ab-bi-šum*

25 *um-ma an-na-an-na-ma*
26 *ba-al-ṭa-*⸢*ti*⸣
27 ⸢ka⸣-inim-ma gír-[tab]

Translation

1–2 Oh brick mould of lapis lazuli, Oh brick board of pure (*lapis lazuli*)!
3–4 The scorpion stung the messenger, son of his god.
5–6 Give the messenger water to drink!
7–8 The traveller should not be detained! Let him continue travelling!
9–11 The incantation is not mine. It is the incantation of Enki, Asalluḫi and Ensigal-Abzu!
12–13 By the command of Enki, Asalluḫi and Ensigal-Abzu,
14–15 may the stricken one be well and the command of Enki be true!
16–19 If the stricken one has come (to you), you place dough in his armpits and groins.
20–26 If the messenger comes to you, you cast an incantation over the water and he drinks it. As follows you will speak to him: "N.N., you are well!"
27 Incantation (against) a scorpion.

Commentary

11/13: For Ensigal-Abzu, see George (2016, 115).
26: For 2. sg. m. stative forms with *-āti* (cf. l. 24), as in JCS 9, 10: 32 (№ 55), see Wasserman (2011, 11 and 2016, 173).

№ 93: CUSAS 32, 49

SEAL No.: 7166
Copy: George 2016 Pl. CXVIII
Tablet Siglum: MS 3060
Photo: George 2016 Pl. CXVII; CDLI P252069
Edition: George 2016, 113f.
Studies: George 2016, 111–113
Collection: Schøyen Collection, Oslo
Provenance: Unknown
Measurements: 7.5 × 4.4 cm
Procedure: No

Introduction

Commencing with a description of the scorpion (perhaps different kinds of scorpions, in plural), the incantation recounts how Sîn was stung by a scorpion (see CUSAS 32, 211 = № 87 and YOS 11, 4b = № 102). By the end, the healer presents himself in the first-person voice. A magician is mentioned in broken context (*wāšip…*, l. 32).

Obverse

1 ⸢*wa*⸣*-ru-uq ša ṣe-*⸢*e*⸣*-*[*ri-*(*im*)]
2 *ṣa-li-im ša bi-t*[*im*]
3 *mu-ut-ta-ap-ri-iš ša-m*[*a-i*]
4 *a-ru-uḫ ša ba-aš-tim*
5 *ša i-na e-pe-er ša-di-š*[*u*]
6 *ba-al-lu*
7 *bu-da-šu li-bi-it-tum*
8 *li-ib-ba-šu na-du-u*[*m*]
9 *li-iḫ-‹ḫe›-pi li-bi-it-tum*
10 *li-iš-ša-ri-iṭ na-du-um*
11 *li-ib-li di-pa-ar*
12 *zi-ib-ba-ti-šu ù qá-an-ni-*[*šu*]
13 ^{d}*Sîn*(EN.ZU) *bi-it-sú i-*⸢*pu*⸣*-uš*
14 [*i-na*] *e-pe-eš bi-ti-šu*
15 [*i-na š*]*u-ba-al-ku-ut a-ma-*[*ri-im*]
16 [*ú-b*]*a-an* ^{d}*Sîn*(EN.ZU) *ṣe-ḫe-*[*er-tam*]

Reverse

17 [*li-bi*]*-tu iz-qú-ut*
18 [x (x)] ⸢x⸣ ti [x]
19 [x x] it *nāru*(ÍD) ⸢x x⸣ [x x]
20 *ru-ku-us li-*[*bi-it-tam*]
21 *i-na qá-an-*[*n*]*i-*[*ša/šu*]
22 *a-a ik-ki-*⸢*ip a*⸣*-*[*na p*]*a-*⸢*a*⸣*-*[*ni-šu*]

23 *a-a ir-ḫi-iṣ a-na wa-a*[*r-ki-šu*]
24 *im-ta-am* is ˹x˺ um [x x]
25 *li-iš-ti* ˹x x˺ ak [x x]
26 *li-*˹*it*˺*-ta-pa-aṣ pa-*˹*ši*˺-[*ru-um?*]
27 *pa-ši-ir-tum* [*l*]*i-*˹*te!*˺*-l*[*i-lu*]
28 *pa-ši-ir* ˹x x x˺*-tim*
29 *i-na zi-*[*ba?*]*-t*[*i*]*-šu*
30 *lu-uṣ-ba-as-súm ka-*˹*ak*˺*-k*[*a-am*]
31 *ša ma-a-*[x (x)]
32 *wa-ši-ip* ˹x x x˺ [x x x]
33 a ˹x x˺ bi [x x x]
34 *ka-ši-ip* [x x x x]
35 ka-inim-[ma gír-tab]

Translation

1–4 It is the yellow of the steppe, it is the black of the house, it is the soaring one of the sky, it is the rushing one of the shrubs.
5–6 The one spread with the dust of its mountain of origin,
7–8 its shoulders – a brick, its middle part – a water-skin.
9–12 May the brick be broken! May the water-skin be torn! May the torch of its tail and its two horns be extinguished!
13–17 Sîn built his house. [While] building his house, while turning over the brick pile, [a bri]ck stung Sîn's little finger.
18–19 […] … […]
20–27 Bind the [brick] by [its] two horns! May it not charge forward! May it not hasten backwards! May it drink (its own) … poison…! May it be crushed! May the male releaser and the female releaser *purify*!
28–29 *The releaser of … in its t*[*ai*]*l.*
30 I will take up a weapon against it.
31–32 … the magician of …
33–34 *is bewitched …*
35 Incantation [(against) a scorpion].

Commentary

1: We read *ṣe-*˹*e*˺-[*ri-*(*im*)] (George has *ṣe-*˹*e*˺-[*tim*]).

1–6: It is possible that, as in some snake incantations (see, esp. TIM 9, 65 = № 110), this incantation starts with a list of different scorpions against which it is supposed to work. The scorpions are distinguished according to their colour and/or habitat, and are arranged along two opposite poles: outside-inside (steppe-house) and up-down (sky-earth). Notable is the use of the sound Š in the middle of each line, welding this thematic unit phonetically: *waruq* ***ša*** *ṣē*[*rim*] / *ṣalim* ***ša*** *bītim* / *muttapriš* ***šam***[*āʾī*] / *aruḫ* ***ša*** *baštim* / ***ša*** *ina eper* ***šadīš***[***u***] *ballu.*

3: Without denying the possible zoological reality of flying scorpions and the mythology woven around such creatures (see George 2016, 113), we understand that the incantation refers to the scorpion in the sky, namely the zodiac sign

Scorpio. The mention of *muttapriš šam[āʾī]* makes it clear that the historiola recounting Sîn's being stung by a scorpion (ll. 13–17) has a stellar setting: the moon taking a position in *Scorpio* next to its tail.

4: For *baštum* > later *baltum*, "thorny shrub" (not "dignity" or "beauty), see George (2016, 113–114).

5–6: George (2016, 114) marked that *eper šadīšu* equals Sum. s a ḫ a r k u r - r a, "crude ore", probably describing the metal tone typical of a scorpion's body.

7–12: These lines are stitched with labials and dentals: ***b**ūḏāšu li**b**iṯṯum* / *li**bb**ašu nāḏum liḫ‹ḫe›**pi** li**b**iṯṯum liššariṭ nāḏum* / *li**b**li ḏi**p**ār zi**bb**aṯišu u qanni[šu]*. Alliteration links this passage to the previous one: *libli* (< *balûm*) in l. 11 echoes *ballu* (< *balālum*) in l. 6.

8: Also in YOS 11, 1: 4 (№ 100), the scorpion's body is compared to a water-skin.

11–12: A torch, a metaphor for his sting, is found also in YOS 11, 35: 6–7 (№ 104).

12: Note the unusual assimilation of *qarnīšu* to *qannīšu*. The same form is found in l. 21.

17: The sign *-tu* after the break suggests *[libit]tu* (see also *li-*[...] in l. 20). It is probably the brick which stung the Moon-god: the scorpion stings so quietly and escapes so quickly that even Sîn can't grasp the agent of the vicious deed (cf. l. 7).

18: A river is mentioned, in broken context, in CUSAS 32, 211: 24' (№ 87).

22: For the scorpion as a goring bull, see RA 88, 161a: 1 (№ 97). George (2003, 112–113) marks the similarity of this description and Ḫumbaba's fighting for his life in Gilg. V 165.

26: For *napāṣum*, cf. commentary to BM 97331a: 10 (№ 84).

№ 94: CUSAS 32, 50a

SEAL No.: 13430
Copy: George 2016 Pl. CXIX
Tablet Siglum: MS 3073
Photo: George 2016 Pl. CXIX; CDLI P252082
Edition: George 2016, 116
Studies: –
Collection: Schøyen Collection, Oslo
Provenance: Unknown
Measurements: 5.8 × 4.9 cm
Procedure: No

Introduction
A short and atypical incantation against scorpions. On the reverse, an incantation for honeybees (CUSAS 32, 50b = № 77).

Obverse
1 [*lu*$^{?}$]-*li-mu ši-pa-as-sú*
2 [x (x) A]NŠE *ra-ma-an-šu*
3 [*ka*$^{?}$-*la*$^{?}$]-⸢*šu*⸣ *ra-ma-ni ú-wa-aš-ši-ip*
4 [tu]-én-é-nu-ru
5 ka-inim-ma gír-tab

Translation
1 A *stag* is his spell,
2 […] (of a) donkey is his body,
3 I enchant my body [*in*] its [*totality*]!
4 [tu]-én-é-nu-ru
5 Incantation (against) a scorpion

Commentary
1: George (2016, 116) suggests alternatively [*ṭù*]-*li-mu* "spleen" and [*sa*]-*li-mu* "friendliness".
3: George (2016, 116): [*ba-lu*]-*šu*.

№ 95: Elamica 10, 65c

SEAL No.: 27434
Copy: –
Tablet Siglum: –
Photo: Krebernik/Wasserman 2020, 65–68
Edition: Krebernik/Wasserman 2020, 48–50
Studies: –
Collection: Private Collection
Provenance: Unknown
Measurements: 9.4 × 6.1 cm
Procedure: Yes

Introduction
This hybrid (Elamite and Akkadian) incantation collective, destined to fight scorpions, is the longest second millennium alloglot magic text known so far. Judging by the ductus – typical of the First Sealand Dynasty – the text can be dated to the later part of the chronological framework of our corpus (note the syllabic use of /qad/ and /lik/ in l. 20 and of /bal/ in l. 29). The Akkadian incantation begins with a historiola describing the building of a house. Although not said explicitly, we assume that – as in other parallel historiolae – it refers to the Moon-god being stung by a scorpion. A rubric designating the purpose of the spell and short procedure seals the text.

Reverse

17 *Bēlet-ilī*(DINGIR.⸢MAḪ⸣) (⸢x⸣) ⸢x⸣ *i-na* ⸢*maḫ-ri*⸣*-ki i-ip-pu-uš bītam*(É?)
18 ⸢*na*⸣*-al-*⸢*ba-at-tum*⸣ *ša kaspim*(⸢KÙ⸣.BABBAR)
19 ⸢*ki*⸣*-is-ki-*[*ir*]*-*⸢*ki*!?⸣ *ša ḫurāṣim*(KÙ.GI)
20 *dipārum*(⸢IZI?⸣.GAR) *i-na* ⸢*na*⸣-[x]-*e i-qad*(-)⸢x *i*?⸣-*na zuqāqipim*(GÍR.TAB) ⸢*lik*?⸣*-šu-ud*
21 ⸢*a*⸣-[*wi*?-*l*]*u*?-*um*?-*ma ta-ri-*⸢*ik*?⸣ *ši-ip-rum*!
22 [DUMU? *š*]*i-ip-ri š*[*a* …]
23 [x] ⸢*e*? x x x *ma i*?⸣-[…]
24 [*l*]*i-ib-lu-*[*uṭ*]

Upper Edge

25 [k]a-inim-ma *ša* gír-⸢tab⸣ [(x)] ⸢x⸣ ⸢lú?⸣
26 [(x)-]⸢x gur?⸣ tab/me!?-kam

Left Edge

27 *awīlum*(LÚ) *ša* ⸢*al*?-x⸣ *ša zuqāqipum*(GÍR.TAB) ⸢x x⸣ […]
28 *me*!-*e i-ša-aq-*⸢*qú*?-*šu*? x x⸣ […]
29 ⸢*i*⸣-*bal-*⸢*lu*⸣-[*uṭ*]

Translation

17	Oh Bēlet-ilī the..., he is building *a house*? in front of you:
18–19	Your brick mould made of silver, board (for bricks) made of gold!
20	A torch in the ... will kindle. May it reach the scorpion.
21	The man has become dark. The work/message,
22	(the … of) the work/message of/which …
23–24	… in order that he would get well.
25–26	An incantation for a scorpion which … a man …
27–29	A man … whom a scorpion … They will make him drink water … and he will get well.

Commentary

See Krebernik/Wasserman (2020).

№ 96: RA 66, 141b

SEAL No.: 7167
Copy: Nougayrol 1972, 141
Tablet Siglum: AO 7682
Photo: –
Edition: Nougayrol 1972, 141–143
Studies: Cunningham 1997 Cat. No. 357; Wasserman 2003 Cat. No. 140; Pientka-Hinz 2004, 389f.; Foster 2005, 993
Collection: Louvre, Paris
Provenance: Unknown
Measurements: 7.5 × 4.4 cm
Procedure: Yes

Introduction

This scorpion incantation follows a syllabic Sumerian spell ("Life! Life! Life! ..."). The reverse contains the procedure.

Obverse

----

7 *wa-ru-uq i-na ba-aš-tim*
8 *ša-ḫur i-na ba-ṣí*
9 *im-ta i-šu i-na na-al-ba-ni*

Reverse

10 *ša li-ib-bi šēri*(UZU-*ri*)
11 *te-le*$^{!?}$*-eq-qé*$^{!}$*-e-ma*
12 *mu-uḫ*$^{?}$*-ḫi*$^{?}$ *zi-iq-ti*
13 *ta-pa-aš-ša-aš-ma*
14 *i-ne-e-iš*

Translation

7–9 It is yellow in the shrubs, it is deadly quiet in the sands, it has venom in the brick mould.
10–14 You will take out what's in the flesh and rub the sting with oil and he will recover.

Commentary

7: For *baštum*, "shrubs", see George (2016, 114) and CUSAS 32, 49: 4 (№ 93).
9: "It has venom in the brick mould" refers elliptically to the story about the scorpion stinging Sîn while he is working on building his house, see CUSAS 32, 211 (№ 87) and CUSAS 32, 49 (№ 93).
10: *ša libbi šēri* reminds of *ša libbi uzun immēri* (YOS 11, 4b: 20 = № 102).

№ 97: RA 88, 161a

SEAL No.: 7168
Copy: Cavigneaux 1994, 161
Tablet Siglum: M. 15289
Photo: –
Edition: Cavigneaux 1994
Studies: Wasserman 2003 Cat. No. 145; George 2010; Guichard 2018, 29–33
Collection: Deir ez-Zor Museum$^{?}$/ Damascus$^{?}$
Provenance: Mari
Measurements: –
Procedure: No

Introduction

A landscape-oriented tablet which holds three incantations: the first, in Akkadian, against a scorpion (ll. 1–r. 4'); the second, against an unknown agent, in non-identified language (ll. r. 5'–9'); the third, in Akkadian, against various diseases (ll. r. 10'–13'). The scorpion is the "bull of the earth" and the "messenger of death" whose origin is in the Apsû.

Obverse

1 *a-la-ap er-ṣé-e-tim e-te-lum*
2 *bu-ru-um ek-du-um mu-na-ki-pu ša-am*$_7$*-ru*
3 *qa-lu*$^{?!}$*-um mu-ug-da-ru-*⸢*um mu-na-*x⸣-[...]
4 *ša-am*$_7$*-rum i-na ki-sa-a*[*l*] ⸢*ir*⸣-[...]
5 *ka-ri-iṣ-ma i-na Ap-si-im ṭi*$_4$-⸢*da-šu*⸣
6 *ul-da-aš-šu a-su-ru-um na-aš-pa-ar mu-ti*$^{?!}$-[*im*]
7 *zi-ba-sú gi-*⸢*ri*⸣*-i ta-ri im-tam*
8 ⸢*qa*⸣-[*ar-ni i*]*-šu qa-qa-da* ⸢*ú*⸣*-ul i-*[*šu*]
9 [x x x x x x x] ⸢x x⸣ ir [...]

Reverse

1' *ki-ma ši*$^{?}$*-it*$^{?}$ [...]
2' *ši-ip-tum ú-ul i-ia-*[*t*]*um ši-pa-a*[*t* ^{d}*Da-mu*$^{?}$]
3' *be-el ši-pa-tim ù* ^{d}*Nin-kar-a*[*k*$^{?}$ ...]
4' *be-el-et ṣé-*[*ri-im* ...]

Translation

1–4 The bull of the earth, noble one, frantic calf, constantly-goring, raging, *swift*, pulling back, ... [...], fierce in the courtyard ... [...]
5–6 In the Apsû its clay was pinched, the footing of the wall bore it – the *messenger* of death.
7–8 Its tail is fire, curled up with poison, [it has] h[orns, it] has no head.
9 ...

1' …

2'–4' The spell is not min[e], it is the spel[l *of Damu*$^{?}$], the lord of spells and of Ninkarra[k …], the lady of *st*[*eppe*$^{?}$].

Commentary

1–2: For more examples of the metaphoric appellation "bull" for a scorpion, see Cavigneaux (1994, 157). Cf. also CUSAS 32, 49: 22 (№ 93). More on *alap erṣetim* referring to scorpions, see Rudik (2003).

3: Reading with Cavigneaux (1994, 155). The scorpion's swift movement backwards is described also in CUSAS 32, 49: 22–23 (№ 93).

5: The scorpion's origin is from the dirt on Enki's fingers also in CUSAS 32, 27c: 17'–18' (№ 90).

6: For the connection of *našpar mūtim* with *gešpar pūtim* in CUSAS 10, 19: 3–4 (№ 86), see George (2010). – The *asurrûm* as the origin of the scorpion, see CUSAS 10, 19: 2–3 (№ 86) and CUSAS 32, 21l: 26' (№ 87).

7: For *tarûm* describing the scorpion's tail, see commentary to BM 97331b: 13 (№ 85).

8: This line can be safely restored with the help of CUSAS 10, 19: 1, 5–6.

№ 98: Semitica 62, 15f.

SEAL No.: 27568
Copy: Guichard 2020a, 17f.
Tablet Siglum: CUNES 49–02–218
Photo: Guichard 2020a, 15f.
Edition: Guichard 2020a, 9–11
Studies: Cavigneaux 2021
Collection: Cornell University Cuneiform Library
Provenance: Larsa area
Measurements: –
Procedure: No

Introduction

A unique incantation which lifts the veil on an unknown magic practice of opposing a threatening scorpion: the magician challenged the arachnid verbally, while holding it in his hands. Another peculiarity of the text is its first-person pl. voice. Are the pl. verbal forms to be understood as "plural of ecstasy", typical of love literature (Paul 1995 and Wasserman 2016, 122/153)? It is more likely that they refer to the magician and his anonymous helpers.

Obverse
1 *e-da qá-ar-na-ka ki-ma ú-ri-ṣi*
2 *ki-ma né-ši-im ša-gi-mi-im*
3 *ta-ri-at zi-ib-ba-at-ka*
4 *e-ez pí-ka ú-šu-⸢um?⸣-ga-al-⸢la?⸣-‹ta/at›*
5 *i-na ši-ip-tim ṣerram*(MUŠ) *ni-ṣa-ba-at*
6 *ù za-qí-qí-ba-am ši-pa-at mu-tim*
7 *ni-im-mé-li-la-aš-šu i-na qa-ti-ni*
8 *šu-ḫu-uṭ qá-ar-ni li-⸢iš⸣-ku-u[n]*
9 *qá-qá-ar-šu ḫu-bi-it zi-ba-at!-ka*
10 *a-na bi-ri-it ḫa-al-li-ka*
11 *a-na-ku lu-ta-wu-ú*
12 *a-na-ku lu-ud-bu-ub at-ta*
13 *ki-ma ì-lí ia-ti*

Lower Edge
14 *du-ug-la-an-ni*

Reverse
15 *ki-ma ṣe-eḫ-ri la-ʾì-im*
16 *e tu-te-ra a-wa!*(PA)*-at-ka*
17 *ki-ma ṭa-ab-tim ù ka-sí-im*
18 *e-li mu-uš-te-mi-ia*
19 *lu ṭa-ba-a-⸢ku⸣ si-ku-ur a-wa-tum*

20 *di-nu-um du-ru*$^{!}$*-um*
21 6 *pu-šu* 7$^{!}$ *li-ša-nu-šu*
22 *li-im-qú-ut du-ru*
23 *li-iš-ta-li-pa*
24 *li-ib-na-tu-šu-ú*
25 *le-ke-ni* ‹‹im›› *ma-ar-ta*
26 *še*$_{20}$*-we e-we-*⸢*ti*⸣*-šu-nu*
27 *ta-ma-ta*$^{!}$(SI) *ṣí-i*
28 *ša a-na i-di-ia at-pa-lu-ú*
29 te-ni-in-nu-ri

Translation

1 Your two horns are pointed like (of) a goat!
2–3 Your tail is curled up like (that of) a roaring lion!
4 Your mouth is furious! (*You are*) a dragon!
5–6 We seize the snake with a (simple) spell, but the scorpion – (with) a spell of death!
7 We play with it (the scorpion) in our hands.
8–9 Slough down (your) horns to the ground!
9–10 *Drag* your tail in between your thighs!
11–12 As for me, I will speak! As for me, I will declare!
12–14 As for you, watch me like a (personal) god!
15–16 Do not dispute with me like a little child!
17–19 May my words (lit. I) be flavourful to my listener as salt and mustard!
19–20 The words – the lock! The verdict – a wall!
21 Six are its mouths, seven its tongues!
22–24 May the wall fall down! May its bricks be overturned!
25–26 Take from me the poison (lit. bile)! Make them *impose* (upon themselves) their *malicious words*!
27 You *are conjured*$^{?}$: go out!
28 That is what I am saying to my arms.
29 te-ni-in-nu-ri

Commentary

1: *kīma urīṣi*: for ovine imagery in scorpion incantations, see *kīma atūdi* in BM 97331b: 12 (№ 85).

4: The curtailed stative *ez*, instead of *eziz* or *ezi* may be intentional, for it plays on the homonym *ezzu*, or *enzu* "she-goat", pairing with *urīṣu* "male goat" in l. 1.
Reading *ú-šu-*⸢*um*$^{?}$⸣*-ga-al-*⸢*la*$^{?}$⸣*-‹ta/ta›* with Cavigneaux (2021, 1–2).

5: Although the text states that "we seize the snake with a (simple) spell", there were snakes who could not be undone by spells, as demonstrated in the phrase *ṣerri lā šiptum* "a snake impervious to spell(s)" (AMD 1, 245 (fig. 5): 13 = № 105; CUSAS 32, 27a: 4 = № 106; OECT 15, 260: 25 = № 109; TIM 9, 65 // TIM 9, 66a: 2 = № 110). – Cavigneaux (2021, 1) translates: "mais le scorpion nous allons jouer avec lui l'incantation de la mort", namely he assumes that playing with the scorpion is connected to the spell. – The epithet "messenger of death" found in BM 97331b: 10 (№ 85).

7: We learn here that the magician was confronting the scorpion while holding it, tossing it in his hands. This scene is echoed in the last line of the spell (l. 28) (Guichard 2020a, 10, differently).

7–9: Against Guichard (2020a, 10), the magic expert in this passage expresses the wish that the predator's attack will be ineffective. Mark the musicality of this phrase, with the alternation of **š** and **k/q**: *nimmelillaššu ina qātīni šuḫut qarni liškun qaqqaršu*. Cavigneaux (2021, 1) parses the lines differently, translating: "Dans notre main enlève les 'cornes', qu'il (les?) mette à terre".

9–10: Dividing the lines differently (ll. 7–8/9/10), Guichard (2020a, 9) takes these lines as describing the scorpion: "Sa (partie) contre le sol correspond à l'abdomen, la queue est petite", having *ribītu* "(a part of the body)" (CAD R, 321) in mind. We follow here Cavigneaux (2021, 1) and read *ḫubbit zibbatka*.

14: The order "look at me!" is typical of love incantations: CUSAS 32, 23b: 16 (№ 132, *amranni*); OECT 11, 11: 4' (№ 133, *amrīnni*); YOS 11, 87: 21 (№ 136, *ittaplasīni*) and ZA 75, 198–204b: 24 (№ 137, *amranni*) (Cf. also YOS 11, 87: 6).

17–19: For another example of the poetic merging between the semantic field of speech and sweet food, see Wasserman (1997). Note the chiastic construction *kīma ṭābtim…lū ṭābâku*.

20: Against Guichard (2020a, 10, *tú-ú-um* "le verdict c'est l'incantation"), we follow Cavigneaux (2021, 1, 2) and read *du-ru*$^{!}$*-um* "la sentence un rempart" (cf. l. 22). Note that *sikkūr awātum dīnum dūrum* creates an elegant chiastic construction.

21: Six mouths and seven tongues are characteristics of a snake (TIM 9, 65 // TIM 9, 66a: 9 = № 110). For the trope "six… seven…" see also the wisdom dialogue between father and son (Foster/George 2020, 40: a i 46 // b i 7).

22–24: An echo of the story in which Sîn, while building a house, was stung by a scorpion.

25: With *martum* "bile", for poison, *lêkum* "to lick" makes better sense than *leqûm* "to take", which, nonetheless, is also possible (so Cavigneaux 2021). This request follows ll. 17–19, where the healer wishes his words to be tasty as salt and mustard. The imperative *lēkenni* is here taken as a double acc. construction with *marta*, cf. § GAG^{3} 145e (The superfluous IM, bridging *lēkenni* with *marta*, is most likely a hearing mistake).

26: Guichard (2020a, 10) translates "Brûlez leur frauds!", but *šaw/mûm* "to roast (trans.)" is barely attested (CAD Š/1, 350), and its collocation with malicious words (*i/ewītišunu*) is also problematic. Cavigneaux (2021, 2) differs and reads *šiwewêtišunu* "de leurs (= ?) jointures (?)" from *šiwītu/šibītu* "suture, seam", admitting that the result is not clear. We suggest, with caution, to parse this form from *ewûm* II "blasten mit" (AHw, 267, only G is attested). If this analysis holds true, then *šēwê* (a by-form of *šūwê*) would mean "make them impose (upon themselves) their (own) malicious words". The result is a tongue twister: *šēwê ewētišunu*.

27: Guichard (2020a, 10) translates *ta-ma-si* as "*Tu as été éliminé*" (italics in original), which points to *mêsum* "to crush, squash, to trample, to destroy, overwhem" (CAD M/2, 35f.). Now, when spells against scorpions speak of "crushing", they regularly use *napāṣum* (see commentary BM 97331a: 10 = № 84), but more importantly, the expected N-form is *tammās*, without the *i*-Auslaut. Cavigneaux (2021, 2) offers *šamāʾē ṣī* “Vers le ciel (?) sors ! (?)”, but scorpions are not expected to depart to the sky and the preposition “to” is also missing. A possible solution to this crux is emending the form to *ta-ma-ta*! “you are adjured!” (the SI sign, clear on the tablet, is not that different than the TA which precedes). And yet, as no deities are mentioned in the text (as in AoF 35, 146: 20–24 = № 150, against the Evil Eye), this emendation is questionable.

28: This line does not allude to divine aid (as suggested by Guichard 2020a, 10), but recapitulates the magic act that took place beforehand (“we play with him in our hands”, l. 7 and “… I will speak! … I will declare!” ll. 11–12). Thus, *ša... atpalu* is a shortened form of *ātappalu*: *apālum* Gt pres. “I am saying to, conversing with” (cf. *anāku lūtawu*, l. 11). The same shortened form appears in Agušaya A: *ša nuppuš libbi lā ta-at-pa-li-i-ši awātim* “Do not say to her words that calm the heart” (= VS 10, 214: vi 44'–45').

№ 99: Semitica 62, 19

SEAL No.: 27569
Copy: Guichard 2020a, 20
Tablet Siglum: CUNES 49–03–357
Photo: Guichard 2020a, 19
Edition: Guichard 2020a, 11–14
Studies: Cavigneaux 2021
Collection: Cornell University Cuneiform Library
Provenance: Larsa area
Measurements: –
Procedure: No

Introduction

A short incantation which begins with a speech of Sîn. The Moon-god is disheartened for not being able to complete the foundations of his house: his little finger was stung by a scorpion. Ea and Asalluḫi are called for help.

Obverse

1 *a-ma-ra-ma-an a-ša-ka-na-am*
2 *li-bi-ta-ma-an*
3 *ú-ši et-na-a-am*
4 *ú-ba-an Sîn*($^{d+}$EN.ZU) *ṣi-ḫi-ir-tam*
5 *zu-qí-qí-pu-um iz-qú-ut*
6 *a-na É-a ù Sa-lu-úḫ*
7 *qí-bi-a-ma*
8 *ú-ba-an Sîn*($^{d+}$EN.ZU) *ṣi-ḫi-ir-tum*
9 *li-ib-lu-uṭ*
10 *ša-ar sà-ka-pa-šu ta-ri*
11 *zi-ba-sú-ú*
12 *pa-ri-ik ḫa-ra-na-am*
13 *ú-qá-a e-eṭ-lam ša il-šu*
14 *la it-ti-šu*

Reverse uninscribed

Translation

1–3 – "Had I only (succeeded) placing a pile of bricks, had (I only succeeded placing) a (single) brick – I would have replaced the foundations!".
4–5 (But) a scorpion stung Sîn's little finger.
6–7 Speak to Ea and (A)salluḫ(i):
8–9 May the little finger of Sîn recover!
10–11 Its (the scorpion's) thrust is a (fierce) wind! It is curled up as to its tail!
12–14 It blocks the road. It waits for the young man, whose god is not with him.

Commentary

1–2: The irrealis particle *-man* is rarely found in the corpus (see also, in a broken context, UET 6/2, 399: 21 = № 117, against anger). For other bi-partite irrealis sentences with *-man*, see Wasserman (2012, 120–124).

3: *ú-ši et-na-a-am* is difficult. Cavigneaux (2021, 3) has *ušetbīam* with no translation.

10–11: For the description of the scorpion raising its threatening tail, see also BM 97331b: 13 (№ 85), with commentary. Cavigneaux (2021, 3) reads *tarṣā kappāšu* "Bras (les pinces) tendus" but *kappum* never designates the scorpion's pincers, only *qarnum*.

12–14: The scene of the dangerous animal awaiting a young man on the road, and the use of *quʾʾûm*, recalls the OA incantation against the black dog (Fs. Hirsch 427 = № 69) which opens with "The dark howling (canine), the black dog is lying on the tell, waiting for (*uqâ*) the spread-out caravan. Its eyes look around for a beautiful lad (*eṭlam damqam*)".

13–14: Cf. BM 97331b: 15–16 (№ 85).

№ 100: YOS 11, 1

SEAL No.: 7170
Copy: van Dijk/Goetze/Hussey 1985 Pl. I
Tablet Siglum: YBC 5620
Photo: cf. SEAL No. 7170
Edition: van Dijk/Goetze/Hussey 1985, 17
Studies: Farber 1985, 60; Cunningham 1997 Cat. No. 368; Wasserman 2003 Cat. No. 223
Collection: Yale Babylonian Collection, New Haven
Provenance: Larsa area
Measurements: 5.4 × 4.4 cm
Procedure: No

Introduction

A small portrait-oriented tablet, whose half obverse is left unwritten, as is its reverse. The scorpion is described in a sequence of nominal sentences.

Obverse

1 *pa-sa-qú-um*$^{!}$(RU) *ga-ba-ra-a*[*ḫ-ka*]
2 *sa-du-um zi-ba-ta-k*[*a*]
3 *sa-du-um qà-ra-na-k*[*a*]
4 *me-e na-di-im ba-a*[*m*$^{?}$]*-ta-ka*
----
5 [tu$_6$]-én-é-nu-ru
6 [ka]-inim-ma gír-tab-ti-la-kam

(*Reverse not inscribed*)

Translation

1 The panic you cause is *choking*.
2–3 Your two tails – smiting, your two horns – smiting.
4 Your thorax is (shining like) water (from) a water skin.
----
5 tu$_6$-én-é-nu-ru
6 Incantation to heal (from) a scorpion's (sting).

Commentary

1: Reading *pa-sa-ku-ru* is difficult. *paskārum* "(a headdress)" is attested only in lexical lists and in Nuzi and EA (CAD P, 221f.). In addition, since mimation is kept in the text, *pa-sa-ku-ru* is less expected. We suggest emending this word to *pa-sa-qú-um*$^{!}$ "to choke$^{?}$" (CAD P, 218), in parallel to *sâdum* in ll. 2, 3. – Instead of *ga-ba-ra-a*[*ḫ-ka*], one could consider *kaparru* "(a barbed whip or goad)" (CAD K, 177f.). This would fit with the next line where the scorpion's tail is described.

Yet, the spelling /kà/ is not easy and the last sign before the break does not sit with this reading.

2–3: The dual form of *qarnu* is expected, but that of *zibbatu* less so. The fact that the predicate of these two lines is the same, *sâdum*, raises the possibility of a scribal mistake.

4: The scorpion's body is compared to a water-skin also in CUSAS 32, 49: 8 (№ 93).

№ 101: YOS 11, 2

SEAL No.: 7171
Copy: van Dijk/Goetze/Hussey 1985 Pl. II
Tablet Siglum: YBC 5090
Photo: cf. SEAL No. 7171
Edition: van Dijk/Goetze/Hussey 1985, 17; Cavigneaux 1999, 265f.
Studies: Cooper 1996, 48f.; Cunningham 1997 Cat. No. 369; Wasserman 2003 Cat. No. 224; Foster 2005, 129; Polinger Foster 2020, 134
Collection: Yale Babylonian Collection, New Haven
Provenance: Larsa area
Measurements: 6.6 × 5.4 cm
Procedure: No

Introduction

Starting with the motif of self-impregnation (Cooper 1996), the spell's strategy is to remove the scorpion – metonymically called "clods of the street, the dirt of the alley" – by means of gushing water. In other words, the water which impregnates the healer will eventually overcome the scorpion and drive it away.

Obverse

1 *a-ra-aḫ-ḫi ra-ma-ni a-ra-*⌜*a*$^{?}$⌝*-ḫi* / *pa-ag-ri*
2 *ki-ma na-ru-um ir-ḫu-ú* / *ki-ib-ri-ša*
3 *ki-ir-ba-an sú-qí-im*
4 *e-pe-er šu-li-im*
5 *še-er-ḫa-an ši-qí-im*
6 *ṣú-um ki-ri-im*
7 *ka-a-nu-ú-ma zú-qí-qí-pu-um*

Lower Edge

8 *i-la-ku-ú-ma*

Reverse

9 *i-na-du-ú-ma*
10 *la i-na-mu-šu-ú*

Translation

1–2 I impregnate myself, I impregnate my body, just as the river has impregnated its own banks!
3–6 Clods of the street, the dirt of the alley, a current of irrigation, the thirst of the garden.
7 The scorpion (stands there) steady;
8–10 When they (the water) come, when they will pour – it (the scorpion) should not set in movement!

Commentary

1–2: Cf. Maqlû VII 22–23 (Abusch 2016, 350): én *arḫḫēka ramānī araḫḫēka pagri kīma* [d]*Šakkan irḫû būlšu* "Incantation. I am impregnating you, my self, I am impregnating you, my body, as Šakkan impregnated his herd…"

3–6: The main section of the incantation is constructed along the alliteration of velars, dentals and labials: … ***ki***_briša_ ***ki***_rbān sūqim eper šūlim šerḫān ši_***qî***_m ṣūm_ ***ki***_rîm_ ***ka***_yyānumma zu_***qiqī***_pum_.

5: *širḫān šiqîm* "current of irrigation" rather than *šerḫān šikkîm* "sinew of a mongoose", although the latter is also possible.

№ 102: YOS 11, 4b

SEAL No.: 7172
Copy: van Dijk/Goetze/Hussey 1985 Pls. IV/V
Tablet Siglum: YBC 4593
Photo: cf. SEAL No. 7172
Edition: van Dijk/Goetze/Hussey 1985, 18 (partial); Krebernik 2018, 37
Studies: Farber 1985, 60; Cunningham 1997 Cat. No. 371; Wasserman 2003 Cat. No. 226
Collection: Yale Babylonian Collection, New Haven
Provenance: Larsa area
Measurements: 8.7 × 5.5 cm
Procedure: Yes

Introduction
After a short Elamite incantation with an Akkadian procedure (see Krebernik 2018, 37), comes this incantation. Its epigraphy hints at an early-OB date (see, MA and LA signs). By contrast, mimation is not consistent and the dissimilation in *ta-na-an-di-i-ma* (l. 22) points to a later date. As in other scorpion incantations, the Moon-god appears, but his role is unclear. The healer, in first person voice, orders the scorpion to go away from the boy's dish.

Obverse
11 ^{d}*Sîn*(⌜ŠEŠ.KI⌝) *i-na* ⌜x⌝ [x x x]-*li*$^{?}$-*im*
12 *ki-a-am* ⌜x⌝ [x x x x]-*ú pí-ia-ma*
13 *ma-a-*⌜*ri*$^{?}$⌝ [*a*$^{?}$-*wi*$^{?}$-*lu*$^{?}$]-*tim ma* ⌜x⌝ tu ⌜ri$^{?}$⌝ *aq-bi-*⌜*kum*$^{?}$⌝
14 *ki-i la ta-am-ta-*[*li*]-*ik*
15 *ta*$^{?}$-*wi-ir te-eṭ-ḫi*
16 *a-na ma-ka-al-ti ša i-ku-lu ṣu-ḫa-rum me-er-sà*
17 *a-li-ik ṣu-ḫa-rum li-ib-lu-uṭ-ma*

Reverse
18 *zu-qí-qí-pu-um li-mu-ut*
19 *ši-pa-at zu-qí-qí-pí-im*
20 *ki-ik-ki-ta-ša ša li-ib-bi u-zu-un i-me-e-ri*
21 *i-na mu-uḫ-ḫi sí-im-mi ta-ša-ka-an-ma*
22 *ši-ip-ta ta-na-an-di-i-ma ba-li-iṭ*

Translation
11 Sîn in the …
12 thus … of my mouth.
13 The person (lit. "son of mankind") … I told you:
14–16 "How, without considering, you came and drew near to the bowl from which the boy ate the pie?
17–18 Go! May the boy live and may the scorpion die!"
19 Incantation against a scorpion.

20–21 Its procedure: place on lesion the substance (taken) from the inner ear of a donkey

22 and recite the (above) incantation, and he will recover.

Commentary

13: Although uncertain, we rely in our reconstruction on a similar line in BM 97331b: 12 (№ 85) where DUMU? *a-wi-lu-tim* appears. The "son of mankind" refers here concretely to the boy, *ṣuḫārum*.

16: This syntax is inelegant. One expects *ana mākalti ṣuḫārim ša īkulu mersa* or *ana mākalti mersi ša ṣuḫārum īkulu.*

№ 103: YOS 11, 4c

SEAL No.: 7173
Copy: van Dijk/Goetze/Hussey 1985 Pls. IV/V
Tablet Siglum: YBC 4593
Photo: cf. SEAL No. 7173
Edition: –
Studies: Cunningham 1997 Cat. No. 372; Wasserman 2003 Cat. No. 227; Cavigneaux 1995, 78 fn. 9
Collection: Yale Babylonian Collection, New Haven
Provenance: Larsa area
Measurements: 8.7 × 5.5 cm
Procedure: No

Introduction

A broken spell. Sîn's finger is bitten by a scorpion while building a house (cf. CUSAS 32, 211 = № 87 and CUSAS 32, 49 = № 93).

Reverse

23 *bi-ri-it* ^{id}*Idiglat*(IDIGNA) *ù* ^{id}*Lagaš*(ŠIR.BUR.LA)^{ki}
24 *uš-ši i-*⸢*na*⸣ ‹*e*›*-pé-ši-im a-ma-*⸢*ri i-n*⸣*a* ⸢*šu-ba*⸣*-al-ku-tim*
25 *ú-ba-an* ^{d}*S*[*în ṣe-ḫe-er-ta*]*m*
26 *zu-*⸢*qí-qí*⸣*-*[*pu-um iz-qú-u*]*t*$^{?}$
27 ⸢x⸣ [… *-t*]*im*$^{?}$
28 ⸢x⸣ […] ⸢x⸣
29 ⸢x⸣ […]

(*broken*)

Translation

23 Between the Tigris and the canal of Lagaš,
24–26 while preparing the foundations, while turning over the brick pile, the scorpion stung Sîn's little finger.
27–29 …

Commentary

23: A reptile (probably a snake) is born and raised by two rivers also is Fs. Wilcke 62: 1–2 (№ 108).
24: *i-*⸢*na*⸣ ‹*e*›*-pé-ši-im* (against CAD N/1, 327 s.v. *napûm* "to sift").
25: In CUSAS 32, 211: 31' (№ 87) *Sîn* is written ^{d}EN.ZU, but on this tablet Sîn is written Nanna(^{d}⸢ŠEŠ.KI⸣) (YOS 11, 4b: 11 = № 102).
25–26: After CUSAS 32, 211: 31' (№ 87).

№ 104: YOS 11, 35

SEAL No.: 7175
Copy: van Dijk/Goetze/Hussey 1985 Pl. LII
Tablet Siglum: YBC 9899
Photo: cf. SEAL No. 7175
Edition: –
Studies: van Dijk/Goetze/Hussey 1985, 31; Cunningham 1997 Cat. No. 400; Wasserman 2003 Cat. No. 256
Collection: Yale Babylonian Collection, New Haven
Provenance: Larsa area
Measurements: 4.5 × 6.5 cm
Procedure: Yes

Introduction
A fragmentary Sumero-Akkadian scorpion incantation followed by a Sumerian subscript and an Akkadian procedure. An unnamed god (probably Sîn) is stung in the brick mould. Anum and Ninkilim are called for help.

Obverse
1 inim an-na inim na-na inim na-na ^{d}Nin-⸢kilim-ma-ke$_4$⸣
2 ⸢*qá*$^?$*-ti*$^?$⸣ *i-li-im zuqiqīpum*(GÍR.TAB) *iz-qú-ut* ⸢*i+na*⸣ *na-al-*[*ba-ni*(*m*)]
3 *A-nu-um bītam*(É) *a-na sà-la-aḫ pa-la-aš qí-bi*$^?$ *a-*[*na*$^?$]
4 ⸢*ša*$^{!?}$*-pa-al*⸣ *bur-tim*
----
5 ⸢ka⸣-inim-ma gír-tab dab$_5$-bé-da-k[am]
6 [*ú*$^?$]*-pu-úḫ di-pa-ra-am le-qé* ⸢x⸣ […]
7 [*a*$^?$*-ḫu*$^?$]*-uz di-*⸢*pa*$^!$⸣*-ra-am*⸣ *l*[*e-qé* …]
8 […] ⸢x x⸣ […]
(*broken*)

Translation
1 (By) the word Anum, (by) the word of *Anum*, (by) the word *Anum*, Oh Ninkilim!
2 The scorpion stung both hands of the god in the br[ick mould].
3 Oh Anum, command *to purify the house, to make a perforation*
4 below the pit!
----
5 Incantation to catch a scorpion.
6 (The procedure:) light a torch, take …
7 [*Ho*]*ld*$^?$ a torch, t[ake …]
8 …

Commentary

1: inim na-na is a corrupted form of inim an-na. For inim an-na, cf. PBS 1/2, 122: r. 18' (№ 147).

3: Note the ungrammatical use of the infinitive forms *sà-la-aḫ* and *pa-la-aš*.

6–7: A torch in analogy to the scorpion's sting, see, e.g., CUSAS 32, 49: 11–12 (№ 93).

2.2.7 Snakes and Reptiles

As with scorpions, ancient Mesopotamians were enthralled by snakes. These menacing and beautiful creatures captured the Mesopotamian imagination and triggered their keen observant eye. No other creature in the entire magic corpus is so minutely described ("the snake looks so-and-do… its colour is so-and-so… it lives in this and that environment" etc.), and no other creature is so richly catalogued (see, e.g., TIM 9, 65 = № 110). Remarkably, clear thematic threads tie the OB group of snake incantations to the first millennium explanatory text *ṣēru šikinšu* "the snake, its form is…" (Mirelman 2015, 177–178). An unnamed snake in *ṣēru šikinšu* is described as typically living in the upper part ("crown") of the tree (*ina iṣi minnam elâ izziz*, Mirelman 2015, 177: 12, trans. different). This description echoes our CUSAS 32, 48: 16–17 (№ 107) and OECT 15, 260: 12–13 (№ 109). The seven-tongued snake in *ṣēru šikinšu* (Mirelman 2015, 177: 18) shows up in AMD 1, 245 (fig. 5): 8 (№ 105) and TIM 9, 65 // TIM 9, 66a: 9 (№ 110). The shining snake in *ṣēru šikinšu* (Mirelman 2015, 177: 23 *melammī litbuš*) finds its parallel in the *nāwirum* "shiny snake" in CUSAS 32, 27a: 13 (№ 106) and in the snake whose "mouth is a flash, his double-tongue – blazes" (*pīšu nablum lišānāšu birbirrum*, VS 17, 4: 3–4 = № 111). And the snake with the "multicoloured eyes" in *ṣēru šikinšu* (Mirelman 2015, 177: 26 *burrumā īnāšu*) is paralleled with the snake whose "eyes are of awful brightness" (*namurrāta īnāšu*, TIM 9, 65 // TIM 9, 66a: 12 = № 110). The long imaginative tradition of real and quasi-mythological snakes went from genre to genre, across the Akkadian literary system.

№ 105: AMD 1, 245 (fig. 5)

SEAL No.: 7176
Copy: Finkel 1999, 245 (fig. 5)
Tablet Siglum: CBS 7005
Photo: CDLI P262058
Edition: Finkel 1999, 223f.
Studies: Wasserman 2003 Cat. No. 98
Collection: University Museum, University of Pennsylvania, Philadelphia
Provenance: Nippur
Measurements: –
Procedure: No

Introduction

This single incantation, on a landscape-oriented tablet, opens with a detailed description of a snake and continues with a list of serpents which the magician (*wāšipum*) managed to control.

Obverse

1 *šu-ut-tu-uḫ la-nam*
2 *da-mi-iq zu-um-ra-am*
3 *sú-um-ki-nu-šu sú-um-ki-in gišimmarim*(^{giš}GIŠIMMAR)
4 *i-na šu-ub-tim i-ra-bi-iṣ ṣerrum*(MUŠ)
5 *i-na šu-up-pa-tim i-ra-bi-iṣ ba-aš-mu*

6 *ša ba-aš-mi-im ši-it-ta*
7 *ka-qá-da-tu-šu-ma*

Reverse
8 *7 li-ša-na-šu 7 pa-ar-ul-lu*
9 *ša ki-ša-di-šu*
10 *am-ha-aṣ*$^{!}$ *pa-ar-ku-ul*{sup. ras}*-la*
11 *ù pa-ra-ku-ul-la*
12 *ša-am-ma-nam ṣerri*(MUŠ) *qištim*(^{giš}TIR)
13 *šu-ba-ṭam ṣerri*(MUŠ) *la ši-ip-tim*
14 *ṣerri*(MUŠ) *karānim*(^{giš}GEŠTIN.NA) *ša it-ti wa-ši-pí-šu*

Lower Edge
15 *im-ta-ah-ṣú*

Translation
1–2 Elongated of form, beauteous in body.
3 His wood chips are a date-palm's wood-chips.
4–5 The snake lurks in the dwelling. The serpent lurks among the rushes.
6–7 As for the serpent, two are his heads,
8–9 Seven his forked tongues, seven the *par᾽ullu*'s of his neck.
10–11 I smote the *parkulla*, even the *parakulla,*
12–13 *Šammānu*, the snake of the forest; *Šubāṭu*, a snake impervious to spell(s),
14–15 (even) the vine-snake, the one who fights with his magician!

Commentary
3: For *sumkīnu*, see Finkel (1999, 225). – The snake's scales are likened to patterns made on the trunk of a date-palm, see George (2016, 111).
10–11: *par*(*a*)*kullu*(*m*) means, with Finkel (1999, 225), "the seal-cutter snake". This designation is echoed in TIM 9, 65: 13// TIM 9, 66a: 26–27 (№ 110) *elītašu ipaṣṣid abnam*, "his (the snake's) upper lip can split stone", and in OECT 15, 260: 3 (№ 109) *allītušu upaṣṣad abnam* "his *upper lip* can cut through rock".
12–13: Neither *šammānum* nor *šubāṭum* are attested elsewhere and are to be taken as proper names for specific types of snakes (Finkel 1999, 225f.). As for a possible explanation of these names, *šammānum* could derive from the verb *šamāmum* "to paralyze" + *-ān* (GAG^{3} §56 r); and *šubāṭu* (not *šubādum* as in Finkel 1999, 226) could be a *PuRāS* nominal form (GAG^{3} §55 k) from *šabāṭum* "to strike".
13: The designation of snakes "that cannot be conjured", is mentioned in Jer. 8: 17 and Ps. 58: 4 (cf. Wasserman 2002, 10).

№ 106: CUSAS 32, 27a

SEAL No.: 7178
Copy: George 2016 Pls. LXXIV/LXXV
Tablet Siglum: MS 2791
Photo: George 2016 Pl. LXXIII; CDLI P251837
Edition: George 2016, 109f.
Studies: –
Collection: Schøyen Collection, Oslo
Provenance: Unknown
Measurements: 15.0 × 7.0 cm
Procedure: No

Introduction
This Akkadian incantation enumerating different serpents is followed by a Sumerian incantation to mend broken bones (George 2016, 139) and another Akkadian spell against scorpions (CUSAS 32, 27c = № 90).

Obverse
1 *e-ti-iq ti-tu-ra-am*
2 *ú-ṣi na-ṣa-ba-am*
3 *aṣ-ba-at ku-ur-ši-da-am*
4 *ṣerri*(MUŠ) *la ši-ip-tim*
5 *ši-in-na-šu mi-ir-me-er-ru-um*
6 *li-ša-*[*a*]*n-šu ḫe-e-ri-nu-um*
7 *pa-ap-pa-al-li-ib-bi-šu*
8 *a-ga-ar-ga-ru-um*
9 *ù li-ib-ba-šu*
10 *pu-lu-úḫ-ta-am ma-lu-ú*
11 *aṣ-ba-at ṣerram*(MUŠ) *na-pi-ša-ni-a-am*
12 *ú-bu-ur-ri-iš i-la-ak*
13 ⸢*ù*⸣ *na-wi-ra-am*
14 [*ṣe*]*rri*([M]UŠ) *la ši-ip-tim*
15 [*a*]*ṣ-ba-at ku-up-pi-a-am*
16 [*s*]*à-bi-a-am a-la-al-ti-a-am*
17 [*d*]*a*$^{?}$*-qá-am ṣerri*(MUŠ) *me-e*
18 [*mu*]*-uš-ta-ḫi-ṭa-am ṣerri*(MUŠ) *gušūrim*(GIŠ.ÙR)
19 [*mu-u*]*t-ta-aḫ-li-il-lam ṣerri*(MUŠ) *a-pa-tim*
20 [*qá-a*]*l-la-am ṣerri*(MUŠ) *bu-li-a-*⸢*tim*⸣
21 [*aṣ-ba-a*]*t ṣa-al-ma-am ṣerri*(MUŠ) *karānim*(GEŠTIN)
22 [*aṣ-ba-a*]*t pi-i šerrī*(MUŠ)$^{ḫi.a}$ *ka-la-ma*
23 [*aṣ-ba-a*]*t zi-ib-ba-ti-šu-nu*
24 [*bi-ri-it*] *ši-ta ur-ba-tim ú-ru-ma*
25 [x (x) x] *ur-ba-tim*

26 [x (x) x] ⌜x⌝-*um ar-ku-us*
27 [x x x x x] ⌜x da⌝ *ba-aš-ma-am*
28 [x x x x x x x x] *a-la-al-tim*
(*broken*)

Reverse
1' [...] ⌜nim?⌝
2' [...] ⌜id?⌝ du š[a?]
3' [x x x x x] ⌜x⌝ *li-bi-it-*[*t*]*um*?
4' [x x x x x] *ša-ḫa-ar-ru-um*
5' [x x x x *l*]*e*?*-mu-*⌜*ut*⌝*-tum*
6' [...] ⌜x⌝-*ti*
7' [...]-*im*
8' [...]-*i*[*a*]
9' [tu$_6$]-én-⌜é⌝-nu-ru
10' [k]a-inim-m[a m]u[š?]-kam

Translation
1–2 He crossed a bridge, came out of a drain-pipe.
3–6 I seized the viper, a snake impervious to spell(s), whose twin fangs are a (lightning) flash, whose tongue is sharp grass.
7–10 His scutes are fish-spawn and his inside is filled with terror!
11–12 I seized a *sniffer* snake (as) he was passing through a green meadow,
13–14 and a shiny snake impervious to spell(s)!
15–16 [I] seized an eel-(snake), a *sabiʾum*-snake, an *alaltiʾum*-snake,
17–18 a little water-snake, an ever-jumping of the (roof) beams,
19–20 an ever-slithering snake of the windows, a little snake of the wood-pile!
21–23 [I seized] a black snake of the vineyard! [I seized] the mouths of all snakes! [I seized] their tails!
24 I led (them) [between] two rushes,
25 [...] rushes
26 [...] I tied [...]
27 [...] the viper
28 [...] *alaltiʾum*-snake

Reverse
1' [...]
2' [...]
3' [...] *mudbrick*
4' [...] *šuḫarrum*-net
5' [...] *wicked*
6' [...]
7' [...]
8' [...]
9' [tu$_6$]-én-é-nu-ru

10' Incantation (against) a snake.

Commentary

7: *pa-ap-pa-al-li-ib-bi-šu* for *pappān libbišu*.

11: For the otherwise unattested *napīšānīʾum*, see George (2016, 111).

№ 107: CUSAS 32, 48

SEAL No.: 7179
Copy: George 2016 Pl. CXVI
Tablet Siglum: MS 3070
Photo: George 2016 Pl. CXV; CDLI P252079
Edition: George 2016, 106f.
Studies: –
Collection: Schøyen Collection, Oslo
Provenance: Unknown
Measurements: 9.0 × 4.4 cm
Procedure: No

Introduction

This beautiful incantation, imbued with mythological scenes and rich in literary devices, divulges the marine origin of the snake. Coming out of the sea, the menacing creature turns to attack the dry land and hides in various trees. A *mannam lušpur* formula follows, mentioning Ningirsu. Unusually, the two subscript lines are on the reverse, which otherwise left unwritten.

Obverse

1 *ra-ap-ša bu-da-šu di-ka na-ṭa-al*
2 *ṣerrum*(MUŠ) *e-bi-ḫa el-lam-me-e*
3 *ša im-ma-ar-ra-tim ib-nu-šu-ma*
4 *i-na ka-ap-pi-im ša É-a* ⸢*uš*⸣*-zi-zu-ni-*⸢*iš-šu*⸣
5 *i-nu-ma iṣ-mu zi-in-na-tim i-nu-uš ki-ib-*⸢*ru*⸣
6 *i-nu-uš-ma ki-ib-rum i-te-ru-ub a-na šu-up-pi-im*
7 *i-na šu-up-pi-im ṣerram*(MUŠ) *a-ṣa-ab-ba-at*
8 *i-na šu-up-pa-tim a-ṣa-ab-ba-at bašmam*(MUŠ.ŠÀ.TUR)
9 *bašmum*(MUŠ.ŠÀ.TUR) 6 *pī*(KA)*-šu*
10 7 *ma-at-nu mu-*⸢*bi*⸣*-lu li-ib-bi-šu*
11 *iš-si-i-ma šadâm*(KUR) *i-ki-ip šadâm*(KUR) *i-ki-ip-*⸢*ma*⸣ *abnam*(NA$_4$) *il*$_5$*-*⸢*te*⸣
12 *abnam*(NA$_4^{!}$: PA$_5$) *il*$_5$*-te-e-ma* ^{giš}*ṣarbatam*(ASAL) *ú-ta-b*[*é*]-⸢*el*⸣
13 *iš-du* ⸢^{giš}⸣*al-la-nim ḫa-ma-du-ri-iš* ⸢*uš-ta*⸣*-li-ik*
14 *ma-an-nam lu-uš-pu-ur ù lu-wa-ḫe-er*
15 *a-na* ^{d}*Nin-gír-su ka-mi ilī*(DINGIR) *ra-bu-tim*
16 *li-iš-si-a-šum-ma i-na bu-ṭù-um-tim*
17 [*l*]*i-ša-ar-ʾì*(ḪI)*-ba-aš-šum i-na* ^{giš}*al-la-nim*
18 [*li-id*]-⸢*ri*⸣*-is-ma ṣerram*(MUŠ) *ki-ma e-bi-ḫi-im*
19 [*li-iš*]*-k*[*u-u*]*n-šu-ma li-it-ba-a-aš-šu*
20 [*a-na*] ⸢*ke-pi*⸣*-ia*

Reverse

21 [é]-en-[n]u-ri

----

22 [x] ⸢x⸣ eš ⸢x⸣ [x x] ⸢x⸣-*ne-en-me-er*

Rest uninscribed

Translation

1–2 Broad of shoulder, dead of glance – a snake, cord of moonshine,

3–4 whom they created in the bitter sea and placed *in the hand* of Ea.

5–6 When he was thirsting for sustenance, the shore shook; the shore shook and he went into the reed-bed!

7–8 I will seize the snake in the reed-bed. I will seize the viper in the rushes!

9–10 The viper, six are his mouths, seven are the tendons that are *moving* in his body!

11 He cried out and approached the mountain; he approached the mountain and split a rock.

12–13 He split a *rock* and dried up a poplar. He made wither away the roots of the oak.

14–15 Whom should I send and dispatch to Ningirsu, who snares (even) the great gods?

16–17 May he cry out to him (the snake) in the terebinth! May he make him tremble in the oak.

18–20 May he (Ningirsu) trample over the snake like a cord. May he (Ningirsu) make him (the snake) … may he *carry* him (*to serve as*) my *skipping rope*!

Reverse

21 [é]-en-[n]u-ri

----

22 …

Commentary

2: For *ebiḫ(a) ellam-mê*, see George (2016, 108).

4: *ina kappim* could be a corruption of *in-nagabbim*, see George (2016, 108). *kappum* "wing" in collocation with sea is found in the Great Šamaš Hymn 69–70 (BWL, 130–131): "You save from the storm the merchant carrying his capital, the… who goes down to the ocean you give a (helping) hand (*tušaškan kappa*)" (Lambert differently).

10: Though not free of problems, we join George (2016, 109) and take *mu-bi-lu* as an unattested part. of *wabālum* D, or, better, a mistake of *mubabbilu*. Alternatively, one may consider *mu-bi-ku* (part. D of *abākum* "to dispatch").

11: A snake splitting a rock is found in parallel snake incantations. Here *ilte* (< *letûm*) is used, whereas in the parallel texts, the same idea is expressed by *elītašu ipaṣṣid abnam*, "his (the snake's) upper lip can split stone" (TIM 9, 65: 13 // TIM 9, 66a: 26 = № 110). The similar sound of *ilte* and *elītašu* is hardly accidental.

16: Ningirsu is called for on account of his connection to rocks and mountains. Just as the snake cried out and split the mountain (l. 11), so Ningirsu is asked to cry out and frighten the snake in the tree.

18: The magical act reached its successful end when the fearsome snake became "like a cord", that is, an object which looks like a snake, but is motionless, devoid of life and will. Let us note, furthermore, that *kīma ebīḫim* creates a closure with *ṣerrum ebīḫa ellam-mê* "cord of moonshine" (l. 2).

19: Here, too, a constructive closure is created: *ina keppim* ↔ *ana kappîm ša Ea* (l. 4).

№ 108: Fs. Wilcke 62

SEAL No.: 7180
Copy: Cavigneaux 2003, 62
Tablet Siglum: Sb 12360
Photo: CDLI P414447
Edition: Cavigneaux 2003, 61f.
Studies:
Collection: Louvre, Paris
Provenance: Susa
Measurements: –
Procedure: No

Introduction
Single incantation on a landscape-oriented tablet with uninscribed reverse. Here, too, an aquatic surrounding – two rivers – are the snake's place of birth. Adad and Nergal are said to account for some of its frightening features. Ištar and Dumuzi are called for help.

Obverse

1	*[Í]d-⸢ug⸣-lá-at*$^{!}$ *ú-li-is-sú*
2	^{íd}*Ù-la-a ú-ra-ab-bi-i-šu*
3	*ša-pa-al šu-up-pa-a-tim na-a-di ki-i ba-aš-mi*
4	*qa-aq-qa-as-sú ki-i e-ṣi-it-ti-im*
5	*[zi]-ib-ba-ta-a-šu ki-i bu-ka-nim*
6	*[id]-di-iš-šum* ^{d}*Adad*(IŠKUR) *ri-gi-im-šu* ^{d}*Nergal*(NÈ.IR[I$_{11}$.GAL])
7	[(x)] ⸢x⸣ bíl *ša* AN *pí-ta-aš-šu-lam id-di-iš-š[um]*
8	*[ú-ta]m-mi-ka* ^{d}*Eš*$_{4}$*-tár ù* ^{d}*Dumu-zi*
9	*[be*$^{?}$*]-ra-a ù ṣú-up-pa-a la qè-e-re-ba-am*
	Reverse uninscribed

Translation

1–2 The river Tigris bore him, the river Ulaya raised him.
3 He is lying like a viper under the rushes.
4–5 His head is like a pestle, his two tails are like a (mortar)-pounder.
6–7 Adad bestowed him with his scream, Nergal the … *of Anum*, bestowed him with crawling.
8–9 I conjure you by Ištar and Dumuzi not to draw near to me (even to a distance of) one league and sixty cubits!

Commentary

1–2: Two bodies of water are said to be the origin place of a reptile, perhaps a scorpion, in YOS 11, 4c: 23 (№ 103): *birit* ^{id}*Idiglat u* ^{id}*Lagaš*.

4: Note the spelling /qa/, typical of Ešnunna, which appears twice in this line. Was this text, infused with snake imagery, brought to Susa from Ešnunna, a city whose main god was in the form of a snake?

5: [*zi*]*bbatāšu*: This dual form could perhaps refer to a double-faced mace, a known symbol of different gods, one of which is Nergal.

6: A screaming snake is found also in CUSAS 32, 48: 11 (№ 107).

7–8: Other gods may also be connected to crawling. In a late hymn to Ninurta we find: *pāšila ina maḫar lāsimu tašakkan*, "you (Ninurta) place the crawling-one in front of the quick-runner (in the battlefield)" (Mayer 1992, 21: 3b). Nergal's rule over crawling creatures is connected to his chthonic nature, shared by snakes.

№ 109: OECT 15, 260

SEAL No.: 1676
Copy: Dalley 2001, 165; Dalley 2005 no. 260
Tablet Siglum: Ashmolean 1932.382
Photo: CDLI P347602
Edition: Dalley 2001, 166f.
Studies: Dalley 2005, 5f. 25
Collection: Ashmolean Museum, Oxford
Provenance: Larsa
Measurements: 9.4 × 5.1 cm
Procedure: No

Introduction

Dalley (2001, 167) suggested at first that the text is related to the Epic of Gilgameš. Later she identified it correctly as an incantation against snakes, with an allusion to Gilgameš VI (the *allallu*-bird, l. 6), adding that it is "probably a school exercise" (Dalley 2005, 25). The text is divided into five thematic units: first, a typical description of the snake (ll. 1–3); then comes a complex historiola involving a snake, a bird, and a tree – recalling the Epic of Etana, rather than Gilgameš (ll. 4–14). The next unit describes the confrontation with the healer, referred to as the "wise physician" *emqum asûm* (ll. 15–16), after which Ištar, Šamaš and Asalluḫi are called for help (ll. 18–21). Finally, the healer, in first-person voice, boasts about having seized different kinds of snakes (ll. 22ff.).

Obverse

1 *dan pa-la-aḫ*
2 *i-na-šu pur-si-tum*
3 *al-li-tu-šu ú-pa-ṣa-*⸢*ad abnam*(NA$_4$⸣)
4 *i-na ša-ap-li er-ṣe-tim*
5 *i-la-ab-bu-ú ma-ru-šu*
6 *al-la-al-lum bitrumu*(SIG$_7$.SIG$_7$)
7 *i-na qí-ša-tim i-ra-bi-ma*
8 *i-na-ka(-)na-ṭa-al*
9 *ir-ta-ḫi-a-am šammam*(Ú)
10 *ir-tam i-ṣab*$^!$*-tu ištu*(TA) *ša*$^!$(ME)*-me*$^!$(ŠA)
11 *uš-ta-ar-dam ú-šal-li-a*[*m* (...)]
12 *al-la-num*$^!$ *ḫa-ma-di-ru-um*
13 *uš-ta-li-ik*
14 *pi*$^{?!}$*-ti-nu-tu*$_4$ *i-la-ku ḫarrānam*(KASKAL)
15 *em-qá-am asâm*(A.ZU) *ṣerrum*(MUŠ) *i-gu*$_5$*-ug*

Lower Edge

16 *em-qù-*⸢*um*$^?$ *i-ṭá*(TA)*-ra*⸣*-ad*

Reverse

17 [*b*]*a*$^{?}$*-ab* ⸢x⸣ [x (x)] ⸢x⸣ [(...)]
18 ^{d}*Ištar*(INNIN) *rē*ʾ*û*(SIPA) [x (x) ⸢x⸣ [(...)]
19 ⸢^{d}⸣*Šamaš*(UTU) *rē*ʾ*i*(SIPA) a ⸢x x x⸣
20 ⸢*šu*⸣*-up*$^{!}$(PA)*-ra-an-ni marṣam*(⸢GIG) x⸣ [x (x)]
21 ⸢^{d}⸣[*Asal-l*]*ú-ḫi šar*(LUGAL) ⸢x⸣ [x (x)]
22 *aṣ*$^{!}$(AT)-[*ba-a*]*t ṣerri*(MUŠ) *mê*(A)
23 MUŠ GAL ⸢x⸣ [(x)] ⸢x⸣ du$^{?}$
24 *mu-*⸢*uš*⸣*-ta-aḫ-*[*l*]*i*$^{?}$*-*[*lam*$^{?}$ *ṣerri*(MU]Š) ⸢*ap-tim*⸣
25 *kur-ṣi-nu-*⸢*um*⸣ *ṣerri*(MUŠ) *la ši-ip-*⸢*tim*$^{!}$(TUM)⸣
26 *i-na* ⸢x⸣ a *pu-*⸢*lu*$^{!?}$⸣*-uḫ libbi*(ŠÀ)
27 bi ⸢š/ta⸣ bi ru [x] ⸢x⸣ [ta]m
28 *ki-ma i-ša-*⸢*tim*$^{?}$⸣
29 *a-na-ku*$^{?!}$(SU)⸢x⸣ [...]

Translation

1–3 He is strong, he is fearful! His eyes are a porous bowl! His *upper lip* can cut through rock!
4–5 Below the earth his sons are howling.
6–7 The colourful *allallum*-bird grows up in the woods.
8 – I am looking at your (the snake's) eyes! –
9–10 He *impregnated* the grass (and) *seized* the chest!
10–11 From heaven it (the bird) made him (the snake) come down (and) it submerged [(...)].
12–13 It (the bird) made him (the snake) go into a withered oak-tree.
14 *The strong ones* were walking on the road.
15 The snake became furious *against* the clever physician.
16–17 The clever (physician) *has sent away. The gate* ...
18–19 "(By) Ištar, ... the shepherd! (By) Šamaš, the shepherd of...!
20 Send the sick one to me! ...
21 (By) Asalluḫi, the king (of) ...
22–25 *I seized* the water-snake, the big snake, ..., an ever-slithering snake of the window, the *kurṣin(d)u*-snake, a snake impervious to spell(s)
26 *with ... terror of the heart.*
27 ...
28 like *fire* ...
29 *I*$^{?}$ ...

Commentary

2: This line recalls eye incantations, where we frequently find the eyes referred to as "bowls of blood" (*pursīt dāmi*), see Zomer (2018a, 262).

3: Based on TIM 9, 65: 13 // TIM 66a: 26–27 (№ 110) which reads *elītašu ipaṣṣid abnam*, we take *al-li-tu-šu* as a faulty spelling of *elītu* "upper lip", perhaps having also *illātu* "spittle" in mind. A rock-cutting snake is found also in CUSAS 32, 48: 11–12 (№ 107).

4–5: The snake's sons crying under the earth is a clear allusion to the Epic of Etana. The snake built his nest in the roots of the tree, in whose top the eagle inhabited. Breaking his oath of friendship with the snake, the eagle descended from the tree and devoured the snake's sons (Etana I: 51–65, see Novotny 2001, 17).

8: This line contains the magician's exclamation, telling the snake that he dares look straight into his frightening eyes (cf. l. 2). Note the Sandhi spelling *īnāka (a)naṭṭal*.

12: The motif of the withered oak is found in other snake incantations as well: *išdū* ^{giš}*allānim ḫamadūriš uštallik* (CUSAS 32, 48: 13 = № 107) and *allānam ḫamadīram uštelqi* (TIM 9, 65: 6–7 // TIM 9, 66a: 11–12 = № 110).

15: The signs in the copy look clear. If the reading is correct, then the most plausible interpretation is that *emqum asû* refers to the healer. No other text in the corpus mentions this profession.

16: *i-TA-ra-ad*: *ittarad* (< *warādum* G pf.) or *iṭarrad* (*ṭarādum* G pres.), or, as we prefer, *iṭṭarad* (*ṭarādum* G pf.).

18: Ištar is not a shepherd, hence probably *rēʾû* which follows refers to a god whose name is now broken: perhaps Dumuzi?

22: *aṣ*$^{!}$(AT)-[*ba-a*]*t*: cf. also in RA 36, 3a: 1 (№ 144).

24: Our reading is based on *muttaḫlillam ṣerri apātim* in CUSAS 32, 27a: 19 (№ 106), but here *aptim* in sg.

25: *kur-ṣi-nu-*⸢*um*⸣: cf. *kursiddam* in TIM 9, 65: 1 // TIM 9, 66a: 2 (№ 110) and *kuršiddam* in CUSAS 32, 27a: 3 (№ 106).

№ 110: TIM 9, 65 // TIM 9, 66a

SEAL No.: 7181
Copy: van Dijk 1976 Pl. LIV
Tablet Siglum: IM 51292; IM 51328
Photo: –
Edition: Finkel 1999, 226–229
Studies: Cunningham 1997 Cat. No. 323a/b; Wasserman 2002; Wasserman 2003 Cat No. 173/174; Kogan 2004; Foster 2005, 192f.; Krebernik 2018, 37
Collection: Iraq Museum, Baghdad
Provenance: Šaduppûm
Measurements: 5.7 × 8.0 cm; 8.5 × 5.0 cm
Procedure: No

Introduction
With its two almost parallel witnesses – not a common phenomenon in the corpus – this incantation presents a long list of different serpents. For the relation of this list to lexical lists, see Wasserman (2002, 5–9). After TIM 9, 66a comes an incantation in Elamite against a scorpion, see Krebernik (2018, 37).

Text A = TIM 9, 65; Text B = TIM 9, 66a

1	A1	*⸢aṣ⸣-ba-at pí ṣé-ri ka-li-i-ma ù ku-ur-si-⸢da⸣-am*
	B1–2	*aṣ-ba-at pí-i ṣerrī*(M[UŠ-*ri*]) *ka-li-ma ù kur-si-d*[*a-am*]
2	A2	*ṣé-ri la ši-ip-ti-im aš-nu-ga-la-⸢am⸣ bu-ru-ba-la-am*
	B3–4	*ṣerri*(MUŠ-*ri*) *la ši-ip-ti-*[*im*] *aš-šu-nu-gal-lam bu-ru-ba-la-a*
3	A3	*ša-⸢nap⸣-ša-ḫu-ra-am ba-ar-ma-am i-ni-in*
	B5	*ab-ša-ḫ*[*u*$^{?}$]*-ra-am ba-ar-ma i-ni*
4	A4	*ku-pí-a-am ṣé-ri zi-zi na-zi-za-am ṣé-ri a-ap-ti-im*
	B6–7	*ku-pí-am ṣerri*(MUŠ-*ri*) *zi-iz-zi na-zi-za-am ṣerri*(MUŠ-*ri*) *a*$^{!}$*-ap-ti*
5	A5	*i-ru-ub ḫu-ra-am ú-ṣí nu-ṣa-ba-am*
	B8–9	*i-ru-ub ḫu-ur-ra-am ú-ṣí na-*[*ṣa*]*-ba-am*
6	A6	*im-ḫa-aṣ ṣa-la-ta-am ṣa-bi-ta-am a-la-na-am ḫa-ma-di-ra-am*
	B10–11	*i*[*m*]-[*ḫ*]*a-*[*aṣ*] *ṣa-la-ta-am ṣa-bi-ta al-l*[*a-na*]*-am ḫa-ma-di-ra-am*
7	A7	*uš-te-il-qí i-na ši-pí-im ṣé-ru-um i-ra-bi-iṣ*
	B12–14	*uš-te-el-qí i-na ši-ip-pí ṣerru*(MUŠ-*r*[*u*]) *i-ra-bi-iṣ*
8	A8	*i-na ši-pa-ti-im i-ra-bi-iṣ ba-aš-mu-um*

B15–16 *i-na šu-pa-tim i-‹‹na››-ra-bi-iṣ ba-aš-mu*

9 A9 *ša ba-aš-mi-im ši-ši-it pí-šu si-b[i-it li-ša-nu-šu]*
B17–19 *ša ba-aš-mi ši-ši-it pí-šu si-bi-it li-ša-nu-šu*

10 A10 *si-bi-it ú si-bi-it [ú-ṣ]ú*$^{?}$ *mi-ma ša li-b[i-šu]*
B20–21 *si-bi-it ú-ṣú*$^{?}$ *mi-ma ša li-bi-šu*

11 A11 *ú-lu-ḫa-am ša-ra-ti-i[m p]a-al-ḫa-am zi-m[i]*
B22–23 *ú-lu-[ḫ]a-am [ša-r]a-tim pa-al-ḫa-am zi-mi*

12 A12 *na-mu-ra-ta i-na-šu i-na pí-šu ú-ṣa-am pu-[lu-uḫ-tum]*
B24–25 *na-mu-ra-ta i-na-šu i-na pí-šu ú-ṣa-am pu-⸢lu-uḫ-tum⸣*

13 A13 *e-li-ta-šu i-pa-ṣí-id ab-na-am*
B26–27 *e-li-ta-šu i-pa-ṣí-id ab-na-am*

14 A14 tu-en-ni-nu-ri
B28 tu-ú-en-ni-nu-ri

Translation

1 I seized the mouth of all snakes, even the *Kurṣindu*-snake,
2 a snake impervious to spell(s), the *Aš(šu)nugallu*-snake, the *Burubalû*-snake,
3 the *Šanapšaḫuru*-snake of spackled eyes,
4 the eel snake, the hissing snake, (even) the hisser, the snake at the window!
5–7 He entered the hole, went out by the drainpipe. He smote the sleeping gazelle, betook himself *to*$^{?}$ the withered oak.
7–8 The snake lies coiled in the roof beams. The serpent lies coiled in the rushes.
9 Six are the mouths of the serpent, seven his tongues,
10 Seven, indeed seven went out, whatever is inside of it.
11–12 He is wild of hair, fearful of appearance, his eyes are of awful brightness, fearfulness issues from his mouth.
13 His upper lip can split stone!
14 tu-en-ni-nu-ri

Commentary

6: For the motif of the sleeping gazelle, cf. Finkel (1999, 227), Wasserman (2002, 9–10), and Kogan (2004).

7: *uš-te-el-qí* with AHw, 545 (*leqû* Š). Note that the early suggestion of CAD A/1, 354,1a to take *uštelqi* for *ušterqi*, was not repeated in CAD R, 175, s.v. *raqû*, "to hide, to remove (oneself)", nor in CAD R, 268, s.v. *rêqu* III, "to remove". Doubts regarding this suggestion were raised already by Finkel (1999, 227). – *ina ši-pí-im* // *ši-ip-pí*: with AHw, 1247 s.v. *šīpu*(*m*) II, "ein Balken an Gebäuden", see also Finkel (1999, 228).

8: *i-‹‹na››-ra-bi-iṣ ba-aš-mu* is a mistake triggered by *i-na šu-pa-tim* which precedes.

9: *ša bašmim šiššit pīšu sib*[*it li-ša-nu-šu*]: anticipatory genitive is uncommon in OB literary texts (see Wasserman 2011, 11).

10: Finkel (1999, 226) read here [*ú-l*]*u-mi-ma ša li-b*[*i-šu*], leaving **ulumīmu* not translated and commenting (1999, 228) that it is "without independent support".

13: Finkel (1999, 227) translates "His very spittle can split stone". In his commentary (1999, 228), he explains that, based on Wilcke 1985, 206, this form derives from *ellītu* (AHw, 372: "Speichel"). But this lemma is pl. tantum and attested only in SB, so we side with AHw, 839 (s.v. *paṣādum*) where our *e-li-ta-šu* is understood as *elītum* "that which is above" (CDA 69f.), namely the snake's upper jaw, or lip, where his two frightening teeth are located.[245]

245 Rabbinic Aggadah (echoed in later Islamic traditions) knows of the mysterious *Shamir* that was able to cut through rocks. According to some traditions, the *Shamir* was a mythological worm that King Solomon used to hew the stones for the temple he built, see Ginzberg 2003, 35.

№ 111: VS 17, 4

SEAL No.: 7182
Copy: van Dijk 1971 Pl. III
Tablet Siglum: VAT 8363
Photo: cf. SEAL No. 7182
Edition: van Dijk 1969, 540f.
Studies: Cunningham 1997 Cat. No 363; Wasserman 2003 Cat. No. 205; Foster 2005, 193
Collection: Vorderasiatisches Museum, Berlin
Provenance: Unknown
Measurements: 4.0 × 6.0 cm
Procedure: No

Introduction

This short incantation presents a mythological snake (collated by NW in 2/2/2011).

Obverse

1 *[u]l*[!]*-lu-úḫ ki-ma gi*₅*-ṣí-i-im*
2 *[w]a-ru-uq ki-ma* ᵈ*Tišpak*
3 *a-pa-šu* ‹‹šu›› *mu-tum pi-šu na-ab-lum*
4 *li-ša-na-šu bi-ir-bi-ir-ru-um*
5 *bi-ir-bi-ir-ru-šu le-a-wu(-)ti-a-am-*‹*tim*›
6 tu₆-en-é-nu-ru
7 ka-inim-ma muš-ti-l[a-kam]

Reverse uninscribed

Translation

1–2 Tufted like a *reed*, green like Tišpak.
3–4 His nose is death, his mouth is a flash, his double-tongue – blazes.
5 His blazes are *the powerful ones of the sea.*
6 tu₆-en-é-nu-ru
7 Incantation to heal from a snake(-bite).

Commentary

1: For *[u]l*[!]*-lu-úḫ*, see AHw, 1552b s.v. *elēḫum* (and CAD M/1, 153a). The vehicle of this comparison is not clear: *kīma gi*₅*-ṣí-i-im*, for *giṣṣim* "like a thorn"? or *ki-sí-i-im* for *kīsum*/*kissum* "(a reed)" (CAD K 433, so Foster 2005, 193)? CAD U/W, 84 s.v. *ulluḫu* has *kīma kizîm* "adorned like a goat(?)", but *kizû* does not mean "goat".

2: The typical green colour of snakes surfaces also in Anzu's description in *Lugalbanda and the Anzu Bird* 124: ti-ti-zu ᵈNirah dar-a-me-en šag₄-sud-zu kiri₆ sig₇-ga u₆-e gub-ba-me-en "Your breast as you fly is like Niraḫ parting the waters! As for your back, you are a verdant palm garden, breathtaking to look upon" (trans. ETCSL 1.8.2.2).

5: *le-a-wu-ti-a-am* is an old crux. Van Dijk's (1969, 541) comment in his *editio princeps* is worth citing in full: "Le plus énigmatique pour moi est l'expression: *li-a-wu-ti-a-am.* Je ne puis pas en extraire une form verbale. Elle ressemble p[l]utôt à l'une des bahuvrihi-constructions traitées par W. von Soden. Il ne semble pas possible de l'analyser comme: *lēʾû* et *petû*. Est-il possible que sous: *ti-a-am* se cache le status absolutus de *tiʾāmu*, תהום, et qu'il faille comparer *lwi* de *lwitn*, לותן, לויתן, pour *li-a-wu / wi / wa* ?". Leaving the Biblical associations aside, van Dijk pointed in the right direction. Recognizing a Sandhi spelling and allowing that one sign was dropped at the end of the line, *le-a-wu-ti-a-am* results in *lēʾut tiām‹tim›* "the powerful-ones of the sea", with the expected grammatical congruence with *birbirrū*, pl. tantum.[246]

246 In AHw, 1363b, s.v. *t/dium*, von Soden suggested reading *li*-ZA$^{!?}$-WU *ti-a-am*, referring to *diʾu* I, or, alternatively, *ti-a-am-*[*tam*].

№ 112: YOS 11, 19b

SEAL No.: 7183
Copy: van Dijk/Goetze/Hussey 1985 Pls. XXII-XXIII
Tablet Siglum: YBC 4601
Photo: cf. SEAL No. 7183
Edition: –
Studies: Cunningham 1997 Cat. No. 395; Wasserman 2003 Cat. No. 249
Collection: Yale Babylonian Collection, New Haven
Provenance: Larsa area
Measurements: 11.6 × 6.3 cm
Procedure: No

Introduction
The second of two incantations (the obverse contains an Akkadian spell against Lamaštu = № 164), this partially preserved text describes the birthplace of the snake in land, and emphasizes the snake's gazing eyes. Mark the unusual repeated first word in each line (*saḫḫum… saḫḫum… ina bamtika… ina bamat īnīka…*). The subscript overtly states that the incantation is for seizing a snake (i.e., it is not meant to heal its bite).

Reverse
18 ⌜*sa*⌝-*ḫu-um* i[d$^{?}$- …]
19 *sa-ḫu-um* ⌜*la* id⌝-[…]
20 *ib-ba-ni i-na*$^{!?}$(UD) AB$^{!?}$.[SÍN$^{?}$ (...)]
21 *i-na* ⌜*ba*⌝-*am-ti-ka* [(…)]
22 *i-na* [*b*]*a-ma-at i-*⌜*ni*$^{?}$⌝-*ka* / ⌜x$^{?}$⌝
23 t[u]$_{6}$-én-é-nu-ru
===
24 ka-inim-ma muš-dib-ba

Translation
18 The meadow will […]
19 The meadow shall not […]
20 It was created *in* […]
21 in your middle [(…)]
22 in the middle of your eyes.
23 t[u]$_{6}$-én-é-nu-ru
24 Incantation to seize a snake

Commentary
18–19: Following the dictionaries, *saḫḫum* "meadow, waterlogged land" (CAD S 56), is not found before the MA period. This is the earliest attestation of the word. The sign before the break, with Farber's coll. in van Dijk/Goetze/Hussey 1985, 64.

20: *ib-ba-ni i-na*$^{?!}$ *šer*[*ʾim*](AB$^{?!}$.[SÍN$^{?}$]), if correctly restored, presents the known notion that snakes and scorpions were created in dump locations, as e.g., in the scorpion spell CUSAS 10, 19: 2–3 (№ 86). See also Wasserman (2005a). Cf. further CUSAS 32, 48: 3–4 (№ 107) and Fs. Wilcke 62: 1–2 (№ 108).

2.2.8 Worms and Leeches

This non-homogenous group of incantations is destined against different sorts of non-specified tubular invertebrates ("worm"). The incantations describe them as piercing different human organs – nose, eyes, ears – and causing pain (see esp. YOS 11, 5b = № 114). Toothache was also considered to be caused by a worm; these incantations, however, are classified under their own category of Toothache. Unsurprisingly, worms were considered creatures that originate from mud (see YOS 11, 5a = № 113). Some of them are referred to as "Daughters of Gula" – perhaps leeches (see Wasserman 2008 and commentary to YOS 11, 41: 6 = № 115).

№ 113: YOS 11, 5a

SEAL No.: 7193
Copy: van Dijk/Goetze/Hussey 1985 Pls. VI-VII
Tablet Siglum: YBC 4616
Photo: https://collections.peabody.yale.edu/search/Record/YPM-BC-018681
Edition: Veldhuis 1993, 45f.; Wasserman 2008, 73f.
Studies: van Dijk/Goetze/Hussey 1985, 19; Cunningham 1997 Cat. No. 373; Wasserman 2003 Cat. No. 228; Foster 2005, 180; Wasserman 2008
Collection: Yale Babylonian Collection, New Haven
Provenance: Larsa area
Measurements: 7.6 × 8.3 cm
Procedure: No

Introduction

An incantation to eradicate a worm which entered a boy's eye (a leech? see Wasserman 2008). For the motif of the chain of creation see Veldhuis (1993) and Wasserman (2021).

1 ^{d}*A-nu ir-ḫi-a-am ša-me-e ša-mu-ú er-ṣe-tam ul-d[u-n]im*
2 *er-ṣe-tum ú-li-id bu-ša-am bu-šum ú-li-id lu-ḫu-ma-a-am*
3 *lu-ḫu-mu-um ú-li-id zu*$^{!}$*-ba*$^{!}$ *zu*$^{!}$*-u[b]-bu ú-li-id tu-ul-tam*
4 *tu-ul-tum mārat*(DUMU$^{!}$.MUNUS$^{!}$) ^{d}*Gu-la lu-ul-lu-um-tam lu-ub-bu-ša-at da-mi ḫa-ab-ra-at*
5 *a-⌈ak*$^{?}$⌉*-[ki*$^{?}$*]-lu da-mi ṣe-eḫ-ri-im ú-pé-el-li-a-am i-ni-i-šu*
6 *id-⌈di ši-ip-tam* ^{d}*Da-mu ù* ^{d}*Gu-la⌉ ú-ni-ra ⌈tu-ul-tam⌉ [e*$^{?}$*-bi*$^{?}$*]-⌈tam*$^{?}$⌉ / *iṭ-bu-uḫ-šu-⌈nu-ti⌉ a-na ṣ[e*$^{?}$*]-eḫ*$^{?!}$*-r[i*$^{?}$*-im*$^{?}$*]*
7 *ip-te pí-i-šu iṣ-ṣa-bat tu-la-a-am iš-ši-i-ma i-ni-šu i-[ni*$^{?}$*-iq*$^{?}$*]*
8 *ši-ip-tum ú-ul ia-a-tum ši-pa-at* ^{d}*Da-mu ù* ^{d}*Gu-la* ^{d}*D[a-m]u [i]d-di-ma a-na-ku el-qé*

Translation

1 Anum begot the sky, the sky bore the earth,
2 the earth bore the stench, the stench bore the mud,
3 the mud bore the fly, the fly bore the worm.
4 The worm, the daughter of Gula, is clad in a *lullumtum*-garment, thick with blood,
5 the de[vour]er of the child's blood is reddening his eyes.
6 Damu cast the incantation and Gula slew the [thi]ck worm, slaughtered them for the (sake of the) c[hil]d.
7 He opened his mouth, took the (mother's) breast, raised his eyes, (began to) s[uck].
8 The incantation is not mine, (it is) the incantation of Damu and Gula. Damu cast (it) and I took (it).

Commentary

See Wasserman (2008, 73f.).

№ 114: YOS 11, 5b

SEAL No.: 7174
Copy: van Dijk/Goetze/Hussey 1985 Pls. VI-VII
Tablet Siglum: YBC 4616
Photo: https://collections.peabody.yale.edu/search/Record/YPM-BC-018681
Edition: Wasserman 2008, 81f.
Studies: van Dijk/Goetze/Hussey 1985, 19; George 1994; Cunningham 1997 Cat. No. 374; Wasserman 2003 Cat. No. 229; Wasserman 2008
Collection: Yale Babylonian Collection, New Haven
Provenance: Larsa area
Measurements: 7.6 × 8.3 cm
Procedure: No

Introduction

Opening with a historiola – Gula was walking with her dogs named *Supplication*(*s*) and *Laughter* while Sîn, coming out of Nippur, was armed with a fly and a scorpion – this incantation is destined to stop worms (leeches?) attacking a young boy. A legitimation formula seals the text.

9 *i-nu-ma* ^{d}*Gu-la il-li-ku mu-tu-tam kal-bu il-li-ku wa-ar-ki-i-ša*
10 *tu-li-a-tum i-dam ia-ši-im su-up-pu ù ṣú-ḫu-um ša il-li-ku wa-ar-ki-ša*
i-[*n*]*u-ma* ^{d}*Sîn*(EN.ZU) *iš-tu Nippur*(NIBRU)^{ki} *ú-ṣi-a-am*
11 *ú-wa-aš-še-e*[*r zu*$^{?}$/*ku*$^{?}$*-u*]*b-ba-am ù zuqiqīpam*(GÍR.TAB) *a-na*
qá-aq-qá-di-im m[*u*$^{!}$*-n*]*am*$^{!}$ *a-na ap-pí ṣe-eḫ-ri-im bé-li it-ta-di*
12 *ṣe-eḫ-rum la i-de-a-am mu-ru-us-su la i-de-a-am ta-ni-ḫi-šu* ⌜*ta-az*⌝*-zi-qí-šu*
13 *ak-nu-uk ap-pa-am ù ḫa-sí-sà-am ak-nu-uk ši-pi-a-tim ša mu-ḫi-i-šu ša Al-la-tum*
ú$^{!}$(I)*-ra-am-mu-šu*
14 *i-di-a-am a-na bi-ri-tu tu-li-ša ši-ip-tum ú-ul ia-a-tum ši-pa-at* ^{d}*Gu-la*

Translation

9 When Gula was walking in bravery, (her) dogs were walking behind her.
10 – "Worms! To (my) side! To me!" – *Supplication*(*s*) and *Laughter* that were walking behind her.
10–11 When Sîn came out of Nippur he released the [*fly*$^{?}$/*ee*]*l*$^{?}$ and the scorpion to the head. My lord threw the larva to the child's nose.
12 May the child not experience (any of) his illness, may he not experience (any of) his distress, (of) his anxiety!
13 I have sealed (his) nose and (his) ear. I have sealed the sutures of his skull that Allatum has loosened.
14 She threw (him$^{?}$ it$^{?}$) in between her breast. This incantation is not mine: (it is) the incantation of Gula.

Commentary
See Wasserman (2008, 81–83).

№ 115: YOS 11, 41

SEAL No.: 26862
Copy: van Dijk/Goetze/Hussey 1985 Pl. LIV
Tablet Siglum: YBC 5638
Photo: https://collections.peabody.yale.edu/search/Record/YPM-BC-019703
Edition: Krebernik 2018, 31f.
Studies: van Dijk/Goetze/Hussey 1985, 33; Cunningham 1997 Cat. No. 443; Krebernik 2018, 31f.
Collection: Yale Babylonian Collection, New Haven
Provenance: Larsa area
Measurements: 4.0 × 6.0 cm
Procedure: No

Introduction

Krebernik (2018, 14 fn. 2) raises the possibility that the alloglot passage which opens this spell is in Amorite. The organ which the worm attacks is not specified (tooth? eye? or belly?).

1 [ku]-ul ki-im-ḫa ku-ul ki-im-ma-ḫa
2 ku-ul si-ḫa-ra ku-ul si-ik-ra
3 ku-li ra-bi-ka
4 ku-li ra-bi-na
5 *ù at-ti bu-ul-ṭi sa*$^{!}$(SÚ)-*aḫ-la-ti*
6 ka-inim-ma zú-muš-e-[gu$_7$]-⸢e⸣

Rest uninscribed

Translation

1 *kul kimha kul kimmaḫa*
2 *kul siḫara kul sikra*
3 *kuli rabika*
4 *kuli rabina*
5 And you (f.) (worm) are piercing my health!
6 Incantation (against) the [consuming] worm.

Commentary

6: The designation zú-muš-e-[gu$_7$]-⸢e⸣ recalls the Sum. equivalent of the demoness *Pašittu*, lit. "consumed by the worm" (see Wiggerman 2000, 225 fn. 44).

2.3 Humans

2.3.1 Anger

Incantations against bursting anger[247] typically use metaphors and similes of wild animals. In some cases, this anger is connected to flaring desire (ZA 75, 198–204h: 78ff, 85ff., 95ff. = № 119). The magical strategy employed in this group of incantations is that of control by overcoming a substitute entity. The magician steps over, or goes through a door, or a threshold, thus overpowering the effects of anger. This magical approach is not restricted to anger incantations; it is found also in incantations that deal with inimical human reactions, as those destined to calm a crying baby (CUSAS 32, 31e: 19–22 = № 121).

№ 116: TIM 9, 72

SEAL No.: 7045
Copy: van Dijk 1976 Pl. LIX
Tablet Siglum: IM 51207
Photo: –
Edition: Whiting 1985, 180f.
Studies: Cunningham 1997 Cat. No. 324; Wasserman 2003 Cat. No. 177; Foster 2005, 186; Groneberg 2007, 104
Collection: Iraq Museum, Baghdad
Provenance: Šaduppûm
Measurements: 6.5 × 4.0 cm
Procedure: No

Introduction

An elaborate example of the anger incantations. Starting with wild animal metaphors to describe the fierceness of the ravaging emotion, the healer proclaims his ability to control anger as he is able to manipulate different domestic utensils.

Obverse

1 ⌜*ú*⌝*-zu-um i-la-ka ri-ma-ni*
2 [*iš*]*-ta-na-ḫi-ṭà-am*
3 *ka-al-ba-ni*
4 *ki-ma nēšim*(UR.MAḪ)
5 *e-zi a-la-ka-am*
6 *ki-ma barbarim*(UR.BAR.RA)
7 *ma-li li-ba-tim*
8 *ta-aš-ba-am ki-ma ás-ku-pa-tim*
9 *lu-ba-ka*

247 In earlier treatments *UZ-ZU*-um was read *ūṣum*, "arrow" (so still in AHw, 529b s.v. *lakûm* III, cf. CAD U/W, 290b).

10 *⌜ki⌝-ma ar-ka-bi-nim*
11 *lu-te$_9$-ti-ka*

Reverse
12 *ki-ma si-pí-im*
13 *lu-uš-qa-li-il*
14 *i-na ṣé-ri-ka*
15 *ki-ma šu-mu-nim*
16 *lu-ne!-eʾ! ki-bi-ís-ka*
17 *lu-še-ṣí i-ša-tam*
18 *ša li-ib-bi-ka*

Translation

1–3	Anger comes like a wild bull. It keeps [ju]mping like a dog.
4–7	Like a lion, it is fierce-ranging. Like a wolf, it is full of rage.
8–9	– "Sit down! Let me walk through you like (over) a threshold!
10–11	Let me pass back and forth through you like (through) an *Arkabinnu*-door!
12–14	Let me hang above you like a lintel!
15–16	Like (with) a restraining-rope, let me curb your step!
17–18	Let me take out the fire of your heart!"

Commentary

1: *i-la-ka* (*illaka* < *alākum*), not as AHw, 529b, and von Soden (1977, 28) suggest: *lakûm* "durchbohren".

5: *e-zi a-la-ka-am* stative of *ezēzum* (not of *ezûm* II "eilig, hastig sein", as AHw, 270a and still in AHw, 1555b. The correct analysis found in GAG^3 § 101d).

8: *tašbam*: imp. *tašābum* (with AHw, 1337b 1; unlike Whiting 1985, 181). A parallel to this form is found in ZA 75, 184: 1' (№ 118).

8–9: For this simile, see Wasserman (2003, 117).

10: The *arkabinnu*-door is equated in Malku = *šarru* II: 173 with *daltum lā qatītum* "Tür, die die Türöffnung nicht ganz bedeckt" (Hrůša 2010, 345). The exact shape of this door is hard to establish (a saloon-like swing-door? a split Dutch door?), but it is clear that the *arkabinnu* allows easy entrance (see also Gilg. VI 34, and George 2003, 832).

15–16: See Wasserman (2003, 114).

№ 117: UET 6/2, 399

SEAL No.: 7046
Copy: Gadd/Kramer 1966 Pl. CCLXXXVI; Whiting 1985, 184 (by I.L. Finkel)
Tablet Siglum: U.16892D
Photo: CDLI P274660
Edition: Whiting 1985, 180f.
Studies: Biggs 1970, 59; Groneberg 1987, 160 fn. 22; Cunningham 1997 Cat. No. 335; Wasserman 2003 Cat. No. 193; Ludwig 2009, 247
http://www.ur-online.org/subject/17807/
Collection: The British Museum, London
Provenance: Ur
Measurements: 7.0 × 4.6 cm
Procedure: No

Introduction
Again, anger is described through wild animal similes and its control is expressed by the stepping-over symbolism. The end is less clear. The subscript refers only to the act of exorcism, without mentioning the object: anger.

Obverse

1 *[ú-zu]-ú-mi ú-z[u-um]*
2 *[i]-la-ka ri-mi-ni-i[š]*
3 *[i]š-ta-na-ḫi-iṭ ka-al-ba-n[i-iš]*
4 *ki-ma né-ši-im*
5 *e-ez a-la-ka*
6 *ki-ma ba-ar-ba-ri-im*
7 *la-ka-ta ma-ad-mi*
8 *is-sú-uḫ ba-aš-ta-am*
9 *ša pa-ni-i-šu-ú*
10 *iḫ-pi qú-li-a-am*
11 *ša li-bi-šu-ú*
12 *ap-ri-iš-šu-ú-ma*
13 *ki-ma ti-tu-ri*
14 *[l]u-ba e-li-šu*

Reverse

15 *ša-pá-al-*‹‹⌜iz/za⌝››*-šu-ú*
16 *[I]-di-ig-la-at*
17 *[na]-ru-um*
18 ⌜*ḫar*⌝*-gu-la ša*$^{?!}$ *ma-tim-*‹‹iz››*-ma*
19 *às*$^{!}$(AN)*-ni-iq-šum*
20 *i-qì-iq-šum*
21 *šum-ma-an* ⌜*la* x⌝ ak ša$^{?}$ ⌜x⌝

22 *lu-ug-ru-šam-*⸢*ma*⸣ *às-*
23 ⸢*na*⸣*-aq-šum*
----
24 [*š*]*a*$^{?}$ *šu-ṣí-im*

Translation

1 Anger! Anger!
2–3 It comes like a wild bull. It keeps jumping like a do[g].
4–7 Like a lion, it is fierce-ranging. Like a wolf, it is quick-running.
8–9 It (the spell) has removed the splendour of his face.
10–11 It broke the *bowl* of his heart.
12 I have blocked it!
13–18 Like a bridge may I cross over it! Beneath it is the river Tigris, *the lock of the land.*
19 *I approached him.*
20 *He paralyzed him.*
21 *Had it no*[*t*$^{?}$ …]
22–23 *I will move towards and approach him!*
----
24 [(Incantation) o]f letting (anger) out.

Commentary

4–7: For these two couplets, see Wasserman (2003, 33).

5: *e-ez a-la-ka*: stative of *ezēzum* G (*pace* AHw, 1555b; see GAG^{3} § 101 d) cf. *e-zi*, in TIM 9, 72: 5 (№ 116).

8–9: As we understand it, the subject of *issuḫ* and *iḫpi* is the magic spell which managed to break and block the force of the anger.

10: *qú-li-a-am* is tentatively derived from *qullium*, "(a bowl)" (CAD Q, 297f.), perhaps resembling a heart shape. Another possibility is a plene-writing of *qullum*, "(a metal fastening device)" (CAD Q, 298). The latter implement is found in Mari, where it was defined as "collier de cou auquel tiennent des anneaux", see Durand (2009, 185).

12: The verbal form *ap-ri-iš-šu-ú-ma* stands for *aprikšu*, although no other example of the assimilation of /kš/ > /šš/ in OB is known to us.

15–17: The correct reading of these lines is verified by ZA 75, 198–204h: 102 (№ 119).

16: The notion that the river Tigris is capable of wiping away strong human feelings and bad actions is found also in a bilingual proverb, whose Sumerian part is almost entirely broken off: *enūma taḫbilu* ^{id}*Idiglat ubbalu* "when you commit a crime, the Tigris will bear away (the guilt)" (BWL, 253: 1–4).

22–23: An enjambment: the first person continues to the next line. Note the unusual vowel of *sanāqum* (i/i).

№ 118: ZA 75, 184

SEAL No.: 7047
Copy: Whiting 1985, 184
Tablet Siglum: Tell Asmar 1930–T117
Photo: –
Edition: Whiting 1985
Studies: Cunningham 1997 Cat. No. 344; Wasserman 2003 Cat. No. 4
Collection: Oriental Institute, Chicago
Provenance: Ešnunna
Measurements: –
Procedure: No

Introduction
A short incantation, partially parallel to TIM 9, 72 (№ 116), starting directly with the healer trying to control anger. As described by Whiting (1985, 179f.), the tablet was originally made of two lumps of clay pressed together. On this method of preparing tablets, see Taylor/Cartwright (2011, 299f.). As for the reverse, Whiting states "The back of the fragment is smooth and shows marks of a cloth. In addition, it shows traces of two parallel vertical wedges and two converging oblique wedges arranged to form the stylized representation of the neck and snout of an animal as in the contemporary ANŠE or AZ signs".

Obverse[?]

1'	TUŠ-*ba*[!](DA)-*ma ki* ⸢*ás-ku*⸣-[*pa-tim*] *lu-ba-k*[*a*]
2'	*ki ar-ka-bi-nim*
3'	*lu-te*$_9$*-te-ka*
4'	*ki-ma ba-ar-ba-ri-*⸢*im*⸣
5'	[*b*]*a-aš-*⸢*tám*⸣
6'	[*ki*] *né-*⸢*ši-im*⸣ *ša-lu-ma-t*[*ám*]
7'	[*lu-ṭ*]*e*$_4$*-er-ka*

Translation

1'	– "*Sit down*! I will walk through you like (over) a threshold!
2'–3'	I will pass back and forth through you like (through) an *Arkabinnu*-door!
4'–6'	Vigor – like (that of) a wolf, splendour – like (that of) a lion
7'	I will take away from you!"

Commentary

1': The enigmatic opening of the incantation TUŠ-*ba*$^{!}$*-ma* is made clear with the parallel *ta-aš-ba-am kīma askuppatim lubāʾka* (TIM 9, 72: 8–9 = № 116). TUŠ-*ba*$^{!}$*-ma* is therefore a mistake for *tašbam*, or a mixed (Sumerogram with a phonetic complement) spelling of *tašbamma*, "sit down!". Even *taš*(UR$^{!}$)-*ba*$^{!}$*-ma* is not excluded.

1'–2': On these comparisons, see Wasserman (2003, 117).

4'–6': See Wasserman (2003, 118).

№ 119: ZA 75, 198–204h

SEAL No.: 7149
Copy: –
Tablet Siglum: IB 1554
Photo: Wilcke 1985, after p. 208
Edition: Wilcke 1985, 202f,: 73–99; Wasserman 2016, 268–270
Studies: Scurlock 1989–1990; Cunningham 1997 Cat. No. 320; Wasserman 2003 Cat. No. 28; Foster 2005, 204f.; Groneberg 2007, 103f.
Collection: Iraq Museum, Baghdad
Provenance: Isin
Measurements: 25.5 × 8.0 cm
Procedure: No

Introduction

This incantation against anger is composed of three passages marked by a separation line (so, perhaps distinct incantations after all?). It ends with a single subscript. Being part of the Isin tablet of love incantations (Wasserman 2016, 257–274), it is clear that 'anger' here is connected to sexual attraction, or better, caused by sexual rejection. The speaker in the first passage (ll. 78–84) seems to be a woman and the addressee, a man.

Reverse

78 *[uz-zu-um] uz-zu-um*
79 *⸢i⸣-t[a$^{?}$-na-za]-az i-na li-ib-bi-šu*
80 *⸢lu-uš-qì-ka⸣ [me]-e ka-ṣú-ú-tim*
81 *lu-uš-qì-ka šu-ri-pa-am ta-ak-ṣí-a-tim*
82 *[l]i-ib-ba-ka ki-ma barbarim*(U[R.B]AR.RA) *ba-aš-tum*
83 *[ki-ma] nēšim*(UR.MAḪ-*im*) *š[a]-l[um-m]a-tum li-ik-l[a$^{?}$]-ka*
84 *še-ḫ[i-i]ṭ uz-zu-u[m š]a ^{d}Na-na-a*
----
85 *uz-z[u-u]m uz-zu-um*
86 *i-i[l-la-ka-am] ri-ma-ni-iš*
87 *iš-t[a$^{!}$-na-ḫi-ṭa-am] ⸢ka-al-ba⸣-[n]i-i[š]*
88 *k[i-ma nēšim*(UR.MAḪ-*im*) *e-ez] a-l[a$^{?}$-ka-am]*
89 *k[i-ma barbarim*(UR.BAR.RA) *la-k]a-ta-am ⸢ú$^{?}$⸣-ša-[ar$^{?}$]*
90 [x x x x x x x] (-) *me-e ka-ba-at-tim*
91 *i[ḫ-pi qú-li-a-am] ša li-ib-bi-šu*
92 *ti-[tu-ra-am lu]-ba e-li-i-šu*
93 *ša-p[a]-a[l-šu] ⸢íd⸣Idiglat na-ru-um*
94 *še-ḫi-iṭ [uz-zu-um] ša ^{d}Na-na-a*
----
95 *uz-zu-um* [(x x x)] *uz-zu-um*
96 *ki-ma as-[k]u-u[p-p]a-t[i]m lu-ka-bi-is-k[a]*
97 *ki-ma qá-aq-[qá-ri-i]m lu-te-et-ti-iq-ka*

98 *še-ḫi-iṭ [uz]-zu-um ša* ^{d}*Na-na-a*

----

99 ka-inim-ma lag-mun-kam

Translation

78 [Anger!] Anger!
79 It keeps s[tand]ing in his heart!
80 Let me give you (m.) cold water to drink!
81 Let me give you (m.) ice and cool drinks to drink!
82–83 May dignity, like (that of) a wolf, (restrain) your heart! May radiance, like (that of) a lion, restrain you (m.)!
84 Jump off, oh anger of Nanāya!

----

85 Anger! Anger!
86–87 It co[mes to me] like a wild bull, it ke[eps jumpin]g at me like a dog.
88–89 Like a lion, it is fierce-ranging; like a wolf, it breaks into a run.
90 […] *water*$^{?}$ of the liver.
91 I[t has broken the *bowl*$^{?}$] of his heart.
92 *With the help* of a b[ridge], let me cross over it!
93 Beneath it is the river Tigris.
94 Jump off, [oh anger] of Nanāya!

----

95 Anger! Anger!
96 Let me trample over you like (over) a threshold!
97 As (over) the soil, let me pass back and forth over you!
98 Jump! oh anger of Nanāya!

----

99 Incantation of the salt-lump.

Commentary

See Wasserman (2016, 268–270).

2.3.2 Baby (Quieting Cry)

What sets the group of incantations destined to pacify a crying baby aside from the rest of the corpus is that the problem it aims to solve is mundane, not medically critical or life-threatening. As such, some refer to them as 'lullabies' (Farber 1989a, 3). Mesopotamian scribes found interest in the use of incantations to pacify a crying baby, and this category shows textual longevity, from the OB and MB periods (note the recently published CUSAS 30, 448 = Zomer 2018a, 354f.) to first-millennium, SB texts (Farber 1989a, 40–91). The main building blocks of this group are: an address to the baby; remembrance of his peaceful behaviour in his mother's womb; description of the domestic suffering caused by the baby's nocturnal cry; a call for a healing agent to pour sleep over the neonate (For the motif of deities not being able to sleep in Mesopotamian literature, see Oshima 2014).

№ 120: AoF 45, 196

SEAL No.: 26519
Copy: Murad/Cavigneaux 2018, 196
Tablet Siglum: IM 160096
Photo: Murad/Cavigneaux 2018, 197
Edition: Murad/Cavigneaux 2018, 193f.
Studies: Murad/Cavigneaux 2018
Collection: Iraq Museum, Baghdad
Provenance: Unknown
Measurements: 10.4 × 5.1 cm
Procedure: No

Introduction

This elongated incantation opens with the curtailed "you", without the explicative "little-one, a human child" (OECT 11, 2: 1–2 = № 122), or "dweller of the House of Darkness" (ZA 71, 62b: r. 1' = № 124). A uniqe variant of the *mannam lušpur* formula, destined to "the shepherds of sheep, cows, and lambs" follows. The text was produced by a non-professional scribe, as proven by the inelegant enjambment of *lušpur*, skipping over from l. 10 to 11, the mistakes in l. 12 and the lack of the DINGIR determinatives in ll. 18, 19.

Obverse

1 *at-ta-ma ta-ta-ma-ar*
2 *ša-ru-ur ša-am-ši*
3 *a-mi-ni* ⸢*i+na*⸣ *li-bi* ⸢*ú*⸣*-mi-ka*
4 *ki-a-am la te-p*[*u*]-⸢*uš*⸣
5 *ar-ri-*⸢*ig-mi*⸣*-ka*
6 *ú-la i-ṣa-*⸢*la-al i*⸣*-li*
7 *bi-ti-i*[*m*] ⸢*ú*⸣*-la i-ṣa-*⸢*làl*$^{?}$⸣
8 *i-ta-ar bi*$^{!}$*-ti-im*
9 *ù-li-ḫa-zí ši-tu*
10 *ma-an-na-am-mi lu-uš-*

11 *pu-ur* ⸢*ù*? *lu-wa-i-ir*⸣
12 *re*?-*i im*-‹‹i››-⸢*mi*⸣-*r*[*i*]
13 *ar-ḫa-ti ú ka*-⸢*lu-ma*⸣-*ti-im*
14 *li-il*$_5$-*qù-ni-mi*
15 *ši-ta ša ar-ḫa-ti*-⸢*im*?⸣
16 *ù ka-lu-ma-ti*
17 [*ši*]-*ip-tum ú-la* ⸢*ia*⸣-[*ti*?]

Reverse
18 [*ši-pa-a*]*t Ni-gi*$_4$-*r*[*i-ma*]
19 ⸢*ù*⸣ *Ni-ka-ra-a*[*k*]

Translation

1–2 You have already seen the beams of the Sun:
3–4 Why have you not done so (i.e., crying) in your mother's womb?
5–7 Through your crying the god of the house cannot sleep!
7–9 The goddess of the house cannot sleep; slumber does not catch her!
10–13 – "Whom should I send and instruct (with orders) the shepherds of sheep, cows, and lambs,
14–16 so that they grab for me the slumber of cows and lambs?"
17–19 The incantation is not mine: it is the incantation of Ningirim and Ninkarrak.

Commentary

2: *šarūr Šamši* is found also in the MB incantation for a crying baby CUSAS 30, 448: 5.
9: *ù-li-ḫa-zí ši-tu* renders, with a Sandhi spelling, *ul iḫḫassi* (< *iḫḫazši*) *šittu*.
11: The silent nocturnal sleep of hoofed ruminant animals is the ideal situation in this group of incantations, cf. OECT 11, 2: 20, 22 (№ 122), where deer and gazelle are mentioned. A parodical takeoff on this motif is found in PRAK 2 Pl. III (C1) (№ 81), an incantation which describes a goat bleating all night, keeping the shepherds awake.

№ 121: CUSAS 32, 31e

SEAL No.: 7053
Copy: George 2016 Pl. LXXXVI
Tablet Siglum: MS 3103
Photo: George 2016 Pl. LXXXVII; CDLI P252112
Edition: George 2016, 145
Studies: Zomer 2018a, 232
Collection: Schøyen Collection, Oslo
Provenance: Unknown
Measurements: 12.5 × 11.5 cm
Procedure: No

Introduction

With no opening addressee, this incantation starts *in media res*: the parents are deprived of sleep because of their baby's crying. The section describing the baby's pre-natal condition (*ḫalpāt rēmam lubbušāt šalītam*, ll.14–15) is unparalleled in other incantations of this group. The incantation terminates with a broken passage where the speaker is said to step over the baby's harsh cry, a magical approach typical of incantations dealing with anger.

iv
8 *ib-ki ṣe-eḫ-ru-um id-da-li-ip*
9 *a-*⸢*ba*⸣*-a-šu*
10 *ḫa-ar-ra-an la ni-lim*
11 *u*[*m*]*-ma-šu uš-ta-li-ik*
12 ⸢*i-nu-ú*⸣*-ma i-na li-ib-bi*
13 [*u*]*m-mi-ka tu-ši-ba-am*
14 [*ḫ*]*a-al-pa-at re-e-ma-am*
15 [*l*]*u-ub-bu-ša-at ša-li-ta-am*
16 ⸢*a*⸣*-mi-i-ni ki-ma i-na-an-na*
17 [*wa*$^?$]-⸢*ṣí*$^?$⸣ *kārim*(KAR) *ḫa-*⸢*il*⸣*-ti*
18 [*la*$^?$ *ta*$^?$*-q*]*ú-lam-ma ki-ma qá-ni pa-da-ni-im*
19 [*lu-ka-a*]*b-bi-is-ka*
20 [*ki-ma*] *as-ku-up-pa-tim*
21 [*lu-te-t*]*i-iq-ka*
22 […] ⸢x x⸣*-di-im*
23 […]*-tim*
24 […] ⸢x⸣

Translation

8–9	The little-one cried: woke up his father.
10–11	He made his mother take the road-of-no-sleep.
12–13	When you sat in the belly of your mother,
14–15	when you were enveloped with the womb, wearing the placenta –
16–18	why [don't you ke]ep silent, once you are out on the quay of labour?
18–19	[I will tr]ead on you like a reed of the path!
20–21	[I will cr]oss over you like (over) the threshold!

Commentary

10: For *ḫarrān lā nīlim* "road-of-no-sleep", see George (2016, 145). In this context, *nīlum* plays both on *niālum* "to lie down, to rest" and on the homonym "semen".

14–15: Note the shortened 2 m. sg. stative forms in *ḫalpāt rēmam lubbušāt šalītam* (for *ḫalpāta* and *lubbušāta*). For such forms in OB literary texts, see Wasserman (2016, 75/118).

18–21: "Treading on... and crossing over..." are phrases typical of incantations against anger (see § 2.3.1). Their appearance here reflects the frustration, even anger, caused by the child's continuous crying.

22–23: Perhaps the end of [… *wi-il-*]*di-im* [*ša a-wi-lu-ú-*]*tim*, see OECT 11, 2: 2 (№ 122).

№ 122: OECT 11, 2

SEAL No.: 7049
Copy: Gurney 1989, 42
Tablet Siglum: Bod AB 215
Photo: –
Edition: Farber 1989a, 34–37; Gurney 1989, 19–21; Wasserman 2011, 4f.
Studies: Farber 1990a; Farber 1990b; von Soden 1989–1990; Cunningham 1997 Cat. No. 353; Wasserman 2003 Cat. No. 112; Wasserman 2011, 4f.; Zomer 2018a, 232
Collection: Ashmolean Museum, Oxford
Provenance: Unknown
Measurements: 7.7 × 5.3 cm
Procedure: No

Introduction
The main interest in this well-written incantation is the expanded historiola alluding to Enkidu and Gilgameš (16ff.), for which see Farber (1990, 303 fn. 35) and Wasserman (2011, 4f.).

Obverse
1 *[a]t-ta-a-ma ṣ[e]-e[ḫ]-ru[m$^{?}$]*
2 *[w]i-il$^{!}$-du-um ša a-wi-lu-ú-[tim]*
3 *lu-ú ta-at-ta-ṣ[i]-a-am*
4 *lu-ú ta-ta-mar* ^{d}*Šamaš*(UTU) *nu-r[a-am$^{?}$]*
5 *a[m]-mi-ni i-na li-ib-bi um-[m]a-ka*
6 *ki-a-am la te-te-ep-pu-uš*
7 *ki-⸢i⸣ ša du-um-qá-am [t]e-pu-šu a-ba-k[a]*
8 *s[u-qá]-am ša ni-ši um-ma-ka tu-uš-bi-ʾu$_5$*
9 *tu-uš-ta-aʾ-di-ir ta-ri-ta-am*
10 *ta-ad-da-li-ip mu-še-ni-iq-ta-am*
11 *i-na ri-ig-mi-ka i-li bi-tim*
12 *ú-ul i-ṣa-al-la-al*
13 *iš-ta-ar bi-tim*
14 *ú-ul i-ḫa-az ši-it-tum*
15 *[m]a-an-na-am lu-uš-pu-ur*

Reverse
16 *a-na En-ki-du$_{10}$*
17 *ša-ki-in ša-la-a-aš-ti*
18 *‹‹a-na›› ma-aṣ-ṣa-ra-tim*
19 *li-iṣ-ba-as-[s]ú-ú-mi*
20 ⸢*ša*⸣ *iṣ-ba-tu-ú ṣabitam*(MAŠ.DÀ)
21 *l[i]-ka-as-sí-[š]u-mi*
22 *š[a] ú-ka-as-sú-ú ar-wi-[am]*

23 ⌈*i*$^{?}$*-na*$^{?}$⌉ *ṣe-e-ri-im li-id-di-i*[*š*$^{?}$*-šum*$^{?}$]
24 [*m*]*é*$^{?}$*-e-ḫi-ru-um ši-na-as-s*[*ú*]
25 *a-li-ik warki*(EGIR) *alpī*(GUD$^{ḫi.a}$) *ši-it-ta-šu*
26 *li-zi-ib-šum*
27 *a-di um-ma-šu i-de-ku-ú-šu*
28 *a-a i-ig-ge-el-ti*
----
29 ka-inim-ma l[ú]-tur$^{!}$(I) ír-šeš$_4$-še[š$_4$-a-kam$^{?}$]

Translation

1–2 Oh you little-one, a human child,
3–4 you have already come out, you have already seen the Sun, the light.
5–6 Why have you not done so (crying) in your mother's womb?
7–8 Instead of doing good to your father, letting your mother pass (quietly) in the people's street,
9–10 you have frightened the nanny, you have deprived of sleep the wet–nurse.
11–12 Through your crying, the god of the house cannot sleep!
13–14 Slumber does not catch the goddess of the house!
15–16 – Whom should I send to Enkidu,
17–18 the creator of the three night watches, (saying:)
19–20 – "He who caught the deer may catch him (too) (i.e., the baby)!
21–22 He who bound the gazelle may bind him (too)!
23–24 May his fellow (i.e., Gilgameš) in the field give him his sleep!
25–26 May (the constellation of) the One-walking-behind-the-cattle leave for him his sleep!".
27–28 Until his mother wakes him up, may he not awake!
29 Incantation for a crying baby.

Commentary

2: *wi-il*$^{!}$*-du-um ša a-wi-lu-ú-*[*tim*] makes better sense than the enigmatic *wu-úr-du-um*.[248]

17–18: *ana Enkidu šākin šalašti ana maṣṣarātim*: The second *ana* in l. 18 is probably a dittography, repeating *ana* in l. 16.

248 The *l*/*r* change does appear sporadically in OB literary texts, see e.g., *šaniat ar-ka-as-su-nu* (< *alkassunu*) *šipiršunu nukkur*, "Different is their way, their activity is strange", Ištar Louvre: ii 17 (Streck/Wasserman 2018, 20). More examples of this phonetic change, see Streck/Wasserman 2018, 11.

№ 123: RA 36, 4a

SEAL No.: 7050
Copy: Thureau-Dangin 1939, 15
Tablet Siglum: –
Photo: –
Edition: Thureau-Dangin 1939, 14f.; Krebernik 2018, 36
Studies: Farber 1989a, 10; Farber 1990b, 306; Cunningham 1997 Cat. No. 341; Wasserman 2003 Cat. No. 137; Zomer 2018a, 124 fn. 440/126 fn. 443
Collection: Deir ez-Zor$^{?}$
Provenance: Mari
Measurements: 9.0 × 4.8 cm
Procedure: No

Introduction

The fragmentary state of the tablet precludes a full understanding, but it probably aims to quiet a baby who is crying because of earache. The reverse contains a spell in Hurrian, see Krebernik (2018, 36).

Obverse

1'–4'	(*broken*)
5'	^{d}*Sîn i-*[…] ⸢x⸣-*ni-šu*
6'	[*l*]*i-bi* […] ⸢x⸣-*ku-ti-šu*
7'	[x] ma […]
8'	[x] ⸢x⸣ […]
9'	[…]
10'	[*m*]*a-n*[*am lu-uš-pu-ur* …]
11'	*a-na* ⸢x x⸣ […]
12'	*me-e* [*ellūtim*$^{?}$ …]
13'	*li-iš-qí-a-*‹*ni*›*-im* […]
14'	*ú-zu-un* […]
15'	*li-im-ḫa-*[*ṣa* …]
16'	*ṣeḫrum*(LÚ.TUR) *li-*[*nu-uḫ* …]
17'	*a-na-ku* […]

Translation

1'–4' (*broken*)
5' Sîn […] him
6' The heart of […] him
7'–9' …
10'–11' – "Wh[om shall I send and instruct (with orders)] *to* [*the Daughters of Anum, seven and seven*?]?"
12'–13' May they offer to drink […] [*pure*?] water […]!
14' The ear of [*the baby*? …]
15' May *they stri*[*ke* …]
16' May the baby r[est …]
17' [*May*] I [*sleep*? …]

Commentary

10'–11': For the *mannam lušpur* formula here, see Farber (1990b, 306).
16': See Farber (1989a, 10).

№ 124: ZA 71, 62b

SEAL No.: 7051
Copy: Farber 1981, 62
Tablet Siglum: BM 122691
Photo: https://www.britishmuseum.org/collection/object/W_1931-0413-4
Edition: Farber 1981, 63f.; Farber 1989a, 43
Studies: Farber 1989a, 10; Farber 1990b, 306; von Soden 1990, 137; van der Toorn 1999, 139–148; Cunningham 1997 Cat. No. 341; Wasserman 2003 Cat. No. 137; Franke 2013, 40; Zomer 2018a, 232
Collection: The British Museum, London
Provenance: Tell Duweihes
Measurements: 8.9 × 6.4 cm
Procedure: No

Introduction
This tablet contains two more spells, against the Evil Eye and against canines. Judging by sign-forms and its grammatical features, this is an early OB incantation. The nocturnal setting of the text is made clear by the mention of the constellation Kusarikkum.

Reverse
1' *ṣe-eḫ-ru-um wa-ši-ib bi-it ek-*[*le-tim*]
2' *lu ta-ta-ṣa-am ta-ta-ma-ar n*[*u-ur* ^{d}*Šamaš*(UTU)]
3' *a-mi-in ta-ba-ki a-mi-in tu-g*[*a*$^{?}$*-ag*$^{?}$]
4' *ul-li-ki-a a-mi-in la ta-ab-*[*ki-*(*i*$^{?}$)]
5' *ì-lí bi-tim te-ed-ki Ku-sa-ri-*[*k*]*u-u*[*m*] / *i-gi-il-tì*
6' *ma-nu-um id-ki-a-ni*
7' *ma-nu-um ú-ga-li-ta-ni*
8' *ṣe-eḫ-ru-um id-ki-ka ṣe-eh-ru-um ú-ga-li-it/-ka*
9' *ki-ma ša-tu-ù ka-ra-ni-im*
10' *ki-ma ma-ar sà-bi-tim*
11' *li-im-qù-ta-šum ši-tum*

12' *ši-ip-tum ša ṣe-eḫ-ri-im nu-ùḫ-ḫi-im*

Translation

1'	Oh baby, (once) a dweller of the House of Darkness,
2'	You have now come out, you have now seen the li[ght of Šamaš]
3'	Why (then) are you crying, why are you screaming?
4'	There, why did you not cry?
5'	You have awoken the god(s) of the house, the Kusarikkum has aroused, (saying):
6'–7'	– "Who has awoken me? Who has aroused me?"
8'	– The baby has awoken you, the baby has aroused you!
9'–10'	Like (over) drinker(s) of wine, like (over) a son of a tavern keeper –
11'	May sleep fall over him.

12'	Incantation to quiet a baby.

Commentary

1': *wāšib bīt eklētim*: The metaphorical linkage between womb and grave – two dark and unfamiliar locations where humans are placed – is found also later, in Biblical and post-Biblical traditions (see, Jer. 20: 17–18 and Job 10: 18–22, as well as in Mishna *Ohalot* 7: 4 and *Sanhedrin* 92a).

3': *tu-g*[*a*$^{?}$-*ag*$^{?}$]: von Soden (1990, 137) suggested instead: *tu*-[*na-ba*].

5': CAD N/1, 106ff. lists only MB and SB examples for *nagaltû*, "to awake, to wake up". This verb, however, is attested already in OB, as proven by this incantation and the lamentation PBS 1/1, 2: 108.

2.3.3 Empowerment

In this category of texts the speaker is the object of his own incantation. He is "enchanting himself", charging ("impregnating") himself with divine power. The purpose of this self-empowering is not entirely clear, but it is likely to be a preparation for a demanding magical procedure. AMD 1, 273a (№ 125) and TIM 9, 73b (№ 129) display the motif of 'self-insemination/impregnation' discussed by Cooper (1996) and Cavigneaux (1999, 264–271). In CUSAS 32, 55 (№ 126), CUSAS 32, 56 (№ 127) and CUSAS 32, 57 (№ 128) the speaker makes analogies with primordial times by alluding to literary works (Lugale, Angim and Atraḫasīs).[249]

№ 125: AMD 1, 273a

SEAL No.: 7158
Copy: Cavigneaux 1999, 273
Tablet Siglum: H 72
Photo: –
Edition: Cavigneaux 1999, 258–261
Studies: Cooper 1996; Wasserman 2003 Cat. No. 101
Collection: Iraq Museum, Baghdad
Provenance: Mēturan
Measurements: –
Procedure: No

Introduction

The Akkadian incantation is followed by a (syllabic) Sumerian incantation – not a procedure, although flour is mentioned – against the evil tongue (ll. 12–18). A late parallel of this incantation is known, see Cavigneaux (1999, 270f.).

Obverse

1 APIN$_{x}$(ak) *er-ṣé-tam i-ra-ḫi*
2 ^{d}*Šákkan ra-ma-na-šu uš-*⸢*ša-ap*⸣
3 *lu-ši-im-ma ra-ma-ni lu-ši-ip ši-ip-tam*
4 *bi-ṣú-ur ka-al-ba-ti-im qí-bi-it* ⸢*ki-bi*$^{!}$(IB)⸣*-ti-im*
5 *bi-ṣú-ur si-ni-iš-ti-im qa*$^{?}$*-mu-um qa*$^{?}$*-am-šu*$^{?}$
6 ^{d}*Šákkan ra-ma-na-šu uš-ša-ap*
7 *lu-š*[*i-i*]*p ra-ma-ni lu-*‹‹ib››*-ši-ip ši-ip-tam*
8 *ki-ma* ^{d}*Šákkan uš-ša-pu ra-ma-an-šu*
9 *aḫ-zu*$^{?!}$ *im-me*$^{!}$*-ru ka-lu-mu*

249 Some first millennium Sumerian incantations integrate passages from Lugale and other Ninurta narratives, see Zomer 2020.

Reverse

10 *aḫ-za ka-lu-ma-tum maḫ?-ri-šu*

11 *ši-pa-at ra-ma-ni-ia ia-ti aḫ-zi-ni*

Translation

1–2 (As) the plow impregnates the earth (and) Šakkan enchants himself,

3 let me enchant myself and let me cast a spell!

4 The vulva of a bitch, *is the order of strength*!

5 The vulva of a woman, *is very much a flame*!

6–7 Šakkan enchants himself: Let me enchant myself and let me cast a spell!

8–11 As Šakkan enchants himself (and then) sheep (and) lambs are seized, she-lambs are seized in front of him, (so), oh my self-conjuration, seize (f.) me!

Commentary

4: Tentative translation with *qibītum* "order" and *kibittu* "strength" in mind. Our suggestion is not better than that of Cavigneaux (1999, 264) who read KI BI-IT? KI IB-*ti-im* as *kī bīt qīptim* "like the container of a consigned good, (??)", commenting (1999, 264): "no more than a guess!".

5: As difficult as the previous line. Cavigneaux (1999, 264): "very obscure".

9–10: With *reḫûm* (l. 1) and *biṣṣūrum* (ll. 4, 5), *aḫāzum* "to seize, take hold of" must carry a sexual meaning (against Cavigneaux 1999, 264: "no sexual connotation").

№ 126: CUSAS 32, 55

SEAL No.: 26866
Copy: George 2016 Pl. CXXV
Tablet Siglum: MS 3388
Photo: George 2016 Pl. CXXIV; CDLI P252329
Edition: George 2016, 162; Krebernik 2018, 42
Studies: George 2016, 160–162
Collection: Schøyen Collection, Oslo
Provenance: Unknown
Measurements: 10.0 × 7.2 cm
Procedure: No

Introduction

The speaker declares his godlike powers, alluding to the mythology of Ningirsu (ll. 7, 11–12) and Atraḫasīs (ll. 15–16). The genre of this exceptional text is not easy to ascertain, but the repeated alloglot passages and the first-person voice indicate that this is an incantation.

Obverse

1 [x x x za]-⸢za-li za-za⸣-li za-al / *ù* za-za-al
2 [x x x] ⸢*ù* za⸣-li-za-al za-li-za-al / *ù* za-za-al
----
3 [x x x x x] ⸢x⸣ [*e-mu-q*]*á*-⸢*am*⸣ *i*-⸢*šu*⸣ *a-ḫa-am* /⸢*e*⸣*-li-a-ku ù gi-it-ma-la-ku*
4 [*a-wa-t*]*i da-an*-⸢*na-at*⸣ *ra-bi-a-at / ù mu-uš-ta-la-at*
----
5 [x x (x)] ⸢x⸣ la ⸢al⸣ ka-al-la mi-ti-na
6 [x x (x)] ši ḫu gud a ⸢x⸣ i-za-al *ù* a-za-al
7 [x x] ⸢x⸣ *e-ez pa-nu-ú*-⸢*a* ^{giš}*kakki*(TUKUL)⸣ ^{d}*Nin-gír-sú / a-na-ku*
8 [*la-a*] *pa-li-ḫi-ka a-ka-ma-ku-um / a-ka-sà-ku ù e-re-de-a-ku-um*

Reverse

9 [ud-d]u-ul ul-⸢la⸣ ud-du-ul-la ul-la
10 [x] ⸢x⸣ la sà-pa la sà-[pa-a]l-sà ù lú-ùlu
11 [*qá-ar*]*-du-um la-sí*-⸢*mu-um ba*⸣*-nu-um ù na-ṣi-ru-um*
12 [*i-n*]*a da-an-nu-ti-ia i-gi-ti-li-a-am / a-du-uk an-du-ra-ar i-li aš-ku-un*
----
13 [x] ḫu-si ḫu-si-si ḫu-si *ù* ḫu-si
14 [(x)] ḫu-uš-ḫu-ús-si$^{!}$ ḫu-si *ù* ú-ús-si
15 *i-nu-ma i-lu ki-ma a-wi-li a-na-ku da-an-na-ku*
16 *ša-di-i* ⸢*ú-ša*⸣*-pa-ku-ma tu-up-ši-ka-am / ú-ša-ad-di*

Translation

1 [… *za*]*zali zazali zal* and *zazal*!
2 […] and *zalizal zalizal* and *zazal*!
----
3 […] I have strength! I am superior of arm and I am perfect!
4 My [wor]d is strong, great and considerate!
----
5 (*unintelligible*)
6 … *izal* and *azal*!
7 […] fierce is my face! I am the weapon of Ningirsu!
8 Those who do not fear you I will bind, arrest and lead (them) to you!

9 [*udd*]*ul ulla uddulla ulla*!
10 … *la sapala sapalsa* and mankind!
11 Heroic one, runner, beautiful one, protector!
12 In my strength I killed the monoculus! I established freedom for the gods!
----
13 … *ḫusi ḫusisi ḫusi* and *ḫusi*!
14 *ḫušḫussi ḫusi* and *ussi*!
15 When the gods were like men, I was the strongest!
16 They were heaping mountains, (but) I made (them) give up (their) labour!

Commentary

12: For the monoculus in Mesopotamian literature, see George (2012).

№ 127: CUSAS 32, 56

SEAL No.: 26867
Copy: George 2016 Pl. CXXVII
Tablet Siglum: MS 3380
Photo: George 2016 Pl. CXXVI; CDLI P252321
Edition: George 2016, 162f.; Krebernik 2018, 43
Studies: George 2016, 160–162
Collection: Schøyen Collection, Oslo
Provenance: Unknown
Measurements: 6.6 × 11.0 cm
Procedure: No

Introduction
This particular spell was apparently commissioned by Sîn-iddinam (and his wife$^{?}$) (l. 16). Similar to CUSAS 32, 55 (№ 126) and CUSAS 32, 57 (№ 128), this incantation also contains various alloglot passages and mythical allusions to a warrior god (l. 6).

Obverse
1 er-me-eš e-ri-me-eš er-me-eš *ù* [er-me-eš]
2 e-ri-me-eš lú-ùlu er-me-eš ⸢*ù*⸣ [er-me-eš]
3 *i-na li-*⸢*ib*⸣*-bu e*[*r-ṣ*]*é-tim* ⸢*ù*⸣ [*ša-me-e ra-bi*]
4 *šu-mi na-ṭi-lum* [*n*]*a-ṣi-ru* ⸢x⸣ [x x *a-na-ku-ma*]
----
5 ap-pa i-na-la-al-la *ù* ⸢la-ap-pa-la⸣ [x x x x]
6 *a-nu-ma ša-di-i e-né-ru*⸣ *ša-*⸢*di*⸣*-*[*i* x x x x x] / *na-ši-a-ku* ta-⸢x⸣-ik-⸢x⸣ [x x x]
----
7 se-er-mi-iš se-ri-⸢mi-iš-šu⸣ [x x x x x x]
8 lú la al ak ka ⸢x x x⸣ [x x x x x x]
9 *i-na e-ze-zi-ia i-ru-ru* ⸢x⸣ [x x x x x x]
10 *it-ta-ak-ṣa-ra* i šu ⸢x x x x x⸣ [x x x x]

Reverse
11 ud il-li lú li-la-a-al-la lú li-la / il-li-lu-la
12 *i-nu-ma mi-e ep-te-a-am i-lu it-ti-ia ú-la il-*[*qú-ú*] / *zi-ta-am ki-ma ka-li-šu-nu*
----
13 ha-al-la ḫa-al ḫi-la *ù* pa-al-la pa-li-li pa-li / pa-al-la ù-ši-in-dab$_5$
14 *a-na se-bi-šu zi-ta-am él-qé i-na qá-ra-du-ti-ia*
----
15 ti-il-la ù nam-ti-il é na-mi-nu-ka za-za-ag-mé-e[n]
16 nam-ti-il ^{d}nanna-ma-an-šúm *ú* nam-ti-il ‹‹*ù*›› *aš-š*[*a*$^{?}$*-ti*$^{?}$*-šu*$^{?}$]
17 *ge-er-re-et ma-ti-im a-na aš-ri-im aš-ku-un ra-bu-u*[*m*] / *šu-mi*
18 *ma-li-ku-um ba-nu-um na-ṣí-ru-um a-na-ku-ma*

Translation

1–2 *ermeš erimeš* and [*ermeš*]! *erimeš* (of) man, *ermeš* and [*ermeš*]!
3–4 In the midst of earth and [heaven] my name [is big]!
Watcher, the protector [(and) … am I]!

----

5 *appa inalalla* and *lappala* […]!
6 When I smote the mountains, the mountains […] I carry […].

----

7 *sermiš serimiššu* [(*and*) …]!
8 (*unintelligible*)
9–10 In my anger they trembled […] was bound together […].

11 *In those days when man was lilalla, (when) man was lila illilula!*
12 When I opened the waters, the gods, like all of them, they did not receive a share with me.

----

13 *ḫalla ḫal ḫila* and *palla palili pali palla after he seized thither,*
14 I received a share seven-fold from my warriorhood!

----

15 Living and life in the house of lordship, I am the *very best*!
16 (For) the life of Sîn-iddinam and the life of [his] wi[fe$^{?}$].
17 The paths of the land I put in place. Great is my name!
18 Advisor, handsome one, protector am I.

Commentary

3: For other examples of the merismus "earth – heaven" (much less common than "heaven – earth"), see Wasserman (2003, 77).

6: Note the unusual *anūma*, whereas l. 12 has *inūma*.

11: ud il-li stands probably for Sumerian u$_{4}$-ul-li-(a-ta) "since distant days". Cf. CUSAS 32, 55: 15–16 (№ 126).

15: za-za-ag-mé-e[n] remains difficult. It may be derived from sag "good" or zag-e$_{3}$ "foremost". Alternatively, one may suspect a corrupt form of a$_{2}$-sag$_{3}$ "Asakku".

№ 128: CUSAS 32, 57

SEAL No.: 26868
Copy: George 2016 Pl. CXXVIII
Tablet Siglum: MS 3334
Photo: George 2016 Pl. CXXVIII; CDLI P252275
Edition: George 2016, 163
Studies: George 2016, 160–162; Krebernik 2018, 43
Collection: Schøyen Collection, Oslo
Provenance: Unknown
Measurements: 5.5 × 10.0 cm
Procedure: No

Introduction
Similarly to CUSAS 32, 55 (№ 126) and CUSAS 32, 56 (№ 127), in this short hybrid spell the speaker boasts of his superhuman power.

Obverse
1' (*traces*)
2' [za-a]l-⸢la⸣ za-al-za-al-la *ù* za-al-l[a]
3' [z]i-la-lam zi-la-lam za-lam *ù* za-la[m]
4' [^{d}*In*]*šušinak*([M]ÙŠ.EREN) ^{d}Sag-kud ^{d}Sag-mes-Unug^{ki}-ga *ki-ma* ^{d}*En-l*[*íl*]
5' [*a-w*]*a-ti ra-bi-at ka-ab-ta-at ù ma-li-ka-a*[*t*]

Reverse uninscribed

Translation
1' (*traces*)
2'–3' *zalla zalzalla* and *zalla*! *zilalam zilalam* and *zalam*!
4' (By) Inšušinak, Sagkud, Mes-sanga-Unug! Like Enlil
5' my command is great, important and cunning!

Commentary
4': Or: “Inšušinak, Sagkud, Mes-sanga-Unug (am I)”, see George (2016, 163).

№ 129: TIM 9, 73b

SEAL No.: 7159
Copy: van Dijk 1973 Pl. LIX
Tablet Siglum: IM 52546
Photo: –
Edition: Cavigneaux 1999, 264f.
Studies: Wilcke 1985, 208; Cooper 1996, 50; Cunningham 1997 Cat. No. 326; Wasserman 2003 Cat. No. 179
Collection: Iraq Museum, Baghdad
Provenance: Šaduppûm
Measurements: 6.5 × 5.0 cm
Procedure: No

Introduction
This incantation, preceded by a spell against a rabid dog, presents another case of the 'self-impregnation' motif (see AMD 1, 273a = № 125).

Reverse
4 [*uš*]-⸢*ša*⸣-*ap-ka ra-ma-ni*
5 *a*-[*ra-a*]*ḫ-ḫi-ka pa-ag-ri*
6 *ki-ma* ^{id}LU.UḪ.DA ⸢x⸣ [x]
7 *ir-ḫu-ú ra-ma-a*[*n-ša*]
8 tu-en-ne-nu-ri
9 *ri-iš ši-ip-ti i-nu-ma*
10 [x] ša ba$^{?}$ ni$^{?}$ i$^{?}$ ⸢x⸣ bu

Translation
4 I will enchant you, my person!
5 I will inseminate you, my body!
6–7 As the river LU.UḪ.DA … has inseminated itself!
8 tu-en-ne-nu-ri
9 The beginning of the incantation "when......".

Commentary
6: Cooper (1996, 50) reads: *ki-ma A-sa-lu-uh* da x [...]. Cavigneaux (1999, 264f.) (based on photos): *ki-ma A-sa-lu-uh uš*$^{?}$-[*pu*$^{?!}$ (*pagaršu*)], translating "As Asalluhi$^{?}$ ... (*wašāpum*$^{?}$) [his body]". This is not free of difficulties, as there is not enough space for [*pa-ga-ar-šu*]. In parallel texts studied by Cooper (1996) and Cavigneaux (1999), the speaker's self-insemination is compared to a god "inseminating" himself (that is what Cooper and Cavigneaux had in mind), or the speaker's self-insemination is compared to a river "inseminating" itself. Our reading – following Wilcke (1985, 208) – prefers the latter option. A river ^{id}LU.UḪ.DA.X [x] is unknown to us.

9: CAD R, 288, 4c and AHw, 1247 take *rēš šipti inūma* … as a scribal remark referring to the incipit of (the following?) incantation. Such a practice of referring to an incantation by its incipit is, however, unknown in the OB corpus of incantations. More plausible is Cavigneaux's (1999, 265) translation: "beginning of the spell, when...", with the following comment (fn. 75): "The subscript… seems to give the circumstances in which the formula was used".

2.3.4 Love and Sexual Attraction

This group of incantations concerns amorous and sexual relationship. As such, these incantations do not target a threat in the strict sense of the word, but try to manipulate and control other people's emotions and desire. As other love-related compositions, the incantations are rich in simile and metaphor. Dialogues between man and woman are common and verbal manipulation widespread (Wasserman 2016).

№ 130: BM 115743

SEAL No.: 7152
Copy: Plate II
Tablet Siglum: BM 115743
Photo: –
Edition: –
Studies: –
Collection: British Museum, London
Provenance: Unknown
Measurements: 6.6 × 4.7 cm
Procedure: No

Introduction

A charm against the lover of a disloyal wife, written in a confident OB hand (but note the mistakes on ll. 7, 11). The reverse is left uninscribed. The cheated husband is slurring his rival, accusing him of ill (physical and probably also moral) odour, while glorifying his own potency. The man hopes that his cheating wife will disenchant the other man, so that the lover will not be able to perform sexually. No subscript is found, but the context leaves no doubt that the text's purpose is magical. The rhythmic alloglot phrases bolster this conclusion.

Obverse

1 ḫa-an-zu-ru mu-ra-li
2 ḫa-an-zu-ru ⸢mu-ra⸣-ra-li
3 *ša aš-ti i-na-ke-e-em*
4 *li-is-*⸢*sú*⸣*-[úḫ…]* li [(x)]
5 *ba-aš-ti a-qá-ra-an šu-mi-iḫ*
6 *mar-ra-ta*
7 *e-ri-šam mu-ur-ru-‹ur›* ⸢mu-ra⸣-li
8 mu-ra-ra-li
9 *pé-ḫi a-aḫ ap-pí* li-iḫ li-iḫ-ḫi
10 *pí-sa* ⸢KU$_4$⸣ *pí-su* GUR-*ma*
11 *wa-a-kam li-is*[!](MA)*-su-úḫ li-/[n]a-di-i*

Reverse uninscribed

Translation

1–2 *ḫanzuru murali, ḫanzuru murarali*

3–4 Whoever is fornicating with my wife – may (s)he remove [(his)] …!

5 I am piling up my sexual dignity. Make (m.) it grow abundantly!

6–7 You (m.) are bitter! Very bitter as of scent!

7–8 *murali, murarali*

9 Seal off the sides of the nose! *liḫ liḫḫi*

10 *May it* (i.e., the bitterness) *enter her mouth*$^{?}$, *(then) may it go back to his mouth!*$^{?}$

11 May she remove *the weak one*$^{?}$! May he be rejected!

Commentary

3: For the OB form *aštum* (instead of the more common *aššatum*), see also CUSAS 10, 9: 13 (Wasserman 2016, 90), a monologue of a woman in love.

4: *lissuḫ* [*la*]-*le*-[*šu/ša*] is tempting, but there is not enough room for that.

5: For *bāštum* + *nasāḫum*, see the love incantation CUSAS 32, 23b: 7 (№ 132) (cf. Wasserman 2016, 248).

9: We understand this line as continuation of ll. 6–7: the husband is mocking the lover on account of his ill odour, forcing one's nose to be closed (for *peḫûm* used for body openings, cf. CAD P, 316b). – *aḫ appi* "side(s) of the nose" is unknown (for the parts of the nose in Akkadian, see Böck 2000, 49, to which add *dūr appi* in Gilg. XI 137, 139 = Wasserman 2020, 110–111). One expects *naḫīrum* "nostrils".

11: Difficult. If understood correctly, *wakâm* is an old form of *akû* "weak, powerless", referring to the lover, or his masculine member. (Paleographically, note that KAM looks very similar to AḪ on l. 9).

№ 131: CUSAS 10, 11

SEAL No.: 7138
Copy: George 2009 Pl. XXXII
Tablet Siglum: MS 2920
Photo: George 2009 Pl. XXXI; CDLI P252006
Edition: George 2009, 69f.; Wasserman 2016, 236–238
Studies: Wasserman 2016, 236–238
Collection: Schøyen Collection, Oslo
Provenance: Unknown
Measurements: 9.5 × 5.4 cm
Procedure: No

Introduction

Addressing a woman, this incantation begins with a description of the sky at dawn. Discriptions of nature are not common in Akkadian literature, but here, as in other love-related compositions, light serves as a metaphor for love (Wasserman 2016, 47ff.).
The incantation ends with the legitimation formula where Ištar and Ea are mentioned (as in № 133). Affinities to YOS 11, 87 (№ 136) are found.

Obverse

1 *[pí-ta-ar-r]a*$^{!}$*-as-si pí-ta-ar-ra-as*$^{!}$*-‹si›*
2 *[ma-r]a-at A-ni-im ni-pí-iḫ ša-me-e*
3 *[u*$_{4}^{?}$*-ma*$^{?}$*]-am ú-ul-li-la-a-ma*
4 *[š]a-me-e ša Anim*(AN.NA)
5 *i-ba-aš-ši ra-mu-um e-li ni-ši i-*⸢*ḫa*⸣*-ap-pu-up*
6 *ra-mu-um li-iḫ-pu-pa-am i-na* ⸢*ṣe*⸣*-ri-*⸢*ia*⸣
7 *lu-ud-di lu-uq-bi lu-ta-wu-ú* ⸢*lu-ra-ʾì*(ḫi)⸣*-im*
8 *ḫu-us-sí-ni-i-ma ki-ma aš-nu-ga-*⸢*a*⸣*-li*
9 *li-iḫ-šu-*⸢*šu*⸣ *pa-nu-ki*$^{!}$(KU) *ki-ma ri-im-ti-i[m]*
10 *e tu-uš-bi a-na mi-li-ik a-bi-*⸢*ki*⸣
11 *e te-el-qé-e mi-li-ik um-mi-k[i]*
12 *šum-ma qá-aš-da-*⸢*at*⸣ *im-da-ša l*[*i*-x-x]
13 *šum-ma na-di-a-*⸢*at*⸣ *bi-bi-il-ša l*[*i*-x-x]
14 *šum-ma* ⸢*ke*⸣*-ez-re-et li-kà-ap-pí-ir / aš-ta-ma-ša e-li-ia li-im-qú-u[t]*
15 *ši-i[p-t]um ú-ul ia-tu*
16 *ši-*⸢*pa-at*⸣ *É-a ù* ^{d}*Ištar*(INANNA) *iš-ku-nu*

Reverse uninscribed

Translation

1 [Keep] her apart! Keep [her] apart!
2–4 [The] Daughters of Anum, the lights of heaven, [*in day-ti*]*me*$^{?}$ purified the sky of Anum.
5–6 Love came about, twittering over the people; May Love twitter over me!
7 Let me cast (a spell), let me speak, let me utter words of love:
8 – "Think of me as an *ašnugallum*-snake!
9 May your face rejoice as a wild cow!
10 Do not wait on your father's counsel,
11 Do not heed your mother's advice!"
12 If she is a hierodule may she [...] her support;
13 If she is a cloister-lady may she [...] her gift;
14 If she is a harlot may she *clean*$^{?}$ her tavern, may she throw herself at me!
15 The incantation is not mine;
16 (it is) the incantation (which) Ea and Ištar have created!

Commentary

See George (2009, 69) and Wasserman (2016, 237f.).

№ 132: CUSAS 32, 23b

SEAL No.: 7139
Copy: George 2016 Pl. LXIX
Tablet Siglum: MS 3062
Photo: George 2016 Pl. LXIX; CDLI P252071
Edition: George 2016, 148; Wasserman 2016, 247
Studies: Wasserman 2016, 247f.; George, *forthcoming*
Collection: Schøyen Collection, Oslo
Provenance: Unknown
Measurements: 12.0 × 4.5 cm
Procedure: No

Introduction

Between a Sumerian incantation to mend a broken bone and an Akkadian incantation mentioning fire, comes this tightly sewn incantation recited by a woman addressing her male lover. No subscript.

Obverse

7	*a-sú-uḫ ba-aš-ta-am*
8	*a-za-ru-ú ka-ra-na-am*
9	*a-na i-ša-tim*
10	*e-ze-tim me-e*
11	*aš-pu-[u]k*
12	*ki-ma pu-‹ḫa›-di-ka*
13	*ra-ma-an-⸢ni⸣*
14	*ki-ma ṣe-e-⸢nim⸣*
15	*na-as-ḫi-ra-am-ma*
16	*am-ra-an-ni*

Translation

7–8	I have torn the thorn, I will be sowing a vine!
9–11	I have poured water onto the fierce fire!
12–13	Love me as your lamb!
14–15	Encircle me as your small cattle!
16	Look (m.) at me!

Commentary

See Wasserman (2016, 248f.).

№ 133: OECT 11, 11

SEAL No.: 7140
Copy: Gurney 1989, 45
Tablet Siglum: Ashmolean 1932.156g
Photo: CDLI P274668
Edition: –
Studies: Wasserman 2003 Cat. No. 115; Cunningham 1997 Cat. No. 345
Collection: Ashmolean Museum, Oxford
Provenance: Kiš
Measurements: 5.7 × 4.8 cm
Procedure:

Introduction

A poorly preserved text from Kiš, an addition to the growing group of love-related texts from this site.[250] Thematic correspondences to other love incantations can be detected.

Obverse

1' ⸢x (x)⸣ […]
2' *i-na* ⸢x⸣ […]
3' *bi*$_4$*-ka-ni-m*[*a*$^?$ …]
4' *am-ri-ni-m*[*a* …]
5' *li-wi-ru* [*pānū*ʾ*a* …]
6' *ki-ma li-it-*[*tim* …]
7' *a-na pa-ni-ia* […]
8' *ki-ma* ^{giš}*bīnim*(ŠINIG) ⸢x⸣ […]
9' *ki-m*[*a*] ⸢x⸣ […]
10' *a-n*[*a*$^?$ …]
11' ⸢x⸣ […]
(*broken*)

Reverse

(*broken*)
1' *ki-m*[*a ṣeḫrim ernittiya*]
2' *lu-uk-š*[*u-ud* …]
3' *ši-ip-tum* [*ul yâti* …]
4' *ši-pa-at I*[*š*$_8^?$*-tár*$^?$ *ù É-a* …]
5' *a-na* wi […]
====
6' ⸢*li*$^?$⸣*-šar*$^?$*-ri* […]
7' [x x (x)] ⸢x⸣ […]

250 For the importance of Kiš in the development of love-related Akk. literature, see Wasserman 2016, 25f.

Translation

1'–2'	… in …
3'–4'	Wail over me (m.) … Look (f.) at me…
5'–6'	May [my face] shine […]. Like a cow […]
7'	Towards me […]
8'–9'	Like a tamarisk? […] Like a […]
10'–11'	To […]
	(*broken*)
r. 1'–2'	Like [a baby] may I achie[ve my desire!]
r. 3'–4'	The spell [is not mine]. It is the spell of I[štar? and Ea?].
r. 5'	To …
====	
r. 6'–7'	May …

Commentary

3': The exact meaning of *bikânni*, imp. of *bakûm* "to weep, to wail", is not clear, especially as this is a masculine form whereas the parallel *amrīnni* in the next line is feminine. Still, BE followed by KA is clear in the copy and is confirmed by photo. UGU is not impossible but it leads nowhere.

4'–5': *amrīnnima ... liwwirū* [*pānūʾa*?] – this phrase is found in ZA 75, 198–204b (№ 137): 24–25: *amrannima kīma pitnim ḫ̮ūdu kīma Seraš libbaka liwwir* "Look at me and rejoice like a harp! Like (through) Seraš may your heart be bright!", and the final word in CUSAS 32, 23b (№ 132): 16: *amranni* "Look at me!".

6': A simile with a cow is found in CUSAS 10, 11 (№ 131): 9, only there, *rīmtum* "wild cow" is found.

8': The tamarisk tree and its by-products figure in many magico-medical texts, but its function in this context is unclear. When referring to face, the simile "like a tamarisk" signifies paleness, anxiety as, e.g., *bīnu būnūka* "(my lord), your face is (as pale as) tamarisk", Atraḫ̮asīs I 93, see Lambert/Millard (1968, 48) with AHw, 1548. Cf. Ištar's Descent to the Netherworld 29, see Lapinkivi (2010, 10).

r.1'–2': In reading these lines, we have in mind the idiom *ernittam kašādum* "to reach victory, i.e., to reach (male) orgasm". The comparable material is found in Wasserman (2016, 38).

r.4': After *šipat*, a deity must follow. The most plausible candidate is Ištar (written *Iš*8-*tár*, without the DINGIR determinative), joined perhaps by Ea (cf. CUSAS 10, 11 (№ 131): 16).

r. 6' Not a subscript, but rather the beginning of a new section, or the opening of another spell.

№ 134: VS 17, 23

SEAL No.: 7141
Copy: van Dijk 1971 Pl. X
Tablet Siglum: VAT 8354
Photo: cf. SEAL No. 7141
Edition: van Dijk 1971, 11; Wasserman 2015, 602; Wasserman 2016, 249f.
Studies: Farber 1981, 56, No. 25; Cunningham 1997 Cat. No. 366; Wasserman 2003 Cat. No. 208; Wasserman 2015
Collection: Vorderasiatisches Museum, Berlin
Provenance: Larsa area
Measurements: 5.0 × 7.0 cm
Procedure: No

Introduction

An incantation to calm the "fire of the heart" of a desired woman, a metaphor for jealousy or amorous alienation.[251] Ingredients for the preparation of eye make-up are listed (Wasserman 2015).

Obverse
1 *pa-ar-ki-i[š n]a-ak-ra-at*
2 *ṣú-úḫ-ḫu-ri-iš gi-ri-im-mi-iš*
3 *ki-ma i-ni-ib ki-ri-im e-li-šu wa-a-ṣi-a-ti*[!](BI)
4 *li-ib-la-ki-im ú-pe-el-li-a-am*
5 *I-di-ig-la-at*
6 *sà-an-gi-i we-ri-a-am a-ba-ri Šu-ši-im*
7 *li-ib-lam sà-an-gi mu-sà-ḫi-la-at i-né-ki*
----
8 ka-inim-ma izi-šà-ga

Reverse uninscribed

Translation

1–2 Barrier-like she is alienated, (entangled) as a tiny berry-fruit.
3 Like an orchard fruit come out over him!
4–6 Let the Tigris carry for you (f.) charcoal, *sangû*, copper, lead of Susa!
7 Let it carry hither *sangû*! Oh you, who pierces your (f.) eyes!
----
8 Incantation (to calm) the fire of the heart.

Commentary

See Wasserman (2015).

251 CDLI P274691: "incantation against fire of the stomach".

№ 135: YOS 11, 21c

SEAL No.: 7142
Copy: van Dijk/Goetze/Hussey 1985 Pls. XXV/XXVI
Tablet Siglum: YBC 4598
Photo: cf. SEAL No. 7142
Edition: Wilcke 1985, 208f. (no translation); Wasserman 2016, 251
Studies: Farber 1985, 65; Cunningham 1997 Cat. No. 399; Wasserman 2003 Cat. No. 253; Wasserman 2016, 251
Collection: Yale Babylonian Collection, New Haven
Provenance: Larsa area
Measurements: 10.4 × 6.7 cm
Procedure: No

Introduction

A woman is speaking, trying to convince a resistant lover to come back to her. This text is preceded by two incantations – one fragmentary, the other to win a court-case – and followed by two more incantations – one in an unidentified language "to *dr*[*ive away*] a mongoose" (*ša šikkê ana ṭ*[*ú-ru-dim*], ll. 31–32) and another "to appease the heart" (*ša* ŠÀ SI.SÁ, l. 33).

Reverse

====

26 *e-ez-ze-ti ša-am-ra-ti ta-al-li-*[*ik*? …] / *nu-úḫ ṣú-ur-ri ki-in iš-di-i-ka ši*? [x]

27 *lu-ta-ad-di a-na libbika*(ŠÀ-*ka*) *šu-ri-pa-am ta-ak-ṣ*[*i-a-tim*]

28 *i-na a-ma-ri-ia ki-ma Sé-ra-aš na-ap-še-ra ki-m*[*a* (x)] / le ⸢az?⸣ *ru-u*[*m*?*-ma*?]

29 *aš-šum wa-aš-ba-ti-ma kam-sà-a-ku az-za-a-zu i-na mu-ú*[*ḫ-ḫi-ka*]

30 *lu-ud-di-kum ši-ip-tam ši-pa-at ṣūd pāni*(IGI.NIGÍN.NA) *lu-ul-qé-a-am-*[*ma*?] / *ša maḫ-ri-*[*ka*]

====

Translation

26 You (m.[sic]) are fierce, you (m.[sic]) are furious, you *we*[*nt*? …]– be at peace my heart! Make firm (m.) your (m.) two foundations ...

27 Let me throw on your (m.) heart ice (and) frost!

28 When you see me – be soothed (m.) like (one who drinks) beer, *like a ... fon*[*dle* (*me*)?]!

29–30 Because you (m.[sic]) are sitting while I am kneeling, (because) I am standing at [your s]ervice, let me cast a spell on you (m.), the spell of vertigo, let me take that which is in front of [you].

Commentary

26/29: For these stative forms, see Wasserman (2016, 251).

27: Pouring cold water into the heart clarifies the meaning of the colophon ka-inim-ma IZI.ŠÀ.GA in VS 17, 23: 8 (№ 134). The fire of heart represents negative emotions (fury or jealousy), and this blaze is put out with cold water (see Wasserman 2016, 251).

30: Our translation differs from Wasserman (2016, 251).

№ 136: YOS 11, 87

SEAL No.: 7143
Copy: van Dijk/Goetze/Hussey 1985 Pl. LXXVII
Tablet Siglum: MLC 1299
Photo: cf. SEAL No. 7143
Edition: van Dijk/Goetze/Hussey 1985, 50 (no translation); Wasserman 2016, 252f.
Studies: Westenholz/Goodnick Westenholz 1977, 206f.; Cavigneaux 1996, 36; Cunningham 1997 Cat. No. 405; Wasserman/Or 1998 esp. 92; Cavigneaux 1998; Wasserman 2003 Cat. No. 263; Foster 2005, 199f.; George 2009, 68; Polinger Foster 2020, 68f.
Collection: Yale Babylonian Collection, New Haven
Provenance: Larsa area
Measurements: 9.5 × 5.5 cm
Procedure: No

Introduction
A despairing lover tries to catch the attention of his beloved – a girl who is busy with her domestic tasks. The text ends with self-glorification of the male's lovemaking. As there is no subscript, the arguments in favour of tagging this pastoral text as an incantation are the opening historiola about the divine origin of the love-charm *irimmum*, and the modal verbal forms ("may her sweetheart perish", "May the dough fall") which epitomise the manipulative aspect of the text.

Obverse
1 *e-re-mu e-re-mu*
2 *qá-ar-na-šu ḫu-ra-ṣum*
3 *zi-ba-sú*$^{!}$(SÍ) *uq-nu-um e-lu-um*
4 *ša-ki-in i-na li-bi-im ša Eš*$_{4}$*-tár*
5 *a-s*[*i*]*-ši-im-*⸢*ma*⸣ *ú-ul i-tu-ra-am*
6 *a-mur-*‹‹ma$^{?!}$››*-ši-i-ma ú-ul i-pa-al-sà-a*[*m*]
7 *š*[*um*]*-ma qá-áš-da-at li-im-qú-u*[*t*]
8 [*d*]*a-du-ša-a*
9 [*š*]*um-ma na-di-a-at mu-pí-ir-ša*
10 *li-im-qú-ut*
11 *ba-tu-ul-tum ma-ra-tu a-wi-li-im*
12 *a-na ri-ig-mi-ia*
13 *a-na* ‹‹ri ig›› *ša-gi-mi-ia*
14 ‹*li*$^{?}$›-[*i*]*m-qú-ut li-šu-um*

Reverse
15 [*ša*$^{?}$] *qá-ti-ša-a*
16 *li-im-qú-ut* [*ṣ*]*ú*$^{!}$*-ḫa-ru-um*
17 *ša a-ḫi-i-ša*
18 ⸢*e*⸣ [*ta-ar*]*-ku-si-im bi-it-ki*

19 *a-na [ri$^{?}$]-ik-si-im [ša$^{?}$] qá-ti-ki*
20 ⸢la$^{?}$/e$^{?}$⸣ *t[a-ap]-pa-[la/al]-sí-i*
21 *ki-ma šu-u[m-m]a-ni-im i-ta$^{?}$-ap$^{?}$-la-si-ni*
22 *ki-ma bu-ri-im lu-i-ki-ni*
23 *a-mi-ni ra-mi ki-ma pa-ar-[ši]-gi-im*
24 *ta-ar-ku-si re-eš-ki*
25 *ki-ma [n]é-ba-[ḫi]-im*
26 *te-z[i$^{?}$-ḫ]i-ma$^{?}$ q[á-ab-l]a-ki*
27 ⸢*ṣí*⸣*-[ḫa-ti]-ia k[i-m]a ša-am-ni-im*
28 *[n]a-ši [i$^{?}$-n]i-ki*
29 *[al-k]i-ma [a-n]a ṣe-ri-ia*
30 [x x x] iš$^{!?}$ im$^{?}$ m[a$^{?}$ *š]u-mi-i[m]*

Translation

1 Love-charm! Love-charm!
2–3 His two horns are gold, his$^{!}$ tail is pure lapis-lazuli:
4 Placed in the heart of Ištar.
5 I raised my voice to her, but she did not turn to me,
6 I gazed (at her) but she did not look at me.
7–8 If she is a hierodule, may her sweetheart perish.
9–10 If she is a cloister-lady, may her provider perish.
11–14 May the nubile girl, a daughter of a gentleman, fall at my cry, at my shout!
14–16 May the dough fall (out) of her hands,
16–17 (as well as) the little one on her arms.
18 Do not attach your house to me!
19–20 Do not look after the task under your hands!
21 Look at me like (a cow held with) a halter!
22 Lick me like (a cow licking) a calf!
23–24 Why, my love, did you cover your head like (with) a *paršīgum*-cover?
25–26 (Why) like (with) a belt did you girdle your loins?
27 My l[ove-making] is (as good) as oil,
28–29 with the raising of your eye(s) come forward, to me!
30 […] name$^{?}$.

Commentary

See Wasserman (2016, 253–256).

№ 137: ZA 75, 198–204b

SEAL No.: 7144
Copy: –
Tablet Siglum: IB 1554
Photo: Wilcke 1985, after p. 208
Edition: Wilcke 1985, 198f.; Wasserman 2016, 257–259
Studies: Scurlock 1989–1990; Cunningham 1997 Cat. No. 315; Wasserman/Or 1998, 93; Wasserman 2003 Cat. No. 3; Foster 2005, 201f.; Groneberg 2007, 92/101f.; Hecker 2008, 66–71, Nr. II
Collection: Iraq Museum, Baghdad
Provenance: Isin
Measurements: 25.5 × 8.0 cm
Procedure: Yes

Introduction
This incantation, infused with mythological references (l. 14) and manipulative language (ll. 24, 30–36), is uttered by a woman trying to attract a male lover (perhaps Erra-bāni, mentioned in l. 30).

Obverse
9 *e-el-li-a-at ka-al-bi-im ṣú-mi-im*$^{?}$ *em-ṣú-tim*
10 *me-ḫi-iṣ pa-ni-im ši-pi-ir tu-ú*[*r*$^{?}$]*-ti i-ni-im*
11 *am-ta-ḫa-aṣ mu-úḫ-ḫa-ka uš-ta-an-ni ṭe-e-em-ka*
12 *šu-uk-nam ṭe-e-em-ka a-na ṭe-e-mi-ia*
13 *šu-uk-nam mi-li-ik-ka a-na mi-il-ki-ia*
14 *a-ka-al-la-ka ki-ma* ^{d}*Ištar ik-lu-ú* ^{d}*Dumu-zi*
15 *Sé-e-ra-aš ú-ka-as-sú-ú ša-a-ti-ša*
16 *uk-ta-as-sí-i-ka i-na pī*(KA)*-ia ša ša-ra-a-tim*
17 *i-na ú-ri-ia ša ši-i-na-tim*
18 *i-na pī*(KA)*-ia ša ru-ḫa-tim*
19 *i-na ú-ri-ia ša ši-i-na-tim*
20 *a i-li-ik na-ak-ra-tum i-na ṣe-ri-i-ka*
21 *ra-bi-iṣ ka-al-bu-um ra-bi-iṣ ša-ḫi-ú-um*
22 *at-ta ri-ta-bi-iṣ i-na ḫal-li-ia*
----
23 *ša i-na mu-ḫi nu-ni-im wa-ar-qí-im a-na ša-am-ni-im i-na-an-di ip-pa-aš-ša-aš*
----
24 *am-ra-an-ni-ma ki-ma pi-it-ni-im ḫu-ú-du*
25 *ki-ma* ⸢*Sé-e*⸣*-ra-aš li-ib-ba-ka li-wi-ir*
26 *ki-ma* ^{d}*Šamšim*(UTU^{-im}) *i-ta-an-pu-ḫa-am*
27 *k*[*i-m*]*a* ^{d}*Sîn*(EN.ZU) *i-di-ša-am*
28 [x x i]g *ù ra-a*[*m-k*]*a li-i-di-iš*
----

29 [*š*]*a-am-ni-im pa-ša-*⸢*a-ši*⸣*-im*

----

30 *lu a-li-ka pu-ri-*⸢*da-ka*⸣ ^{I}*Èr-ra-ba-ni*
31 *qá-ab-la-ka li-im-mu-š*[*a*]
32 *lu re-du-ú še-er-ḫa-nu-ka*
33 *li-iḫ-du-ú li-ib-bu-ú-ki*
34 *li-iḫ-šu-ša ka-ab-ta-ta-ki*
35 *lu-ú-bi ki-ma ka-al-bi-im*
36 *ki-ma šu-mu-un-ni-im ḫu-bu-ú-ša-ki e ta-at-bu-ki-im*

----

37 ka-inim-ma ki-ág-gá-kam

Translation

9 (*With*$^{?}$) saliva of a dog, of *thirst*$^{?}$, of *hunger*$^{?}$,
10 (*with*$^{?}$) a blow on the face, (*with*) "turning of eyes",
11 I have hit your (m.) head, I have changed your (m.) mood.
12 Place your (m.) mind with my mind!
13 Place your (m.) decision with my decision!
14 I hold you (m.) back just like Ištar held back Dumuzi,
15–18 (Just like) Seraš binds her drinkers, (so) I have bound you (m.) with my hairy mouth, with my drooling mouth.
20 May the enemy-woman not come to you!
21 The dog is lying, the boar is lying –
22 you lie forever in between my thighs.

----

23 What is on the green fish will be thrown into the oil; it will be smeared.

----

24 Look at me and rejoice like a harp!
25 Like (through) Seraš may your heart be bright!
26 Shine on me regularly like Šamaš!
27 Renew (yourself) on me like Sîn!
28 … and may your love be new!

----

29 […] rubbing (with) oil.

----

30 May your (m.) two legs walk, Erra-bāni!
31 May your (m.) loins move!
32 May your ligaments follow!
33 May your (f.) heart rejoice!
34 May your (f.) mood be happy!
35 May I swell like a dog!
36 Your (f.) two curves are like a halter – do not throw (them away) from me!

----

37 Incantation of the lover.

Commentary
See Wasserman (2016, 259f.).

№ 138: ZA 75, 198–204c

SEAL No.: 7145
Copy: –
Tablet Siglum: IB 1554
Photo: Wilcke 1985, after p. 208
Edition: Wilcke 1985, 200f.; Wasserman 2016, 261
Studies: Scurlock 1989–1990; Cunningham 1997 Cat. No. 316; Wasserman 2003 Cat. No. 24; Foster 2005, 202; Groneberg 2007; Hecker 2008, 66–71, Nr. III
Collection: Iraq Museum, Baghdad
Provenance: Isin
Measurements: 25.5 × 8.0 cm
Procedure: No

Introduction
A curse-like incantation addressed against a rival woman. The speaker is the female lover rejected by the man.

Obverse
38 *di-il-pi mu-ši-i-ta-am*
39 *ur-ri e ta-aṣ-la-li*
40 *mu-ši e tu-uš-bi*
----
41 ka-inim-ma *ša* ki-ág-kam

Translation
38 Be (f.) awake at night-time!
39 At day-time may you (f.) not sleep!
40 At night-time may you (f.) not sit down!
----
41 Incantation of the lover.

Commentary
39: The wish "may you not find sleep" is found also in the love dialogue ZA 49, 168–169: ii 8–9: *kīma yâti lā ṣalālum* [*lū emissi*] *kali mūšim likūr* [*lidlip*] "May she, like me, [be afflicted] with sleeplessness! May she be dazed and [restless] all night long!" (Wasserman 2016, 176/179).

№ 139: ZA 75, 198–204d

SEAL No.: 7146
Copy: –
Tablet Siglum: IB 1554
Photo: Wilcke 1985, after p. 208
Edition: Wilcke 1985, 200f.; Wasserman 2016, 262f.
Studies: Scurlock 1989–1990; Cunningham 1997 Cat. No. 317; Wasserman 2003 Cat. No. 25; Foster 2005, 202f. (e); Groneberg 2007, 104f.; Hecker 2008, 66–71, Nr. IV
Collection: Iraq Museum, Baghdad
Provenance: Isin
Measurements: 25.5 × 8.0 cm
Procedure: No

Introduction
A desiring female lover trying to stop her rival, perhaps the lawful wife, from approaching her paramour.

Obverse

42	*na-ra-mu-um na-ra-mu-um*
43	*ša iš-ku-nu-ka É-a ù* ^{d}*En-líl*
44	*ki-ma* ^{d}*Ištar i-na pa-ra-ak-ki-im wa-aš-ba-at*
45	*ki-ma* ^{d}*Na-na-a i-na šu-tu-mi-im wa-aš-ba-at*
46	*a-la-mi-ka e-né-e-tum ma-aq-li-a-am e-ra-am-ma*
47	*aš-ša-a-tum mu-te-ši-na i-ze-er-ra*
48	*bu-ut-qá-am ap-pa-ša ša-qá-a-am*
49	*šu-uk-na-am ap-pa-ša ša-pa-al še-pí-ia*
50	*ki-ma ra-am-ša iš-qù-ú e-li-ia*
51	*ra-mi li-iš-qá-a-am e-li ra-mi-ša*

52	ka-inim-ma ki-ág-gá-kam

Translation

42–43	Loved-one! Loved-one! – whom Ea and Enlil have created.
44–45	You (m.) sit like Ištar in (her) dais; You (m.) sit like Nanāya in (her) treasury.
46	I will encircle you!
46–47	The *ēntu*-priestesses love the burning; the wives hate their husbands.
48–49	Cut down her haughty nose! Place her nose under my foot!
50–51	Just as her love is higher than me, may my love get higher than her love!

52	Incantation of the lover.

Commentary
See Wasserman (2016, 263).

№ 140: ZA 75, 198–204e

SEAL No.: 7147
Copy: –
Tablet Siglum: IB 1554
Photo: Wilcke 1985, after p. 208
Edition: Wilcke 1985, 200f.; Wasserman 2016, 265
Studies: Scurlock 1989–1990; Cunningham 1997 Cat. No. 318; Wasserman 2003 Cat. No. 26; Foster 2005, 203; Groneberg 2007; Hecker 2008, 66–71, Nr. V
Collection: Iraq Museum, Baghdad
Provenance: Isin
Measurements: 25.5 × 8.0 cm
Procedure: No

Introduction
A woman is talking to her beloved, encouraging him to make love to her. The "loosening" in the subscript could refer to sexual relief.

Obverse
53 *am-mi-ni da-an-na-ti ki-ma mu-ur-di-nu qí-iš-tim*
54 *am-mi-ni ki-ma ṣe-eḫ-ri-im la-ʾì-im er-ni-it-ta-ka le-em-né-et*
55 *a[m]-mi-ni za-a-wa-nu pa-nu-ú-ki*
56 *[am-m]i-ni ḫa-al-qá-ku la a-ba-aš-ši*

Lower Edge
57 *⸢i⸣-na li-ib-bi-ka ni-il ka-al-bu-um*
58 *ni-il ša-ḫi-ú-um*
59 *at-ta i-ti-lam-ma lu-na-as-sí-ḫa-am za-ap-pi-ka*
60 *ša qá-ti-ka le-qè-a-am-ma a-na qá-ti-ia šu-ku-un*
----
61 ka-inim-ma *pi-ṭi-ir-tum*

Translation
53 Why are you (m.) harsh like a bramble (bush) of the forest?
54 Why is your (m.) triumph-cry as bad as (that) of a little child?
55 Why is your (f.) face inimical?
56 Why am I lost? Do I not exist (for you)?!
57–58 In your (m.) heart lies a dog, lies a boar –
59 You (m.), lay with me so that I may pluck your bristles!
60 What is in your (m.) hand take for me and place in my hand!
----
61 Incantation for *Loosening*[?].

Commentary
See Wasserman (2016, 265).

№ 141: ZA 75, 198–204f

SEAL No.: 7148
Copy: –
Tablet Siglum: IB 1554
Photo: Wilcke 1985, after p. 208
Edition: Wilcke 1985, 202f.; Wasserman 2016, 266f.
Studies: Scurlock 1989–1990; Cunningham 1997 Cat. No. 319; Wasserman 2003 Cat. No. 27; Foster 2005, 203f.; Groneberg 2007; Hecker 2008, 66–71, Nr. VI
Collection: Iraq Museum, Baghdad
Provenance: Isin
Measurements: 25.5 × 8.0 cm
Procedure: No

Introduction
A woman trying to persuade an indifferent male lover to look at her. Love-making is metaphorically compared to bread and beer – the basic Mesopotamian nutriment pair (ll. 68–69).

Reverse
62 *a-i-iš li-ib-b[a-k]a* [(x x)] *i-il-la-ak*
63 *a-i-iš i-na-[aṭ-ṭa-la] i-na-*⸢*a*$^{?}$*-ka*$^{?}$⸣
64 *ia-ši-im l[i-]* ⸢x x⸣ [...] ⸢x⸣
65 *ia-ti l[i-ip-lu-u]s* ⸢x x⸣ [...] ⸢x⸣
66 *[am-r]a*$^{?}$*-an-ni k[i-m]a*$^{?}$ ⸢x x⸣ [...]
67 ⸢*i*⸣*-ta-ap-la-sà-an-ni* ⸢x⸣ [x x] ⸢x⸣ ka ši [x x x]
68 *ki-ma a-ka-li-im [(te*$^{?}$*)-le*$^{?}$*]-mi-*⸢*a*$^{?}$⸣*-an-ni*
69 *ki-ma ši-ka-[ri-im (te*$^{?}$*)-le*$^{?}$*/la*$^{?}$*]-am-ma-an-ni*
70 *ti-da-ab-ba-a[b*$^{?}$ x x x] ⸢x x x x⸣*-bi-im*
71 *i-na pī*(KA) x x x x *[u]m*$^{?}$*-ma-at* ⸢zi x x⸣ ma ni [(x)]
----
72 ka-ini[m-ma ki-ág-g]á-[kam]

Translation
62–63 Where goes your (m.) heart? Where to l[oo]k your (m.) eyes?
64–65 To me [may your (m.$^{?}$) heart go!] At me [may your eyes look!]
66 Look at me as ...
67 See me ...
68 [(You will) cons]ume me like bread,
69 [You will cons]ume me like beer.
70 Speak with me continually ...
71 In the mouth ...
----
72 Incanta[tion of the lov]er.

Commentary

See Wasserman (2016, 267).

№ 142: ZA 75, 198–204i

SEAL No.: 7150
Copy: –
Tablet Siglum: IB 1554
Photo: Wilcke 1985, after p. 208
Edition: Wilcke 1985, 204f.; Wasserman 2016, 271f.
Studies: Scurlock 1989–1990; Cunningham 1997 Cat. No. 321; Wasserman 2003 Cat. No. 29; Foster 2005, 205; Groneberg 2007; Hecker 2008, 66–71, Nr. VIII
Collection: Iraq Museum, Baghdad
Provenance: Isin
Measurements: 25.5 × 8.0 cm
Procedure: No (but cf. the subscript where a *maštakal*-plant is mentioned)

Introduction

The tone of this incantation, addressed to a man called Iddin-Damu, is scornful, but its end denotes that the incantation is meant to make him docile and ready for love-making (ll. 106–107).

Reverse
100 *ra-ap-ša-am pī*(KA)-⸢*i-im*⸣ *la-wi-a-am uz-ni-in* ^{I}*I*-⸢*din*-^{d}*Da*⸣-*mu*
101 *pi-te pī*(KA)-*i-ka ki-ma* KIN^{ku6}-*im*
102 *li-i*[*b-b*]*a-ka za-as-sà-ru-um*
103 *aš-lu-pa-am* [(x)] *i-qì-ib-ka*
104 *él-qè* [x x b]i *li-ib-bi-*[*i*]*m*
105 *e-si-ir p*[*u*$^{?}$*-ri*]-⸢*di*⸣-*i-ka*
106 *ku-uz-zi-ba-an-ni k*[*i-ma mi*$^{?}$]*-ra-ni-im*
107 *ki-ma ka-al-bi-im* ⸢*a-ta*⸣-*la*$^{?}$*-ak*$^{?}$ ⸢*e*$^{?}$*-li*$^{?}$⸣-*ia*
----
108 ka-inim-ma ^{ú}i[n-nu-uš-kam]

Translation

100 Big-mouth, curled-ears, Iddin-Damu!
101 Open your mouth like a KIN-fish,
102 Your heart is a *zassarum*-plant,
103 I pulled out$^{?}$ your heel,
104 I took the … of your heart,
105 I locked your thighs,
106 Fawn over me like a puppy,
107 keep coming$^{?}$ on me like a dog.
----
108 Incantation [of the] *ma*[*štakal*-plant].

Commentary

See Wasserman (2016, 272).

№ 143: ZA 75, 198–204j

SEAL No.: 7151
Copy: –
Tablet Siglum: IB 1554
Photo: Wilcke 1985, after p. 208
Edition: Wilcke 1985, 204f.; Wasserman 2016, 273f.
Studies: Scurlock 1989–1990; Cooper 1996; Cunningham 1997 Cat. No. 322; Wasserman/Or 1998, 93; Wasserman 2003 Cat. No. 30; Foster 2005, 205f.; Groneberg 2007, 103/105; Hecker 2008, 66–71, Nr. IX
Collection: Iraq Museum, Baghdad
Provenance: Isin
Measurements: 25.5 × 8.0 cm
Procedure: No (but cf. the colophon where a sherd of the crossroad is mentioned)

Introduction

Starting with a woman expressing her wish to sexually control her male lover (ll. 109–111), the text continues with a man encouraging himself to ejaculate (ll. 112–116). It ends with a woman telling a man called Erra-bāni that she is ready for love-making.

109 *am-ta-ḫa-aṣ mu-úḫ-ḫa-ka ki-ma* ⸢x⸣ [(x)] ki [x x] / *ta-ap-ta-na-aš-ši-lam qá-aq-qá-*[*ra-am*]
110 *at-ta ki-ma ša-ḫi-i-im qá-aq-qá-ra-am* [x x x]
111 *a-di ki-ma ṣé-eḫ-ri-im e-le-eq-qú-ú er-ni-*[*it-ti*]
----
112 *ù šu*$^{?}$*-mu-um i-na-ši pa-la ra-ma-ni-šu*
113 *ù al-pu-um i-na-ši pa-la ra-ma-ni-šu*
114 ⸢*ki*⸣*-ma na-ru-um ir-ḫu-ú ki-ib-ri-i-ša*
115 [*a*]*-ra-aḫ-ḫi ra-ma-ni-ma*
116 *a-ra-aḫ-ḫi pa-ag-ri*

Upper Edge
117 *up-te-et-ti-ku-um se-bé-et ba-bi-ia* ^{I}*Èr-ra-ba-ni*
118 [*qá*$^{?}$*-aq*$^{?}$*-q*]*á*$^{?}$*-ad*$^{?}$*-sú* ka ri ka ta am *uš-ta-ad*$^{?}$*-di*$^{?}$*-ir*
119 [x (x) g]a am *ap-ta-ša-ar ša-a-ti*
120 [*a-t*]*a-ku-ul li-ib-bi-ka šu-ta-aq-ti-a-am i-na ṣe-ri-ia*

Left Edge
mu-šid 2.0;0 (= 120)
an mul ki mul-mul
an mul an mul-mul
----
ka-inim-ma šika e-sír-ka limmú

Translation

109 I have hit your (m.) head; you keep crawling on the ground towards me like ….

110–111 You, like a boar, [*lay*$^{?}$] on the ground, until I gain my victory like a child!

112–113 Indeed, even the garlic plant carries its own staff! Indeed, even the bull carries its own staff!

114–116 Just like the river had flowed over its bank, so I will engender myself! (So) I will engender my body!

117 I have opened for you (m.) – Oh Erra-bāni – my seven gates!

118 His *h*[*ead*$^{?}$]...

119 … I have released him$^{?}$.

120 Let the constant consummation of your (m.) desire (lit. heart) come to completion in me!

The line number – 120.
Sky, star, earth, stars!
Sky, star, sky, stars!

Incantation of the sherd of the crossroad.

Commentary

See Wasserman (2016, 274).

2.3.5 Trial

The spells in this section aim to control personal rivalry in favour of the speaker. The setting of the texts is presumably a legal process. A group of similar texts is the Egalkurra, known mostly from the first millennium, but also from an OB tablet to be published by Finkel (*forthcoming*) (№ 179–181, see also Zomer 2018a, 230f.).

№ 144: RA 36, 3a

SEAL No.: 7186
Copy: Thureau-Dangin 1939, 12
Tablet Siglum: –
Photo: –
Edition: Thureau-Dangin 1939, 10f.; Krebernik 2018, 10–13
Studies: Cunningham 1997 Cat. No. 340; Wasserman 2003 Cat. No. 136; Foster 2005, 175; Guichard 2018, 24; Zomer 2018a, 126 fn. 443; Mertens-Wagschal 2018, 165f.
Collection: Deir ez-Zor Museum, Deir-ez-Zor$^{?}$
Provenance: Mari
Measurements: 7.0 × 5.5 cm
Procedure: No

Introduction

The incantation serves to overcome the protagonist's rival. Mertens-Wagschal (2018, 166) presented parallels between this text and the Late Babylonian tablet AMD 8/1, 8.12 (VAT 35), suggesting that RA 36, 3a could have been accompanied by a procedure in which a manipulation of a figurine representing the opponent took place. The reverse contains a different incantation in Hurrian.

Obverse

1 *aṣ*$^{!}$(AT)*-ba-at-ka ki-ma a-*[…]
2 *uk-ta-as-sí-ka ki-ma i*[*m-ba-ri-im*]
3 *ad-di-ka šu-bu-ur-*[*ka*$^{?}$]
4 *el-qé ma-at-na-am uš-ta-pu ša-ap-ti-*[*ka*]
5 *ki ba-ar-ba-ri-im uš-ta-aḫ-ḫi-iṭ-ka*
6 *ki né-ši-im ru-pu-uš-ti e-li-ka ad-di*
7 *lu-uq-bi-ma qí-bi-ti el qí-bi-ti-k*[*a*] *lu e-*[*la*$^{?}$*-at*$^{?}$]
8 *lu-ut-wi-ma ti-wi-ti el ti-wi-ti-ka lu ḫa-ab-r*[*a-at*]
9 *ki-ma bu-lu e-li ša-am-ka-ni ḫa-ab-ra-at*
10 *ki-im qí-bi-ti el qí-bi-ti-ka lu ab-ra-at*
11 *ki-ma ša-mu-um el qa-aq-qa-ri-im ḫa-ab-ra-at*
12 *ki-im qí-bi-ti el qí-bi-ti-ka lu ḫa-ab-ra-at*
13 *ta-as-ni-ib ap-pa-ka aq-qí-na-ti-ka*
14 *a-ki la am-ta-ḫa-aṣ le-et-k*[*a*]

Translation

1 I have seized you as a […].
2 I have enveloped you like a f[og].
3 I have thrown you down (on) your buttocks!
4 I have taken a bowstring; I have *fastened* your lips.
5 I have attacked you like a wolf,
6 I have thrown my excrement over you like a lion.
7 When I speak, may my command be more e[*levated*$^{?}$] than your command!
8 When I utter a word, let *my utterance* be louder than *your utterance*!
9 Just as the masters are superior to the servants,
10 may my words be superior, in the same way, to your words!
11 Just as the rain is superior to (lit. heavy on) the land,
12 may my words be superior, in the same way, to your words.
13 You have tied your nose into buttocks,
14 so that I cannot strike your cheek!

Commentary

1: *aṣ*$^{!}$(AT)-*ba-at-ka* is probably a scribal mistake (repetition of the AT sign), but the same form in OECT 15, 260: 22 (№ 109) (*aṣ*$^{!}$(AT)-[*ba-a*]*t ṣerri mê*) which may indicate that this spelling is not accidental but reveals a phonetic variant of *aṣbat.*

2: Restitution after CAD K, 253c.

4: The speaker uses *matnum* "a sinew or a bowstring" (CAD M/1, 412, 2 and CAD Š/1, 484, 2' without translation) to fasten his opponent's lips and to stop his words. Hence, logically, *uš-ta-pu* is an OB attestation of *šapûm* B "to wrap, to fasten with laces" (CAD Š/1, 490). But the vocalization of this verb is (i) and all its attestations are late. This leads one to derive *uš-ta-pu* from *šapûm* C "to be silent, to remain silent", which in the D-stem means "to silence, to subdue" (CAD Š/1, 490f.). A contamination between *šapûm* B (i) and *šapûm* C (u) probably took place here.

5: For *uš-ta-aḫ-ḫi-iṭ-ka*, see CAD Š/1, 92a and AHw, 1131 (D only here).

7–8: For this couplet, see CAD T, 302 s.v. ***tawû*, and CAD T, 440 s.v. *tīwītu*. (See also AHw, 1363), but note the criticism by Mayer (2009, 432).

2/5/6/11: For the similes in these lines, see Wasserman (2003, 113). For the comparatives in this text, see Wasserman (2003, 151).

9: *bu-lu*, not to be emended to *be-lu* (against CAD Š/1, 314, s.v. *šamkānu*), see Wasserman (2003, 90 fn. 128).

9–10: For this couplet, see Wasserman (2003, 119 with previous literature).

11: *ša-mu-um* is rain, not sky, see Wasserman (2003, 77).

11–12: Another example of this line of argument ("the words of X are superior/stronger/overcome the words of Y"), cf. the NA proverb discussed in Livingstone (1988, 185f.).

13–14: Some parallels to such vulgar expressions (cf. also l. 3) can be furnished, e.g., the Sumerian Diatribe against Engar-dug (ETCSL 5.4.1.1: 12f.): "Engar-dug, blocked at the anus, … speech, … *vomit*$^{?}$! A man without …, a tail stuck in its mouth".

14: Mertens-Wagschal (2018, 165f.) understands this line as a rhetorical question, i.e., "Did I not strike your cheek?"

№ 145: YOS 11, 21b

SEAL No.: 7187
Copy: van Dijk/Goetze/Hussey 1985 Pls. XXV/XXVI
Tablet Siglum: YBC 4598
Photo: cf. SEAL No. 7187
Edition: Wilcke 1985, 209 (no translation)
Studies: van Dijk/Goetze/Hussey 1985, 27; Cunningham 1997 Cat. No. 398; Wasserman 2003 Cat. No. 252
Collection: Yale Babylonian Collection, New Haven
Provenance: Larsa area
Measurements: 10.4 × 6.7 cm
Procedure: No

Introduction
Although this incantation displays strong similarities to love incantations, specifically those from Isin (ZA 75, 198–204), the legal terminology (ll. 17/19/20) suggests that the text deals with winning a legal case.

Obverse
13 *wa-aš-[t]a-a-ti ki-ma [ṣeḫrim*$^{?}$]
14 *le-em-ne-et er-ni-i[t-ta-ka …*]
15 *a-na mi-i-nim ḫu-um-mu-*[…]
----
16 *ra-bi-iṣ kalbum*(UR.GI$_7$) *ra-bi-i[ṣ šaḫûm*$^{?}$]
17 *i-na dīnim*(DI.KU$_5$) *ù awātim*(INIM-*t*[*im*]$^{?}$) […]
----
18 *aṣ-ba-at qí-im-ma-a[t-ka*$^{?}$ …]
19 *ap-ta-ṭa-ar ri-i[k]-sà-a[m*] ⸢x⸣ […]
----
20 *i-na di-nim ù a-wa-tim e[l]-q[é*$^{!}$ *er-ni-it-ti*$^{?}$]
----
21 ^{d}*Sîn*(EN.ZU) *ip-ti-il* ^{d}*Ni[n- …*]
22 [x x (x)] la a ka ši […]

Reverse
23 *qāt*(ŠU$^{?}$) ^{d}*Šamaš*(UTU) *ku-tu-um-mi* ^{d}*Ištar*(INAN[NA])-*ma*$^{?}$ ^{d}*Ni[n-gi]r-gi*$_4$-[*lum*] / *ù* ^{d}*Nin*-MAŠ *wa-e-ru la te-ṭe-eḫ-ḫe-e e-li-*[…]
----
24 *ṣe-e-nu pa-aš-šu-ru-*[*um*]
25 *pe-e-ti ba-ab-šu ma-am-ma-an ú-ul ú-ša-a-ar-*[*šum*$^{?}$]
====

Translation

13 You (f.?) are harsh like [*a baby*?],
14 [Your vic]tory (cry) is bad:
15 Why is …

----

16 A dog is lying, a boar is lying:
17 in the trial and the legal case...

----

18 I have caught [your l]ock of hair,
19 I have released the contract …

----

20 I have gained [*my victory*?] in the trial and legal case!

----

21 Sîn *twisted*?, Ni[n-…]
22 …
23 The hand of Šamaš is my protection, Ištar, *Ningirgi*[*lum*?],
24 and Nin-MAŠ are the *commanders*? – you will not approach to …

----

24 The table is loaded,
25 his gate is open, (but) no one goes straight to [him].

Commentary

13–14: For this tentative restitution, see ZA 75, 198–204e: 53–54 (№ 140) and ZA 75, 198–204j: 111 (№ 143).

16: The sequence 'dog – boar' is found also in ZA 75, 198–204e: 57–58 (№ 140).

18: The lock of hair must refer to the effort of the magician to have in his possession an object, an article of clothing, or even better, a lock of hair of his adversary which will enable him to control the opponent (as in PBS 1/2, 122: 4–6 = № 147, against witchcraft).

20: Restitution after ZA 75, 198–204j: 111 (№ 143).

21: The verbal form can be read *ib-ṭì-il* (< *baṭālum*, "to cease, to abandon") or *ip-ti-il* (< *patālum*, "to twist"), but since ṬI is used in l. 23, reading *ip-ti-il* seems preferable.

23: *kutummum* is attested here for the first time with clear metaphorical meaning, similar to *andullum*. The protecting hand of Šamaš, the god of justice, is another indication that the incantation deals with success in court.

24: *ṣe-e-nu pa-aš-šu-ru*-[…] can be understood as *ṣēnū*, "evil ones", and *paššurū*, Assyrian/Mari stative form of *pašārum* D, "to release" (said of evil), resulting in "the evil one(s) are released". But the Babylonian form *puššurū* is expected.

2.3.6 Witchcraft

This group of incantations is destined to neutralise malicious acts whose agents are (female) witches and (male) wizards. Contrary to later Mesopotamian magic literature, in the OB corpus this category is varied and still not standardized.

№ 146: AMD 1, 287b

SEAL No.: 7189
Copy: Hallo 1999, 287
Tablet Siglum: MLC 1614
Photo: cf. SEAL No. 7189
Edition: Hallo 1999, 278f. (no translation)
Studies: Wasserman 2003 Cat. No. 105
Collection: Morgan Library Collection, New Haven
Provenance: Unknown
Measurements: 7.8 × 4.8 cm
Procedure: No

Introduction

This incantation follows a Sumerian incantation against Lamaštu on the obverse of the tablet. It begins by a solemn address to an unnamed god, most probably Enki/Ea (l. 4). The broken subscript does not allow one to determine the sex of the evil-doer, but the client is a male (note the masculine possessive suffix *-ka* in l. 3 and l. 6).

Reverse$^{?}$

1 *etellum*(NIR.GÁL) *tukultum*(NIR) *etellum*(NIR.GÁL)
2 *etellum*(NIR) *tukultum*(NIR.GÁL)
3 EN-*ka tukultum*(NIR.GÁL)
4 ABZU N[UN^{ki} (x)]
5 *ši*$^{!}$(SI)-*tas-si*$^{!}$(ŠI) ki ⸢ib x x⸣
6 *mu-ub-bi*$^{?!}$*-ra-ti-*[*k*]*a*$^{?}$
7 ^{d}*É-a* ^{d}*Asal*$^{!}$(LÚ)-*lú*$^{!}$(ASAL)-*ḫi*
8 *li-taš-ši-ra-an-ni*
9 te-e$^{!}$-en-nu$^{!}$-ri-e
10 [*ši*]-*pa-at ka-*⸢*ša*$^{?}$*-pí*$^{?}$*-ia*$^{?}$ or: *ša*$^{?}$*-ap*$^{?}$*-ti*$^{?}$*-ia*$^{?}$⸣

Translation

1 The pre-eminent one, the aegis, the pre-eminent one,
2 the pre-eminent one, the aegis,
3–4 the aegis is your lord *in the Apsû of E*[*ridu*!]
5–6 Keep calling out … *of your accusers* (f.)!
7–8 Oh Ea (and) Asalluḫi release me forever (from witchcraft)!
9 te-e$^{!}$-en-nu$^{!}$-ri-e
10 Incantation against [*my wi*]*tch*.

Commentary

6: *mubbirātika* in this line (omitted by Hallo 1999, 278) is participle f. pl. of *abāru* D. This verb is found in a context of accusations of witchcraft. Alternatively, one could read *mu-up-pa*$^{?!}$*-ra-ti-*[*k*]*a*$^{?}$, (*mupparrātim*), a participle f. pl. of *parārum* N "to be scattered, disperse". This verb in the N- and Ntn-stems refers to roaming demons, or to their description as being smashed and scattered (AHw, 830 s.v.).

№ 147: PBS 1/2, 122

SEAL No.: 7190
Copy: Lutz 1919 Pls. CXXVIII-CXXIX; Abusch/Schwemer 2016 Pls. 23–24
Tablet Siglum: CBS 332
Photo: Falkenstein 1939 Pls. V-VI; CDLI P257778
Edition: Wilcke 1973, 10–13; Geller 1989; Abusch/Schwemer 2016, 112–134
Studies: Falkenstein 1939; Geller 1989; Cunningham 1997 Cat. No. 313; Wasserman 2003 Cat. No. 121; Zomer 2018a, 129f.
Collection: University Museum, University of Pennsylvania, Philadelphia
Provenance: Unknown
Measurements: 15.9 × 7.2 cm
Procedure: No

Introduction

A long and elaborate bilingual incantation. The Akkadian translation is not complete. Certain words and phrases, even lines, are left untranslated: they were probably deemed obvious to the translator who found no need to convert them to Akkadian. Lilītum and the Evil Eye are mentioned, but the incantation as a whole deals with sorcery (*rušû*). Asalluḫi and Enki are called for help and Gilgameš, Nergal and Ningišzida – chthonic gods – also referred to. Since the Sumerian and the Akkadian show significant variation, both are translated below. For OB/MB unilingual Sumerian duplicates of this incantation, see Zomer (2018a, 388 no. 244). Restorations follow the duplicates.

Obverse

1 [ḫul-gá]l ⸢igi⸣ ḫ[ul dumu ḫa-lam-ma-ke$_4$]
li-li-tum ša ⸢*i*⸣-[*in-ša lem-ne-et* …]

2 uš$_7$-zu uš$_7$-ri š[u dag-dag-ge nita-líl-lá-àm ì-bu-bu]
ki-iš-pu ru-ḫu-ú it-t[*a*$^{?}$*-na*$^{?}$*-ag*$^{?}$*-ga*$^{?}$*-šu*$^{?}$ …]

3 ki-sikil guruš [šu-dù-a á lá-e-dè]
eṭ-lam ù wa-ar-da-t[*am* …]

4 ì-gen im$^{!}$ abzu ḫabrud-da ^{siki}ḫamanze[r-re šu im-ma-ab-ti]
il-li-ik-ma ṭi-da-am i-na Apsîm(ABZU) *i-na ḫu-u*[*r-ri-im* …]

5 alan mu-un-dím ^{siki}ḫamanzer šu i[m-ma-an-gur]
i-pu-uš-ma mu-ša-ṭe$_4$ […]

6 munsub-a-né lú ba-an-g[ir$_{11}$-gir$_{11}$(-re)]
i-na ša-ra-ti-šu (*vacat*) *r*[*a*$^{?}$*-ki-is*]

7 uš$_7$ i-ni-in-dé ki-a [bí-in-túm]
ru-uḫ-tam id-di-ma i-na er-ṣe-tim i[*q-bi-ir*]

8 uš$_7$ du$_{11}$-du$_{11}$ níg-gu$_7$-gu$_7$ [gá-gá]
ki-iš-pí i-pu-uš-ma i-na ma-ka-lim ⸢*is*$^{?}$⸣*-r*[*u*$^{?}$*-uq*$^{?}$]

9 [u]š$_7$ kaš-e dé-a eme-gar ḫul g[i$^{!?}$-ga]
ru-uḫ-tam$^{!}$(TIM) *ši-ka-rum id-di-ma lem-ni-iš* […]

10 [lú-ùl]u pap-ḫal-la ki nu-zu-a ⸢ba⸣-[an-gen or: ba-ab-dib]

[a-wi-lam m]u-ut-ta-al-li-kam i-na la i-du-⸢ú⸣ [...]
11 ⸢lú⸣-ùlu-bi á-šu-gìri-ni ⸢sa-ad-nim⸣ [im-šub]
(*vacat*) *i-na ma-na-ni-šu [ša$^{!}$]-⸢áš-š[a-ṭam id-di]*
12 zag-še im-gúr-gúr ⸢á$^{!}$⸣-gig-ga$^{!}$ [...]
a-ḫa-a-šu (*vacat*) ⸢*ku$^{!}$-us-sà*⸣-[(*a*) ...]
13 ^{d}Asal-lú-ḫi igi [i]m-ma-an-[sì]
14 a-a-ni ^{d}En-ki-ra é ba-ši-in-ku$_{4}$ [gù mu-na-dé-e]
15 a-a-gu$_{10}$ ḫul-gál igi ḫul dumu ḫa-⸢lam⸣-m[a-ke$_{4}$ ...]
16 a-rá-min-kám-ma-aš ù-ub-da a-na ba-ni-ib-g[i$_{4}$-g]i$_{4}$
17 $^{d+}$En-ki-ke$_{4}$ dumu-ni ^{d}Asal-lú-ḫi mu-na-ni-íb-g[i$_{4}$-g]i$_{4}$
18 dumu-gu$_{10}$ a-na-àm na-e-zu a-na-àm a-ra-ab-daḫ-⸢e⸣
19 ^{d}Asal-lú-ḫi a-na-àm na-e-zu a-na-àm a-ra-ab-daḫ-e
20 níg gá-e ì-zu-a-gu$_{10}$ ù za-e in-ga-⸢e⸣-zu
21 ù za-e in-ga-e-zu gá-e ì-zu
22 gen-na dumu-gu$_{10}$ ^{d}Asal-lú-ḫi
23 a kar-sikil-la-ta ^{dug}sáḫar ù-ba-e-ni-si
me-e kar-ri el-lim i-na (*vacat*) *mu-ul-li-ma*
24 ^{giš}šinig ^{ú}in-nu-uš ⸢naga-si⸣ gi-šul-ḫi
(*vacat*)
25 ^{giš}li [^{giš}eren-bab]bar-ra (šà-bé ù-me-ni-gar)
bu-ra-ša [...] (*vacat*)
26 ⸢^{na4}x x x ^{na4}⸣nir$_{7}$ [...] ^{na4}za-muš-[gír$^{?}$ ...]
27 [nam-šub eridu^{ki}-ga ù-me]-⸢šúm$^{!}$⸣
(*broken*)

Reverse

(*broken*)
1' ⸢^{d}Bil$_{4}$⸣-[ga-mes-e k]a-⸢kéš⸣-[bi] ⸢ḫu-mu-du$_{8}$⸣
(*vacat*) *ki-iṣ-ri-šu li-pa-aṭ-ṭe$_{4}$-er*
2' ⸢uš$_{7}$⸣-zu uš$_{7}$-ri-a né amar-di$_{4}$-di$_{4}$-⸢lá⸣-gin$_{7}$
(*vacat*) *ru-ša ki-ma wa-at-mi ṣe-eḫ-ḫe-ru-tim*
3' lú-ad$_{6}^{!}$ uš$_{7}$-ri-a né ^{giš}sa-šú-uš-gal ḫu-mu-šú
ša-lam-ti ka-aš-ša-ap-ti šu-a-ti (*vacat*) *[l]i-is-ḫu-up*
4' AN-MUŠ-gin$_{7}$ šà-bi-⸢šè⸣ ḫé-en-sur-re-eš
ki-ma (*vacat*) *libbašu*(ŠÀ-*šu*) *a-ia i-né-eš*
5' dumu gír-tab-ba-gin$_{7}$ uš$_{7}$-ri-a né uš$_{7}$-zu-e-ne ḫé-š[ub-b]u-uš
ki-ma (*vacat*) *ša$^{!}$* (*vacat*) *ka-ša-ap-tam šu-a-ti ki-iš-pu-ša li-ša-am-qí-tu-ši*
6' sa-UD ^{giš}gazinbu-gin$_{7}$ uš$_{7}$-zu-e-ne ḫé-b[a]l-uš
ši-ir-a-ni-ša ki-ma ga-ši-ši-im ka-ša-ap-tam šu-a-ti [l]i-iḫ-ru-ú
7' uš$_{7}$-zu ní-te-na-šè šu ḫa-ba-ab-zi
ki-iš-pu-ša a-na ra-ma-ni-ša li-⸢in⸣-na-ad-ru
8' akan á-kùš-a-na ⸢zú⸣ ḫé-ku$_{5}$-ku$_{5}$-e
ṣé-re-es-sà i-na am-ma-t[i-š]a li-ba-ṣí-ir
9' šu-si-ni ga-àr-gin$_{7}$ [ḫé]-⸢túkur⸣-e
(*vacat*) *ša ki-ma ba-*⸢x⸣ [...]

10' ^{uzu}a-ú-na [mùrgu-a] ⸢x⸣ [x x] ḫa-ba-laḫ$^{la-aḫ}$
⸢*i-na*⸣ *li-iq pí-ša* ⸢x⸣ […]
11' [^{d}N]ergal([N]È.IRI$_{11}$.GAL) en-gal kur-[ra x x x x-b]i hé-a
(*vacat*) [… *ana ka-ša-ap-ti*]*m*$^{?}$ *šu-a-ti*
12' [^{d}N]in-urta ur-sag ka[la-ga mas-su x x x] hé-a
13' ⸢$^{d!}$Utu di-ku$_{5}$⸣ gal dingir-re-⸢e⸣-[ne-ke$_{4}$ kar-gal an-ki …] ⸢x⸣ ḫé-a
14' ⸢^{d}Nin⸣-giš-zi-da gu-[za-lá …] ḫé-a lu ka ⸢di$^{?}$⸣ ⸢x⸣ [(x)]
15' ^{d}Gibil$_{6}$ súr […] ḫé-a lu ⸢x⸣ [(x x x)]
(*vacat*) *ez*-⸢*zu*⸣ […]
16' ⸢ur-sag⸣ ^{d}Íd-lú-r[u-gú …] ḫé-a
17' ^{gi}èn-bar-gin$_{7}$ ⸢uš$_{7}$⸣-[ri$^{?}$-a$^{?}$ …] ⸢x⸣
[*k*]*i*$^{!}$*-ma* (*vacat*) ⸢*ka*$^{!?}$⸣-[*aš-ša-ap tam* …]
18' inim an-na inim ⸢$^{d!}$En-ki-ga⸣-[…]
i-na […]
19' lú-ùlu dumu dingir-ra-na [ḫé-sikil ḫé-kù ḫé-dadag]
(*vacat*) *šu*-[*ú* …]
20' ^{na4}bur-šagan-gin$_{7}$ [ù-me-ni-luḫ-luḫ-ḫe]
21' ^{na4}bur-ì-nun-na-gin$_{7}$ [ù-me-ni-su-ub-su-ub-su-ub]
(*vacat*) *ki-ma pu-ri* […]
22' ^{d}Utu sag-kal dingir-re-e-ne-⸢ke$_{4}$⸣ [šu-na ù-me-ni-šúm]
a-na ⸢x⸣-[…]
23' ^{d}Utu sag-kal [silim-ma-na]
24' šu sa$_{6}$-ga dingir-ra-ni-šè [ḫé-en-ši-in-gi$_{4}$-gi$_{4}$]
(*left blank*) [(…)]
25' dingir lú-ba-ke$_{4}$ $^{d+}$En-ki ^{d}A[sal-lú-ḫi …]
i-li awīlim(LÚ) *šu-a-ti ù* […]
26' lú ba-an-⸢dab⸣ […]
⸢*šu-ú*⸣ […]
27' ⸢inim $^{d+}$En-ki⸣-ga-ke$_{4}$ [ḫé-kù$^{?}$ (…)]
[x x x] ⸢x⸣ *l*[*i*$^{!}$*-li-il*]
(*broken*)

Translation

Obverse

1 Sum: Evil one, [evil] eye, child of destruction,
Akk: Lilītum whose e[ye is evil, …]
2 Sum: is r[oaming around] (with) sorceries and witchcraft, [chasing around like a *lilû*-demon].
Akk: Witchcraft (and) sorceries are *r*[*oaming around*, ...]
3 Sum: [In order to bind the ensnared] young girl (and) the lad,
Akk: The young lad and girl […]
4 Sum: she went and took clay of the Apsû from a hole (in the ground) (and) collected loose hair.
Akk: She went and [took] clay from the Apsû out of a hole (in the ground).
5 Sum: She made a figurine (and) wrapped it with the combed-out hair,

	Akk:	she made (a figurine) and the loose hair […],
6	Sum:	(so that) the man is bound with his own hair.
	Akk:	with his (own) hair he is b[ound].
7	Sum:	She spat on it and buried it in the earth.
	Akk:	She spat (on it) and b[uried] it in the earth.
8	Sum:	Uttering witchcraft, putting (them) in food,
	Akk:	she performed witchcraft and *spr*[*inkled*? (it) over the food].
9	Sum:	Pouring witchcraft into beer,
	Akk:	she put witchcraft into beer, malevolent […]
10	Sum:	The troubled man [was walking about] without knowing his destination.
	Akk:	She […] the troubled man in [*a place*?] he does not know.
11	Sum:	She cast the *sadnum*-disease on the limbs of that man.
	Akk:	[She cast] the *šaššaṭum*-disease on his muscles.
12	Sum:	She twisted (his) shoulders. The sick arms […]
	Akk:	His arms are *bou*[*nd* …]
13	Sum:	Asalluhi took note.
14	Sum:	He entered the house of his father Enki, [saying]:
15	Sum:	"My father, the evil one, the Evil Eye, the child of destruction, […]"
16	Sum:	After he said for a second time "What can make him recover?"
17	Sum:	Enki answered his son Asalluḫi:
18	Sum:	"My son, what is it that you do not already know? What can I add to it?
19	Sum:	Asalluḫi, what is it that you do not already know? What can I add to it?
20	Sum:	Whatever I know you also know!
21	Sum:	Whatever you kow, I know!
22	Sum:	Go, my son, Asalluḫi!
23	Sum:	After you have filled a saḫar-vessel with water from the pure quay,
	Akk:	Fill (a saḫar-vessel) with water from the pure quay and
24	Sum:	(after you put) tamarisk, innuš-soapwort, 'horned' alkali, šulḫi-reed,
	Akk:	(*left blank*)
25	Sum:	li-juniper (and) white cedar,
	Akk:	*burāšu*-juniper, […]
26	Sum:	… -stone, nir-stone, zamušgir-stone (in it),
27	Sum:	[after you] cast [the spell of Eridu],
		(*broken*)

Reverse

1'	Sum:	May Gil[gameš] undo its bond!
	Akk:	May he undo its knots.
2'	Sum:	The witchcraft *of that witch* may be like small hatchlings:
	Akk:	(Her) witchcraft may be like small hatchlings:
3'	Sum:	may a great net cover the corpse of that witch!
	Akk:	may (a great net) cover the corpse of that witch!

4'	Sum:	Like … may *they press* on her heart!
	Akk:	Like (…) may his heart not weaken!
5'	Sum:	May witchcraft cast that witch down like the young of a scorpion!
	Akk:	May her (own) witchcraft cast that witch down like (…) of (…)!
6'	Sum:	May the witchcraft dig (into her own) muscles like a pole!
	Akk:	May (the witchcraft) dig into the muscles of that witch like a pole!
7'	Sum:	May the witchcraft rise against herself!
	Akk:	May her witchcraft rage against herself!
8'	Sum:	May she bite (her) breast in her arms!
	Akk:	May she tear off her breast in her forearm(s)!
9'	Sum:	May she chew her fingers like cheese!
	Akk:	her (fingers) […]
10'	Sum:	May her *saliva*? dry up in her palate [*from anger*!]
	Akk:	In her palate … […]
11'	Sum:	May Nergal, the great lord of the Netherworld, be […]!
	Akk:	[… *to*] that *w*[*itch*!]
12'	Sum:	May Ninurta, the mighty hero, [*the leader*] be […]!
13'	Sum:	May Utu, the great judge of the gods, [*the great quay of heaven* (*and*) *earth*] be […]
14'	Sum:	May Ningišzida, the thr[one-bearer …] be […]!
15'	Sum:	May the furious Gibil […] be […]!
	Akk:	[May] the furious (Gibil) […]!
16'	Sum:	May the hero Idluru[gu …] be […]!
17'	Sum:	Like a reed the *w*[*itch*? …]
	Akk:	Like (a reed) the *w*[*itch*? …]
18'	Sum:	By the command of Anum (and) the command of Enki […]
	Akk:	By […]
19'	Sum:	[may] the man, the son of his god, [become pure, clean (and) bright!]
	Akk:	That [man …]
20'	Sum:	[After you clean him] like a perfume flask,
21'	Sum:	[after you rub him] like a ghee bowl,
	Akk:	like a bowl […]
22'	Sum:	[after you entrust him] to Utu, the foremost of the gods,
	Akk:	to [Šamaš …]
23'–24'	Sum:	so that Utu [may let him return safely] to the benevolent hand of his god!
25'	Sum:	The god of that man, Enki (and) A[salluḫi …]
	Akk:	The god of that man and […]
26'	Sum:	The man *was seized* […]
	Akk:	That [man …]
27'	Sum:	By the command of Enki [may he *be purified*?!]
		(*broken*)

Commentary

2: Geller (1989, 194) reads *it-t*[*a-na-ar-pu-ud*], but *rapādum* is not attested in the N stem. Perhaps a form of *nagāšum*? While the first two substantives seem to serve as the direct object in the Sumerian version (see Geller 1989, 199), they are in the nominative case in the Akkadian translation. Against the copy, we read uš$_7$ (KA×LI) following Wilcke (1973, 12).

9: *šikārum*: loc. adv. (Sumerian: kaš-e).

1'–2': For the image in this couplet, Gilgameš with the running chicks, see Wasserman (2003, 154).

2': *ru-ša*, stands here for *rusû* (*rušû*), a type of witchcraft, CAD R, 425f.

3': For this line, see Michalowski's collation in CAD S, 31a, lex. sec.

5': The idea expressed here is that sorceries are transmitted from generation to generation, at times attacking their own kin, at other times simply multiplying (see the opening lines of YOS 11, 15 // YOS 11, 29b = № 149).

9': Geller (1989, 197/203) suggests *ba-á*[*š*?*-li*?…], but *bašlu* is otherwise not paired with ga-àr.

14'–15': For a different interpretation, see Geller (1989, 198ff.). The signs at the end of the line are probably Akkadian glosses.

№ 148: UET 6/2, 193a

SEAL No.: 7203
Copy: Gadd/Kramer 1966 Pl. CCXXIX
Tablet Siglum: –
Photo: CDLI P346278
Edition: Cavigneaux/Donbaz 2007, 332f.
Studies: Farber 1981, 55f.; Cunningham 1997 Cat. No. 334; Wasserman 2003 Cat. No. 184; Ludwig 2009, 178f.; Charpin 2020
Collection: British Museum, London
Provenance: Ur
Measurements: 7.7 × 6.5 cm
Procedure: no

Introduction

Similarly to YOS 11, 15//YOS 11, 29b (№ 149), this spell is to expel witchcraft from the household. Exact times to perform the magic procedure are mentioned. The reverse contains a Sumerian incantation mentioning a snake and a scorpion.

1' [...] ⸢x⸣
2' [...] ša?
3' [...] su? [...] ⸢x⸣
4' [...] ⸢x⸣ [x x] ⸢x⸣-*i?-im?*
5' ⸢x⸣ [...] ⸢x x x⸣ *i?*⸣-[*n*]*a?* [*su?-pu?-r*]*i? al-pi-im*
6' *i-na* [x-*i*]*m* ⸢*i?*⸣-[*na bi*]-*ib-bu-li-im*
7' *i*-⸢*na*⸣ [*wa*]-*ar-ḫi-im i-na se-bu-tim*
8' *ù šapattim*(U$_4$.15.KAM) *pa?-še?-er ki-iš-pi-i*
9' *di-pa-ra-am ṣa-ḫa-ra-am*
10' *ki-ib-re-e-*[*e*]*t am-ma-aš-ta-ka-al*
11' *i-ṣi pi-iš-ri-i-im*
12' [*q*]*á-an ša-la-la-am bīnam*(^{giš}ŠINIG)
13' *suḫuššam*(^{giš}GIŠIMMAR.TUR)⸢x⸣ [(x)]
14' [(x) *e*]*l?-lu-tum i-ba-a-*[(x)]
15' [*a?-na?*] *bīt*(É) *a-wi-lim pu-*[*uš?-šu?-ri?-im?*]
16' [*li?*]*-še-ṣi ki!-i*[*š?-pi?-i?*]
17' [t]u-ú-e[n-ni-nu-ri]

Translation

1'-4' (*traces*)
5' [... in the *tr*]*ack?* of the bull
6' in [the ...], on the day of the disappearance of the moon,
7' on the first day of the moon, on the seventh day,
8' and on the fifteenth day (of the moon) release the sorcery!

9'–13' A torch, mottled barley, sulfur of a *maštakal*-plant, the 'magic-stick'-plant, the *šalālum*-reed, tamarisk, a young date palm –

14'–16' The pure ones (= the above *materia magica*) will come along [in order] to re[lease] the house of the man, [so that] the *so*[*rcery*?] will [c]ome out.

17' [t]u-ú-e[n-ni-nu-ri]

Commentary

5': ⌜x⌝ [...] ⌜x x x⌝ *i*?]-[*n*]*a*? [*su*?-*pu*?-*r*]*i*? *al-pi-im*: For this conjectural restitution (different from Cavigneaux/Donbaz 2007), cf. YOS 11, 14a: 2–4 (№ 185).

7': Reading follows Cavigneaux/Donbaz (2007, 332) and is confirmed by photo.

8': *pa*?-*še*?-*er ki-iš-pi-i*: since *kišpī* is certain and the verb *pašārum* appears probably also in l. 15', reading ZI-*ir*, as suggested by Cavigneaux/Donbaz (2007) is unlikely (the translation "toile? *zīru* (qui protége) des sortileges" is not convincing). The form *pa*?-*še*?-*er* is either the imperative of *pašārum*, or the constr. state of *pāširum*, "undoer, exorcist", not attested yet in OB (see CAD P, 253 s.v.).

9': *ṣa-ḫa-ra-am*, from *ṣaḫḫarum*, "mottled barley", seems preferable to Cavigneaux/Donbaz (2007, 332) *sà-ḫa-ra-am*, "faire le tour (de la maison) avec la torche", which is difficult syntactically. Admittedly though *ṣaḫḫarum* is documented only in late, post-OB records.

14': Reading follows Cavigneaux/Donbaz (2007, 332). A similar enumeration of plants serving as *materia magica* appears in Mīs pî VI-VIII: 33b–35b, see Walker/Dick (2001, 216).

15': Reading follows Cavigneaux/Donbaz (2007, 332) but also possible is [d]*É-a wa-ši-pu*[*-um*] (note the partial parallel to the title d*Ea wāšipu* in Mīs pî VI-VIII: 16 (Walker/Dick 2001, 212f.): a-a-gu10 maš-maš // *a-bi maš-maš-šu*).

16': Cavigneaux/Donbaz (2007, 332) have *di*-⌜*i*?⌝-[*ḫa-am*], "[l'affliction diʾu (?)]". The incantation, however, is destined against a general evil that attacks the man's house, not against a personal disease. Reading *ki*!-*i*[*š-pi-i*], "sorcery" (as in l. 8') is more likely in our eyes.

№ 149: YOS 11, 15 // YOS 11, 29b

SEAL No.: 7191
Copy: van Dijk/Goetze/Hussey 1985 Pl. XVII; Pls. XLVII/XLIX
Tablet Siglum: YBC 4588; YBC 4597
Photo: https://collections.peabody.yale.edu/search/Record/YPM-BC-018653
https://collections.peabody.yale.edu/search/Record/YPM-BC-018662
Edition: Abusch/Schwemer 2016, 154f.
Studies: van Dijk/Goetze/Hussey 1985, 30; Cunningham 1997 Cat. No. 391a–b; Wasserman 2003 Cat. No. 244/255; Schwemer 2010, 63; Mertens-Wagschal 2018, 166f.
Collection: Yale Babylonian Collection, New Haven
Provenance: Larsa area
Measurements: 6.2 × 7.7 cm; 9.3 × 7.9 cm
Procedure: Yes

Introduction
This spell – containing gnomic, wisdom-like sayings on evil – is destined to ward off domestic witchcraft. Text A is probably of late-OB date, as seen by the verbal form in *inneppušū* (rather than *inneppešū*, l. 20) and the unusual use of Sumerograms (esp. DIŠ = *šumma* in l. 21).

Text A =YOS 11, 15; Text B =YOS 11, 29b

1	A1	*e-pi-iš le-em-né-tim le-em-né-tu-šu ú-ul i-še-et-ta-ša*
	B23	⸢*e-pi*⸣*-i*[*š*$^{!}$ *le-em-n*]*é*$^{!}$*-t*[*i-šu*] *ú-ul i-še-et-ta-šu*
2	A2	*lu-mu-un-šu pi-ri-iḫ-šu ú-ul ú-wa-aš-šar*
	B23	*lu-mu-un-šu pi-ri-iḫ-šu ú-ul ú*$^{!}$*-wa-šar*
3	A3	*za-a-ri lum-nim i-iṣ-ṣi-da qá-ta-*[*šu*]
	B24	*za-ri lu-um-nim i-ṣi-da qá-ta-šu*
4	A4	*awāt*(INIM-*a-at*) *uṣ-ṣi-a ú*$^{!}$*-š*[*a*$^{!}$]*-a*[*n*$^{!}$*-nu*]*-ú*$^{!}$ […]
	B24	*awāt*(INIM-*a-at*) *uṣ-ṣi-a-am ú-ša-an-nu-ú ap-lu-šu*
5	A5	*ú-ul i-ḫa-di bar-ba-ra-*[…]
	B25	*ú-ul i-ḫa-ad-di ba-ar-ba-ru i-mi-ṣi-ni*
6	A6	*ù ne-ša-am ša-gi-*[*ma-am* …]
	B25	*ù né-ša-am ša-gi*$^{!}$*-ma-am id-mu-*[*um*$^{?}$] *ia-a-tim*
7	A7	*ú-ul ú-šal-lam*$^{!}$ d[a$^{!}$ …]
	B26	[…] ⸢x⸣ b/pu-ul$^{!?}$ ši-r[a x]

8	A8	*ú-ul ú-*[…]
	B26	[…] *na-zi-iq-tim*
9	A9	*a-na ḫa-ab-*[*li*$^{?}$*-im*$^{?}$ …]
	B27	[…] *ša ki* ⸢x⸣ […]
10	A10	*a-na* […]
	B27	[…] i-di-im-[(x)]
11	A11	*ḫa-ab-*[*lu/li-um/im...*]
	B28	[…]
12	A12	ù$^{!}$ t/ša […]
	B28	[…]*-at*
13	A13	*a-na li-*[…]
	B29	[…]
14	A14	ga ⸢x⸣ […]
	B29	[…] ar
15	A15	*na-ši* […]
16	A16	iš ⸢x⸣ [x x (x) x] *i-na ma-a-at* ⸢x⸣ […]

		(*blank line*)
17	A17	8$^{?}$ *ḫallūrī*(GÚ.GAL) 7 *kiššēnī*(GÚ.NÍG.ḪAR.RA) 9 *šegušš am*(ŠE.MUŠ$_{5}$)
18	A18	7 *uṭṭat*(ŠE) *sikillam*(Ú.SIKIL) *billatam*(KAŠ.Ú$^{!}$.SA$^{!}$) (Text: SA.Ú) *ù ṭābā*[*tam*](A.GEŠTI[N.NA])
19	A19	*i-na ṣi-ir-ri daltim*(^{giš}IG) *te-te-me-e*[*r*]
20	A20	*ki-iš-pu ša a-na bīti*(É)*-šu i-né-pu-šu*$^{!}$ *p*[*a*$^{?}$*-aš*$^{?}$*-ru*$^{?}$]

21	A21	*šumma*(DIŠ) *it-ta-na-ad-la-aḫ ù du*$^{!}$*-bu-ub*$^{!}$*-tum*
22	A22	*ša-ak-na-sú li-bi-it-tam ša askuppi*(I.LU)*-šu*
23	A23	*i-na-sà-aḫ a-na ki-nu-nim i-ša-ka-an-ma*
24	A24	*du-bu-ub-ta-šu in-na-sà-aḫ*

Translation

1 The evildoer, his evil deeds will not leave him (Text A: her),
2 his wickedness will not leave his offspring.
3 He who sows wickedness, his hands will reap (it).
4 The word which came out against me – his (the evil-doer's) sons will repeat$^{?}$.
5 The torn-eyed wolf shall not rejoice,
6 and as for the roaring lion – he will moan to me.
7 The […] will not be well […]
8 […] will not […] the howling […]

9 To the *wro[nged person?* …] *who like* […]
10 To the […] *hand?* […]
11 The *wro[nged person?* …]
12 […]
13 To the […]
14 […]
15 He who *carries?* […]
16 […] in the […]
----
17 8 *ḫallūrum*-peas, 7 *kiššēnum*-peas, 9 (grains of) *šeguššum*-barley,
18 7 grains of *sikillum*-plant, beerwort and vinegar
19 you will bury in the socket of a doorpost –
20 The witchcraft that was done against this house will be *u[ndone]*.
----
21 If he is constantly troubled and worry is set upon him –
22–23 He will tear out a brick from his threshold and place it in his stove;
24 then his troubles will be torn out as well!

Commentary

4: INIM-*a-at*, read *awāt* or pl. *awât*, seems to us better than *ka-a-ad*, suggested by Schwemer (2010, 63: 3: "the ... from which he escapes, his sons will *double* (it)"), cf. YOS 11, 12c: 37 (№ 47): *a-wa-tum a-wa-at bu-[ul?-ṭim?]*. The line states that the evil words will be repeated by his sons (similarly in l. 2).

25: *i-mi-ṣi-ni* is a Sandhi spelling of (*ḫ*)*imiṣ īni*, for which see OB Lu B iv 48–49: [lú.igi.x.x] = *ša ināšu nasḫā*, "whose eyes have been torn out", [lú.igi.x.x] = *ša ināšu ḫamṣā*, "whose eyes have been torn out", and AfO 18, 65: 20 (OB omen) *šumma awīlum na-ap-lu-sú ḫa-mi-iṣ mūt ḫinqi imât*, "If a man's way of looking is oblique: he will die of constriction". For the grammatical construction of (*ḫ*)*imiṣ īni*, see Wasserman (2003, 53).

2.4 Supernatural Entities

2.4.1 Evil Eye

The incantations against an envious probing eye show considerable variation, but the setting is mostly fixed: the eye is described as causing bedlam in the house and in the yard, harming animals and stopping different domestic activities. Usually, the eye is described as a separate entity, but in some cases, it seems to be part of another hostile being – Lamaštu (Fs. de Meyer 86, 20' = № 156 and CUSAS 32, 31c = № 154), or a witch (CUSAS 32, 7g // CUSAS 32, 8c: 40' = № 151). Interestingly, the Evil Eye may find an echo in the description of the bad wife in the Laws of Hammurapi (§§ 141/143). Both the Eye and the wife "scatter the household" (*bīssa usappaḫ*).

№ 150: AoF 35, 146

SEAL No.: 7221
Copy: –
Tablet Siglum: Kt 94/k 520
Photo: Barjamovic/Larsen 2008, 146
Edition: Barjamovic/Larsen 2008, 145–147
Studies: Zomer 2018a, 61 fn. 203
Collection: Anadolu Medeniyetleri Müzesi, Ankara
Provenance: Kaneš
Measurements: –
Procedure: No

Introduction

This OA incantation is closer to the OB incantations of its group than to the MA incantation against the Evil Eye published by Geller (2004), proving the dependency of OA magic lore on Babylonian material. The dittography by the end of l. 8 and the gawky separation of lines suggest that the text was copied from an unknown, probably Babylonian, origin. A long legitimation formula seals the text.

Obverse
1 *e-nu-mì* | *e-nu-um* | *e-nu-um*
2 *a-lu-ší-tum* | *ki-ša* | *bi-ru-um*
3 *la-am-nu-um* | *ki-ša* | *ší-tum*
4 *a-bi-ik-tum* | *tí-ru-um*
5 *bēt*(É) *a-wi-lem* | *ká-nu-nam*
6 *pá-ḫu-ra-am tù-sà-pí-iḫ*
7 *bé-tám* | *ša-gi*$_4$*-ma-am* | *tí-li-šu*
8 *ta-áš-ku-un* | ‹‹*ta-ḫu-uz*››
9 *alpam*(GU$_4$) | *i-na ú-ri-im ta-ḫu-uz*
10 | *immeram*(UDU) | *i-na ma-áš-qí-e*

11 *ta-ḫu-uz | eṭ-lam | i-na*
12 *sú-pu-em | ta-ḫu-uz*
13 *wa-ar-da-tám | i-šu-wa-ri-im*

Lower Edge
14 *[t]a-ḫu-uz | ṣú-ùḫ-ra-⸢am⸣*
15 *⸢i⸣-bu-ud | ta-ri-tim*

Reverse
16 *ta-ḫu-uz | e-nu-um*
17 *la-mu-tum | a-tí | ší-ip-tum*
18 *la i-a-tum | ší-pá-at*
19 *É-a | be-el ší-pá-tim*
20 *ta-mu-a-tí | A-nam*
21 *ù A-na-tám | Lá-aḫ-ma-am*
22 *ù ⸢Du⸣-ra-am | er-ṣa-tám*
23 *⸢ù⸣ na-i-le-ša | la ta-tù-/ri-ma*
24 *la ta-ṣa-bi-tí-ší-ni*

Translation

1–4 Eye, eye, *a-lu-ší-tum* eye! Truly, bad *vision*; Truly, robbed sleep; *mud.*
5–6 As for the man's house – she scattered the gathered hearth;
7–8 She turned the house full of (happy) noise into a ruin; ‹‹She seized››
9 She seized the ox in the stable;
10–11 She seized the sheep in the watering place;
11–12 She seized the young man in *prayer*;
13–14 She seized the maiden while dancing;
14–16 She seized the little-one from the lap of the nurse;
16–17 An Evil Eye – are you!
17–19 The incantation is not mine, it is the incantation of Ea, the lord of incantations.
20–24 You are adjured by Anum and Anatum, (by) Laḫmum and Dūrum, (by) the earth and its watercourses: You shall not return! You shall not snatch her!

Commentary

1–2: *ēnum a-lu-ší-tum*: a comparison to other incantations against the Evil Eye (Ford 1998) suggests that the unknown adj. *a-lu-ší-tum* designates a colour, or another physical quality of the Evil Eye.[252] – For the particle *kīša*, see Wasserman (2012a, 138–153).

2–3: *bi-ru-um lamnum*: *bīrum*, "divination" (CAD B, 264ff.), here probably with a concrete meaning "vision" (similarly Barjamovic/Larsen 2008, 148 connected it to *birratu*, "a filmy condition of the eye").

252 With Barjamovic/Larsen 2008, 147, *alušûm*, "eine Menschenklasse?", AHw, 39b is a ghost lemma, corrected in CAD A/1, 391b and AHw, 1543a to *kulûm*.

4: *tí-ru-um*: Barjamovic/Larsen (2008, 148) suggest "an affliction", or "trembling" (from *tarāru* "to tremble"). Another possibility is *ṭērum* "mud, silt" (CAD Ṭ, 105; no OA attestations) which fits the notion of unclear sight. The Evil Eye is connected to unclear sight also in CUSAS 32, 7g // CUSAS 32, 8c: 1–4 (№ 151), where the Eye is related to a cloud covering the sun.

5–6: As in the OB parallels (ZA 71, 62a: 10' = № 157 and CUSAS 32, 31c: 6 = № 154).

11–12: *tāḫuz eṭlam ina sú-pu-em*: Barjamovic/Larsen (2008, 149) concluded that *suppuʾum* in l. 12 "proves that *šullûm* in the OB texts clearly has to represent a phonetic variant of *sullûm* 'prayer'". But, with George (2016, 132), the parallel OB passages (YOS 11, 11: 8 = № 35; YOS 11, 19a: 9–10 = № 164; and CUSAS 32, 7o // CUSAS 32, 8i: 13–14 = № 19) prove the opposite, namely that the Assyrian scribe read, or heard, *šullûm*, "street" with the Assyrian pronunciation *sullûm*, and mistook it for the homonym "prayer".

23: *erṣatam ù na-i-li-ša*: Barjamovic/Larsen (2008, 149) translate: "the Underworld, and those who lie in it". *niālum*, "to lie down", is used to describe the dead (cf. MDP 18, 255: 2), but the inhabitants of the underworld are the *eṭemmū* or *mītūtu*. Moreover, they are not called for as guarantors in oaths. Following Lambert (1959–1960, 117: 32) and CAD N/1, 150b, we take *naʾilu* to denote a "watercourse". An oath invoking the netherworld together with a body of water is found in YOS 11, 12a: 8 (№ 36): *uttamīka erṣetam u ḫa-am-mé-e*, "I conjure you by the earth and the lakes".

24: *lā taṣabbitīšini*: Note that the incantation is destined for a female client (as YOS 11, 14c = № 39).

№ 151: CUSAS 32, 7g // CUSAS 32, 8c

SEAL No.: 7104
Copy: George 2016 Pl. XXIII; Pl. XXVIII
Tablet Siglum: MS 3097; MS 3085
Photo: George 2016 Pl. XXI; CDLI P252106; Pl. XXVII; CDLI P252094
Edition: George 2016, 93f.
Studies: George 2016, 94–96
Collection: Schøyen Collection, Oslo
Provenance: Unknown
Measurements: 25.0 × 24.0 cm (MS 3097); 16.5 × 9.3 cm (MS 3085)
Procedure: No

Introduction

Two duplicates of this incantation are found on incantation collectives (followed by the same dog incantation, see George 2016, 93). Here the eye is not causing disorder and discord, but has an ability to 'seize', that is, to paralyze different victims in the domestic realm: animals and humans alike. The 'seizing'-motif is known from incantations against the magic 'heart-plant' (YOS 11, 11 = № 35; YOS 11, 12a = № 36; CUSAS 32, 7o // CUSAS 32, 8i = № 19), only that here *aḫāzum*, not *ṣabātum* is used. By the end, where the text is broken, a *kaššaptum* is mentioned, pointing at the possibility that the Evil Eye serves as the sorceress' agent.

Text A = CUSAS 32, 7g; Text B = CUSAS 32, 8c

1	A iii 21'	*i-nu-ma i-nu-um i-ḫu-zu [a-ḫ]i-⸢za-am⸣*
	B i 24'	*i-nu-ma i-nu-um i-ḫu-⸢zu⸣ a-ḫi-za-am*
2	A iii 22'	⸢*ù*⸣ ^{d}*En-ki a-*⸢*ḫi*⸣*-za-am i-ḫu-uz*
	B i 25'	*ù* ^{d}*En-ki a-ḫi-za-am i-ḫu-uz*
3	A iii 23'	⸢*i*⸣*-ḫu-*⸢*uz*⸣ *ib-ba-ru-*⸢*um*⸣
	B i 26'	*i-ḫu-uz ib-ba-ru-um*
4	A iii 24'	[*i-in* ^{d}*Šamši*(UTU]⸢^{ši}⸣) *il*$^{?}$⸣*-mi*
	B i 26'	*i-in* ⸢^{d}⸣*Šamši*(UTU^{ši})
5	B i 27'	*ù i-nu-um bi-it a-wi-lim i-*⸢*ḫu*⸣*-uz*
6	B i 28'	⸢*iz*⸣*-zi-iz-ma i-na ba-ab a-wi-lim*
7	B i 29'	[*e*]*-ri-ba-am ik-bu-us wa-ṣi-a-am ik-bu-/*[*u*]*s*
8	B i 30'	[*sà*$^{?}$]*-ar-ru-ti*$^{!}$*-i*[*š*$^{?}$ x x x x] ⸢x⸣ [x]
9	B i 31'	[*za-a*]*b-bi-lam*$^{!}$ [*i-na*] ⸢*su*⸣*-pu-ri-*[*im*]
10	B i 32'	[*al-pa*]*-am ša-di-da-am ik-l*[*a*]
11	B i 33'	[*ša-ḫa*]*-a-am da-an-n*[*am*]
12	B i 34'	[*ú-na-a*]*s-sí-ḫa-am ši-e-pi-i-*⸢*šu*⸣

13	B i 35'	[*ik-sí*$^{?}$*-m*]*a mu-uš-ta-ap-ṣa-am*
14	B i 36'	[*i-na*] *i-di-šu*
15	B i 37'	[*ik-sí*$^{?}$ *la*]*-sí-ma-am i-na bi-*⸢*ir*⸣*-ki-šu*
16	B i 38'	[x x x] *i-nam le-mu-ut-ta-am*
17	B i 39'	[x x] ⸢x⸣*-zu*$^{?}$*-nim*
18	B i 40'	[(x) *k*]*a-aš-ša-ap-ta-am*
19	B i 41'	[x x x] ⸢x⸣*-bi ṣe-e-re-sà*
20	B i 42'	[x x x] ⸢x⸣*-de-e ù* ⸢x⸣*-di-ša*
21	B i 43'	[(tu$_6$) én]-é-nu-ru

22	B i 44'	[ka-ini]m-ma *i-nu-um*

Translation

1–2	When the Eye seized the Seizer – Enki seized the Seizer.
3–4	Mist seized the Eye of the sun (A: enfolded (it)) (B: and the Eye seized man's household).
5–7	(The Eye) stood at the man's door: she trampled over the one who enters, she trampled over the one who goes out.
8–9	Deceitfully she [*misled*] the carrier.
9–10	In the cattle-fold she held back the draught-ox,
11–12	she ripped out the mighty pig's legs,
13–14	she tied up the wrestler in his hands,
15	she tied up the messenger in his knees.
16–17	… the Evil Eye!
18–20	[…] the witch […] her teat […] her […]!
21	[(tu$_6$)-én]-é-nu-ru

22	[Incan]tation (against the Evil) Eye.

Commentary

1: *inūma īnum* "When the Eye…" plays on *īnummi īnum* "Eye! Eye!", the common formula which opens different incantations (*uzzummi uzzum*; *erṣetummi erṣetum*; *qānummi qānum* etc., see Wasserman 2012a, 189).

2: The dynamics of the magic is clear: The Eye seizes an unknown seizer, and Enki, in his turn, seizes the seizer. In other words, both the Eye and Enki have the power to seize, but Enki, mentioned last, prevails. For the alliterative construction *inūma īnum īḫuzu āḫizam u Enki āḫizam īḫuz*, see § 1.7.2.

10: Cf. YOS 11, 20: 8 (№ 165).

15: The quick running messenger blocked by the Eye is mentioned also in CUSAS 32, 31c: 8–9 (№ 154).

№ 152: CUSAS 32, 21f

SEAL No.: 7100
Copy: George 2016 Pls. LXIII, LXV
Tablet Siglum: MS 3084
Photo: George 2016 Pls. LXII/LXIV; CDLI P252093
Edition: –
Studies: –
Collection: Schøyen Collection, Oslo
Provenance: Unknown
Measurements: 18.5 × 9.5 cm
Procedure: Yes

Introduction

A badly damaged incantation with a subscript indicating it as a spell against the Evil Eye. Preliminary edition was sent to us by George.

Reverse

1' [...] ⸢x x⸣ [...]
2' [...] ⸢ir⸣ [x x x] ⸢x x x x⸣ [...]
3' [...] *er-ši-ša ṣe-eḫ-ra-am i-*⸢x⸣-[...]
4' [...] *ke-e-nu-nam pu-*⸢*úḫ*⸣*-ḫu-ra-am ú-*⸢*sà*⸣*-a*[*p-pi-iḫ* (x x x)]
5' [...] ⸢x x⸣*-am iš-ku-*⸢*un*⸣ *al-pa-am a-li-ka-am* ⸢*i*⸣-[*ka-al-la*]
6' [...] ⸢x x x⸣ *ba-ab re-*⸢*e*⸣*-i-im i-ku-*⸢x⸣ [(x)]
7' [... *ba*]*-ab iš-pa-*⸢*ri*⸣-[*im* (x)] *is*-[(x) x]
8' [...] x*-ri-im* [(x)] *ri-*⸢*iš*$^{?}$⸣ *is*-[(x) x]
9' ⸢x x⸣ [...] ú ⸢ri⸣ ⸢x⸣ [(x)] *is*-[(x) x]
10' ^{giš}KIRI$_6$ [...] ⸢x x x x⸣ [(x)] ⸢x x⸣ [...]
11' *i-nam le-*[*em-nam ...š/t*]*a-am* ⸢x x⸣ [x]
12' *ši-pa-ra-am* ⸢x⸣ [... *pu*]*-ur-sí-ta-am* ⸢*ša ú*⸣-[x] x [x (x) x]
13' *šu-uk-na-a-ma* ⸢*i-na*⸣ [x] ⸢x x x x x⸣ ba ni ⸢x x⸣ na ku ⸢up pi⸣ me [x x x]
ka-inim igi-[(kam)]

Translation

1'–2' (*unintelligible*)
3' [... from] her bed the little-one.
4' [...] she scattered the gathered hearth
5' [... the ...] she placed; the walking ox [she holds back]
6' [She] ... the gate of the shepherd
7' [... the ga]te of the weaver she has ...
8'–9' ...
10' The orchard ...
11' The E[vil] Eye ...
12' The *work*$^{?}$ [... the off]ering bowl which ...

13' Place (pl.) in …
Incantation (against) the (Evil) Eye.

Commentary

5': *ikalla* in the end of the line, after YOS 11, 20: 8 (№ 165): [*al*]*pam*([G]U_4[!]) *a*[!]-*li*[!]-*ka i*[!]-*ka-a*[*l*[!]-*la*] (cf. also CUSAS 32, 31c: 9 = № 154).

12'–13': These lines belong to the procedure. 2 pl. imperatives are found also in the Evil Eye incantation ZA 71, 62a: 15'–16' (№ 157).

№ 153: CUSAS 32, 31b

SEAL No.: 7101
Copy: George 2016 Pls. LXXXV
Tablet Siglum: MS 3103
Photo: George 2016 Pl. LXXXIV; CDLI P252112
Edition: –
Studies: –
Collection: Schøyen Collection, Oslo
Provenance: Unknown
Measurements: 12.5 × 11.5 cm
Procedure: No

Introduction
The first of three consecutive incantations against the Evil Eye, this incantation is almost entirely broken, save for *muṣṣabram* "very bad" (l. 6'); *īnišu* (l. 7'); *ṣērum* (l. 18') and perhaps *ramānim* (l. 5'). The subscript, however, makes it clear that this spell is against the Evil Eye.

Obverse

ii
1' [...]-*ni*$^{?}$
2' [...]-*li-im*
3' [...]-⸢*i*⸣-*im*
4' [...]-*i-šu*
5' [...] *ra*-⸢*ma*$^{?}$⸣-*nim*
6' [...] ⸢x⸣-*na-šu mu-uṣ-ṣa-ab-ra-am*
7' [...] ⸢x⸣ *i-ni-šu*
8' [...] ⸢x x⸣-*a-bu*
9' [...] ⸢*ka-la-a-ma*⸣
10' [...] ⸢x x x⸣ di
11' [...] ⸢x x⸣
12' [...] ⸢x⸣-*ia*
13' [...] ⸢x⸣-*ib*
14' [...]-*ni*
15' [...] ⸢x⸣-*ia*
16' [...]-*am*
17' [...] ⸢x⸣-*a-am* [x] ⸢x⸣
18' [... *ana*] *ṣe-ri-*[*im*]
19' [ka-inim-m]a igi-ḫul-a-[kam]

Translation
(*Too fragmentary*)

Commentary

18': [… *ana*] *ṣe-ri-*[*im*]: The open country, *ṣērum*, is mentioned in Fs. de Meyer 86: 14' (№ 156), another Evil Eye incantation.

№ 154: CUSAS 32, 31c

SEAL No.: 7101
Copy: George 2016 Pl. LXXXV/LXXXVII
Tablet Siglum: MS 3103
Photo: George 2016 Pl. LXXXIV/LXXXVI; CDLI P252112
Edition: George 2016, 96
Studies: George 2016, 94–96
Collection: Schøyen Collection, Oslo
Provenance: Unknown
Measurements: 12.5 × 11.5 cm
Procedure: No

Introduction
The second of three consecutive incantations, this spell against the Evil Eye resembles in part YOS 11, 20 (№ 165), a Lamaštu incantation. Another connection between the Evil Eye and Lamaštu is found in Fs. de Meyer 86 (№ 156).

Obverse

ii	
20'–22'	(*missing*)
23'	[...]-*pu-um*
24'	[...]-*im*
25'	⸢*i-ba-a*?⸣ *i-nu-*[*um*]
26'	*i-mu-ur-ma al-pa-am*

Reverse

iii	
1	*iš-te-bi-ir ni-ir-*[*šu*]
2	*i-mu-ur* {ma} *i-me-ra-am*
3	*ṣé-re-et-ta-šu uš-ta-ad-di*
4	*i-mu-ur bu-ki-na-am*
5	*mu-de-a-am* ⸢*ú*⸣-[*ma*]*r-ri-*⸢*ir*⸣
6	*ke-e-nu-na-am pu-úḫ-ḫu-ra-am*
7	*ú-*⸢*sà*⸣*-ap-pi-iḫ i-nu-um*
8	*i-na ur-ḫi-im la-sí-ma-*⸢*am*⸣
9	*i-*⸢*ka*⸣*-al-la*
10	*ṣe-eḫ-ra-am i-ša-aq-qí-a-am*
11	*me-e pi-iš-ri-im*
12	*iš-tu ke-e-nu-ú-na-am*
13	*ú-sà-ap-pi-*⸢*ḫu-ú-ma*⸣
14	*il-li-ik ip-*[*s*]*ú-sà-am*

15 *i-ši-ir-ti bi-*⸢*i*⸣*-tim*
16 *am-ti bi-tim i-na sa-ba-ṭi-im*
17 *i-na-am li-še-*‹*ṣi*›*-a-*[*a*]*m*
18 *a-na sú-ú-qí-*⸢*im*⸣
19 *i-li bi-tim i-na-am li-še-ṣi-a-*[*a*]*m*
20 *a-na ki-di-im*
21 ka-inim-ma igi-ḫul-a-kam

Translation

ii 20'–iii 1 … the Eye has passed by. When she saw the bull, she broke its yoke.
2–3 She saw an ass, made it throw its leading rope;
4–5 She saw the trough, embittered an acquaintance.
6–7 The Eye scattered the gathered hearth.
8–9 She holds back the messenger on the road.
10–11 She gives the baby amniotic fluid to drink.
12–15 After she has scattered the hearth, she went and destroyed the chapel of the house.
16–18 May the maiden of the house, while sweeping, throw the Eye out to the street!
19–20 May the god of the house throw the eye out to the outside!
21 Incantation (against) the Evil Eye.

Commentary

iii 2: The erased {ma} after *i-mu-ur* is erroneously carried from ii 26' (*i-mu-ur-ma*).

iii 4–5: *īmur bukīnam mu-de-a-am umarrir*: George (2016, 96) translates "it saw a bucket, turned an acquaintance (*mūdâm*) bitter", interpreting this unusual sentence as playing on *bukīnum* and *pû kīnum* "loyal talk" (George 2016, 95). But how does the bucket cause this destabilizing effect? Beyond the possible pun here,[253] we suggest a physical explanation. The bucket, or trough, full of water, looks like a mirror, retaining the passing Eye. When an accidentally passing-by victim looks at it, the Eye's glance attacks him. Somewhat similar is the description in the love-related text A 7478: i 5–17 (Wasserman 2016, 65/69), where an infatuated woman looks at the water in a washbasin (*murammiktum*), recalling the unexpected arrival of her beloved.

iii 6–7: The scattering of the gathered hearth symbolizes the break of familial bonding and harmony (George 2016, 95). An action which reminds one of Lamaštu.

iii 8–9: See CUSAS 32, 7g // CUSAS 32, 8c: 15 (№ 151).

iii 10–11: Choking babies (or old people) by making them drink amniotic fluid is also typical of Lamaštu (see Or. 66, 61: 13–16 = № 162 and YOS 11, 20: 10–12 = № 165).

253 *bukīnam mu-de-a-am umarrir* could play on *mû… murrurum* "making the water (of the trough) bitter".

№ 155: CUSAS 32, 31d

SEAL No.: 7103
Copy: George 2016 Pl. LXXXVII
Tablet Siglum: MS 3103
Photo: George 2016 Pl. LXXXVI; CDLI P252112
Edition: George 2016, 96
Studies: George 2016, 94–96
Collection: Schøyen Collection, Oslo
Provenance: Unknown
Measurements: 12.5 × 11.5 cm
Procedure: No

Introduction
A partially broken incantation. After a legitimation formula, an unexpected expelling order comes: the eye must return to her father and mother (cf. *īnum litūr ana bēli*[*ša*], Fs. de Meyer 86: 20' = № 156).

Reverse

iii
22 *i-nu-um le-em-né-et*
23 ⸢*i-nu-um*⸣ *al-lu-ḫa-ap-pa-at*
24 [*i-nu-u*]*m mu-uṣ-ṣa-ap-ra-at*
25 [x x x *t*]*a*$^{?}$-*al*-⸢*pu-ut*$^{?}$⸣ *ṣe-el-ta-am*
26 [x x x] ⸢x ka x x x⸣ gi ⸢x⸣
27 [x x x x x x x] ⸢x⸣ [x]

(*gap*)

1' [*ši-ip-tum ú-ul ia-tum*]
2' [*ši-pa-at* ^{d}*En-ki*]
3' [*ù* ^{d}*Nin-girim*$_{x}$]

iv
1 [*b*]*e-le-*⸢*et*⸣ *ši-pa-a-tim*
2 *a-*[*š*]*a-ar a-na-*⸢*ad-du*⸣*-ú*
3 ⸢*lu-ú*⸣ *bu-ul-ṭù-um*
4 ⸢*i-ni*⸣ *a-bi-i-ka ù um-mi-i-ka*
5 ⸢*lu-ú sa*⸣*-am-*‹*ḫa*$^{?}$›*-ti-i-ma*
6 *i-na* ⸢*bi*⸣*-ti-ka lu*$^{!}$ *eḫ-le-et*
7 ka-nim-ma igi-⸢ḫul⸣-a-kam

Translation

22–24	The Eye is evil, the Eye is a hunting-net, [the Ey]e is malicious.
25–26	She touched the …, she [*caused*] quarrel (in the…).
27	…
1'–iv 3	[The incantation is not mine: it is the incantation of Enki and Ningirim], the lady of incantations. Wherever I cast it – there is healing.
4–5	May you (f.) rejoin the eye(s) of your (m.) father and mother!
6	May you (f.) be tied up in your (m.) house!
7	Incantation (against) the Evil Eye.

Commentary

iii 23: The comparison to a net is found also in Fs. de Meyer 86: 1' (№ 156), where the Evil Eye is called *šaškallum*.

iii 24: Discord (*ṣēltum*) in the familial surrounding caused by the Eye is found also in ZA 71, 62a: 5' (№ 157).

iv 4–6: Note the grammatical alternation between f. and m. forms in these lines: the eye, as expected, is referred to as f. forms (*samḫāti*, *eḫlet*), but when talking of her family members and her house, m. pronouns are used (*abika*, *ummika*, *bītika*), cf. Fs. de Meyer 86: 9' = № 156).

№ 156: Fs. de Meyer 86

SEAL No.: 7105
Copy: Cavigneaux/Al-Rawi 1994, 86
Tablet Siglum: IM 90648
Photo: –
Edition: Cavigneaux/Al-Rawi 1994, 85f.
Studies: Wasserman 1995b; Cavigneaux 1996; Ford 1998, 207 fn. 15/249 fn. 164; Wasserman 2003 Cat. No. 150
Collection: Iraq Museum, Baghdad
Provenance: Sippar
Measurements: –
Procedure: No

Introduction
The Evil Eye is winged. It hurts the animals around the house. By the end, the Eye is called to return to its "owner". Some parallels to ZA 71, 62a (№ 157), also against the Evil Eye, are found.

Obverse

1 *īnum*(IGI) b u - u r *ša-aš-ka-al-lum*
2 ⸢*ḫu*⸣-*ḫa-ru-um*$^?$ *mu-sa-aḫ-ḫi-iš*$^?$*-tum*
3 ur ⸢x⸣ [x x] *ta-ab-ba-a-ku-um*
4 ša a ab nu [x x] ⸢x⸣ *el*$^?$*-ni* ⸢x⸣ [...] ⸢x⸣
5 *im-ḫa-aṣ alpam*(GU$_4$) *iš-te-b*[*i-ir nīršu*]
6 *im-ḫa-aṣ šaḫâm*(ŠAḪ) *iḫ-te-pí ḫu-u*[*l-šu*]
7 *it-ru-uṣ ka-ap-pí-i-ša*
8 *uš-pa-ri-ir i-di-ša*
9 *i-ši-i-ma i-ni-ka*
10 *i-na pu-ut ki-nu-ni-im i-na i-še-er-tim*
11 *ši-na at-ḫa-a wa-aš-ba-a-ma*

Reverse
12 ⸢*ú*$^?$⸣-[*u*]*l*$^?$ *im-ta-ag-ga-ra*
13 *ku-si-a-ti-*⸢*šu*$^?$⸣*-nu ú-sa-ap-pí-iḫ*
14 *ṣí-li-*⸢*šu*$^?$⸣*-nu ú-ma-al-li ṣēram*(⸢EDIN.NA⸣)
15 *īnam*(IGI) *ku-ši-da* [*ī*]*nam*([I]GI) *ṭú-ur-da*
16 *īnam*(IGI) *šu-ṣí-*⸢*a*⸣ *a-na* [x]-⸢x⸣*-ka*
17 *īnam*(IGI)$^!$ ⸢x x⸣ [...] ⸢x⸣
18 [...] ⸢ma⸣ [x]
19 *šu*$^?$*-li* ⸢x⸣ li$^?$ da ⸢x⸣ [x x]
20 *īnum*(IGI) *li-tu-ur a-na be-lí-*[*ša*]
21 t u - e - e n - n e - n u - r i

Lower Edge
22' *ši-pa-at īnim*(IGI)

Translation

1 The *staring* Eye is a net,
2 a bird-snare, an incessantly swooping-down catcher,
3–4 … who pours out, who …
5–6 She stroked the ox, smashed [its yoke], she stroked the pig, broken [its] *neck-[ring]*.
7–8 She stretched her wings, spread out her arms.
9 Raise your (m.) eyes (and see):
10–12 In front of the fireplace, in the chapel, two companions are sitting, not agreeing with each other.
13–14 She scattered their robes; she filled the steppe with their shadows.
15–16 Chase away the Eye! Drive away the Eye! Make the Eye go out to your (m.) …!
17 The *Eye* …
18–19 …
20 May the Eye go back to its own[er!]
21 tu-e-en-ne-nu-ri
22 Incantation against the (Evil) Eye.

Commentary

1: IGI bu-ur: With Cavigneaux (1996, 38f.) and Ford (1998, 207 fn. 15), this compound stands probably for Sum. igi-bar "regard perçant" which could play also on *būrum* "pit, well, pond, pool" (CAD B, 342f.; already Cavigneaux/Al-Rawi 1994, 86).

2: *mussaḫḫištum*, the participle of *saḫāšum* Gtn, is so-far only lexically attested (CAD S, 54b, see with Ford 1998, 207 n. 15). The form could be the attribute of *īnum* (f.), or of *ḫuḫārum* whose grammatical gender is unknown (pl. *ḫuḫārātum*).

3: *tabbākum* is a PaRRāS of *tabākum* (unattested): "one who pours out, spatters, discharges (terror, blood, etc.)".

6: If *nīrum*, "yoke" in the previous line is right (Cavigneaux/Al-Rawi 1994, 85), then *ḫullum*, "neck-ring", is possible, although this implement is typically used for dogs. In CUSAS 32, 7g // CUSAS 32, 8c: 11–12 (№ 151) the Eye breaks the pig's legs.

9: *išīma īnīka* addresses the client? or the healer?

10–11: Cf. AoF 35, 146: 5–6 (№ 150) and ZA 71, 62a: 10' (№ 157).

11–12: See Wasserman (1995a).

20: The "owner" of the Evil Eye seems to be the demoness Lamaštu (Wasserman 1995a, followed by Ford 1998, 209f. fn. 32). A similar link between the Evil Eye and Lamaštu is detected in CUSAS 32, 31c (№ 154).

№ 157: ZA 71, 62a

SEAL No.: 7106
Copy: Farber 1981, 62
Tablet Siglum: BM 122691
Photo: https://www.britishmuseum.org/collection/object/W_1931-0413-4
Edition: Farber 1981, 61f.
Studies: Farber 1984, 69–71; Farber 1990a; Cavigneaux/Al-Rawi 1994, 85 fn. 19; Wasserman 1995a; Cunningham 1997 Cat. No. 327; Ford 1998, 205–211; Wasserman 2003 Cat. No. 266
Collection: The British Museum, London
Provenance: Tell Duweihes
Measurements: 6.3 × 9.0 cm
Procedure: No

Introduction
The first of three-incantations (the second – to calm a baby, the third – against canines). Judging by sign-forms and grammatical features, this is an early-OB text. Parallels to Fs. de Meyer 86 (№ 156), against the Evil Eye, are found.

Obverse
1' *[i-n]u-⸢um ip-pa-la-ás it-ta-na-ap⸣-[ra-ar]*
2' *ša-aš-ka-lum sà-ḫi-ip-tum*
3' *ḫu-ḫa-ru-um sà-ḫi-ìš-tum*
4' *ba-ab la-ʾì i-ba-ma*
5' *i-na be-ri la-ʾì ṣe-[e]l-ta-am iš-ku-un*
6' *ba-ab wa-li-[d]a-ti-im i-ba-ma*
7' *še-ri-ši-na u*$_4$*-ḫa-ni-iq*
8' *i-ru-ma a-[n]a [b]i-it qè-e*
9' *ši-pa*$^{?!}$*-sa-am [i]š-bi-ir*
10' *ki-nu-na-am pu-⸢ḫu*$^{!}$*⸣-ra-am ú-sa-pi-iḫ*
11' *bi-ta-am ša-gi-[m]a*$^{?}$*-am*$^{?}$ *ti-li-ša-am iš-ku-un*
12' *im-ḫa-aṣ-ma i-še-er-ta-am*
13' *i-ta-ṣi ì-lí bi-tim*
14' *ma-aḫ-ṣa-ma le-e-sà sú-ḫi-ra-ši / a-na wa-ar-ka-*‹‹da››*-tim*
15' *i-ni-ša mu-li-‹a› ṭa-ab-ta-am*
16' *pāša*(KA-*ša*) *mu-li-a di-ig-ma-a[m]*
17' *il bi-ti-im li-tu-r[u*$^{?}$*]*

Lower Edge
18' *ši-ip-tum ša i-ni-[im/in]*

Translation

1'	The [E]ye is looking, she is [roa]ming about!
2'–3'	A swooping-down net! An entrapping bird-snare!
4'–5'	Passing through the tots' door, she brought about quarrel between the tots;
6'–7'	Passing through the door of the birthing women, she strangled their babies.
8'–9'	She entered the vessels' storeroom, broke the sealing bullae;
10'	She scattered the gathered hearth;
11'	She turned the house full of (happy) noise into a ruin;
12'–13'	Having struck down the chapel, the god of the house went out.
14'	Strike her cheek! Make her turn back!
15'	Fill (pl.) her eyes with salt!
16'	Fill (pl.) her mouth with ashes!
17'	May the god of the house *return*?!
18'	Incantation (against) the (Evil) Ey[e].

Commentary

1':	Reading with Ford (1998, 205) (improving on Cavigneaux/Al-Rawi 1994, 85 fn. 19).
3':	*ḫuḫārum sāḫšitum*, cf. *ḫuḫārum mussaḫḫištum* (Fs. de Meyer 86: 2 = № 156).
5':	For the collation, see Wasserman (1995a).
10':	Farber reads *pu-zu*?*-ra-am*, but leaning on parallels (AoF 35, 146: 5–6 (№ 150) and CUSAS 32, 21f: 4' (№ 152) with Fs. de Meyer 86: 10–11 (№ 156)), and re-examining the photo, we read here *pu-*⸢*ḫu*!⸣*-ra-am*.
15'–16':	The incantation strives to reverse the damage the Eye caused. In ll. 8'–9', the Eye broke the bullae in the storeroom and in l. 15' salt, perhaps stored in those jars, is used against her. In l. 10', the eye scattered the fireplace and in l. 16' ash is used to oust her. – Note that the Eye has her own eyes, which could be used as an argument that the Evil Eye belongs to Lamaštu.
17':	The last sign could be -*r*[*u*], but *litūrū* is hard as the subject is sg., *ili bītim* (cf. l. 13').
18':	For the subscript, see Farber (1984, 70); Farber (1989a, 9 fn. 1) and Ford (1989, 205 fn. 9).

2.4.2 Lamaštu

The most notorious villain of Mesopotamian incantations is Lamaštu.[254] This sinister demoness is described as a wet nurse turned rogue, devouring the infants instead of nursing them. As such, Lamaštu is seen as responsible for miscarriage, infant death and still birth.[255] Numerous amulets, often with the demoness' depiction, are known from the third millennium onwards, demonstrating the fear this murderess inculcated.[256] In the present corpus, only one amulet against her is found, Or. 66, 61 (№ 162, without graphic depiction). Lamaštu is unique in that the texts supply a mythical etiology for her actions: for her wrong behaviour, when young, she was banished from heaven (BIN 4, 126 = № 160). Her evil nature is therefore an innate quality. She is, in a way, the personification of evil.

A typical incantation in this group would start with the horrifying look of the demoness, describe her *mode opératoire*, and end with calling upon her to go away. Not much, it seems, can be done against her.

№ 158: AMD 1, 286a

SEAL No.: 7130
Copy: Hallo 1999, 286
Tablet Siglum: YBC 8041
Photo: https://collections.peabody.yale.edu/search/Record/YPM-BC-022109
Edition: Hallo 1999, 276f.
Studies: Wasserman 2003 Cat. No. 103
Collection: Yale Babylonian Collection, New Haven
Provenance: Unknown
Measurements: 5.2 × 3.8 cm
Procedure: Yes

Introduction

Nothing but the procedure is left of this incantation which is followed by an incantation against a dog bite (№ 63).

Obverse
1 [...] ⸢x⸣
2 [...] ⸢x⸣-ma$^{?}$
3 ki ⸢x⸣ [...] ⸢x⸣
4 tu-⸢ú-e-ni⸣-in-nu-ri
5 *ši-pa-at Lamaštu*(^{d}DÌM.ME)
6 *ki-ki-ṭa-ša ki-ir-ba-an ṭābtim*(MUN)
7 *i-na lu-ba-ri-im ta-ra-ak-ka-as*$^{!}$
8 *i-na ki-ša-di-šu ta-ra-ak-ka-a*[*s*]

254 For the possible Sumerian reading ^{d}kamad-me instead of ^{d}dìm-me, see George 2018.
255 On the destructive aspects of Lamaštu: Farber 2007b.
256 An overview of amulets in the second millennium is found in Zomer 2018a, 20–23.

9 *ba-li-iṭ*

Translation

1–3 …
4 tu-⌜ú-e-ni⌝-in-nu-ri
5 Incantation (against) Lamaštu.
6–7 Its procedure: you tie up a lump of salt in a piece of cloth.
8 You tie (it) on his neck.
9 He will be well.

№ 159: BIN 2, 72

SEAL No.: 7131
Copy: Nies/Keiser 1920, Pl. XXXIII
Tablet Siglum: NBC 1265
Photo: cf. SEAL No. 7131
Edition: von Soden 1954, 337–344; Farber 2014, 260/280f./315–317
Studies: Landsberger 1958, 57; Farber 1981, 72; Cunningham 1997 Cat. No. 346; Veldhuis 1999, 42–45; Wiggermann 2000, 231f.; Wasserman 2003, 34/ 47/159/163/Cat. No. 41; Edzard 2004, 542–544; Foster 2005, 173f.; Zomer 2018a, 192f.; Polinge Foster 2021, 132
Collection: Yale Babylonian Collection, New Haven
Provenance: Ešnunna$^{?}$
Measurements: 6.7 × 4.5 cm
Procedure: No

Introduction

This spell describes the demoness' features and actions. The lack of mimation (ll. 6/13/5), the dative pronoun *-ki*, not *-kim* (l. 14), the sign /lab/ (l. 2), and the mention of the three paths of the sky (ll. 1–2, see below), are indications of a relatively late dating.

Obverse
1 *Anum*(AN) *ib-ni-ši* ^{d}*É-a ú-ra-bi-ši*
2 *pa-ni lab-ba-tim i-ši-im-ši* ^{d}*En-líl*$^{!}$
3 *i-ṣa-at ri-ti*$^{!}$*-in* [*a*]*-ra-ka-at*
4 *ú-ba-na-tim ṣú-up-ra-tim*
5 *ar-ra-ka-at a-ma-*⸢*ša bu*$^{?}$*-lu*$^{?}$⸣*-la*
6 *bāb*(KÁ) *bi-ti i-ru-u*[*b*]$^{!}$
7 *i-ḫa-lu-up ṣé-ra-am*
8 *iḫ-lu-up ṣé-ra-am i-*[*t*]*a-m*[*a*]*r ṣeḫram*(LÚ.TUR)
9 *i-na em-ši-šu a-di* 7 *iṣ-ba-sú*

Lower Edge
10 *ús-ḫi ṣú-up-ri-ki*
11 *ru-um-mi i-di-ki*

Reverse
12 *la-ma ik-šu-da-ki*
13 *ap-kal-lam ši-pí-ir É-a qar-du*
14 *ra-pa-aš-ki ṣé-rum pu-ta-a dalātum*(IG^{meš})
15 *al-ki-ma a-ta-la-ki i-na ṣé-ri*
16 *ep-ra-am pí-ki*
17 *ta-ar-bu-ʾa_4-am pa-ni-ki*
18 *saḫlê*(ZÀ.ḪI$^{?}$.LI-*a*) *da-qa-tim*
19 *ú-ma*$^{!}$*-lu-‹ú› i-ni-ki*

20 *ú-ta-mi-ki ma-mi-it É-a*
21 *lu! ta-at-ta-la-ki*

Translation

1–2 Anum created her, Ea brought her up, a face of a lioness Enlil fixed for her.
3–5 She is short of hands, very long of fingers, as to her nails she is very long, her two forearms are *smeared?*.
6–7 She entered the door of the house, slipping through the door socket.
8–9 Once slipped through the door socket, she saw the child. She seized it seven times in its abdomen.
10–13 Take off your nails, drop off your arms, before he has reached you, the wise-of-work, Ea the hero!
14–15 The door socket is wide (enough) for you, open are the doors: Go, walk about the steppe!
16–19 With dust your mouth, with a whirl-wind your face, with cress seeds finely ground I will verily fill your eyes!
20 I conjure you by the oath of Ea!
21 You must go away!

Commentary

1: The creation of Lamaštu – referred to as *pāšittum* – by Enki/Ea is found in Atraḫasīs III vii:1 (Lambert/Millard 1969, 103). Her astral origins are also found clearly in the OA incantation BIN 4, 126 (№ 160), where Anum is mentioned. Note that the short historiola in these lines echo the three paths of the sky – Anu, Enlil and Ea – known in Mesopotamian astronomy only since the Kassite period (see Horowitz 1998, 254–255).

2: Von Soden (1954, 340), read *kal-ba-tim*, claiming that the reading *labbatim* is difficult, as the sign /lab/ is not used in OB. But although she had dog's teeth (cf. Farber 2014, 230), iconographic and textual evidence clearly depict Lamaštu with a lioness' head (see Farber 1980–83, 444, and CBS 10455: 5' which say explicitly: *qaqqassa qaqad ne!-*[*e-ši-im*]). With this evidence, we follow Veldhuis (1999, 42), and Foster (2005, 173), and opt for "lioness".

3: With von Soden (1954, 338), Veldhuis (1999, 42) and Edzard (2004, 543) we read *i-ṣa-at ri-ti!-in* "short of hands" (Wiggermann 2000, 232 fn. 107 and Foster 2005, 173 had *i-za-at* for *ezzat*). – Reading [*a*]*rrakat* follows von Soden (1954, 338), Veldhuis (1999, 42), Edzard (2004, 543) and Foster (2005, 173f.). Wasserman (2003, 34 fn. 34) proposed to read [*w*]*a!-ra-qà-at*, "very pale as to her hands", but since the text uses /qa/ (l. 18), and *arrakat* yields a good chiasm ([*a*]*rrakat ubānātim ṣuprātim arrakat*), this proposal is now rejected.

3–5: [*a*]*rrakat* / *ubānātim ṣuprātim* / *arrakat*: a clear and purposeful enjambment.

5: For Lamaštu's affinity to dung and mud, cf. Farber (1980–1983, 444). Note the shortened dual form *ammāša* (not *ammatāša*). The signs after *a-ma-*⌜*ša*⌝ are difficult to read: only *-la* by the end of the line is clear.

6–7: Against von Soden (1954, 339/341) and Veldhuis (1999, 43), who analyse *i-ru-u[b]*$^{!}$ as present tense, *īrub–iḫallup* is a sequence of preterite–present (cf. Streck 1999, 65–67).

12: A similar warning to the maleficent agent is found in YOS 11, 14b: 5 (№ 41): [*ṣ*]*i-i maškadum lāma ikšudūka ṣurrū naglab*[*u* (*ša*) ^{d}]*Gula*, “Go out *maškadum* before the flint razors of Gula will reach you!”.

15: *atallakī* is Gtn (von Soden 1954, 339: “geh herum”, Veldhuis (1999, 42: “roam”), Edzard (2004, 543: “tummle dich”), not Gt as understood by Foster (2005, 173: “be gone into”). From this follows that *ṣé-ri* is probably “steppe”, not “door socket”.

18: ZÀ.ḪI$^{?}$.LI-*a* (or as AHw, 1009b 1 reads: ZÀ.ḪI.LI.A) is a pseudo-Sumerogram, a back-formation from Akk. *saḫlû*. The form *saḫlâ* is a mistaken sg. m. acc., as seen by the incongruence with the adjective *daqqātim*. The pl. *saḫlê* is expected.

19: For the interpretation of *umallû* as an assertive subjuntive denoting the speaker’s oath mentioned in the following line, see Wasserman (2003, 163); GAG^{3} §81e. See further Foster (2005, 175).

№ 160: BIN 4, 126

SEAL No.: 7224
Copy: Clay 1927 Pl. LII
Tablet Siglum: NBC 3672
Photo: https://collections.peabody.yale.edu/search/Record/YPM-BC-006647
Edition: von Soden 1956; Wiggermann 1983, 297; Foster 1993, 59; Wilson 1994, 72–74; Farber 2014, 259/280f./314f.
Studies: Cunningham 1997 Cat No. 347; Wasserman 2003 Cat No. 42; Michel 2003, 137; Hecker 2008, 64f.; Zomer 2018a, 192f./330.
Collection: Yale Babylonian Collection, New Haven
Provenance: Kaneš
Measurements: –
Procedure:

Introduction

This single incantation on a square tablet offers the earliest account of Lamaštu being thrown out of heaven. The demoness is described and her malicious actions related, but no remedy or counteraction is mentioned.

Obverse

1 *iš-t[í]-a-at e-lá-at*
2 *a-pu-la-at*
3 *mu-uš-ta-ba-⸢ba⸣-at!*
4 *ù-tù-kà-at*
5 *lam-na-at bu-un-/tù*
6 *i-le-em*
7 *ma-ar-tù | A-ni-im*
8 *a-na ṭé-mì-⸢ša⸣ lá dam-qé-/[em]*

Lower Edge

9 *ma-al-ki-š[a]*
10 *pá-ru-em A-nu-um*

Reverse

11 *a-bu-ša | iš-tù*
12 *ša-ma-e | i-pu-ṣa-ší*
13 *qá-qá-ar-šu-um*
14 *a-na ṭé-mì-ša lá dam-qé-/em*
15 *ma-al-ki-ša sà-aḫ-i-/⸢im⸣*
16 *pè-ra-sà | wa-ša-ra-/at*
17 *da-du-ša ša-aḫ-ṭù*
18 *a-na be-el lá i-le-em*

Upper Edge

19 *i-ša-ru-um*

20 *té-šé-er* I *šé-er-ʾa*$_4$*-an*

Left Edge

21 *lá-áb-i-im tù-ra-mì*

22 *šé-er-ʾa*$_4$*-an ṣú-ḫ̮a-re-/em*

23 *ù*$^{!}$(WA) *lá-i-im*

24 *ta-áš-šu-‹uš*$^{?}$*›-ma*

Translation

1–2 She is unique! She is a *goddess*! She is late (born)!

3–5 She keeps flashing! She is an *utukku*-demoness! She is evil!

5–7 A daughter of a god, the daughter of Anum.

8–10 Because of her malevolent intention(s), her blasphemous decision(s),

10–13 Anum, her father, smashed her down to earth from heaven.

14–15 – Because of her malevolent intention(s), her rebellious decision(s)!

16–17 Her hair is loose. Her garments are stripped off.

18–20 She goes straight for the godless person(s)!

20–21 She slackens the lion's muscles!

22–24 She *catches* the muscles of a child and the infant!

Commentary

2: Following Wiggermann (1983, 297), we assume a corrupt form for *illat*. Cf. *i-lá-at* in the other OA Lamaštu incantation Or. 66, 61: 2 (№ 162). Less likely, one could interpret *ellat* 'she is pure'. For a discussion on *ellu* in this difficult context, see Wilson (1994, 74).

5/7: *buntu ilim* (5) and *martu Anim* (7): archaic *status constructus* ending with *-u*.

12: The verb *napāṣum* describes Lamaštu's banishment from heaven also in a MA incantation AS 16, 287f.d: 23, see Zomer (2018a, 330). In the SB Lamaštu-series, (*w*)*arādu* Š is used, see Zomer (2021, 174).

23: As remarked by von Soden (1956, 141), the copy BIN 4, 126 has left out the penultimate line. The transliteration of ll. 23–24 follows Von Soden (1956).

24: This line remains difficult. Farber (2014, 259) reads ta áš šu ku. CAD R, 207a, notwithstanding Farber (1981, 72), follows von Soden (1956, 143), reading *ta-ra*$^{?}$*-šu*$^{?}$. We suggest a form of *ašāšum* "umfassen" (AHw, 79–80), although this verb shows a/u vocalization.

№ 161: Fs. de Meyer 89

SEAL No.: 7132
Copy: Cavigneaux/Al-Rawi 1994, 89
Tablet Siglum: CBS 10455
Photo: CDLI P265667
Edition: Cavigneaux/Al-Rawi 1994, 88f.
Studies: Wasserman 2003 Cat. No. 152
Collection: University Museum, University of Pennsylvania, Philadelphia
Provenance: Nippur
Measurements: –
Procedure: No

Introduction
A broken text, describing Lamaštu's appearance. CDLI P265667 comments that this text joins CBS 10454 + 10455 + 10460.

Obverse$^{?}$
1' ⸢*da-du*⸣-*š*[*a*$^{?}$*šaḫṭū*$^{?}$ …]
2' *e-en-zu* ba$^{?}$-⸢x⸣-[…]
3' *ki-ma nu-nim tu-uk-k*[*u-up zumurša*$^{?}$]
4' *ki-ma še-er-še-ri-im le-e*[*s-sa*] / *wa-ar-qá-a*[*t*]
5' *qá-qá-as-sa qá-qá-ad ne*$^{!}$-[*e-ši-im*]
6' [*ši-i*]*n-na-ša ši-in-na-at imērim*(A[NŠE])
7' [*x x*]-*ri ka-al-bi-im e-l*[*a*$^{?}$ …]
8' [x x x] *i-na ḫur*$^{?}$-*ri* […]
9' [x x x] ⸢x⸣ […]
(*broken*)

Reverse$^{?}$
1' [x x] ni$^{?}$ ša ši […]
2' [*li-i*]*b*$^{?}$-*ba-ša* am ⸢x x x⸣ […]
3' *e tu-ur-ri* ma ⸢x⸣ [...]
4' *i-me-ra-am* pa ta a […]
5' *ša iṣ-ba-tu* uš x […]
6' *ṣa-ab-ti* ⸢x⸣ […]
7' *ri*-⸢x⸣ […]
8' *iḫ*-[…]
(*broken*)

Translation

1' H[er] *breasts* are [*stripped off* …]
2' A *goat* is … […]
3' Like a fish [*her body is do*]*tted.*
4' Like *šaršerru*-paste [her ch]eek is pale.
5' Her head is a lion's head,
6' Her teeth are donkey's teeth.
7' … of a dog …
8' … in a *hole* …

1' …
2' Her [h]eart …
3' Do (f.) not return! …
4' The donkey …
5' That she has caught …
6' Catch (f.) !
7'–8' …

Commentary

Obv.2': The spelling *e-en-zu* for *ezzu*, "furious" (so Cavigneaux/Al-Rawi 1994, 89) is difficult, see Farber (2014, 319). The occurrence of a goat in this context remains obscure.

Obv.5': Cavigneaux/Al-Rawi (1994) read *qá-qá-ad ka-*[*al-ba-tim*], but the last sign before the break is probably /ne/, see BIN 2, 72: 2 (№ 159): *pa-ni lab-ba-tim i-šim-ši* ^{d}*Én-líl*$^{!}$ and the MB Lamaštu incantation MC 17, 443ff.: 11 *qaqqad*(SAG.DU)*-sa qaqqad*(SAG.DU*-ad*) *ne-e-ši ši-in-na-at imēri*(ANŠE) *ši-in-*[*n*]*a-a-ša*.

№ 162: Or. 66, 61

SEAL No.: 7225
Copy: Michel 1997, 61
Tablet Siglum: Kt 94/k 821
Photo: Michel 1997, pl. I
Edition: Michel 1997, 59–64; Farber 2014, 74f., 149, 201–205
Studies: Ford 1999; Wasserman 2003 Cat. No. 117; Michel 2003, 138; Mayer 2003, 232/241, Hecker 2008, 64; Barjamovic 2015; Zomer 2018a, 21 fn. 56/190
Collection: Anadolu Medeniyetleri Müzesi, Ankara
Provenance: Kaneš
Measurements: 5.3 × 5.0 cm
Procedure: No

Introduction

A clay amulet-like tablet (*tabula ansata*), without pictographic rendering. Found in a private house together with the archive of the merchant Šalim-Aššur, son of Issu-Arik, see Barjamovic (2015, 68). Lamaštu is described and her dreadful actions listed, but no solution is offered.

Obverse

1 *e-za-at pu-ul-ḫa-at*
2 *i-lá-at na-ma-ra-at*
3 *ba-ar-ba-ra-tum*
4 *ma-ra-at A-né-em*
5 *i-na sà-sé-em*
6 *mu-ša-*‹‹mu››*-bu-ša*
7 *i-na el-pé-tem*
8 *ru-*‹‹du››*-ba-sà*
9 *eṭ-lá-am lá-sí-ma-am*

Lower Edge

10 *ta-kà-lá*
11 *pá-ra-am ar-ḫa-am*

Reverse

12 *ta-na-sà-ḫa-am*
13 *zi-ba-sú ṣa-ḫu-ru-tem*
14 *na-pu-ṣú-um tù-na-pí/-iṣ*
15 *ší-bu-tem ta-ša-/qí-a-mì*
16 *me-e bi-iš-re-em*
17 *ší-ip-tum lá ia-tum*
18 *ší-pá-at Ni-ki-li-il*$_5$
19 *be-el ší-pá-tem*

20 *Ni-kà-ra-ak*
21 *ta-dí-ší-ma*
22 *a-na-ku al-qé-/ší*

Translation

1–2 She is fierce! She is fearsome! She is a goddess! She is radiating!
3–4 She is a she-wolf! The daughter of Anum!
5–6 In the grass is her dwelling,
7–8 in the *alfafa*-grass is her lair.
9–11 She holds back the agile young man.
12–13 She tears off the tail of the quick mule.
13–14 She smites entirely the little ones.
15–16 She gives the old ones amniotic fluid to drink – so they say.
17–19 The spell is not mine, it is the spell of Ninkilil, the lord of spells!
20–22 Ninkarrak cast it, I received it.

Commentary

14: The use of the *napāṣum* is otherwise used to denote Lamaštu's expulsion from heaven, cf. BIN 4, 126: 12 (№ 160).

№ 163: TIM 9, 63d

SEAL No.: 7133
Copy: Van Dijk 1976, 63
Tablet Siglum: IM 21180$_{x}$
Photo: –
Edition: Tonietti 1979, 305/307
Studies: Farber 1981, 67; Cunningham 1997 Cat. No. 359; Wasserman 2003 Cat. No. 172
Collection: Iraq Museum, Baghdad
Provenance: Unknown
Measurements: 10.5 × 7.0 cm
Procedure: No

Introduction

Incantation collective containing three Sumerian Lamaštu spells. On the left edge, the remains of an Akkadian Lamaštu incantation.

Left Edge

i 1 [*a-a i-t*]*u-ru*
i 2 ⸢x⸣ *a-a i-tu-ur*
i 3 ⸢x x ti$^{?}$-la$^{?}$⸣
----
ii 1 ka-inim-ma ^{d}*Lamaštu*(DÌM.ME)

Translation

i 1 [May *they*$^{?}$ *not*] *return*!
i 2 … may she$^{?}$ not return!
i 3 … *life*$^{?}$
----
ii 1 Incantation (against) Lamaštu

№ 164: YOS 11, 19a

SEAL No.: 7134
Copy: van Dijk/Goetze/Hussey 1985 Pls. XXII/XXIII
Tablet Siglum: YBC 4601
Photo: https://collections.peabody.yale.edu/search/Record/YPM-BC-018666
Edition: van Dijk/Goetze/Hussey 1985, 25f.; Farber 2014, 260
Studies: van Dijk/Goetze/Hussey 1985, 26; Cunningham 1997 Cat. No. 394; Wasserman 2003 Cat. No. 248
Collection: Yale Babylonian Collection, New Haven
Provenance: Larsa area
Measurements: 6.3 × 2.8 cm
Procedure: No

Introduction
This text, the first of two spells (on the reverse, an Akkadian incantation against snakes), focuses on the treacherous behaviour of Lamaštu. She pretends to be helping, but actually kills her victims. Unlike other texts, the incantation ends on a happy note: through divine intervention, the demoness is expelled and tied to a far-away tree.

Obverse
1 *ez-ze-et* ⌜*bi*$^{?}$⌝*-ša-at* [... *-a*]*t*
2 *mu-ut-ta-ad-ri-ra-at šerrī*(TUR$^{?}$*-r*[*i*$^{?}$]) [...]
3 *ú-ul a-sà-a-at ú-ra-ak-k*[*a-as abunnatam*$^{?}$]
4 *ú-ul ša-ab-sà-at ú-ka-ap-pa-ar š*[*e*]*-er-ra-am*
5 *wa-ra-aḫ e-ri-a-tim im-ta-na-an-nu*
6 *ba-ba-am ša wa-li-it-tim sa-an-da-a*[*k*] *pa-ri-ka-at*
7 *ki-ib-sà-at būlim*(MÁŠ.ANŠE) *ir-te-né-di*
8 *i-na uz-zi-im ša li-li-im i-ḫi-a-ar ma-tam*
9 *i-ṣa-ab-ba-at eṭ-lam i-na šu-li-im*
10 *wardatam*(KI.SIKIL) *i-na me-lu-li-im*
11 *ṣé-eḫ-ra-am i-na bu-ud ta-ri-tim*
12 *i-mu-ra-ši-ma i-la-an ki-la-al-la-an*
13 *ú-še-ṣi-a-ši a-pa-ni*
14 *ú-ša-aḫ-li-pa-aš-ši ṣé-er-re-*ni_{7}(nim)
15 *ir-ku-sú-ni-iš-ši i-na* ^{giš}*bīni*$^{!}$(ŠI[NI]G) / [*i-n*]*a*$^{!}$ *qá-ba-al ta*$^{!}$*-a*[*m*$^{!}$*-tim*]
16 [...] *A*$^{!}$*-ra*$^{!}$*-a*[*ḫ*]*-tim* [... / ...] ⌜x ši$^{?}$⌝ [...]

Lower edge
17 [ka]-inim-ma ^{d}*Lam*[*aštu*](D[ÌM.ME.KAM]) / (...) *še*$^{!}$*-er*$^{!}$*-*[*ri-im*]

Translation

1 She is fierce, she is *evil*?, she is...
2 She is roaming around *the c*[*hildren*? (…)]
3 Although she is not a physician, she bandages [*the umbilical cord*?].
4 Although she is not a midwife, she wipes off the new-born,
5 She keeps counting the months of the pregnant women,
6 She is blocking regularly the gate of the woman who is giving birth.
7 She keeps accompanying the stride of the livestock.
8 She is examining the land in a demon's rage:
9–11 she takes hold of the young man in the street, of the young woman in the dance, of the little-one on the shoulder of the nurse.
12–14 When the two gods saw her, they threw her out of the window, they made her slink through the door socket.
15 They have tied her to a *tamarisk*? in the middle of the sea.
16 ... *in the Araḫtum-canal*...
17 Incantation (against) Lamaštu... babi[e(s)].

Commentary

1: We prefer ⌜*bi*?⌝-*ša-at* (with Farber 2014, 260) rather than *gap-ša-at* or *ga-ša-at* (from *gâšum*, as in VS 10, 214: ii 1, Agušaya A).

2: Foster (2005, 174) reads: *i*!-*l*[*a-at*]?, and translates "she is un[canny]", probably based on *i-la-at* in YOS 11, 20: 2 (№ 165).

3–6: A *hysteron-proteron*, namely an inverse temporal order of events, from the moment when the baby is born back to the pregnancy and the birth itself (see Wasserman 2005b).

6: For *sandak*, see Farber (2014, 318).

7: See Mayer (2003, 236).

8: See George (1987, 360).

11: For *bu-ud ta-ri-tim* in this line, cf. Wasserman (2003, 88).

13–14: For the terminative adverbials *apāni*... *ṣerrēni*, "through the window... through the door socket", see Mayer (1995, 184). Cf. further YOS 11, 8: 8 (№ 58) *e-l*[*i*] *š*[*a*]-*ma-n*[*i*?] (Wasserman 2003, 116 fn. 105).

№ 165: YOS 11, 20

SEAL No.: 7135
Copy: van Dijk/Goetze/Hussey 1985 Pl. XXIV
Tablet Siglum: YBC 9846
Photo: cf. SEAL No. 7135
Edition: van Dijk/Goetze/Hussey 1985, 26; Farber 2014, 74f./194/201–204
Studies: Farber 1985, 65; Cunningham 1997 Cat. No. 396; Wasserman 2003 Cat. No. 250; Zomer 2018a, 191f.
Collection: Yale Babylonian Collection, New Haven
Provenance: Larsa area
Measurements: 5.2 × 7.3 cm
Procedure: No

Introduction

A single incantation on a landscape-oriented tablet. Note the curious position of the rubric tu-en-nu-ru. Lamštu's nefarious actions are described: no course of treatment is offered.

Obverse
(*line 13b precedes*)
1 *e-ze-et pa-al-ḫa-at*
2 *i-la-at a-mu-ra-at*
3 *ù ši-i ba-ar-ba-ra-tum*
4 [*m*]*a-ar-ti A-ni-i*[*m*]
5 [*s*]*a-sa-a-ti*$^{!?}$ *na-ar-b*[*a-ṣú*$^{?!}$*-ša*$^{?}$]

Lower Edge
6 ⌜id$^{?}$⌝ ri [x (x)] ra [x x x]

Reverse
7 [*ina as-ku*]*-pa-ti ma-za-*[*zu-ša*]
8 [*al*]*pam*([G]U$_4$$^{!}$) *a*$^{!}$*-li*$^{!}$*-ka i*$^{!}$*-ka-a*[*l*$^{!}$*-la*]
9 *i*$^{!}$*-mi*$^{!}$*-ra šu-u*[*r*]*-bu-ṣú* ú [x x]
10 *ṣé-eḫ-ru-tim ḫu-nu-qú*
11 *ú-ḫa-an-na-aq ra-ab-bu-*[*t*]*im*!
12 *i-ša-qi-a-am me-e pí-iš-ri*
13a tu-

Obverse
13b en-nu-ru

Translation

1–2	She is fierce, she is frightening, she is a goddess, *she has awe-inspiring radiance*$^{?}$.
3–4	Indeed, she is a she-wolf, the daughter of Anum,
5–7	*the grass is* [*her la*]*ir*$^{?}$, … [in the th]reshold is [her *lo*]*cation*$^{?}$,
8–9	*She is ho*[*lding back*$^{?}$] *the walking* [*b*]*ull*$^{?}$, [*she is forcing*$^{?}$] the donkey to sit.
10–12	She strangles the small-ones, she compels the big ones to drink the amniotic fluid.
13	tu-en-nu-ru

Commentary

2:	Based on later Lamaštu incantations, we take *a-mu-ra-at* for *na-mu-ra-at*, "she has awe-inspiring radiance" (see, e.g., SpTU 3, 84: 62: ÉN *ezzet šamrat ìl-at na-mur-rat u šī barbarat mā*[*rat* ^{d}*A-nu*]).
5/7:	For this restitution, see Lamaštu II 121 GIŠ.GI *manzassa sassatu*(Ú.KI.KAL) *rubussa* (Farber 2014, 113).
9–12:	For *mê b/pišri* "amniotic fluid", see Wasserman (2003, 89).
11:	For *ra-ab-bu-*[*t*]*im*$^{!}$, see Mayer (2003, 23f.).
13a–b:	Curiously, the scribe began to write the rubric on the last line of the reverse and finished it on the first line of the obverse (so, already Farber 1985, 65). If not merely due to scribal clumsiness (cf. Farber's remark: "very crude script", and the mistake in l. 2), this practice could perhaps be explained as a purposeful attempt to seal the text, i.e., to prevent further writing on the beginning of the obverse.

2.4.3 Wardat-lilî

In Mesopotamian thaumaturgy there existed two pairs of spectres who died young, before they could express their sexuality: *(W)ardat-lilîm* (ki-sikil-líl-lá) "phantom young woman" and *Eṭel-lilîm* (guruš-líl-lá) "phantom young man", and *Lilītu* (munus-líl-lá) "female phantom" and *Lilû* (lú-líl-lá) "male phantom". The haunting character of these creatures is engendered by their sexual deprivation and frustration. A first-millennium compendium of incantations against (W)ardat-lilî and Eṭel-lilî is known (Lackenbacher 1971), but for the second millennium only two spells are known: YOS 11, 92 (below) and the MB Studies Jacobsen 210 = BM 54716 (see Zomer 2018a, 227).

In the following text, Wardat-lilîm is depicted as a succubus, slipping through the window into people's houses, looking for a male victim to serve as a substitute groom.

№ 166: YOS 11, 92

SEAL No.: 7188
Copy: van Dijk/Goetze/Hussey 1985 Pl. LXXXI
Tablet Siglum: YBC 9841
Photo: cf. SEAL No. 7188
Edition: Farber 1989b, 16–22
Studies: van Dijk/Goetze/Hussey 1985, 51; Farber 1989b; Cunningham 1997 Cat. No. 406; Wasserman 2003 Cat. No. 264; Marchesi 2006, 35–38; Zomer 2018a, 227; Polinger Foster 2020, 132f.
Collection: Yale Babylonian Collection, New Haven
Provenance: Larsa area
Measurements: 11.0 × 5.0 cm
Procedure: No

Introduction

A rare case in which the subscript is found at the head of the text, becoming a superscript, a header. Wardat-lilî is a wind-like demoness that is related to Erra, the god of plague and death. The incantation relates that she died in "her prime like a fresh fruit", before she had any sexual experience. Sexually hungry, she is trying to find a man to satisfy her unfulfilled urges. Pointing at Wardat-lilî's youth as a reason for her wicked behaviour is similar to how other incantations relate to another female demoness: Lamaštu, who also behaved badly in her early days.

Obverse

1 ka-inim-ma *[W]a-ar-da-at li-li-i-im*
2 *re-e-di-it i-li-im Èr-ra*
3 *ba-a-ki*$^{!}$(DI)*-a-at ka-lu ša-ri-im*
4 *ša ki-i-ma in-bi-im*
5 *e-eš-ši-[i]m i-na la*$^{?}$*-li-[š]a*
6 *qá-a[t*$^{?!}$*-p]a*$^{?!}$*-at*

7 *a-na me-lu-l*[*i*]*-i-im*
8 *ri-i-*[*qá*]*-a-ma*
9 *i-im-me-l*[*e*]*-el-la*
10 *u*$_{4}$*-mi-ša-am*
11 *i-iš-ta-na-aḫ-ḫi-ṭa ka-da-aš-ša-am*
12 *i-na ri-ig-mi-ši-i-na i-ḫa-al-lu-ul sú-q*[*u*]*m*
13 *ú-ul i-ip-te* [*ḫ*]*a-wi-*[*i*$^{?}$*-ru-u*]*m*
14 *bu-di*$^{!}$(UD)*-i-*[*š*]*a*
15 *ša-ap-ti še*$_{20}$*-er*$^{!}$*-ri-i-*[*i*]*m*
16 *ra-ab*$^{!?}$(BA)*-ba-ta-am ú-ul* [*i*]*-ši-iq*
17 *na-ki-i-la-at*$^{!}$(LA) *bi-i-it abim*$^{?}$([A].BA)
18 *ú-ṣi*$^{?}$*-am-ma*
19 *qá-la-a-la-at-ma ú-ul* [*ú*$^{?}$*-li*$^{?}$*-id*$^{?}$]
20 *še*$_{20}$*-e-er-ra-a*[*m*]
21 *i-iṣ-ṣa-ab-tu-ú-ma*
22 *mu-us-sà nu-úḫ-ḫu-ul-lu-*[*um*]
23 *ú ši-i zi-qí-i-qù-u*[*m*]
24 *i-ra-ap-pu-du ṣe-e-ra-*[*am*]
25 *ú-ta-am-*[*m*]*i-i-ki*$^{!}$
26 *A-na-am ú An-ta-am*
27 *E-en-še*$_{20}$*-e-da ù Ḫa-da-ni-i-iš*
28 [*b*]*i-i-it e-er-ru-bu*
29 [*l*]*a te-er-ru-bi-i-ma*
30 [*ašar*$^{?}$] *ru-uʾ-ti a-ad-du-ú*
31 [*la tu*]*-la-ap-pa-ti-i-ma*

Reverse uninscribed

Translation

1 Incantation (against) Wardat-lilî.
2–3 The guide of the god Erra, the *weeper*$^{?}$ of all winds,
4–6 who was cut-off in her prime like a fresh fruit.
7–12 The (girls) spend (f.) time in dancing every day, the (girls) keep twirling in celebration. At their shout, the street *shuts away*.
13–14 A bridegroom did not deflower her.
15–16 She did not kiss the lip(s) of a baby, so tender.
17–18 She was canny, she left her *parental* house.
19–20 She was despised for not [*giving birth to*] a child.
21–24 And so, her husband, an evil storm, and she, a phantom, are roaming in the steppe.
25–27 I conjure you (f.) by Anum and Antum, Enšēda and Ḫadaniš:
28–29 You will not enter to the house which I enter!
30–31 [Where] I spit you will not touch!

Commentary

2: Cf. Mayer (2003, 236).

12: Since the vocalization of *i-ḫa-al-lu-ul* is (u), one tends to derive this form from *ḫalālum* II, "to pipe, murmur" (attested in post-OB sources). Still, the context leads one to consider *ḫalālum* I, (a/u), "to confine, shut away" (OB): the joyful cries of the dancing girls make the entire street stop its activities (so also Farber 1989b).

13–14: The idiom *būdam petûm* stands for the more common *sūnam* (or even *irtam*) *petûm*.

15: Note the grammatical incongruence between *šapi/ī* and *rabbatam*.

17–20: These lines accuse the demoness, in her pre-demonic stage, of breaking a marriage agreement by running away from her father's house after being betrothed.

30: Cf. Deller/Mayer/Sommerfeld (1987, 196).

2.5 Inanimate Objects

2.5.1 Bitumen

Bitumen was one of the rare raw materials available in ancient Mesopotamia proper. Unsurprisingly, the only incantation comprising this category deals probably with sealing and caulking.

№ 167: CUSAS 32, 20d

SEAL No.: 7200
Copy: George 2016 Pl. LXI
Tablet Siglum: MS 3086
Photo: George 2016 Pl. LX; CDLI P252095
Edition: George 2016, 151
Studies: George 2016, 150f.
Collection: Schøyen Collection, Oslo
Provenance: Unknown
Measurements: 15.5 × 6.5 cm
Procedure: No

Introduction

According to George (2016, 150f.), this incantation – found in an incantation collective – is the Akkadian version of the Sumerian spell CUSAS 32, 43. Although some phrases are parallel in the two incantations, their similarity is only partial. CUSAS 32, 20d is focused on bitumen and is concerned with sealing and waterproofing, whereas the Sumerian incantation does not mention this substance at all. The text begins probably with a short historiola.

Obverse
14' [...] ⸢x⸣ *a-na Urim*$_5^{ki}$ *i-te-*⸢*li*⸣ [x x x] ⸢x⸣-⸢ki$^?$⸣
15' [...]-⸢ur$^?$⸣ *a-ba-ra-ka-tim iṭ-ṭù-um iš-nu kar-r*[*a*$^?$-(*am*$^?$)]
16' [...]-⸢x⸣-*am a-na pi-šu šu-uk-na-ma le-sú ma-aḫ-ṣa-m*[*a*]
17' [...] ⸢x⸣ *li-it-ta-ra-ad* ka-inim-ma *iṭ-ṭù-*[*um*]
====

Translation

14' [When$^?$ (s)he] went up to Ur ...
15' [(s)he ...] the stewardesses. Bitumen *soaked the qu*[*ay*$^?$].
16' "Place (pl.) the [...] into his mouth and slap (pl.) his
17' cheek, so that [...] he goes down again and again!"
Incantation for bitumen.

Commentary

14': The first line is probably a short historiola, as in YOS 11, 5b: 9 (№ 114): *inūma Gula illiku mutūtam* "When Gula was walking in bravery".

15': We derive the verbal form *iš-nu* from *šanû* "to soak with water, to rinse" (AHw, 1167: "abspülen"). – The final word, opening with *kar-* could be *karṣum* (so George 2016, 151), but *karrum*, a by-form of *kārum* "quay" fits the context better.

16': The dominating act of striking one's cheek is found in ZA 71, 62a: 14' (№ 157, against the Evil Eye); RA 36, 3a: 14 (№ 144, trial).

2.5.2 Foods and Drinks

A small group of non-standardized incantations for obtaining food and drink and for enabling the preparation thereof.

№ 168: CT 42, 6e

SEAL No.: 7110
Copy: Figulla 1959 Pl. 13
Tablet Siglum: BM 15820
Photo: https://www.britishmuseum.org/collection/object/W_1896-0612-40
Edition: –
Studies: Farber 1981, 72 n. 3; Cunningham 1997 Cat. No. 349; Wasserman 2003 Cat. No. 62
Collection: British Museum, London
Provenance: Unknown
Measurements: 10.9 × 9.1 cm
Procedure: No

Introduction

Found with Sumerian and alloglot spells in an incantation collective, the setting of this compact text is nocturnal, for stars are mentioned. The hungry speaker's tone is agitated. Having no other option to get food, he calls for no less than a cessation of the entire universe until he receives his ration.

Reverse
iv

2	*kakkabū*(MUL^{meš}) *a-ka-al-la-ku-nu-ti*
3	*šamû*$^{?}$(AN.NA) *a-ka-al-la-ku-nu-ti*
4	*er-ṣe-tum a-ka-al-la-ki*
5	*An-nu-um a-ka-al-la-ka*
6	^{d}*En-líl a-ka-al-la-ka*
7	*a-di e-le-eq-qú-ú*
8	*ma-*[*á*]*š*$^{?}$*-t*[*i*]*-it-ti ù ku-ru-um-ma-ti*
9	[*šamû*$^{?}$(AN.NA) *šamû*$^{?}$(AN.N]A) *šamû*$^{?}$(AN.NA) *šamû*$^{?}$(AN.NA)
10	[tu$_{6}$-én]-é-nu-ru

Translation

2–4	Stars, I detain you! Heavens, I detain you! Earth, I detain you!
5–6	Anum, I detain you! Enlil, I detain you!
7–8	(You are detained) until I receive my drink and food rations!
9	[Heavens! Hea]vens! Heavens! Heavens!
10	[tu$_{6}$-én]-é-nu-ru

Commentary

7–8: A similar phraseology is found in an oath in the OAkk. letter RA 23, 25 (AO 4419 = Kienast/Volk 1995, 53f.).

8: CAD K, 578, 3a brings this line, reading [*mal-ti*]-*it-ti u ku-ru-um-ma-ti* (SB inc.), but, with Farber (1981, 72 fn. 3), we take this text as an OB incantation.

9: Following a photo (against the copy).

№ 169: JEOL 47, 58a

SEAL No.: 7222
Copy: Kouwenberg 2018–2019, 58
Tablet Siglum: Kt 91/k 502
Photo: Kouwenberg 2018–2019, 58
Edition: Kouwenberg 2018–2019, 59–66
Studies: Michel 2003, 138; Barjamovic/Larsen 2008, 145/147/149; Barjamovic 2015, 50f.
Collection: Anadolu Medeniyetleri Müzesi, Ankara
Provenance: Kaneš
Measurements: 4.8 × 4.8 cm
Procedure: No

Introduction
"Brewing pot" (*diqārum*) is a known metaphor for a bloated belly (similar to *namzītum*), thus one could place this incantation in the section dealing with gastrointestinal problems (as its succeeding incantation JEOL 47, 58b = № 31, cf. Kouwenberg 2018–2019, 69f.). However, since no reference to *libbum*, or "wind", or any pain is mentioned directly, we interpret this incantation literally, as a magical aid for the preparation of beer in a brewing pot.

Obverse
1 | *dí-qá-ru-mì dí-qá-ru-um*
2 | *ku-ub-ta-ki*$^{!}$(DI) *tí-lu-ma*
3 | *e-pá-ki ma-lá ga-ni-nem*
4 | *ma-ú-ki tí-am-tum*
5 | *pá-pá-sà-tù-ki*
6 | *ma-lá kà-sé-em*
7 | *ta-at*$^{?}$*-tí-ki ku-*⸢*ru*⸣*-ma*
8 | *ta-mu-a-tí* | AN *ú* AN-*tám*
9 | *La-aḫ-ma-am ú Du-ra-/am*
10 | *er-ṣa-tám ú na-*⸢*i-le*⸣*-/ša*
11 | *ta-mu-a-tí* | *a-*⸢*dí*⸣

Lower Edge
12 | *kà-ku-sà-am*
13 | *ù pì-tí-il*$_5$*-tám*
14 | *a-na-*⸢*dí-ú-ke*⸣*-ni*

Reverse
15 | *la ta-pá-šé-ri*

Translation

1	(Brewing) pot, Oh (brewing) pot!
2–3	Your heaviness is (like) a tell, your massiveness is as much as a storeroom!
4–7	Your water is (like) the sea, your *pulp* is as much as a (full) cup, your dripping is choice beer!
8–10	You are conjured by Anum and Antum, (by) Laḫmum (and) Dūrum, (by) the earth and her watercourses!
11–15	You are conjured: until I put a plug and cord in you, you shall not come loose!

Commentary

2: The *tīlum* "tell, (ruin) mound", is an image that appears in another OA incantation: *kalbum ṣalmum ittīlim rabiṣ* "a black dog is lying on the tell" Fs. Hirsch 427: 2–4 (№ 69).

7: We suggest the second sign in this line is AT, resulting in *ta-at*[?]*-tí-ki*, namely *tattīkki* (cf. *tattīku* "dribble, dripping", CAD T, 299f., attested in Bogh. and in SB texts) (Kouwenberg 2018–19, 59: *ta*-x-*DÍ-ki* and *ta-DU*[??]*-DÍ-ki* on p. 63). The next word is understood as *kurunma* "choice beer/wine" (an option raised by Kouwenberg 2018–2019, 63f.).

12: With Kouwenberg (2018–2019, 66) *kà-ku-sà-am* "may refer to a kind of lid, plug, or stopper". For *purussu* in OB incantations, see CUSAS 32, 32a: 9, 12 (№ 27).

2.5.3 Reeds

Reeds were a common material, utilized for a plethora of daily uses. The exact purpose of the sole incantation in this category is not clear.

№ 170: NABU 1996/30

SEAL No.: 7226
Copy: Hecker 1996, 21
Tablet Siglum: Kt a/k 320
Photo: –
Edition: Hecker 1996
Studies: Balkan 1953, 21; Veenhof 1996, 425; Farber 1996; Cunningham 1997 Cat. No. 336; Wasserman 2003 Cat. No. 108; Michel 2003, 137; Barjamovic 2015, 66
Collection: Anadolu Medeniyetleri Müzesi, Ankara
Provenance: Kaneš
Measurements: 3.0 × 4.0 cm
Procedure: No

Introduction

This text was found in the house of Uzua in a lot containing an incantation against a dog (Fs. Hirsch 427 = № 69), two copies of a royal inscription from Assur and a short economic document (see Barjomovic 2015, 66).

Obverse
1 *qanûm*(GI)-*mì qanûm*(GI) [(x)]
2 *qanûm*(GI) *bu-uk-ru*
3 *a-pè-em ša-ap*$^{!}$-*li-iš*
4 *er-ṣa-tum ú-ra-sú*
5 *e-li-iš ša*$^{!}$-*ra-ta-šu*

Reverse
6 *i-ḫ̮a-ni-*⸢*ma*⸣
7 [x-x-(x)]-ba-at
8 [x-x-(x)]-ze-e
9 [x-x-(x)]-⸢sí⸣-in
(*broken*)

Translation
1 Reed! Oh Reed!
2–3 Reed! Descendant of the reed-bed!
3–4 Below on earth is its plot of land!
5–6 Above its 'hairs' are abundant!

(*Rest too fragmentary for translation*)

2.6 Miscellaneous

This section contains incantations whose designation is unclear, but which are still readable. The rubric in these texts is either non-specific (tu-e-en-ne-nu-ri, Fs. de Meyer 87: 9' (№ 172) or entirely missing.

№ 171: CUSAS 32, 58

SEAL No.: 26869
Copy: George 2016 Pl. CXXIX
Tablet Siglum: MS 3323
Photo: George 2016 Pl. CXXIX
Edition: Alster 2007, 52–54; George 2016, 163; Krebernik 2018, 43
Studies: George 2016, 160–162
Collection: Schøyen Collection, Oslo
Provenance: Unknown
Measurements: 7.2 × 8.0 cm
Procedure: No

Introduction
Alster (2007, 9) identified this text as a bilingual proverb. As the present interpretation stands, this is an Akkadian incantation with Sumerian passages against an unknown illness with a symptom of 'losing water', perhaps heat exhaustion, which could be remedied with salt. The fact that we find a correction gloss kúr in l. 4 suggests that this tablet belongs to a school context.

Obverse
1 é-a laḫ$_4$ lú a$^!$ sur(-ra) la-ba-an-laḫ$_4$
2 *i-na bi-ti-ia al-li-ik-šum-ma*
3 *i-na ša-di-i ut-te-ra-aš-šu*$^!$
4 me-luḫ-ḫa ù-luḫ-ḫa ‹‹sag$^{?!}$›› ḫé-gál-la$^!$(AB)
kúr
5 *ki-ma ú-te-ra-aš-šu ḫi-iṣ*$^!$(IŠ)*-ba-am na-ši-i*
6 *ḫé-gal-la ša ṭá-ab-ti-im*

Translation
1 (Sum.) From the house they brought (him). They could not bring the person *who was losing water*.
2–3 I went from my house towards him and sent him back to the East.
4 (Sum.) – In Meluḫḫa *saplings* are abundant! –
5–6 Since I sent him back, he was carrying opulence, plenty of salt.

Commentary

1: lú a sur(-ra) is understood as a description of the patient's condition. Note that a – sur usually means "to urinate" (Civil 1964, 81).

1–2: Alternatively, é-a may be interpreted as the deity $^{(d)}$Ea.

3: With Meluḫḫa in l. 4, *šadî* refers to the cardinal point "East (Wind)", not "mountains".

4: For the equation of ^{giš}ù-luḫ = *pirḫum* "sapling", see OB Diri Nippur 221 (MSL 15, 20). For a spelling ^{giš}ù-luḫ-ḫa, see Civil (2010, 67). A wordplay between me-luḫ-ḫa and ù-luḫ-ḫa is probably at work here.

4–6: Goods are brought from far away countries also in VS 17, 23 (№ 134, for love).

5: For constructions similar to *ḫiṣbam naši* see Wasserman (2003, 54).

№ 172: Fs. de Meyer 87

SEAL No.: 7198
Copy: Cavigneaux/Al-Rawi 1994, 87
Tablet Siglum: IM 90647
Photo: –
Edition: Cavigneaux/Al-Rawi 1994, 87f.
Studies: Wasserman 2003 Cat. No. 151
Collection: Iraq Museum, Baghdad
Provenance: Sippar
Measurements: –
Procedure: No$^{?}$

Introduction
Very little can be understood of this badly written and confused text (Cavigneaux/Al-Rawi 1994, 87: "quel imbroglio!"). First-person speech can be identified (ll. 1/5), and different objects, whose commonality is unclear, are listed (l. 4). Precious metals are also mentioned (ll. 6/7). The incantation ends probably in line 9, with the paratextual term *awātum* "spell" (lit. "word").

Obverse

1	*ia-ú sa-am-ku-um ti-bí-ia* ⸢*ki*$^{?}$*-ma*$^{?}$⸣
2	IM ŠE.GA bi *ma-ri ki-*⸢*iš*$^{?}$⸣ […]
3	*a-‹bu-ul›-la-am* ‹‹bu-ul›› *ḫa-ri-pu-um* [(x)]
4	*ḫa-al-ḫa-‹la*$^{?}$*›-tum ma-ia-al* ⸢x⸣ [x x]
5	im ma pa ab nu ki *a-na-ku*$^{?}$ [(…)]
6	ta ḫal$^{?}$ *ku-di-im kaspam*(KÙ.BABBAR) *ki-la-ma*
7	*ḫurāṣum*(KÙ.GI) *ki-la ša ki-ma* [x]
8	*ti-iṣ-ba*$^{?}$*-ta ki-la* ⸢x⸣ ú
9	⸢*a*⸣*-wa-tum pa* ⸢*ra* x x⸣ […] / ⸢x⸣ (x) […]

Reverse

1'	⸢x⸣ […]
2'	al ga […]
3'	pa e […]
4'	ki ḫi l[i …]
5'	KI.SIKIL ⸢x⸣ […]

Lower Edge

6'	[(x) *e*]*l mu* ⸢x x⸣ *ša-ra*
7'	*bīt*(É) ^{d}Nin-DU ud a ka ni ma me

Left Edge

8' a ka ma ni

9' tu-e-en-ne-nu-ri

Translation

1–2 Mine is …, my rising [is like] a *pleasant wind, the son of* …

3–4 *At the gate* – a lamb, a drum, a bed of …

5 … am I.

6–7 … hold (pl.) the silver! Hold (pl.) the gold which is like … !

8 Enclose (pl.)! hold (pl.)!

9 A word …

1'–4' (*broken*)

5' A girl …

6' …

7' The temple of NinDU …

8' …

9' tu-e-en-ne-nu-ri

Commentary

1: We refrain from translating *sa-am-ku-um*. Naturally, *samku* "spiteful?" (CAD S, 118) is possible, but it is attested only in NA and makes little sense here. Cavigneaux/Al-Rawi (1994, 87) parsed the line differently: *ia-ú sa-am* "le mien est rouge" which is also unclear.

3: Cavigneaux/Al-Rawi (1994, 87): "il est peut-être d'une statue", having in mind A.LA.AM as phonetic writing of ALAM = *ṣalmum* (or *ṣa*!-*la-am*). We take a different path and suggest reading *a-‹bu-ul›-la-am* ‹‹bu-ul››, a muddled form of *abullam*.

9: If *awātum* denotes here "spell" (as in YOS 11, 12c: 37 = № 47), then this line marks the end of the incantation, and the continuation (on the reverse and the edges) belongs to another text, probably in syllabic Sumerian (note: pa-e, ki-sikil).

7': The deity ^{d}NinDU is known from the god list An = Anum I 104f., attested with ^{d}EnDU, see Cavigneaux/Krebernik (1998–2000, 339).

8': One may tentatively read *a-ka-ma-ni* > *ana kamāni* "to the sweet cake?". Possibly repeated in the garbled ending of l. 9' in a ka ni ma.

№ 173: YOS 11, 12d

SEAL No.: 7207
Copy: van Dijk/Goetze/Hussey 1985 Pls. XIII/XIV
Tablet Siglum: YBC 4625
Photo: cf. SEAL No. 7207
Edition: van Dijk/Goetze/Hussey 1985, 23 (no translation); Krebernik 2018, 40
Studies: Cunningham 1997 Cat. No. 437; Krebernik 2018
Collection: Yale Babylonian Collection, New Haven
Provenance: Larsa area
Measurements: 17.2 × 7.6 cm
Procedure: No

Introduction
After an alloglot opening comes an Akkadian incantation against a disease which seems to darken the patient's face.

Reverse

-----
38 [š]u ba-an-da-aḫ ⌜šu$^{?}$ ba$^{?}$-an$^{?}$-da$^{?}$⌝-ah ši-in-da-aḫ
39 ši-in-da-da-aḫ ši-in-da-[aḫ]
40 e-ri-PI-ni-GAR-ri ù-pa-ri-in-[x]
41 [*ú*$^{?}$]-*ba-la-am ki-ma na-ri-*[*im*]
42 *i-ka-ap-pu-ša ki-ma tiāmtim*(A.AB.⌜BA⌝)
43 ⌜*ù*⌝ *ú-pi-il-li-a pa-ni-šu ip-šu-u*[*š*]
====
(*Rest uninscribed*)

Translation
38–39 *šubandaḫ labandaḫ šindaḫ*, *šindabaḫ šindaḫ*
40 …
41 [It] is carrying away like a river.
42 [It] is abundant like the sea.
43 Verily, it darkened (lit. smeared) his face (as with) charcoal.

Commentary
41: Less likely but not impossible is [*i*$^{?}$]-*ma-la-am*.
43: As we take it, this line describes a symptom caused by the unnamed disease. It may, however, refer to a procedure.

№ 174: YOS 11, 16a // YOS 11, 77b

SEAL No.: 7210
Copy: van Dijk/Goetze/Hussey 1985 Pls. XVIII/XIX; Pl. LXXII
Tablet Siglum: YBC 5328; YBC 9898
Photo: https://collections.peabody.yale.edu/search/Record/YPM-BC-019392
cf. SEAL No. 7210
Edition: van Dijk/Goetze/Hussey 1985, 24 (no translation)
Studies: Cunningham 1997 Cat No. 392a–b; Wasserman 2003 Cat No. 245/261
Collection: Yale Babylonian Collection, New Haven
Provenance: Larsa area
Measurements: 6.8 × 5.3 cm (YBC 5328); 7.5 × 5.0 cm (YBC 9898)
Procedure: No

Introduction

The incantation might be addressed against a scorpion, a creature which, according to CUSAS 10, 19: 4 (№ 86), lives in the *asurrûm*. The order to keep away is also typical to incantations against scorpions.

Text A = YOS 11, 16a; Text B = YOS 11, 77b

1	A1	[*ṣe*$^{?}$]*-et er-ṣe-tim* / *ṭà-ab*
	B10	[...]*-ṣe-tim ṭa-ab*
2	A2	*ṣe-et a-sú-ri-im* / *na-pi-ša-am i-šu*
	B11–12	⸢*a*⸣*-sú-ri na-pi-ša-am*$^{!}$ [*i*]*-šu-ú*
3	A3	*it-ta-ṣe-a-ku-um tu-ú*$^{!}$ {x} / *ša a-wi-lu-tim du-up-pi-ir*
	B13–15	*lu-ta-di-ku ta-a ša a-wi-lú-ti du-up-pi-ir* tu-ú-en-nu-ri

Translation

1 [*The gro*]*wth*$^{?}$ of the earth – (how) good it is!
2 The growth of the footing of the wall has a (pleasant) smell:
3 The spell of mankind has come out towards you – stay away!
(Var.:) Let me cast the spell of mankind on you – stay away!
tu-ú-en-nu-ri

Commentary

1: In view of A2 it is tempting to restitute [*ṣe*$^{?}$]*-et er-ṣe-tim ṭà-ab*, but *ṣītum* (or *ṣētum*) is a f. noun, a fact which precludes *ṭāb* from being its predicate. The provisional translation offered here tries to accommodate this difficulty by splitting the line to a quasi-cleft sentence.

3: The duplicates differ here slightly: in text B the magician introduces himself in the first-person voice.

№ 175: YOS 11, 67a // NABU 2019/43a

SEAL No.: 7212
Copy: van Dijk/Goetze/Hussey 1985 Pl. LXVI; Wagensonner 2019b
Tablet Siglum: MLC 640; MLC 334
Photo: cf. SEAL No. 7212
Edition: Cavigneaux/Al-Rawi 1994, 81f.; Wagensonner 2019b
Studies: van Dijk/Goetze/Hussey 1985, 44; Farber in van Dijk/Goetze/Hussey 1985, 44; George 1987, 360; Cavigneaux/Al-Rawi 1994, 81f.; Cunningham 1997 Cat. No. 284; Wasserman 2003 Cat. No. 257; Rendu-Loisel 2018, 104
Collection: Yale Babylonian Collection, New Haven
Provenance: Larsa area
Measurements: 5.53 × 8.31 cm; 5.43 × 6.6 cm
Procedure: Yes

Introduction

These parallel texts contain two incantations each. The first, mainly in syllabic Sumerian, ends with an Akkadian address to Enlil and an Akkadian procedure. The second, entirely in Sumerian, presents the well-known sevenfold appellation to heaven and earth, and to different officials.[257] Interestingly, the reverse of NABU 2019/43 is oriented at 90° to the obverse, i.e., the lines are arranged as columns.

Cunningham (1997 Cat No. 284) suggested that YOS 11, 67a is "possibly directed against evil daimons". Van Dijk (1985, 44) seems to have taken it as an incantation against dogs, for he read ^{d}En-líl muḫ-ur-gi$_7$-ra-ka (ll. 5, 6). As we read these two lines, they contain an Akk. exclamation *muḫur zērâka* "*appeal to* your begetter!", a formula which is unknown from other incantations and is more typical of a prayer. The text can be safely tagged as an incantation, albeit lacking a subscript, as seen in the rubric *kikkittaša/kikkiṭṭaša* (l. 7) and the exclamations on the reverse. The designation of this text remains unclear.

Text A = YOS 11, 67; Text B = NABU 2019/43

Obverse

1 A1 al ⌜mu-mu⌝
B1 al ⌜mu-mu⌝

2 A2 ki ⌜mu-mu⌝
B2 ki$^!$ mu-⌜mu⌝

3 A3 al-⌜ma⌝ ^{d}En-ki-⌜ke$_4$⌝
B3 al-ma ^{d}En-ki-⌜ke$_4$⌝

257 For seven-times repetitions, see Farber in van Dijk/Goetze/Hussey 1985, 44. See, more recently, Murad 2016: 8–9 and Wagensonner 2019b ad ll. 11–16.

4 A4 *ki-ma* ⸢^{d}⸣En-ki-ke$_4$
B4 *ki*$^{!}$*-ma* ^{d}En-ki-ke$_4$

5 A5 ^{d}*En-líl mu-ḫu-ur ze-*⸢*ra-ka*⸣
B5 ^{d}*En-líl mu-ḫu-ur ze-ra-ka*

6 A6 *mu-ḫu-ur ze-*⸢*ra*⸣*-*[*ka*]
B6 ⸢*mu*⸣*-ḫu-*⸢*ur*⸣ *ze-ra-ka*

7 A7 *kikiṭṭašû*(KI.KI.BI) 2 *an-ni-a-tim* ⸢*i-na*$^{?}$ É$^{?}$⸣ [x]
B7 *kikiṭṭašû*(KI.KI.BI) 2$^{!}$ *an-ni-a-tum i-na* ⸢x-*nim*⸣ [...]

8 A8 *la-bi-ri-im* ⸢*pa-ni* ⸢x⸣-[x-x]
B8 *la-bi-ri-im pa-ni* ⸢x-x⸣-[x]

9 A9 *ta-*⸢x⸣-[...]
B9 *te*$^{?}$*-ṣí-ir-ma i-na bi-ti* [(...)]

10 A10 (r.1) *ù* ⸢*il*$^{?}$*-ta-nim i*$^{?}$⸣-[*ba*$^{?}$*-lu*$^{?}$*-uṭ*$^{?}$]
B10 [*ù*$^{?}$] *il-ta-nim i-ba-l*[*u*$^{?}$*-uṭ*$^{?}$]

Translation

1–2 The *heaven*$^{?}$ is growing! The earth is growing!
3–4 The *heaven*$^{?}$ ... by Enki! The earth ... by Enki!
5–6 Oh Enlil! *Appeal to* your begetter! *Appeal to* [your b]egetter!
7–10 Its procedure: You will *draw*$^{?}$ these two in the old ... the face of [...], as well as in the house, [– in its *south side*$^{?}$] and north side. He will be w[ell].

Commentary

1–2: mu-mu is understood as a syllabic reading for mú-mú "to grow", and the couple al ... ki... is cautiously taken as a variant of an... ki... found on the following incantation (ll. 11–12).
3–4: ma is understood as syllabic reading for ma$_4$, a variant of mú(SAR).
7: In B7 the sign before *-nim* (seen clearly on the photo) cannot be deciphered (perhaps la$^{?}$).
8: For this line in text A, Cavigneaux/Al-Rawi (1994, 82) suggested *pāni a*[*wīlim*].
10: The line may end with the promise *iballuṭ* "he will be well", although it is not clear what the malevolent agent is, nor who is the patient.

List of Excluded Texts

№ 176 **AMD 1, 243 (fig. 2)b**

SEAL: No. 7184
Tablet Siglum: BM 79938
Copy: Finkel 1999, 243 (fig. 12)
Provenance: Tell ed-Dēr$^{?}$
Edition: Finkel 1999, 218f.
Measurements: 4.7 × 5.7 cm
Studies: Finkel 1999, 213–250
Photo: https://www.britishmuseum.org/collection/object/W_1889-1014-486
Remarks: –
Subscript: –

№ 177 **AMD 1, 247 (fig. 12)**

SEAL: No. 7195
Tablet Siglum: U.30503
Copy: Finkel 1999, 247 (fig. 12)
Provenance: Ur
Edition: –
Measurements: 10.3 × 4.7 cm
Studies: Finkel 1999, 235f.; Shaffer 2006, 26; Charpin 2020
http://www.ur-online.org/subject/52760/
Photo: –
Remarks: Contains the phrase: "The incantation is not mine, (it is) the incantation of Ningirim". Signs of a dating are found on the lower edge.
Subscript: –

№ 178 **CUSAS 32, 20a**

SEAL: No. 7199
Tablet Siglum: MS 3086
Copy: George 2016 pl. LXI
Provenance: Unknown
Edition: –
Measurements: 15.5 × 6.6 cm
Studies: –
Photo: George 2016 pl. LX; CDLI P252095
Remarks: Final rubric preserved: [tu$_6$-é]n-é-nu-ru
Subscript: k[a-inim-ma …]

№ 179 **Finkel (*forthcoming*)/a**

SEAL: –
Tablet Siglum: Private Collection
Copy: –
Provenance: Unknown
Edition: –
Measurements: –
Studies: Zomer 2018a, 231
Photo: –
Remarks: Final rubric preserved: tu$_6$-én-é-nu-⸢ru⸣
Subscript: ka-inim-ma é-gal-ku$_4$-ra

№ 180 **Finkel (*forthcoming*)/b**

SEAL: –
Tablet Siglum: Private Collection
Copy: –
Provenance: Unknown
Edition: –
Measurements: –
Studies: Zomer 2018a, 231
Photo: –

Remarks: Incipit: *zittum ilat u šarrat*
Subscript: ka-inim-ma é-gal-ku$_4$-ra

№ 181 **Finkel (*forthcoming*)/c**

SEAL: –
Copy: –
Edition: –
Studies: Zomer 2018a, 231
Photo: –
Remarks: Incipit: *baštum ilat baštum šarrat*
Subscript: ka-inim-ma é-gal-ku$_4$-ra

Tablet Siglum: Private Collection
Provenance: Unknown
Measurements: –

№ 182 **TIM 9, 67a**

SEAL: No. 7169
Copy: van Dijk 1976 Pl. LVI
Edition: –
Studies: Farber 1981, 57 (no. 29); Cunningham 1997 Cat. No. 360; Wasserman 2003 Cat No. 175
Photo: –
Remarks: Mostly obscure (with possible non-Akkadian phrases inserted). In fact, the clearest part of it is the final rubric [t]u-é[n]-é-nu-ru (l. 18). Its designation – against a snake or a scorpion – is only conjectural (following van Dijk, TIM 9, catalogue). Very likely a student training text (note the repeated *-kunu* possessive suffixes in ll. 5, 6, 7 and the phrases *abum*/*ummum* in ll. 8, 9, 10, 11).
Subscript: [muš/gír-tab da]b$_5$-bé-da

Tablet Siglum: IM 21180, 21
Provenance: Unknown
Measurements: 10.0 × 7.0 cm

№ 183 **TIM 9, 67b**

SEAL: No. 7291
Copy: van Dijk 1976 Pl. LVI
Edition: –
Studies: Farber 1981, 57 (no. 29); Cunningham 1997 Cat. No. 361; Wasserman 2003 Cat No. 176
Photo: –
Remarks: The only reason for labeling this text an incantation is the fact that the obverse of this tablet includes an incantation (according to its colophon). However, as said in the commentary to TIM 9, 67a, it is very likely that the obverse is a student training text. If so, it is most likely that the reverse is also a training text, and hence perhaps not an incantation.
Subscript: –

Tablet Siglum: IM 21180, 21
Provenance: Unknown
Measurements: 10.0 × 7.0 cm

№ 184 **YOS 11, 12b**

SEAL: No. 7206
Copy: van Dijk/Goetze/Hussey 1985, no. 12
Edition: –
Studies: Cunningham 1997 Cat. No. 385; Wasserman 2003 Cat No. 238
Photo: cf. SEAL No. 7206
Remarks: –
Subscript: –

Tablet Siglum: YBC 4625
Provenance: Larsa area
Measurements: 17.2 × 7.6 cm

№ 185 **YOS 11, 14a**

SEAL: No. 7208
Copy: van Dijk/Goetze/Hussey 1985 no. 14
Edition: –
Studies: Cunningham 1997 Cat. No. 388;

Tablet Siglum: YBC 4599
Provenance: Larsa area
Measurements: 7.5 × 10.6 cm

	Wasserman 2003 Cat No. 241		
Photo:	cf. SEAL No. 7208		
Remarks:	–		
Subscript:	–		

№ 186 YOS 11, 21a

SEAL:	No. 7211	**Tablet Siglum:**	YBC 4598
Copy:	van Dijk/Goetze/Hussey 1985, no. 21	**Provenance:**	Larsa area
Edition:	–	**Measurements:**	10.4 × 6.7 cm
Studies:	van Dijk/Goetze/Hussey 1985, 27; Cunningham 1997 Cat. No. 397; Wasserman 2003 Cat No. 251; Krebernik 2018, 19		
Photo:	cf. SEAL No. 7211		
Remarks:	Contains accompanying procedure introduced with KIN.KIN.BI.		
Subscript:	–		

№ 187 YOS 11, 77a

SEAL:	No. 7213	**Tablet Siglum:**	YBC 9898
Copy:	van Dijk/Goetze/Hussey 1985 no. 77	**Provenance:**	Larsa area
Edition:	–	**Measurements:**	7.5 × 5.0 cm
Studies:	van Dijk/Goetze/Hussey 1985, 47; Cunningham 1997 Cat. No. 403; Wasserman 2003 Cat. No. 260		
Photo:	cf. SEAL No. 7213		
Remarks:	Final rubric preserved: [tu-ú-en]-nu-ri		
Subscript:	–		

№ 188 ZA 75, 198–204g

SEAL:	No. 7214	**Tablet Siglum:**	IB 1554
Copy:	–	**Provenance:**	Isin
Edition:	Wilcke 1985, 202 (ll. 73–77)	**Measurements:**	25.0 × 8.0 cm
Studies:	Cunningham 1997 Cat. No. 320; Wasserman 2003 Cat. No. 28; Hecker 2008, 66–71 (Nr. VIII)		
Photo:	Wilcke 1985, after p. 208		
Remarks:	–		
Subscript:	–		

Bibliography

Abusch, T. 2016: *The Magical Ceremony Maqlû* (= AMD 10), Leiden/Boston.

Abusch, T./Schwemer, D. 2011: *Corpus of Mesopotamian Anti-Witchcraft Rituals. Vol. I* (= AMD 8/1), Leiden/Boston.

— 2016: *Corpus of Mesopotamian Anti-Witchcraft Rituals. Vol. II* (= AMD 8/2), Leiden/Boston.

Ali, M./Geller, M.J. 2020: *utukkū lemnūtu* (udug-hul) in a New Text from the Iraq Museum, *Iraq* 82, 1–11.

Al-Rawi, F.N.H./Dalley, S. 2000: *Old Babylonian Texts from Private House at Abu Habbah, Ancient Sippir* (= Edubba 7), London.

Alster, B. 1972: A Sumerian Incantation against Gall, *Or.* 41, 349–358.

— 2007: *Sumerian Proverbs in the Schøyen Collection* (= CUSAS 2), Bethesda.

Arbøll, T.P. 2018: Tracing Mesopotamian Medical Knowledge: A Study of maškadu and Related Illnesses, in: G. Van Buylaere/M. Luukko/D. Schwemer/A. Mertens-Wagschal (eds.), *Sources of Evil. Studies in Mesopotamian Exorcistic Lore* (= AMD 15), Leiden/Boston, 261–284.

— 2019: A Newly Discovered Drawing of a Neo-Assyrian Demon in BAM 202 Connected to Psychological and Neurological Disorders, *JMC* 33, 1–31.

Balkan, K. 1953: Ein kurzer Bericht über die neuen Tafeln aus Kültepe, in: Z.V. Togan (ed.), *Proceedings of the Twenty Second Congress of Orientalists held in Istanbul, September 15th to 22nd, 1951*, Istanbul, 18–21.

Baragli, B. 2019: Abracadabra Incantations: Nonsense or Healing Therapies?, *KASKAL* 16, 293–321.

Barjamovic, G. 2015: Contextualizing Tradition: Magic, Literacy and Domectic Life in Old Assyrian Kanesh, in: P. Delnero/J. Lauinger (eds.), *Texts and Contexts: The Circulation and Transmission of Cuneiform Texts in Social Space* (= SANER 9), Berlin/Boston, 48–86.

Barjamovic, G./Larsen, M.T. 2008: An Old Assyrian Incantation against the Evil Eye. *AoF* 35, 144–155.

Barrett, C.E. 2007: Was Dust Their Food and Clay Their Bread? Grave Goods, the Mesopotamian Afterlife, and the Liminal Role Of Inana/Ishtar, *JNER* 7, 7–65.

Bartelmus, A. 2016: *Fragmente einer grossen Sprache. Sumerisch im Kontext der Schreiberausbildung der kassitenzeitlichen Babylonien* (= UAVA 12), Boston/Berlin.

Bergmann, C.D. 2008: *Childbirth as a Metaphor for Crisis Evidence from the Ancient Near East, the Hebrew Bible, and 1QH XI, 1-18* (= BZAW 382), Berlin/New York.

Biggs, R.D. 1967: *ŠÀ.ZI.GA: ancient Mesopotamian potency incantations* (= TCS 2), Locust Valley.

— 1970: Review of C.J. Gadd and S.N. Kramer, UET 6/II, *JNES* 29, 58–59.

Black, J.A./Al-Rawi, F.N.H. 1987: A Contribution to the Study of Bird Names, *ZA* 77, 117–126.

Blaschke, T. 2018: *Euphrat und Tigris im Alten Orient* (= LAOS 6), Wiesbaden.

Bloch, G./Francoy, T.M./Wachtel, I./Panitz-Cohen, N./Fuchs, S./Mazar, A. 2010: Industrial apiculture in the Jordan Valley during Biblical times with Anatolian honeybees, *PNAS* 107, 11240–11244.

Böck, B. 2000: *Die babylonisch-assyrische Morphoskopie* (= AfO Beih. 27), Horn.

— 2007: *Das Handbuch Muššuʾu "Einreibung". Eine Serie sumerischer und akkadischer Beschwörungen aus dem 1. Jt. v. Chr.* (= BPOA 3), Madrid.

— 2009: Proverbs 30:18–19 in the Light of Ancient Mesopotamian Cuneiform Texts, *Sefarad* 69, 263–279.

Böhl, de Liagre, F.M.T. 1934: *Mededeelingen uit de Leidsche verzameling van spijkerschrift-inscripties II. Oorkonden uit de periode van 2000–1200 v. Chr.*, 1–6 (= 23–28).

— 1954: Zwei altbabylonische Beschwörungstexte: LB 2001 und 1001 (Tafel II), *BiOr* 11, 81–83.
Bottéro, J. 1985: *Mythes et rites de Babylone*, Paris.
Cagni, L. 1969: *L'Epopea di Erra* (= Studi Semitici 34), Rome.
Cammarosano, M./Weirach, K./Maruhn, F./Jendritzki, G./Kohl, P.I. 2019: They Wrote on Wax. Wax Boards in the Ancient Near East, *Mesopotamia* 54, 121–180.
Campbell, D.R.M./Fischer, S. 2018: A Hurrian Ritual Against Tootache: A Reanalysis of Mari 5, *RA* 112, 31–47.
Carter, J.G. 1990: *Herbal Dentistry: Herbal Dental Remedies From Ancient Times to the Present Day*, Chapel Hill.
Cavigneaux, A. 1994: Magica Mariana, *RA* 88, 155–161.
— 1995: La pariade du scorpion dans les formules magiques Sumériennes, *ASJ* 17, 152–158.
— 1996: Notes Sumérologiques, *ASJ* 18, 31–45.
— 1998: YOS 11 n° 29: 19-21 // n° 87: 18-20: séduction et thérapie!, *NABU* 1998/74.
— 1999: A Scholars Library in Meturan?, in: T. Abusch/K. van der Toorn (eds.), *Mesopotamian Magic: Textual, Historical, and interpretive Perspectives* (= AMD 1), Groningen, 251–273.
— 2003: Fragments littéraires susiens, in: W. Sallaberger/K. Volk/A. Zgoll (eds.), *Literatur, Politik, und Recht in Mesopotamien. Festschrift für Claus Wilcke* (= OBC 14), Wiesbaden, 53–62.
— 2020: Les traditions littéraires Suméro-Akkadiennes à Susa. Fragments littérraires Susiens (Suite), *RA* 114, 63–102.
— 2021: Scorpions insaisissables, *JMC* 37, 1–3.
Cavigneaux, A./Al-Rawi, F.N.H. 1994: Charmes de Sippar et de Nippur, in: H. Gasche/M. Tanret, C./Janssen/A. Degraeve (eds.), *Cinquante-deux reflexions sur le Proche-Orient Ancien offerts à Léon de Meyer* (= MHEO 2), Leuven, 73–89.
— 2002: Liturgies exorcistiques agraires, *ZA* 92, 1–59.
Cavigneaux, A./Donbaz, V. 2007: Le myth du 7.VII: Les jours fatidiques et le Kippour mésopotamiens, Or. 76, 293–335.
Cavigneaux, A./Krebernik, M. 1998–2000: ^{d}Nin-DU, *RlA* 9, 339.
Charpin, D. 1987: Notices prosopographiques, 2: les descendants de Balmunamḫe, *NABU* 1987/36.
— 2005: Chroniques bibliographiques 5. Economie et société à sippar et en babylonie du nord à l'époque paléo-babylonienne, *RA* 99, 133–176.
— 2020: En marge d'Ecrit Ur, 8 : l'incantation de Ningirim U.30503, *NABU* 2020/6.
Civil M. 1964: A Hymn to the Beer Goddess and a Drinking Song, in R.D. Biggs/J.A. Brinkman (eds.), *Studies Presented to A. Leo Oppenheim*, Chicago, 67–89.
— 1974: Medical Texts from Nippur, *JNES* 33, 329–338.
— 2010: *Lexical Texts from the Schøyen Collection*. (= CUSAS 12), Bethesda.
Clay, A.T. 1927: *Babylonian Inscriptions in the Collection of James B. Nies, vol. 4: Letters and Transactions from Cappadocia* (= BIN 4), New Haven.
Cohen, M. 1976: Literary Texts from the Andrews University Archaeological Museum, *RA* 70, 129–144.
Cohen, S. 1976: Studies in Sumerian Lexicography I, in: B.L. Eichler (ed.), *Kramer Anniversary Volume. Cuneiform Studies in Honor of Samuel Noah Kramer* (= AOAT 25), Neukirchen-Vluyn, 97–110.
Cohen, Y. 2018: An Old Babylonian List of Sheep Body-parts (BM 29663), in: S.V. Panayotov/L. Vacín (eds.), *Mesopotamian Magic and Medicine. Studies in Honor of Markham J. Geller* (= AMD 14), Leiden/Boston, 131–148.
Collins, T.J. 1999: *Natural Illness in Babylonian Medical Incantations*, PhD thesis University of Chicago.
Cooper, J.S. 1996: Magic and M(is)use: Poetic Promiscuity in Mesopotamian Ritual, in: M. E. Vogelzang/H.L.J. Vanstiphout (eds.), *Mesopotamian Poetic Language: Sumerian and Akkadian* (= CM 6), Groningen, 47–57.

Corfù, N.A./Oelsner, J. 2018: Beschriftete Hundestatuetten aus Mesopotamien, in: P. Attinger/A. Cavigneaux/C. Mittermayer/M. Novák (eds.), *Text and Image. Proceedings of the 61ᵉ Rencontre Assyriologique Internationale, Geneva and Bern, 22-26 June 2015* (= OBO 40), Leuven/Paris/Bristol, 131–138.

Couto-Ferreira M.E. 2014: She Will Give Birth Easily: Therapeutic Approaches to Childbirth in 1st Millennium BCE Cuneiform Sources, *Dynamis* 34, 289–315.

— 2018: Putting Theory into Practice: Kiṣir-Aššur's Experiment between Textual Knowledge and Practical Experimentation, in: S.V. Panayotov/L. Vacín (eds.), *Mesopotamian Magic and Medicine. Studies in Honor of Markham J. Geller* (= AMD 14), Leiden/Boston, 149–166.

Crane. E. 1999: *The World History of Beekeeping and Honey Hunting*, New York.

Cunningham, G. 1997: *"Deliver me from Evil": Mesopotamian Incantations, 2500–1500 BC* (= St. Pohl SM 17), Rome.

Dalley, S. 2001: Old Babylonian Tablets from Niniveh and possible Pieces of early Gilgamesh Epic, *Iraq* 63, 155–167.

— 2005: *Old Babylonian Texts in the Ashmolean Museum: Mainly from Larsa, Sippir, Kish and Lagaba* (= OECT 15), Oxford.

deJong-Ellis, M. 1986: Review: The Archive of the Old Babylonian Kititum Temple and Other Texts from Ishchali, *JAOS* 106, 757–786.

Deller, K./Mayer, W.R./Sommerfeld, W. 1987: Akkadische Lexikographie: CAD N, *Or.* 56, 176–218.

Delnero, P. 2019: Archives and Libraries in the Old Babylonian Period, in: K. Ryholt/G. Barjamovic (eds.), *Libraries before Alexandria: Ancient Near Eastern Traditions*, Oxford, 168–191.

van Dijk, J. 1969: Vert comme Tišpak, *Or.* 38, 539–547.

— 1971: *Nicht-kanonische Beschwörungen und sonstige literarische Texte* (= VS 17), Berlin.

— 1972: Une variante du thème de «L'Esclave de la Lune», *Or.* 41, 339–348.

— 1973: Une incantation accompagnant la naissance de l'homme, *Or.* 42, 502–507.

— 1976: *Cuneiform Texts: Texts of Varying Content* (= TIM 9), Wiesbaden.

van Dijk, J./Goetze, A./Hussey, M.I. 1985: *Early Mesopotamian Incantations and Rituals* (= YOS 11), New Haven.

Durand, J.-M. 1988: *Archives épistolaires de Mari* I/1 (= ARM 26/1), Paris.

— 2009: *La nomenclature des habits et des textiles dans les textes de Mari: Matériaux pour le Dictionnaire de Babylonien de Paris*, 1 (= ARM 30), Paris.

Durand, J.-M./Guichard, M. 1997: Les rituels de Mari (textes no. 2–5), *FM* 3, 19–74.

Dyckhoff, C. 1999: *Das Haushaltsbuch des Balamunamḫe*. Unpublished Dissertation, Münich.

Edzard, D.O. 1997: Old Babylonian Incantation Against Cattle Disease (1.121), in: W.W. Hallo (ed.), *Context of Scripture I*, Leiden, 426.

— 2004: Altbabylonische Literatur und Religion, in: D. Charpin/D.O. Edzard/M. Stol (eds.), *Mesopotamien. Die altbabylonische Zeit* (= OBO 160/4), Fribourg/Göttingen, 485– 640.

El-Ashry, E.S./Rashed, N./Salama, O.M et al. 2003: Components, therapeutic value and uses of myrrh, *Pharmazie* 58, 163–168.

Falkenstein, A. 1931: *Haupttypen der sumerischen Beschwörung: literarisch untersucht* (= LSS NF 1), Leipzig.

— 1939: Sumerische Beschwörungen aus Boğazköy, *ZA* 45, 8–41.

Faraone, C.A. 1988: Hermes but No Marrow: Another Look at a Puzzling Magical Spell, *Zeitschrift für Papyrologie und Epigraphik* 72, 279–286.

— 1995: The Mystodokos and the Dark-Eyed Maidens: Multicultural Influences on a Late-Hellenistic Incantation, in: M. Meyer/P. Mirecki (eds.), *Ancient Magic and Ritual Power*, Leiden, 297–334.

Farber, W. 1980–1983: Lamaštu, *RlA* 6, 439–446.

— 1981: Zur älteren akkadischen Beschwörungsliteratur, *ZA* 71, 51–72.

— 1984: Early Akkadian Incantations: Addenda et Subtrahenda, *JNES* 43, 69–71.

— 1985: Comments and Collations, in: van Dijk, J./Goetze, A./Hussey, M.I. 1985: *Early Mesopotamian Incantations and Rituals* (= YOS 11), New Haven.
— 1987: Rituale und Beschwörungen in akkadischer Sprache, in: O. Kaiser (ed.), *Rituale und Beschwörungen* I (= TUAT II/2), Gütersloh, 212–281.
— 1989a: *Schlaf, Kindchen, Schlaf: Mesopotamische Baby-Beschworungen und Rituale* (MC 2), Winona Lake.
— 1989b: (W)ardat-lilî(m), *ZA* 79, 14–35.
— 1990a: Magic at the Cradle: Babylonian and Assyrian Lullabies, *Anthropos* 85, 139–148.
— 1990b: *Mannam lušpur ana Enkidu*: Some New Thoughts about an Old Motif, *JNES* 49, 299–321.
— 1996: qanu'ummi qanu'um, *NABU* 1996/80.
— 2007a: Lamaštu and the dogs, *Journal for Semitics* 16, 635–645.
— 2007b: Lamaštu – Agent of a Specific Disease or Generic Destroyer of Health? in: I. L. Finkel/M. J. Geller (eds.), *Disease in Babylonia* (= CM 36), Leiden/Boston, 137–145.
— 2014: *Lamaštu. An Edition of the Canonical Series of Lamaštu Incantations and Rituals and Related Texts from the Second and First Millennia B.C.* (= MC 17), Winona Lake.
— 2018: Two Old Babylonian Incantation Tablets, Purportedly from Adab (A633 and A704), in: S.V. Panayotov/L. Vacín (eds.), *Mesopotamian Magic and Medicine. Studies in Honor of Markham J. Geller* (= AMD 14), Leiden/Boston, 189–202.
Figulla, H.H. 1959: *Cuneiform Texts from Babylonian Tablets in the British Museum, part 42* (= CT 42), London.
Figulla, H.H./Martin, W.J. 1953: *Ur Excavation Texts: Letters and Documents of the Old-Babylonian Period* (= UET 5), London.
Finkel, I.L. 1976: *HUL.BA.ZI.ZI. Ancient Mesopotamian Exorcistic Incantations.*Unpublished Dissertation Birmingham.
— 1980: The Crescent Fertile, *AfO* 27, 37–52.
— 1998: A study in Scarlet: Incantations against Samana, in: S. Maul (ed.), *Festschrift für Rykle Borger zu seinem 65. Geburtstag am 24. Mai 1994* (= CM 10), Groningen, 71–106.
— 1999: On Some Dog, Snake and Scorpion Incantations, in: T. Abusch/K. van der Toorn (eds.), *Mesopotamian Magic: Textual, Historical, and interpretive Perspectives* (= AMD 1), Groningen, 213–250.
— 2000: On Late Babylonian Medical Training, in: A.R. George/I.L. Finkel (eds.), *Wisdom, Gods, and Literature. Studies in Assyriologie in Honour of W.G. Lambert*, Winona Lake, 137–224.
— 2011: Drawings on Tablets, *Scienze dell'Antichità* 17, 337–344.
— 2018: Amulets Against Fever, in: S.V. Panayotov/L.Vacín (eds.), *Mesopotamian Magic and Medicine. Studies in Honor of Markham J. Geller* (= AMD 14), Leiden/Boston, 232–271.
Fish, T. 1939: Miscellanea, *Iraq* 6, 184–186.
Ford, J.N. 1998: "Ninety-Nine by the Evil Eye and One from Natural Causes": KTU_2 1.96 in its Ancient Near Eastern context, *UF* 30, 201–278.
— 1999: The Old Assyrian Incantation against Lamaštu kt 94/k 821, lines 11–13a, *NABU* 1999/56.
Foster, B.R. 1993: *Before the Muses: An Anthology of Akkadian Literature* (1st edition), Bethesda.
— 2005: *Before the Muses: An Anthology of Akkadian Literature* (3rd edition), Bethesda.
Foster, B.R./George, A.R. 2020: An Old Babylonian Dialogue between a Father and his Son, *ZA* 110, 37–61.
Frame, G. 1995: *Rulers of Babylonia: From the Second Dynasty of Isin to the End of Assyrian Domination* (= RIMB 2), Toronto.
Franke, S. 2013: Wiegenlied, in: S. Franke (ed.), *Als die Götter Mensch waren. Eine Anthologie altorientalischer Literatur*, 40.
Frassanito, P./Pettorini B. 2008: Pink and Blue: The Color of Gender, *Child's Nervous System* 24/8, 881–882.
Gabbay, U. 2019: Akkadian *gadādu*, "lacerate", *Or.* 88, 306–316.

Gadd, C.J./Kramer, S.N.: *Ur Excavation Texts VI. Literary and Religious Texts Second Part* (= UET 6/2), London.
Gager, J.G. 1992: *Curse Tablets and Binding Spells from the Ancient World*, New York/Oxford.
Gasche, H. 1994: Une figurine d'envoûtement paleo-babylonienne, in: P. Calmeyer (ed.), *Beiträge zur altorientalischen Archäologie und Altertumskunde. Festschrift für Barthel Hrouda zum 65. Geburtstag*, Wiesbaden, 97–102.
Geller, M.J. 1989: New Piece of Witchcraft, in: H. Behrens/D. Loding/M.T. Roth (eds.), *DUMU-E$_2$-DUB-BA-A. Studies in Honor of Åke W. Sjöberg* (= OPKF 11), Philadelphia, 193–206.
— 2002: Sumer, Incantations et magie, in: J. Briend/M. Quesnel/H. Cazelles (eds.), *Supplément au Dictionnaire de la Bible*. Paris. 269–283.
— 2004: Akkadian Evil Eye Incantations from Assur, *ZA* 94, 52–58.
— 2007: Incantations within Akkadian Medical Texts, in: G. Leick (ed.), *The Babylonian World*, New York/London, 389–399.
— 2010: *Ancient Babylonian Medicine. Theory and Practice*, Chicester.
— 2016: *Healing Magic and Evil Demons. Canonical Udug-hul Incantations* (= BAM 8), Boston/Berlin.
Geller, M.J./Wiggermann, F.A.M. 2008: Duplicating Akkadian Magic, in: R.J. van der Spek (ed.), *Studies in Ancient Near Eastern World View and Society. Presented to Marten Stol on the Occasion of his 65th Birthday*, Bethesda, 149–160.
de Genouillac, H. 1925: *Premières recherches archéologiques a Kich. Mission d'Henri de Genouillac 1911-1912. Notes archéologiques et inventaires, fac-similés, dessins et photographies, Tome II* (= PRAK II), Paris.
George, A.R. 1987: Review of J. van Dijk, Early Mesopotamian Incantations and Rituals (= YOS 11), *BSOAS* 50/2, 359–360.
— 1993: *House Most High. The Temples of Ancient Mesopotamia* (= MC 5), Winona Lake.
— 1994: tazzîqum, «vexation», *NABU* 1994/27.
— 1995: Ea in hiding, *NABU* 1995/68.
— 1999: The Dogs of Ninkilim: Magic against Field Pests in Ancient Mesopotamia, in: H. Klengel/J. Regner (eds.), *Landwirtschaft im Alten Orient. Ausgewählte Vorträge der XLI. Rencontre Assyriologique Internationale Berlin, 4-8.7.1994* (= BBVO 18), Berlin, 291–299.
— 2003: *The Babylonian Gilgamesh Epic: Introduction, Critical Edition and Cuneiform Texts*, Oxford.
— 2009: *Babylonian Literary Texts in the Schøyen Collection* (= CUSAS 10), Bethesda.
— 2010: Babylonian Literary Texts in the Schøyen Collection, Nos. 18 and 19, *NABU* 2010/5.
— 2012: Nergal and the Babylonian Cyclops, *BiOr* 69, 421–425.
— 2016: *Mesopotamian Incantations and Related Texts in the Schøyen Collection* (= CUSAS 32), Bethesda.
— 2018: Kamadme, the Sumerian Counterpart of the Demon Lamaštu, in: G. van Buylaere/M. Luukko/D. Schwemer/A. Mertens-Wagschal (eds.), *Sources of Evil. Studies in Mesopotamian Exorcistic Lore* (= AMD 15), Leiden/Boston, 150–157.
— (*forthcoming*): "Be My Baby" in Babylonia: An Akkadian poem of Adolescent Longing, in: A. Alshaer (ed.), *Poetry and Love in Middle Eastern Literatures*, London.
Gesche, P.D. 2001: *Schulunterricht in Babylonien im ersten Jahrtausend v. Chr.* (= AOAT 275), Münster.
Ginzberg, L. 2003: *Legends of the Jews*, vol. I, Philadelphia.
Goetze, A. 1955: An Incantation against Diseases, *JCS* 9, 8–18.
— 1957: Review of the Assyrian Dictionary of the Oriental Institute of the University of Chicago vol. 6. H, 5. G, *JCS* 11, 79–82.
Goodnick Westenholz, J. 1997: *Legends of the Kings of Akkade* (= MC 7), Winona Lake.

Goodnick Westenholz J./Westenholz A. 2006: *Cuneiform Inscriptions in the Collection of the Bible Lands Museum Jerusalem. The Old Babylonian Inscriptions* (= CM 33), Leiden.
Greengus, S. 1979: *Old Babylonian Tablets from Ishchali and Vicinity* (= PIHANS 44), Leiden.
— 1986: *Studies in Ishchali Documents* (= BiMes 19), Malibu.
Groneberg, B. 1987: *Syntax, Morphologie und Stil der jungbabylonischen "hymnischen" Literatur* (= FAOS 14), Stuttgart.
— 1997: *Lob der Ištar. Gebet und Ritual an die altbabylonische Venusgöttin* (CM 8), Groningen.
— 2007: Liebes- und Hundebeschwörungen im Kontext, in: M. T. Roth/W. Farber/M. W. Stolper /P. von Bechtolsheim (eds.), *Studies Presented to Robert D. Biggs, June 4, 2004* (= AS 27), Chicago, 91–107.
Guichard, M. 2018: Incantations à Mari, *CIPOA* 3, 23–40.
— 2019: De Larsa à Mari (I): nouvelles incantations paleo-babyloniennes, *Semitica* 61, 5–14.
— 2020a: De Larsa à Mari (II): nouvelles incantations paléo-babyloniennes, *Semitica* 62, 5–20.
— 2020b: Écrire à ses morts: une lettre-supplique akkadienne datant de l'époque d'Isin-Larsa (env. 2000-1800 av. n. è., *JA* 308, 151–165.
Gurney, O.R. 1989: *Literary and Miscellaneous Texts in the Ashmolean Museum* (= OECT 11), Oxford.
Hallo W.W. 1999: More Incantations and Rituals from the Yale Babylonian Collection, in: T. Abusch/K. van der Toorn (eds.), *Mesopotamian Magic: Textual, Historical, and interpretive Perspectives* (= AMD 1), Groningen, 275–290.
— 2010: *The World's Oldest Literature. Studies in Sumerian Belles-Lettres* (= CHANE 35), Leiden/Boston.
Hecker, K. 1993: Schultexte vom Kültepe, in: M.J. Mellink/E. Porada/T. Ozgüc (eds.), *Aspects of Art and Iconography: Anatolia and its Neighbors. Studies in Honor of Nimet Özgüç*, Ankara, 281–291.
— 1996: Schultexte aus Kültepe: ein Nachtrag, *NABU* 1996/30.
— 2008: Texte aus Mesopotamien, 2. Rituale und Beschwörungen, in: B. Janowski/G. Wilhelm (eds.), *Omina, Orakel, Rituale und Beschwörungen* (= TUAT NF 4), Gütersloh, 61–127.
Heeßel, N.P. 2000: *Babylonisch-assyrische Diagnostik* (= AOAT 43), Münster.
— 2014: Amulette und ‚Amuletform': zum Zusammenhang von Form, Funktion, und Text von Amuletten im Alten Mesopotamien, in: J.F. Quack/D.C. Luft (eds.), *Erscheinungsformen und Handhabungen heiliger Schriften*, Berlin/Boston, 53–77.
Heimpel, W. 1998–2000: Nanše.A, *RlA* 9, 152–160.
Hinz, W. 1976–1980: Inšušinak, *RlA* 5, 117–119.
Hirsch, H. 1972: *Untersuchungen zur altassyrischen Religion. 2. Auflage* (= AfO Beiheft 13/14), Osnabrück.
Horowitz, W. 1998: *Mesopotamian Cosmic Geography* (= MC 8), Winona Lake.
Hrouda, B. 1987: *Isin - Išān Baḥrīyāt. 3. Die Ergebnisse der Ausgrabungen 1983 – 1984*, Münich.
Hrůša, I. 2010: *Die akkadische Synonymenliste malku = šarru. Eine Textedition mit Übersetzung und Kommentar* (= AOAT 50), Münster.
Huehnergard, J./Pat-El, N. 2012: Third-person possessive suffixes as definite articles in Semitic, *Journal of Historical Linguistics* 2, 25–51.
Kämmerer, T. 1995: Die erste Pockendiagnose stammt aus Babylonien, *UF* 27, 129–168.
Kinnier Wilson, J. 1994: The sāmānu Disease in Babylonian Medicine, *JNES* 53, 111–115.
Kienast, B./Volk, K. 1995: *Die sumerischen und akkadischen Briefe des III. Jahrtausends aus der Zeit vor der III. Dynastie von Ur* (= FAOS 19), Stuttgart.
Kilmer A.D. 1987: The Symbolism of Flies in the Mesopotamian Flood Myth and some further Implications, in: F- Rochberg-Halton (ed), *Language, Literature, and History: Philological and Historical Studies Presented to Erica Reiner*, New Haven, 175–180.

Klan, M. 2007: *Als das Wünschen noch geholften hat oder: wie man in Mesopotamien Karriere machte. Eine Untersuchung zur 'dunklen Seite' der akkadischen Beschwörungsliteratur des 1. Jh. v. Chr*, Hamburg.
Kogan, L. 2001: *ǵ in Akkadian, *UF* 33, 263–298.
— 2004: Sleeping Deer in Mesopotamia and in the Bible, in: L. Kogan (ed.), *Babel und Bibel: Ancient Near East, Old Testament and Semitic Studies* (= Babel und Bibel 1), Winona Lake, 363–368.
Kossmann, M. 2011: The Names of King Antef's Dogs, in: A. Mettouchi (ed.), *Parcours berbères. Mélanges offerts à Paulette galand-Pernet et Lioned Galand pour leur 90e anniversaire* (= Berber Studies 33), Cologne, 79–84.
Kouwenberg, N.J.C. 2010: *Akkadian Verb and its Semitic Background* (= LANE 2), Winona Lake.
— 2017: *A Grammar of Old Assyrian* (= HdO 118), Leiden/Boston.
— 2018–2019: The Old Assyrian Incantation Tablet kt 91/k 502, *JEOL* 47, 57–72.
Kouwenberg, N.J.C./Fincke, J.C 2013: A "New" Old Assyrian Incantation, *JEOL* 44, 141–146.
Krebernik, M. 1984: *Die Beschwörungen aus Fara und Ebla. Untersuchungen zur ältesten keilschriftlichen Beschwörungsliteratur* (= TSO 2), Hildesheim.
— 1993–1995: Müttergöttin. A. I, *RlA* 8, 502–516.
— 1998–2001: Nin-girima. I, *RlA* 9, 363–367.
— 2001: *Tall Bi'a - Tuttul II. Die altorientalischen Schriftfunde* (= WVDOG 100), Saarbrücken.
— 2018: Eine neue elamische Beschwörung aus der Hilprecht-Sammlung (HS 2338) im Kontext alloglotter Texte der altbabylonischen Zeit, in: B. Mofidi-Nasrabadi/D. Prechel/A. Pruß (eds.), *Elam and its Neighbors. Recent Research and New Perspectives* (= Elamica 8), Hildesheim, 13–48.
Krebernik, M./Wasserman, N. 2020: An Elamite Magical Text against Scorpion Bite with an Akkadian Procedure, *Elamica* 10, 47–68.
Kritsky G. 2015: *The Tears of Re. Beekeeping in Ancient Egypt*, Oxford/New York.
Kryszat, G. 2015: Old Assyrian Writing and the Secret of the Kültepe Eponym List A, Subartu 35 (= KIM 1), 111–115.
Lackenbacher, S. 1971: Note sur l'Ardat-lilî, *RA* 65, 119–154.
Lambert, W.G. 1959–1960: An Address of Marduk to the Demons: New Fragments, *AfO* 19, 114–119.
— 1969: A Middle Assyrian medical text, *Iraq* 31, 28–39.
— 1976: An Old Babylonian Letter and Two Amulets, *Iraq* 38, 57–64.
— 1991: Another Trick of Enki?, in: D. Charpin/F. Joannès (eds.), *Marchands, diplomates et empereurs: études sur la civilisation mésopotamienne offertes à Paul Garelli*, Paris, 415–419.
— 2013: *Babylonian Creation Myths* (= MC 16), Winona Lake.
Lambert, W.G./Millard, A.R. 1969: *Atra-ḫasīs. The Babylonian story of the Flood*, Oxford.
Landsberger, B. 1958: Corrections to the Article "An Old Babylonian Charm against Merḫu", *JNES* 17, 56–58.
— 1969: Über Farben im Sumerisch-Akkadischen, *JCS* 21, 139–173.
Landsberger, B./Jacobsen, T. 1955: An Old Babylonian Charm against Merhu, *JNES* 14, 14–21.
Lapinkivi, P. 2010: *The Neo-Assyrian Myth of Ištar's Descent and Resurrection* (= SAACT 6), Helsinki.
Larsen, M.T. 1976: *The Old Assyrian City-State and its Colonies* (= Mesopotamia 4), Copenhagen.
Lauinger, J. 2012: The Old Babylonian Tablets from Adab in the Collection of the Oriental Institute Museum, in: K.L. Wilson (ed.), *Bismaya: Recovering the Ancient City of Adab* (= OIP 138), Chicago.
Leichty, E./Finkelstein J.J. /Walker, C.B.F. 1988: *Catalogue of the Babylonian Tablets in the British Museum. Vol. VIII: Tablets from Sippar 3*, London.

Lenzi, A. 2008: The Uruk list of kings and sages and late Mesopotamian scholarship, *JANER* 8, 137–169.
— 2010: Šiptu ul yuttun. Some reflections on a closing formula in Akkadian incantations, in: J. Stackert/B. N. Porter/D. P. Wright (eds.), *Gazing on the Deep. Ancient Near Eastern and Other Studies in Honor of Tzvi Abusch*, Bethesda, 131–166.
Livingstone, A. 1988: At the Cleaners: Notes on humorous Literature, in: G. Mauer/U. Magen, *Ad bene et fideliter seminandum* (= AOAT 220) 175–187.
Ludwig, M.-C. 2009: *Literarische Texte aus Ur. Kollationen und Kommentare zu UET 6/1–2* (= UAVA 9), Berlin.
Lutz, H.F. 1919: *Selected Sumerian and Babylonian Texts* (= PBS 1/2), Philadelphia.
Manekin-Bamberger, A. 2020: Who Were the Jewish 'Magicians' behind the Aramaic Incantation Bowls?, *Journal of Jewish Studies* 71, 235–254.
Marchesi G. 2006: *LUMMA in the Onomasticon and Literature of Ancient Mesopotamia* (= HANES 10), Padova.
Marello, P. 1992: Vie Nomade, in: J.-M. Durand (ed.), *Florilegium marianum: Recueil d'études en l'honneur de Michel Fleury* (= Mémoires de NABU 1), Paris, 115–125.
Maul, S.M. 1994: *Zukunftsbewältigung: Eine Untersuchung altorientalisches Denkens anhand der babylonisch-assyrischen Lösungsrituale (Namburbi)* (= BaF 18), Mainz.
— 2009: Die Lesung der Rubra DÙ.DÙ.BI und KÌD.KÌD.BI, *Or.* 78, 69–80.
May, N.N. 2018: Exorcists and Physicians at Assur: More on their Education and Interfamily and Court Connections, *ZA* 108, 63–80.
Mayer, W.R. 1976: *Untersuchungen zur Formensprache der Babylonischen "Gebetsbeschwörungen"* (= St. Pohl SM 5), Rome.
— 1992: Ein Hymnus auf Ninurta als Helfer in der Not, *Or.* 61, 17–57.
— 1995: Zum Terminativ-Adverbialis im Akkadischen, *Or.* 64, 161–186.
— 2003: Akkadische Lexikographie: CAD R, *Or.* 72, 231–242.
— 2005: Das Gebet des Eingeweideschauers an Ninurta, *Or.* 74, 51–56.
— 2009: Akkadische Lexikograpie: CAD T und Ṭ, *Or.* 78, 423–439.
Mazar, A. 2020: Socioeconomic, Historical and Ethnographic Aspects of the Apiary, in: A. Mazar/N. Panitz-Cohen (eds.), *Tel Reḥov. A Bronze and Iron Age City in The Beth-Shean Valley, Volume II: The Lower Mound: Area C and the Apiary* (= Qedem 60), Jerusalem, 639–658.
Mertens-Wagschal, A. 2018: The Lion, the Witch, and the Wolf: Aggressive Magic and Witchcraft in the Old Babylonian Period, in: G. van Buylaere/M. Luukko/D. Schwemer/A. Mertens-Wagschal (eds.), *Sources of Evil. Studies in Mesopotamian Exorcistic Lore* (= AMD 15), Leiden/Boston, 158–170.
Michalowski, P. 1978: Review of OECT 5, *JNES* 37, 343–345.
Michel C. 1997: Une incantation paléo-assyriene contre Lamaštum, *Or.* 66, 58–64.
— 2003: *Old Assyrian Bibliography of Cuneiform Texts, Bullae, Seals and the Results of the Excavations at Aššur, Kültepe/Kaniš, Acemhöyük, Alişar and Boğazköy* (= Old Assyrian Archives, Studies 1; PIHANS 97), Leuven.
— 2004: Deux incantations paléo-assyriennes. Une nouvelle incantation pour accompagner la naissance, in: J.G. Dercksen (ed.), *Assyria and Beyond. Studies Presented to Mogens Trolle Larsen* (= PIHANS 100), Leiden, 395–420.
Michel, C./Wasserman, N. 1997: Du nouveau sur *šumma zikar a-li-da-ni šumma sinnišat na-ap-TA-ar-ta-ni*, *NABU* 1997/64.
van de Mieroop, M. 1987: The Archive of Balmunamḫe, *AfO* 34, 1–29.
Mirelman, S. 2015: Birds, Balaĝs, and Snakes (K. 4206+), *JCS* 67, 169–186.
Mittermayer, C. 2009: *Enmerkar und der Herr von Aratta. Ein ungleicher Wettstreit* (= OBO 239), Fribourg.
Morier, H. 1989: *Dictionnaire de poétique et de rhétorique*[4e], Paris.

Murad, A. 2016: [IM-160562] Charme de Larsa contre les divins trépassés, *NABU* 2016/8.
Murad, A./Cavigneaux, A. 2018: IM 160096: un charme pour calmer un bébé qui pleure, *AoF* 45, 193–198.
Nies, J.B./Keiser, E. 1920: *Historical, Religious and Economic Texts and Antiquities* (= BIN 2), New Haven.
Nougayrol, J. 1972: Textes Religieux (II), *RA* 66, 141–145.
Novotny, J.R. 2001: *The Standard Babylonian Etana Epic* (= SAACT 2), Helsinki.
Novotny, J./Jeffers, J. 2018: *The Royal Inscriptions of Ashurbanipal (668-631 BC), Aššur-etel-ilāni (630-627 BC), and Sîn-šarra-iškun (626-612 BC), Kings of Assyria, Part 1* (= RINAP 5/1), Universt Park.
Ohgama, N/Robson, E. 2010: Scribal Schooling in Old Babylonian Kish: The Evidence of the Oxford Tablets, in: H.D. Baker/E. Robson/G. Zólyomi (eds.), *Your Praise is Sweet. A Memorial Volume for Jeremy Black from Students, Colleagues and Friends*. London.
Oshima, T. 2014: "Let us Sleep!" The Motif of Disturbing Resting Deities in Cuneiform Texts, *Studia Mesopotamica* 1, 271–289.
Panayotov, S.V. 2018: Magico-medical Plants and Incantations on Assyrian House Amulets, in: G. van Buylaere/M. Luukko/D. Schwemer/A. Mertens-Wagschal (eds.), *Sources of Evil. Studies in Mesopotamian Exorcistic Lore* (= AMD 15), Leiden/Boston, 192–222.
Parpola, S. 1997: *Assyrian Prophecies* (= SAA 9), Helsinki.
Paul, Sh. M. 1995: The "Plural of Ecstasy" in Mesopotamian and Biblical Love Poetry, in: Z. Zevit/S. Gitin/M. Sokoloff (eds.), *Solving Riddles and Untying Knots: Biblical, Epigraphic, and Semitic Studies in Honor of Jonas C. Greenfield*, Winona Lake, 585–597.
Pientka-Hinz, R. 2004: Aus der Wüste ins Schlafzimmer – der Skorpion, in: C. Nicolle (ed.), *Nomades et sedentaires dans le Proche-Orient ancien* (= Amurru 3; CRRAI 46), Paris, 389–403.
Pinches, T.G. 1898: *Cuneiform Texts from Babylonian Tablets in the British Museum* 4 (= CT 4), London.
Polinger Foster, K. 2020: *A Mesopotamian Miscellany* (= Gorgias Studies in the Ancient Near East 15), Piscataway.
Reiner, E. 1956: Lipšur Litanies, *JNES* 15, 129–149.
— 1960: Plaque Amulets and House Blessings, *JNES* 19, 148–155.
— 1985: *Your thwarts in pieces, your mooring rope cut: Poetry from Babylonia and Assyria*, Michigan.
— 1995: *Astral Magic in Babylonia* (= TAPS 85), Philadelphia.
de Ridder, J.J. 2019: Review of N.J.C. Kouwenberg, *Grammar of Old Assyrian*, *BiOr* 76, 126–132.
Rittig, D. 1977: *Assyrisch-babylonische Kleinplastik magischer Bedeutung vom 13.-6. Jahrhunderts v. Chr*, München.
Robson, E. 2008: *Mathematics in Ancient Iraq: A Social History*, Princeton/Oxford.
Röllig, W. 1985: Der Mondgott und die Kuh. Ein Lehrstück zur Problematik der Textüberlieferung im Alten Orient, *Or.*54, 260–273.
Roth, M.T. 1995: *Law Collections from Mesopotamia and Asia Minor* (= WAW 6), Atlanta.
Rudik, N. 2003: *alap erṣetim* and *nēšu ša qaqqari*: Animals of the Ground or Beast of the Netherworld?, in: L. Kogan (ed.), *Studia Semitica Orientalia. Papers of the Oriental Institute, Issue III* (= Fs. Militarev), Moscow, 378–388.
— 2015: *Die Entwicklung der keilschriftlichen sumerischen Beschwörungsliteratur von den Anfängen bis zur Ur III-Zeit*. PhD-thesis. Friedrich-Schiller Universität Jena.
Sallaberger, W. 2002: Der ‚Ziqqurat-plan' von Nippur und exorzistische Riten neusumerischer Zeit, in: O. Loretz/K.A. Metzler/H. Schaudig (eds.), *Ex Mesopotamia et Syria Lux: Festschrift für Manfred Dietrich zu seinem 65. Geburtstag*, Münster, 609–618.

Sanders, S. 2001: A Historiography of Demons: Preterit-Theme, Para-Myth, and Historiola in the Morphology of Genres, in: T. Abusch *et al.* (eds.), *Proceedings of the XLV Rencontre Assyriologique Internationale: Historiography in the Cuneiform World*, Bethesda, 429–440.

Schramm, W. 1981: ka-inim-ma, *RA* 75, 90.

Schuster-Brandis, A. 2008: *Steine als Schutz- und Heilmittel. Untersuchung zu ihrer Verwendung in der Beschwörungskunst Mesopotamiens im 1. Jt. v. Chr.* (= AOAT 46), Münster.

Schwemer, D. 2007: *Abwehrzauber und Behexung. Studien zum Schadenzauberglauben im alten Mesopotamien*, Wiesbaden.

— 2010: Entrusting the Witches to Ḫumuṭ-tabal, *Iraq* 72, 63–78.

— 2013: Gauging the influence of Babylonian magic: The reception of Mesopotamian traditions in Hittite ritual practice, in: E.C. Cancik-Kirschbaum/J.W. Klinger/G.G.W. Müller (eds.), *Vielfalt und Normierung/Diversity and Standardization. Perspektiven altorientalischer Kulturgeschichte*, Berlin, 145–172.

— 2014: 'Form follows function?' Rhetoric and Poetic Language in First Millennium Akkadian Incantations, *WO* 44, 263–288.

— 2020: Any Evil, a Stalking Ghost, and the Bull-Headed Demon, *ZA* 110, 141–160.

Scurlock, J.A. 1989–90: Was there a "love hungry" Ēntu-priestess named Eṭirtum?, *AfO* 36–37, 107–112.

— 1991: Baby-snatching Demons, Restless Souls and the Dangers of Childbirth: Medico-Magical Means of Dealing with some of the Perils of Motherhood in Ancient Mesopotamia, *Incognita* 2, 137–185.

Shaffer, A. (with a contribution by M.-C. Ludwig) 2006: *Ur Excavations Texts VI. Literary and Religious Texts, Third Part* (= UET 6/3), London.

Sibbing Plantholt, I. 2017: Black Dogs in Mesopotamia and Beyond, in: D. Kertai/O. Nieuwenhuyse (eds.), *From the Four Corners of the Earth: Studies in Iconography and Cultures of the Ancient Near East in Honour of F. A. M. Wiggermann* (= AOAT 441), Münster, 165–180.

Sigrist, M. 1987: On the Bite of a Dog, in: J.H. Marks/R.M. Good (eds.), *Love & Death in the Ancient Near East: Essays in Honor of Marvin H. Pope*, Guilford, 85–88.

Simkó, K. 2014: Überlegungen zu den symbolischen Rollen der Steine in Mesopotamien, *AoF* 41, 112–124.

Stadhouders, H. 2018: The Unfortunate Frog: On Animal and Human Bondage in K 2581 and Related Fragments with Excursuses On BM 64526 and YOS XI, 3, *RA* 112, 159–176

Stadhouders, H./Steinert, U. 2018: Two rituals to postpone an ill-omened childbirth: an edition of KAR 223 and duplicates, *JMC* 32, 56–76.

Steinert, U. 2013: Fluids, rivers, and vessels: metaphors and body concepts in Mesopotamian gynecological texts, *JMC* 22, 11–13.

— 2017a: Cows, Women and Wombs. Interrelations between Texts and Images from the Ancient Near East, in: D. Kertai/O. Nieuwenhuyse (eds.), *From the Four Corners of the Earth: Studies in Iconography and Cultures of the Ancient Near East in Honour of F. A. M. Wiggermann* (= AOAT 441), Münster, 205–258.

— 2017b: Concepts of the Female Body in Mesopotamian Gynecological Texts, in: J.Z. Wee (ed.), *The Comparable Body. Analogy and Metaphor in Ancient Mesopotamian, Egyptian, and Greco-Roman Medicine* (= SAM 49), Leiden/Boston, 275–357.

— (*forthcoming*) *Women's Health Care in Ancient Mesopotamia: An Edition of the Textual Sources*. (= BAM 11), Berlin.

Steinert, U./Vacín, L. 2018: BM 92518 and Old Babylonian Incantations for the "Belly", in: S.V. Panayotov/L. Vacín (eds.), *Mesopotamian Magic and Medicine. Studies in Honor of Markham J. Geller* (= AMD 14), Leiden/Boston, 698–744.

Steinkeller, P. 2005: Of Stars and Men: The Conceptual and Mythological Setup of Babylonian Extispicy, in: A. Gianto (ed.), *Biblical and Oriental Essays in Memory of William L. Moran* (= Biblica Et Orientalia 48), Rome, 11–47.
Stol, M. 1987–1990: Lugal-Marada, *RlA* 7, 148.
— 1989: Old-Babylonian Ophthalmology, in: M. Lebeau/Ph. Talon (eds.), *Reflets des deux fleuves. Volume de mélanges offerts à A. Finet* (= Akkadica Beih. 6), 163–166.
— 1992: The Moon as Seen by the Babylonians, in: D.J.W. Meijer (ed.), *Natural Phenomena. Their Meaning, Depiction and Description in the Ancient Near East*, Amsterdam, 245–277.
— 1993: *Epilepsy in Babylonia* (= CM 2), Groningen.
— 1996: Suffixe bei Zeitangaben im Akkadischen, *WZKM* 86 (= Fs. Hirsch), 413–424.
— 1998: Einige kurze Wortstudien, in: S. Maul (ed.), *Festschrift für Rykle Borger zu seinem 65. Geburtstag am 24. Mai 1994* (= CM 10), Groningen, 343–352.
— 2000: *Birth in Babylonia and the Bible: Its Mediterranean Setting* (= CM 14), Groningen.
— 2007: Fevers in Babylonia, in: I. L. Finkel/M. J. Geller (eds.), *Disease in Babylonia* (= CM 36), Leiden/Boston, 1–39.
Streck, M.P. 1999: *Die Bildersprache der akkadischen Epik* (= AOAT 264), Münster.
— 2004: Dattelpalme und Tamariske in Mesopotamien nach dem akkadischen Streitgespräch, *ZA* 94, 250–290.
— 2006–2008: Salz , Versalzung, *RlA* 11, 592–599.
— 2017: The Terminology for Times of the Day, in: Y. Heffron/A. Stone/M. Worthingdon (eds.), *At the Dawn of History. Ancient Near Eastern Studien in Honour of J.N. Postgate*, Winona Lake, 583–610.
Streck, M.P./Wasserman, N. 2018: The Man is Like a Woman, The Maiden is a Young Man. A New Edition of Ištar-Louvre, *Or.* 87, 1–38.
Sullivan, B.B. 1980: *Sumerian and Akkadian Sentence Structure in Old Babylonian Literary Bilingual Texts*, PhD thesis Hebrew Union College-Jewish Institute of Religion, Ohio (microfilm, Ann Arbor).
Taylor, J./Cartwright, C. 2011: The Making and Re-making of Clay Tablets, *Scienze dell'Antichità* 17, 297–324.
Thavapalan, S. 2020: *The Meaning of Color in Ancient Mesopotamia* (= CHANE 104), Leiden/Boston.
Thomsen, M.-L. 2018: Die Fliege und der Tod: Beschwörungen gegen Tiere, in: S.V. Panayotov, L. Vacín (eds), *Mesopotamian Magic and Medicine. Studies in Honor of Markham J. Geller* (= AMD 14), Leiden/Boston, 771–778.
Thureau-Dangin, F. 1939: Tablettes ḫurrites provenant de Mâri, *RA* 36, 1–28.
Tonietti, M.V. 1979: Un incantesimo sumerico contro la Lamaštu, *Or.* 48, 301–323.
van der Toorn, K. 1999: Magic at the Cradle: A Reassessment, in: T. Abusch/K. van der Toorn (eds.), *Mesopotamian Magic: Textual, Historical, and interpretative Perspectives* (= AMD 1), Groningen, 139–148.
Tsukimoto, A. 1999: "By the Hand of Madi-Dagan, the Scribe and Apkallu-Priest"- A Medical Text from the Middle Euphrates Region, in: K. Watanabe (ed.), *Priests and Officials in the Ancient Near East*, Heidelberg, 188–200.
Ungnad, A. 1915: *Babylonian Letters of the Hammurapi Period* (= PBS 7), Philadelphia.
— 1920: *Altbabylonische Briefe aus dem Museum zu Philadelphia.* Stuttgart.
Veenhof, K.R. 1996: An Old Assyrian Incantation against a black Dog (kt a/k 611), *WZKM* 86 (= Fs. Hirsch), 425–433.
— 2005: *Letters in the Louvre* (=AbB 14), Leiden/Boston.
Veldhuis, N. 1989: The New Assyrian Compendium for a Woman in Childbirth, *ASJ* 11, 239–260.
— 1990: The Heart Grass and Related Matters, *OLP* 21, 27–44.
— 1991: *A Cow of Sîn* (= LOT 2), Groningen.

— 1993: The Fly, the Worm, and the Chain: Old Babylonian Chain Incantations, *OLP* 24, 41–64.
— 1999: The Poetry of Magic, in: T. Abusch/K. van der Toorn (eds.), *Mesopotamian Magic: Textual, historical, and interpretative Perspectives* (= AMD 1), Groningen, 35–48.
Vilozny, N. 2017: *Lilith's Hair and Ashmedai's Horns. Figure and Image in Magic and Popular Art: Between Babylonia and Palestine in Late Antiquity*, Jerusalem.
von Soden, W.F. 1954: Eine altbabylonische Beschwörung gegen die Dämonin Lamaštum, *Or.* 23, 337–344.
— 1956: Eine altassyrische Beschwörung gegen die Dämonin Lamaštum, *Or.* 25, 141–148.
— 1961: Review of H.H. Figulla, CT 42, *BiOr* 18, 71–73.
— 1966: Aramäische Wörter in neuassyrischen und neu- und spätbabylonischen Texten. Ein Vorbericht. I (agâ- *mūš), *Or.* 35, 1–20.
— 1977: Review of CAD L, *OLZ* 72, 27–30.
— 1989–1990: Review of O.R. Gurney, *Literary and Miscellaneous Texts in the Ashmolean Museum* (= OECT 11), *AfO* 36–37, 118–120.
—1990: Review of W. Farber, Schlaf Kindchen Schlaf: Mesopotamische Baby-Beschwörungen und Rituale (= MC 2), *ZA* 80, 136–138.
von Weiher, E. 1971: *Der babylonische Gott Nergal* (= AOAT 11), Neukirchen-Vluyn.
Wagensonner, K. 2019a: Larsa Schools: A Palaeographic Journey, in: E. Devecchi/J. Mynářová/G.G.W. Müller (eds.), *Current Research in Cuneiform Palaeography 2. Proceedings of the Workshop organised at the 64th Rencontre Assyriologique Internationale*, Innsbruck 2018, Gladbeck, 41–86.
— 2019b: A new duplicate of a Sumero-Akkadian incantation, *NABU* 2019/43.
— 2020: Expelling Demons by the Use of a Fish and Bird, *Akkadica* 141, 115–125.
Waller, D.J. 2014: Echo and the Historiola: Theorizing the Narrative Incantation, *Archiv für Religionsgeschichte* 16, 263–280.
C. Walker/M. Dick 2001: *The Induction of the Cult Image in Ancient Mesopotamia. The Mesopotamian Mīs Pî Ritual* (= SAALT 1).
Wasserman, N. 1994: A Neo-Babylonian Imposture of an Old Babylonian Amulet?, *RA* 88, 49–57.
— 1995a: Concerning two Incantations against Lamaštu's evil Eye, *NABU* 1995/70.
— 1995b: Sîn Goes to Fishing, *NABU* 1995/71.
— 1999: Eqlam naṣārum: Pests and Pest Prevention in Old-Babylonian Sources, in: H. Klengel/J. Renger (eds.), *Landwirtschaft im Alten Orient: Ausgewählte Vorträge der 41. Rencontre Assyriologique Internationale* (= BBVO 18), Berlin, 341–354.
— 2002: Dictionaries and Incantations: Cross-Generic Relations in Old-Babylonian Literature, in: N. Wasserman (ed.), *Wool from the Loom: The Development of Literary Genres in Ancient Literature*, Jerusalem, 1–13.
— 2003: *Style and Form in Old Babylonian Literary Texts* (= CM 27), Leiden.
— 2005a: Offspring of Silence, Spawn of a Fish, Son of a Gazelle…: Enkidu's Different Origins in the Epic of Gilgameš, in: Y. Sefati/P. Artzi/C. Cohen/B.L. Eichler/V.A. Hurowitz (eds.), *An Experienced Scribe Neglects Nothing. Ancient Near Eastern Studies in Honor of Jacob Klein*, Bethesda, 593–599.
— 2005b: The Rhetoric of Time Inversion: Hysteron-Proteron and the 'Back to Creation' Theme in Old Babylonian Literary Texts, in: S. Shaked (ed.), *Genesis and Regeneration: Essays on Conceptions of Origins*, Jerusalem, 13–30.
— 2007: Between Magic and Medicine - A Propos of an Old Babylonian therapeutic Text against *Kurārum* Disease, in: I.L. Finkel/M.J. Geller (eds.), *Disease in Babylonia* (= CM 36), Leiden/Boston, 40–61.
— 2008: On Leeches, Dogs, and Gods in Old Babylonian Medical Incantations, *RA* 102, 71–88.

— 2010: From the Notebook of a Professional Exorcist, in: D. Shehata/ F. Weiershäuser/K. Zand (eds.), *Von Göttern und Menschen. Beiträge zu Literatur und Geschichte des Alten Orients. Festschrift für Brigitte Groneberg* (= CM 41), Leiden/Boston, 329–349.
— 2011: The Distant Voice of Gilgameš: The Circulation and Reception of the Babylonian Gilgameš Epic in Ancient Mesopotamia. A Review Article of A.R. George, The Babylonian Gilgamesh Epic: Introduction, Critical Edition and Cuneiform Texts, *AfO* 52, 1–14.
— 2012a: Most Probably: *Epistemic Modality in Old Babylonian* (= LANE 3), Winona Lake.
— 2012b: Maškadum and Other Zoonotic Diseases in Medical and Literary Akkadian Sources, *BiOr* 69, 426–436.
— 2014a: What you see is what you get, in: D. Bawanypeck/A. Imhausen (eds.), *Traditions of Written Knowledge in Ancient Egypt and Mesopotamia* (= AOAT 403), Münster, 47–70.
— 2014b: Old-Babylonian, Middle-Babylonian, Neo-Babylonian, Jewish-Babylonian? Thoughts about Transmission Modes of Mesopotamian Magic through the Ages, in: U. Gabbay/S. Secunda (eds.), *Encounters by the Rivers of Babylon. Scholarly Conversations Between Jews, Iranians and Babylonians in Antiquity*, Tübingen, 255–269.
— 2015: Piercing the Eyes: An Old Babylonian Love Incantation and the Preparation of Kohl, *BiOr* 72, 601–612.
— 2016: *Akkadian Love Literature of the Third and Second Millennium BCE* (= LAOS 4), Wiesbaden.
— 2018: Labour Pains, Difficult Birth, Sick Child: Three Old Babylonian Incantations from a Private Collection, *BiOr* 75, 14–25.
— 2019: The Susa Funerary Texts: A New Edition and Re-Evaluation and the Question of Psychostasia in Ancient Mesopotamia, *JAOS* 139, 859–891.
— 2020a: *The Flood: The Akkadian Sources. A New Edition, Commentary, and a Literary Discussion* (= OBO 290), Leuven.
— 2020b: “Talking to Doors”: Paraklausithyron in Akkadian Literature, in: A. Azzoni/A. Kleinerman/D.A. Knight/D.I. Owen (eds.), *From Mari to Jerusalem and Back: Assyriological and Biblical Studies in Honor of Jack Murad Sasson*, University Park, 305–318.
— 2020c: A Hybrid Magical Text from the Böhl Collection, *BiOr* 77, 446-458.
— 2021: Lists and Chains: Enumeration in Akkadian Literary Texts, in R. Lämmle/C. Scheidegger Lämmle/K. Wesselmann (eds.), *Lists and Catalogues in Ancient Literature and Beyond. Towards a Poetics of Enumeration* (= Trends in Classics – Supplementary Volumes 107). Boston/Berlin, 57–79.
Wasserman, N./Or, A. 1998: Babylonian Love Poetry, *Helicon. Anthological Journal of Contemporary Poetry* 27, 86–96 (in Hebrew).
Westenholz, A./Goodnick Westenholz, J. 1977: Help for rejected suitors. The Old Akkadian Love Incantation MAD V 8, *Or*. 46, 198–219.
Whiting, R.M. 1985: An Old Babylonian Incantation from Tell Asmar, *ZA* 75, 179–187.
Wiggermann, F.A.M. 1983: Enige Lamaštu-Bezweringen uit de Oud-Babylonische en Nieuw-Assyische Tijd, in: K.R. Veenhof (ed.), *Schrijvend Verleden. Documenten uit het Oude Nabije Oosten. Vertaald en Toegelicht*, Leiden, 294–300.
— 1996: Scenes from the Shadow Side, in: M.E. Vogelzang/H.L.J. Vanstiphout (eds.), *Mesopotamian Poetic Language: Sumerian and Akkadian* (= CM 6), Groningen, 207–230.
— 2000: Lamaštu, Daughter of Anu. A Profile, in: M. Stol, *Birth in Babylonia and the Bible: Its Mediterranean setting* (= CM 14), Groningen, 217–252.
Wilcke, C. 1973: Sumerische literarische Texte in Manchester und Liverpool, *AfO* 24, 1–18.
— 1985: Liebesbeschwörungen aus Isin, *ZA* 75, 188–209.
— 1989: Die Emar-Version von “Dattelpalme und Tamariske” – ein Rekonstruktionsversuch, *ZA* 79, 161–190.

Wilhelm, G. 2019: Mari Hurr. No. 8, in: G. Chambon/M. Guichard/A.-I. Langlois (eds.), *De l'argile au numérique. Mélanges assyriologiques en l'honneur de Dominique Charpin* (= PIPOAC 3), Leuven/Paris/Bristol, 1181–1188.

Wilson, E.J. 1994: *"Holiness" and "Purity" in Mesopotamia* (= AOAT 237), Neukirchen-Vluyn.

Woolley, L. 1976: *The Old Babylonian Period* (= UE 7), London.

Worthington, M. 2020: *Ea's Duplicity in the Gilgamesh Flood Story*, London/New York.

Wu, Y. 2001: Rabies and Rabid Dogs in Sumerian and Akkadian Literature, *JAOS* 121, 32–43.

Zilberg, P./Horowitz, W. 2016: Medico-Magical Text from the Otage Tablets, Dunedin New Zealand, *ZA* 106, 175–184.

Zomer, E. 2013: KUB 4, 13: 15'-23' revisited, *NABU* 2013/27.

— 2017: Zauberei (Witchcraft), *RlA* 15, 222–224

— 2018a: *Corpus of Middle Babylonian and Middle Assyrian Incantations* (= LAOS 9), Wiesbaden.

— 2018b: 'The Physician is the Judge!'— A Remarkable Divine Dialogue in the Incantation: ÉN ur-saĝ ^{d}asal-lú-ḫi igi-bé ḫé-pà saĝ-ḫul-ḫa-za ḫé-pà, *JMC* 31, 38–42.

— 2019: Some Observations on the Prism KBo 1.18", in Y. Hazırlayan/A. Süel (eds.), *Acts of the IXth Hittitology Congress, Çorum 2014/ IX. Uluslararası Hititoloji Kongresi Bildirileri, Çorum 08-14 eylül, 2014*, Çorum,1257–1266.

— 2020: Review of A.R. George/J. Taniguchi, Cuneiform Texts from the Folios of W.G. Lambert. Part One (= MC 24), *JNES* 79, 357–359.

— 2021: Demons and Tutelary Deities from Heaven. The Hyleme-Pattern "X Descends from Heaven" in Akkadian Incantation Literature, in: A. Zgoll/C. Zgoll/G. Gabriel/B. Kärger (eds.), *Was vom Himmel kommt. Stoffanalytische Zugänge zu antiken Mythen aus Mesopotamien, Ägypten, Griechenland und Rom* (= Mythological Studies 4), Berlin/Boston, 161–187.

— (*forthcoming*): Negotiating with Evil. The Rhetorical Strategy of Epiplexis in Mesopotamian Magic, in: N.P. Heeßel/E.Zomer (eds.), *Legitimising Magic: Strategies and Practices in Ancient Mesopotamia*.

Indices

I. Texts

Besides the Corpus

Akkadian and Sumerian

II. Personal and Divine Names (Selection)

III. Geographical and River Names (Selection)

IV. Index of Words Discussed (Selection)

Akkadian

V. Grammatical, Literary and Other Terms (Selection)

Grammatical

Literary

Other

PLATES

Plate I

BM 97331

Obverse

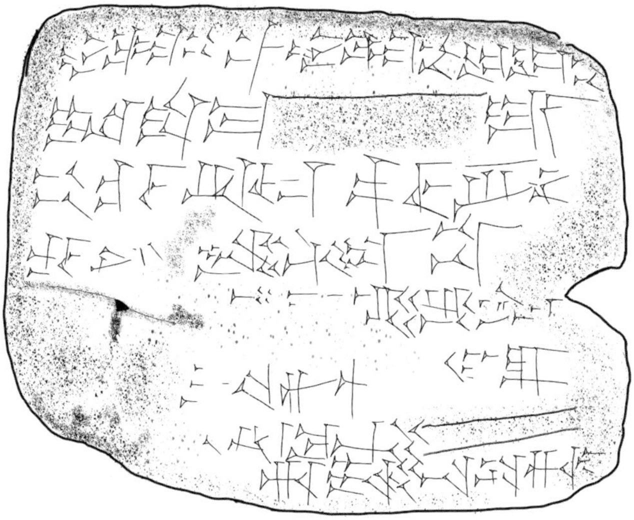

Lower Edge

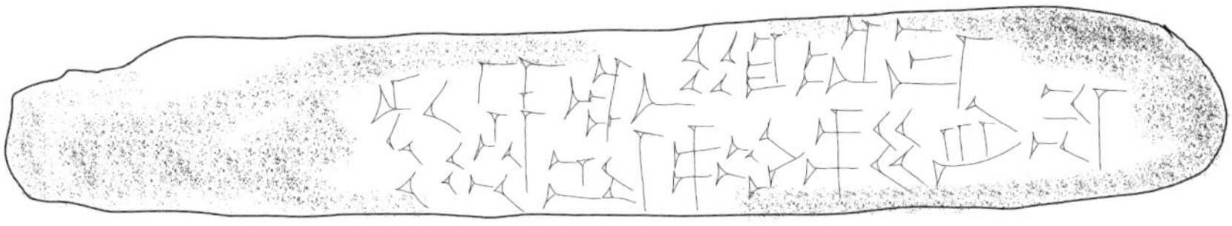

Reverse

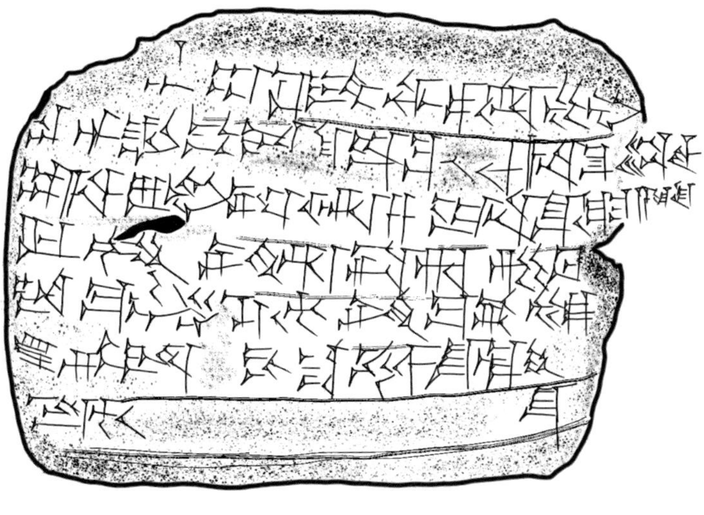

BM 115743

Obverse

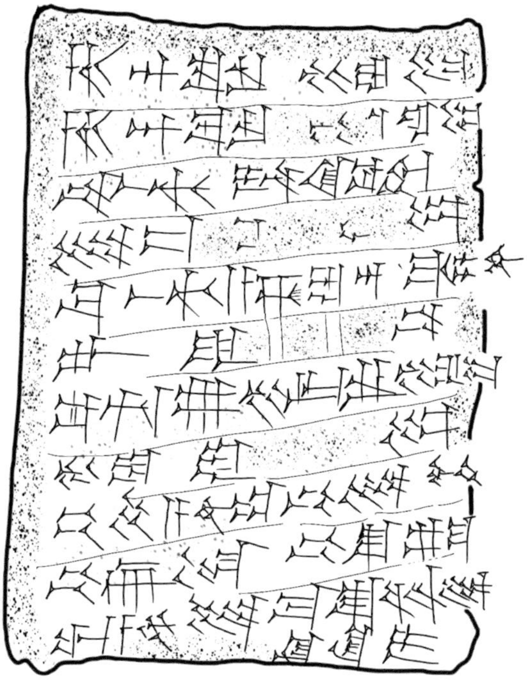

Leipziger Altorientalistische Studien

Herausgegeben von Michael P. Streck

8: Jacob Jan de Ridder

Descriptive Grammar of Middle Assyrian

*2018. XXVIII, 628 pages, 3 diagrams,
3 ill., 2 maps, 73 tables, hc
170x240 mm
ISBN 978-3-447-10979-6* *€ 98,– (D)*

The Middle Assyrian period (ca. 1500–1000 BCE) is characterized by the transformation of the former city state of Ashur into an expansive empire. Over the last couple of decennia, the text corpus has grown considerably due to many archaeological excavations of archives in Syria.

This grammatical description of Middle Assyrian seeks to improve our knowledge of the language of these texts. It takes into account recently published texts, including the archives from Tell Aš-Šēḫ Ḥamad, Tell Ḫuwīra, Tell Ṣabī Abyaḍ and Tell Ṭābān. The result serves as a long overdue supplementation to Mayer's *Untersuchungen zur Grammatik des Mittelassyrischen* (1971). The monograph consists of an introduction to the corpus and its historical context, followed by discussions on orthography, phonology, morphology and syntax. Non-Assyrian influences on orthography and grammar are also subject of discussion. In addition, comparisons are made between the different stages of the Assyrian language in order to put Middle Assyrian into context of its intermediate stage between Old Assyrian (ca. 1900–1700) and Neo-Assyrian (ca. 1000–600). Thus, the monograph is aimed at Assyriologists as well as Semitists.

9: Elyze Zomer

Corpus of Middle Babylonian and Middle Assyrian Incantations

*2018. XXIV, 470 pages, 1 diagram,
1 map, 3 plates, 237 tables, hc
170x240 mm
ISBN 978-3-447-11041-9
⊙E-Book: ISBN 978-3-447-19635-2* *each € 84,– (D)*

The present volume is the first systematic treatment of the *Corpus of Middle Babylonian and Middle Assyrian Incantations*. It comprises an exhaustive and detailed catalogue of all magical material in cuneiform texts in Sumerian and Akkadian from the Middle Babylonian and Middle Assyrian periods (ca. 1500–1000 BCE).

The work begins with a typology of the different subgroups of incantations, the physical properties of the tablets, an innovative survey of the text formats, a discussion of drawings on magical texts and a critical discussion of the different paratextual comments, followed by an overview of the geographical and archival setting and an examination on the social context of the corpus. The circulation of magical texts during the Late Bronze Age is investigated by outlining the corpus itself: its thematic grouping of incantations, division of unilingual and bilingual texts, local scribal traditions and their influences. With respect to the question of whether the standardization of incantations took place in Mesopotamia during the Second Millennium, an extensive chapter provides a comparative analysis of the incantation corpora of the Third and Second Millennium against the standardized ritual series of the First Millennium. Furthermore, fifty cuneiform texts have been edited and translated, accompanied by a thorough philological commentary.